THE
Beecher
SISTERS

THE
Beecher
SISTERS

Barbara A. White

Yale University Press
NEW HAVEN AND LONDON

Frontispiece: Beecher family, c. 1859. Left to right: Isabella Hooker,
Thomas, Catharine, William, Lyman, Edward, Mary Perkins, Charles, Harriet
Stowe, Henry Ward. Left insert (in China): James. Right insert: George (1843).
Courtesy Harriet Beecher Stowe Center, Hartford, Conn.

Designed by Gregg Chase
Set in Albertina type by Achorn Graphic Services, Inc.
Printed in the United States of America by Vail-Ballou Press

Library of Congress Cataloging-in-Publication Data
White, Barbara Anne.
The Beecher sisters / Barbara A. White.
p.   cm.
Includes bibliographical references and index.
ISBN 0-300-09927-4 (cloth : alk. paper)

1. Beecher, Catharine Esther, 1800–1878. 2. Stowe, Harriet Beecher, 1811–1896.
3. Hooker, Isabella Beecher, 1822–1907. 4. Perkins, Mary Beecher, 1805–1900.
5. Beecher family. 6. Sisters—United States—Biography. 7. Women—United States—
Biography. 8. Feminists—United States—Biography. 9. Authors, American—19th century—
Biography. 10. United States—Social life and customs—19th century. I. Title.
CT274.B43W48   2003
920.72′0973—dc21   2003010630

A catalogue record for this book is available from the British Library.

The paper in this book meets the guidelines for permanence and
durability of the Committee on Production Guidelines for Book Longevity
of the Council on Library Resources.

10 9 8 7 6 5 4 3 2 1

To the memory of my parents,
Betty Busacker White (1919–1979) and
Frank L. White (1912–1995)

Contents

Preface

THIS BOOK IS A JOINT biography of the famous Beecher sisters, who lived and worked in nineteenth-century America. Daughters of the well-known evangelist Lyman Beecher, the three sisters were not allowed to follow their father and seven brothers to college and into the ministry. Yet they all had successful careers at a time when few women entered the public sphere. Catharine Beecher (1800–1878) became a pioneer educator. She founded the Hartford Female Seminary in the 1820s and devoted her life to improving women's schooling; she wrote some thirty books on education, religion, and health. Harriet Beecher Stowe (1811–1896) became world-famous in 1852 as the author of the explosive anti-slavery novel *Uncle Tom's Cabin*. She went on to write a series of novels about New England, initiating the women's tradition of local-color realism in the United States. The youngest Beecher sister, Isabella Beecher Hooker (1822–1907), devoted herself to her husband and children until middle age. After the Civil War she began to speak out on women's rights and quickly found herself a leader in the movement. She was a friend and colleague of Elizabeth Cady Stanton and Susan B. Anthony. In her suffrage work Hooker became associated with the flamboyant feminist Victoria Woodhull, also known as "Mrs. Satan." This connection ignited a major quarrel among the sisters.

There was a fourth Beecher sister. Mary Beecher Perkins (1805–1900) remained solely a housewife and mother throughout her long life. She was the most conventional sister, hardly changing her conservative views as time passed. Because she was not a public figure, less information is available about her; her experiences are included in the biography so far as sources allow. The strongest emphasis is on Isabella Beecher Hooker because plenty of primary material is available but no existing biography (several biographies of Catharine Beecher and Harriet Beecher Stowe have been published).

The lives of the Beecher sisters span the entire nineteenth century, from the birth of Catharine in 1800 to the death of Isabella in 1907. It was an exciting time in American history, a time of cataclysmic change. The sisters' careers provide a vivid illustration of the social, economic, and religious changes during that century and the issues, such as abolition, women's rights, Spiritualism, and health reform, that engaged nineteenth-century Americans. *The Beecher Sisters* tells the story of the sisters' individual lives and their interactions with prominent people of the time and with one another—how they supported one another, how they disagreed, and how they influenced one another's private lives and public careers.

Acknowledgments

THIS BIOGRAPHY COULD NOT HAVE been written without the assistance of numerous librarians and archivists. I especially want to thank the Reference, Interlibrary Loan, and Loan departments of the University of New Hampshire Library. I am grateful to Josephine Donovan for her thorough and valuable reading of the manuscript. Thanks also to Mara Witzling for the longtime loan of a book and to Mary M. Moynihan for discussions about Charlotte Perkins Gilman. I am indebted to Harvey Epstein for taming the computer and accompanying me on several research trips. Finally, I thank friends and family for moral support during a lengthy process, particularly Ellie Epstein-White, Susan Franzosa, Annette Tischler, and Herbert Tischler.

Beecher Sisters Genealogy

Plus signs mean "married." Asterisks set off spouses subsequent to the first.

Lyman Beecher 1775–1863
+Roxana Foote 1775–1816
Catharine Esther Beecher 1800–1878
William Beecher 1802–1889
+Katherine Edes ?–1870
Edward Beecher 1803–1895
+Isabella Porter Jones 1807–1895
Mary Foote Beecher 1805–1900
+Thomas Perkins 1798–1870
Frederick 1828–1899
Emily 1829–1912
Charles 1832–1917
Catherine 1836–1879
Harriet Beecher 1808–1808
George Beecher 1809–1843
+Sarah Buckingham 1817–1902
Harriet E. Beecher 1811–1896
+Calvin Stowe 1802–1886
Harriet B. 1836–1907
Eliza 1836–1912
Henry 1838–1857
Frederick 1840–1870?
Georgiana 1843–1890
Samuel 1848–1849
Charles 1850–1934
Henry Ward Beecher 1813–1887
+Eunice Bullard 1812–1897
Charles Beecher 1815–1900
+Sarah Coffin 1815–1897

*2d Wife of Lyman Beecher
+Harriet Porter 1790–1835
Frederick Beecher 1818–1820
Isabella Homes Beecher 1822–1907
+John Hooker 1816–1901
Thomas 1842–1842
Mary 1845–1886
Alice 1847–1928
Edward 1855–1927

Thomas Beecher 1824–1900
+Olivia Day 1826–1853
*2d Wife of Thomas Beecher
+Julia Jones 1826–1905
James Beecher 1828–1886
+Ann Goodwin Morse ?–1863
*2d Wife of James Beecher
+Frances Johnson 1832–1903

*3d Wife of Lyman Beecher
+Lydia Beals Jackson 1789–1869

1

Calvinist Childhoods,
1800–1837

THE BEECHER SISTERS had the good fortune (or misfortune, depending on one's perspective) to be born into one of the most famous and controversial families of the nineteenth century. Lyman Beecher, the family patriarch, was an energetic Puritan minister who dedicated his life to defending religious orthodoxy. An aggressive and outgoing man, he was widely loved and hated. In addition to his four daughters, Catharine, Mary, Harriet, and Isabella, he had seven sons—William, Edward, George, Henry, Charles, Thomas, and James. All seven would follow their father into the ministry. Henry Ward Beecher outdid Lyman as an orator, ending up the most famous preacher in America. Even the lesser known Beecher boys became college presidents, scholars, or authors; by 1860 the Beechers had written some forty books.

Perhaps Lyman Beecher fathered so many children because he himself grew up as an only child. He came from a long line of blacksmiths, his father, grandfather, and great-grandfather having practiced their trade in New Haven, Connecticut. Lyman's father, David, although physically very strong, was known as a man of ideas who read widely. He married five times, a large number even in the nineteenth century. Lyman was the son of David's third wife, Esther, who is described as a "tall, fair and lovely woman." Shortly after Lyman's birth in 1775 she died of consumption, the nineteenth-century killer that would later be known as tuberculosis. David immediately left the baby with his childless aunt and uncle, the Lot Bentons, who lived on a farm in nearby Guilford. Although David Beecher remarried and had other children, he never sent for Lyman. He did help the Bentons pay the cost of Lyman's education at Yale, once Uncle Lot decided that Lyman was too absentminded to make a farmer.

Lyman found Yale still under the influence of the rationalism and religious skepticism of the Age of Enlightenment; when he arrived at the college, there were two different societies named for the radical Thomas Paine. In Lyman's second year, however, the Rev. Timothy Dwight became president of the college. Dwight, the grandson of the Puritan divine Jonathan Edwards, author of *Sinners in the Hands of an Angry God*, turned the college back toward Calvinism and converted Lyman Beecher in the process. Calvinists believed that human beings were born in a state of sin, which they called "natural depravity." The fate of humans was predestined—either God had elected them to receive the gift of grace and be saved or He had condemned them to everlasting Hell. People could not ensure their salvation; they could only avoid sin and prepare themselves for "conversion," an experience of God's grace that was a sign of being elected.

After graduating from Yale in 1797, Lyman spent a year in Yale Divinity School under the tutelage of Reverend Dwight. He then became minister of the Presbyterian Church in East Hampton, Long Island, across the Long Island Sound from Connecticut. He brought with him his new wife, Roxana Foote, daughter of a well-off Revolutionary War veteran who lived at Nutplains, a two hundred–acre farm outside Guilford, Connecticut. Roxana was a good match for Lyman. She had experience in the household tasks of cooking and sewing and also spoke French, grew flowers, and painted miniature portraits on ivory. The Footes were Episcopalians, but from Lyman's point of view Roxana's best quality was her quiet submissiveness: she "entered into my character entirely," as he put it.

Less than a year after their marriage, Roxana and Lyman's first child was born. Catharine Esther arrived on September 6, 1800, named Catharine after Lyman's foster mother, Aunt Benton, and Esther after his birth mother. Lyman was charmed. He said he would never forget his feelings when Grandmother Foote first put Catharine in his arms—"Thou little immortal!" he exclaimed. Catharine and Lyman were always very close. Her earliest memories were of riding in his carriage as he traveled from farm to farm making pastoral visits. Catharine's biographer Kathryn Kish Sklar suggests that as Lyman Beecher was the most powerful person in the isolated region, Catharine learned from him "to feel the confidence that power brings." Psychologists would probably emphasize her birth order position as the oldest child. She identified strongly with her parents and became, like a typical firstborn, ambitious, achievement-oriented, and domineering.

When Catharine discussed her own childhood, she stressed other issues. She noted her father's nurturing qualities, writing that he possessed "that passionate love of children which makes it a pleasure to nurse and tend them, and which is generally deemed a distinctive element of the woman." Her mother, by contrast, had very little of that passion and did not fondle and caress the children as Lyman did. Roxana was doubtless preoccupied with constant childbearing and trying to make ends meet. She spent what little spare time she had trying to bring "civilization" to their Long Island outpost. All her daughters remembered her famous carpet, the first in East Hampton, which consisted of a piece of woven cotton she had painted in oils "with a border all around it, and bunches of roses and other flowers over the centre." The carpet lasted to Catharine's adulthood and was one of Harriet Beecher Stowe's earliest memories.

By the time Catharine's first sister, Mary Foote Beecher, was born in 1805 Roxana had given birth to four children in five years. Mary was named after Roxana's younger sister, Mary Foote Hubbard, who lived with the Beechers during much of their time in East Hampton. Mary Hubbard had a tragic clash with the inhumane practice that would touch the lives of all the Beechers, chattel slavery. At age seventeen she married a merchant and went to live on his slave plantation in the West Indies; she had no idea what to expect. Harriet later wrote of her: "What she saw and heard of slavery filled her with constant horror and loathing. She has said that she has often sat by her window in the tropical night, when all was still, and wished that the island might sink in the ocean, with all its sin and misery, and that she might sink with it."

Mary Hubbard finally left her husband and returned to East Hampton. She soon died of consumption, but before her death she helped Roxana run a small boarding school for girls in an attempt to meet the family expenses. Roxana taught English composition, French, drawing, painting, and embroidery. Catharine would remember how her mother and Aunt Mary studied chemistry and did some "ludicrous" experiments in order to impart the new science to their pupils. In Catharine's view a better school was the intellectual atmosphere created by her father as he read his sermons to her mother and Aunt Mary. "By this intellectual companionship our house became in reality a school of the highest kind, in which he was all the while exerting a powerful influence upon the mind and character of his children."

Roxana's school was successful but not lucrative enough to compensate for Lyman's low income. After Mary, another child was born (George). A salary of four hundred dollars plus firewood was not enough to support such a large family—this would be a continual problem in Lyman's ministerial career and those of most of his sons. By this time, however, Lyman's name was becoming recognized—as his sermons against dueling and drinking had been published—and he easily found another position. In 1810 the Beechers moved to Litchfield, Connecticut, in the northwest corner of the state, where Lyman became minister of the Congregational Church. Litchfield was a prosperous town, a Federalist stronghold with genteel and educated residents. It could boast of two well-known schools, the Litchfield Law School and the Litchfield Female Academy. The academy was one of the first schools for women in the United States, having been started by Sarah Pierce in 1792. It had an excellent reputation and Miss Pierce was one of Lyman's parishioners. In return for his help and advice, Catharine recalled, she gave his children free schooling. Catharine, age ten, was enrolled immediately.

In Litchfield three more children were born, Harriet, Henry Ward, and Charles. Harriet arrived on June 14, 1811. She was named for another of her mother's sisters, the one considered the smartest and wittiest of the Foote girls. Roxana had given the same name to an earlier baby who had died of whooping cough at the age of one month. The new Harriet was the Beechers' sixth child and third daughter to survive infancy. As the famous author Harriet Beecher Stowe, she would later write in her novel *Poganuc People* (1878) that the first child is pure poetry but the later ones are prose. Dolly, the character Stowe based on herself, entered the family "at a period when babies were no longer a novelty, when the house was full of the wants and clamors of older children, and the mother at her very wits' end with a confusion of jackets and trousers, soap, candles and groceries, and the endless harassments of . . . a poor country minister's wife." Harriet thus emphasized her birth position. As a middle child, she had to compete for her parents' attention with both older and younger siblings.

But even Harriet's distracted mother was taken from her when she was only five. Roxana died in 1816 at the age of forty-one. Like Lyman's mother and her own younger sister Mary, she was felled by consumption. By all accounts, Lyman and the children were devastated and immediately set about turning Roxana into a saint. As Forrest Wilson, one of Harriet's biographers, notes, "Roxana became pure spirit with them all, an ideal . . . the symbol of all that was most perfect in womanhood." This ideal, Harriet said, influenced the children toward good more than the living presence of other mothers. Henry, who was just two when she died and could hardly remember her, would in middle age tell his congregation that his mother was to him what the Virgin Mary means to a devout Catholic.

The holy mother is a hard act to follow and perhaps Lyman Beecher's second wife, the mother of the youngest Beecher daughter, Isabella, was doomed to failure from the beginning. Lyman went to Boston hunting for a wife less than a year after Roxana's death and found Harriet Porter from Portland, Maine. Like Roxana, Harriet P. was a devout Christian from a distinguished family far above Lyman Beecher's. Her father was a successful doctor, and her mother's brothers included members of Congress, senators, ambassadors, and a governor of Maine. Harriet P.'s family led a fashionable life in Portland and Boston, and she had once been a belle. After conversion she was predisposed to admire an evangelist, even if he struck her family as being, in one writer's words, "an outlandish, threadbare country minister." Also, Harriet P. may have accepted Lyman because when they met she was twenty-six, old enough to be considered a spinster.

At first, the marriage seemed successful. Catharine felt displaced, having been allowed to leave school at her mother's death and take on the maternal role in the family. But when she wrote a stilted letter of welcome, Harriet P. replied in a pleasant manner. She assured the children that she intended not to take the place of their mother but to be a new friend. The children's first reaction to her was positive, as expressed years later by Harriet Beecher Stowe:

> I was about six years old, and slept in the nursery with my two younger brothers. . . .
>
> We heard father's voice in the entry, and started up in our little beds, crying out as he entered our room, "Why, here's pa!" A cheerful voice called out from behind him, "And here's ma!"
>
> A beautiful lady, very fair, with bright blue eyes, and soft auburn hair bound round with a black velvet bandeau, came into the room smiling, eager, and happy-looking, and, coming up to our beds, kissed us, and told us she loved little children. . . .
>
> Never did mother-in-law [sic] make a prettier or sweeter impression.

In letters to her sister, the new Mrs. Beecher praised the children. She thought Catharine "a fine-looking girl, and in her mind I find all that I expected. She is not handsome, yet there is hardly any one who appears better." Mary would make a good woman, she believed, and was more handsome than otherwise. "She is twelve now, large of her age, and is almost the most useful member of the family." Harriet, who always seemed to be hand-in-hand with brother Henry, was amiable, affectionate, and bright. Harriet P. also noted the refined society of Litchfield and the beauty of the town, with its surrounding hills and wide, tree-lined streets. Her new husband might be only a country minister but in 1818 he was presented with an honorary doctorate from Middlebury College.

But before long Harriet Porter Beecher became less cheerful, and the teenage Mary could write that she was unwell and no longer laughed. Harriet P. had a difficult time recovering from the death at age two of Frederick, her first child, and like her predecessor had to manage a house and many children on her husband's low ministerial salary. Eventually, she sank into a permanent state of melancholy. Lyman himself was more hindrance than help, as he fell into a deep depression the year before his youngest daughter's birth. He had experienced such a collapse earlier in East Hampton, likening it to his father's attacks of "dyspepsia" or chronic indigestion, which were accompanied by depression. According to Milton Rugoff, in the best book on the Beecher family, these attacks would become a sort of "family malaise," reappearing in later generations. Rugoff thinks that Lyman's "violent alternations of despair and hope" might today be diagnosed as manic depression.

Isabella thus had a troubling heritage of mental illness from both her parents. But at her birth on February 22, 1822, observers noted only that she had inherited her mother's beauty, her "finely chiseled features and fair, delicate coloring." Isabella would be considered the prettiest of the four Beecher sisters. As one of the youngest children, she was a favorite and, even by her own admission, was much petted and praised. The family called her "Belle" or "Bella," and she was given the middle name "Homes," after the married name of one of her mother's sisters.

Catharine, now age twenty-two, was home in Litchfield when Isabella was born (the previous year she had gone to New London to teach). For the first few weeks she assumed the care of the new mother and baby. The year 1822 would be a crucial one in Catharine's life, and her experiences would affect her and her sisters for years to come. According to a letter she wrote to her aunt, her father was still sick, little Charles had punctured his knee with a nail, and Aunt Esther, Lyman's spinster step-sister, who was spending the winter with them, was feeble. Catharine's status as the only healthy adult in the extended family, servants and all, lasted only a short time. By April 1822 her father was writing that Catharine had been sick for three days, "the first in acute distress . . . she was seized with the most agonizing pain."

Catharine's agonizing pain came not from dyspepsia or manic depression but from another family illness, conversion anxiety, as her father had been "addressing her conscience not 20 minutes before" the painful attack. Catharine had become engaged at the beginning of the year to Alexander Fisher, a brilliant scientist who had earned a Yale professorship at the young age of twenty-four. Fisher was sailing to England to visit European universities at the time of Catharine's April attack, and when he returned they were to marry. This meant that Catharine should experience conversion, for it was considered unlikely after marriage when worldly cares intervened. Thus her father put pressure on her, as he eventually did all his children, whom he loved dearly and never wished to see as sinners in the hands of an angry God.

Catharine resisted. She could not feel her own sin deeply enough and could not fully accept the concept of a God who got angry. When Fisher died in a shipwreck, she felt even more alienated from the Calvinist religion. He had never been saved and, according to her father, would spend his afterlife burning in Hell. Catharine wrote her brother Edward that it was not so much the "ruined hopes of a future life" that afflicted her as fear and apprehension for Fisher's immortal soul: "Oh, Edward, where is he now? Are the noble faculties of such a mind doomed to everlasting woe, or is he now with our dear mother in the mansions of the blessed?" A few months later she told her brother that the doctrine of original sin filled her with despair: "When I look at little Isabella, it seems a pity that she ever was born, and that it would be a mercy if she was taken away."

All this Calvinist doom and gloom might suggest that the Beecher sisters had bleak childhoods, but in general they recalled their early years as lively and happy. According to Marie Caskey, the shy Harriet had some "vaguely unhappy" memories of Litchfield "because she was made to feel unimportant in a crowded household," but the other girls were more social and enjoyed sibling visits and family events. As an adult visiting home, Isabella was more likely to complain when the house was *not* crowded. She recalled fondly the evening hymn singing and prayers, noting that "there is the strongest and most interesting combination in our family of fun and seriousness." The religious exercises were almost always leavened by humorous stories, practical jokes, and Lyman's old-time fiddle tunes; occasionally, he took off his shoes and danced in his socks, exhibiting the steps he learned as a boy before dancing was frowned on as too worldly.

Lyman Beecher's children denied the anti-Calvinist view of their father as the grim warden of a "Puritan penitentiary" who paid little attention to his offspring. There was Catharine's comment about his passionate love of children, along with Harriet's recollections of family fun. Harriet, one of the children who helped her father write his "autobiography" during old age when he had lost his memory, recalled the family tradition of the youngest child being sent to wake Lyman in the morning. This child would be told to "take him by the nose, and kiss him many times before the heaviness in his head would go off so that he could lift it."

> Oftentimes he would lie in bed after his little monitor had called him, professing fears that there was a lion under the bed who would catch his foot if he put it out, and requiring repeated and earnest assurances from the curly head that he should be defended from being eaten up if he rose; and often and earnestly the breakfast-bell would ring before he could be induced to launch forth. Great would be the pride of the little monitor, who led him at last gravely into the breakfast-room, and related in baby phrase the labors of getting him up.

In March 1826, when Isabella had just turned four, her father accepted a call to Boston and the Beechers moved. Again, Lyman's salary had not kept pace with the growth of his family. He also wanted to educate his sons, who, he explained to his Litchfield parishioners, he had promised God would be ministers of Christ. Unless he earned more money he would have to take his son George out of college. Lyman and Harriet P. had other reasons for preferring Boston. Harriet P. cheered up at the prospect of living near her relatives in a cultural center; Lyman was enthusiastic about battling the Unitarians in their own citadel, for ironically Boston had fallen away from its Puritan past and become an anti-Calvinist stronghold. Lyman felt that by his efforts "victory will be achieved, and Unitarianism cease to darken and pollute the land." The only Beecher affected at all negatively by the move to Boston was Isabella because she did not get to follow Catharine, Mary, and Harriet to the Litchfield Female Academy; even some of the boys—George, Henry, and Charles—had been allowed instruction from Miss Pierce and her most talented teacher, her nephew John Brace.

In 1826 Boston was a city of only fifty thousand and transportation was by stage, the railroads not yet having transformed the city. The Beechers took a "new, airy and delightful" house in the North End. Unlike the Litchfield house it had no rats scurrying around in the walls—as adults, all the Beecher sisters would remember Aunt Esther's famous rat stories. The location of the new house pleased Lyman greatly, as it bordered on the old Copp's Hill cemetery, wherein lay many of the Puritan founders. As Harriet P. put it dramatically, "This soil was pressed by the feet of the Pilgrims, and watered by their tears, and consecrated by their prayers. Here are their tombs, and here are their children who are to be brought back to the fold of Christ." The Beecher household was considerably smaller than at Litchfield. The oldest son, William, was at Andover, and Edward and George were in college at Yale. Catharine, Mary, and Harriet were residing in Hartford, Connecticut, with Aunt Esther heading the household. Only the four youngest children were at home: Henry (thirteen), Charles (eleven), Isabella (four), and Thomas (two).

The family outpost at Hartford dated from 1822, the year of Isabella's birth and Catharine's tragedy. Edward (born 1803), the second oldest son and the most scholarly of the Beechers, graduated from Yale as valedictorian of his class. Although he would stay only a year before leaving to train for the ministry, he took a position in 1822 as headmaster of the Hartford Grammar School. Unlike Catharine, he managed to convert ("Oh, my dear son," wrote Lyman, "*agonize* to enter in. You *must* go to heaven; you *must not* go to hell!"). Edward's position in Hartford was useful to Catharine when she decided to start a school for girls. Her father made it clear that she could not stay home but needed to earn money, and she must have thought of her mother's and Miss Pierce's schools. Edward helped her obtain pupils and tutored her in chemistry and Latin, for Catharine wanted her academy to be more intellectually respectable than a mere finishing school. The Hartford Female Seminary opened in May 1823, with Catharine as administrator and Mary, who had earned the highest grades of any of the Beechers at the Litchfield Female Academy, doing most of the teaching.

Although Catharine deliberately chose education as her vocation, it was simply one of the few choices available to women; she did not care for teaching, which she described to her father as "drudgery." Indeed, it could be argued that before Catharine found herself a renowned pioneer in American women's schooling she was simply devising an elaborate rationale for correcting the defects in her own education. She told her father that all the knowledge she possessed "has as it were, *walked into my head*, without any exertion to acquire or any care to arrange it." In addition to chemistry and Latin, she began to study logic, arithmetic, algebra, and geometry.

Catharine's school had a profound effect on all her sisters. She brought both Mary and Harriet to Hartford with her. The latter was only twelve when Catharine was put in charge of her education. Harriet had been an indifferent student overall at the Litchfield Female Academy but excelled in composition. She recalled in the family autobiography a time when one of her papers was read aloud and her father was gratified to learn she had written it. "It was the proudest moment of my life. There was no mistaking father's face when he was pleased, and to have interested *him* was past all juvenile triumphs." Harriet thus decided she wanted to be a poet, but at the Hartford Female Seminary Catharine demanded she give up writing blank verse to read exciting texts like *Analogy of Religion, Natural and Revealed, to the Constitution and Course of Nature*, by Joseph Butler. In Hartford Mary met Thomas Clap Perkins, a successful lawyer, and left the seminary in 1827 to marry him. Catharine then promoted Harriet to student teacher.

Isabella was too young to attend the Hartford Female Seminary when her sisters taught there. With the ill luck that plagued her educational efforts throughout her youth she in effect lost her older sisters, upon whom she depended for instruction, to the seminary. Isabella did have one significant educational experience in Boston, the only Boston memory she mentions in her short memoir, "The Last of the Beechers: Memories on My Eighty-Third Birthday." She notes that every Beecher child began singing soon after birth. She was sent to Lowell Mason's "first juvenile class in Boston and learned to sing by note about as soon as I had learned to read—blessed be his memory." Lowell Mason (1792–1872) was a music educator who would become the leading composer of church music in America. He published his first songbook, *The Boston Handel and Haydn Society Collection of Church Music*, in the year of Isabella's birth and probably started instructing her in 1827, when she turned five and he began to serve as organist and choir director at her father's Boston church. In return for the use of church facilities, Mason often taught free of charge, an arrangement that greatly suited Lyman Beecher.

Music was always a source of enjoyment and self-esteem for Isabella; she had an excellent voice and learned to accompany herself on both the piano and the guitar. Her music could gratify the one person a Beecher child wanted most to please—her father. On a family visit soon after her marriage, Isabella wrote her husband that she had sung for company and "my own father said to me in the afternoon, while I was playing, 'Belle I like your playing & singing better than any one's I have heard—it seems to come so spontaneously—& from the heart—as if it was composed & poured forth at the moment' & I was delighted." Isabella and her half brother Charles, seven years older, were the Beechers who were most serious about music (Charles once tried to pursue a career in church music). Both Catharine and Mary were also accomplished pianists, and Harriet loved to sing hymns.

When Isabella was in grammar school, at the time when the family might have been preparing to send her to the Hartford Female Seminary (Henry went at age eleven), the Beechers began to consider leaving the East. Although Lyman and Catharine were outwardly successful and growing in fame, they were both inwardly dissatisfied. The Hartford Female Seminary was a tremendous success, having expanded from a handful of students to several hundred. In place of the single rented classroom Catharine started with, there was a brand new building replete with ten rooms and Grecian-style pillars in front. The school ranked with Emma Willard's in Troy and Zilpah Grant's in Ipswich as one of the outstanding academies for women. Catharine's instructional staff had grown from one to eight, making her teaching duties less onerous. She had time to initiate in 1829–1830 the first Beecher campaign for a social cause, organizing a protest against the Cherokees' being driven out of Georgia. Yet she had not accomplished one of her major goals—creating a permanent endowment for the school and thus a secure financial base for herself. Mary Beecher Perkins's defection ended Catharine's briefly fulfilled dream of having her own household, and Catharine and Harriet were soon boarding with the Perkinses, Catharine in a "broken down" state. Isabella also spent a year living with her sisters there.

Lyman's situation was uncannily similar to Catharine's. In 1830 his church burned, the Boston Fire Department reportedly making no effort to save the building. An oft-repeated Lyman Beecher anecdote holds that the day after the fire "as the church committee met glumly in Pierce's Bookstore, in skipped Beecher and, referring to the jug-shaped steeple, blithely announced, 'Well, my jug's broke; just been to see it,' and proceeded to encourage the members to build a new church." But building a new church meant another strenuous fundraising campaign and fewer chances of Beecher's improving his always faltering personal finances. Unitarianism had not been defeated in Boston and there were increasing doctrinal controversies, causing rifts among New England's Calvinists. By July Lyman was thinking about the West and writing Catharine that he contemplated "going over to Cincinnati, the London of the West, to spend the remnants of my days in that great conflict, and in consecrating all my children to God in that region who are willing to go." The "great conflict" was between Protestants and Catholics for the soul of the West, as Lyman had already rationalized the move; in his usual manner he dramatized it also: "If we gain the West, all is safe; if we lose it, all is lost."

It seemed a good omen that family members had already started moving to the Ohio valley. Uncles John and Samuel Foote, Roxana's brothers, were living in Cincinnati, and in December 1830 Edward Beecher left his church in Boston to become president of the new Illinois College in Jacksonville, Illinois. When the trustees of the Lane Theological Seminary of Cincinnati offered Lyman the presidency of the newly organized school, he was eager to accept as soon as he could fulfill his obligations in Boston. In spring 1832 Lyman and Catharine visited Cincinnati to explore it as a place to settle. The city, founded only a few decades earlier and now boasting a population of thirty thousand, still had rough edges: the riverfront was tough and squalid, and pigs roamed the streets. Uncle Samuel, a sophisticated former sea captain who had traveled the world, thought Cincinnati a beautiful city, however, and beauty was what Lyman and Catharine were determined to see (Catharine had resigned from the Hartford Female Seminary *before* the trip).

Catharine wrote Harriet that Walnut Hills, the site of Lane Seminary, some two miles from the city, was "very beautiful and picturesque" and "so elevated and cool that people have to come away to be sick and die, it is said." Already planning her new school, Catharine confided that she had met the local ladies and found them intelligent. Cincinnati, she thought, wrongly as it would turn out, was a New England sort of city. The Second Church, she told Harriet in conclusion, would invite Lyman to be their minister; they understood that he would give them the time he could spare from the seminary.

The Beechers moved from Boston to Cincinnati in October and November 1832. Although most Cincinnati residents no longer considered themselves "pioneers," the trip West was still a long and heroic production. Several of the Beecher children described it later in life, and the trip dominates Isabella's short account of her childhood. Nine of the family made the journey: Lyman and Harriet Porter Beecher, Aunt Esther, Catharine, George, Harriet, Isabella, and the two youngest brothers, Thomas and James. "Noah, and his wife, and his sons, and his daughters, with the cattle and creeping things," wrote Harriet. (Mary remained in Hartford with her husband, while the older boys were employed or in college.) Isabella describes the journey thus: "We went to Philadelphia, and were all quartered on the town somewhere for a week, as missionaries bound to a foreign land. . . . After a week in Philadelphia we chartered a big, old-fashioned stage, with four great horses, for Wheeling, Virginia, and spent a week or more on the way, crossing the Alleghenies, before even a railroad was thought of, and enjoyed every minute of the way. At least we children did, with brother George on the box shouting out the stories he got from various drivers, and leading us all in singing hymns and songs. . . . Arrived at Wheeling, we were distributed again for a week, because the Ohio River was so low no boat could be had." And because, the adults were informed, Cincinnati was enduring an outbreak of cholera. It appeared that people could die there after all.

The Beechers first lived inside the city while their house in outlying Walnut Hills was being built next to the seminary. At age eighty-three Isabella remembered settling into a comfortable house in town, but her sister Harriet described it at the time as "the most inconvenient, ill-arranged, good-for-nothing, and altogether to be execrated affair that ever was put together." The kitchen could not be reached from anywhere in the house without going outside first, and since it was November Harriet P. had to put on her coat and hat every time she entered the kitchen. Harriet Porter Beecher's feelings on having to leave her beloved Boston for this crude outpost might be compared to Elizabeth Cady Stanton's a decade later when she and her husband left Boston for western New York. In her autobiography Stanton notes that as a young wife and mother in Boston she met all the famous thinkers and "attended all the lectures, churches, theaters, concerts, and temperance, peace, and prison-reform conventions within my reach. I had never lived in such enthusiastically literary and reform latitude before, and my mental powers were kept at the highest tension." But in Seneca Falls, New York, her situation was comparatively isolated and depressing, as her husband was away much of the time and she became responsible for an increasing number of children and household duties. Stanton's "general discontent . . . with woman's portion as wife, mother, housekeeper, physician, and spiritual guide" led to a historic meeting in Seneca Falls in 1848. Harriet Porter Beecher must have worn the demeanor Stanton resented, "the wearied, anxious look of the majority of women." But Harriet's protest was purely personal: she sank further into melancholy and ill health.

Near the end of 1833 the Beechers moved into the newly built president's house adjoining the seminary at Walnut Hills. This house *was* comfortable, a two-story brick building with a long "L" running back into a grove of beech, black oak, and elm trees. The yard offered flower and vegetable gar-

Beecher home at Walnut Hills, Ohio. Courtesy Harriet Beecher Stowe Center, Hartford, Conn.

dens, chickens, and a barn complete with horse and cow. In her memoir Isabella recalled "the magnificent . . . forest trees that ran between us and the Seminary." One of her favorite pastimes was "to climb to the very top of one and another of these trees and sway with the branches in a heavy wind." The only disadvantage of living close to nature was Lyman's fondness for shooting living things. He always kept a double-barreled shotgun in his study, loaded and ready for use, and "once when a great flock of pigeons, with a mighty rush, lighted on our great forest trees, I ran out to enjoy the sport with him and when he brought down five at first shot I hastened to pick them up— but oh the revulsion of feeling, when those tender eyes looked up to mine! I dropped the birds, and have always hated guns ever since, and never could understand why the masculine race could call hunting a sport."

Isabella was able to attend school at her sisters' new academy, the Western Female Institute, which opened in spring 1833. Catharine and Harriet were supposed to be associate principals and Mary Dutton, a talented teacher whom Catharine enticed from the Hartford Female Seminary, would do most of the actual instruction. Harriet was soon pressed into teaching, however. Isabella remembered that she did so "with a quiet fervor that was most attractive," but Harriet herself was ambivalent. She believed in Catharine's mission—"to turn over the West by means of *model schools*," but teaching consumed too much of her life. She wrote a friend that "my school duties take up *all* my time—so that I cannot visit much nor read for amusement or write half what I wish to." Harriet did publish *Geography for Children* (1833), with Catharine's name added to the title page, and she joined her older sister in the Semi-Colon Club, a literary society that met once a week to critique the members' compositions. Gradually Harriet branched out to publish tales and sketches in various periodicals. Her "A New England Sketch" (1834) announced her lifelong subject matter and won a prize of fifty dollars.

But the most influential learning that the Beecher sisters experienced in Cincinnati came not from the Western Female Institute or the Semi-Colon Club but from the family dinner table. The new Beecher household was a large one numbering thirteen, with the original nine who traveled from Boston, two female servants, one Welsh and one Irish, and brothers Henry and Charles, who had graduated from college and entered Lane Seminary. The children who wrote Lyman's "autobiography" called life at Walnut Hills "an exuberant and glorious life while it lasted." The atmosphere of the household was "replete with moral oxygen—full charged with intellectual electricity. Nowhere else have we felt anything resembling or equaling it." In his account of the Beechers, Milton Rugoff questions this "rhapsodic tribute," noting brother Thomas's description of long, long discussions, lasting until midnight and resumed at every meal, of such topics as "free agency" and "sovereignty." Rugoff sees these discussions as "theological indoctrination" leading to the Beechers' ailments: he notes that after a visit in 1833 a Foote relative wrote that Catharine had a "bilious fever" and George had dyspepsia "all the time dreadfully. Mrs. Beecher is always sick and Aunt Esther is suffering from a sore mouth . . . and they all have nerves."

The theological arguments were not always so deadly serious, though. One, saved for posterity, was in the form of a "circular" or round-robin letter, a type the Beechers started sending in fall 1833 to keep Mary, William, and Edward in the family loop. This letter, written in 1836, begins with Charles criticizing George's doctrine of "perfectionism"—can a Christian really be perfect? Next Edward's wife, Isabella Jones Beecher, describes the dying agonies of her little daughter and reminds the family that she and Edward have lost three of six children; Henry goes back to the doctrine of perfectionism—he really doesn't care either way; Harriet, whom one suspects of mockery, asks George what soil is best for planting dahlias; Catharine (characteristically) sets down rules—no one can delay a circular letter longer than a week; Lyman begs William to write; Calvin Stowe, who was teaching at Lane Seminary, returns to the doctrine of perfectionism; and George thanks his brothers for their advice.

The theological disputes—about free will, regeneration, heaven, and hell—were interspersed with discussions of political and social questions, such as "the United States Constitution, fugitive slave laws, Henry Clay and [the] Missouri Compromise." Isabella states directly that "I date my interest in public affairs from those few years between eleven and sixteen, when our family circle was ever in discussion on the vital problems of human existence." In the 1830s in New England the question of slavery could seem as remote and abstract as Christian perfectionism; but the Ohio River separated "North" and "South," and just one trip from Cincinnati into Kentucky furnished Harriet with key scenes for *Uncle Tom's Cabin*.

When the Beechers had been in Ohio slightly over a year, they found themselves in the midst of their own battle over slavery. The instigator was Theodore Weld, a student leader of the first class of forty seminarians at Lane. When Lyman Beecher and Calvin Stowe were in the East raising funds for the seminary, Weld, an eloquent speaker, organized an eighteen-day "meeting" to debate the slavery issue. After nine days devoted to the abolitionist stance and nine to colonization, or returning the slaves to Africa, the students voted against colonization and for immediate abolition. The conservative trustees of the seminary were outraged and changed the school rules, prohibiting meetings and abolitionist societies. Upon his return Lyman "found all in a flurry." He felt that if he had arrived earlier, he could have effected a compro mise, but it was too late. The recalcitrant students left Lane and were eventually accepted at a new department of theology at Oberlin College. Lane's reputation suffered and in the next few years its classes averaged only five students.

Isabella described this Lane incident in her memoir as having broken her father's heart, "for he loved the young men as if they were his own sons" and had great hopes of what they could do in evangelizing the West; he declared Weld and Henry B. Stanton to be the most gifted young men he had ever known: "I can see him now, joining them in the little log house just opposite ours—pleading, remonstrating, with tears and almost with groans. I was but a child, but was in such sympathy with his distress that I never could forgive the young men for departing from such a loving guide and friend." The family autobiography also highlights Lyman's misery and interprets the event as an instance of Lyman's being caught between radical students and conservative trustees. It must be said, however, that Lyman Beecher would inevitably have come in conflict with Weld because he was never an abolitionist. The basic Beecher family position, held by all the most famous Beechers, was against slavery but not for abolition. Slavery should not be extended into the territories but should be allowed to die out gradually; colonization was one way of accomplishing this. Abolition was too radical— would inflame the South and inevitably lead to violence.

Catharine argued this position in her *Essay on Slavery and Abolitionism with Reference to the Duty of American Females* (1837). Ever since she had become known as an educator of women and had published books on education—*Suggestions Respecting Improvements in Education* (1829) and *An Essay on the Education of Female Teachers* (1835)—Catharine was accepted as a commentator on national affairs. In another version of the Beecher–Weld conflict she addressed her essay on slavery to Angelina Grimké, the Quaker abolitionist who would soon marry Theodore Weld. Grimké wrote back a series of letters published first in newspapers and then in book form as *Letters to Catherine [sic] E. Beecher* (1838). Grimké defended abolitionist tactics and theory on the basis of natural rights, that of slaves to their persons and women "to have a voice in all the laws and regulations by which she is to be governed." The "duty of American females" was not, as Catharine Beecher thought, to exercise their moral influence in the home but the same as the duty of American males—to end slavery. Grimké considered colonization a direct result of race prejudice: "Surely you never want to 'get rid' of people whom you *love*." But even as late as 1852 Harriet Beecher Stowe would disappoint her abolitionist readers by sending runaway slave George Harris to Africa at the end of *Uncle Tom's Cabin*.

As a teenager Isabella adhered to the Beecher family position on slavery, but the seeds were sown then for her conversion to abolition as she entered womanhood. In the mid-1830s there were not only the arguments rehearsed by the seminarians but also the views of the three oldest Beecher brothers, William, Edward, and George, who all insisted on joining abolitionist societies. William firmly rejected his father's advice that he wait and not commit himself as a partisan on either side of the issue. Lyman assured William that if he were patient, the abolition of slavery would eventually come about. He aired his fear that his sons would become "he-goat men," those "who think they do God service by butting every thing in the line of their march which does not fall in or get out of the way. They are . . . made up of vinegar, aqua fortis, and oil of vitriol, with brimstone, salt petre, and charcoal, to explode and scatter the corrosive matter." At about the same time, Edward switched from the colonizationist to the abolitionist position and the year after Catharine's *Essay on Slavery* published his very different *Narrative of Riots at Alton [Illinois]*, an eyewitness account of the mob shooting of an abolitionist editor. It was Edward's wife, Isabella, who suggested to Harriet that if she had her writing talent she would depict the sufferings of the slaves.

Just a few weeks before Lyman Beecher wrote his son William about the "he-goat men," he was himself being tried for heresy in Cincinnati (thus perhaps giving rise to the comparison of abolitionists to exploding theologians). The trouble had begun as soon as the Beechers arrived, when a Dr.

Wilson, who had been on the hiring committee, decided the committee had made a mistake and employed a dangerous radical (though, of course, many thought Lyman a dangerous conservative). The main issue was the same over which Lyman and Catharine had clashed—original sin, only in this case Lyman was accused of being soft on human depravity and implying that sinners might use their free will to save themselves. People said Dr. Wilson resembled Andrew Jackson, but he was no match for Lyman Beecher.

Although Beecher's trial before the Presbytery must have been stressful, it is hard to avoid the conclusion that he enjoyed the fight. The trial took place in his church, where he gathered all his books and sat on a stair of the pulpit. "I looked so quiet and meek, my students were almost afraid I shouldn't come up to the mark. . . . But when I had all my references, and had nothing to do but extemporize, I felt easy. I had as much lawyer about me as Wilson, and more. I never got into a corner, and he never got out." The young Isabella remembered the trial as an incomprehensible spectacle: "[W]ell do I remember sitting in the choir gallery of the church listening to the jolly comments of young men and maidens, led by my brother Henry, all on the proceedings below. It seemed a strange thing to me, even then, that ministers of the Gospel should be found fighting such a good man as my father, and I have never changed my mind."

The next important event for the Beecher sisters was the death of Harriet Porter Beecher in July 1835, just weeks after Lyman had been acquitted. Although Lyman hinted that he thought the heresy charges caused her death, it seems that Harriet P.'s health had been declining for some time. When they first arrived in Cincinnati, she shared the household duties with Aunt Esther and helped supervise the servants hired to assist with student boarders; but gradually she sank to her bed. The account in the Beecher family autobiography does not mention the cause of Harriet P.'s death at age forty-four— consumption again—but rather implies that she died of gloom: "Constitutionally less inclined than some to look on the bright side of things, her mind had been gradually losing that elasticity and brilliancy which was the charm of her early youth," and she was "dimmed by a melancholy depression of spirit." This report, written by Harriet, inappropriately includes a long description from a letter by Harriet Porter Beecher describing the death the year before of her friend Eliza Stowe, Calvin's first wife. The effect is to contrast the good behavior of Eliza, who greeted death joyously, with the somber parting of Harriet, who "shivered" as she entered the valley of the shadow of death.

The portrayal of Harriet Porter Beecher as cold and rejecting, as well as melancholy, originated with Harriet. She initiated the kind of oppositional thinking she and brother Henry always used in regard to their stepmother when she concluded the description quoted earlier of the advent of a beautiful woman with auburn hair in a black velvet bandeau: "The next morning, I remember, we looked at her with awe. She seemed to us so fair, so delicate, so elegant, that we were almost afraid to go near her. We must have been rough, red-cheeked, hearty country children, honest, obedient, and bashful. She was peculiarly dainty and neat in all her ways and arrangements; and I remember I used to feel breezy, and rough, and rude in her presence. We felt a little in awe of her, as if she were a strange princess, rather than our own mamma." "We" undoubtedly means Henry and her, for the older boys reacted positively to Harriet Porter. Henry Ward Beecher would always speak bitterly of his stepmother: "She was polished; but to my young thoughts she was cold. As I look back I do not recollect ever to have had from her one breath of summer. Although I was longing to love somebody, she did not call forth my affection." Henry continually contrasted her with a much idealized image of his birth mother.

What Isabella thought of her mother's death and her siblings' reaction is hard to determine, for she was so affected as seldom to be able to talk about her mother directly. Even in her memoir, written seventy years after Harriet P.'s death, she approaches the event obliquely, noting that her mother's death led ultimately to her being sent back to New England, and "that was the last of my living at home with my father." The emphasis here is squarely on the father. Isabella did later record a recurrent dream about her mother—that she was alive and Isabella was prevented from seeing her. "Forbidden" is the word she uses, though she does not say by whom. It may be that Isabella felt constrained to separate from her mother's example in order to develop herself as a real person. Milton Rugoff characterizes Harriet Porter Beecher's life as "a shadow life, the remote, passionless, resigned existence characteristic of many of the daughters of upper-class New England families of the nineteenth century." She was fit only for the life of a daughter in the type of family she grew up in: she had a difficult time handling "sexual love, children, a household not amply staffed, or any of the world's work that a woman might do." It could not have helped Isabella see her mother as anything more than a shadow that Lyman often forgot about her. After her death he frequently referred to Roxana Foote Beecher as though she were also the mother of his second family.

Harriet Porter Beecher left Isabella her books and dresses, plus a more lasting legacy, a letter written to Isabella when she was seven. The letter was formally presented to Isabella by Aunt Esther on her fourteenth birthday, a half year after her mother's death. According to Isabella, her mother entrusted her two younger brothers to her care (the letter was written when the youngest Beecher, James, was a year old and Harriet perhaps felt she had fulfilled her earthly responsibilities and might die any time). Although Isabella was touched to have a token of her mother's regard, the letter also proved to be a source of pain. Isabella felt, in her words, "haunted with the thought of her anxieties for us—& the responsibility that she laid on me in regard to my brothers." The responsibility did not come with any corresponding power, and both brothers, Thomas and James, were exceedingly odd and troubled, even for Beechers; Thomas would settle down after a restless youth, but James committed suicide in his fifties. Isabella confessed to Aunt Esther, "I have cried & cried again & again, over that letter of my mother's, that you gave me on my fourteenth birthday."

Isabella thought her younger brothers did not feel the same sense of "deprivation" she did at her mother's death because of their relative youth. But they loved her memory and Isabella "as her representative as well as their sister." Interestingly, the boys felt more acutely their separate status as Lyman's second family; they did not consider the older half siblings their true brothers and sisters. This may have been in part the result of the older Beechers having left home before Thomas and James were born. When Lyman succeeded in getting all eleven children to Cincinnati in summer 1835, after his trial and bereavement, some children had never met each other before. Mary, for instance, had met Thomas only once and had never seen James; James was born in 1828, the same year as her oldest son, Frederick. Isabella had a very different attitude, much more conciliatory than that of her brothers. It may have stemmed from her gender and the need to identify with her sisters. She revered her older half siblings as she did her father, and if she felt out of touch with someone, as happened with William, the oldest brother, she visited and got to know him better.

To a certain extent, though, Isabella's mother's letter consigned her to a separate family, and her father's quick remarriage reinforced this effect. Again he hardly managed to wait the expected year before traveling to Boston for a new wife. In summer 1836 Lyman returned to Cincinnati with Lydia Jackson, a widow, and her two children Joseph and Margaret (her older children had already married). Lydia was a "fine looking woman," in Catharine's words, and by all accounts more energetic than Harriet Porter Beecher. But this does not mean that Catharine approved. She soon quarreled with the latest stepmother to the point where she felt she couldn't come home to visit; Harriet later complained to Catharine that Lydia "never loved or trusted us." Isabella tried to get along with Joseph and Margaret but followed her sisters' example in blaming her stepmother for attitudes and decisions that were more likely her father's, such as the early end to her education.

After her mother's death, Isabella continued to attend Catharine's Western Female Institute, boarding during the week in downtown Cincinnati.

There were three terms of fourteen weeks each and four teachers in the school—Mary Dutton and Elizabeth Lyman, both of whom Catharine had hired from Hartford; Anne Tappan, who taught composition; and Harriet Beecher. In 1835 Isabella studied geography, arithmetic, Latin, English grammar, spelling, composition, and penmanship; she also took piano lessons and sang in the choir. She worked hard, striving and usually succeeding in being "perfect" in her recitations. Still, the schoolgirl compositions she saved show no evidence of sister Harriet's writing talent. They are awkward and stilted, as in her description of a scene "where from joy to joy the raptured eye hurries, and is hid beneath the fair protrusion which yellow Autumn spies." By the end of the year the first difficulties with the school were appearing, and Ms. Dutton wrote Catharine complaining of a dearth of teachers. "It is out of the question," she added, "for Harriet to stay in school any longer—she is so bent on matrimony." In February 1836 Harriet indeed married Calvin Stowe, whom she had gotten to know through their mutual mourning of his first wife.

The Western Female Institute moved along without Harriet, but in 1836 the main problem became low enrollment rather than lack of teachers. Catharine, in a bitter letter to the editor of the Cincinnati *Gazette*, blamed the city for educational backwardness and lack of interest in educating its daughters. But as her biographer has pointed out, other female academies in the area were thriving: "Catharine's school failed because she alienated her constituency" by her aggressive manners, New England chauvinism, and transparent social climbing. She tried and failed, for instance, to gain the backing of the Cincinnati aristocrat Edward King, who was distantly related to Harriet Porter Beecher. He wrote his wife to "Tell Catharine Beecher" that she was a guest and not a "director" in their home. Furthermore, he objected to the idea of "*cousin*," as he sarcastically called her, urging Cincinnati to imitate the superior education of the Yankees. This time the leading citizens not only refused to contribute to the fund Catharine set up to endow the Western Female Institute but also failed to send their daughters to the school.

One of Isabella's occasional assignments as a composition student of Anne Tappan was to keep a journal, which revealed a marked change in attitude toward school from 1835 to 1837. As Isabella entered adolescence, she became increasingly dissatisfied and critical of her oldest sister's school:

> Monday morning—rose early—studied my Geography Lesson until 7, 7 to 8 ate my breakfast & prepared for school—Took a pie Sally made me for luncheon—enjoyed it very much. Like to have been ran over by a bakers cart. Arrived at school just before the ringing of the second bell. Came very near missing my Geogra-

phy lesson after all my study—did not however. Was perfect in all my lessons during the day—learned nothing new except some dry facts in Philosophy. Tired of school wish it was vacation. . . . did not study any in the afternoon or evening—went to bed early. Slept soundly—dreamed of long lessons & bad marks.

By Friday of that week Isabella was piqued at having been scolded by "prosaical people" for laughing too much in class and decided to skip school. "The Spirit of Rebellion," as she now entitled a composition, seemed to be breaking out in her—if the long lessons weren't shortened, she and her friends would refuse to study.

This did not mean, however, that Isabella wanted to see the lessons end altogether. In her last composition written in Cincinnati, "Retrospective View of the W.F. Institute," Isabella sounds distressed that the school was closing. The Panic of 1837 finished it off, as hundreds of banks failed and even Uncle Samuel Foote went bankrupt. Catharine and Harriet were not unhappy to see the end of the Western Female Institute. Harriet did not want to teach again, even if she could (women were expected to give up teaching when they married). Catharine thought the institute had plagued her more than "all I suffered in Hartford." But the fifteen-year-old Isabella had a problem—how and where could she finish her education? Years later, as a thirty-seven-year-old wife and mother, she read an anonymous article in the *Atlantic Monthly* entitled "Ought Women to Learn the Alphabet?" This essay, by abolitionist and women's rights advocate Thomas Wentworth Higginson, prompted Isabella to pour out years of buried resentment over her truncated education to a Hartford friend and neighbor. She would rather have written these pages than any other she ever read: "There's not a vital thought there, but I have had for my own, and spoken it too, in a whisper and in my blundering way and it is only my lack of this very Alphabet that has given this favored mortal (man or woman is it?) such a precedence before the world."

She could have said everything in the article, and just as skillfully too, Isabella went on, if she had had a boy's training. "At fifteen my dear good father (instigated of course by his new wife) came to me and suggested that I should begin to teach school now and support myself. I, who had never been to school in earnest, for two years together in my whole life." After being granted one year ("one blessed year") at the Hartford Female Seminary, her education came to an end. "At sixteen and a half, just when my brothers began their mental education, mine was finished. . . . Till twenty three, their father, poor minister as he was could send them to College and Seminary all *six*—cost what it might, but never a daughter cost him a hundred dollars a year, after she was sixteen."

Such a direct criticism of her father was unprecedented for a Beecher daughter, and of course Isabella tries to deflect some of the blame onto her stepmother. She had come to think of Lyman Beecher as "filling the place of my own mother." Following Catharine's lead, she said she never knew a man so nurturing, one who exhibited toward his children all the tenderness a mother would. A description of the 1835 family reunion by a family friend gives the same impression: "When the children gathered, the old doctor was almost transported with joy." He tried to pray but could only weep, as the children joined hands and sang hymns. Edward preached in his father's pulpit in the morning, William in the afternoon, and George in the evening. Monday they assembled in a circle while Lyman made an "affecting speech" and gave each a farewell kiss.

But he was also a patriarch, as shown by the choice of Edward and the not very successful William and George to preach. Why not Catharine, who was the only Beecher child nationally known in 1835? But Lyman was always conservative when it came to "woman's place." Not for him the innovations of the great revivalist preacher Charles Grandison Finney, who allowed women to pray in public. "[A] greater evil, next to the loss of conscience and chastity, could not befall the female sex," Lyman intoned. "[No] well educated female can put herself up . . . to the point of public prayer, without the loss of some portion at least of that female delicacy, which is above all price."

Lyman's sexism caused difficulties for the three of his four daughters who aspired to public careers. Much of the animosity that Catharine inspired, both inside and outside her family, stemmed from the ban on women speaking in public and conducting their own business affairs. If she was manipulative, as all the brothers and brothers-in-law complained, it was partly because she had to have men as committee members and spokespeople for her causes. The same rules that gave Calvin Stowe a welcome share of Harriet's *Uncle Tom's Cabin* limelight, as he had to deliver speeches and negotiate contracts for her, enraged him when Catharine pushed him into serving as figurehead president of one of her educational organizations. He fulminated to Harriet, "Cate has neither conscience nor sense—if you consent to take half a pound, she will throw a ton on to your shoulders, and run off and leave you, saying— *it isn't heavy—it isn't heavy at all, you can carry it with perfect ease.*" He would never do business with her again, any more than he would with the Devil. Catharine's half brother Thomas felt much the same way after he had escorted her around the country on a speaking tour delivering her public lectures "as a kind of live marionette."

Harriet was eleven years Catharine's junior, enough younger to be less hampered by the traditional restrictions against women speaking in public; she would even go on the lecture circuit in the 1870s. But her reminiscences of childhood are full of wistful accounts of differential treatment, of waiting impatiently for her brothers to return from hunting and fishing excursions and other adventures with her father. Although she wasn't allowed to chop wood, she could pile it up and was "sucked into the vortex of enthusiasm by father's well-pointed declaration that he 'wished Harriet was a boy, she would do more than any of them.'" Interestingly, Isabella included in her indictment of her education the physical, as well as mental, training she received. She had gained whatever physical strength she had, she told her friend, "only thro' a determined preference, for boy's games and out door sports, that added not at all to my general reputation." At least Isabella and Harriet had the benefit in this respect of Catharine's ideas on physical education, which she had learned from Miss Pierce. Isabella took a course in calisthenics at the Western Female Institute and was encouraged to spend time outdoors. Catharine was a skilled horsewoman and insisted that her sisters ride, as well as walk, for exercise.

If Isabella exaggerated the deficiencies of her physical education, she did not exaggerate when it came to academics. Some writers on the Beechers have implied or stated that Isabella's truncated education was her own fault. Rugoff, for instance, suggests that when Isabella complained, "she was conveniently forgetting how many less serious interests she had when she was fifteen years old." One might also mention her mysterious headaches and other maladies that seemed to arise when it was time to study. But Isabella's main point is well taken, that her father *expected* all his sons to get a good education and whipped them into shape until they did. Six of the seven Beecher sons graduated from college and seminary. The only exception was the oldest, William, who lacked the scholastic aptitude; Lyman had to pull strings to get him licensed to preach. If the boys lost motivation, did poorly in school, or became ill, as all but Edward sometimes did, their father might approve a break from school, but the goal of graduation was never relaxed, any more than its twin, conversion. Sometimes the boys rebelled. Both George and James were suspended from college, and Charles lost his faith and left seminary. But all the boys ultimately finished their educations, and the fact that every one became a minister shows whose plan they were consciously or unconsciously following. As one writer says of Lyman Beecher, "He valued boys immeasurably more than girls because they could grow up to be ministers."

It could be argued of the Beecher sisters that the very constraints of their educations pushed them into pioneering new vocations for women in education, literature, and women's rights. However that may be, Catharine, Harriet, and Isabella were all adversely affected by their lack of intellectual training. As teachers, Catharine and Harriet were usually only a few lessons ahead of their students, and after they became famous, they sometimes seemed lacking in culture to people they wanted to impress, such as parents of prospective students and the Europeans Harriet met on her trips. Although some of this difficulty was class-based—Catharine and Harriet were "middle-brow" partly because they were middle class—a college education would have prepared them better for their leadership roles. Literary critics have always complained of Harriet's disinterest in aesthetics and lack of intellectual curiosity. As for Isabella, the early end to her education damaged her self-confidence and ability to act in the world. She needed to wait many years before she could do more than whisper. The "bare bones" of the argument in "Ought Women to Learn the Alphabet?" had been in her mind for a long time. Had she been able to clothe them "with the flesh and drapery of historic literature as this Author has done (he is a man I think, by his gallantry and alas! by his learning) you might have seen something more than a skeleton."

Educated or not, Isabella would eventually follow her older sisters onto the public stage. If her father valued boys more than girls and accepted the gender conventions of his day, how did three of his four daughters manage to circumvent those conventions and become atypical women? The answer would seem to lie in the customs and values governing the Beecher family circle. The "electricity" that sparked the family dinner table was competition. If Catharine had not been the oldest child, the girls might have been silenced, but as it was, she participated from the beginning and the younger girls had to be given a turn. Yes, Lyman valued boys but what he esteemed most was excellence and achievement. Harriet learned early on that she could attract her father's attention with a well-written paper. Lyman's behavior in regard to Catharine's first school is also instructive. It was he who pushed her into the Hartford Female Seminary project in the first place and he who warned her to take it seriously: "I should be ashamed to have you open, and keep only a commonplace, middling sort of school. It is expected to be of a higher order; and, unless you are willing to put your talents and strength into it, it would be best not to begin." In other words, Lyman Beecher's daughters were disadvantaged in being girls, who could not be ministers—but this was no excuse for becoming commonplace and middling. The Beecher sisters had to show that they were "of a higher order."

2

Marriage and Motherhood,
1837–1852

ISABELLA BEECHER DID GET the one more year of education she asked her father for at the Hartford Female Seminary, the school Catharine had founded. Her father's original plan was for Isabella to teach and study at a school in Batavia, Ohio, where George was preaching. George had married Sarah Buckingham, a woman from a well-to-do family who offered to board Isabella. After the girl arrived in Batavia, it turned out that the school had no openings. Harriet intervened on her sister's behalf; as a middle child she often acted as negotiator between parent and sibling or between older and younger siblings. She wrote Lyman that the best place for Isabella was the Perkinses in Hartford, where Mary and Aunt Esther could watch over her. Harriet used an argument well suited to persuading her father—that Cincinnati was "exerting a very deletirious [sic] influence" on Isabella's character. "She is very much I think under the influence of companions with whom dress and accoutrement are the absorbing topics and who may lead her farther and farther from all serious and profitable habits." George agreed, and Isabella promised to study hard and help Mary, who now had four children. Thus it was that Isabella went to join Mary in Hartford, Connecticut. Years later Harriet would follow and Catharine would be a constant visitor.

When Isabella arrived at the Perkins home in Hartford, the household was in turmoil. Mary Perkins and her husband, Thomas, were generally thought of as well-to-do and refined people, Thomas earning a good living from his law practice. Angelina Grimké, on a visit to the Hartford Female Seminary in 1831, characterized the Perkinses in her diary as "very genteel" and "quite the gentleman & lady in their deportment." If there is a touch of disapproval in the description, Grimké was a Quaker and plain woman. Angelina admired Mary's organization of the household. Though twelve students as well as Catharine and Harriet were boarding in 1831, the house was "as quiet as though there were neither young children nor boarders in it." But the Panic of 1837 hit Hartford as well as Cincinnati. Thomas Perkins, who

Mary Beecher Perkins. Courtesy Schlesinger Library, Radcliffe Institute, Harvard University.

was a speculator and had failed financially several times in life, had to turn over his assets to his creditors—assets that included not only land, Aunt Esther reported, but also the parlor furniture and Mary's piano. As the servants were reduced from "two girls and a man" to "one girl and no man," Isabella's advent was timely.

Being Beechers, Mary and Isabella were used to financial reversals, and Isabella's time at the seminary and the Perkins home was a happy one. Thomas Perkins was the first man she liked almost as much as her father and brothers, and Mary she loved devotedly. "Oh what a sister—she has been to me," she wrote. She had come to revere the Christian life she felt Mary was leading and hoped her own character would improve under her influence. The Beechers thought it did, for one of the first things Isabella achieved in Hartford, in the first few months of 1838, was conversion. She lacked her most important religious mentor, sister Harriet, who had given her a "sacred" gift for her twelfth birthday, a "charming little English edition of the Bible" that Isabella preferred to all others; Harriet had been her sister's religious teacher at the Western Female Institute, and Isabella always felt, even during their later estrangement, that Harriet was the most truly religious person she knew.

But being separated from Harriet meant being separated from their father and the hectoring interrogations to which he had subjected Catharine and the other children over the state of their souls. Isabella was treated comparatively gently by Mary, Aunt Esther, and the Rev. Joel Hawes, pastor of the First Church of Hartford and the Perkins family minister. Instead of questioning her, Mary sent encouraging notes. Brother Thomas wrote often, and brother Charles, who was having his own conversion problem, counseled his sister to be humble and depend on God. Isabella felt that her own efforts amounted to little. She had sought Christ unsuccessfully, she later told a friend, but "all at once He seemed to descend into my consciousness & I could no more ignore his presence than I could my own." Fortunately for her, she was able to convince Reverend Hawes of her sincerity—he had questioned the genuineness of Harriet's conversion at age thirteen because of her youth. An exultant letter arrived from Lyman Beecher: the news of his youngest daughter's salvation "rendered the goodness of God like the bursting out from darkness of an effulgent sun." He wept with joy.

As her year at the Hartford Female Seminary came to an end, Isabella met her husband-to-be, John Hooker, a clerk in Thomas Perkins's law office. John was a well-educated and progressive man six years older than Isabella. His father, Edward Hooker, had a large farm in the pretty town of Farmington, Connecticut, near Hartford. According to John in his autobiography, *Some Reminiscences of a Long Life* (1899), Edward Hooker was the fifth in direct descent from Thomas Hooker, the author of the first written constitution and founder of Connecticut. John's mother, Eliza Daggett, was related to more than one governor of Connecticut, and John had a younger brother, Edward, and a sister, Eliza. After attending the district school until he was ten, the oldest son of Edward Hooker then entered the well-regarded Farmington Academy. He also received private instruction from his father, a Yale graduate, "who was a rare classical scholar for that day, and who began to drill me in Latin and Greek at quite an early age." John went to Yale at age sixteen but was taken ill with typhoid fever midway through his college career. His efforts to study hard and catch up with his class caused an eye injury that forced him to discontinue his studies. Yale later granted him a degree, listing his name with his graduating class in 1837.

Prevented from using his eyes in close work, John did something more adventurous than his mild character would suggest but not uncommon for nineteenth-century New Englanders—he went to sea. His first voyage was on a ship bound to Spain for wine and fruit. Soon after his return in 1836 he shipped on board the *Marblehead* sailing from New York to Canton, China. This voyage lasted over a year and provided John with stories for a lifetime, including an instance of the ship's being boarded by pirates. Hooker then finished out a friend's term teaching at the Farmington Academy and began to study law with Thomas Perkins. According to Isabella's memoir, she and John got engaged soon after they met, before she turned seventeen (in February 1839), whether or not her family knew about the engagement then. The couple reached an understanding that if either of them decided they had made a mistake, they could break the engagement without recriminations.

In August 1839 Isabella left the Perkins household to visit her brothers in central New York and then go home to Cincinnati. She planned to return to Mary's but in the event was reluctant to leave her "aged father" (who, at age sixty-four, was a decade away from retirement from Lane). For the next nearly two years, until Isabella returned to Hartford to prepare for marrying John, the two carried on a voluminous correspondence. As postage was charged according to distance, it was expensive to exchange letters each week, and John recalled that it cost him half a dollar "where now the postage would be but four cents. Still, I think it was a good investment." In some ways letter writing was more satisfactory than visiting; it certainly advanced the couple's knowledge of each other. At the Perkinses they had been too shy and embarrassed to seek privacy. Isabella refers to "the few & miserably constrained evenings we have passed together at Sister Mary's—when I could not think of leaving the room for a moment—under Mr. P[erkins]'s—searching eye—& you stood equally in awe of his ridicule." They could use letters to explore each other's feelings, goals, and suitability for marriage.

Isabella and John's courtship correspondence was very conventional; in terms of the topics they discussed, it could have been Harriet and Calvin Stowe's correspondence when they parted soon after marriage (he went to Europe to buy books for Lane Seminary). With both couples there was much religious jousting—who was more religious than whom, who could do better in advancing their partner's spiritual state. One might think Harriet would refuse to enter the lists with Calvin the Bible expert, but she did—nineteenth-century spouses were expected to exhort each other in religious matters. Still, Isabella was irritated by John's assumption that he was more religious than she. Maybe he was questioning her conversion, for he suggested she read the classic accompaniment of conversion, Philip Doddridge's *The Rise and Progress of Religion in the Soul.* Isabella replied tartly that John might benefit from reading it himself. She countered that John cared more about settling down in ease with his family and friends than he did about doing good for others. Whatever the state of John's soul, this was a penetrating statement of his life goals.

The second conventional topic for letters was character analysis. Harriet and Calvin carried it on ad infinitum after their marriage. "There are certain points in which we are so exactly unlike," he wrote her, "that our peculiarities impinge against each other and sometimes produce painful collisions." He was highly methodical, for instance, while she lacked system and order; she was dreamy and given to fits of abstraction. During their engagement Isabella and John followed suit in dissecting each other's personalities. Isabella was frank about her willfulness, which her family considered her main character flaw: "This is a thing that has been cultivated rather than subdued in the course of my education—all the way up—the opinions & tastes of Miss Bella have been consulted by her parents & *sisters* . . . until she learned to feel pretty extensively her own importance." Catharine wrote John directly that "Bell is formed by nature to *take the lead*" and would learn more each year of her power to influence others.

Because John felt that he was lacking in decisiveness himself and he hoped to gratify Isabella's wishes, he was not worried. He might have concerned himself more with a fault Mary told him about and he would soon discover for himself, Isabella's being, as Mary put it, "susceptible to the least reproof." Her lifelong habit when criticized was to rationalize first and consider later. This trait ultimately harmed herself more than others. Her fear of criticism often prevented her from pursuing her goals. For instance, Isabella's dislike of writing letters (and, later, essays) seems to have stemmed from hypersensitivity to criticism; even in making journal entries she agonized between quickly catching up to the present date and taking the time to write more elegantly for the eyes of others.

In her courtship correspondence with John, Isabella revealed a trait that would go a long way toward softening the sharp edges of her personality. She told John that her feelings had "long been accustomed to show themselves" and urged him to write freely also, even if she did not always approve of what he said. It was probably her father who had taught Isabella to avoid bottling up feelings. Lyman, in spite of his mood swings, had some emotionally healthy habits and reportedly told a seminary class, "You will have troubles, young gentlemen, go where you will; but when they come, *don't dam them up, but let them go down stream,* and you will soon be rid of them." Isabella was unable to follow this advice when it came to large central issues like her education and her mother's death, but she did heed it on a daily basis, which allowed her and John (and later their children to some extent) to express themselves openly and stay in close touch with each other's feelings.

Isabella's encouragement of such expression made her a favorite of her brother Charles, the youngest of her half brothers, who was seven years older than Isabella and four years younger than Harriet. Charles and Isabella had always felt a bond in their love of music; when Charles graduated from college, he was an accomplished violinist and student of music theory. Dutifully, he entered Lane Seminary but soon lost his faith and fled to New Orleans. Although his father deplored his stubbornness, Charles managed to support himself as a clerk and penned a series of highly emotional letters. Influenced by Byron, Rousseau, and Goethe, he saw himself as a Romantic wanderer, a sensitive rebel stifled by the dull world of business. He suffered from a mostly fantasized love affair and wrote Isabella: "You have never stood by the dark cave of Insanity—& looked with horror in at the dark door—& down the frightful chasms." Nor had she heard "the hideous noises—the shrieks & the laughter—feeling meanwhile your own brain boil."

In a calmer moment Charles compared his sisters Isabella and Harriet as correspondents (it was he who supplied Harriet with stories of New Orleans slavedrivers, including the original of Uncle Tom's persecutor, Simon Legree). He told Isabella: "Nobody writes such letters as you write. All else are in comparison cold and awaken only an emotion of disappointment. Harriet tis true wrote some beautiful letters. . . . Nevertheless—she doth not as you do satisfy herself with the artless expression of spontaneous emotions. She is not in her letter pouring forth feeling merely *because she feels* it but planning by the combination of such & such feelings or thoughts to produce a given effect." Harriet would have agreed with this analysis. In fact, she once wrote that she could hardly keep her letters from turning into sermons. "I was made for a preacher," she admitted. "It is as much my vocation to preach on paper as it is that of my brothers to preach viva voce."

At the time of Charles's letter the preaching Beechers were campaigning to change John Hooker's vocation from the law to the ministry. (The next best thing to being a minister was marrying one, as Harriet was well aware.) The idea that John should become a minister originated less from Isabella than from her father and sister Catharine. Lyman thought any being possessing brains and a penis should enter the ministry. As Isabella quoted him to John in October 1839, four days after she had arrived home in Cincinnati, "Every young man with the means of education & *common sense* is *called* to be a minister." Lyman himself had considered becoming a lawyer, and the relish with which he defended himself at his heresy trial suggests the attraction. When he graduated from Yale in 1797, sixteen of his classmates became lawyers and fifteen ministers, showing the rise of the legal profession from its earlier low status in American history and the fall of the clergy, which had formerly been the dominant profession in the country. Indeed, by 1797 Connecticut no longer had a state religion. But Lyman had scorned what he considered the dishonesty and tricks of legal courtroom practice. For Catharine, the inferiority of the law lay in its failure to be socially useful. Lawyers were calculating, dedicated to the "clashing views & interests of selfish men," whereas ministers devoted themselves to helping others.

Catharine started in on Isabella as soon as the latter left Hartford in August 1839 to visit her brothers George (in Rochester, New York) and William (in Batavia, Ohio) on the way to Cincinnati; Catharine was also visiting George and accompanied Isabella on the rest of her trip. Isabella's engagement seems to have triggered a desire in Catharine to have her little sister follow her path and live out the dream, cut short by Alexander Fisher's death, of marriage to a promising young minister. The argument Catharine used that was most effective with both Isabella and John was the law's greater amount of temptation to worldliness. As the couple tried to prove their religious fitness, they were particularly vulnerable to charges of being too much of the world. John saw the truth of Isabella's (perhaps originally Catharine's) insight that he wished only to settle down in comfort. Isabella realized that she *was* worldly, in fact; her skills were more practical than spiritual or intellectual, and she had to fight materialism. She wrote John, "We have both erred in looking forward to a happy instead of a useful life."

John Hooker reacted ambivalently to the Beecher attempt to redirect his career. On the one hand, he was put off by Catharine's long, intense letters. He protested to Isabella that he did not want to get into an argument with Catharine because the correspondence would soon be published in the *Biblical Repository* (as had Catharine's earlier letters, arguing fatalism and free will with a noted clergyman). The Beecher brothers often complained to their father about Catharine's bent for religious dispute. John's parents and Mary Beecher Perkins were outraged at the Beechers' interference and advised him to stick to the law. But he was moved by the content of Catharine's arguments at the same time he objected to their form, and March 1840 found him enrolled at Yale Divinity School. After a month John quietly returned to Hartford and the law; interestingly, he does not mention this divergence in his autobiography. As for Isabella, she was accepting and even somewhat relieved. Although Catharine saw the position of preacher's wife as one of power for Isabella, where she could use her strong will to influence people, Isabella may have recalled her mother's poverty and ill health. She was also taken aback at John's father's opposition—how could she counsel John to go against his father's wishes? Isabella started backtracking after her initial letter and left the decision to John.

Once John decided his vocation, he began to pressure Isabella to marry him. The time was ripe for him—he was the proper age, he planned to open his own law office and make a good living, and his parents had room in their attractive Farmington home for him to bring a bride. But why Isabella should want to marry when she was still in her teens is less clear—probably because she had no good alternative choices. Her father had promised her one more year of schooling in Hartford, and the year was up. The only vocation open to her was teaching, which she had never been interested in and which Catharine and Harriet had disliked. Spinsterhood would mean a peripatetic life like Aunt Esther's, serving whichever household needed her most. If she tried to be independent, she had Catharine's example; at age thirty-nine Catharine had no home of her own and was reduced to fighting Harriet for pennies in the Western Female Institute financial settlement. By contrast Mary Perkins's life may have looked good. Like Catharine, Mary seems to have wanted to claim Isabella, encouraging her to marry John and become more like herself.

If there were many good reasons to marry, Isabella was still reluctant—increasingly so as the day of her "immolation," as she put it, approached. Several writers on the Beechers have concluded that Isabella did not return John Hooker's affection. Marie Caskey notes in her book on religion and the Beecher family that John considered Isabella his "angel," but "for her part, Isabella did not reciprocate this rapturous devotion." Yet she assured John in her letters that she objected to the institution of marriage and not to him. She argues that the feelings she recently expressed to him "are such, as, to a *certain* degree, would come to the mind of every thoughtful, delicate woman on first contemplating *seriously* the change of relation & situation, which wedded life presents—for engagement is one thing & marriage quite a different thing—requiring specific thought & attention implying as it does [illegible word] obligations—duties & responsibilities."

A favorite anecdote in Beecher lore, started by Isabella herself, has

her as a young wife reading with John the commentaries of Sir William Blackstone, famous explicator of English law. She was horrified to learn that according to the law a wife's identity was collapsed into her husband's. By marriage husband and wife became one person, and that person was the husband.
A wife could not independently own property or enter into a contract; if she
behaved badly, her husband, as the responsible party, could be sued or pun-
ished. As her grandnephew Lyman Beecher Stowe later dramatized Isabella's
story, the young couple read in idyllic peace until they came to Blackstone's
chapter on domestic relations. "'Is that the justice which your Law furnishes
to us women?' exclaimed the beautiful bride, her eyes flashing with indignation."

There is a basic truth to this story—Isabella was probably shocked
to read Blackstone's actual words. But the force of the anecdote depends on
an incredibly naive young wife. Intelligent women of the time knew that
marriage involved loss of identity for the woman. That is why so many
women resisted it. The women's rights advocate Lucy Stone, who would become head of the American Woman Suffrage Association, the rival group to
Elizabeth Cady Stanton's and Susan B. Anthony's, viewed her approaching
marriage to Henry Blackwell as "putting Lucy Stone to death." Even sister
Harriet, no feminist, had felt uneasy about marrying Calvin Stowe. Her choice
of her father's colleague was guaranteed to please him, but marriage might
make her "cease to be Hatty Beecher and change to nobody knows who."
Isabella was particularly irritated by what she called the wife's "duty of submission etc." According to one of her letters, she thought the love of power
was innate in humans and most men would take advantage of their position.
"I don't know how it can be otherwise but galling to a sensible woman—
especially when she is eminently the one to be consulted as to have her wishes
gratified during an engagement and the early part of married life—to find in
a few months that one whom she has heretofore looked upon as an equal—
a companion and friend wishes to assume the appearance and manner of a
superior—a master."

In the same letter Isabella confided that if she thought their married
life would be like those she had seen in her family, she would break her
engagement. She might be referring to her brother William, whom she had
just mentioned in the letter and who was unhappily married, but the comment could also apply to Lyman's union with her mother or with Lydia. As
an adult, Isabella came to think Thomas Perkins did not properly confide in
Mary, and she felt the Stowes were inharmonious, saying she never envied
Hattie her Calvin. (He was twenty years older than Isabella, and she could
never get past her awe at his professor status.) Isabella hoped her relatives
had conflicted because of naturally irreconcilable dispositions or selfish failure

to consider the other's feelings. She and John would start right by resolving from the beginning to practice self-sacrifice.

Isabella returned to Hartford in March 1841. John was admitted to the bar and opened his law office in Farmington. As they were still separated, albeit by less distance, they continued to write. Isabella still had doubts about their approaching marriage but felt more reconciled. She consoled herself with the prospect of their studying together in winter. The idea was that she would read at night, saving his eyesight, and he would improve her education by reading to her during the day; she wrote that she looked forward to the influence of his superior knowledge. At first the couple planned a romantic evening wedding with the party riding out to Farmington on horseback, but the timing of the full moon intervened.

The wedding actually took place in the evening of August 5, 1841, at the Perkins's house. Dr. Joel Hawes, the minister who had presided over Harriet's and Isabella's conversions, performed the ceremony. The maid of honor and best man were Harriette Day and John Putnam, friends of Isabella's from Cincinnati, who themselves married the following year. The guest list included Father and Mother Hooker; John's sister Eliza and her husband, Francis Gillette, and their son Frank; Mary and Thomas Perkins and their four children; Mrs. Robinson, who was Isabella's teacher during her year at the Hartford Female Seminary, and her son; and John Brace, Catharine's successor as principal of the seminary, and his daughter. Brace was actually related to Isabella, having married a sister of Harriet Porter Beecher. In her journal entry on her silver wedding anniversary Isabella could not recall if Aunt Esther had been at the wedding or had gone back to Cincinnati. Catharine had planned to be present, but Isabella does not name her as a guest.

If Catharine missed the wedding, it may have been to avoid arousing painful feelings she could not express about her past bereavement; she was also absent at the last minute when Harriet married. But Catharine readily vented her fears about Harriet's rapid childbearing. Married in January 1836, Harriet gave birth to twin daughters in September. Calvin had not even returned from his European trip and was surprised to come home to two babies instead of one. Harriet had named them "Eliza" and "Isabella," but Calvin changed "Isabella" to "Harriet" in order to have his daughters named for his two wives. Two boys soon followed, Henry (born 1838) and Frederick (born 1840). Thus Harriet had four children in four years. "Poor thing, she bears up wonderfully well," Catharine wrote Mary, "and I hope will live through this first tug of matrimonial warfare, and then she says she shall not have any more *children, she knows for certain* for one while." If the Stowes were practicing any form of birth control beyond abstinence, it didn't work, for this letter was written before the advent of Henry and Frederick.

The large number of children not only made for a hectic household, especially as Harriet lacked Mary's organizing abilities, but also strained the Stowe finances. Calvin felt frustrated that, despite his great reputation as a scholar, the trustees of Lane Seminary often didn't see fit to pay him his full salary. The saving grace was that both Harriet and Calvin had grown up in families strapped for money. Calvin had lost his father at about the same age as Harriet lost her mother; he was sent to Bowdoin College (where he became valedictorian of his class) and Andover Theological Seminary by a group of ministers in his hometown of Natick, Massachusetts.

In spite of her burgeoning family, Harriet had not given up her dream of becoming a writer. At the end of 1838 she wrote a former colleague: "I also have made a new arrangement—I have realized enough by writing one way and another to enable me to add to my establishment a stout German girl who does my housework leaving to Anna [Smith, her long-time servant] fulltime to attend to the children so that by [this] method in disposing of time I have about three hours per day in writing and if you see my name coming out everywhere—you may be sure of one thing, that I *do* it for *the pay*—I have determined not to be a mere domestic slave."

But if the new arrangement allowed Harriet to write, it also had its drawbacks. Joan Hedrick notes that even in her best-laid plans she resembled a tiger chasing its tail. Harriet "wrote to get money to hire help to enable her to write (to get money to hire help, and so on)." At times she felt guilty for taking time away from her children. Was it wrong to divide her attention by her literary efforts, she asked her husband. Although he could be difficult in many ways, Calvin always supported Harriet's vocation as a writer. "You must be a *literary woman*," he wrote. It was fated to be so. She should make all her plans accordingly, improve her health, and "drop the E. out of your name, which only encumbers it and stops the flow and euphony, and write yourself only and always, *Harriet Beecher Stowe*." (Heretofore, she'd been "Mrs. H. E. Beecher Stowe.")

What Calvin called fate was probably his sense that Harriet couldn't stop writing even if she wanted to. If her father was the published author, the deep source of her fiction (and the drawing and painting she engaged in all her life) was clearly her lost mother. In autumn 1841, soon after Isabella's wedding, Harriet's maternal grandmother, Roxana Foote, died at Nutplains; she was ninety-one. This news caused Harriet to reflect nostalgically, as she would at intervals throughout her life, on the Foote homestead she associated so closely with her mother. She never forgot her childhood visits there, particularly the one right after her mother's death when she was loved and comforted by her grandmother and her namesake aunt. As Hedrick notes, "Nutplains was the maternal home" and as such it had a powerful hold on Harriet's imagination. Her "love affair with the New England past was in some sense a literary transformation of her love affair with a distant mother." After her grandmother's death Harriet began gathering together the New England stories and sketches she had published in such journals as *Western Monthly Magazine* and *Godey's Lady's Book*, the popular women's magazine. The resulting collection, *The Mayflower; or, Sketches of Scenes and Characters among the Descendants of the Pilgrims* (1843), became Harriet's first published book of fiction.

As Harriet began her writing career, Isabella was experiencing new happiness as a bride. She wrote Aunt Esther six months after the wedding that John made an excellent husband. She spent her afternoons at his office knitting while he read to her from his law books, and evenings she would read literature to him or they would visit with her in-laws; unlike Harriet, who suffered her mother-in-law, Isabella particularly liked John's mother and praised her highly to Aunt Esther. Isabella clearly felt that John was living up to his promise to spend time in study and further her education. In her "Memories" article she notes that her "interest in the woman question" began soon after her marriage with her consternation at reading Blackstone. She and John continued their reading program for four years (that is, until children intervened) and "to it I owe my intelligent interest in public affairs and a certain discipline of mind—since I never attended school or college after my sixteenth year."

The only worry Isabella could come up with in her letters to Aunt Esther was feeling *too* happy and not properly resigned to death, either John's or her own. She had feared during their engagement that John might die; perhaps she was identifying too closely with Catharine and her loss of Alexander Fisher. Now, after marriage, Isabella had fallen in love with John. This change of feeling is obvious from a perusal of her letters, which became more romantic and affectionate in tone, and she later confessed it outright to her children. Her separations from John that she had once found stimulating now seemed onerous. She adhered to a fairly consistent schedule of visiting, staying with the Perkinses in Hartford every few months and visiting at least once a year her sister-in-law's family in Bloomfield, Connecticut, and her own family and friends in Boston or New York. But she felt lonely and unhappy, complaining that she and John were "too much *one* ever to be separated." On a trip to Boston in 1843 to attend a cousin's wedding, she announced that it was the last visit she would ever make without him: "I never desire to leave you again—or to be left." Sometimes prosaic friends and relatives considered this devotion extreme, as when Isabella refused an invitation one Christmas in case John got home early from a trip. John's father "ridiculed" this act as "childish," and Isabella concludes her letter to John, certain of being understood, "I wonder if there are many people in the world who love as we do."

One significant event of the Hookers' early married life was Isabella's conversion to abolitionism. John had been converted in 1840, probably by his brother-in-law, Francis Gillette, who had graduated valedictorian of his class and Phi Beta Kappa from Yale and eventually became a U.S. senator. This change was not easy for John because he was essentially a conventional, peace-loving man who cared deeply what his neighbors thought and hated being driven by principle to be part of a radical minority. In addition, his father, though anti-slavery, feared the wrath of the South and advised John against becoming an open abolitionist; a lawyer relative warned that he would endanger his fledgling law practice.

Yet John was enraged not only at slavery in the South but also at the "universal disregard of the rights of the colored people" up North. He could not forget the sight of a well-dressed black man in the stage for New Haven being forcibly removed to make room for a white man or the shocked reaction of his Farmington neighbors when he invited a visiting "colored man" to sit in his church pew. The visitor was the Rev. James W. C. Pennington of Hartford, who, it turned out, was a fugitive slave. Although Pennington had run away over twenty years earlier, John was able to negotiate with his old master and buy and free him. Hooker was also involved with the Flora slave case in 1845, taking depositions from people who recalled that Flora had been free (and thus her descendants suing in Virginia should be free). In the year of the Hookers' marriage, 1841, John was following the *Amistad* case, in which the U.S. Supreme Court decided that fifty-three African men who had taken control of a slave ship were free on the basis of the international law prohibiting the slave trade; John invited the defendants to Farmington and helped raise money for their return to Africa.

John had started working on Isabella's attitudes before their marriage but to no avail. She had adopted the cautious, conservative views of the family members to whom she was closest—her father and sisters—instead of the abolitionist ideas of her older brothers. She was too defensive to give the subject a fair hearing, and John was outraged that she refused to read about slavery. Soon he cleverly persuaded her to do some reading. In an essay on woman suffrage written twenty years later, Isabella recalled "the wise procedure of a certain young gentleman I knew once—who, having married a spicy, young girl, who hated abolitionists more than she did slavery, begged her in the long winter evenings of the first year to read aloud, out of pity to his weak eyes 'The Life of Wilberforce'" (Wilberforce (1759–1833) was an English reformer who led the battle to end the British slave trade).

John "surreptitiously laid on her table" some books on West Indian emancipation. He also countered one of Isabella's main complaints about abolitionists—the vituperative language they used. She found their discourse mean, coarse, and filled with contempt for their opponents. John responded with a clever argument comparing Lyman Beecher's sermon against dueling. He urged her to reread it and notice that almost every argument against the language used by abolitionists also applied to that sermon. He never knew a slaveholder more severely abused than the duelists were by Lyman Beecher. Within a year and a half of their marriage John had won Isabella over and could point to her conversion as the finishing touch to their "perfect happiness" in one another. "How I thank God that you are a whole souled abolitionist."

But this change created conflict between Isabella and her sisters, particularly Mary, whom she saw most often. In December 1842 she wrote to John from a visit to the Perkinses that they had a "little" abolition talk at the dinner table. Mr. Perkins had asked sardonically about "the progress of the good cause," and Isabella responded equally sarcastically, describing a recent meeting that showed everyone in Connecticut was converted except himself. "I talked very pleasantly—but could not help, after all, feeling somewhat hurt inwardly to have the whole subject treated so lightly by so many sensible & dear friends—for I find my sympathies more strongly enlisted in that cause, than I am aware, until opposition or ridicule call them into action. I suppose they talk here very much as I used to—but it does not strike me either pleasantly or as becoming intelligent, reading, christian [sic] people."

However much she tried to minimize them as "little," the arguments over abolition caused Isabella some anguish. She thought Mary and Aunt Esther could change if they had better information and drew Mary aside for serious talk on abolition. But Thomas Perkins was "hopeless." In another dinner table argument he claimed that northerners knew nothing—"absolutely nothing"—of slavery, any more than they did of "Hindoo idolatry," and should keep their mouths shut about both so-called sins. Mary was more easily influenced by her husband than her sister. Although Isabella told herself she was making gradual progress, on a later visit she was "wounded" by a slighting comment Mary made about abolition.

With this background of conflict, it seems a bit harsh to accuse Isabella, as Harriet Beecher Stowe's recent biographer does, of "smug self-congratulation" in noting Harriet's late arrival to the abolitionist ranks. After the publication of *Uncle Tom's Cabin*, Isabella wrote John as follows:

> It is amusing almost to see how Hatty is coming strait onto our Anti slavery platform—she has been you know a father & Mr. Stowe abolitionist [i.e., no abolitionist at all] heretofore—but she said to me here, the other day, when some little talk had been going on, 'Belle, what do you think, or what does John do about

this matter'—I smiled & said, why just as he always has done, vote for nobody who is in any wise committed to slavery—'Well'[,] said she, so shd. I—there is no other way'—& yet she was so absorbed in the dawn of her own ideas, she did not once remember that in common with others of our family she *had* doubted the wisdom of such practice.

By this time, John had been elected by the abolitionist voters of Farmington to the state House of Representatives and had influenced Isabella to support the anti-slavery Liberty Party. If she dared not break the rules and speak at meetings, she could help John plan anti-slavery gatherings and, before their children were born, accompany him on his lecture tours around the state. John needed considerable encouragement. "How strange," he mourned, "that in *this country*—and among the sons of Pilgrims, *such* a cause should be unpopular."

Mary Beecher Perkins feared, as she saw her newly married sister getting involved in politics, that Isabella would become a "public woman" like Harriet and Catharine. She wrote to Isabella, "I could not perform any of my duties if I gave way to my feelings and allowed myself to attend meetings and become as much interested as I easily could." It is not clear how Mary, the fourth Beecher child and five years younger than Catharine, became as conservative as her older sister and more conventional in her enactment of prescribed female roles. Alfred Adler, the psychologist who pioneered birth order theory, sees the oldest child as understanding the importance of power and authority: "When [s]he grows up, [s]he likes to take part in the exercise of authority and [s]he exaggerates the importance of rules and laws. Everything should be done by rule and no rule should ever be changed. Power should always be preserved in the hands of those who are entitled to it. We can understand that influences like these in childhood give a strong tendency towards conservatism."

Certainly Catharine possessed that tendency. Frank J. Sulloway, a historian of science, mentions her in his book arguing that later-born scientists have been more open to new ideas and paradigms than firstborns. He notes that Catharine worked for change in women's education but "her reformist inclinations had limits" because she was "motivated to reform by high moral conscience, not by rebellion against the status quo." He claims that "firstborn women have tended to reject radical reforms and have generally confined their own reforming efforts to improving the system, not to overthrowing it."

By contrast, later-borns like Harriet and Isabella have been able to "empathize with other downtrodden individuals and generally support egali-

tarian social change." American abolitionism especially attracted a large proportion of later-borns. Harriet often seemed torn between identifying with her
older sisters' caution and being willing to take risks, but she usually supported
change. Isabella would eventually become the radical of the family. As for
Mary, her conservatism would probably be explained by birth order theorists
as a by-product of a second daughter's attempt to "find a valued family niche
that avoids duplicating the one already staked out by the parent-identified
firstborn." In other words, whereas Catharine went into education, became
nationally known, and decided not to marry, Mary did the opposite—quit
teaching, married, and adopted her husband's identity.

At this point Isabella was more interested in having a family than
pursuing social change. On September 30, 1842, she gave birth to her first
child. Thomas Beecher Hooker, named for John's distinguished Hooker ancestor and for Isabella's brother Tom, died before December. The Hookers did
not mention him in their correspondence; the only reference is Isabella's request, written from her first visit after the baby's death, that John return "that
breast pump" to his sister Eliza in Bloomfield. Like all nineteenth-century
mothers, Isabella knew several parents who had lost babies. Her brother Edward and his wife had been unlucky enough to lose three of their six children;
Eunice Beecher, Henry's wife, had just had her second baby stillborn. Isabella
perhaps recalled her mother's severe depressive illness after the death of two-
year-old Frederick and determined to avoid depression. (Isabella's dream that
her mother was alive, but she was not allowed to see her, occurred during
the period between baby Thomas's death and the birth of the Hookers' next
child.) Some thoughtful person gave Isabella and John a puppy, which they
named Fido and showered with affection during their period of mourning.

Isabella was particularly satisfied with John when she compared him
to other husbands. Her cousin's new husband did not come up to John's
standard, and on a visit to their wedding attendants, the Putnams, Isabella
disliked their noisy home—the Hookers' quiet household seemed a paradise
in comparison. Worse, she had introduced her local friend and companion
Charlotte Cowles, with whom she went horseback riding, to Joseph Hull, a
friend of John's (both Isabella and John were inveterate matchmakers). Charlotte and Joseph married and had a baby. But, Isabella wrote John, who was
away in Hartford, "Joe beat his wife so unkindly this morning in my presence
and mother's that I could not get over it all day. I cannot like him since." She
felt grateful, she continued, to have John as a husband. Before their next child
was born, they continued their pattern of quiet study and companionable
horseback rides. They also socialized frequently, as they would all their lives,
for both were fun-loving to the core. Their neighbor and abolitionist ally,
John Pitkin Norton, confided to his diary that Isabella was an enchanting

hostess. At a boating party for her sisters she sang duets on the water with Norton; during a party game "Mrs. Hooker, indeed, acted like a perfect witch, she was entirely carried away, by excitement and fun."

In September 1843, a year after baby Thomas's birth, the Beechers had another family reunion. It began in Hartford, with Lyman visiting old friends, and continued in the Boston area. They had one of their typical rambunctious times, full of jokes and laughter, but the underlying occasion for the reunion was a sad one. On July 4 brother George had committed suicide or, as the Beechers would have it, accidentally shot himself in the mouth. Since the time Catharine and Isabella had visited him on their way home to Cincinnati, George had accepted a parish in Chillicothe, Ohio. The day after Catharine arrived for a visit he took his double-barreled shotgun into the garden, presumably to drive away birds that were stripping his fruit trees, and was later found dead. The coroner's verdict was accidental death, though as Milton Rugoff notes, "No one publicly pointed out how curious it was that George had overlooked the fact that the gun was loaded and that he happened to pull the trigger just as he put the muzzle to his face." Presumably it was too shocking to consider that a minister of God would take his own life. George had always experienced the Beecher mood swings and mysterious illnesses requiring periods of rest. The effect of his death on his all-too-similar siblings may be imagined. Harriet said years later that George's sudden death "shook my whole soul like an earthquake." The month after his suicide she gave birth to her fifth child, whom she named Georgiana after her dead brother and her childhood friend, Georgiana May.

George Beecher had probably waited until Catharine's arrival to kill himself so that she could take charge and assist his wife and children. She did, of course, and she even published a memorial volume the next year entitled *The Biographical Remains of Rev. George Beecher* (1844). Despite her competence, Catharine was in many ways the Beecher most deeply affected by George's death. She saw too many parallels between her life and George's. They had both striven to please their father and internalized his expectations, which they felt unable to live up to. As Kathryn Sklar points out, they could not escape Lyman's influence but neither could they be happy in careers modeled after his example. Now in her forties, Catharine had carved out a place for herself as a writer and national commentator. But her life was still a tangle of contradictions. Sklar states, "She was an expert on domestic economy, but had no home of her own; she was a writer on the moral education of children, but had no children herself; she was a competent religious writer, but had never experienced conversion; and she urged young women to become teachers, but was herself not willing to teach."

The Beecher sisters had to worry about another brother during this time, the next to youngest boy, Thomas. It was déjà vu. Like Charles, he had decided he did not want to be a minister and had fallen in love with an unattainable woman. By 1843, the year of the family reunion, Thomas was writing Isabella in the following vein: "My dear Sister I will not disguise from you—that I feel terribly unsettled in my religious constitution. Tis what I have long feared—& I know not, nor can any one predict save the Omniscient, where my resting place will be. I am in darkness on the philosophy of religion—the reality of it & the practice of it." Thomas had always held a dark view of life. Whether or not he absorbed as a child some of his mother's pessimism, he considered happiness an illusion and thought it an affliction to be a Beecher. If there were anyone likely to follow in George's footsteps, it was Thomas. A month after his "I am in darkness" letter he was suspended from college for being disorderly in chapel.

The youngest Beecher, James, was also a problem. Isabella found him "wayward" even before her marriage when he was only thirteen. She felt he wouldn't improve in the West "under *home influences*" and wanted him to come to Hartford. But, although Isabella took seriously her mother's charge, she had no power to enforce her ideas, particularly when they conflicted with her father's. Nothing came of the Hartford plan because Lyman wanted his sons at home with him as long as possible. According to Thomas's reminiscences in Lyman's "autobiography," his father begged him to remain home for a while after leaving college. He "put both hands upon my shoulders, looked me full in the face, and said, with broken utterance, 'Tom, I love you; you mustn't go 'way and leave me.'" Tom stayed. He acted as his father's secretary until he could leave with Lyman's blessing.

At the family reunion Isabella thought her father looked tired, worn out, and depressed. He had retired from his ministry (though not Lane Seminary) earlier in the year, and she feared that not having a church would cause him distress. But if she was right to worry about her brothers, she underestimated her father's strength. The next year Charles became the prodigal son with a vengeance; he not only returned to Christianity but also was ordained as a minister in Fort Wayne, Indiana. Lyman made a celebratory gesture typical of him. Henry wrote: "Father got here the Saturday night before I did. He is you know 70 years old. When he got to St. Mary's on Friday night . . . he had 69 miles to ride, the road terrible . . . [so he] rode all night and all day Saturday—and Sunday preached twice and is hearty as a buck!"

In summer 1845 Isabella awaited the birth of the Hookers' second child. She felt uncomfortable in body and spirit, she told John, and disliked her increasing dependence on him. (This was the first mention of a complaint that would become more insistent as the years passed.) More disturbingly, she feared dying in childbirth. Like all women of the time, Isabella knew relatives and friends who had lost their lives in this way. Also, both Isabella and Harriet were anxious about dying young because their mothers had. One of Stowe's biographers notes that Harriet lived to be eighty-five, but until she was past the age at which her mother died (age forty-one) she believed her life would end soon. Her reply to the urging of Edward's wife that she write a book exposing slavery was "I will if I live." A few days before Isabella gave birth she and Harriet spent a quiet day together with Harriet resuming her old role as her sister's spiritual counselor. Harriet always showed a special sensitivity to her younger sister, perhaps remembering how it felt to be "unimportant" in a crowded household.

On August 15, 1845, Isabella gave birth to a "darling baby" girl, whom the Hookers named Mary, after Mary Beecher Perkins. They worried about her health, of course, but her babyhood proved relatively disease-free. Isabella reported years later that a longtime friend from Farmington had called and reminisced about the good old days. She "vividly remembered" John calling out in "a voice of ecstasy, 'Oh, Isabella—do come here—& see Mary—was there ever any thing so cunning' [nineteenth-century parlance for "cute"]." Before the end of the year John's father died; John and Isabella were grateful that he had gotten to see the baby. In December Isabella recorded in her journal that since Mary's birth she had hardly found a moment to write about the baby or her own feelings about her. This journal was the one Isabella later dubbed her children's journal. She had begun it two weeks before Mary's birth with the entry about her fear of childbirth and Harriet's helpful visit, and she kept it for ten years until September 1855, when her youngest child was baptized. The children's journal has an interesting form, being a cross between the typical baby scrapbook of today and a personal diary. Isabella used it to preserve the children's cute or precocious sayings and doings, record their physical and moral development, vent her feelings about motherhood, and analyze the children's characters.

The children's journal had a very twentieth-century child-centeredness. Isabella seems not to have discussed the journal outside her immediate family; many of her contemporaries would have thought it a waste of paper. But if she needed validation, it was close to home in the person of sister Catharine. Catharine had just become her century's combination of Martha Stewart and Dr. Spock. In 1841 she published A Treatise on Domestic Economy, the first book to cover all aspects of the home, from how to design and build it to how to cook, sew, and bring up children. The Treatise was enormously successful, being reprinted almost every year in the forties and fifties and giving Catharine some financial independence at last. She followed up with the also popular Miss Beecher's Domestic Receipt-Book (1842), a collection of healthful recipes. One reason for the extensive sales of the Treatise was its widespread use as a textbook; one educator called it "the first text-book in Home Economics." Catharine connected her writings on domestic economy and her writings on education by arguing that proper housewifery should be taught as a branch of study in girls' schools. At one time academic subjects took a backseat to domestic skills, but now, she complained, many young women knew how to make oxygen and hydrogen better than how to make a bed.

A *Treatise on Domestic Economy* dealt not only with the sundry details of housekeeping, such as ironing, dressing an infant, administering first aid, or folding a gentleman's coat. It also presented an overarching philosophy beyond the domestic details, the idea that motherhood was supremely important. Dedicating the *Treatise* to American mothers, Catharine claimed that "the mother writes the character of the future man . . . whose energies may turn for good or for evil the destinies of a nation." The woman who rears a family of children is an agent in accomplishing "the greatest work that ever was committed to human responsibility." To Catharine motherhood was a profession, not just a biological relationship. Perhaps she had to make such an argument to shore up her own credibility; she was well aware of the type of criticism expressed in the sardonic comment of one of her married Foote cousins on the *Treatise*: "If it were not for these maiden ladies instructing the married ones how to keep house and take care of children I don't know what would become of us." Catharine therefore expanded the definition of "mother" to cover all women who interacted closely with children, including teachers and nurses.

Catharine did not suggest that mothers keep a record of their children's lives, but Isabella's journal is much in line with the *Treatise*'s philosophy. Isabella was also discovering for herself one of the keystones of Catharine's theory—maternal self-sacrifice. Mothers could be entrusted with forming the characters of children simply because, Catharine thought, they were capable of denying themselves and focusing continually on the welfare of others. Isabella's first few entries in her journal are more about her self-denial than about Mary. In the December entry about not having time to write a line she concludes that she has been so occupied with the physical care of the baby, she hasn't been able to realize any self-improvement. It was a vicious circle: she needed to start living a "holy life" before Mary was old enough to follow her example, but Mary's care left no energy to develop her spiritual side.

Isabella made her next entry on August 1, 1847, exactly two years after she had commenced the journal and in the same circumstances. She was pregnant, expecting to deliver that month, and afraid of dying. How could she leave her darling Mary to the care of others? Isabella looked back on her two years of motherhood and marveled at how different they had been from her expectation. She enjoyed little Mary more than she had foreseen, but maternal duties and responsibilities were more overwhelming than she had anticipated. Isabella had never intended to be solely a wife and mother. Although she appreciated her sister Mary's advice and gentle influence on her character, she always expressed some reservations about her wholly domestic life, as in her statement to John that Mary "has *in some things* been to me a model [my italics]." She felt that the circumstances of Mary's life had been such as to "preclude other developments that are equally important with those which she so beautifully exhibits." Little Mary was only a year old when Isabella expressed to Aunt Esther some of her frustration over her lack of education. When John traveled to New Haven for a college reunion, Isabella confessed, "I almost wish I were a man, that I might go to college & have such stirring times."

Isabella's cares and responsibilities as a mother were, of course, increased with the birth of Alice on August 26, 1847. Alice, "as sweet a little puss as ever breathed the breath of life," was an easier baby than Mary. She seldom cried, was easily trained (the opposite of her sister, Isabella noted), and from the beginning nursed only once during the night. Isabella breastfed her for about a year, as she had done with Mary. During Alice's infancy and often during the children's illnesses, Isabella had the assistance of an older woman, "Aunty Smith," who took care of the baby and brought her to Isabella to be nursed at night. But if Alice was a pliant baby, Mary was a strong-willed two-year-old. Why did God create will, Isabella asked John plaintively, if it only had to be subdued? Isabella was the designated subduer, to her dismay, and she had to struggle with the issue of corporal punishment.

One day little Mary had an "obstinate fit" in front of a visiting cousin. Isabella persistently asked the child to hand her a book, but every time she asked, Mary would throw it on the floor and stomp on it. "I never whipped her half so hard in all her life before," Isabella wrote John. Lyman Beecher believed that whipping was a necessary tool in bringing up children, and Catharine stated emphatically in the *Treatise* that submission of the will was the most important habit to teach young children; she predicted dire consequences for "lack of government," or even worse, "unsteady," or inconsistent, punishments and rewards. Isabella felt instinctively that corporal punishment was wrong but had no authority she could point to for that position.

Her dilemma is shown clearly in a long entry dated March 17, 1852, when Mary was almost seven: "It pains me greatly to make the entry which I now must in Mary's Journal—not so much because she has been so very naughty—but I did so truly mean a long time since never to whip her again &

it fairly shocks & mortifies me to think I have done so." The problem was the same—persistent fits of obstinacy. At the next instance,

> I started up, seized the long handled brush & proceeded after the usual fashion of administering regular whippings—she was frightened horribly & tho' half choked & violently struggling, said very plainly 'I want Alice to go out' thus showing her sense of shame to be uppermost. I sent Alice out & whipped pretty hard—but the pain was nothing to the mortification I think. The effect has been excellent in every aspect—yet I feel mortified every time I think of it—just as I shouldn't have my husband or brother flogged on board ship. I always have entertained the greatest horror of physical punishments administered to *grown* people—& Mary has for a long time seemed to me to belong to that class.

Isabella gradually realizes the absurdity of this last and admits that Mary is still a child. Finding no way out of her predicament, she turns to the children's dental problems and devotes several pages to her exertions to get them to brush their teeth.

This entry may illustrate the reason why more parents haven't kept, or at least preserved, honest children's journals. Posterity is unforgiving, and critics have portrayed Isabella as crazed or cruel. Marie Caskey calls Isabella's relations with her children "troubled." Nothing could be further from the truth. In general, she was an attentive, loving parent and the children adored her. If she felt it her duty to whip them, she also showered them with hugs and was capable of apologizing to them when she was wrong. She was relatively open for the times and tried to answer all the children's hard questions, even on topics not usually discussed, such as why wasn't Aunt Esther married? During Aunt Eliza Gillette's pregnancy Isabella told the eight-year-old Mary the origin of babies, although she confessed in the journal that she couldn't help being evasive when Mary inquired further about the role of Uncle Francis. The girls' affection for their mother led to another difficulty that Isabella admits in the journal: "The literal fact is that my two dear little girls, do *quarrel* quite often." Alice had even bitten Mary. Both girls wanted to be the favorite and plagued their mother with their "everlasting jealousy."

One may wonder why Isabella did not enlist her husband's aid with her child-raising quandaries. There were two related reasons. First, John was away a lot when the children were young. He often spent the week in Hartford and returned to Farmington only on weekends; Isabella complained that he was becoming hardened by business. In 1849 and 1850 he traveled to New Haven, where the Connecticut legislature met. He decided not to run again for office because he disliked being parted from his family. Second, John delegated responsibility for the children to Isabella. When she told him Mary needed a stronger hand and she wished he would help with the discipline of the children, he expressed his complete faith in his wife. To some extent this arrangement was a good one for Isabella, whether she would admit to it or not, for she liked control and had much invested in her maternal role; she would not have to argue with John over how to raise the children. But what if she should inadvertently harm them? She confided to the journal her fear of making self-reliance "the rock on which I may make shipwreck of my children—the danger of this is strengthened by my husband's entire confidence in me, insomuch that he does not in the least assist or advise concerning the children."

Lacking John's help, Isabella naturally turned to her sisters for advice. But motherhood was like marriage in the models provided by the family. Mary Beecher Perkins, who had sunk her identity into marriage and motherhood, was having trouble with her children. She asked Harriet's advice when her oldest child, Frederick, was arrested in a street brawl. Fred Perkins would go down in history as the delinquent father of Charlotte Perkins Gilman, the turn-of-the-century feminist; his abandonment of his family led to Charlotte's having to move nineteen times during her poverty-stricken childhood. Mary's younger daughter, Caty, caused her "much anxiety and unhappiness," and the older girl, Emily, precipitated at least two family crises.

Although Emily was by all accounts a charming young woman and would be friends with Isabella in the 1860s, she had trouble choosing a mate. First she got engaged to Frederick Law Olmsted, who would become a famous landscape architect and the designer of New York City's Central Park. Within weeks she grieved her parents by breaking the engagement and offending the illustrious Olmsted family; not even her aunt Harriet could convince her to wed Olmsted. Then Emily decided to marry Edward Everett Hale. Hale, a minister from a distinguished family, would gain fame as author of the short story "The Man without a Country." The problem? He was a Unitarian, one of the horrid breed Lyman had dedicated himself to saving Boston from. Isabella reported to John that "my poor dear father is *distressed* & I suspect he & Mary had some talk . . . for she looked miserably [sic] when I met her at Emily's & said she had not slept all night."

Isabella thus bypassed Mary and turned to sister Harriet for childrearing advice. By now Harriet had seven children and an article in the Cincinnati *Journal* entitled "Bring Up Your Child in the Way He Should Go." Isabella was nonetheless skeptical of Harriet's mothering skills (and this before the Stowe children grew up to have problems). In July 1849 she wrote Harriet a tactless letter saying she hoped to learn something from "your experience in obstinate, irritable children—I do think Mary is very much like Georgy as I remember her here when I used to think Anna was too hard sometimes." She often despaired at Mary's lack of docility and truthfulness. What is reasonable to require of such a child, what kinds of punishment are most effective? This letter was very unfortunately timed, as Isabella hadn't yet heard that Harriet had just lost her youngest and favorite child, the one-and-a-half-year-old Samuel Charles, to typhoid fever. "My Charley—my beautiful, loving, gladsome baby," she mourned to Calvin. The next year she had another son, her last child, whom she named Charles Edward. The grief she felt over the first Charley she poured into the actual or threatened separations of mothers and children in *Uncle Tom's Cabin* (1852).

The late 1840s and early 1850s were low points in the Beecher sisters' relations with one another and their brothers. Mary and Isabella were still arguing over slavery. Although Isabella tried to rely on Mary as she used to, she felt alienated from her sister and her brother-in-law. In January and February 1847 Isabella moved into the Perkins home in Hartford to care for the children while Mary went to a health resort and enjoyed a break from her domestic routine. Such an arrangement was not at all unusual for the times, though John joked to Mary that they should write each other love letters since his wife and her husband were keeping house together. But Isabella and Thomas Perkins no longer got along. She wrote John, "I am perfectly conscious of not being as pleasing to him as formerly—I am very apt to say things to him, which I afterwards regret—then if we get into a debate he's sure to vex me beyond endurance—he is so provoking."

Mary showed no signs of wanting to come home, and Isabella's patience was soon taxed to the limit. She finally resolved the situation by securing Mary's permission to bring the children home to Farmington with her. There is some indication that Perkins's behavior toward Isabella was what today would be called sexual harassment. As a young woman, she had enjoyed his attentions, but in the 1850s, on another visit when Mary was away, she confessed to John that "I do hate to be admired so extensively & repeatedly." Although Thomas's behavior toward her would make her "cross" with him, she would feel sorry for him in his loneliness. "I abate a little & then he takes advantage again."

In the late 1840s all three of the younger Beecher sisters were annoyed with Catharine, who was meddling with the lives of others in an embarrassingly public way. Catharine had come to rely heavily on friendships with women, and she had met a former Hartford Female Seminary student, Delia Bacon, and renewed their intimacy. Delia pursued a successful career as a lecturer and teacher of young women on Shakespeare, Puritan history, and other literary and historical topics. When Catharine and Delia took up their relationship, Delia was seemingly being courted by Alexander MacWhorter,

Catharine Beecher, c. 1848. Courtesy Schlesinger Library, Radcliffe Institute, Harvard University.

a wealthy minister about ten years her junior. Catharine took it upon herself to inquire about MacWhorter's intentions, whereby his friends at Yale Divinity labeled Delia a frustrated old maid who was chasing MacWhorter. Delia's brother Leonard, a Congregational minister and professor of theology, had MacWhorter charged with slander and brought to ecclesiastical trial.

Yale closed ranks, with the defense being led by Dr. Nathaniel Taylor, an old friend of Lyman Beecher's. Catharine supported Delia during the trial and, when MacWhorter was found guilty of nothing more than "imprudence," refused to give up. She ignored the opposition of all the Beechers and Bacons, including Delia herself, who pleaded, "I am tired of being a 'victim.' I do not wish to be a 'heroine.'" Catharine wrote an attack on MacWhorter and the clerical establishment, entitling it *Truth Stranger than Fiction: A Narrative of Recent Transactions involving Inquiries in regard to the Principles of Honor, Truth and Justice which Obtain in a Distinguished American University* (1850). In the book Catharine exposed the efforts of her family, particularly her brothers (Lyman tried to stay in the background), to stop her publishing; she spoke of her "various brothers in full pursuit, some of them fancying an insane hospital my only proper residence." Perhaps Harriet and Isabella should have been listening, as they would encounter the same treatment when they tried to defend women accused of being sexually aggressive.

On the issue of slavery Catharine and Harriet were drawing closer to Isabella's position. The catalyst was the passage of the infamous Fugitive Slave Law, part of the Compromise of 1850. It obliged northerners to turn in runaway slaves instead of helping them escape. Even famous ex-slaves like Frederick Douglass, even free black people who couldn't readily prove they were *not* slaves, were in danger of capture. The conservative Catharine, who had once cautioned "ladies" to avoid abolitionism, now felt outraged. Harriet wrote her that "it did my heart good to find somebody in as indignant a state as I am about this miserable wicked fugitive slave business—why I have felt almost choked sometimes with pent up wrath that does no good."

In spring 1850 Harriet traveled East with her three oldest children, Eliza, Hattie, and Henry, in order to set up housekeeping in Brunswick, Maine; Calvin had accepted a position at Bowdoin College, his alma mater, and would begin teaching there when his Lane term ended. On the way to Maine Harriet stopped in Hartford to visit Mary and Isabella and then in Boston to see her brother Edward; it was on this visit that Edward's wife suggested Harriet might write a book showing the wrongs of slavery. In March 1851 she informed Gamaliel Bailey, the editor of the *National Era,* that she had begun a "series of sketches" on the topic; they might fill two or three numbers of the magazine. Until this year she had avoided writing about the subject, but she now felt "the time is come when even a woman or a child who can speak a word for freedom and humanity is bound to speak." The first installment of *Uncle Tom's Cabin* appeared in the *National Era* in June 1851.

That year the next to youngest Beecher brother, Thomas, married Olivia Day (known as Livy), the daughter of Yale's president. Tom had gone into teaching but came under the influence of Horace Bushnell, the most famous minister in Hartford. He was the one whose church the Perkinses and Hookers pointedly did *not* attend, for Lyman Beecher considered his theology too vague and liberal. Bushnell's emphasis on "Christian nurture," rather than Calvinist doctrine, rekindled Tom's religious impulses and made him decide to become a minister. In 1851 he was ordained and the next year became pastor of the new Congregational Church formed in Williamsburgh, New York. Henry Ward Beecher preached nearby at the Plymouth Church in Brooklyn.

Isabella could thus breathe a sigh of relief that her mother's charge was finally settled, even though she knew she did not understand Thomas and probably never would. When Livy fell ill during pregnancy and died, Thomas shocked his sisters by refusing to mourn and insisting that everyone should rejoice in Livy's release from the tribulations of life. Mary Beecher Perkins was particularly upset, complaining to Isabella that she found Tom's manner and language wholly repugnant. His explanation for his behavior was even more incomprehensible. He claimed that for Livy to have survived and become a mother "would have been as foul an incongruity as it would have been for Undine [a water sprite in folklore] to have been transformed into a steady dutch vrow, nursing her children through the measles." Neither Mary nor Isabella, who had just nursed little Mary through whooping cough, would have been capable of understanding the sexist preference for an unreal nymph over a nurturing mother. It was too much like saying the only good woman is a dead one.

If Thomas seemed odd, he was at least mild-mannered. James, the youngest brother, had a nasty temper. He had been a holy terror at Dartmouth and was eventually suspended for assaulting another student. According to the college president, he was generally "rude, ungoverned . . . [and] impatient of discipline." Only his family name gained him readmission, allowing him to graduate. In 1849 Jim defied his father and went to sea. He wrote a worried Isabella from Hong Kong, where he was engaged in the East India trade. She next saw him in summer 1852. She was repulsed by his cynicism and wrote John that

> He is an odd fish & troubles me continually—I wish I could forget him or he could annihilate himself for five years or more—if he would then come out strait & good. I can't tell where the fault

is—but somehow I don't love him much—or any body else, who is always ridiculing every body & every thing.

If it were not for our Mother, I could shirk him entirely—& find perfect rest & comfort in my own husband & children. But I am haunted with the . . . responsibility that she laid on me in regard to my brothers—I am so thankful Tom is moored at last.

Despite her criticism, the opening of Isabella's letter suggests that historians may be correct in viewing Jim as a "pampered" youngest child: "Jim has just come in & is sitting on a trunk reading," she wrote, "while 'Belle' & Mary are fussing over his hair—one on each side." The sisters thought Jim handsomer than ever (he was considered the best looking of the Beecher boys). The occasion for Isabella, Mary, and Jim's being together was a gathering of the Beecher sisters (plus Jim and Charles) at the Stowe household in Brunswick, Maine, in June 1852. Catharine had been there for some time, having moved in with her sister and organized the household so that Harriet could finish the serial version of *Uncle Tom* (the few sketches had ballooned to a massive novel). The book came out in spring 1852 and created an uproar in the nation and in Harriet's life: she was suddenly rich (comparatively, at least), famous, and infamous. She had thought of her book as a peacemaker that would attract southern moderates, but a storm of vituperation erupted in the South. Harriet was under siege. Mary gathered her two daughters, Isabella took little Mary, and they all hurried to Brunswick to help.

3

In the Wake of *Uncle Tom's Cabin,*
1852–1859

IN BRUNSWICK WITH HER sisters, Harriet Beecher Stowe seemed stunned by the reception of *Uncle Tom's Cabin.* She was no less equipped to handle sudden wealth and fame than the average person, but the situation would have been overwhelming for any fledgling author. The first printing of the novel sold out in a few days—and this without advance promotion. Before any reviews appeared, additional printings had sold. A Boston newspaper noted that the publisher kept three mills going to make the paper, three power presses running twenty-four hours a day, and a hundred bookbinders at work; yet the demand for the book exceeded the supply. By the end of the year three hundred thousand copies had been sold in the United States and a million in Great Britain.

The Stowes could have been economically fixed for life, but they made a bad business decision. The publisher, John P. Jewett, had offered a choice between sharing evenly in the costs and profits or taking a ten percent royalty on each copy sold. The Stowes chose the latter option. There were also few royalties on the British sales, as there was no international copyright. Still, Harriet received a check that summer for ten thousand dollars for three months' royalties. Her husband or father could not have earned that sum in years.

Southerners did not at first react to *Uncle Tom's Cabin,* but when it became clear how influential the book was going to be, the novel was effectively banned in the South (a British visitor noted that when he gave a copy to a young southerner he was threatened and run out of town). Initially the attacks on *Uncle Tom's Cabin* targeted the veracity of the portrayal of slavery—Harriet's portrait simply wasn't true. But the criticism quickly became more vitriolic and directed toward Harriet personally. She was not only a liar but also a "loathesome" person. According to the *Southern Quarterly Review,* Stowe's foul imagination had produced a book "whose touch contaminates with its filth." Poor Harriet became a "vile wretch in petticoats." The southern novelist

William Gilmore Simms even peeked underneath, claiming "Mrs. Stowe betrays a malignity so remarkable that the petticoat lifts of itself, and we see the hoof of the beast." Strong stuff for a minister's mate, a housewife and mother who had always been treated like a "lady"!

But in some ways the blame was easier to take than the praise. As Forrest Wilson asks, "How could a plain Brunswick housewife, dicing potatoes and onions in her kitchen for a chowder, remain precisely calm when her husband brought from the post office such a letter as this:

> I congratulate you most cordially upon the immense success and influence of *Uncle Tom's Cabin*. It is one of the greatest triumphs recorded in literary history, to say nothing of the higher triumph of its moral effect.
>
> With great regard, and friendly remembrance to Mr. Stowe, I remain,
> Yours most truly,
> Henry W. Longfellow

More privately, the famous poet confided to his diary: "At one step she has reached the top of the staircase up which the rest of us climb on our knees year after year." Longfellow's tribute was echoed by the great in every country—Prince Albert in England, George Sand in France, Heinrich Heine in Germany, Leo Tolstoy in Russia. Harriet was now an international celebrity.

Her brother Edward, for one, worried that all the adulation would go to Harriet's head and ruin her character. She, however, took refuge in her humble housewife persona. To the letter of a female author of children's books she replied, "So you want to know something about what sort of a woman I am!" Well, she was "a little bit of a woman—somewhat more than forty, about as thin and dry as a pinch of snuff; never very much to look at in my best days and looking like a used-up article now." Harriet sometimes refused to take all the credit for writing the book. Her friend Susan Howard, one of Henry Ward Beecher's wealthy parishioners in Brooklyn, once shared a guest room with Harriet at Mary Beecher Perkins's house. Howard said that Harriet undressed at bedtime and sat down cross-legged on the floor. Going into one of the dreamy reveries she was known for, she started brushing her hair. Finally she talked about her brother Edward's fears: "She dropped her brush from her hand and exclaimed with earnestness, 'Dear soul, he need not be troubled. He doesn't know that I did not write that book.' 'What!' said I. 'you did not write *Uncle Tom?*' . . . 'No,' she said, 'but it all came before me in visions, one after another, and I put them down in words.'" Harriet sometimes said more directly that God had written *Uncle Tom's Cabin*.

While Harriet coped with her great success, the Beecher men sought their own limelight. According to one observer, the early 1850s "marked the climax of the family's achievement and fame." Lyman's collected sermons appeared in the same year as *Uncle Tom's Cabin*. He was on the verge of senility and seemed unaware that he had passed from being the great Lyman Beecher to "Harriet Beecher Stowe's father." Lyman's sons by his first wife were just reaching their stride. Henry was drawing phenomenal crowds to his Sunday sermons in Brooklyn, and even Charles gained an audience when his sermon attacking the Fugitive Slave Law lost him his pastorate. In 1853 appeared Edward Beecher's masterwork, *The Conflict of Ages*. In this book Edward, or Dr. Beecher since he had been awarded an honorary Doctor of Divinity degree, developed his theory of the preexistence of souls. He defended Calvinism's central doctrine, original sin, against the protests of critics like his sister Catharine by postulating a time before birth when souls had an opportunity to choose right or wrong. Thus God was not arbitrary and people were responsible for their own damnation. Edward's book made a splash in theological circles, though some reviewers agreed with his father's assessment: "Edward, you've destroyed the Calvinistic barns, but I hope you don't delude yourself that the animals are going into your little theological hencoop."

It is possible to read some envy into Edward's concern about Harriet's becoming vain. Henry was obviously jealous of his sister's accomplishment; he even wrote a novel (*Norwood*, 1867) that he hoped would equal hers. But for the most part the gulf between male and female was so great in Lyman Beecher ideology that the boys competed with the boys and the girls with the girls. The two Beechers most profoundly affected by Harriet's grand stroke were Catharine and Isabella (Mary had presumably adjusted to a solely domestic life). As the sisters gathered in Brunswick, Catharine was being meddlesome again in interfering with Harriet's publishing arrangements. She had originally tried to get her latest publisher to bring out *Uncle Tom*, but he had refused for fear of losing southern trade. Now Catharine burst into anger at John P. Jewett for reaping most of the profits from Harriet's book. She began waging a campaign against Jewett, threatening him and trying (unsuccessfully) to get him to alter the terms of his contract with the Stowes. Sister Mary wrote Lyman that the siblings feared Catharine would go public and write "another book after the manner of 'Fact Stranger than Fiction' [sic— she is referring to the Delia Bacon book]."

Isabella attributed Catharine's actions to her single status: she didn't have enough to do. In a statement that would have made her cringe if she recalled it a decade later, she wrote John, "The fact is all women do need a domestic circle of their own to *manage*—then [they] won't have to 'go abroad.'" Amusingly, she inserted as an afterthought the words "& husband" after "domestic circle." But Catharine's behavior was more likely a way of dealing with Harriet's sudden fame. Catharine presented herself as the architect and protector of Harriet's career. There was some reason to this. She had, in fact, supported her sister's writing when she was better known than Harriet; she had even written an introduction to her first collection of stories. For the rest of her life Catharine would let no one forget that she had been her sister Harriet's mentor.

As for Isabella, she had never resigned herself to being solely a wife and mother. Forrest Wilson describes her thus in his biography of Stowe: "Harriet found an accumulation of mail so formidable that she brought up her half sister Isabella to help her with it as secretary. Isabella, a lush brunette, aged thirty, was married to John Hooker, who had been a law clerk in Thomas Perkins's office in Hartford." Dealing with the mail was not easy; the next envelope in the pile might contain a letter of praise from European royalty or, as Calvin Stowe reportedly found, the severed ear of a slave. But Isabella was having the greatest difficulty handling her own emotions in view of Harriet's stunning achievement. Here she was thirty years old with nothing to keep the world from categorizing her in terms of physical appearance and husband's occupation.

Ordinarily Isabella was too gregarious to feel self-conscious, but with her family in Brunswick she experienced a new feeling, "forever *conscious*," as though she were constantly watching herself. This behavior in turn made an unfortunate contrast with what Isabella saw as Harriet's selflessness, her great Christian charity. Isabella wrote John, "At first I was melancholy—on seeing the evidences of genius all around me here—my own bitterness fairly stared me in the face—but I am calming down considerably & begin to think my bump of order & housekeeping capacity are worth something in this working, matter of fact world." John would have to be comforted for her lack of Harriet's brilliance, she went on, by realizing that if she had it, she wouldn't be half as good a wife and mother. On this trip Isabella gave up for good her idea of asking Harriet for childrearing advice. At Brunswick she found Georgie a "romp" and worried she was turning little Mary "wild." For the time being she would concentrate on her own domain. She would bide her time managing her domestic circle, but Harriet's success could be considered the first move in her own quest for an identity beyond the home.

Harriet spent the 1850s adjusting to her new roles as anti-slavery leader and world-famous writer. First, the Stowes moved again, as Calvin accepted a better job as chair of sacred literature at Andover Theological Seminary in Andover, Massachusetts. This position came with a good salary and a free house on campus. Once the house was renovated, Harriet threw herself into completing her next book, *A Key to Uncle Tom's Cabin* (1853). The book was a compilation of documents her sisters had helped her collect at Brunswick. Harriet proposed to show, by means of laws, court records, newspaper articles, and accounts by ex-slaves, that she had not exaggerated the evils of slavery as the southern press accused her of doing. One of the stories in *A Key* concerned the Edmondson family of Virginia. The mother, Milly Edmondson, appealed to Harriet when her remaining slave children were about to be sold (Henry Ward Beecher had earlier persuaded his congregation to ransom two of Milly's daughters). Harriet started an "emancipation fund" and succeeded in raising enough money to buy the freedom of all the Edmondsons; later she paid for the sisters to study at Oberlin College.

Now that Harriet was looked upon as the spokesperson of the antislavery movement, whether she wanted to be or not, she was invited to England by British abolitionists (*Uncle Tom's Cabin* had sold even better there than in the United States). Before going abroad she duly acquainted herself with the American abolitionist leaders, such activists as Frederick Douglass and William Lloyd Garrison. Douglass had escaped from slavery to become an influential speaker, writer, and editor; Garrison had started his newspaper the *Liberator* in 1831 and painted Lyman Beecher as pro-slavery in the Lane Seminary controversy. Harriet tried to stay neutral amid the internal quarrels of the abolitionists, for instance, the quarrels between Garrison and Douglass and between Garrison and such men as Henry Stanton, who disagreed with his avoidance of political parties.

But inevitably her lack of knowledge of the movement and lack of interaction with African Americans got her into trouble. When she was finishing *A Key* in preparation for going to Europe, Harriet received a letter from Amy Post, an abolitionist and early women's rights advocate from western New York. Post wrote at the behest of her friend Harriet Jacobs, a former slave who was working as a nursemaid in the household of the journalist Nathaniel Willis and his wife. Jacobs wanted literary advice in telling the story of her life in slavery and eventual escape to the North; she also thought Stowe might let her daughter Louisa accompany her to England, for "Louisa would be a very good representative of a Southern Slave" for the English to meet.

The approach to Stowe was hard for Jacobs to make because Louisa's father was a married white man, an embarrassing fact Jacobs had not told even the Willises. As Jacobs said, "Slavery is terrible for men; but it is far more terrible for women." Stowe's response to Amy Post's letter was insensitive at best. She forwarded it to Mrs. Willis, asking whether the story were true and if she could use it in her *Key* to corroborate the character of Cassy as portrayed in *Uncle Tom's Cabin*. According to Jacobs, when Stowe learned that Jacobs planned to write her own story, she failed to answer her subsequent letters. Eventually Jacobs published her compelling narrative under the title *Incidents in the Life of a Slave Girl* (1861). As for Louisa, Stowe told Mrs. Willis that if the English discovered Louisa had once been a slave, she would be more "petted and patronized" than would be healthy for a young girl. Outraged, Jacobs complained to Amy Post that "Mrs. Stowe thinks petting is more than my race can bear[;] well what a pity we poor blacks cant [sic] have the firmness and stability of character that you white people have."

Harriet was probably thinking of her own spoiled daughters instead of being racist, and she was also under pressure to finish *A Key* before leaving for Europe in spring 1853. But her experience in England and Scotland, where she was petted by the aristocracy and hailed by huge crowds, unfortunately confirmed the idea that she could "speak for" the slaves. The British seemed to expect it. Bizarrely, though, she could not as a woman speak out loud. Calvin and brother Charles, whom she brought along as secretary, had to read her speeches for her. In general, Harriet's trip was a success. She made valuable contacts, raised money for the anti-slavery cause, and felt broadened by her "grand tour" of Paris, the Swiss Alps, and Germany. She would make two more European trips in the 1850s, ostensibly to establish copyright for her books, but staying longer on each occasion. This time she was back in Andover by fall, organizing, along with Garrison, an anti-slavery lecture series.

Harriet's trip provided material for a travel book, *Sunny Memories of Foreign Lands* (1854). In 1856 she published *Dred*, her last anti-slavery novel. Dred, a fugitive, is a more aggressive character than Uncle Tom; Harriet makes him the son of Denmark Vesey, who led a slave rebellion in the 1820s. But the plot and style of the book suffer greatly from the haste with which it was composed. If the title character is more palatable than Tom to modern readers, the novel is practically unreadable today. It did sell. After reading an unfavorable review, Harriet wrote Calvin that one hundred thousand copies had sold in four weeks. "After that who cares what critics say?"

In terms of books published, Catharine kept pace in the 1850s with her now more famous sister. She published five books during the decade, the same number as Harriet, and her *Letters to the People on Health and Happiness* (1855) was very popular. Catharine spent much of her time in travel, moving back and forth from the East to the Midwest where she had founded her third school, the Milwaukee Normal Institute (later Milwaukee Female College and Milwaukee-Downer College). After visiting the Milwaukee school, the Swedish novelist and traveler Frederika Bremer wrote: "An important reformation in female schools is taking place in these Western States at the present time under the guidance of a Miss Beecher . . . who is a kind of lady-abbess in educational matters."

In the East the lady-abbess often stayed with her siblings as she lectured and raised funds for an endowment for the Milwaukee school and her new organization, the American Woman's Educational Association (AWEA). The purpose of the AWEA, as she later described it, was "to establish *endowed* professional schools, in connection with literary institutions, in which woman's profession should be honored and taught as are the professions of men, and where woman should be trained for some self-supporting business." Catharine emphasized teaching as "woman's true profession." Her idea was that women in the East, where paid work for middle-class women was lacking, should be trained to teach and sent to the West, where more teachers were desperately needed.

To Harriet this idea was a brilliant one. As she read Catharine's recent books, she realized that she hadn't properly appreciated her sister's goals and motives during the past several years. "I considered her strange, nervous, visionary and to a certain extent unstable," she wrote her father and Henry. Now she finally saw that Catharine's work, far from being a series of individual failures (such as the failure of the Western Female Institute), formed a consistent whole unified by her idea of preparing women to educate the country. Harriet's recognition of her sister's aim was perceptive, and Catharine would eventually be credited for her achievements by historians of American education.

But recognition did not pay the rent. A key word in Catharine's statement of the AWEA's purpose was the one she emphasized: "endowed." She did not succeed in getting an endowment for her Milwaukee school, any more than she had in Hartford and Cincinnati. Furthermore, the trustees of the Milwaukee Normal Institute did not go along with her plan to have a house built for her on the seminary grounds. She managed to raise half the cost, thinking the trustees would cover the rest, but they firmly refused to finance a home that would be used primarily by her. No doubt Catharine thought enviously of the free house provided by Andover Theological Seminary for the use of her brother-in-law Calvin Stowe. She was now back to square one—she still had no home of her own and no place to retire in her old age. Angrily, she ended her relationship with the Milwaukee college and withdrew from the AWEA.

For Isabella, the 1850s was a decade of preparation rather than public achievement. She moved her household from Farmington to Hartford, starting the Nook Farm community there, gave birth to her last child, began to educate herself regarding women's status, and dealt with her health problems in preparation for venturing into the public world. By 1850 Hartford had grown from the small town Catharine knew when she established the Hartford Female Seminary. It was now a bustling and prosperous city of fourteen thousand; it was already known for its insurance industry and would soon expand economically with the advent of life insurance.

In 1851 John Hooker, with his brother-in-law, Francis Gillette, purchased a hundred-acre farm lying just outside the western limits of the city. The heavily wooded property was called Nook Farm because a river—originally the Hog or Meandering Swine River, renamed the Park—curved about the farm so as to leave thirty or forty acres within a nook. Kenneth Andrews, in his book *Nook Farm: Mark Twain's Hartford Circle* (1950), assumes that the Hookers moved because they found life in the village of Farmington too simple and rustic. But Isabella and John were always nostalgic about life in Farmington and often spent summers there. They moved because John's legal business took him increasingly to Hartford and it was inconvenient to travel back and forth, especially in the winter; the last few years before the move the Hookers boarded in Hartford during the winters.

The original Nook Farm had only one dwelling house, and that was occupied by the Gillettes, while the Hookers built a substantial brick house on a street they opened and called Forest Street. They settled in the new place in 1853, and a few years later the Gillettes built an even larger house nearby. As John notes in his autobiography, a "curious thread of relationship" soon ran through the neighborhood. In 1855 Mary and Thomas Perkins built a house around the corner on Hawthorn Street (in the twentieth century this would be the childhood home of actress Katharine Hepburn). Then in the 1860s the Stowes built Oakholm, an expensive white elephant of a house, on another part of the farm; ultimately they would sell it and buy a simpler house on Forest Street. John's widowed mother, Elizabeth Daggett Hooker, had a "cottage" built next to the Hookers. Then John's niece, Elizabeth "Lilly" Gillette, married George H. Warner, a businessman, and settled nearby. Warner attracted his sister-in-law, Susan Lee Warner, a talented musician, and his brother, Charles Dudley Warner, an editor and literary man who would be close to Mark Twain. Twain (Samuel Clemens) did not build his Nook Farm house until the 1870s; the thread of relationship here is that Isabella was an intimate friend of the Langdons of Elmira, New York, Clemens's in-laws.

The Nook Farm neighborhood was thus close-knit. As John explained, they lived "like a little society by ourselves—each of us making free of the others' houses, and each keeping open house, and all of us frequently gathering for a social evening or to welcome some friendly visitor, often some person distinguished in political, literary, or philanthropic life." One innovation Isabella introduced, now that she had a large enough house, was dancing. Although dancing was looked down upon by strict Calvinists and Lyman Beecher had once chastised a dancing Cincinnati family, she had come to consider it an acceptable amusement. After exchanging gifts at the Hookers' New Year's party in 1854 (holiday gift exchange being another non-Calvinist custom), the Perkins and Hooker families danced. There was plenty of cake and oysters, so Thomas and John invited some law students and lawyers from their office buildings. "Montgomery, the Irishman who works for us, came up in his shirt sleeves & played Irish jigs so fast on his violin we had to fly to keep any sort of step," Isabella wrote. She and John had learned the Virginia Reel, she and Aunt Esther could play popular tunes on the piano, and Grandma Hooker would "stand up once in a while to complete the figure."

A few years later the Calvinist prohibition against the theater fell away also. When Isabella was a teenager, Mr. Putnam, who would be John's best man, asked her opinion of attending the theater; she replied that it lowered the moral standards of the community (and added that Mr. Putnam was surely injuring himself by reading Bronson Alcott and other Transcendentalist philosophers). At the age of thirty-five Isabella went to the theater for the first time in her life. While visiting in Boston, she was taken to see *Hamlet*. The identical thing happened to Harriet, who was persuaded at about the same time to attend a performance of *Uncle Tom's Cabin* at the National Theatre in Boston. Previously Calvin had been so anti-theater that he would not let the twins go to the opera. From this point on, the Stowes and the Hookers not only attended the theater but also produced amateur theatricals and played charades at their parties at home. The Gillettes' son William, schoolmate of the Hookers' son, would become a celebrated actor and playwright.

These changes in lifestyle have been viewed as signs that "Victorian aspirations were replacing Calvinist standards." Whether it resulted from their interest in reform or the growing sophistication of their social circle, the Hookers' old Puritan sense of sin seemed dated. It was not that John and Isabella were no longer religious. In Farmington they worshipped under the Rev. Dr. Noah Porter, a distinguished minister who held his pastorate for over fifty years. When they moved to Hartford, they joined the Fourth Congregational Church under the Rev. William Patton and John became a deacon. (John had a second opportunity to change his occupation and again rejected it. As he left for Hartford, the Farmington church tried to persuade him to give up the law and become assistant pastor to Dr. Porter.) In his autobiography John notes that about the time he went to Hartford he began to have serious doubts about certain Calvinist doctrines, such as election (certain people being elected to be saved) and everlasting punishment. He started to think that people might be saved by good character.

Likewise, Isabella's injunctions to herself in the children's journal to provide an example of holiness gave way to Bible instruction; she read and discussed with the children the pictures and stories from a monthly magazine,

Scriptural History. In the 1870s, when looking over her journal of twenty-five years earlier, Isabella made some annotations. Most were corrections of sexist language—"he and she" substituted for "he"—but next to an entry lamenting the children's failure to be "holy" she wrote, "What a fool!" Both Isabella and John were more concerned with the children's moral character. Isabella had them visit a poor family, for instance: "I took them to see a family just come into town & lodged in a cellar—buying a loaf of bread on the way, with a five cts. of each [child]. They could not stay long—from the darkness & crowded state of the cellar—but they were much impressed & were more ready than ever to pray for the poor." But although the Hooker children were baptized, sent to church and Sunday school, and given religious instruction at home, they were never expected to go through the conversion process that had scarred so many of their aunts and uncles.

The religious transformations of the Hooker family were paralleled in the Beechers at large and the country as a whole. By the time Lyman Beecher retired from Lane Seminary in 1850, most of his children, ministers or not, had strayed from his Calvinist faith. Edward had burned the Calvinist barns, in Lyman's view, as he tried to shore them up, and William and Charles followed Edward, Charles even being tried for heresy. Henry and Thomas became what Marie Caskey calls, in her religious classification of the Beechers, "christocentric liberals." Completely uninterested in theological doctrines, they emphasized Christ's love for humanity. Lyman once said of Henry that he "had no business to tell sinners of the Love of God without telling them of the wrath of God."

As for the Beecher sisters, Mary had long been a convert to Reverend Bushnell's liberal doctrine of "Christian nurture." She first tried to resist it, out of loyalty to her father, but ultimately gave in. From the time she was a girl she had the same problem as Catharine with the wrathful God of the Calvinists. Although she managed to convert, she confided to brother Edward that religion seemed a joyless "task" to her—"if I ever go [to pray] with feelings of pleasure, I soon become wearied and cold." Mary felt disappointed when her son Frederick turned out to be anti-religious. Still, like Isabella, she did not try to force conversion on her children. Mary's and Isabella's private falling away from Calvinism was nothing compared to the deliberate public attacks Catharine and Harriet made on the religion in the 1850s. The two had been critical in their writings before, but the fading of their father's mind in the middle of the decade allowed them to express their views without fear of hurting him.

Catharine directly confronted the religion of her childhood in two books, *Common Sense Applied to Religion* (1857) and *An Appeal to the People on Behalf of Their Rights as Authorized Interpreters of the Bible* (1860). Neither of these titles would have made sense to the famous Puritan minister Jonathan Edwards—he who portrayed sinners as dangling over the pit in his sermon "Sinners in the Hands of an Angry God." Edwards thought only ministers were authorized to interpret the Bible. Catharine's attack was partly on Calvinist doctrine and partly on the authority of the ministry. She took apart the theories of predestination, original sin, and conversion. Most Americans no longer believed, she said, that their fate was predestined, that they were born horribly corrupt and had to seek God's grace in a conversion experience. These notions were perversions of Christianity introduced long ago by St. Augustine. They would no longer be influential if it were not for the power of the clerical establishment, what Catharine called the "vast array of wealth, position, influence, and ecclesiastical power" of institutionalized Protestantism.

Catharine would not, of course, replace Calvinist ideas with self-indulgence, as her nephew Frederick Perkins was inclined to do. She simply believed that moral leadership was passing to secular elements in American society. Social influence would now discourage vice and lead people to virtue. People would be motivated by what she considered the highest morality, the principle of self-sacrifice. In the early 1860s, before her father died but long after he was mentally incompetent, Catharine joined the Episcopal Church, the church of the Footes of Nutplains. She did not leave the symbolism of that act for her biographers to interpret. She wrote Delia Bacon's brother straightforwardly, "I have only stepped from my father[']s house into my mother[']s."

Harriet also made the switch, and she too attacked the clerical establishment in her writings. A reviewer of *Dred* sighed over the number of characters who were unsympathetic Calvinist ministers and wished the author had put at least one good clergyman in the book. She did so but also aired her doubts in her next novel, *The Minister's Wooing* (1859), based on a tragic event in her personal life. In June 1857 Harriet returned from her second trip to Europe. The Hookers met her in Andover, having brought Georgie, who had stayed with them during her mother's absence. Harriet and Fred then went to Hartford to visit the Hookers and the Perkinses and consider moving to Nook Farm. In July the news came that Henry Stowe, who was nineteen and attending Dartmouth College, had drowned during a swimming party. Harriet told Isabella that "Henry was the only one of our children that we had begun not to feel anxious for & to hope to rely on him ourselves." The Stowes had, however, worried about his relation to Christianity; even if they had not insisted on conversion, they wanted Henry to adopt a religious path. Whether he had so chosen was not certain, and Harriet found herself in an agony similar to Catharine's when her fiancé drowned thirty-five years before. Like

Catharine, she searched desperately for signs that her beloved had become a Christian before he died.

After Henry's death Harriet sank into a deep depression for two years. She wrote Georgie that she was like a leafless tree: "I am cold, weary, dead; everything is a burden to me. . . . I let my plants die by inches before my eyes, and do not water them." As Harriet was a dedicated horticulturist, like her mother, this was a frightening admission. But she was also a professional author now and so made use of her situation to write *The Minister's Wooing*. The minister in the book is based on the real Puritan minister Dr. Samuel Hopkins (Aaron Burr appears in the novel also). Dr. Hopkins woos Mary Scudder, the Catharine Beecher character, who was in love with James Martyn, a young man lost at sea. The author says of Hopkins: "These hard old New England divines were the poets of metaphysical philosophy, who built systems in an artistic fervor, and felt self exhale from beneath them as they rose into the higher regions of thought. But where theorists and philosophers tread with sublime assurance, woman often follows with bleeding footsteps,—women are always turning from the abstract to the individual, and feeling where the philosopher only thinks." Mary Scudder and Martyn's mother, the character based on Harriet herself, walk with bleeding footsteps because Martyn was unconverted when he died. In fiction, unlike life, there could be a happy ending to this situation, so Martyn did not drown after all and returns home a believer.

The Minister's Wooing introduces Candace, the Martyns' black slave (whom they free in the course of the book), to represent a Christianity more benign than Calvinism. Described as "a powerfully built, majestic black woman," Candace was also modeled after a real person—Sojourner Truth, the great abolitionist and women's rights advocate, whom Harriet had recently met. Candace refuses to believe in original sin, arguing that *she* never ate the apple. She is the only person who can comfort Mrs. Martyn when Jim is reported missing. She cradles her in her arms and says, " 'Why, de Lord a'n't like what ye tink,—He *loves* ye, honey! . . . He died for Mass'r Jim,— loved him and *died* for him." For Harriet, a true religion had to be based on love. At about the same time that Catharine Beecher joined the Episcopal Church, Harriet gave permission for her three daughters to be confirmed as Episcopalians; once Calvin had retired from Andover Theological Seminary she quietly followed. The Hookers thought the Stowe girls became "absorbed in crosses" but were just as disapproving when their minister started preaching Calvinist sermons during the next decade.

As Harriet lost a son, Isabella gave birth to one—her last child, Edward. Harriet visited shortly before his birth; this assumption of a mother's role had become a tradition. Eddie was born prematurely on the 26th of

Harriet Beecher Stowe and twin daughters, Harriet and Eliza Stowe, c. 1850. Courtesy Harriet Beecher Stowe Center, Hartford, Conn.

February 1855, while his sisters slept in the next room. Isabella noted that she was "so stupefied by the morphine taken to prevent the premature birth that I did not hear the children's first expressions of delight—or know much about what they said & did for two or three days. Indeed the baby was so puny & feeble, we had but little hope that he would live." He weighed three and a half pounds, only half of what Alice had weighed, and looked like a "poor little unfledged bird." Yet he lived, and finally began to nurse, until at eight months he weighed as much as Alice at the same age.

Isabella did not recover as quickly from childbirth as she had earlier. She experienced a general prostration and suffered from severe headaches and problems with her eyesight. She had trouble breast-feeding now. After nursing Eddie her breasts felt tired and were pierced by sharp pains. She wrote that "my health is so feeble it seems as if the milk must be poor—yet he grows more & more fond of nursing & will not *now be denied*. He is even refusing to be fed from a spoon—which he enjoyed from his birth till now— so what can we do?" Aunty Smith, who came to help with the baby, recalled that Alice too had evinced a passion for nursing. As they were walking one day they saw a little colt nursing its mother. "Alice was perfectly delighted & called out 'Oh Aunty, see the little baby horse, sucking his mother horse & *so happy!*'"

"Aunty" Anna Smith was a middle-class woman in her forties who coincidentally had the same name as the Stowes' governess in Cincinnati. Harriet's Anna was an English immigrant slightly younger than Harriet and very devoted to her. Isabella's was an older woman with children of her own. She spent about three months at the Hookers after the birth of each baby; she would get up after the middle-of-the-night feeding and take the baby from Isabella into her bed. When the children were older Aunty Smith would occasionally come simply to visit or to care for the children when they were ill. In the fifties the Hookers usually had a full complement of domestics. In addition to a nursemaid, they had a cook/maid, a part-time chauffeur, and occasional tutors for the children. Montgomery, the Irishman who played at the Hookers' dances, divided his time evenly between Isabella and John and the Perkinses as chauffeur and gardener. Many of the household workers in Hartford were Irish, as was typical in the antebellum North; in New York City at midcentury almost two-thirds of domestic servants were Irish. It is common to find anti-Irish sentiment in letters and diaries of women of the time, along with complaints about their service and the difficulties in general of finding and keeping domestic workers. One of the worst offenders in published writing was Catharine, who referred to "the influx into our kitchens of the uncleanly and ignorant." She considered foreign domestic help to be thriftless and frequently dishonest as well.

Isabella, however, had excellent relationships with her workers. She tended to keep them a long time and to praise, rather than criticize, when she referred to them in letters. There was undoubtedly an element of the Lady Bountiful in some of her traditions, such as lining up the servants formally to receive their Christmas presents, but she showed real concern for their lives. Her letters to John when she was away from home often contained personal messages to the servants and hints for improving their health. When Eddie came down with whooping cough when she was absent, she instructed John to hire someone to sleep with him at night "but not Bridget," their cook and maid, because it might harm her health and "her good constitution is all the wealth she has." Isabella treated Bridget Doran kindly many years later when she was seduced and impregnated by William, a short-lived Hooker chauffeur, against whom Isabella had warned her. In the mid-fifties, when another maid, Clara, left to get married, Isabella hosted her wedding at Nook Farm, including a reception for forty guests.

The Hookers were financially well off during the 1850s and could afford such gestures. Isabella tended to feel guilty about their relative wealth. She compared herself to brother Charles, who had been driven from his pastorate and had five little children and no income. The Hookers, of course, joined the Stowes in helping Charles financially, but Isabella still wondered to Harriet whether it was right for them to spend so much money when others were poor. Harriet advised her to accept her prosperity as sent by God, and if Isabella could have seen into the future, when the Hookers would have to rent out their house because they couldn't afford to live in it, she might have taken this characteristic Puritan advice. As it was, her attempts to get her children to remember the poor show a continuing uneasiness.

In the children's journal Isabella frequently analyzed her offspring's characters and personalities. Each was very different from the others. Mary tended to be quiet and reserved, Isabella noting that she was already exhibiting "her father's & Grandma's *caution* as to personal exposures of any kind." Her willfulness had been subdued, and her mother thought she had a capacity for spirituality. Although Mary was intelligent, she was slower in her studies than Alice; she had a good sense of humor and, as she grew older, would emulate her father in being a wit and jokester. Isabella felt that "if she lives" she would make a lovely, pious woman. The worried "if she lives" reflected her deep fears for Mary's health. Because Mary coughed at night throughout her childhood, Isabella thought she might not live past it: "Sometimes I fear her lungs may become irritable & *early consumption her fate.*"

Alice Hooker was more lively and affectionate than her sister. Isabella likened her to Pearl, the daughter of Hester Prynne in Nathaniel Hawthorne's *The Scarlet Letter* (1850). But Alice showed a weaker will than Pearl (or Mary); she was gregarious and anxious to please and thus presented less of a discipline problem. In a lengthy journal entry in 1852 Isabella compares her daughters and her own reactions to them. The entry begins with her worries about Mary's dying:

> [M]y soul seems to rest on hers so much that I know not how to sustain myself alone—she seems a part of myself—& to lose her, would be to find myself dis-membered—
>
> Towards Alice I feel differently in this—that I desire to live myself to take care of her—to guide, & guard—without expecting so much in return—not but that she is generous—& more affectionately demonstrative than Mary—but somehow I do not rely upon her & cannot yet feel that I ever shall—She seems to me more a fancy piece to amuse & please than a solid article for daily use & comfort.

Isabella thought Alice more like herself and thus easier to predict, but she identified more closely with Mary. She seemed to feel and understand every emotion Mary had before it was expressed in words; "every thing she says & does, finds an echo in my own bosom." This strong identification would make it hard for Isabella to let Mary separate from her in later years.

There is less in the children's journal about Eddie, as he was the youngest child, born eight years after Alice and ten after Mary. What his mother does say about him makes him appear that rarity, the "easy child." He seemed to be naturally loving, obedient, unselfish, and smart. His only problems in childhood were his tendency to catch every possible childhood disease, including scarlet fever, and to be timid and whiny around other boys. One day when Eddie was nine and looking sad, Isabella questioned him. It was "the same old story" of big boys teasing littler ones—they had made fun of his short hair and small nose. Isabella and John suggested some retaliatory actions, but Willie Gillette, his slightly older cousin and best friend, had told him he would never be as good as the big boys, and Eddie believed it. "The little darling—so pure—& honest & lovely as he is—so generous, high minded & obliging—I just smothered him with kisses & told him it would take all the good in ten common boys to make one so dear & lovely as he." The high points of Eddie's childhood were the large and elaborate birthday parties his mother orchestrated, with fifteen to thirty children as guests. There would be outdoor games and, as the years progressed, dancing. At one party Isabella served biscuits and dried beef, macaroons, lemon ice, birthday cake, and over three pounds of candy.

The education of the Hooker children was rather haphazard. Typically, they began district school in Farmington or Hartford at age five or six and attended only in the mornings, even as they grew older. But the girls' attendance would quickly become occasional as they were plagued by headaches and colds. In December 1854, for instance, Mary and Alice were enrolled half days in a Miss Richmond's school in Hartford, yet by the next February they had stopped going because of illness and the difficulty of travel through the snow. The Hookers did supplement the children's education at home. They would occasionally hire a governess, Mary Doyle, to tutor the children in various subjects, and Isabella herself read Isaac Taylor's *Home Education* and other works on education. When the girls were not in school, she built study time into their daily routine. In 1854, before attending Miss Richmond's school, they would take a sponge bath upon rising, eat breakfast, make their beds and straighten their rooms, and at 9:30 go outside for an hour. Sometimes their Uncle Francis (Gillette) would take them into the woods on a horse sled so they could slide on the river while he gathered wood. At 11:00 Isabella listened to the girls read and spell, and after midday dinner they practiced writing and sewing.

There is nothing unusual for the time about this desultory education. It was much the same as that received by Mary's and Harriet's daughters. The Perkins girls were quite openly educated for marriage. The Stowe girls attended some good schools, such as Abbot Academy in Andover and a boarding school in Paris, but they were never urged to work very hard; Mary Perkins wrote her husband of the twins that "I never saw girls who were so bright & intelligent who so hated to study & apply themselves." Mary and Harriet simply followed Beecher family tradition in paying more attention to the education of their sons, who went to college. Isabella's similar attitude toward her daughters' schooling is puzzling, though, given her conscious resentment of her own lack of formal education. Her assertion in the 1859 letter to her neighbor that she had never been to school for two years together in her life could also apply to her daughters. Isabella explains in the children's journal that neither girl could obtain an education "in the regular way." Because of their delicate health they could study only one or two subjects at a time. She states her priorities directly when she notes that she has found just the school for Mary and Alice, featuring "a very kind, indulgent teacher—who regards health & ventilation as the first thing to be looked after—& study secondary."

In her ambitions for her daughters Isabella differed markedly from other women's rights advocates in the nineteenth century. Leaders such as Elizabeth Cady Stanton, Lucy Stone, and Ida Wells-Barnett all pushed their daughters beyond their own educational attainment: Harriot Stanton Blatch received a master's degree from Vassar, Alice Stone Blackwell attended top schools before graduating from Boston University, and Ida Wells-Barnett's daughter Alfreda Duster earned her bachelor's degree at the University of

Chicago. Later in life Isabella wrote her daughter Alice wistfully of Harriot Stanton Blatch's continuation of her mother's work, but she never prepared her own girls for this eventuality.

All the women's rights leaders mentioned above were "strong-minded," to use the nineteenth-century word for "feminist," *before* they had children. Their greater knowledge no doubt explains the discrepancies in Isabella's behavior. Although she clearly had feminist tendencies in her youth when she complained about the institution of marriage, she did not start reading and thinking about women's rights and applying the insights of movement leaders until the 1860s. In 1859 when Isabella read Thomas Wentworth Higginson's "Ought Women to Learn the Alphabet?" Mary was already fourteen and Alice twelve.

Several events occurred in the 1850s that were crucial in leading Isabella to her eventual public career. The first, of course, was the publication of *Uncle Tom's Cabin* and Isabella's feelings of inferiority when she compared herself to Harriet and other achieving family members. The second was her husband's six-month trip to Europe in 1857. John, whom she considered her "Siamese twin," had wanted to tour Europe ever since the Stowes went in 1853. When Isabella refused to go with him, having no desire to travel, he set off by himself, planning to meet Mary Beecher Perkins, who was accompanying the Stowes on their second trip. Isabella surprised herself by feeling devastated at John's departure. She had long been regretting her increased dependence on him, describing the funicular effect that F. Scott Fitzgerald would make the central metaphor of his *Tender Is the Night* (1934); as one spouse went up, the other came down. Isabella had written John in 1853 that "I do believe that I have less self-reliance, in its best sense too, than I had six or eight years ago [before the birth of the children]. You have more[;] as I seem to lose you gain."

Interestingly, the metaphor of the funicular applied also to the marital experience of Harriet and Calvin Stowe. When the two were separated, as they were about a third of the time during her childbearing years, Harriet often felt an influx of strength. For example, her health improved both physically and psychologically when she spent a whole year away from home at a Vermont sanitarium. Calvin acknowledged that Harriet had been dangerously weak before she left, but when he visited he was furious at being made to sleep in a separate bed. He informed her that their separation had put him in "a sad state physically and mentally." The only solution for him was "if your health were so far restored that you could take me again to your *bed and board*." If, however, Harriet took him to her bed she risked another pregnancy, and she had already borne seven children and suffered at least two miscarriages. As Mary Kelley concludes, "In the end, they could not help each other: one's needs clashed with the other's; one's cure brought the other's illness."

After John left for Europe, Isabella cried frequently and felt herself drained of energy. Eventually she began to think of a cure and pulled herself together enough to visit her friends Hattie Putnam and Charlotte Hull in the Boston area. She seems to have devised a long-range plan to become more independent and stronger by improving her health. In Boston she consulted a Mrs. Binney about her tipped uterus, which she thought was causing her backaches. She may also have had, after years of childbirth, a prolapsed uterus (in which the muscles and ligaments that hold the uterus in place become stretched, causing the vagina to bulge and sag). Mrs. Binney found, as Isabella reported to John, "severe inclination of the neck of the uterus and the same old displacement." Her treatment consisted of applications of silver nitrate. During her stay in Boston, Isabella considered studying with Mrs. Binney and then practicing the treatment of "female complaints" in Hartford. Her son Eddie, however, was only two years old at the time.

The idea of making money became increasingly important to Isabella. In January 1860 she wailed to John, "Oh my *soul*—if you could only teach me how to earn money—but there's no use in hoping—I can't write a book—nor draw pictures—nor do any other productive work—I have always told you, that you overestimated your wife." At the time of this letter she was staying with brother Henry in Brooklyn, and the immediate occasion was her inability to afford a painting by a protégé of Henry's. As the Hookers' financial situation worsened during the 1860s and John felt nervous and overworked, Isabella wished more and more to help.

That she also connected earning money with independence of action is shown in her essay "Shall Woman Vote? A Matrimonial Dialogue," which she wrote in February 1860. In this dialogue Mrs. Smith tells Mr. Smith that if she found him on the wrong side of any political issue, she would subscribe to a newspaper that took the right position and would read it to him nightly. Instead of answering her argument directly, Mr. Smith takes a detour: "You mentioned, I think, that you should pay for your charming paper—permit me to inquire, if you please, where you would procure the necessary funds?" Mrs. Smith replies that she would give a lecture—"fifty dollars for one night." That would pay for several papers and leave something over for his birthday present.

In another decade Isabella would indeed be lecturing for pay, but in 1860 she was far from that point. She was just becoming interested in women's rights, the catalyst being the article she read in the February 1859 *Atlantic Monthly*, "Ought Women to Learn the Alphabet?" This was the essay that prompted her to think about the past and write bitterly about the contrast between her brothers being pushed to attend college and her own truncated education. Isabella was right in guessing that the anonymous author of the essay was a man—she could tell "alas! by his learning." The article was (and still is) a brilliant summary of historical attitudes toward women's education and argument for allowing women the alphabet. It is full of wit and erudition, including both ancient and modern languages and an impressive knowledge of women's history. No wonder Isabella envied the author his ability to expose the twisted logic of conventional ideas about women, for instance, "that it is right to admit girls to common schools, and equally right to exclude them from colleges,—that it is proper for a woman to sing in public, but indelicate for her to speak in public,—that a post-office box is an unexceptionable place to drop a bit of paper into, but a ballot-box terribly dangerous."

When Isabella discovered the author was Thomas Wentworth Higginson, a Boston abolitionist, she wrote him a fan letter. The letter has been lost, but Higginson remembered it forty years later as a great compliment. He responded to Isabella's letter with comments that would prove prophetic regarding her eventual involvement in women's rights. It made him indignant, he wrote, to be thanked by women for telling the truth when those same people often rejected "the *women* who, at infinitely greater cost, have said the same things. It costs a man nothing to defend woman,—a few sneers, a few jokes, that is all; but for women to defend themselves, has in times past cost almost everything." He cited the bravery of Lucretia Mott, Elizabeth Cady Stanton's mentor, and Lucy Stone, the first female graduate of Oberlin College. Then he exhorted Isabella to rise above the mass of women who revile their own defenders and seek a "mean safety" by sacrificing those who have made a heroic start. Isabella was not yet ready to risk seeking out the pioneers of women's rights, but when she did she would follow Higginson's prescription.

Thomas Wentworth Higginson was one of the founders of the *Atlantic Monthly* and thus acquainted with Harriet, who had published *The Minister's Wooing* in the new journal. The soon-to-be prestigious magazine was established in 1857 by such New England literary lights as Ralph Waldo Emerson and James Russell Lowell with the conscious purpose of bringing culture to the masses. In fact, the twentieth-century split between "high" and "low," or "popular," culture has often been traced to the time of the founding of the *Atlantic*. Harriet was at first a highly desirable contributor. As Calvin wrote her, all the founders and editors were saying that she should give them a serial to start the first year and then Hawthorne would follow in the second. *The Minister's Wooing* was the perfect serial, for it contributed, in Joan Hedrick's words, to "the mythification of New England so central to the *Atlantic's* mission." But soon women's books, especially those having social and political agendas as Harriet's did, were demoted to the lower categories of literature; works by women were too "sentimental" and "melodramatic," to use the *Atlantic*'s code words.

Even at the beginning women were not fully integrated into the *Atlantic* circle. The men conducted literary business during dinners at Boston taverns and hotels, and no women were present at the founding dinner. Hedrick notes that although Harriet "should have been included in these social business meetings," she was invited to only one, which turned out to be uncomfortable. In July 1859 Harriet and a number of other female contributors to the *Atlantic* were invited to a farewell dinner at the Revere House (the Stowes were about to embark on their third trip to Europe). Harriet asked whether wine would be served and was assured it would not. She was no teetotaler and had drunk wine with meals in Europe, but apparently she had heard rumors of the heavy drinking that sometimes took place at the *Atlantic* dinners.

The Stowes appeared at the event anticipating some memorable conversation because Lowell and Oliver Wendell Holmes were known to be witty. According to Higginson, Harriet was "quietly dressed in a Quakerish silk, but with a peculiar sort of artificial grape-leaf garland round her head" (the poet Henry Wadsworth Longfellow wrote in his diary that this wreath was very becoming). Only one other woman showed up, the shy young Harriet Prescott (later Spofford), and the women were left to languish in a separate parlor while the men socialized in another room. When dinner was finally announced, the two Harriets were placed at opposite ends of the table, with Emerson, Lowell, Holmes, Higginson, Longfellow, John Greenleaf Whittier, and the other men scattered between. There was "a visible awkwardness," Higginson recalled, as the women remained silent and the men whispered to each other jokes and complaints about the lack of wine. Finally, the men's water glasses were handed to the waiter and came back "suffused with a rosy hue." The discourse reached the level of Holmes's arguing that all swearing originated in the pulpit and Lowell's claiming that *Tom Jones* was the greatest novel ever written. Calvin and Harriet later confessed to Whittier that the conversation hadn't quite met their expectations.

Were women really unfit for public life, as the Boston Brahmins seemed to think? Henry Ward Beecher argued in a speech entitled "Woman's Influence in Politics" that women's participation would reform public affairs. It was an attack on this idea by the editor of the *Independent* that pushed Isabella to write "Shall Women Vote? A Matrimonial Dialogue." She has Mr. Smith argue the editor's position, that women should stay out of public affairs. Mrs. Smith agrees in the case of mothers who are rearing a family but uses as the crux of her argument her sister Martha, whose children are married and gone, leaving her with nothing to do. Isabella now introduces an argument that would become central to her women's rights theory—that mothers have had life experience qualifying them for public work, if not actually making them superior to men. Mrs. Smith notes of Martha "what maturity of thought, real wisdom there is in her—gained in this most motherly way of discriminating between her own children—adapting influence & government according to character & bringing out a harmonious whole, from so many discordant or at least different elements." The phrasing here sounds much like the children's journal—and like Catharine Beecher. Though Isabella's argument was rather obviously self-serving, providing her with a ready-made résumé and justification for entering the public sphere, it also owed something to Catharine's conception of the female teacher. As Harriet once summarized this conception, men might have more knowledge than women but "they have less talent at communicating it, nor have they the patience, the long-suffering, and gentleness necessary to superintend the formation of character."

But if Catharine had been asked, "Shall Women Vote?" she would have answered an emphatic no rather than Isabella's qualified yes. She had published early in the decade *The True Remedy for the Wrongs of Woman* (1851), in which she acknowledged that women had indeed endured wrongs but rejected suffrage as a solution. Women had been wronged because they were neither educated for nor honored and appreciated in their profession as "the conservators of the domestic state, the nurses of the sick, . . . and the educators of the human mind." The true remedy was, of course, Catharine's educational scheme. Women in general should receive more education, including instruction in the domestic arts and the principles of good health, and many women should be educated as teachers. As Catharine pointed out, her goal had always been "to secure a *liberal education* and *remunerative employ* to our own sex." Certainly this aim was not opposed to woman's rights; it was not in today's parlance an "anti-feminist" goal. Unlike many of the nineteenth-century "antis" (that is, anti-suffrage women), Catharine kept her focus squarely on women and consistently aimed to raise their status. She never approved, for instance, when wealthy women gave money to benefit men. In *A True Remedy* she scolds women for financially supporting men's educational institutions and providing scholarships for male students only.

Catharine also fought the numerous prejudices against unmarried women. Why did every woman have to marry? Why was it unthinkable that a single woman could have a home of her own? Many of her beliefs are held by women who call themselves feminists today—for instance, that women should be economically independent, that "posts of honor and emolument" should be open to them, that the work of housewives and mothers is terribly underrated. Catharine's grandnephew Lyman Beecher Stowe once told a revealing anecdote about her. In her later years she spent an evening with Nook Farm neighbors of her sisters'. The company was singing hymns and someone suggested one with the chorus "I am nothing, Lord." Catharine immediately objected, declaring "I am *not* nothing!" Maybe this assertion reflected her large ego and personal vanity, as Lyman Beecher Stowe seemed to think; or perhaps it was instead a protest that had become second nature for Catharine, an objection to women's being treated like "nothing" and erased from history.

But if Catharine sometimes sounded like a feminist, she also insisted that women remain in their own "sphere" of action. They were limited to their one "profession" (Catharine always uses the singular) as domestic guardians, nurses, and teachers. While her definition was in one way expansive, broadening the actual roles of women at the time, it was also restrictive. Women should not try to poach on "masculine employments," which consisted of everything outside woman's profession. In particular, women should stay out of the public arena, leaving politics and civic responsibilities solely to men. It was not that women weren't competent to vote or undertake public duties, but participation in politics might corrupt them, weakening their special qualities. Even worse, men might start to view them as competitors. Catharine had a strong fear of men's power. Whether her fear stemmed from growing up with a domineering father and seven brothers or from losing the Delia Bacon battle, she always kept in mind the fact that men ruled the world. Her main objection to the women who fought for women's rights was that their methods were unsafe—that is to say, they directly confronted men instead of trying to influence them from the sidelines.

Surprisingly, Catharine had a much greater knowledge of the emerging movement for women's rights than did Isabella. At this point neither Isabella nor Harriet had heard of the gathering at Seneca Falls, New York, in 1848 in which women issued a declaration of their rights. Catharine, however, had obviously read this "Declaration of Sentiments" because she responds point by point in *The True Remedy*. She writes, for instance: "Is it claimed that there are civil laws which are unjust and unequal, and contrary to the Bible rights of our sex? Let every intelligent woman use her influence with the lawmakers, and in *an acceptable manner,* and these laws would speedily be changed. Is it claimed that, in social customs, the guilty woman is treated with overbearing cruelty, and the guilty man with shameful leniency [the double standard]? Let all virtuous women decide that they will treat both sexes alike, and the unjust custom will speedily pass away." If it were claimed that women were deprived of "remunerative employ," as the declaration does, Catharine's answer was to raise the status of woman's profession instead of "rushing into the political arena to join in the scramble for office."

Isabella did not agree that women should stay out of politics. She has Mrs. Smith say that if you take middle-aged mothers like Martha who have already reared their children, and then take all the widows and childless women, and all the single women, and all the women who would be single if they did not fear boredom—"taking all these, there is material enough I am sure, for a very respectable Congress—respectable in point of character & ability too, as well as numbers." It may be this vision of an all-female Congress that prompted Thomas Wentworth Higginson to label Isabella's article "radical" when she sent it to him for comment. She actually comes to a conservative conclusion, having Mrs. Smith declare that if she had absolute power, she would not open the polls to women until public opinion demanded it.

From a modern standpoint the most radical part of the essay is Isabella's contention that women should serve on juries; although women won the vote in 1920, they did not routinely become jurors until the 1970s. Higginson wrote Isabella that it would be practically impossible to get paid for an article so radical. "To do great good & make money at the same time was the lot of Uncle Tom's Cabin [sic], but a rare one." He agreed to forward "Shall Women Vote?" to the *Atlantic Monthly* but made clear his expectation that it would be rejected. Isabella should not be discouraged from further writing, because she would have failed only in making her very first article palatable to conservative editors.

In a long essay on Isabella Beecher Hooker, Anne Throne Margolis says that Higginson's assessment of the dialogue could only have had a demoralizing effect on her. His reference to her sister's success could not have helped, nor his joking promise not to print her praise of his article as "the opinion of an anonymous lady, of distinguished family." As Margolis notes, "Ironically, it was precisely when she measured herself against the accomplishments of her distinguished family that Isabella felt herself to be most anonymous." Yet she was not completely demoralized, and she had already faced her lowest point when John went to Europe. Since then Isabella had proved she could express her thoughts in a competent, if not distinguished, essay; she had also made the firm decision to try anything available to improve her health. The ghost of Harriet Porter Beecher seemed always at her heels, and Isabella could not allow herself to sink into illness or depression. She dreaded becoming a "useless" and bedridden invalid, she told John, "a trial to my husband—& children—a nervous, fidgetty [sic] old woman causing gloom in the house instead of sunshine." Thus, a month after receiving Higginson's letter Isabella checked in to the Gleasons' water cure establishment in Elmira, New York, to try a course of treatment recommended by her sisters.

4

Water Cure and Civil War,
1860–1865

By 1860 WATER CURE, or hydropathy, was nothing short of a craze. Although water cure establishments predominated in New York and New England, they existed all over the United States. The cure at Brattleboro, Vermont, which had opened in 1845 with fifteen guests, now had six hundred to eight hundred a year. Elmira boasted patients from fourteen states, two territories, and Canada. It had all started in Austria in the 1820s when Vincenz Priessnitz cured his broken ribs by wrapping them in wet bandages. He came to believe that the external application and drinking of pure soft water (not mineral water), combined with fresh air and exercise, could prevent and even cure disease. In *Letters to the People on Health and Happiness* (1855) Catharine describes her treatment at Brattleboro thus: "At four in the morning packed in a wet sheet; kept in it from two to three hours; then up, and in a reeking perspiration immersed in the coldest plunge-bath. Then a walk as far as strength would allow, and drink five or six tumblers of the coldest water. At eleven A.M. stand under a douche of the coldest water falling *eighteen feet, for ten minutes*. Then walk, and drink three or four tumblers of water. At three P.M. sit half an hour in a *sitz*-bath (i.e. sitting bath) of the coldest water. Then walk and drink again."

Cold wet sheets notwithstanding, it is easy to see how this treatment could be effective. For one thing it avoided the more extreme practices of the traditional medicine of the day, such as application of leeches and harsh chemicals. Exercise, fresh air, and water drinking are considered health-improving today. Water cure was also allied to movements and causes now considered relatively healthy, such as temperance and vegetarianism. Above all, there was rest from the patient's usual routine, or what the water cure theorists thought of as the ills of an overcivilized society—fast pace, overwork, sedentary habits, late hours, and rich food and drink. Some people disliked the constant dressing and undressing to prepare for the baths but, as Isabella wrote John, "It is such a relief—to have nobody to care for—nothing that *must* be done."

Catharine was an early advocate of water cures. She constantly looked for ways to improve her health since her first "nervous breakdown" in Hartford. She noted in *Letters to the People on Health and Happiness* that as a child she was never sick. Her family "obeyed the laws of health, not from *principle,* but from *poverty.*" In other words, they had simple food and clothing; there was no coffee or tea available for the young. None of the Beechers' houses was built well enough to be poorly ventilated, and the children spent most of their time outside exercising in the fresh air. It was not until Catharine had to earn her living teaching and was confined to the schoolroom that her health became a problem. Her eyes grew sore, and any slight wound, bruise, or sprain to a limb would lead to semi-paralysis. (When she first went to Brattleboro, her foot was so nearly paralyzed she could hardly walk.) Catharine was willing to experiment widely with the isms of the day to find a cure. She tried mesmerism (hypnosis), galvanism (electric shock), magnetism, and spiritualism (attempts to contact the spirits of the dead). She found water cure the most restorative treatment because it was the least drastic. "The great advantage of Water Cure," she wrote "is that the process is so *slow* that no great harm can be *suddenly* effected, while the indications of mistaken treatment can be obeyed before any evil is done."

Catharine gradually extended her concern about her own health to the poor health of American women generally. So many women seemed to be chronically ill. She started gathering statistics in an informal and impressionistic way. As she explains in *Letters to the People,* she asked women she met in the course of her travels to write down the initials of the ten "married ladies" they knew best and then their impressions of the health of each one. She obtained statistics from about two hundred places and recorded them like this: "*Milwaukee, Wis.* Mrs. A. frequent sick headaches. Mrs. B very feeble. Mrs. S well, except chills. Mrs. L. poor health constantly. Mrs. D subject to frequent headaches. Mrs. B very poor health. Mrs. C. consumption and a cough. Mrs. B always sick. Do not know one perfectly healthy woman in the place." She put the information into tables, such as the following:

Residence.	Strong and perfectly healthy.	Delicate or Diseased.	Habitual Invalids.
Hudson, MI	2	4	4
Castleton, VT	Not one.	9	1
Bridgeport, "	4	4	2
Dorset, "	Not one.	1	9 . . .
Greenbush, NY	2	5	3

Catharine recommended a variety of solutions for women's invalidism: better diet, more exercise, and teaching as a profession. She also boosted water cures as the best of the thirteen health establishments she had resided at in the past decade. Of course, being Catharine, she also criticized water cures and included several pages of suggestions for improvement; they should provide better ventilation in their lodgings, formal health instruction, and calisthenics as well as walks for exercise. But overall she paid tribute to the methods of water cure: "I have seen approaching blindness and deafness entirely remedied; neuralgia, with its thousand agonies, conquered; a great variety of skin complaints and bad humors cured, and multitudes of internal organic disorders and displacements remedied."

From the beginning of her experience with water cure Catharine tried to get her sisters involved. In 1847, only two years after the founding of the Brattleboro cure, Catharine, Mary, and Harriet all stayed there together (Isabella was taking care of Mary's children). After Harriet returned home Calvin went and remained over a year. Both Isabella and John had made short visits to closer establishments in Massachusetts—John to Northampton and both Hookers to Florence. Isabella chose the Gleason cure in Elmira for a longer stay because Catharine thought it one of the best. Also, brother Thomas was now preaching in Elmira. He was friendly with the Gleasons and had actually lived at the water cure establishment for a while with his second wife, Julia; she had been a friend and mourner of his first wife and married him under the same circumstances as Harriet wed Calvin Stowe. Mrs. Gleason finally had to tell Tom that a hotel for invalids was not the best place to settle a healthy young wife.

Silas O. and Rachel Brooks Gleason had established the Elmira Water Cure in 1852. Both were physicians, he having graduated from a Vermont medical school and she from a new institution founded by the New York State Eclectic Medical Society in central New York. Rachel Gleason received her medical degree along with four other women in 1851, only two years after Elizabeth Blackwell became the first female physician in the United States. Catharine thought so highly of Dr. Gleason that she included an article by her as an appendix to *Letters to the People*.

Isabella's attitudes toward health and medicine fit in perfectly at Elmira. She had for a long time distrusted traditional medicine. The Hookers had a traditional doctor in Hartford, Dr. Curtis, whom Isabella gave his due and sometimes praised for helping her children; she credited him with saving Eddie's life when he had whooping cough. But she remained skeptical. Once she noted in the children's journal that Eddie was given powders of belladonna and ipecac for his cold, "but whether the cure came by these or kind nature, I am not able to say." As much as possible she withheld the strong medicines prescribed by Dr. Curtis, such as calomel, a mercury-based drug, and first tried milder homeopathic remedies. (Too bad she did not prescribe for her sister

Harriet, as Joan Hedrick thinks Harriet and other Stowes may have contracted mercury poisoning from the omnipresent calomel pills; Harriet's headaches and trouble concentrating were symptoms of chronic mercury poisoning.)

In her growing feminism, Isabella was also bound to appreciate the connections between the water cure movement and women's rights. Although a slight majority of the patients were male, the water cures recruited and supported women as doctors, health workers, and lecturers on health. It has been estimated that between a fifth and a third of hydropathic practitioners in the United States were female; this is in 1860, when only a handful of women had graduated from orthodox medical schools. A woman like Rachel Gleason, who became successful in her profession, had a husband and child, and sympathized with the problems and aspirations of other women, was a powerful role model for Isabella and other ailing wives.

The water cures were also female-friendly in taking seriously what traditional medicine dismissed as "female complaints." Gynecological care was a major concern of hydropathy, and discussions of menstruation, childbirth, and disorders of the reproductive organs filled the pages of the *Water Cure Journal*. Pregnant women were common at the cures and often delivered there. Hydropathists believed that pregnancy was a natural process, not a disease. They encouraged exercise for the whole nine months, massage and warm baths during labor, and a quick return to ordinary routines after delivery. In her article on hydropathy Kathryn Kish Sklar speculates that water cures may also have given women information about contraception and abortive remedies. She concludes that hydropathy's "sympathy for the special medical problems of women stood in stark contrast to the hostility and indifference characteristic of traditional contemporary medicine." At Elmira in particular Dr. Rachel Gleason and her sister, Zipporah Brooks, were advertised by the water cure as specialists in "the chronic diseases of women." Isabella thus had another reason for choosing Elmira.

At age thirty-eight Isabella suffered not only from *prolapsus uteri* but also from inflammation of the neck of the uterus, which Mrs. Binney had found, and from menorrhagia, or unusually heavy and prolonged menstrual periods. Isabella would occasionally write John expressing relief that her "monthly has ceased at last," and she worried incessantly about bleeding to death. Unfortunately, Dr. Gleason supported her in this mistaken idea, suggesting that if she did not have treatment beforehand "there was quite a possibility of flowing to death" as menopause approached. (According to current medical wisdom, the risk of menorrhagia is developing iron-deficiency anemia, which Isabella may well have had.)

Dr. Gleason thought her patient could be "cured" in three months. Midway through her stay, Isabella gave John the diagnosis: "The neck &

mouth of the uterus is (or was) very much enlarged—hard almost as a bony surface—& very red & angry looking—the body of the uterus was also heavy & distended & prolapsed—both were tender to the touch & so engorged as to cause not only the sensation of weight which has been so oppressive to me for years—but the profuse menstruation of the last year—which has been *fearful*." Dr. Gleason treated her twice a week "with instruments" and application of silver nitrate. Water cure per se was only a supplement to the main treatment. The baths she took, Isabella noted, were intended as a soothing accompaniment to Dr. Gleason's work on her uterus. In fact, the baths could have had a damaging effect. In the middle of June she wrote John that she and Dr. Gleason now thought the cool baths designed to stop her flow had stimulated it instead.

Dr. Gleason introduced one other water cure staple in her care of Isabella—dress reform. The dress question was another strong link between the water cure and women's rights movements. Hydropathists saw a strong connection between fashionable clothing and middle-class women's notoriously poor health. Catharine noted in *Letters* that "pernicious customs of dress" that deformed the body were carried by dressmakers and "still more by the miserable fashion-plates in our literature" from the city to the country. Women wore whalebone or steel corsets and at midcentury very wide skirts; it was common to wear six, eight, or even more underskirts. Dr. Gleason thought uterine prolapse and other displacements stemmed from the pressure exerted by this extra weight. She advocated dressing loosely and making sure all the weight of one's clothing rested on the shoulders.

Shortly after arriving at Elmira, Isabella had her sister-in-law Julia Beecher get her a "Bloomer dress." This costume consisted of a short dress reaching about to the knees and worn over trousers. Isabella had had a bloomer for exercise since the early fifties. The writer Gail Hamilton (the pseudonym for Mary Abigail Dodge) wrote her brother in 1855 that she had gone to Mrs. Hooker's for tea and been given "a dress which she had made several years ago, in order to practice in at a gymnasium. It is a kind of bloomer, full Turkish trousers, etc." The outfit was originated by Elizabeth Cady Stanton's cousin, Elizabeth Smith Miller, and named for Amelia Bloomer, a women's rights and temperance worker who wore and advocated the new attire.

Stanton notes in her autobiography that she and her friends wore the bloomer for a few years but eventually gave it up, "for the physical freedom did not compensate for the persistent persecution and petty annoyances suffered at every turn." Not the least of these annoyances were crowds of teasing street boys. They would surround the bloomer-wearer and follow her, joking, laughing, and chanting rhymes. A favorite, quoted by Stanton, went thus:

Heigh! Ho! In rain and snow,
The bloomer now is all the go.
Twenty tailors take the stitches,
Twenty women wear the breeches.
Heigh! Ho! In rain or snow,
The bloomer now is all the go.

Fortunately, the water cures were free of this ridicule, and female doctors and patients continued to wear the bloomer outfit. Isabella informed her daughters that after going without hoops for a month, she had no desire to resume "the burden of long dresses."

In addition to her gynecological problems, Isabella had other ailments she hoped to have cured at Elmira. Backaches she traced to her uterine displacement, and frequent colds and cough she felt were constitutional, inherited from her mother. But she also had headaches, sore eyes, problems with her throat, and weak and often swollen ankles. She had injured her ankle in a carriage accident in 1849. The ankle only worsened at the water cure. One evening while returning to her room in the dark, she fell down a flight of stairs and sprained both ankles; this accident caused her to spend about a month longer at the cure than she had originally planned.

The prospects for improvement of her throat were brighter because Elmira advertised treatment of "Catarrh, throat diseases, loss of Voice and Bronchitis." The first three of these Isabella complained of, along with attacks of quinsy, an infection of the tonsils. She had also lost much of her sense of smell and thus taste, a condition known today as anosmia. The water cure's location on top of a hill provided the bracing air thought necessary for treating throat and lung disease. The main treatment was inhalation of cold or warm water spray. Elmira prided itself on having imported the latest French and German instruments for atomizing and vaporizing water and medicinal substances. Isabella was able to write her daughter Mary in the middle of June that her ability to smell and taste was improving.

This improvement made Isabella more aware of the water cure's "poor food—badly cooked." She wrote John that they had a curious way of cooking steaks. "They put them into the oven—after first pounding out all the good juices—& dry them up to a chip—& no gravy." Isabella bought herself some Porterhouse steaks and had them broiled, though she felt twinges of conscience about enjoying them while others had to "chew & chew." It may be that the Hookers were used to richer food than the Elmira cure provided; perhaps it was overrich food that the hydropathists thought contributed to people's ill health, or perhaps the cook had problems. Isabella suggests as much to her daughters when she writes that Dr. Gleason raved about the bread the Hookers' Bridget had sent. She wanted Isabella to teach the cook how to make this bread, but Isabella refused. She felt that the cook was already overworked and not strong enough to do all the kneading by herself; she had two other kinds of bread to make and only one young assistant to help. Isabella's reaction was characteristic, as she was always attentive to servants. Of course, it was also characteristic for her to claim a privilege others lacked (her own special steaks) and then feel guilty that others missed what she enjoyed.

The food was the only aspect of water cure culture Isabella didn't like. She would have objected to getting up at 4 A.M. to be wrapped in a wet sheet like Catharine at Brattleboro (she always hated getting up early), but the Gleasons prescribed a good night's sleep instead. Isabella loved the exercise at Elmira—the long walks and horseback rides through the beautiful hilly scenery. The nearby glen, she wrote Mary, was a wild, rocky, and romantic place. It reached up into the mountains and offered gorgeous views. She also appreciated the leisure time for letter writing and catching up on her reading. At Elmira she read the latest novels, including *The Mill on the Floss* by Harriet's friend George Eliot, Charles Dickens's *A Tale of Two Cities*, and Nathaniel Hawthorne's *The Marble Faun*. Just as she had once compared her daughter Alice to Hawthorne's Pearl, she now saw Eddie as his Donatello. Isabella had a compatible roommate at the cure, her friend Harriet (Hattie) Foote Hawley, a cousin from the Foote family of Lyman Beecher's first wife. Isabella and John had introduced Hattie to Joseph Hawley, John's junior law partner, and prided themselves on making a solid match. Friends and sisters often went to water cures together.

In the evenings there was time for socializing. One couple had experience in amateur theater and directed readings of Shakespeare's *The Merchant of Venice* and other plays. Isabella, who had recently attended the theater for the first time, found herself acting an English housekeeper in a play they staged. The Gleasons' scientific interests also provided material for conversation and recreation. Isabella was excited to look at human blood specimens through a microscope. Writers on the Beechers have made fun of her enthusiasm as another of her faddish "notions" and "fancies," but microscopy was then a science in its infancy and might be expected to interest the general public. Dr. Silas Gleason founded in Elmira a society for the study of microscopy.

One of the strictest rules of water cures was the ban on admission of children except as patients. Otherwise, mothers would not have been able to rest from their daily routines and concentrate on their own health. No doubt many women were prevented from seeking the cure unless they had someone to care for their children—as, for instance, Isabella did for her sister

Mary when Mary went to Brattleboro. Isabella's girls were teenagers when she stayed at Elmira in 1860, and she had at home the loyal Bridget and Aunt Esther's replacement, Aunt Sarah (Sarah was Harriet Porter Beecher's sister), to look after Eddie. Still, Isabella did not achieve much distance from the household. Her guilt over leaving home is obvious in her constant rationalizations for her absence. To John she writes about his opportunity to get closer to the children, and to Alice she boosts her chance to get better acquainted with her father. Isabella felt that she had acted for a long time in the "double capacity" of father and mother, and now John could try it for a few months. Not surprisingly, she soon took back these brave words, worried that John would break down. He had never stayed home before without a wife.

In actuality, Isabella could not resist trying to run the household from Elmira. She wrote long, detailed letters with instructions for having the children's clothes made and treating their illnesses (Eddie came down with whooping cough). She sent Thomas, the handyman, directions for planting the gardens with the help of sister Mary and the girls; then the girls had to help maintain the gardens and transplant the strawberries. Isabella so missed her flowers and was so frustrated at her daughters' inability to describe the blooms that she finally had them send dead blossoms to Elmira for her inspection. But the skill the Hooker family missed most was her peacemaking and smoothing of relations among the children. She was continually called upon to intervene in the girls' quarrels. If one sister picked leaves from her mother's plants in a thoughtful way, Isabella wrote, the other ought not to criticize. "But if No. 1 leaves her things 'kicking about' I think No. 2 may *gently* admonish—at least suggest a better way—& No. 1 ought to take it patiently & try to do better immediately."

In dealing with her children Isabella could be considerably more tactful and considerate than she was with adults. When Alice complained about Mary's sending her on too many errands, their mother replied as follows: "[Y]ou have so long been full of life & activity & cheerful readiness, we all get used to depending on you—& are in some danger of abusing you, a little I fear—so we must all look to it—especially as you are just coming to an age when you won't feel so much like jumping & running as you did—I shall hope too that Mary will be quite ready to come to the rescue, as fast as she grows stronger—& repay you in kind for the many steps you have taken for her in days past." Isabella often had to reassure Mary and soothe her hurt feelings as she compared herself to her more effervescent sister: "Your character is as lovely & attractive as hers, though in a different way."

At the Elmira water cure Isabella was occupied with mending relations with one of her own siblings, her brother Thomas. After the unpleasantness over his reaction to his first wife's death, their meetings were awkward.

Isabella felt that he lacked respect for her. She was probably right in this judgment, as Tom admired only a few of his relatives—his father, Henry (although he believed him an adulterer), and Harriet. Always fond of comparing his sisters, Tom had as a young man written Isabella that she and Mary were "true Yankees" compared to Harriet. They were "too pragmatical, looking at apparent *things*, judging by them, making them essential to . . . happiness; [and] neglecting . . . the inward soul, & moving spirit—as the only just criterion of character & action. I cannot refer you to a better illustration of the points I am laboring to enounce, than you can find in a careful comparison of yourself or Mary with Harriet." These words must have hurt all the more because they were written before *Uncle Tom's Cabin* and because Isabella believed them to be true. (Catharine, of course, did not even enter into the equation—she was worldly and difficult besides.)

At first, Isabella saw less of Tom than she had expected. "He is very pleasant, however," she assured John, "& we avoid all sharp speeches as if by instinct." She went to hear him preach on Sunday and praised his sermons to brother Henry, probably knowing it would eventually get back to Tom; she made friends with his new wife and praised her too. Eventually, as they went out riding together, they drew closer. They found some areas of agreement on religious matters, and Isabella hoped either to "modify his treatment of me, or to overlook it so thoroughly as to love him in the way I wish to love my own dear mother's son." Tom was becoming more manageable, she wrote her husband, and if John came for a visit, he needn't fear meeting him ("don't scratch this out," she added, knowing John's reluctance to have it be known that he disliked someone).

One circumstance that had to improve the big sister–little brother relationship was Tom's popularity among his parishioners; he was a big fish in the small Elmira pond. Isabella thus had to respect him instead of viewing him solely as a cross to bear. Of course, the other side (for Isabella) of respecting a sibling was feeling a sense of her own inferiority. She wrote John that it was gratifying to see how useful Tom had become and how much he was beloved. But "it is funny, how, everywhere I go—I have to run on the credit of my relations—no where, but at home can I lay claim to a particle of individuality—to any distinction of goodness—smartness or anything else whatever." In Elmira she was Tom Beecher's sister.

The time spent with Tom had some lasting effects on Isabella. First, he provided an example that one did not have to write *Uncle Tom's Cabin* or be the greatest orator of the day to be both personally successful and helpful to others. Unlike his brother Henry, Tom sought not fame or wealth but only a place to live his life as a Christian. He never became well known outside Elmira but showed that a Beecher could be important and do good on a local level. Second, Tom introduced Isabella to his parishioners, the Langdons, with whom the Hooker family became friendly. Jervis Langdon was the father of Olivia (Livy), who would marry Mark Twain. He was a deacon of Tom's church, the Park Church, which had been founded in 1846 by abolitionist seceders from the pro-slavery Presbyterian Church. Langdon had made his fortune in lumber and coal mining. Once, he and his wife took Isabella to Pennsylvania by train to visit his large lumberyard. More often, they invited her to their home for tea or sent a carriage to the water cure to take her to church and afterward to Sunday dinner. After the meal they talked and sang. Jervis Langdon, whom Isabella called "one of the best men in the whole world," thought Isabella treated Tom just right and did him good; the rest of the family who had visited Elmira bore down too hard on him. Isabella wrote John that Langdon's mere presence revived her and made her feel stronger and happier. She never changed her view that he was one of the best men.

During the last month of her stay at the water cure Isabella's room-mate, Hattie Hawley, took a turn for the worse and required a private room. Isabella then roomed with the fourteen-year-old Livy Langdon, whom she described as a "sweet young girl" the same age as Mary but in very delicate health. Typically, she blamed Livy's weakness on her education, for she had been sent to a good private school and then enrolled in the college prepara-tory branch of Elmira College. "Oh dear—how blind mothers are," Isabella complained to John, "& what miserable work they make of educating daugh-ters." This formulation was probably influenced by Dr. Rachel Gleason, who despite her general feminism taught that girls should avoid "mental excite-ment" at puberty because "mental application . . . results often in invalidism." Interestingly, Catharine never held this theory that would become so damag-ing to girls' education later in the century. In this case her promotion of education for women took precedence over her rejection of the movement for women's rights. She admitted that girls in boarding schools were often ill but refused to blame female physiology. Instead, she pointed out the mis-takes of the schools—lack of ventilation and exercise, provision of strong tea and coffee and animal food.

Isabella ended up staying four months at Elmira, a month longer than originally planned. She even had the so-called water cure crisis, a tempo-rary turn for the worse that patients anxiously awaited as a sign of returning health; the idea was that the body had to purge itself of the harmful residue of poisons taken as allopathic (traditional) medications. Isabella's crisis was a brief "bilious turn" with pain in her stomach and bowels. When she left Elmira, Isabella felt restored and looked forward eagerly, she told her daughter Mary, "to live for others once more—& not in this eternal bondage to self." But was her health truly improved from visiting the Gleason water cure? Her nose and throat maladies soon returned, but the problems with her uterus seem to have been permanently alleviated. She had also found time to think about the future and was ready to step off "the treadmill of self analysis" she had been on for the past few years. Isabella hadn't made any definite decisions. She again thought about studying with Mrs. Gleason and specializing in gynecological problems in Hartford, but Eddie was only five years old and could not be left for long. So when she arrived home in late August 1860, Isabella was still in a holding pattern but readier than she had been to take up some sort of public work.

As Isabella came home to Hartford relaxed, Harriet was in Andover trying to write two novels at once. She had just returned from her third trip to Europe and an extended stay in Italy. There she met the up-and-coming publisher James T. Fields and his young wife, Annie, and began a lifelong friendship with the couple. She also started an Italian story, a novel entitled *Agnes of Sorrento*, about a young orange-seller. Harriet convinced Fields, who was just taking over the editorship of the new magazine the *Atlantic Monthly*, to serialize this novel. But feeling the need to boil the pot and refurbish her finances after the European trip, she sold a series of articles on ways to beautify American homes to Theodore Tilton, brother Henry's protégé and editor of the journal *Independent*. Tilton then asked for fiction and Harriet recalled a Maine story, "The Pearl of Orr's Island," which she had begun while living in Brunswick. When she sent Tilton the second installment of "Pearl" in December 1860, she realized she had yet another novel in progress just as *Agnes of Sorrento* was due to start in the *Atlantic*. Harriet much preferred her Italian story. At about the time Abraham Lincoln was being inaugurated as president of the United States, Harriet was writing Fields, "I have a pleasure in writing 'Agnes of Sorrento' that gilds this icy winter weather. I write my Maine story with a shiver, and come back to this as to a flowery home where I love to rest."

Readers then and now have disagreed entirely with Harriet's estimate of her two novels. Most critics have regretted the time and energy she put into the slight *Agnes of Sorrento* (1862) while she neglected *The Pearl of Orr's Island* (1862), which could have been her New England masterpiece. Of course, Harriet did not know that she would be remembered not only for having written *Uncle Tom's Cabin* but also as having "pioneered the women's tradition of local color realism in this country." In *The Pearl* she portrayed her childhood self in the dreamy and sensitive orphan, Mara, who wistfully learns embroidery while her friend Moses embarks on his first fishing voyage. But in spring 1861 she stopped working on *The Pearl* in order to finish *Agnes* and did not resume it until the end of the year. When she took up the novel again, she dropped the growing-up-gendered theme and advanced the ages of Mara and

Moses to adulthood. The novel became a sentimental love story, with its rich texture thinned and the issues brought out in the first half of the book never resolved. Even so, the book was a favorite of the Quaker poet John Greenleaf Whittier, who called it "the most charming New England idyll ever written."

The Pearl may have been a casualty of the Civil War more than anything else. While Harriet pursued her two novels, a national crisis put everyone's life on hold. Lincoln had sought to conciliate the South, but on April 15, 1861, the Confederacy fired on Fort Sumter and the Civil War began. As Harriet wrote Theodore Tilton in excuse for discontinuing *The Pearl*, "Who could write on stories that had a son to send to battle, with Washington beleaguered and the whole country shaken as with an earthquake?" The son was Frederick Stowe, now age twenty-one, who had been trying to please his parents by attending medical school. As soon as war was declared, he left Harvard and enlisted in the 1st Massachusetts Volunteer Infantry. Harriet wrote an editorial urging that if war were an evil, it was a lesser evil than a shameful peace. Like everyone else, she had no idea just how terrible the war would be. When Fred first enlisted she went to Boston every week to visit him and his regiment at the Armory, "little dreaming for what earnest and bloody work they had gone in and how few of them should ever return."

The general mood was evident at a dinner Isabella hosted in Hartford a few weeks after war broke out; she would later call the event her "Lincoln supper." The occasion was the departure for war of the Hookers' abolitionist friend Joseph Hawley. Hawley, John's former law partner, had helped him shelter fugitive slaves. He was now editor of the Hartford *Evening Press*, the first Republican daily newspaper in the state. He left Hartford a company commander and returned a general. At the farewell dinner the guests, not anticipating that the war would last for years and entail tragic losses, made hilarious fun of Lincoln's appearance, manners, and politics. There were endless jokes about how such an awkward-seeming creature would behave in the White House. Lincoln's manners, John had written Isabella, were those of "a Maine logger or a half-civilized back-woodsman, almost a boor."

The Nook Farm community was basically committed to the president, however. John added that "he is honest and fearless, and after all the corruption and subserviency that have prevailed I think we can get along with the want of courtly manners." Joe Hawley had just been to Washington in January to check out rumors that the Lincoln inauguration would be prevented; he was appalled at the rampant corruption there. Thus, jokes aside, the Nook Farmers supported and defended Lincoln. They also began to see the personal consequences of the war. In summer 1861 Edward Hooker, John's younger brother who had followed him to sea and stayed in the merchant service, joined the U.S. Navy. A few months later the thirty-eight-year-old

Edward was severely wounded while acting master on the gunboat *Louisiana*. He survived to fight in other naval battles and even be promoted for gallantry in action. But the Hookers worried that while their relatives were risking their lives, the war could end without the slaves being freed.

When, if ever, would Lincoln get around to emancipation? Hawley rebuked the radical Wendell Phillips for calling the president "a slave hound and a knave." He replied, "I know Mr. Lincoln. He is not quite up to my standards, but he has always been ahead of his neighbors." Even so, the Hookers knew that, as abolitionists, they were in a minority. In Connecticut the so-called Peace Democrats were holding large outdoor meetings (after his first term of military service, Joe Hawley led a group of veterans in breaking them up). Even their old friend the Hartford minister Joel Hawes proclaimed loudly that the abolition of slavery was not a war aim. As 1861 crawled on, the Hookers and the Stowes bombarded President Lincoln with letters.

In November, for instance, Isabella used a legal argument. When one party does not fulfill its part of a contract, she began, the other party is exempt from the terms; thus the Union had no obligation to allow fugitive slaves to be returned to the rebel states. Military law should take precedence over constitutional law, and the president as commander of the armed forces had the right to proclaim emancipation whenever it would aid the war effort. So far so good, but Isabella could not help revealing Nook Farm's greatest fear— that Lincoln had somehow been bought off. She knew he was subject to "insidious temptation" in the corrupt Washington atmosphere, she wrote, but he mustn't "betray his sacred trust." Northerners were willing to sacrifice in order to end slavery, she concluded, but not for other reasons.

A month later Isabella wrote brother Henry with another constitutional argument. Henry Ward Beecher had always been one of her favorite brothers, and they basically agreed about the progress (or lack of progress) of the war. Henry had stated in a sermon haranguing Lincoln that only the president, not Congress, could emancipate the slaves. Why not Congress, asked Isabella, if Congress is a war making power and emancipation a military necessity? (This species of argument actually worked in the District of Columbia, as Congress voted to abolish slavery in a district over which it had full jurisdiction.) A long year passed, however, and the rest of the slaves were still not free.

In fall 1862 Harriet turned her attention to the question of an emancipation proclamation. She was furious that the British government stood on the verge of recognizing the Confederacy, apparently for economic reasons (Great Britain's need for Confederate cotton). The women of Britain had not protested, even though half a million of them had signed an anti-slavery document ("Affectionate and Christian Address from the Women of Great Britain") and sent it to Harriet after her triumphal tour of England and Scotland in 1853. Harriet began composing a late reply to that address, rebuking the women for allowing their government to support slaveholders. But she needed to be able to say that the Union was definitely going to free the slaves.

In late September 1862 the newspapers published President Lincoln's draft Emancipation Proclamation, which he said would take effect on January 1, 1863, unless the belligerent states returned to the Union. Harriet wanted to know, before she finished her "Reply," whether this proclamation was more than a political ploy. Thus she decided to speak to Lincoln directly. "I am going to Washington," she wrote James Fields, "to see the heads of department myself & to satisfy myself that I may refer to the Emancipation Proclamation as a reality & a substance not to fizzle out at the little end of the horn." Harriet had another motive, perhaps even more compelling, for visiting Washington—Frederick, now a lieutenant in the Union army, was stationed nearby at Fort Runyan. She told the twins, "I *must* see Fred." Ever since she heard that his doctor was prescribing whiskey for his ague, she had had no rest. The Stowe family would always claim publicly that Fred's drinking problem stemmed from the trauma of being at Gettysburg, but in fact he was an alcoholic before the war. The Stowes sent him to the Gleason Water Cure in Elmira to dry out under Thomas Beecher's supervision as early as 1857 when he was seventeen. "Sister Hattie has a very hard lot in many respects," Mary Perkins once wrote Isabella. "I would not take her burden with all her trials even if the money & the fame came too."

Harriet asked brother Henry to accompany her to Washington. When he refused she turned to Isabella, who was eager to meet with Lincoln and see the youngest Beecher brothers, Thomas and James; Tom was a chaplain and Jim a lieutenant colonel in the same regiment near Washington. In the middle of November Harriet and Isabella met at Henry's in Brooklyn. Their brother had good news. The president had written, assuring him that he would stand by the proclamation. Henry claimed to receive information directly from military headquarters and announced that twelve major generals had asked to be relieved rather than serve any longer under the unpopular Gen. George McClellan. Harriet and Isabella decided to adhere to their original plans, and Harriet called on Mary Lincoln, who was staying in New York. Although she succeeded in getting an invitation to the White House, she did not think much of the president's wife, whom she described to Calvin as "a good hearted weak woman fat, & frank." Isabella confided to John that Harriet found Mrs. Lincoln "an old goose & a gobbler at that."

The day before they left for Washington Harriet and Isabella visited their aged father. Lyman Beecher was staying with Lucy Jackson White, his wife's daughter, and had by this time lost his memory completely. Isabella wrote John as follows: "He looked perfectly lovely—with his long soft grey hair floating over his shoulders[,] his face white & smooth & plump as a baby. He did not exactly recognize us—but our presence seemed very soothing & pleasant to him & when we sat one on each side & sang hymns—old ones that he used to love, he leaned back in his chair & sung too—in a humming tone—& when we stopped brightened up & said distinctly & with much animation 'well *that* is good.'" Isabella wanted to bring him home but was told he shouldn't be moved. This was the last time the sisters saw their beloved father.

The Beecher party now included Harriet's daughter Hatty, whom she had chosen to come along because Hatty was the oldest child. They traveled by train and stopped overnight in Philadelphia, reaching Maryland just as Tom and Jim's regiment was about to move. While Harriet and Hatty departed to find Fred at Fort Runyan, Isabella caught up with her brothers. Jim had spent a fairly successful five years as a missionary in Canton and Hong Kong. He had set up a floating chapel among the docks and, in the manner of his father, started revivals among the sailors. His wife, Annie, however, the former Ann Morse of Newburyport, Massachusetts, had become an alcoholic in the Far East. She came home for treatment in 1859 (under Tom's supervision at the Gleason Water Cure) but was committed to an asylum the next year. Jim returned in 1861 and enlisted in the army. Henry got him a post as chaplain in the First Long Island Regiment, but he was impatient at the lack of action and through Tom's influence was appointed lieutenant colonel of his regiment, the 141st New York Volunteers. Isabella thought Jim's suffering over his wife's condition had ennobled him, and she and Harriet shared a proud moment when he marched by their Washington boardinghouse at the head of his regiment. Jim looked resplendent in uniform as he saluted his sisters with his sword. As usual, though, he was harder to take close up. Isabella tried to talk politics and found him "infected with Tom's pernicious absurdities [anti-reform ideas] & dropped the whole subject."

Isabella, Harriet, and Hattie visited hospitals and went sightseeing. They saw the patent office, the dead letter office, and the State Department. Fred Stowe, for whom Harriet had gotten a pass, took them on a tour of the Capitol, which Harriet found equal to any building in Europe. One day they visited the Treasury, where the son of a Hooker acquaintance was head. "For once I took the lead of Mrs. Stowe," Isabella reported, "which was quite refreshing by way of variety." She could not forget that on this trip she was secondary to "her highness," as she called Harriet in a letter to daughter Mary. Harriet was given three cheers by the contraband (former slaves who had escaped to the Union side) when she visited their barracks for Thanksgiving dinner. For Isabella—the lover of music—this occasion, more than the meeting with Lincoln, was the highlight of the trip. She wrote that "The contraband choir sang the Moses Song ["Go Down Moses"]—a negro Marsellaise—which is forbidden to them down South." She loved the "slow, solemn plaintive music," as the freedmen sang hymns in harmony. "I never heard such before—& would come all the way here for that alone." Another memorable day was December 1, when President Lincoln read the Emancipation Proclamation on the opening day of Congress. Isabella was sitting in the gallery with Harriet and concluded, "Yes I think 25 years hence I shall mention this fact with some exultation." Clearly, however, the sisters were more impressed by the "magnificent" and "imposing" senator Charles Sumner, who came over to speak with Harriet, than they were by the president.

Mrs. Lincoln kept her promise to invite Harriet and her party to tea, and on the evening of December 2 Harriet, Hatty, and Isabella went to the White House. They were accompanied by Henry Wilson of Massachusetts, the Stowes' senator, who would later become vice president under Ulysses Grant. Harriet herself did not describe the meeting but wrote Calvin that she would tell him about it when she got home. Hatty wrote her twin sister only that the encounter was so funny they could barely keep from disgracing themselves by laughing out loud. When they returned to their rooms, "we perfectly screamed" with "pent-up laughter." Isabella's account in a letter to John confirms this impression and explains what was funny. "I must tell you our introduction. The pavilion entrance was really fine under the brilliant lamps & all looked well enough till we mounted to the Pres. private room or office—here Mr. Wilson stuck his head in the door & out again."

Meanwhile the Beecher party contemplated an ugly tin water cooler painted green and resting on a marble table. Under its spout sat

> an old battered, rusty tin pan—much worse than those Eddie is accustomed to feed his chickens from. . . . This was a premonition to be sure—but hardly prepared us for such—a rough, scrubby—black—brown withered—dull eyed object as advanced to meet us—on entering—I can give you no idea of the shock—sister Hattie immediately became so engaged in silent observation of the unexpected apparition—there was no conversation to be expected from that quarter—so I put in vigorously in behalf of the charming open wood fire—& started various topics—till at last Mr. Lincoln—was 'reminded of a man out west'—& then I collapsed & enjoyed myself vigorously—tho' quite internally—so we all did. . . . [P]retty soon Hattie [i.e., sister Harriet] waked up & told a story—& then the Pres. had his term of enjoyment—& such a shaking—& wiggling up of his indefinitely long nose I never before beheld. On the whole—it was a bewildering sensation—from first to last—the discrepancies all about one—in furniture & ap-

pointments & character were too much for one half hour—it seemed as if we must get by ourselves & have a little blow out.

Isabella's impressions were not entirely negative, as she added the following:

> I will say however that the Pres. sincerity & pathos of character were both visible—through his indifferent speech & rustic manners—& when he told us he felt quite sure he should not last long after all this was over—we felt quite touched & ready to say we hoped this might not be the case.
>
> We looked into his reception room & then descended to Madame's—where she received us with rather better grace than I anticipated—& was dressed in altogether better taste than usual according to report—but I will keep further details till we meet.

Most twentieth-century accounts of the Lincoln visit mention the presence of Charles Stowe, Harriet's youngest son. Harriet, Hatty, and Isabella, however, do not refer to him in any of their letters from Washington. Isabella wrote John from Brooklyn that no one was going on the trip "save the original *three*" (Harriet, Hatty, and Isabella). She alludes to the difficulties of traveling without men: "We are so helpless *in* & *of* of [sic] our three selves; spite of being somewhat strong minded women." When Charles wrote his first biography of his mother, published in 1889, he did not mention the Washington trip. The second biography, written jointly with his son Lyman, has Harriet visiting Lincoln by herself with no Hatty or Isabella; she is introduced to Lincoln by William Seward, the secretary of state. Charles and Lyman attribute the remark about the fire to Lincoln, with Lincoln showing poor grammar by saying he liked an open fire "to home" instead of "at home." The biography does *not* say that Charles was present. This must have been a later interpretation by Lyman.

Charles Stowe was the source of the story, often considered apocryphal, that Lincoln said to his mother, "So this is the little lady who made this big war." Isabella's version of the meeting casts additional doubt on whether Lincoln actually made this comment. She concluded: "I think by the way that owing to Mr. Wilson's perfectly unsophisticated manner of introducing, that father Abe. had no conception who Mrs. Stowe was—& will not have till Mrs. Lincoln instructs him on the subject in her own peculiar manner." In other words, Lincoln did not realize that the woman he was meeting was the famous Mrs. Stowe who had written *Uncle Tom's Cabin*. By contrast, Isabella noted, a brigadier general who was just leaving Lincoln's office when they arrived evidently recognized Harriet and stared rudely.

Isabella Beecher Hooker, c. 1866. Courtesy Harriet Beecher Stowe Center, Hartford, Conn.

Back home from her Washington adventure, Harriet experienced another triumph. She was attending a New Year's Jubilee at Boston Music Hall on January 1, 1863, when news came that President Lincoln had signed the Emancipation Proclamation. The crowd jumped to its feet applauding and, as Forrest Wilson describes the scene, began to call out Harriet's name: "Mrs. Stowe! Mrs. Stowe! Mrs. Stowe!" People knew she was sitting in the balcony and called for her to come to the rail, "this woman who had put down slavery." As the audience shouted and waved, she bowed and wiped tears from her eyes. Wilson concludes: "Thus in great triumph ended the cycle that had begun with her vision [of Uncle Tom's death] in a Brunswick church. The play was over, the curtain falling, and the star would never hear such salvos for herself again."

Just ten days later, the curtain came down for good on Lyman Beecher's life. As Henry put it, "The old oak finally fell." He was eighty-seven. All four Beecher sisters (and all the brothers save Edward and James) attended the funeral at Plymouth Church in Brooklyn. The siblings held a family prayer service at which there occurred "an unpremeditated outburst of memories." To Harriet the very air around them in the church seemed saturated by the past, "full of bright visionary faces of those *called* dead, but who live more truly than we do." The funeral eulogy was given by the Rev. Dr. Leonard Bacon of Yale, who around this time made his famous comment that the nation was inhabited by three types of people—saints, sinners, and Beechers. After the scandal involving his sister, Bacon remained a friend and correspondent of both Catharine and Harriet. Poor Delia Bacon had come to a sad end. She grew increasingly obsessed with her theory that Francis Bacon wrote Shakespeare's plays and finally went mad. She had to be hospitalized at the Hartford Retreat for the Insane and died before the start of the Civil War.

When Isabella returned from Washington, she worked with the Women's Sanitary Commission, which aided the Union hospital and medical services. Her son Eddie was fascinated by the war, and the Hookers followed the battles and army routes on their own map. Only a short time elapsed before word came that James Beecher had broken down in Washington. As Tom had resigned from the regiment and gone back to Elmira, he was not there to help. In fact, Jim and Isabella blamed him in part for the breakdown. It seems that there had been irregularities in the process by which Tom had gotten Jim into the regiment. Several of the officers resented this and treated Jim poorly; Jim wanted to resign but felt that doing so would be accepting the truth of the charge against his brother. As Isabella put it later, "Tom got him into a hornet's nest—all so innocently—& then left him there to be stung to death." In addition to the regimental politics, there was Annie's worsening alcoholism and Jim's growing attraction to Frances "Frankie" Johnson, a young woman from Guilford, Connecticut. Jim finally took chloroform to try to sleep, was drugged with morphine by an army surgeon (he claimed), and ended up in the hospital "out of his head." Isabella rushed to Washington to find that Annie was staying with her husband in the hospital, but "Jim loathes her—her breath is pestilence itself—& he could not endure it." He sent Annie back to Elmira "with his last cent."

Before she could bring Jim home, Isabella had to extract him from his regiment. Here she relied on a contact she had made on her previous Washington trip. She and Harriet had stopped to talk with Edwin M. Stanton, Lincoln's secretary of war, about the progress of the war. Stanton recalled their visit and on hearing Isabella's story granted Jim an honorable discharge. Isabella promptly brought her brother to a new Catharine Beecher discovery in New York City, the Taylors' Institute of the Swedish Movement Cure. The Taylors, George and Charles, were brothers and physicians who specialized in therapeutic exercises and orthopedics. Dr. George Taylor had apprenticed at water cures and had a practice similar to the Elmira Gleasons' (there was a water cure facility at the institute). Dr. Charles Taylor, a specialist in spinal disorders, had studied the Ling method of movement, or the "Swedish Movement Cure," invented by Dr. Peter Henry Ling of Stockholm. This method used exercise to cure disease. The patient was given several exercises relating to the afflicted area and shown how to stretch and bend the body. Livy Langdon had been at the Taylors' for a year and would remain another year; she apparently suffered from Pott's Disease, a curvature of the spine for which she was successfully treated.

Jim Beecher stayed at the Taylors' for two weeks in March 1863. He was "very blue," except during the visits of his sweetheart, Frankie, who boarded nearby, and he admitted that taking chloroform had been a suicide attempt. He still felt suicidal, talking about wanting to die and cease troubling his friends. Catharine visited Jim along with Isabella and acted as a "real comfort" to the family during this period. The two sisters thought Jim should live with his various siblings in New York and Connecticut and gradually get back into the ministry by filling vacant pulpits nearby. He should not, as he wanted, go back into the army. "He is too excitable to be in the army," Isabella wrote home, and "too much worn down by sorrow & anxiety to be so isolated." He needed to be near his friends, "loved & petted"—Isabella's solution for just about any problem.

She had to deal also with brother Tom, who was "fearfully excited" and quarreling by letter with both Jim and Isabella. The latter got herself into trouble by showing Jim a letter Tom had written her blaming him for the regimental troubles and accusing him of wanting to be dependent on his siblings. Although letters were much less private in the nineteenth century than they are now and people often read them aloud or copied them to others, Isabella had a tendency to be unusually free with the letters of others. Once she sent her husband a copy of one of Jim's letters to Tom and instructed him to read it aloud in a low, pathetic voice and see if the style didn't remind him of Dickens. Milton Rugoff concludes, not unreasonably, that Isabella viewed life "as a drama that she is helping to direct."

The current Jim-Tom-Isabella-Henry brouhaha (Henry got involved because Isabella copied all the letters to him also) ended fairly amicably. Tom promised Isabella they would work together for Jim's good and assured Jim that he would no longer lecture him or criticize him in letters to others; he did add that Jim should not "let Belle tamper too much" in his affairs. Tom and Isabella still disagreed over whether Jim should try to get a divorce—she consulted a lawyer, while Tom looked on disapprovingly. The issue was settled when Annie died of delirium tremens in late April. Against his siblings' advice, Jim rejoined the army and was allowed to recruit a black regiment in North Carolina. By June he had his men equipped and trained. He boasted to Frankie that if skeptical people at home (those who believed that former slaves wouldn't fight) could see his regiment, they would "talk less nonsense about negro inferiority." In September Jim wrote his commanding officer to protest his regiment's being ordered to lay out camps for white soldiers on Morris Island, South Carolina. Having to do menial work—leveling ground and digging wells—for whites, Jim argued, "reduces them to the position of slaves again." He must have enlisted Isabella in his cause, for she wrote again to Edwin Stanton, asking the secretary of war to punish anyone treating black soldiers differently from white.

As the war dragged on, it took its toll on the Beecher relatives serving in the army. The sisters' nephews Robert (William's son) and Harry (Henry's son) escaped injury, but Willie, Henry's younger son, caught a bullet in the knee; two years after the war ended he bent his knee and was unable to straighten it, the bullet having slipped into the joint. Frederick Beecher, Charles's son, was wounded at Gettysburg and not expected to live; he did survive, only to be killed later in the decade fighting Indians in the West. Fred Stowe, who had been promoted to captain, was also wounded at Gettysburg. A fragment of a shell entered his ear. Apparently Calvin set off by train to find him, only to have his pocket picked, fall ill, and slink home ignominiously without Fred. Later, when Fred's wound failed to heal properly, Harriet followed Isabella in obtaining a discharge from Secretary of War Stanton.

While the men were wounded in war, tuberculosis continued to strike the women. In 1864 Isabella was shocked when Charlotte Hull, her friend since youth, died of the disease; she was forty-six and left four children. The worst Hooker family tragedy occurred in 1865 when the war was almost over. Robert Gillette, son of John Hooker's sister, was killed in battle. Robert's father, Francis, John's business partner and the man who converted him to the abolitionist cause, was inconsolable. Also toward the end of the war James Beecher was seriously wounded. He had been allowed to marry Frankie and have her join him at his headquarters in the South. During a battle at Honey Hill, South Carolina, Jim was shot three times and spent months recuperating in the officers' hospital in Beaufort, South Carolina; his thigh wound required him to walk thereafter with a cane. Another wounding sent Isabella on her third trip south during the war. The injured was Henry Eugene Burton, who had gotten engaged to Mary Hooker before he joined the army.

Henry Burton, or "Eugene," as he was known, entered the Hookers' lives in 1857 when his older brother Nathaniel became their new preacher. Isabella and John were on the hiring committee and befriended the Reverend Nathaniel and Rachel Burton when they arrived in Hartford (Rachel was the friend to whom Isabella confided her regrets about her education). At various times the Burtons rented rooms and boarded at the Hooker home. The relationship between Mary and the shy, withdrawn Eugene began as early as 1860, when Mary was only fifteen. Isabella wrote her from the Elmira water cure, "I am glad to hear that Eugene Burton has walked out of his shell at last. . . . It *is* a little funny, that such a shy one as you, should take the lead in such a development." Make sure you don't get a reputation as a flirt, she concluded, and then added an odd postscript—"Who is Gene? You mention him but don't identify him." She continued to turn a blind eye to the growing romance until August 1863, when the pair got engaged prior to Eugene's becoming a lieutenant in the army. Isabella did not feel ready to give up her daughter, and her reaction (or strategy, if it was conscious) was to shower Eugene with affection and try to absorb him into the family. She referred to him as her "son" and urged him to call her "mother." He became Eddie's "big brother," and John received Christmas presents from "his *four* children."

Thus, when word came that Eugene had been wounded in the battle of Olustee, Florida, but no one knew his condition or exact location, Isabella rushed to the rescue. Undeterred by Calvin Stowe's experience after Gettysburg, Isabella possessed a more practical temperament and was joined for part of the trip by her brother James. On March 3, 1864, in New York they boarded the steamer *Fulton* heading for Hilton Head, South Carolina. Their destination was the officers' hospital in nearby Beaufort where Jim had recuperated and Eugene might be. The boat trip took five days because the steamer had to tow a supply vessel for the army, and Isabella was warned of the possibility of Confederate torpedoes. She spent much of the trip seasick but was heartened by Jim's positive attitude. He conducted church services in the ship cabin, talked at length with his sister, and pledged to stop chewing tobacco in deference to her theory that the tobacco might be causing his mood swings. At Hilton Head they had good news. A lieutenant from the 55th Massachusetts who knew Eugene Burton said he was among the first of the fifteen hundred wounded men to be brought in. He had undergone surgery that was painful but not dangerous and would not lose his leg. Eugene had indeed been sent to the hospital at Beaufort, as they suspected. Jim had to leave with his regiment for Jacksonville, South Carolina, so Isabella took another steamer without him to Beaufort. There she learned that Eugene had already been escorted north by her friend Harriet Hawley, who had been living with her officer husband in the area.

Isabella did not regret the wasted trip, she wrote her daughter Mary, and made up her mind to relax and enjoy the beautiful scenery. She also clearly enjoyed the attentions of young, handsome soldiers, many of whom she described in detail in twenty-page letters to Mary. It was a social time. She breakfasted with Joseph Hawley and visited Jim's camp in Jacksonville; there she watched the black color guard perform and again heard the soldiers sing their moving hymns. "I am living such an intense life of eye & ear," she wrote. At Beaufort hospital, making sure that Eugene had really gone north, she met some wounded black soldiers who knew both Jim and Eugene. Isabella also visited Folly Island, which the Union forces had occupied the year before, and saw Fort Wagner, the object of a long and costly Union attack. This was the campaign in which Joseph Hawley made his mark and the black regiment most famous today, the 54th Massachusetts, suffered heavy losses; its leader, Col. Robert Shaw, was killed in the assault on the fort.

Isabella heard the rumor that one of the commanders present at the attack on Fort Wagner, Gen. Truman Seymour, had said, "We will put those damned niggers in front." Seymour was also the commanding officer at Olustee, the man who, in Isabella's words, "led 4500 of our tired men against twice their number." A week before that fight Jim's regiment was about to feast on Florida beef when Seymour canceled the dinner for fear of the men somehow disturbing the peace. Isabella thought Seymour was a racist and should be removed from authority over black regiments. She told John she planned to speak to Quincy Gillmore, the general in command; as she once stayed next to his headquarters at Beaufort, she may actually have done so.

The occasion of Isabella's proximity to General Gillmore was a visit to the beach shanty of a new friend she made in South Carolina, Caroline Severance. Severance was not a southern woman. She and her banker husband, Theodoric Severance, were Bostonians until he was appointed customs collector at the Union-occupied sea islands. Before Boston they had lived in Ohio, where Caroline worked with pioneer feminist Frances Dana Gage and became involved in the women's rights movement. In fact, Severance could be called a pioneer herself, having attended in 1851 the famous Akron convention addressed by former slave Sojourner Truth. The next year she attended the convention in Syracuse, New York, where she met Elizabeth Cady Stanton, Lucretia Mott, and other women who had started the movement in 1848 at Seneca Falls. After moving to Boston, Severance presided over a women's rights convention there and delivered abolitionist lectures in Massachusetts and Rhode Island until the outbreak of the war.

Isabella wrote daughter Mary enthusiastically that Caroline Severance was "a jewel of a woman—thinks just as I do about, homeopathy & health—anti-slavery—religion—[illegible word] housekeeping etc.—*as far as we have talked*—(we slept together last night) & they have the most comfortable *shanty* at the Head." Severance accompanied Isabella on the rest of her travels—to the Beaufort hospital and on board the steamer *Cosmopolitan* to visit Jim's camp and Folly Island. Meeting Caroline Severance turned out to be the most significant occurrence of Isabella's trip south in 1864, having a lasting effect on her life. Severance provided Isabella with a model far different from her more conservative sisters. She was a respectable and even genteel happily married woman with several grown children; yet she had dedicated her life to reform and actually associated with such infamous radicals as Elizabeth Cady Stanton and William Lloyd Garrison. The Severance home in Boston was a gathering place for women's rights leaders, temperance workers, advocates of health reform, abolitionists, and other "extremists." Isabella and Caroline became fast friends and after the war would visit back and forth in Boston and Hartford.

By spring 1865 the war was finally coming to an end. As usual, the Beechers played a prominent role. While James was made a brevet brigadier general and given half of Charleston to command, Henry accepted Lincoln's invitation to deliver the oration at the raising of the U.S. flag over Fort Sumter. To celebrate the war's end Harriet reread *Uncle Tom's Cabin*. No matter what happened to her in the rest of her life, she felt, she would always know that she had helped bring an end to slavery. She wrote her British friend the Duchess of Argyle that "[W]hen I read that book scarred & seared & burned into with the memories of an anguish & horror that can never be forgotten & think it is all over now!—all past!—& that now the questions debated are simply of more or less time before granting legal suffrage to these who so lately were held only as articles of dead merchandise—When this comes over me—I think no private or individual sorrow, can ever make me wholly without comfort."

5

The Gilded Age,
1865–1868

LESS THAN A WEEK after Robert E. Lee surrendered at Appomattox Court House, officially ending the war, President Abraham Lincoln was assassinated. By this time the Beecher sisters and many other northerners were sorry for the way they had ridiculed Lincoln. They realized they had underestimated him and elevated lesser men above him simply on the basis of looks and manners. Harriet and Isabella probably remembered the evening Lincoln told them he wouldn't last long after the war was over. Catharine was speechless, no doubt for the first time in her life. Her grandniece Charlotte Perkins Gilman recalled Catharine visiting in Providence, Rhode Island, when the streets were hung with black. "Aunt Catherine [sic] with her little gray curls, and my mother facing her, sat speechless—Lincoln was dead!" Harriet reacted by writing a tribute to the late president: "He has been a marvel and a phenomenon among statesmen, a new kind of ruler in the earth. There has been something even unearthly about his extreme unselfishness, his utter want of personal ambition, personal self-valuation, personal feeling." Stirring praise—but Milton Rugoff thinks the poignancy of these lines is diminished by Harriet's accompanying suggestion to her publisher that he could combine this tribute with a piece she had written on Andrew Johnson. A "little book with mourning decorations" might sell thousands of copies.

The Stowes were again in need of money, for during the inflationary war times they had built a very large and expensive house at Nook Farm. Once Calvin retired they did not need to stay in Andover. The Hartford site consisted of four and a half acres of woods on the bank of the Park (formerly Hog) River. The land lay on the south branch of the river, a considerable distance from the other Nook Farm residences, but Harriet had pleasant memories of walking there with her friends when she attended Hartford Female Seminary. The house, which the Stowes came to call "Oakholm," was based on dwellings Harriet had seen in Italy. The same architect designed it who had planned the Hooker house, but Oakholm was much fancier. In building her dream house Harriet did not stint on gables, ornate columns, balconies, and bay windows; inside were several varieties of wood paneling and intricately carved mantelpieces. She wrote James Fields enthusiastically, "Tell Mrs. Fields that my house with *eight* gables is growing wonderfully, and that I go over every day to see to it. I am busy with drains, sewers, sinks, digging, trenching, and above all, with manure!"

An inveterate gardener like her sisters Mary and Isabella, Harriet looked at the manure heaps on her lawn and saw grapes and pears and roses. The pièce de resistance of Oakholm was the round two-story conservatory containing plants and a fountain. (Mark Twain would imitate this feature when he built his Nook Farm house.) Charlotte Perkins Gilman's memories of childhood visits to her great-aunts in Hartford were centered around the conservatory. Most of the rooms at Oakholm, including the dining room and back parlor, opened onto it. "Aunt Harriet used to sit at a small table in that back parlor, looking out on the flowers and ferns and little fountain, while she painted in water-colors." According to the reminiscences of Caroline Severance, Charlotte's grandmother Mary Beecher Perkins was the pioneer among the sisters in using plants for home decoration. Mary's house was "made bird-like and beautiful by ivy vines. These were rooted in a pretty conservatory on the south, climbed freely through a bay window into the long library-parlor and made a living frame for the portraits and paintings on its walls. Mrs. Perkins was the first traveler to introduce the English ivy for house decoration into this country. Mrs. Stowe had imitated her in growing and using it in the same pretty fashion in her home."

Summer 1865, just after the war ended, the Stowes depleted their bank account still further to marry their youngest daughter off in style. Georgie had always worried her parents with her Lyman Beecher–like moods. She seemed to have inherited his manic depressive tendencies and acted, in Harriet's words, like "a poor drooping bird half the time & then *too* excited & too frolicsome the rest." But she was making an excellent marriage—to Henry F. Allen, a handsome young Episcopal minister who had a parish in western Massachusetts. Again, Harriet did not stint on cost. Georgie's wedding reception at Oakholm was said to be one of the most lavish events Hartford had ever seen.

The Stowes were now able to join the fun as Nook Farm resumed its busy social life, which had been held in abeyance. In January 1866 the Hookers hosted their first party since the "Lincoln supper" before the war. They had thirty guests and a larger area for receiving them because just as the war was starting they had made an addition to their house. They now possessed a brand new kitchen, which delighted Bridget, a new parlor, and a large bedroom for the girls with its own bath and dressing rooms attached.

Hooker house, c. 1870. Courtesy Harriet Beecher Stowe Center, Hartford, Conn.

At the January party the main activity was charades, while at others they danced the polka and the Virginia Reel. Isabella later wrote Alice, when she was away visiting, that they'd had a "gay old frolic" like before the war. Although the temperature outside was fifteen degrees below zero, the Nook Farmers danced the night away. The year 1866 was also a time for obligatory social events. The Hookers celebrated their twenty-fifth wedding anniversary in August, and Mary and Eugene were married in October.

The silver anniversary celebration was something she could never forget, Isabella wrote her niece in Cincinnati. They invited over two hundred people, though they were unsure how many actually came; John and Harriette Putnam, the original wedding attendants, were detained by a sudden illness.

All the Beecher sisters and most of the Hookers' relatives and Nook Farm friends were present. Isabella wore a gray silk dress and a silver pin given her by the Hawleys. Other meaningful gifts were a portrait of Aunt Esther (given by Harriet) and the engraved golden rings the Hookers presented each other as they renewed their vows. The guests sat outside on the piazza and dined on "Bridget's best biscuit & rare coffee," orange ices, and cake. Caroline Severance remembered watching the Beecher family at a long table on the lawn. "Here were gathered that gifted family of brothers and sisters—a noticeable group, anywhere. Off duty now, each seemed conscious only of the old time home atmosphere and the exchange of bon mot and repartee was almost as rapid and incessant as the flash of light artillery in action." Or were the siblings *on* duty? Severance's description sounds like the competitive dinner table of the Beecher youth in Cincinnati.

Mary Hooker and Eugene Burton were married in October by two ministers: Nathaniel Burton, their Hartford minister, and Henry Ward Beecher. Alice was a bridesmaid and Eddie an usher. Except for the young friends of the wedding couple, the guests were nearly all relatives. Mary and Isabella were especially excited that Mary's aged grandmother, Mrs. Hooker, was still alive and could be present. Isabella always had a good word for Grandma Hooker, whom she thought "serene & beautiful" and for whom she felt a great affinity. It was tempting to cry at the wedding but Isabella restrained herself. She was delighted with people's praise of the event, especially when the whole thing cost less than three hundred dollars, including the band, the food, and the servants. This was in sharp contrast to Georgie Stowe's luxurious wedding the year before.

The concern with cost was new for the Hookers in the 1860s. The first mention in Isabella's writings of financial problems occurs in her letters from the Elmira Water Cure in 1860. She often asks John for money in a rather passive-aggressive way. She either apologizes profusely for asking ("my *poor husband*") or plays the martyr ("If I had as much money as you have I would send for an easy coach . . . but I am too poor"). She informs her husband that Dr. Gleason has agreed that room and board payments do not have to be immediate. While preparing to leave the water cure, Isabella wrote Alice that she was coming home full of ideas for more frugal living. Alice should not laugh at her or try to discourage her small attempts.

Soon economizing would become more than a game. Isabella began to mention their debts in her journal and gradually reduced her wardrobe. She sought financial advice from the wealthy Jervis Langdon, who suggested selling real estate and buying government securities. The Hookers started to keep a "covered sleigh" instead of a more expensive carriage; although the sleigh was perfectly respectable in Isabella's view, the girls were embarrassed and often refused to ride in it. John made a healthy salary for the time—in 1858 he had become reporter of the state Supreme Court. The family should have been able to afford some luxuries, such as carriages or visits to water cures; these establishments were usually in range of middle-class families, as room, board, and treatment averaged between five and ten dollars a week. John earned between ten and fifteen thousand dollars a year.

The expenses of living at Nook Farm, however, were gradually creeping upward. Everyone in the neighborhood experienced financial difficulties at one time or another. The authors, Harriet Beecher Stowe and Mark Twain, had to write frantically to maintain their standards of living (and in Twain's case, this was *before* he poured money into the typesetting machine and other inventions). The Gillettes, Burtons, and both sets of Warners (Charles Dudley and Susie, George and Lillie) also had money problems. Kenneth R. Andrews suggests that Nook Farm was attracted beyond its economic means by a wealthier class with which it associated—at the time Hartford could boast the highest per capita wealth among American cities. "The luxury prevailing among the wealthy and the standards of expensive comfort by which the well-to-do governed their expenditures seem to have drawn Nook Farm into conspicuous consumption that it could not afford."

Andrews's statement certainly applies to the Stowes. Harriet seems to have thought she had to maintain "standards of expensive comfort" as part of her position as famous author. Calvin, now that he no longer received a salary, felt uneasy about the extravagances of Oakholm. Unlike Isabella, however, he could supplement the income of the main breadwinner. His *Origin and History of the Books of the Bible* (1867) was more than a scholarly success—he earned ten thousand dollars in royalties. Harriet had to manipulate the situation to get him to finish the book. She wrote Fields that when Calvin brought part of the manuscript to Boston, he should pretend to begin printing it and Calvin would "immediately go to work and finish up the whole; otherwise, what with lectures and the original sin of laziness, it will all be indefinitely postponed." But if Calvin could hold his own—earn as well as spend, the younger generation was more inclined to imitate the wealthier classes of Hartford in earning little and spending lots.

The Perkins children, Mary Hooker, and Georgiana Stowe had all married and left home by the end of 1866, the year after the war ended. But the Stowe twins and Alice Hooker tested the limits of their Puritan parents' forbearance. The United States was entering the period Mark Twain and Charles Dudley Warner would soon christen "the Gilded Age" in their novel with that title. After the war many Americans felt justified in indulging themselves to make up for years of sacrifice. Also, as Rugoff notes, merchants and financiers used the tools of the industrial revolution and "took over the world.

The nation's industries and wealth increased apace but so did political corruption, extravagance and the relaxing of moral and religious standards."

Oakholm was a sign of the times, but the symbolic occurrence closest to the Beecher sisters was an episode involving Harriet's and Isabella's friends, the Howards of Brooklyn. Because Henry Ward Beecher's wife, Eunice, resented his family and was often inhospitable, Harriet and Isabella had taken to staying with John and Susie Howard when they visited New York. They could then "enjoy Henry without alloy," as Isabella put it. Before the end of the war the Howards' son Joseph got in trouble for trying to manipulate the stock market. He forged a presidential proclamation calling for a fresh draft of troops, caused a panic on Wall Street, and made a killing on the market. Joe soon found himself in a federal prison and was released only when Henry Ward Beecher interceded personally with Lincoln (God forbid that a Beecher friend should rot in jail!).

The Stowe and Hooker daughters weren't unethical but strove anxiously to follow the latest fashions. A relative remarked disapprovingly of the twins, "Hatty & Eliza grow more & more so, as they grow older. They are dressed as usual in expense of the worst & most exaggerated fashion." Their parents made noises about their being too concerned with appearances but hesitated to rein them in. Harriet did begin to insist that the twins contribute some work toward the family upkeep. Although they were disinclined to give up their lives of leisure, their mother warned them that if her health failed, the family's economic foundation would crumble. She scolded them as follows: "[T]he energy with which you often say that you detest housekeeping, that you hate accounts & cant keep them[,] that you dont like to write letters & cant write them—that you hate sewing—that you cant take care of sick people[,] all these leave a load upon me which if you were differently inclined you might take off." The twins finally assumed most of the housekeeping but were content to stay dependent on their mother. As Joan Hedrick notes, Harriet had been trained by her sister Catharine to lead an independent life. Yet, distracted by work, family, and her own variable temperament, she did not pass this heritage on to her daughters.

Like her cousins, Alice Hooker at age eighteen aspired to be, in her mother's words, "rich & handsome, stylish & fashionable." She kept late hours partying with a wealthier set and developed a taste for finer clothes than the Hookers could furnish. Isabella, writing in her journal in February 1865, noted that there had recently been "a certain infelicity in our family life" difficult for everyone. Their yearly income was less than they needed to support their standard of living, and so they had to cut back. Isabella felt caught in the middle trying to negotiate between John's "old-fashioned notions" of economy and the children's "extravagant newer ones." The immediate question was whether they could afford to send Alice to the Taylors' Institute of the Swedish Movement Cure in New York.

Although Alice did go, Isabella continued to worry about John's overexerting himself at work. Any pressure tended to make him anxious, depressed, and ill. Then he would have to let up on work and money would be shorter, creating more pressure and thus a vicious circle. Many of John's ailments seem today to have been psychosomatic. In spring 1866, for instance, when he was hiding the severity of their financial problems from Isabella, he developed paralysis in one of his hands; she thus had to help him with his writing for the court. (This paralysis is reminiscent of Catharine's problem with her foot that originally sent her to the water cures.) The Hookers started keeping boarders to earn money, and this was the year in which Isabella produced scaled-down versions of an anniversary party and a wedding. She stayed within her budget and made all the table decorations herself for both celebrations.

These economies, however, were not enough to avert a crisis in spring 1867. The Hookers' financial difficulties were not simply a matter of spending too much but had to do also with bad investments and poor judgment in endorsing notes for other people. John's business partner, his brother-in-law Francis Gillette, was especially naive concerning the latter and the Hookers wished they could separate from him. In March John could not pay their monthly bills. When he broke down, Isabella intervened, seeking and receiving advice from Jervis Langdon; she went to talk with a Mr. Bartholomew, who owed John money, and convinced him to borrow the money to pay. John went with Pastor Nathaniel Burton to recover in Florida. He promised to stay out of the stock market—having bought "Adams' stock," which promptly went down, he sold it at a loss and bought railroad stock. The new stock, of course, went down and Adams back up. Isabella hoped that ill luck would keep John out of "such dangerous business" in the future.

On their trip south, Hooker and Burton stayed with the Stowes, who had just discovered the joys of Florida. The previous autumn Fred Stowe had met some veterans in a bar who were trying to grow cotton on a plantation bordering the St. Johns River near Jacksonville. Land was cheap and ex-slaves a ready source of labor, but the men needed further financing. Harriet and Calvin jumped at the chance for Fred to work as a distraction from alcohol. His disease had progressed since the war, and he had become an embarrassment not only to himself but also to the Beecher sisters in Hartford. It was not uncommon for him to suddenly disappear from a family gathering and be gone for days on a bender. "Poor Hattie—& poor [Fred's] sisters," Isabella wrote John. "They are all heart broken—it seems to have come to them at last, that he is hopelessly bound to this habit & they are in despair."

Harriet and Calvin thought the opportunity to work outdoors away from Hartford and the responsibility of managing a plantation might turn their son around; they thus agreed to finance the operation in Florida and put Fred in charge. The next March the Stowes went to visit and became instant snowbirds. Harriet was enchanted at the idea of stepping from Hartford winter to Florida summer with birds and flowers everywhere. She soon discovered the pretty village of Mandarin on the other bank of the St. Johns River, along with a piece of property with a house and its own orange grove. Fred seemed better, but no sooner had the Stowes returned to Hartford in the summer when he showed up out of control. This time Catharine found an institution for him in Binghamton, New York, near Elmira; there he was locked in his room while he went through withdrawal under a doctor's care. From a twenty-first-century point of view, this course of treatment would seem more promising than running a cotton plantation staffed with drinking men. The treatment had no lasting effect, however, and once Fred returned to Florida he fell off the wagon. When his mother arrived the next winter, she found a dissipated son and no bales of cotton ready to be sold. She withdrew from the cotton venture and sent Fred to dry out again on a Mediterranean voyage with Calvin.

However painful Fred's failure, Harriet took solace in the presence of her youngest son, Charles, now eighteen, who accompanied her on the Florida trip. He had had a difficult adolescence, much like that of his maternal uncles. Sent at age fourteen to a strict boarding school because of his habitual lying, he ran away to sea. Harriet and Calvin, to their credit as parents, did not panic but remembered the trials of the Beecher brothers. After a few years at sea Charles returned to prepare for Harvard. Eventually—of course—he became a minister. As for Florida, the Stowes bought the Mandarin property and hired cousin Spencer Foote, one of the Guilford Footes, to expand and manage the orange grove. This venture was successful, and the Stowe family spent the next twenty years wintering in Mandarin.

John Hooker was much less impressed with Florida, as he was bothered by mosquitoes. He returned from the Stowes' more depressed than before and actually began to talk of suicide. It was finally Jervis Langdon's lending the Hookers money without security that saved them from bankruptcy. John perked up enough to stop taking the "harmless" medicine prescribed by Dr. Curtis for his hand and suddenly recovered. Isabella sent him off to the Green Mountains in Vermont. Interestingly, the funicular effect she had described years before (one partner up while the other was down) occurred again during the financial crisis. Earlier she had sensed John grow stronger as she weakened and became more dependent. Now as John felt suicidal Fred Stowe told Isabella he had never seen her look so young and handsome; she admitted to Alice that "I never was happier in my life than now—nor so well since I can remember."

The Hookers' arrangement with Jervis Langdon was confidential and not known to the rest of the family or most of their friends. It comes to light today because of Isabella's frank correspondence in 1867 and 1868 with a family friend, Robert W. Allen. Robert Allen was close to Eugene Burton and had spent considerable time in the early 1860s staying with the Hookers. He had endeared himself to Isabella by being kind to Eddie and entertaining him when he had scarlet fever. Allen had fought in the war, been an usher at the Burtons' wedding, and was romantically interested in Alice (she did not reciprocate). In 1867 he was a naval attaché in Europe. Isabella wrote Allen initially to ask him to intervene in a dispute with Eugene. She found his letters sympathetic and, although he was thirty years old and only fifteen years younger than she, began referring to him as her dear boy and signing her letters "Mamma." Much of their correspondence has to do with Allen's buying luxury items such as lace and silk dresses and sending them duty-free to the Hookers and their friends. Typically, Isabella felt "little twinges of conscience" about defrauding the government but took advantage of the situation. She also discussed with Robert Allen topics too sensitive to bring up with her family, such as the Hooker financial situation and, most especially, her deteriorating relationship with her son-in-law, Eugene Burton.

Isabella began complaining of Eugene's cold and contemptuous treatment of her just a few months after he and Mary were wed. It is not clear whether Eugene deliberately waited to show his true feelings until Mary was legally his or whether he began to dislike Isabella at this time. The two were bound to conflict eventually, as they were opposites in every way. Isabella was outgoing and demonstrative, demanding shows of affection in return; Eugene was shy, withdrawn, and secretive. One of their ongoing quarrels had to do with visitors. Eugene kept to his room when guests came, and if they stayed overnight, he wanted to go out to a hotel. He also refused to share his letters with the rest of the family in the usual way of the time. Isabella wanted to convert Eugene, for she was still religious even if her religion had become a watered-down version of her father's. She sought to make him more like his clergyman brother, while he rejected religion entirely. Isabella was no doubt correct when she wrote Alice that "He is tired of my praying & tired of me."

There were also the questions of rights for black men and for women. Eugene had a "childish prejudice against the negro" that his mother-in-law wanted to eradicate, and as Isabella stood on the threshold of becoming a national leader in the women's movement, Eugene opposed suffrage for women. He believed that the only argument in favor of women voting was that it might benefit men. Isabella wrote Alice sarcastically, "[S]o the argument stands thus—'They [women] have no rights in the matter—they are singularly incompetent—they will cease to be women & become monsters, nevertheless it will so humanize us men to have them in our midst on election day, we will think of it.'"

Eugene Burton was thus poor material for the loving adopted son Isabella envisioned having. Her imaginings in this regard are quite outrageous. She had a daydream in which "I felt his gentle hand stroking my thin cheeks, as I did my mother's once, when I was an old woman even & his eyes & voice saying—'my pretty mother—I love you so dearly—you look sweeter than ever to me & you never will change, to my eye. It isn't because you are Mary's mother that I love you—but for yourself & all that you have been to me—& that you are my ideal mother—the ones boys ought always to have born to them' & much more." Isabella wrote Alice that "I never knew the possibilities of a mother's heart till I knew him & gave myself to him with an absolute consecration." Eugene, however, had broken her heart. "One whole long year have I been waiting for the one blessed word mother from his lips—& it has not come—& I am sobbing this moment as I write." This effusion is the first indication, despite Isabella's heritage of mental illness, of feelings beyond what might be thought normal for the era.

Even so, the dominant chord of her outpouring—the sentimentality attached to motherhood—was harmonious with the times. It was not just sisters Catharine and Harriet who glorified motherhood. Even the feminists or "strong-minded" women who would soon become Isabella's colleagues saw motherhood as the pinnacle of women's existence. "That function gives women such wisdom and power as no male ever can possess," said the ordinarily unsentimental Elizabeth Cady Stanton. In her autobiography she presents herself as a kind of supermother, stressing the ease with which she bore and cared for children. She is full of kindly maternal advice and anecdotes about her curing sick babies on trains; clearly Stanton made use of a maternal image to soften and legitimize her radical social philosophy. In his history of the women's movement William O'Neill contends that motherhood was so revered in the Victorian age that "the temptation to exploit rather than resist the current of opinion was irresistible," even though accepting the maternal mystique led feminists back to the domesticity they had hoped to escape.

What distinguishes Isabella's yearning to hear the "blessed word mother" is the intensity of her longing and of her suffering at Eugene's defection. In her letters to Robert Allen and her daughter Alice she obsessively returns to the subject of Eugene and the pain he causes her. Why, one might ask, did she feel the need for another son when she already had one who was nearly perfect from a parental point of view? If one assumes an element of the erotic in her feelings toward Eugene, along with anxiety about facing menopause and losing her looks (she was forty-five when she aspired to be "pretty mother"), why weren't the attentions of men her own age sufficient? She had an adoring husband *and* a devoted admirer in the person of Jervis Langdon. Isabella had been attracted to Langdon since the Elmira water cure days. Their friendship was "sacred," she confided to Robert Allen, as she had always been "affected by him *magnetically*." To Alice she wrote that "our intimacy has been very great—far greater than you can realize." No doubt they were too proper to have an affair, but Langdon seems to have returned Isabella's warm feelings. Besides lending the Hookers money with no strings attached, he was assiduous in arranging pleasure trips on which Isabella would accompany his family—to Saratoga, to Niagara Falls, to New York City to hear Charles Dickens read. The death of Jervis Langdon in 1870 from stomach cancer was a great blow to Isabella.

However one might interpret Isabella's "magnetic" attraction to Langdon, her description of Eugene Burton as "round & plump as a big partridge" does not sound very erotic. Maybe her obsession had to do primarily with her attachment to motherhood. That is to say, her identity was so bound up in being a mother, she could not face the approaching end of active mothering. This end also reminded her of her own mother, as shown in the reference to stroking her mother's cheeks, and likely took on all her unresolved feelings about Harriet Porter Beecher's death and the death of her first baby boy. Isabella's mother had died at age forty-four, just short of forty-five, Isabella's age at the time of the "pretty mother" letter. Once fully developed, Isabella's obsession with claiming Eugene as her son was hard to dislodge. She could have benefited from a late-twentieth-century advice book on the gender-based commitment struggle—his to stay free of committing himself to another person, hers to force him to commit; the harder she pushes, the faster he withdraws.

One of Isabella's difficulties in getting over Eugene was her inability to express anger. Anger was not part of the Victorian gentlewoman's equipment; it was "unladylike" and had to be suppressed at all cost. Thus Isabella felt the need to write pages to Robert and Alice describing Eugene's behavior toward her and detailing her hurt feelings before she could reveal any hostility. Usually she simply rededicates herself to helping him and winning him over. Only at the end of the long "pretty mother" letter does she conclude that Mary does not understand her true feelings; according to Isabella, Mary thinks her mother is satisfied with Eugene's slightly improved manner while in reality she nearly hates him.

Alice Hooker was understandably upset by her mother's irrational letter about Eugene. When she accused her mother of grasping for love, Isabella replied calmly, "I think it is not love—of which I am so greedy—as the assurance that I can be of real service to those I tenderly love. There is a restlessness in me—& always was, to be doing something of importance— to reach moral results—& in the cases we spoke of—I have failed—partially at least—& have lost ground in E[ugene]'s, that once seemed gained." She realized she had gone too far in pouring out her feelings to her daughter, apologized, and drew back. "I have nothing to complain of—am sorry rather that I have tried to draw you into my confidence so deeply."

At the time of these letters, September 1867, Isabella and Alice were somewhat at odds in their own relationship. Alice had in no way abated her craving to be rich and fashionable. She was, in Isabella's words, "filled with desires after a gay life." Against her better judgment, Isabella at first tried to gratify her daughter. She provided dancing lessons, gymnastic lessons (to improve the figure), stays at the Taylors' institute in New York, parties, and private theatricals. She fussed over Alice's dresses and capitulated to her insistence that Bridget, their cook, start waiting on table ("we are growing genteel I fear," Isabella remarked). When these actions simply whetted Alice's appetite for high society, Isabella sent her on a long trip, even though Mary had just gone on her honeymoon and Isabella feared being lonely. Alice spent seven months visiting friends in Connecticut and New York, ending up at the Taylors' cure with Livy Langdon and then Elmira for a long stay. Although Alice enjoyed reading and studying with Livy, whom she admired, the Langdon house (or rather, mansion) was not the place for shedding an attraction to wealth. "Oh Mother what a nice thing it is to have plenty of money!" Alice enthused. "They spend money very fast and freely here."

Her parents' response may be imagined, for this was the time of the Hookers' financial panic. When Alice was informed of the money problems, she wrote back in anger, upset that her parents would "resort to keeping boarders for a living." This unrealistic attitude, plus Alice's restlessness when she returned home and found a scarcity of servants and decent carriages, convinced Isabella that there was more at issue than her own anti-materialism based on her Puritan upbringing. She confided in the children's journal in December 1867 that she was arguing the question with Alice, who was trying hard to "overcome the spirit of worldly ambition" within her. By then it was too late. Isabella concluded: "It is surprising however how deep is her fear of the remark of the multitude—how great her reverence for wealth—how critical her observation of the defects of a moderate & economical household. I find myself lecturing her too much I fear—yet where to stop is the question."

This month was a significant one for the future of Nook Farm because Samuel Clemens, who was becoming known to the world as Mark

Twain, met his wife-to-be, Livy Langdon, in New York. Twain had been on a tour of the Holy Land (written up later as *Innocents Abroad*) with Livy's brother Charles, who introduced them. Present were Isabella and Alice Hooker, whom the Langdons had invited to stay with them at their hotel. The occasion was Charles Dickens's visit to New York to read from his work. Isabella, a great fan of Dickens, found him an only moderately good interpreter of his *David Copperfield*. As is well known, Mark Twain was entranced by Livy Langdon at this first meeting. Still, he had eyes to notice that Alice was also a "beautiful girl," and apparently Isabella noticed him noticing. She went back to Hartford after the reading, leaving her daughter with the Langdons, and promptly wrote Alice, "I wish you would not go in public with Clemens till I see you again—there are opinions of him I did not know & you ought not to go with him again." In a supreme irony, Twain would return the favor a mere five years later when Isabella's reputation was tarnished through her work in the women's movement; at that point he forbade Livy to see Isabella.

Back in 1868, it was probably rumors Isabella heard about Twain's wild frontier past that prompted the Hookers to treat him less forthrightly than they ordinarily would have. In late January he stayed with them in Hartford while he conducted business with his new publisher, Elisha Bliss of the American Publishing Company. Part of his reaction to the Hookers was pure Mark Twain— comic exaggeration of the differences between himself and his surroundings. Thus he wrote the following report for the *Alta California*, the newspaper that had him under contract: "At the hospitable mansion where I am a guest, I have to smoke surreptitiously when all are in bed, to save my reputation, and then draw suspicion upon the cat when the family detect the unfamiliar odor. . . . So far, I am safe; but I am sorry to say that the cat has lost caste."

Twain wrote a friend that he had to "walk mighty straight" at the Hookers' because he wanted to "have the respect of this sterling old Puritan community." His anxiety about "the Puritans" (referring apparently to John's Hooker heritage) and sense of being an outsider are shown in his inscription in Isabella's visitors' book:

> Samuel L. Clemens
> San Francisco 1/24/68
> Forget the Pilgrims, if you will, but I beg that as long as they
> shall deserve it you will remember kindly 'the Others.'

Something went wrong during the visit. Clemens ultimately wrote Livy that the Hookers had "humiliated" him. "I am afraid I never shall feel right in that house . . . I let my trust & confidence go out to them as I seldom do with new acquaintances, & they responded by misunderstanding me." In a riff on the word "acquaintance," he explained that he disliked being treated ceremoniously as a visiting acquaintance and being poked and prodded with polite attentions. Yet Twain did not extend his negative feelings from the Hookers to Nook Farm as a whole. He and Livy would move there in fall 1871. They rented the Hooker house that he did not "feel right" in while their own was being built nearby.

While her friend Livy Langdon was being courted by Mark Twain, Alice Hooker was juggling suitors as one of the leading belles in Hartford. As she had been with Mary, Isabella seemed oblivious to the fact that Alice was twenty years old with no plans for the future. When she was staying with the Langdons in Elmira, Alice even asked her mother what she should "do in the world." The best Isabella could come up with was that she stay home a year and study natural philosophy. By contrast, Eddie (or Ned, as he was now called) had his vocation decided at age twelve. After he had fetched some medications for Hattie Hawley, who was ill, he said he would like "to become a Doctor—It does seem as if one only studies into these things he *could find* ways to cure so much suffering & do so much good." Isabella pledged to help him. The children's journal ends in 1868 with her plans for Ned's future: he would finish his high school course by age nineteen and take a collegiate and medical course together, emphasizing homeopathy and omitting subjects not relevant to his career. At age twenty-three or twenty-four he would travel in Europe and at twenty-five or twenty-six marry and launch his practice, helped financially by his parents. In its broad outlines this scenario became a reality.

As for Alice, she got engaged. In spring 1868 she was becoming "quite a society belle" and continually provoking her mother. Just as Isabella was writing another suffrage article and thinking she might convert Alice and Mary to the cause, Alice accepted a part in a play entitled "The Coming Woman." The play satirized women's rights. Isabella confided to Robert Allen that nothing could have induced her at Alice's age to lend herself to anything that "brought contempt on woman." Alice seemed to lack her mother's "pride of womanhood." Worse, the man who would become her fiancé was an older man her parents disapproved of. He was John Calvin Day, a corporate lawyer from a wealthy Hartford family. Isabella and John, who knew him only slightly, thought him conservative, cold, and sarcastic, "all manners & polish" and no substance.

The crisis came when Isabella and Mary went to the railway station to see Alice off on a trip to New York. As Alice arrived, who should be with her but John Day? Isabella gave a vivid description of the scene. She was shocked, she wrote Alice, "seeing you glide out of the station, with that fox at your side & you so manifestly at one with him & so far apart from your mother & sister, who could only stand by, as in a dream." Alice seemed mesmerized by the fox or, as her mother saw it, under a kind of spell. Alice later apologized for keeping her family in the dark, explaining that she could not admit her true feelings for Day until she knew he was serious about her also. Isabella and John gradually reconciled themselves to Alice's engagement, though they were never enthusiastic about her choice. Their main objection, that he had not fought in the war, Day addressed. He had wanted to go, he said, but his invalid mother begged him to stay home. Other negative features were that he did not belong to a church and did not want to, nor did he believe in women's rights. Still, what seemed to be coldness and cynicism in his character could be reinterpreted as shyness. Isabella thought he improved on further acquaintance and was delighted when he referred to her, when speaking to Eliza Stowe, as "my new mamma."

If Isabella's feelings about Alice's engagement seemed to echo her earlier reaction to Mary and Eugene, Harriet was also caught up in a déjà vu situation in spring 1868. She was trying to finish for James Fields the book she intended to be her masterpiece, *Oldtown Folks* (1869). This novel had been conceived back in 1864 but, as had happened before, Harriet's need for ready cash (for the Florida ventures and Fred's treatments) tempted her to accept competing projects. She started to write for the growing children's book market and also committed herself to a collection of biographical sketches of famous men. The collection was to be published by the Hartford Publishing Company, which put out subscription books. As Harriet wrote Fields, Hartford was becoming a huge publishing mart, the center of a booming subscription book (book-of-the-month club) business. Hartford Publishing had first secured Calvin Stowe, promising to sell at least one hundred thousand copies if he would put together a book from his old sermons and lectures. Then Harriet succumbed to the idea of publishing as a book some biographical sketches she had written for journals. The catch was that she had to compose more sketches to produce a thick enough volume. According to Forrest Wilson, Hartford Publishing asked Harriet to include a biography of brother Henry. When she refused, they offered her a thousand dollars in cash in addition to her royalties, and "that argument overcame her scruples."

Neither Harriet nor Calvin ended up being pleased with the bargains they had struck with Hartford Publishing. Harriet wrote a long letter of complaint to biographer James Parton, the husband of her friend and former student Fanny Fern: "I live in a great centre where I see immense fortunes being daily & constantly made *out of us*, in which *we* have scarcely any share. There are four or five houses here with their agents who choose some subject, of deep common interest—hire well known authors who ask them only ordinary magazine prices for their work & then *make* for themselves a clear profit of fifty or a hundred thousand dollars." She claimed she would be receiving only twelve cents per copy for her collection, and the time she had to spend writing and revising was not worth it. Finally she hired her nephew Fred Perkins as secretary and fulfilled her obligation. *Men of Our Times* came out in 1868, freeing her to finish *Oldtown Folks*.

Harriet described *Oldtown Folks* as a novel about "New England life in the age after the revolutionary war & before rail roads had destroyed the primitive flavor of our life—the rough kindly simple religious life of a Massachusetts town in those days when the weekly mail stage was the only excitement." She made use of Calvin's memories of growing up in Natick, Massachusetts, and employed him as narrator under the name "Horace Holyoke." Horace is also a fatherless boy with scholarly tendencies. As Harriet's description indicates, an air of nostalgia permeates the book. Many readers have seen it as a retreat on the author's part to a better past, a tranquil time before industrialization and the rampant money-getting of the Gilded Age. Horace Holyoke thinks old New England, "that simple, pastoral germ-state of society[,] is a thing forever gone. Never again shall we see that union of perfect repose in regard to outward surroundings and outward life with that intense activity of the inward and intellectual world, that made New England, at this time, the vigorous, germinating seed-bed for all that has since been developed of politics, laws, letters, and theology, through New England to America, and through America to the world. The hurry of railroads, and the rush and roar of business that now fill it, would have prevented that germinating process."

If this statement seems a bit simplistic (as well as jingoistic in its familiar Lyman and Catharine Beecher–like glorification of New England), Harriet makes the world of the novel more complex. Among the kindly rustics in Oldtown are two characters almost villainous (as reflected in their names)—Old Crab Smith and Miss Asphyxia. This brother and sister take the work ethic too far and in their greed mistreat the orphans who come into their care; Miss Asphyxia is even compared to a steam engine or power loom in her zeal for efficiency, the "golden calf" the region worships. In other words, the seeds of rabid materialism always existed in New England (for perfection Harriet has to invent the Utopian community of Cloudland, where the children go away to school). Perhaps her creation of Miss Asphyxia is an admission that she, too, was implicated in the excesses of the Gilded Age.

As Harriet finished *Oldtown Folks,* she was also collaborating with Catharine on *The American Woman's Home,* which also came out in 1869. The work on this book was not onerous. It is basically a condensation of parts of *A Treatise on Domestic Economy* with sections on gardening and decorating added by Harriet. Earlier in the 1860s she had written a series on housekeeping for the *Atlantic Monthly,* so she had plenty of material available. The sisters drew closer together as Catharine spent more time in the latter part of the decade staying at Oakholm. It was much the pattern of the sisters' relationship that they would grow a bit distant but then come closer when they had a joint project to work on—earlier in life it was teaching and now it was writing.

For some years Catharine had not been welcomed enthusiastically in the various family homes. In her youth her father had protected her and intervened with the brothers and sisters, but now he was gone. Brother Charles wrote of Catharine as follows: "Now I know she has peculiarities that repel some from her. And yet it seems sad to me to see her cast out as it were from the family circle by Mary, and Hatty and you [Henry]—Not that she is really cast out—but—something virtually pretty near it. Yet she is sincere, and kind, and benevolent. . . . Cannot she be made to feel more of the warm sympathy of fraternal affection in her loneliness?"

Catharine *was* sincere and benevolent. She was well-intentioned and hardly ever nasty. But her absorption in her own projects and inability to consider other people made her a dreaded houseguest. Edward Everett Hale, her nephew by marriage, told a story that illustrates the behavior Catharine could indulge in. Once when she was visiting the Hales he came home from work and found his wife and daughters toiling away in the kitchen. It seems that Catharine had been there earlier in the day trying out recipes for one of her books. When the cook and maids lost patience and objected to the experiments, Catharine promptly fired them! Hale went to her room, where she was quietly writing, and called, "Aunt Catharine, your visit is over! Pack up your things. A hack will call for you first thing in the morning!"

Catharine angered Isabella when she wrote announcing she would be in Hartford for a committee meeting on a certain day and would stay with the Hookers. She didn't give Isabella time to respond, nor did she ask if the date were convenient. As Isabella noted in a letter of complaint to Catharine, "[Y]ou habitually violate these [standard] courtesies." When Catharine arrived at Nook Farm, she told a neighbor (but not the Hookers) she intended to stay for a month. Isabella also complained that her older sister disrupted family harmony. Although Catharine meant well, she freely repeated what she heard from one household to another and thus started quarrels. If her intent was to heal wounds, in nine cases out of ten, "you really *make* the wound you are striving to heal." Isabella did not often invite Catharine to visit when her children were young, she said, in order to protect them from this behavior. In conclusion, Isabella suggested that her sister find a good boarding house in Hartford. With this advice she claimed she was expressing the opinion of every one of her brothers and sisters.

One major issue that caused conflict between Catharine and her siblings was money. Although she had repeatedly been admonished to save for sickness and old age, she always refused to do so and gave whatever extra funds she had to her educational projects and charities. She relied on her siblings to support her if necessary. Except for Henry, however, all the siblings occasionally had trouble making ends meet. The ultimate effect, Isabella asserted in her complaining letter, was that Catharine got to choose for everyone, whereas all should have the right to select their own charities for themselves. Catharine's devotion to her causes made her completely blind to such criticism; she and Isabella argued the point for years. Or perhaps it was less devotion to causes than the typical Beecher belief that she had the ability (and the right) to make decisions for everyone. Before the war, for instance, brother Edward had financial problems and Catharine set about raising money from the rest of the family. Instead of contacting family members and asking them to contribute, she promised Edward a certain amount, divided it up equally among the family members, and in effect sent each a bill for their share. Isabella complained at that time also. Sister Mary, she noted, wanted to help Edward but thought Catharine's fundraising "injudicious as to manner."

However annoying Catharine could be, she did not hold grudges. Perhaps her relatives felt so free to criticize her because they knew she wasn't vindictive. As she grew older, she tended to become more easygoing. The Edward Everett Hale story has a sequel. A couple of years after he expelled Catharine from his house he encountered her on Boston Common, sitting on a bench reading. Embarrassed, he tried to retreat and pretend he hadn't noticed her, but she called out, "Edward, do come and see the wonderful books I have just bought at that second-hand store on Tremont Street." Hale was so touched by her friendliness to him that he invited her to visit and she stayed without incident for two weeks.

This anecdote is told by Harriet's grandson Lyman Beecher Stowe and, like his Lincoln story, might be embellished from the original. But Catharine's written response to Isabella's strongly worded criticisms was quite mild, perhaps reflecting a softening of her edges. She concluded the following:

> When I had a home of my own, my sisters always found a welcome and I aided them to an education and means of support. I think you for some months had a gratuitous board and tuition in my family years ago. I believe all of you are as good and sisterly as ever I could be and I know many other friends that would rejoice to contribute to sustain my declining years. . . . I love you and trust you as one anxious to do right in all things.
>   Your affectionate
>   Sister Catharine

This letter may have aggravated Isabella further because it distorted reality to a large degree. Catharine had aided Mary and Harriet in their education and occasionally supported them, but not Isabella. She had a home of her own in Hartford for about a year (1826–1827) when Isabella was four years old; it was Mary who had offered free room and board to the youngest Beecher sister. Catharine used ambiguous language in her letter—"you are as good and sisterly as ever I could be" (how sisterly is that?), I "trust you as one anxious to do right" (but I don't trust you to actually do right?). Yet if Catharine's wording was indirect and she did not really answer her sister's criticisms, neither did she defend herself in an angry, hostile way.

By the late sixties Catharine had not changed her attitude toward women's rights. She included a letter to her countrywomen at the end of the household manual she edited with Harriet, *The American Woman's Home* (1869). Entitled "An Appeal to American Women by the Senior Author of This Volume," it repeats what she wrote in *A True Remedy for the Wrongs of Women* back in the early 1850s. Catharine catalogs the wrongs of women and the dangers to the American family, including woman suffrage as one of the new dangers. If women gained the ballot, she argues, what good measures could they enact that men wouldn't grant to a "united petition" of women? Wouldn't men allow women what they requested "very much sooner than they would give power and office to our sex to enforce these advantages by law? Would it not be a wiser thing to *ask* for what we need, before trying so circuitous and dangerous a method? God has given to man the physical power, so that all woman may gain, either by petitions or by ballot, will be the gift of love or of duty." The American Woman's Education Association had a better chance of improving women's lot, Catharine predicted, because "the ballot never will be accorded till benevolent and conscientious men are the majority—a millennial point far beyond our present ken."

But Isabella was rapidly becoming involved in the movement her older sister thought unsafe. As she described it to Robert Allen, "I am deep in reform matters." She did not engage in organizational work on the national level until 1869, when she met Susan B. Anthony and Elizabeth Cady Stanton. But her work for women really began two years earlier, after her older daughter Mary was wed. It was the same spring (1867) of the Hookers' financial crisis. Isabella was alone a good deal—John went to Florida with Pastor Burton and Alice stayed in New York and Elmira with Livy Langdon. Mary, wrote Isabella, "grows more & more to her own husband & plans & I feel more alone in consequence." Her loneliness, or more accurately a combination of loneliness and stimulation by her new feminist friends, pushed her into action.

One friend who helped propel her toward the women's movement was Caroline Severance. The other was Anna Dickinson, the orator, whom

Isabella had also met during the war. Although she was only Mary Hooker's age, Dickinson had been hired by the Republican Party in the early sixties to speak for their candidates in New England. In her memoir Isabella notes that she and John were apprehensive when Dickinson came to Hartford. They feared a young girl might injure the abolitionist cause and worried about "the speaker who would have to encounter so much adverse criticism in our conservative and prejudiced city." But a few minutes after Dickinson began talking, "we found ourselves, with the rest of the large audience, entranced by her eloquence. At the close of the meeting we went with many others to be introduced and give her the right hand of fellowship. She came home with us for the night, and after the family retired she and I communed together, heart to heart, as mother and daughter."

The Hartford *Press* declared Dickinson's speech to have saved the state from the Democrats, and she was likened to Joan of Arc. The occasion also inaugurated a long-lasting friendship. Dickinson, sometimes accompanied by her mother and/or siblings, would make frequent visits to the Hookers in Hartford. As was common at the time, Isabella shared her new acquaintance with friends and relatives, and Dickinson also became friendly with Harriet and with the Langdons of Elmira. Her high energy level tired Isabella (after one visit she wrote Alice that Anna "always uses me up"), but was also rewarding. In her memoir Isabella credits Dickinson with leading her to the women's movement. Although Dickinson was too busy with her political speeches to be involved in the day-to-day activities of the movement, she knew its history and was close to some of its leaders, particularly Lucretia Mott and Susan B. Anthony. Isabella wrote: "It was she who brought me to the knowledge of Mrs. John Stuart Mill and her remarkable paper on the 'Enfranchisement of Women' in the *Westminster Review*. She told me, too, of Susan B. Anthony, a fearless defender of true liberty, and woman's right of public speech; but I allowed an old and ignorant prejudice against her and Mrs. Stanton to remain until . . . I met Mrs. Caroline Severance . . . who confirmed what Miss Dickinson had told me of Miss Anthony, and unfolded to me the whole philosophy of the woman suffrage movement."

Anna Dickinson visited in early February 1867. Her stay was typically intense, involving much political talk and affectionate display. Although she had male suitors, she enjoyed the close, physically expressive relations with women that were typical in the nineteenth century. Isabella wrote Alice that Aunt Harriet had been staying with her when Dickinson arrived. Thereupon Harriet "slept with" Hattie Hawley and she with Anna: "I am enjoying Anna after the old fashion in my lovely bed room alone together." Such language was by no means unusual. At about the same time, Susan B. Anthony was looking forward to a visit from Anna, promising a "snuggle" in her big double bed. After Dickinson departed, Isabella traveled to Boston and stayed with her niece, Emily Perkins Hale. She visited old friends, such as her cousin Miranda Homes Southgate and her wedding attendant Harriette Putnam; time had miraculously made Harriette's husband "stout and a judge."

The highlight of the trip was a visit to Caroline Severance at her new house in West Newton. Isabella did not leave a record of what they talked about, but she suddenly began to discuss women's rights in letters to Alice. "The truth is when young girls wish they were young men it is not their sex that they wish to change at all—but they want the innocent privileges of the other sex which custom not nature denies them." Emily Hale, to whom Isabella was drawing closer, did not think she wanted to vote herself but resented being told she lacked the right and wasn't competent to vote. Some good men, Isabella explained to Alice, fancied that women would be contaminated by entering public life and so allied themselves with the brutal men who simply wanted to keep their power. Twenty years ago she had "shut my teeth with a snap" and resolved not to argue with men who opposed women's equality. Lately she had been thinking about the subject a great deal and could hardly keep herself out of the fray. Perhaps it helped that Eugene Burton was one of the men who scorned women's voting; the "shut my teeth" letter is the same one in which Isabella satirizes his views.

In April she responded in writing to an article by a Rev. Dr. Todd that appeared in the Boston *Congregationalist*. Entitled "Fashionable Murder," the article condemned married women who had abortions. Their motive, Todd asserted, was their selfish wish to live in fashionable ease and avoid the pains of childbirth. In her reply Isabella points out that fathers were just as responsible, in fact more responsible, than mothers in conceiving children out of passion rather than a desire for offspring. As a general rule, she argues, "Women are feebly endowed with this passion [i.e., sexual desire], and . . . men are by nature and training (or by lack of it, perhaps) overstocked." The husband is given to "inordinate indulgence of animal passion," while the wife submits through love of her husband. Isabella suggests that men learn restraint if they want to prevent abortion, and that each mother teach her son to consider the health of his wife and children to be.

The examples Isabella uses probably came from her own life. She tells of a boy who happened to encounter "a case of criminal intercourse between two servants in his own house." She has the mother explain the facts of life to the boy using the analogy of chickens, which her son Ned kept. Bringing an unwanted baby into the world "is just as if you should put one of your little pets into a snow-bank the moment it has pecked its way out of the shell; and how could you ever do that, do you think?" Ned at age ten had seen a young friend expose himself in the Hooker house. He may also have witnessed "criminal intercourse" between servants, as at the time of Isabella's writing their servant Bridget Doran was pregnant but unmarried. She had been impregnated by William, the Hookers' handyman whom they had let go. He finally agreed to marry Bridget but only a week before their baby was born. No doubt Isabella had her servant's situation in mind when she replied to the Rev. Dr. Todd's diatribe.

In her response Isabella also referred to her father's experience: "I have heard of one New England minister, the father of many children, whose word to his daughter on her approaching marriage was, 'You must instruct your husband, my dear, that he do not allow you to have children too often. If I had known what I now know earlier in life, your mother, of blessed memory, might be living to this day. The drain upon her vitality, in giving birth to all those children, and the incessant care of them through many years of poverty and trial, were more than human strength could endure, and disease coming to her at last, she sank under it, with no power to rally.'" If Lyman did actually say this to Isabella, "your mother" would have been Roxana Foote, not Harriet Porter Beecher, and he would have again confused his children's mothers; at least he had the grace to feel remorseful. One wonders what he knew at the point of his youngest daughter's marriage that he had not known earlier. Was he talking about the need for male restraint or for birth control?

Isabella's reply to Todd's article has the mother who expounds the facts of life to her son tell him that he will need the kind of self-restraint rarely practiced these days. There is a divine intimation of its necessity in the old Jewish law that has fallen into neglect. The old law, she explains, held the wife apart from her husband for nearly half of every month, not only the period of her menses but also that of her "more probable maternity." Modern science, in the person of certain Frenchmen, Isabella continues, holds a similar "theory of generation." In other words, she is advocating the rhythm method of birth control. Unfortunately for nineteenth-century women, the science of the time switched the more and less probable times of the month for conception to take place.

It was probably Isabella's assertion that women were less endowed than men with "animal passion" that led a twentieth-century writer to disparage the Hookers' sex life. Actually, Isabella's beliefs were consistent with the feminist thought of the time. Most people did think women felt less sexual desire, or at the least, as Isabella's letter suggests, were better trained to suppress it. Rather than advocating birth control devices or choice of abortion, "strong-minded" women called for male restraint. The fact that this position seems odd at the turn of the twenty-first century shows how successfully the idea was combated in the twentieth century that men should, or even could, control their sexual behavior. Isabella's reply to the Rev. Dr. Todd was not published in the Boston *Congregationalist;* instead the editor ran a follow-up article by Todd. He perhaps felt that women should not speak out on such "indelicate" matters, though Isabella argued that if anyone be allowed to write about these crucial topics, why not mothers and grandmothers? In any case she was unwilling, because of her daughters, to have the article published with her name. She circulated her response to Todd privately among her friends and co-workers until 1873, when she included it under the title "Motherhood" in her book *Womanhood: Its Sanctities and Fidelities.*

In May, the month after she wrote to the *Congregationalist,* Isabella was busy organizing a "Womens [sic] Christian Association" in Hartford. The association, she wrote Robert Allen, would "take care of young women who are earning their own support—make social evenings for them—& a Christian Home ultimately." Isabella threw herself enthusiastically into building up the association, devoting "all my time & strength" because "I see a life work in it just suited to my desire." But as she would soon find in the woman suffrage movement, there were basic disagreements among the founders. Presumably the organization was a branch of the YWCA (Young Women's Christian Association), which had been started in 1858, lay dormant during the war, and was rising again. The national association was not yet strong enough to impose regulations, and the local groups made their own. In Hartford a bunch of "old fogies," in Isabella's words, insisted on making church membership a condition for joining the group. Isabella fought against this requirement but was outvoted eleven to two. She stayed with the association for a while but found it too conservative and eventually dropped out.

It may have been her involvement with the Women's Christian Association, along with Alice's return home from her long sojourn, that prevented Isabella from attending the May 1867 meeting of the American Equal Rights Association (AERA) in New York. This association had been established the previous May at the first national women's rights convention since before the war. Anna Dickinson had spoken at the founding convention of the AERA, and Caroline Severance was elected corresponding secretary of the new organization. Isabella's brother Henry Ward Beecher gave the keynote address, a speech asserting that women not only possessed the right to vote but also had a positive duty to do so. Henry thus formally entered the women's movement before Isabella. But she may have helped Severance write resolutions for the AERA founding conference, as she wrote Alice before the meeting that Uncle Henry "much approved our Convention resolutions."

The AERA was essentially a reaction to the introduction into Congress of the Fourteenth Amendment to the Constitution. This amendment ensured freedmen their rights as citizens but at the same time specifically denied these rights to freedwomen: it introduced the word "male" into the

Constitution. The leaders of the women's movement were shocked. During the war, they had postponed their own cause to form the National Women's Loyal League, gathering four hundred thousand signatures on a petition to abolish slavery. Now the same man who had proudly accepted their petition on the Congress floor (Senator Charles Sumner) claimed he could not compose a fourteenth amendment without referring to "male" citizens.

As historian Eleanor Flexner explains the situation, the women's rights leaders expected to be rewarded at the end of the war for their patience in dropping their own issues to work for abolition. "[T]hey were totally unprepared for the opposition of the Republican politicians. The latter had their eyes fixed on a windfall of 2,000,000 potential male Negro voters in the South, which they had no intention of jeopardizing by stirring up an unnecessary tempest over woman suffrage. Nor did the women reckon on desertion of their cause by the abolitionists, long their staunch allies." The AERA declared itself for universal suffrage, but the cracks in its unity were obvious even at the first conventions. Some members, like Susan B. Anthony, were already saying they would not work for black male suffrage alone, while others thought "this was the Negro's [i.e., the Negro man's] hour."

Not having attended these conventions, Isabella was blissfully unaware of the women's plight and the storms to come over the Fourteenth and Fifteenth Amendments. She even believed for a time that the increasing participation in the movement of leading "good men," such as her brother Henry and John Stuart Mill of England, would obviate the need for her own involvement. Mill, during a brief term (1866–1868) in Parliament, introduced an amendment to the Second Reform Bill to extend the vote to female property owners (and thus taxpayers). Isabella, hearing of Mill's act from Anna Dickinson, recommended his May 20, 1867, pro-woman suffrage speech in the House of Commons to Robert Allen, concluding, "I am so relieved that any speech or thinking of mine are quite unnecessary now."

In her 1905 memoir Isabella notes that her friend Anna had also introduced her to an essay by Mill's wife, Harriet Taylor, entitled "The Enfranchisement of Women," which had appeared in the *Westminster Review* of 1851. This article, reprinted several times as a pamphlet, became one of the bestselling tracts of the American women's movement. It was as much about the United States as about England because Taylor quoted the Declaration of Independence and pointed out the contradictions in denying women equality in education, property law, work opportunities, and political rights. She also included some history of the American movement, listing the most important resolutions and demands of the 1850 Worcester Convention, the first self-consciously national woman's rights convention (it followed the 1848 convention at Seneca Falls).

In summer 1867 Isabella met one of the organizers of the Worcester Convention, the pioneering feminist Lucy Stone. Stone had fought hard for an education, graduating from Oberlin College, and been an abolitionist speaker before branching out into women's rights. She married Dr. Elizabeth Blackwell's brother, Henry, but refused on principle to relinquish her name and take his; when they wed, they issued a stirring memorial on the subject. Stone and Blackwell spoke on woman suffrage in July before the Connecticut legislature. They had just come from stumping in Kansas, which was having state referenda in the fall on woman and Negro suffrage. Isabella's resistance to the movement was still strong. Even though Stone and Blackwell brought the latest news from Kansas and Stone was reputed to be a charismatic speaker, Isabella did not join her friends in going to hear them. She feared "being irritated," she wrote Alice, who was away on vacation. Isabella would have missed them altogether had not Stone and Blackwell called at the Hookers the next day in search of Harriet. They had a good conversation, Isabella reported to her daughter. "Mrs. Blackwell is exceedingly intelligent & well informed—but talks too fast—her husband is a *gentleman* & agreeable very, & their harmony of feeling & action is charming—they go together & speak on different parts of the same subject & defer to each other in perfect good breeding."

If she sounds as though she is shopping for a pair of racehorses, Isabella also failed to understand Lucy Stone's refusal to be known as "Mrs. Blackwell." Yet in the same letter to Alice she complains at length about an anti–woman suffrage article she read in the *Nation*. Isabella's struggle between her growing feminist beliefs and her fear that the movement leaders might not be proper ladies and gentlemen was not at all unusual for the time. Just as many married women waited until their children were grown before becoming active, many women hesitated to risk their good reputations. Charlotte Wilbour, a suffragist and later president of Sorosis, one of the first women's clubs, wrote a recruit as follows: "I do see the gulf between us and the rest of womankind. My dear Mrs. Blake, it is a fearful thing to be different from other women today. . . . A mission that takes you out of their circle makes you thenceforth a curiosity to be tolerated as a tamed lion or a bear."

"Mrs. Blake" was Lillie Devereux Blake, a society matron who entered the movement around the same time as Isabella and eventually became a leader. Her husband, Grinfill Blake, suggested that she act upon her beliefs by joining the woman suffragists, although her friends and birth family were opposed. Blake said she spent days walking back and forth past the offices of the National Woman Suffrage Association in New York before she gathered courage to enter. When she did, she found Elizabeth Cady Stanton looking "charming and high-bred," Susan B. Anthony in an attractive gray traveling suit, and Charlotte Wilbour wearing "black lace and a handsome black lace hat." According to her daughter, Blake was bubbling over with enthusiasm when she informed her husband that night, "Grinfill, I went to the Woman Suffrage Headquarters today—and Grinfill, *they're ladies!*"

Isabella might have said the same thing to John when *she* met Stanton and Anthony the next year. Not only did the leaders of the women's rights movement qualify as ladies, but they would also expand Isabella's conception of what a "lady" could do and who might qualify to be one. As befitting a lady Beecher, she entered the movement from the top, quickly becoming a national leader. Finally, in her late forties, Isabella began to do the work and achieve the recognition she had always longed for. Yet her conservative sister Catharine may have had a point about the "dangers" of the suffrage movement. Isabella also stood on the verge of learning that fame can be a double-edged sword.

6

Suffrage Arguments,
1868–1870

IN SPRING 1868 Isabella wrote another article, which she entitled "A Mother's Letters to a Daughter on Woman Suffrage." This was a longer and more developed version of her earlier essay "Shall Women Vote?" The letter format was less awkward and more flexible than the "matrimonial dialogue" of the first essay. The main point was the same—that mothers have a special capacity for the art of government because of their experience in the family. They are uniquely fit to debate such questions as whether state prison discipline should be penal or reformatory, whether divorces should be restricted or freely granted, and whether children with disabilities should be educated at home or in institutions. Mothers would bring to politics "a habit of *calculating possibilities in the management of human beings.*"

Isabella does not say what role single women would play (should they even vote?), nor does she anticipate the objection that some mothers are bad mothers, lacking any ability to manage others. She also does not argue here a position she would come to later, that women are more moral than men and would bring higher ethical standards to government. She says instead, "I am not in the least of the opinion that if women alone bore the responsibilities of government, there would be greater faithfulness or higher patriotism than now; but rather that each sex needs the stimulus of the other to the right performance of every duty." The nation is analogous to the family in needing both men and women as leaders. Thus Isabella concludes, following brother Henry, that women have a duty as well as a right to vote and participate in government along with men.

At this stage in the development of her thought on women, Isabella was still adhering to the strict egalitarian view of the sexes she had held since her youth. She once told John, for instance, that her brother Edward's wife was "another demonstration of my theory that there is no sex in minds— that women can do anything that men can do—& vice versa." The "vice versa" is key here, and Isabella honored it when she wrote the letter complaining about her unequal education. In a postscript she noted that her brother-in-law Mr. Gillette had just come in and offered his opinion that women are superior to men when they have equal opportunity. I don't agree, wrote Isabella, "they are cut from the same *batch*." The reason women often seemed to be smarter or more perceptive is that they had been driven by oppression to sharpen their wits.

The special-capacity-of-mothers argument does not necessarily contradict the egalitarian view. The reason a mother has this capacity, Isabella maintains, is not because she grows life in her womb but because she enacts the social role of bringing up her children. Still, the mother argument seems rather partial in its obvious reflection of Isabella's own situation. One historian of the nineteenth-century women's rights movement attributes "power and glory of motherhood" language to activists of a certain age. She says this rhetoric struck mothers of about fifty who were soon to become grandmothers, not young women actually engaged on a daily basis with small children. Isabella was forty-six and two years away from grandmotherhood.

Isabella's personal situation is also reflected in the concluding argument of "A Mother's Letters." Apparently her remark to Robert Allen that men would bring about woman suffrage and obviate her need to get involved was more than a passing fancy. She contends that women must inevitably suffer if left alone to fight for their rights, whereas men can confer these rights without sustaining any loss of reputation. "[N]othing could be much more trying to a woman of delicacy and sensibility than such assertions of herself as are commonly stigmatized as immodest, unfeminine, unnatural, and the like; especially if she be the mother of sensitive children, on whom the recoil of rebuke may fall so heavily as to more than double her own pain. And does not this become the best of reasons why men should prepare the way for herself?" She thus determines to "call upon man" to step in chivalrously and open the doors to women's equality. A short time hence this wishful thinking would seem impossibly naive to Isabella. It also makes for a poor conclusion to her essay. Again, as with "Shall Women Vote?," Isabella weakens her writing by intruding personal concerns likely to be unfathomable to the reader instead of following her argument to its logical end.

The "mother of sensitive children" did not dare tell her daughters that she was composing "A Mother's Letters to a Daughter on Woman Suffrage." Instead, as she worked on the essay, she wrote Robert Allen in confidence: "You know a little of my deep interest in this suffrage question & the whole matter of the relation of the sexes—but you never knew how intense & sometimes devouring, my feeling has been in the matter, because I never would let that out to any one. . . . But now, the times are ripening fast & discussion is making converts rapidly." She talked over her ideas with the family minister, Nathaniel Burton, and he encouraged her to contribute to the public discussion. "Thus encouraged I have given a good many hours to writing—& have experienced the richest happiness of my life, perhaps in so doing." In part, Isabella simply felt relief in releasing her pent-up thoughts, just as her sisters had so often done before her. Writing was good for her health, she told Robert, because once she saw her thoughts in black and white they ceased to bother her so much. Also, she felt she had succeeded in expressing her ideas in such a reasonable manner that no one could be offended. John approved wholeheartedly and joined Burton in urging her to publish.

This time she found a publisher easily, and the article was printed in the November and December 1868 issues of *Putnam's Magazine*. The author's name was not included. By remaining anonymous, Isabella avoided two sore spots. She would rather the essay "make its own way, than be helped by my Beecher name" and "my daughters would not relish any publicity." She finally read the paper to Mary and Alice, who were resigned if not pleased. "A Mother's Letters" was well received in movement circles and for a time was attributed to one of the Massachusetts group. Both Julia Ward Howe of the Bay State and Mary Livermore entered the woman suffrage movement about the same time as Isabella; they both had daughters and were "ladies." Eventually, Isabella's essay was published with her name in pamphlet form as a tract of the Connecticut Woman Suffrage Association.

Until this point Isabella had participated in the woman movement solely through her writings, but after she finished "A Mother's Letters" she finally plunged into organizational work. In July 1868 she visited Caroline Severance in West Newton, Massachusetts, and helped write the call for the formation of the New England Woman Suffrage Association. She attended its convention in Boston in November, writing her son Ned that she overcame homesickness by listening to noble women. She met such anti-slavery stalwarts as William Lloyd Garrison and Julia Ward Howe and became reacquainted with Lucy Stone. This time Isabella heard Stone speak and was thus more favorably impressed; in her judgment Stone was "an orator beyond Anna [Dickinson]." Most important, Isabella made a new friend at the conference. Caroline Severance introduced her to Paulina Wright Davis (1813–1876), a woman ten years older than they who had been a founder of the movement. She helped organize and presided at the first national Woman's Rights Convention in Worcester in 1850. In the fifties she published a feminist monthly magazine, the *Una*, and in the sixties served as president of the Rhode Island suffrage association.

Davis was consistently described by her contemporaries as "beautiful and charming." This was also Isabella's emphasis. In her memoir she notes that "I met Paulina Wright Davis, whose mere presence upon the platform, with her beautiful white hair and her remarkable dignity and elegance, was a most potent argument in favor of woman's participation in public affairs." The two women took to each other immediately and even found a family connection—Davis had boarded in Washington with the Hooker in-laws, the Gillettes, when her husband was a congressman. Isabella wrote Ned that she had "fallen in love" with Davis and would exchange visits with her in Providence and Hartford the week after the convention.

In "The Last of the Beechers," written when she was eighty-three, Isabella says she confessed to Davis her prejudice against Elizabeth Cady Stanton and Susan B. Anthony and was invited to meet them at Davis's home "a few weeks" after the convention. Actually the few weeks were several months, as shown by the women's correspondence. During the period before they met Isabella exchanged letters with both Stanton and Anthony. Her letters were mainly criticisms—of Anthony for administrative errors such as getting the names wrong in a convention call, of Stanton for radical ideas in her magazine, the *Revolution*. Isabella also complained of Stanton's association with George Francis Train, the flamboyant and racist Democrat who was bankrolling the *Revolution*.

As they were understandably anxious to snare a Beecher for the movement and perhaps through her *the* Beecher (Harriet), Stanton and Anthony responded mildly enough to Isabella's criticisms. Anthony even asked for help. She attributed her mistakes to overwork and being saddled by others with last-minute details. She praised their mutual friend, Anna Dickinson, and thanked Isabella for the work she was beginning to do. The pioneers needed and deserved some assistance from other women. "Oh if the women who have sat silent lookers on these twenty years could begin to realize how good a word of recognition from them feels to us—*to me at least*—I am sure they would not fail to give it." Stanton claimed to welcome criticism, even though she was being battered from all sides at the time, and took a position somewhat above it. Outsiders might see much to blame that she never even noticed, she wrote, because her eye was focused on the creation of a better society. Regarding Train, she would work with anyone who helped obtain freedom for women; once they found financial support elsewhere they could dispense with his aid.

The women finally met, in August 1869, at Paulina Wright Davis's Providence estate. Stanton and Anthony were just a little older than Isabella. Elizabeth Cady Stanton at fifty-four was short and roly-poly with a motherly demeanor. Indeed, she'd had seven children with Henry Stanton, the abolitionist leader whom Isabella knew in her childhood—he was one of the firebrands who left Lane Seminary in the fight over slavery. At the time of the Providence meeting Elizabeth had been a reformer for almost thirty years. In

Elizabeth Cady Stanton (right) and Susan B. Anthony (left), 1870. Courtesy Schlesinger Library, Radcliffe Institute, Harvard University.

1840 she accompanied her husband to the World Antislavery Convention in London; when the women were barred from speaking, she and Lucretia Mott vowed they would "form a society to advocate the rights of women." In 1848 they organized the historic first woman's rights convention at Seneca Falls, New York. Stanton had been a leader of the woman movement ever since. An excellent speaker and writer, she was witty, confident, and bold.

Stanton's colleague, Susan B. Anthony, complemented her in looks as well as style. A thin and angular spinster, she had been brought up a Quaker and supported by her family in her activism in the abolition and temperance movements. When she met Stanton shortly after Seneca Falls, she became the Napoleon of the women's rights movement, as one contemporary put it. Stanton says in her autobiography that Anthony was "always pushing and goading me to work. . . . I forged the thunderbolts and she fired them." In other words, Anthony became the organizer and day-to-day manager of the movement. In 1869 she was forty-nine years old; the next year Isabella would make a speech at her fiftieth birthday celebration. Isabella describes herself in her memoir as sitting at the feet of Stanton and Anthony at Davis's Providence home. She says she spoke to them as follows: "While I have been mourning in secret over the degradation of woman, you have been working through opposition and obloquy to raise her to self-respect and self-protection through enfranchisement, knowing that with equal *political rights* come equal social and industrial opportunities. Henceforth, I will at least share your work and your obloquy."

In a long letter to Caroline Severance written at the time of the meeting she calls Elizabeth Cady Stanton "a noble woman, a magnificent woman & the truest womanliest woman of us all." For three days Isabella engaged in "the most intense heart-searching debate" she had ever undertaken. "I have handled what seem to me her errors [regarding marriage and divorce] *without gloves* & the result is that I love her also, just as I do you." As for Susan B. Anthony, she might sometimes fail in judgment but never in good intentions; she has no equal in loyalty and unselfishness. "She is a woman of incorruptible integrity." After studying Susan carefully under the shadow of Stone's and Severance's letters criticizing her and after attending her convention, "I am obliged to accept the more favorable interpretation of her that prevails here, rather than that of Boston."

Here Isabella refers to the recent split in the movement between the Boston and New York camps or between Lucy Stone and Stanton and Anthony. She had seen the fault lines at the New England convention in November, though she did not understand the full implications. She wrote Robert that Frederick Douglass had warned the New Englanders not to petition for a constitutional amendment enfranchising women until one had been obtained for black men. (The Fourteenth Amendment had been ratified by this time, but the Fifteenth, guaranteeing black men the vote, had not.) "Lucy Stone showed him the error of his ways in this—& made such a splash." Isabella did not know at this point that Stanton and Anthony had deliberately not been invited to the New England convention. In fact, Stanton had received an invitation by mistake and then been asked by abolitionist Stephen Foster to please *not* attend. The New England group was incensed at Stanton and Anthony's refusal to support the Fourteenth and Fifteenth Amendments and at their association with the racist Train. Stanton and Anthony had succeeded Stone and Henry Blackwell in Kansas in 1867, speaking on behalf of black and female suffrage. Train spoke with them for woman suffrage, supporting them when the eastern Republicans were silent on the question of women voting. As it turned out, both Kansas referenda lost. Stanton and Anthony thought Train had helped gain Democratic votes, but Stone and Blackwell felt he had cost them overall.

The simmering disagreements boiled over at the May 1869 meeting of the American Equal Rights Association. Elizabeth Cady Stanton gave a rousing keynote address, urging the conferees to organize around a sixteenth amendment enfranchising women. But Stephen Foster then asked Stanton to relinquish her office in the organization because she had "repudiated the principles of the society [i.e., universal suffrage]." She had published in the *Revolution* an article by Train entitled "That Infamous Fifteenth Amendment." Douglass chimed in with a speech on the urgency of giving black men the ballot: "With us, the matter is a question of life and death. . . . When women, because they are women, are hunted down through the cities of New York and New Orleans; when they are dragged from their houses and hung upon lamp-posts; when their children are torn from their arms, . . . when they are objects of insult and outrage at every turn . . . then they will have an urgency to obtain the ballot equal to our own."

Someone asked whether that situation were not true of black women, and Douglass replied yes, "but not because she is a woman, but because she is black." Stanton might have related a story she told in her autobiography about Anthony's helping an abused wife escape with her child from a husband who had had her incarcerated in an insane asylum, though she was not insane. Anthony broke the law in refusing to give up the runaways to their "owner." Although white women were not hung from lampposts, they *were* dragged from their houses with their children torn from their arms. The arguments continued. Lucy Stone concluded that Mrs. Stanton "will, of course, advocate the precedence for her sex" and Mr. Douglass for his race, and "both are perhaps right." But she thanked God for the Fifteenth Amendment and hoped it would be adopted. "I will be thankful in my soul if *any* body can get out of the terrible pit."

Finally, the delegates passed a wishy-washy resolution declaring that while they approved the Fifteenth Amendment, they regretted that Congress had not submitted a parallel amendment giving women the vote. They did not mobilize behind such an amendment, and the convention ended with nearly everyone feeling disappointed and frustrated. The American Equal Rights Association was defunct. Two days after the convention adjourned Stanton and Anthony founded the National Woman Suffrage Association. Stone, Blackwell, and many of their followers had already left New York and would charge that Stanton and Anthony deliberately excluded them. Stanton and Anthony claimed that the formation of what Ellen Carol DuBois calls "the first national feminist organization in the United States" was a spontaneous act. At any rate, Stone, Blackwell, Howe, and Higginson reacted by organizing a convention in November 1869 to found the American Woman Suffrage Association. The woman movement thus split in two, and it would stay split for over twenty years, until 1890.

What, exactly, were the reasons for the division? One major cause is clear from the proceedings of the last few AERA meetings. Some members were willing to see black men climb out of the "terrible pit" before women, and others were not. Or some, namely Lucy Stone and the Boston-based abolitionists, accepted the Fourteenth and Fifteenth Amendments and others, namely Stanton and Anthony, opposed the amendments. Beyond this difference, historians of the women's movement have identified various reasons for the split. Robert E. Riegel catalogs them as follows in his article "The Split of the Feminist Movement in 1869": conservative versus radical ideas, personal antagonisms, disagreements over proper form of organization, and conflicting ideas concerning the role of men in the movement.

It is true that the reformers who formed the Boston group tended to be more conservative personally than those who went with "New York," or Stanton and Anthony. But the terms "conservative" and "radical" might better be altered to "safe" and "daring" because what was considered conservative or radical could and did change. Stanton was fond of reminding people that when she included a woman suffrage plank at Seneca Falls, it was considered a wildly radical idea; even her mentor Lucretia Mott was shocked and urged her to drop it. Twenty years later in 1869 suffrage seemed a more conservative demand, and Lucy Stone and her supporters wanted to exclude other "extraneous" and "radical" issues, such as divorce and labor reform, issues that could be divisive and that Stanton and Anthony were bent on pursuing. Stanton could be "conservative" herself, as in her growing advocacy of educated suffrage, but she was never safe. Because she was a bold thinker, and because she was disinclined to reject potential supporters (like George Francis Train) on the basis of reputation alone, she was considered a loose cannon.

Personal antagonisms also played a big role in causing the split and especially in perpetuating it. The main problem was between Stone and Anthony, though Stone did not care much for Stanton either. Anthony got along with a wide variety of women but could not forgive Stone's having publicly accused her of mismanaging money—Anthony was said to lack the proper receipts for her expenses in Kansas. Both Stone and Anthony were constantly accusing each other of bad faith, and their friends lined up behind them. Both women claimed to want union of the two sides but sabotaged any such attempt and blamed the other for its failure.

The additional reasons historians have offered for the split—conflicts over form of organization and the role of men—were essentially ex post facto. That is to say, they occurred after the breakup and were used to justify it. The American Woman Suffrage Association, or "Boston," prided itself on being representative, having organized itself as a national delegate society with state affiliates. The National Woman Suffrage Association, or "New York," kept in touch with the rest of the country through constant travel and speaking tours, seeing no need for rigid organization. The American welcomed men as members and officers and often elected a well-known man as president, though Stone and Blackwell remained the powers behind the throne. The National believed that the cause of woman suffrage had been betrayed by men, particularly by the Republican old-time abolitionists, like William Lloyd Garrison and Wendell Phillips, who affiliated with the American. They did not bar men from their association as the American accused them of doing, and in fact retained Parker Pillsbury as an editor of the *Revolution*, but for several years they were wary of men and promoted women for leadership positions.

In 1869 both new organizations were actively recruiting members. They probably would have courted Isabella Beecher Hooker even if she hadn't been a Beecher and a link to the bigger prize, Harriet Beecher Stowe. Isabella entered the movement just at the point of the split. In fact, her first convention, the one in Boston in 1868, could be considered an opening salvo in the battle of the suffragists. Alarmed by the growing influence of Stanton and Anthony and their *Revolution,* Lucy Stone decided to form a regional organization composed of her supporters and under her control; she therefore did not invite Stanton and Anthony to that convention. Isabella's joining the movement under the auspices of the people who eventually formed the American Woman Suffrage Association, including her friend Caroline Severance, would seem to have assured her allegiance to the American. All logic supported it. Though Isabella could have gone either way on the question of black men's versus women's suffrage if she had been forced to choose, she was definitely on the conservative side of any conservative–radical split.

Isabella deplored as much as Stone and Blackwell the idea of easier divorce and wanted like they did to exclude questions of marriage and the family from public discussion. Even though she had loved wearing the less restrictive clothing of the Elmira water cure, she was shocked at Stanton's (tongue-in-cheek) suggestion in the *Revolution* that women should dress like men. She thought men were essential to the movement, and one of the men prominent in the American was Thomas Wentworth Higginson, her earlier idol. The women in the American, such as Severance and Howe, were indubitably "ladies." In fact, Susan B. Anthony would label them "sick unto death" with propriety. Henry Blackwell, in one of the long letters he wrote Isabella trying to attract her to the American, summed up the feelings of the Boston group when he said that by her tastes, principles, and social position she belonged to their side.

Unquestionably so. But a Beecher was never so simple as his or her outward tastes and principles might indicate. After maintaining her neutrality for a time and trying to make peace between the two warring groups, Isabella ultimately aligned herself with the Stanton-Anthony faction. Some historians have seen this choice as inexplicable; one writer concludes that she must have been motivated by family rivalry, wanting to disassociate herself from her brother Henry, who was affiliated with the American, and be the only Beecher in the group. This explanation overlooks the fact that Isabella at the time believed she could draw her sisters Harriet and (much more unrealistically) Catharine into the movement. In addition, she was on excellent terms with Henry and had never felt the same sort of competition with her brothers as with her sisters. After all, she knew the boys had had unfair advantages; why should she have to measure up?

There were some personal reasons, though, for Isabella's choice. First, she had friends in the National as well as the American. Olympia Brown, the Universalist minister who became Isabella's Connecticut co-worker and lifelong friend, was so staunchly anti-Boston that she would bitterly oppose the union of the two associations in 1890. Isabella's new friend Paulina Wright Davis bewailed what she thought of as Boston's treachery and defended Stanton and Anthony in a series of letters addressed more informally than customary to "dear sister" and signed "lovingly yours." Caroline Severance seems to have been jealous of Isabella's relationship with Davis. At least Isabella felt it necessary to write her, in August 1869, comparing the two friendships. She had "fallen in love" with both women and subsequently learned that they were reform speakers and believers in woman's rights. Although both friends drew Isabella to the woman movement, she had a "peculiar fellowship" with Davis once she found her similar in religion (Severance was Unitarian).

The second personal consideration that influenced Isabella was the personalities of the leaders themselves. Isabella always responded to warmth and affection, and she found it in Stanton and Anthony. Lucy Stone was a more reserved person who had never forgotten her poverty-stricken childhood and could not be comfortable in "society." She may have felt intimidated by Isabella, for she delegated the task of her recruitment to her husband Henry and various women in Connecticut. If she had interacted personally with Isabella, she might have been able to overcome some of the latter's prejudices. Isabella wrote Caroline Severance that she had heard Lucy speak and "was quick to hand in my allegiance to her as an orator." But she still misunderstood the significance of Stone's retaining her birth name: "Lucy has hurt the woman's cause in refusing to accept her husband's name, in just the same way that Susan has by her reputed carelessness & indiscretions & Mrs. Stanton by the expression of her too deep (or too superficial I should say) views of the marriage question. The Kansas trip of the latter with Mr. Train. . . . is no worse to my eye nor that of the public in general than the trips of Mrs. Lucy all over the country, proudly putting her name on hotel registers as Mrs. Stone & then frequenting the room of Mr. Blackwell." Isabella then quotes a friend of Paulina Davis, who complained that many people didn't believe Stone and Blackwell were really married. (They could have asked Thomas Wentworth Higginson, who performed the ceremony.)

Whatever the effect of personal considerations on Isabella's decision to back Stanton and Anthony, she herself thought she made the choice on the basis of her research into the causes of the split. She interviewed people on both sides and sifted through a mass of correspondence about the quarrel. Some of her research has turned out to be historically significant. Kathleen Barry argues in a biography of Susan B. Anthony that Isabella's notes and letters provide the key to what really happened in Kansas and why George Francis Train suddenly appeared there when he did. Isabella took notes on a conversation she had with Henry Blackwell in November 1869 and the next month summarized Blackwell's statements in a confidential letter to her Brooklyn friend Susan Howard, who had been trying to warn her away from Stanton and Anthony. Blackwell told her, she wrote, "that Mr. Train went to Kansas on the invitation of one Wood, a republican, to lecture to whomever would hear on Woman Suffrage among other things . . . Mr. Blackwell & Gov. Robinson & two or three others who were conducting the W.S. [woman suffrage] campaign thought it might be well for Susan to accompany Train & so get democratic votes—while at the same time she could perhaps keep him straight on the negro question—Train being there against negro suffrage. *They accordingly advised & promoted her Kansas trips with Train* and she went as General Agent of the Equal Rights Association & with their full approval on that whole Kansas campaign."

Being aware that the eastern Republicans blamed the association of Train with the woman movement entirely on Anthony, claiming that she had invited him to Kansas, Isabella was shocked. "I could hardly believe my ears when Mr. Blackwell quietly told me this, the beginning of the story." She waited a bit and then asked him if she had understood him correctly. He said yes and went on to explain that the affair had worked out poorly, that they had probably lost more Republican votes for woman suffrage by Train's advocacy than they gained Democratic. She could see how Henry and Lucy might have wanted Train in Kansas and not in the East, Isabella concluded, "but I cannot think they were honorable in throwing the whole blame on Mrs. Stanton & Susan, when they themselves initiated the enterprise." Others would have agreed, but Isabella did not use this information publicly to defend the National against the aspersions of the American. After their talk Blackwell wrote Isabella a nervous letter, reminding her that his statements were confidential; she answered promptly, assuring him that she understood. She said she now felt fully possessed of the positions of both sides and would not use for ill any confidences bestowed on her. Instead, she used the bits of history she ferreted out to make up her mind.

In doing so, Isabella was interested not only in the history of the split but also in the current attitudes of the participants. She hated the truculent behavior at recent conferences of William Lloyd Garrison, the great abolitionist. The long letter he wrote her arguing the case of the American and criticizing Stanton and Anthony backfired. Isabella wrote Susan Howard that he was a man of prejudice, passion, and bad judgment. He made her "realize anew how patient & tolerant reformers should be of each other—the very stuff that makes them reformers, will make them persecutors also if they are not always on their guard." Lucy Stone also failed in this respect, Isabella concluded, as she went on to tell the story of Stanton and Anthony being blamed for the Train fiasco.

She looked at letters from Stone discussing Anthony and vice versa and found "the spirit of love" in Anthony's but not in Stone's. She wrote Caroline Severance that Stanton and Anthony "*speak* of Mrs. Lucy with tenderness & regard." They ascribed her criticisms of them to her being menopausal and thought she would later change her mind. Partisans of the Stone faction might question whether Stanton and Anthony really felt so charitable and really wanted to stay in one organization any more than Stone did; it could be said that they more successfully maintained the facade of wanting union than Stone and Blackwell were able to do. They did, however, refrain from trying to blacken Stone's and Blackwell's reputations. Isabella was indignant that Lucy Stone, who had known and worked with Stanton for years, "*since that break* has begun to accuse her of holding free love doctrines." Isabella ended her researches by concluding that the American was more to blame for the split and more against reuniting than the National was.

She could thus believe, in joining Stanton and Anthony, that right was on her side. But Isabella's strongest reason for choosing the National over the American was her desire to be of service. At the turn of the twenty-first century the desire to serve is often interpreted as cant and translated as the desire to advance oneself. However Isabella's motives might be dissected today, she had been taught as a Beecher and consistently expressed throughout her life the need to serve. In her view Stanton and Anthony needed her help in improving their image. If she affiliated with the other side, she would be just another lady. Her letters to friends explaining her choice stress the assistance she could render in smoothing Stanton and Anthony's rough edges. As she wrote Caroline Severance, "The truth is, the more people are mistaken and going in a wrong way, provided they are *good and noble* people, the more I am inclined to keep company with them in the hope of using with them what influence I may have, towards a right way."

On the one hand, Isabella was correct in thinking that if she steered Stanton and Anthony in the right direction, they could attract large numbers of conventional women to the movement. It was twenty years since the Seneca Falls convention, and the idea of women having rights, even the right to enter the public sphere and vote, no longer seemed so radical; yet respectable matrons could be put off by Anthony's oversights and Stanton's attacks on marriage. On the other hand, Isabella was making a typical new convert's mistake. The rightness of the cause becomes so obvious that the convert assumes everyone would see this rightness if it weren't for the errors of the leaders. Airbrush the leaders and the cause will triumph. At this point in her career Isabella had no inkling of the strength of the opposition to feminist ideas. She would soon find out in the most painful ways.

Elizabeth Cady Stanton and Susan B. Anthony were also aware that the time was ripe for attracting ordinary women to the movement. Moreover, they needed new recruits if they were to maintain themselves apart from the American association. They thus held conventions in July and August 1869 at the upper-class summer "watering holes," Saratoga Springs, New York, and Newport, Rhode Island. Isabella attended both conventions, perhaps in reaction to her daughter Alice's marriage that June. She rejected Caroline Severance's charge that the summer meetings lacked organizational authority. They were not "state affairs," she argued, but fruitful organizing devices—"much precious seed was sown." Always attentive to financial matters, Isabella noted

Isabella Beecher Hooker in middle age, 1868. Courtesy Harriet Beecher Stowe Center, Hartford, Conn.

that they took in three hundred dollars at Newport, which after paying expenses left one hundred dollars in the treasury. She confided to her friend that Saratoga and Newport had also given her an idea—she would sponsor a Connecticut convention in the fall and organize a state society for suffrage. This convention would be eminently respectable; either she or her sister Harriet would give a reception the day before to "bring out the fastidious ones to the meeting." It would also be an attempt to unite the two factions of the woman movement. Isabella would invite *all* the leaders equally, and the state society to be organized would be independent of any national association.

Isabella could confidently assert that Harriet would give a reception because in August 1869 it appeared that she too was embracing the woman movement. Harriet had always stood somewhere between Catharine and Isabella on the question of women's rights, but after the war she leaned increasingly toward Isabella's side. In a series of sketches in the *Atlantic Monthly* (later published as *House and Home Papers*) she had her persona, Christopher Crowfield, discuss with his family the changing roles and status of women. Crowfield's commentary makes it clear that Harriet had departed from Catharine's view that women should stick to their one "profession" and try only to "influence" men in the public sphere. She retained Catharine's premise—that the most important gain for women would be to elevate the status of wives and mothers. Sometimes she sounded like her older sister, as when she advocated teaching domestic economy in the schools and increasing the "dignity" of household labor in the eyes of working-class girls. But Harriet was more willing than Catharine to allow women expanded roles. In terms of employment she went beyond teaching and nursing. Women might enter the arts—"authorship, painting, sculpture, with the subordinate arts of photographing, coloring, and finishing"—and they could be architects and landscape gardeners. Women could study bookkeeping and accounting and work in the business world. There were in addition needlework, manufacture of cloth, and the new occupation of typesetting.

Like Catharine, Harriet emphasized women's duties over their rights, but she also accepted the idea that women had certain abstract rights. Christopher Crowfield lists them as follows: "1. The right of every woman to hold independent property. 2. The right of every woman to receive equal pay with man for work which she does equally well. 3. The right of any woman to do any work for which, by her natural organization and talent, she is peculiarly adapted." It was a short step from these rights to the right of women to participate in public affairs, which was anathema to Catharine. If the principle of no taxation without representation is correct, Crowfield argues, and if female property holders are taxed, it follows that they should be represented in government by their votes.

The rights argument was not particularly congenial to Harriet, though. She goes on to make a more Beecher-like argument from expediency—that the public sphere needs women's voices: "I think that a State can no more afford to dispense with the vote of women in its affairs than a family. Imagine a family where the female has no voice in the housekeeping! A State is but a larger family, and there are many of its concerns which equally with those of a private household would be bettered by female supervision." Here she sees women less as individuals with rights that cannot be abrogated by gender than as wives and mothers who could clean up politics. As the authors of *The Limitations of Sisterhood* note, Harriet incorporated suffrage into her (and Catharine's) "ideology of domesticity." She "legitimated" suffrage by this ideology.

Four years later, in 1869, Harriet had begun to put more emphasis on the natural rights of women. To discuss "The Woman Question" she used the pages of *Hearth and Home*, a domestic magazine she was co-editing at the time. The focus of her series of three articles was squarely on rights. The position of married women, she instructed her readers, is under English common law "precisely similar to that of the negro slave." She enumerated the civil rights the married woman lacked, including the right to her own body; the wife had "neither privacy nor retreat from her husband if he proves disagreeable to her." Harriet had also moved closer by 1869 to the organized women's movement. Back in Christopher Crowfield days, she showed her ambivalence by using a metaphor comparing the women's movement to the ocean. Just as the waves "bring with them kelp, sea-weed, mud, sand, gravel, and even putrefying debris, which lie unsightly on the shore, and yet, on the whole are healthful and refreshing,—so the Woman's Rights movement, with its conventions, its speech-making, its crudities and eccentricities, is nevertheless a part of a healthful and necessary movement of the human race towards progress." It would seem that she considered the conventions and speech-making, apart from any particular content, as "crudities" in themselves.

But in the *Hearth and Home* articles Harriet insists that the women's rights leaders be given credit. Do you know, she asks, to whom the women of America owe any improvements in their legal status? "They owe them to these reformers often ridiculed as the Woman's Rights party." The reformers were women living in happy homes who were motivated by their love for justice and feeling for women less fortunate than themselves. Instead of leaving "putrefying debris" in their wake, these reformers compiled "the record of a calm, composed, dignified movement, inspired by noble motives, and appealing directly and logically for its support to the Declaration of Independence." (The "Declaration of Sentiments" issued at Seneca Falls was modeled after the Declaration of Independence.) Far from being crude and eccentric, the women's rights pioneers exemplified "what a true woman and true lady should be." This admission was Harriet's version of Lillie Devereux Blake's discovery, "Grinfill, *they're ladies!*"

What had happened between 1864 and 1869 to change Harriet's mind about the woman movement? In a word, Isabella. It was not that Harriet easily accepted Isabella's new ideas based on her arguments supporting them; after all, Harriet had Catharine as a countervailing influence. Also, as older sisters neither Harriet nor Catharine ever seemed to grant Isabella much credibility. She was always "the baby," the much younger sister to be guided and instructed by them, and they tended to underestimate her intelligence. In the case of women's rights, however, Isabella's new ideology provided an explanation for certain events that were troubling Harriet. For instance, in fall 1868 the young magazine the *Nation* viciously attacked Anna Dickinson. The venue was a review of Dickinson's first novel *What Answer?* (1868), which featured an interracial marriage as an answer to the "race problem." The *Nation* reviewer entitled his essay "Injurious Works and Injurious Criticisms" and argued that Dickinson was ignorant of all the "scientific" implications of miscegenation. In his view, Harriet Beecher Stowe and Lydia Maria Child should not have publicly praised the novel. Significantly, the reviewer did not limit himself to the novel but also lambasted Dickinson's speeches. He claims she didn't know her subjects and should "hold her tongue" until she was more thoroughly educated.

Isabella promptly wrote a letter of protest to the editor of the *Nation*. She praised Dickinson's novel for its criticism of "the spirit of caste" and pointed out that Dickinson had to support her mother and siblings and did not have the luxury of a thorough education. Isabella thought the magazine was really objecting to Dickinson's being an outspoken woman. Harriet may or may not have agreed at the time, but in June 1869 she saw that Isabella was right. The *Nation* published a completely negative review of *Oldtown Folks*. The reviewer complained that the book was less a novel than "a series of pictures of life" (an apt description of all Harriet's works). Faults in "literary workmanship" abounded, and it was a mistake to use Horace Holyoke as narrator. Mrs. Stowe consistently failed in the depiction of character, as the characters were simply stereotypes being put through tedious time-worn incidents. These criticisms were not unreasonable. *Oldtown Folks* has had the most mixed reception of all the author's works. Some of her contemporaries (John Greenleaf Whittier, Gail Hamilton) loved it, while others (Lydia Maria Child) found the long book tedious. Even today, opposite opinions emerge. While Josephine Donovan calls *Oldtown Folks* Stowe's "culminating masterpiece," Joan Hedrick finds it "labored" and lacking the author's usual zest.

The problem with the *Nation* review was its thoroughgoing negativity. The reviewer did not identify any good points about the book or show respect for the author's previous accomplishments. He employed a nasty and waspish tone throughout. There was also a disconcerting emphasis on gender. The reviewer disliked Horace Holyoke as narrator because he was really just a "dreamy little female" and claimed the book included "no male personage with a real existence of their own as individual men." Apparently Calvin Stowe failed to qualify as a "real man." Harriet did not suffer this review in silence. She wrote in protest to Nation editor E. L. Godkin, who was remotely related to her through the Foote family. The letter indicted the obvious—the discourtesy of the review. She stated: "Rudeness & heedless discourtesy, an assumption of supercillious [sic] contempt I think are just as much out of place in literary criticism as in a private parlor." Godkin apologized, saying he had not seen the review until it was too late. In fact, however, the Nation would routinely publish negative reviews of Harriet's work for the rest of her career.

"Just like a woman!" Henry James might have responded to Harriet's comment on incivility in book reviewing. The young James had the year before published in the Nation a rude attack on novelist Rebecca Harding Davis. He deplored the social and political content of her Dallas Galbraith (1868), preferring the "objective novel," which was more artistic and appealed to the reader's sense of beauty. Typically, he zeroed in on the male characters. Davis's hero was a "sentimentalist . . . worse than a woman's man—a woman's boy." He was "like nothing in trousers" and behaved "like a hysterical school-girl." Harriet could not have predicted how thoroughly women writers would be devalued by the new critical ethos being promulgated by the Nation and her own Atlantic Monthly. But she did realize, with the help of sister Isabella, that there was a backlash in progress against female writers (and speakers); her own literary reputation and livelihood could be jeopardized.

It isn't possible to trace with certainty the impact Isabella's feminist ideas had on Harriet. When Harriet discusses women's education, for example, in her Hearth and Home series, she repeats Isabella's complaint that women's education ends when men's begins. As the boy enters college and spends his hours in intellectual pursuits, the girl "fritters away [her time] in what is called society" and forgets everything she learned earlier. But Harriet could be drawing here on her own memory and reading and not just Isabella's experience. In addition, her own feminist friends influenced her. There was her former student Fanny Fern, a newspaper columnist and strong advocate of rights for women. There was also fellow writer Mary Abigail Dodge ("Gail Hamilton"), who maintained friendly relations with both Harriet and Isabella. The sisters read her Woman's Wrong (1868), and Harriet especially noted her comments on the "fine, subtle, impalpable, but real" prejudice against women writers. As Isabella became acquainted with the current leaders of the woman movement, she would discuss them and introduce them to Harriet (and sometimes her other sisters). She would occasionally pass on the women's letters, as she did Elizabeth Cady Stanton's when Harriet was in Florida in 1869.

Isabella had the greatest effect on Harriet in passing along her new knowledge of the history of the women's movement and the issues of its contemporary phase. Harriet began to refer in her articles not only to Seneca Falls but also other conventions—and not just as crudities or putrefying debris. She concluded her "What Is and What Is Not the Point in the Woman Question" by listing approvingly the resolutions passed at the national woman's rights convention in Worcester, Massachusetts, in 1850. One of the resolutions called for the obliteration of "all the barbarous, demoralizing, and unequal laws relating to marriage and property." Just as Harriet had sympathized with the plight of slave mothers in *Uncle Tom's Cabin,* she deplored the laws that denied married women rights to their property and guardianship of their children.

Much of Harriet's knowledge of women's legal rights came from Isabella, who with John's help was developing a specialty in that area. In 1869 they were busily drafting a married women's property act. Isabella notes in her memoir, "In 1870 I presented a bill to the Connecticut Legislature making husband and wife equal in property rights." Harriet was excited about the bill. She wrote enthusiastically to George Eliot, the English novelist, with whom she had recently begun to correspond: "We are busy now in the next great emancipation—that of woman. This session I trust Connecticut will repeal *the whole of the old unjust English marriage property laws as regards women and set her free* and then I shall be willing to claim Connecticut as my mother. Massachusetts has half done this work—New York *half*—but if the amendments just drafted by my brother in law John Hooker and now before the house pass [they didn't], Connecticut will . . . recognize the absolute equality of *woman in the marriage relation.*"

Isabella also introduced Harriet to the work of the English philosopher John Stuart Mill and his wife Harriet Taylor. A few years earlier Isabella had written Mill asking him to send an article for the American press and he had replied that he was too busy finishing a book. In summer 1869 he sent her a copy of that book, *The Subjection of Women* (1869). Isabella urged it on her daughters and sisters. Catharine was unimpressed; she would grumble in her next book that the "doctrine of Stuart Mills [sic] and his followers is in direct opposition to the teachings both of common sense and Christianity." But Harriet read Mill avidly. He was perhaps the best persuader Isabella could have chosen. A clear and careful writer, he was eminently logical and never wavered from his focus on the natural rights of women.

Unlike many rationalist Enlightenment thinkers, Mill did not restrict himself to discussion of the public sphere and neglect private life. He felt that the family taught tyranny and needed reform just as much as politics did. Harriet began to quote him in her articles, as in "John Stuart Mill says all popular reforms have to go through three stages—Ridicule, Discussion, Acceptance." The question of woman's rights, she thought, was just passing out of the ridicule stage into that of discussion. She wrote her friend Fanny Fern of Mill's book, "It has wholly converted me—I was only right *in spots* before[;] now I am all clear." And then: "Yes I do believe in Female Suffrage. The more I think of it the more absurd this whole government of men over women looks."

Ironically, just as Harriet was being confirmed in an equal rights point of view, Isabella veered toward a "women, especially mothers, are more moral than men" philosophy that was more characteristic of the younger Harriet. The ease with which the sisters switched places was not atypical in the century. Women often moved from one to the other rationale or lived in contradiction, trying to hold both perspectives simultaneously. Isabella entered into a correspondence with Mill in which she tried to explicate her evolving women's rights philosophy. After thanking him and praising his book, she admitted that she did disagree on one point, the "comparative endowment of the sexes." She continued, "For many years I have contended, privately I mean, that men were, by nature, capable of as high moral excellence as women, and, under the same outward circumstances, would develop the same moralities. But of late I have been impressed more and more with the close likeness to the divine nature which woman seems to bear, in that she is more sensibly, if not more truly, a creator than man is." Add to this her more intimate relationship with her child before and after birth, and she has a "moral advantage" men can never possess.

In his reply Mill expressed his gratitude for Isabella's perception of the influence of his wife on his work (this influence was often denied, much to Mill's dismay). He also agreed that a child is definitely closer to its mother than to its father. He then took issue with Isabella's conclusion: "But I do not perceive that this close relationship gives any ground for attributing a natural superiority in capacity of moral excellence to women over men. I believe moral excellence to be always the fruit of education and cultivation, and I see no reason to doubt that both sexes are equally capable of that description of cultivation."

Despite this rebuke Isabella continued to hold and develop her theory of maternal superiority. This theory had practical consequences for her behavior as an activist in the women's movement. One of the weaknesses of the Stanton-Anthony leadership she felt she could compensate for was

Anthony's having never been married. When she wrote to adherents of Lucy Stone trying to defend Anthony from their charges, she openly argued that Anthony's errors should be excused as coming from a spinster. Happily, she herself had joined the movement late in life, she wrote Mary Livermore, for "what injury to so dear a cause might have resulted, had I earlier been called to a public advocacy—(especially had I lacked that *home constituency* ever ready to call a mother to account for misdeeds & misjudgements)." To Henry Blackwell she emphasized his and Lucy's good fortune in having each other to keep them from misjudgments and mistakes. She, Isabella, owed to her husband and "home constituency" her spirit of caution and habit of considering carefully the feelings of others. "[A]s Susan has never had the benefit of such close companionship, such friendly & unselfish advice [what about Stanton?], my heart warms to her—& until she throws me off, I shall undoubtedly cleave to her with a strong & patient heart." Anthony and Stanton were to some extent aware of Isabella's blind spot regarding marriage—as a very happily married woman she failed to see the full oppressiveness of that relation to some women; if they had known the extent to which Isabella was patronizing Anthony, they might well have thrown her off.

Instead, the two women were impressed by Isabella's leadership skills at her Hartford convention in October. The convention was held at the Roberts Opera House and lasted two days. In terms of respectability it was a grand success. On the platform were Harriet and Calvin Stowe, Catharine, Henry, Francis Gillette, and Nathaniel Burton, the Hookers' minister. Catharine Beecher and Francis Gillette did not even advocate woman suffrage but believed the question should be publicly discussed. Elizabeth Cady Stanton made an effort to keep her promise to Isabella that her "dress, manners, and speech shall be worthy of a place in the opera House [sic] of Hartford." She had a white traveling dress with point lace for evening and a black silk for morning; she would give her hair an extra curl and wreathe her face in its sweetest smile. More pertinently, she toned down her speech. Stanton later described the occasion with the irony she often employed in writing to or about Isabella: "Mrs. Hooker wrote each [speaker] a letter of instructions re dress, manners, and general display of all the Christian graces. I did my best to obey orders, and appeared in a black velvet dress with real lace, and the most inoffensive speech I could produce; all those passages that would shock the most conservative were ruled out, while pathetic and aesthetic passages were substituted in their place. From what my friends said, I believe I succeeded in charming everyone but myself and Susan who said it was the weakest speech I ever made. I told her that was what it was intended to be."

The only people to behave badly were the volatile William Lloyd Garrison and Isabella's friend Paulina Wright Davis, who praised Stanton and

Anthony too warmly and recommended the *Revolution* and the National Woman Suffrage Association. Davis's comments, Garrison explained in a letter to his wife, made him lose his temper and champion the Boston women. In terms of Isabella's second goal, of uniting the two factions, the Hartford conference was a failure. The Bostonians attended, perhaps because of all the Beechers involved, and the leaders sat, albeit uncomfortably, on the same platform as Susan B. Anthony. But it was too late. The battle lines had hardened and the Boston group had already announced their forthcoming convention in Cleveland to launch a rival national organization. Although Isabella kept her promise to make the state society she founded independent, both sides simply redoubled their efforts to capture Isabella and the newly formed Connecticut Woman Suffrage Association and Society for the Study of Political Science.

The conference did establish beyond a doubt Isabella's credibility and usefulness to the movement. Everyone, even her sisters, praised her executive ability. As Isabella herself noted in her memoir, she managed to pay all the expenses of the convention, all the speakers and the entertainment (the Hutchinson family singers), out of the receipts. Never one to be modest, Isabella concluded in her memoir, "This practical organizing ability has stood me in good stead all these intervening years, and has enabled me, with the help of my husband, to work for thirty odd years for the enfranchisement of [women]." When she left the stage of the Opera House after speaking at the convention, Nathaniel Burton, who had been elected president of the new Connecticut association, said, "If such women don't vote before I die—well . . . I won't die till they do." (When he died in 1889, Isabella still couldn't vote.)

After the Hartford convention Isabella made a few more attempts to unite the quarreling factions. When Mary Livermore of the American wrote praising brother Henry's conference speech, Isabella replied with the suggestion that the two societies unite under Henry. (He had just been asked to run for president of the new society formed at Cleveland.) He would be a good peacemaker, she thought. Elizabeth Cady Stanton wanted to leave office anyway, and even if Susan B. Anthony weren't the most prudent person ever, she would be only one officer among many from both groups. When nothing came of this proposal, Isabella resigned herself to the split. Anthony wrote her that she was glad her friend had given up the idea of union. Surely more could be accomplished by converting new women to the cause. Isabella thus substituted other goals for the aim of uniting the two suffrage societies. During the remainder of 1869 she devoted herself to a double mission—initiating her reform of Stanton and Anthony and bringing her sisters, especially Harriet, firmly into the woman movement. Perhaps she sensed that even on the personal level Abraham Lincoln's comment held true: a house divided against itself cannot stand.

Isabella combined her new goals by suggesting that she and Harriet become editors of the *Revolution*. (This idea was originally John's.) Stanton and Anthony's magazine was a thorn in Isabella's side; it was the thing about them that, in her view, most needed reform. The *Revolution* suffered not only from its association with the odious George Francis Train but also from Stanton's radical ideas. A definite pattern was forming: the *Revolution* would publish a radical article and Isabella would be bombarded with complaints from her friends and relatives about her new associates. The McFarland-Richardson scandal was one example. Abby McFarland separated from her abusive husband, and he accused her of having an affair with Albert Richardson. When she managed to get a divorce, the jealous McFarland shot Richardson, who stayed alive just long enough to be married to Abby McFarland on his deathbed. To the feminist Stanton, Abby functioned as an object of exchange. Stanton compared her in the *Revolution* to a fugitive slave. The court took the side of the "master" in the most blatant way, declaring McFarland innocent by virtue of insanity and then granting the madman custody of the couple's child!

Isabella and her relatives and friends saw the case differently from Stanton. Abby McFarland shouldn't have divorced in the first place, especially when she had a child. Besides, how could she have transferred her affections to another man so quickly? In this particular case Susan B. Anthony defended the *Revolution* article, telling Isabella she agreed with it and claiming "you are the only one who's spoken of it other than approvingly." Generally, however, she accepted Isabella's criticisms of the magazine and promised to do better, as she hoped to see Isabella and Harriet become associate editors. "I really have come to lean on you ever so much," Anthony wrote in December.

The first thing the Beecher sisters wanted in regard to the *Revolution* was to be paid for their editorial services. Stanton and Anthony agreed, even though they were not paid themselves and the paper was almost broke. Anthony wrote Paulina Wright Davis that the movement needed literary women, and "if *Cash will bring Mrs. Stowe* to the Rev. with her *deepest holiest Woman, wife & Mother Soul struggle*—clothed in her *inimitable story garb*—then *it is cash that must be.*" Mrs. Stowe had not yet given the world her very best because she hadn't written directly from her own experience. Her story on woman, Anthony envisioned, would be serialized in the *Revolution*, published as a book, and have the same galvanizing effect on the nation as *Uncle Tom's Cabin*. Stanton had her own fantasy—that the Beecher sisters would take over the cause and she would be able to escape all the responsibilities and movement in-fighting and retire to a quiet life of writing. "We are through the wilderness," she wrote Davis, "and now if Mrs. Hooker and Mrs. Stowe will take it up, and one of them be President of the National Association and one editor of 'The Revolution' no one would rejoice more than I."

But the Beecher editorship of the *Revolution* was not to be, for Harriet became involved in a controversy that deeply frightened her, showing how much power men really had. Like the McFarland-Richardson scandal, this one involved marriage, motherhood, and separation. In June 1869, just after the *Nation* attacked *Oldtown Folks,* Harriet traveled to Canada to establish British copyright for the novel. She happened upon a newly published book, *My Recollections of Lord Byron,* by Byron's last mistress, the Countess Guiccioli. This memoir depicted Byron's estrangement from his wife as solely the fault of the cold-hearted and mercenary Lady Byron. Harriet remembered having heard the same story in her youth. When she was a girl discovering Byron's poetry, the couple had separated and Lady Byron was blamed. By this time, however, Harriet had met Lady Byron (on her first trip to Europe in 1853). Through correspondence and further visits the two became friends and confidantes. Harriet admired the slight, intellectual Englishwoman and developed strong feelings for her. Josephine Donovan calls their relationship a "romantic friendship," the intense bonding that often took place between nineteenth-century women. There is much language in the women's correspondence to support this interpretation. For instance, Harriet wrote after her second trip to England: "I left you with a strange sort of yearning, throbbing feeling; you make me feel quite as I did years ago, a sort of girlishness quite odd for me."

On that second trip in 1856 Harriet and her sister Mary had stayed at Lady Byron's country house. While Mary chatted with the other guests, Lady Byron took Harriet aside and confided a shocking secret—the cause of her separation from her husband was his incestuous liaison with his half-sister; a child had resulted from the affair. Lady Byron wanted Harriet's advice. Should she continue her silence, even when an impending new edition of the poet's works would revive the old false story of their marriage? Harriet's first impulse was that the truth should be revealed, but after she told Mary the story and they stayed up all night discussing it, she asked for time to think. The cautious and conservative Mary was totally opposed to any disclosure of the incest story. It was only a few years after Catharine had exposed Delia Bacon's secrets against Mary's advice, and look what happened then—the man had been exonerated and Delia and Catharine tarred. For the time being Harriet listened to Mary and wrote Lady Byron her considered advice—she should leave the story with discreet friends, who, after Lady Byron's death, would satisfy the demands of justice by publishing the truth.

By the time Countess Guiccioli's recollections were published Lady

Byron had died and justice still hadn't been achieved. Harriet was furious at the Countess's aspersions. Since Lady Byron's death and her own growing feminism, she had come to see her friend as, in Josephine Donovan's words, "a symbol of women's oppression." She wrote, "I consider Lady Byron's story as a type of the old idea of woman: that is, a creature to be crushed and trodden under foot whenever her fate and that of a man come in conflict." Had the brilliant Lady Byron been a man, she might have influenced the thought of all England, but instead she spent her life in quiet sacrifice. Someone needed to set the record straight. Stowe thus composed at white heat "The True Story of Lady Byron's Life."

Ever since the furor over *Uncle Tom's Cabin*, Harriet had in general been cautious about attracting publicity. She was very circumspect, for instance, about the school she had established in Mandarin, Florida. Although her goal was not to have the two races taught together in the classroom, knowing the white parents wouldn't allow integration, she still kept a low profile. She asked a British supporter not to talk about her contribution to the school because "it would be sure to get over here and set the country all in a flame. It is astonishing how everything I say and do gets in the papers, often in the most absurd and untrue ways." But even though she anticipated some negative press, Harriet in her indignation allowed the Byron exposé to appear in the *Atlantic Monthly* for September 1869. She was in no way prepared for the storm to come.

What followed was, in today's terms, a media "feeding frenzy." The bait was not Lord Byron, of course, but Lady Byron and Harriet Beecher Stowe herself. The press thought Lady Byron was at best "deluded" on this one topic and at worst completely insane. Stowe was so starstruck by British royalty (a valid criticism) that she would believe anything—or maybe she misunderstood her friend in her Beecher "craving for notoriety," her "prurience," and her "repulsive eagerness to publish." She was also accused of publishing the story solely for financial gain. A nasty cartoon showed a tiny Harriet trying to climb a huge white statue of Byron, leaving dirty footprints everywhere.

As she had done during the controversy over *Uncle Tom's Cabin*, Harriet called her sisters Isabella and Catharine to her side to help her prepare a book by way of rebuttal, in this case *Lady Byron Vindicated* (1870). The book did little better than the article, however. Although Stowe's version of the Byron situation is accepted by today's scholars as substantially true, she had no documentary proof of Lady Byron's allegations. As the Beecher sisters might have learned from Catharine's earlier attempt to champion Delia Bacon, trying to defend a "wronged woman" in a sex scandal was a losing proposition. Some voices were raised in Stowe's favor, but nowhere near the number who praised *Uncle Tom's Cabin*. Almost all Harriet's supporters were women who wrote for a women's periodical. Elizabeth Cady Stanton wrote an editorial for the *Revolution* in which she noted that the very wrath of the male press showed that Stowe's charges against Byron were true. The press was furious at her demolition of the theory that men were women's natural protectors. Stanton felt that Harriet's exposé of "the abominations of our social life," coming at the same time as John Stuart Mill's book on the subjection of women, might lead thinking people to reexamine the position of women.

Although Stanton had good reason to think that the furor over the Byron article might push Stowe into the woman movement, the opposite turned out to be true. Harriet, it seems, was more frightened than angered by the brouhaha. Events had shown that at least one of sister Catharine's main arguments against women's rights was true: men possessed all the power in society. As Catharine put it, "men have the physical power that can force obedience; in most cases they have the power of the purse, and in all cases, they have the civil power." Men also have the power of the press, she might have added. "They can not be forced by the weaker sex to resign this power. It must be sought, then, as the gift of justice and benevolence."

Catharine apparently convinced Harriet that editing a magazine with the fiery title of *Revolution* would be too militant. Was the revolution in question a rebellion against men? Backtracking quickly, Harriet made a new condition for her editorship—the name of the journal would have to be changed. Susan B. Anthony considered the proposal for some weeks, for it was hard to relinquish the dream of Stowe writing and serializing a feminist *Uncle Tom's Cabin* for a wide audience. Finally she was convinced that a title change would harm the struggling paper. Stanton wrote with some asperity: "The establishing of woman on her rightful throne is the greatest revolution the world has ever known or will know. To bring it about is no child's play. . . . A journal called the *Rosebud* [Harriet and Isabella had actually suggested the *True Republic*] might answer for those who come with kid gloves and perfumes to lay immortal wreaths on the monuments which in sweat and tears others have hewn and built; but for us . . . there is no name like the *Revolution*."

By the end of December it was settled that Harriet and Isabella would contribute articles to the *Revolution* without any formal relationship. Isabella promptly sent in an article. In "Happy New Year" she characteristically addresses the *Revolution* as her adopted child. She also pleads for tolerance. There may be advocates of suffrage whose views disagree, but "since we cannot be sure that all wisdom" is ours, we must be patient with one another. One is reminded of her comment on Garrison's excesses, that reformers should be patient and tolerant. Clearly this is a role Isabella wanted to adopt for herself—hence her efforts to unite the two factions of the women's movement.

Although Anthony pressed Harriet for contributions to the *Revolution*, Harriet was silent. Perhaps she had sincerely intended to write for the magazine, but the timing was off. January 1870 marked the first issue of a paper Henry Ward Beecher had bought and renamed the *Christian Union*. Christian union was more to Harriet's liking than revolution, and she and Calvin promised to write three columns a week for the new magazine. Harriet confessed to her brother the ambitions of a female Beecher: "I have all my life but especially lately gone with a gospel burning in my bosom which I longed to preach but could not because I was a woman." At the same time, Isabella saw contributing to the *Revolution* as "my opportunity to preach Christ." She was irritated by the attempts of friends and relatives to limit her free speech, to insist that "I should avoid all connection with that paper & refuse to write for it because the views of its Editor & Publisher are in some respects not quite my own." Thus Isabella and Harriet, so alike in their burning desire to preach, went their separate ways, which would increasingly diverge.

7
"Foes in Your Own Household,"
1870–1871

NOW THAT SHE OWNED a winter home in Florida Harriet had a place to escape to when there were problems in the North. After she mailed the Byron story to the *Atlantic* she suffered a "sinking turn" that left her weak all over. She went to Georgiana's in Stockbridge, Massachusetts, to recover and when the press onslaught began sought refuge at the Taylors' cure in New York. There Calvin joined her, along with her friend Susie Howard and sister Catharine. Always a useful person in a crisis, Catharine assumed the role of nurse so that Harriet could finish *Lady Byron Vindicated*. Both Catharine and Isabella worried over her health; Isabella even wrote Harriet's publishers about her sister's exhaustion. At last, in January 1870, the Lady Byron book was published and the Stowes fled south. Harriet explained her poor health and low spirits to Florida friends by saying she'd suffered "a fall"—certainly the truth metaphorically if not physically.

The Stowes arrived in Mandarin laden with china, silver, and other amenities for their new home. They had decided to start spending the entire winter and spring seasons in Florida and thus began to improve the house. This was originally a "hut," as Harriet described it to George Eliot, "built close to a great live-oak twenty-five feet in girth, and with overarching boughs eighty feet up in the air, spreading like a firmament." The Stowes added lath, plaster, and paper and then built a wide veranda around the house to serve as their living room. The twins worked out a housekeeping arrangement this year that would be long-standing—Hatty would keep house in Mandarin and Eliza in Hartford. Harriet rested. She wrote Annie Fields that she would read nothing relating to the Byron controversy; instead, she tried to occupy herself in "being chatelaine of a Florida farm." She entertained visitors, picnicked, and sailed in her neighbors' boat. When a nearby house burned to the ground, she directed the relief effort, gathering money, food, and clothing for the homeless family. Harriet would write only if she felt like it. Her current project was a collection of stories about Oldtown that she hadn't had room for in

Oldtown Folks. The stories appeared in the *Atlantic Monthly* in the latter half of 1870 and were eventually published as *Oldtown Fireside Stories* (1872).

While Harriet recuperated in Florida, Isabella helped organize the National Woman Suffrage Association (NWSA) convention held in Washington, D.C., in January 1870. This was the second convention to meet in Washington; it made sense to convene there to lobby for a sixteenth amendment. Susan B. Anthony agreed with Isabella that members of the American should be invited, not only Stone, Blackwell, and Livermore but "even Higginson and Garrison." The National could not afford to be spiteful. No one from the Stone group attended, of course, but a letter was read from Robert Purvis, a black officer of the American Anti-Slavery Society who supported a sixteenth amendment. He might be criticized for inconsistency, Purvis wrote, in approving a movement whose leaders opposed the Fifteenth Amendment, but if he were a woman, black or white, he would resist any measures based on the "infamous assumption of superiority of sex."

The convention passed four resolutions. Besides asking Congress to submit to the state legislatures a sixteenth amendment giving women the vote, the NWSA wanted it to do the following: enfranchise the women of Utah as a step in abolishing polygamy; amend the federal employment laws so that women received equal pay for equal work; and strike the word "male" from laws governing the District of Columbia. On behalf of this third request Elizabeth Cady Stanton spoke in front of the Senate and House Committee on the District of Columbia. For the first time she used the argument the suffragists would come to call the "New Departure"—the idea that the Constitution had already given women the vote via the Fourteenth Amendment. The argument was formulated by Francis Minor, a Missouri lawyer, and his wife, Virginia, president of the state suffrage society. The Minors had contended at a St. Louis convention in October 1869 that the Constitution declared all persons born or naturalized in the United States to be citizens and the Fourteenth Amendment prohibited any state from abridging the privileges of citizens; therefore state laws excluding women from the vote violated the Constitution.

After Stanton's speech other women were invited to make brief additions, and Isabella had her moment (actually, five minutes) of glory. Speaking from her seat, she said "the fifth commandment, 'Honor thy father and thy mother,' can not be obeyed while boys are taught by our laws and constitutions to hold all women in contempt. I feel it is not only woman's right, but duty to assume responsibility in the government." Isabella found the conference exhilarating. She stayed for ten days with Senator and Mrs. Samuel Pomeroy from Kansas (Pomeroy had introduced the proposed sixteenth amendment into Congress) and was continually in the thick of things. In addition to the excitement of the hearing, there were large parties (Mrs. Pomeroy gave a reception attended by three hundred young women who had attended the convention and were said to favor woman suffrage). Of the NWSA meeting itself, Isabella wrote that interest grew so fast it had to be extended from two days to three. "Yesterday morning Lincoln Hall jammed, even aisles full. I never heard better speaking in my life." For the remainder of her women's rights career Isabella would prefer the Washington lobbying conventions to all others. She would plan to stay longer and longer, sometimes for the first three months of the year.

It was at the 1870 convention that Isabella first met Olympia Brown, the suffragist and Universalist minister. Brown spoke twice for over an hour to between twelve hundred and fifteen hundred people, and Senator Pomeroy considered her the best female orator. Isabella wrote her family that "Olympia Brown is wonderful; she talked Christ and His Gospel just [as] I should have done with her voice and practice; can't enlarge, but she surely is a remarkable woman." In her autobiography Brown, or "Brownie," as her friends called her, remembered her first meeting with Isabella. It was the beginning of a long friendship and a decade of working together for suffrage in Connecticut, for Brownie had a church in Bridgeport. Brownie recalled Isabella as "then very beautiful, tall and slender, charmingly dressed, with keen bright eyes sparkling, while her refined manners won the admiration of all who saw her." She was well-informed, original, stimulating, and full of "rare moral courage." Brownie concluded her discussion of Isabella with a remarkable compliment—remarkable because she knew Stanton, Anthony, and most of the famous women of the day: "I have learned more and enjoyed more from association with her than with any other woman outside my own family with whom I have ever been associated."

In Washington in 1870 Isabella must have felt a little envious. Here was a woman thirteen years younger who had done something the achieving Beecher sisters wanted but were born too soon to accomplish—Olympia Brown was a full-fledged minister. She had been ordained in 1863, the second woman to be ordained as a Protestant minister in the United States. "I do so long to preach Christ," Isabella confided after the conference to her niece Lillie. She saw religion and suffrage as one and the same, "the liberty wherewith Christ has made us all free." She had been "patiently dumb so long"; she wished she could conduct a Sunday service for mothers and children. Isabella harkened back to an old theme—if she could earn an income, John would be relieved of some responsibility.

Olympia Brown had another advantage, besides ordination, over her new friend from Hartford—she was an excellent orator. Isabella, like most women just entering the public sphere, had no experience or inclination in

Olympia Brown, c. 1863. Courtesy Schlesinger Library, Radcliffe Institute, Harvard University.

that realm. Yet she knew that ministers and leaders of a sociopolitical move-ment had to be able to speak; times had changed since Charles Beecher needed to read Catharine's speeches and Calvin Stowe speak for Harriet. One could not expect to stay forever behind the scenes writing resolutions. Nor would there be many opportunities to give five-minute talks from one's seat. Isabella shared her fears about speaking with other women in the movement. She wrote Caroline Severance after her very first speech, at the Newport conven-tion in 1869, that she doubted she would speak any more because of the strain on her nervous system. She had been too nervous to have her speech publicized in advance and delivered it only after heavy persuasion. Severance had her own fears. She accepted Isabella's invitation to the Hartford conven-tion but asked her not to announce that she would speak because she was worried about the size of the hall. Paulina Wright Davis wrote that she had gotten used to speaking but could not do so if her husband happened to be in the audience.

Stanton and Anthony were by this time accustomed to the ner-vousness of new recruits. After all, they had gone through it themselves. At the first convention in Seneca Falls no woman, not even the normally intrepid Stanton, dared preside. James Mott, Lucretia's husband, had to assume the chair. Stanton and Anthony not only pushed newcomers to speak at conven-tions (this was one purpose of the conventions), but also set up an informal school in New York for the purpose of helping recruits hone their oratorical skills. Elizabeth B. Phelps, a well-off suffragist, owned property on East Twenty-third Street that she allowed to be used as a Woman's Bureau. The editorial offices of the *Revolution* were there, and meetings were held every week that provided opportunities for new speakers. As Stanton and Anthony (and their co-editor, Matilda Joslyn Gage) described it in the *History of Woman Suffrage,* the Woman's Bureau was "a kind of ladies' exchange, where reformers were sure to meet each other. . . . This was the school where Lillie Devereux Blake, Dr. Clemence Lozier, Isabella Beecher Hooker, and others made their first attempts at oratory."

There was another school, and a tougher one, that Stanton, Anthony, and Olympia Brown had all attended and no doubt urged on Isabella—the speaking tour of the Midwest or West. In fall 1870 she set out to improve her skills. Isabella spoke at an NWSA convention in Chicago, where she gained national attention. She stopped in Cincinnati, her old home. Usually she criticized the city of her youth, but this time she was impressed by the politics of the people, who seemed less conservative than the residents of Hartford. No one opposes suffrage here, she wrote her family. Isabella traced her way from Chicago to Galesburg, Illinois, to Kansas City, and as far West as Des Moines, Iowa; then she returned to Chicago and made her way home

through Indiana, Ohio, and New York. Although the lecture tour was successful, Isabella did not take to this staple of postwar suffrage work the way she
did to the Washington lobbying conference. She wrote her son that she was
tired of riding alone on trains at night. She never succeeded in becoming a
good traveler. Walking was difficult because of her weak ankles. She and John
had had carriage accidents, leading her to distrust carriage horses. Trains had
mishaps too, and every now and then she would vow to stop taking the risk
of riding them. The idea of crossing the ocean on a ship terrified her. Isabella
would continue to go on speaking tours, but she generally restricted herself
to Connecticut.

Back home, she began thinking about the next NWSA convention.
She had missed the last two important conferences, the "Decade Meeting,"
or twentieth anniversary of the 1850 Worcester convention, at which Paulina
Wright Davis presided, and the annual May meeting. The anniversary event
Isabella missed for a happy reason—she wanted to be in Hartford when she
became a grandmother. At the beginning of May Alice gave birth to Katharine
Seymour Day. Although Alice was a "terrible sufferer" for a few hours and
her father had to be called in to help with the chloroform, she recovered
quickly and Isabella was delighted with the baby. Coincidentally, Harriet became a grandmother for the first time shortly after Isabella. Her daughter
Georgiana gave birth to Freeman Allen. Harriet was present for the birth in
Stockbridge and stayed on several months to help. Although Georgie and the
baby were physically healthy, Georgie had gone into an "excitable state" before the birth and then suffered from postpartum depression. This may have
been the natural course of her manic-depressive disease, or perhaps she was
already showing signs of the morphine addiction that would plague her later.
The baby, though, was perfect and Harriet enjoyed being "first lady-in-waiting
on his new majesty."

When Elizabeth Cady Stanton sent Isabella congratulations on becoming a grandmother, she also said she was devoting the summer to her
own family "so you will have no more shocks for at least three months." As it
happened, Stanton was wrong in her prediction and would produce a shock.
Isabella, not having the advantage of hindsight, had not quite realized the
extent to which she was moving away from her sisters by getting involved
in the NWSA. After all, both Catharine and Harriet cared about the status of
women, and both had supported her by sitting on the platform at the Hartford
convention; the three sisters had worked together on Lady Byron Vindicated.
But in summer 1870 something happened that made the true situation clearer,
accentuating the splits in the sisters' united front.

An article appeared in the Revolution praising the ideas of French
novelist George Sand (pen name of Aurore Dudevant, 1804–1876). The femi-

nist Sand was quoted as calling marriage a "barbarous institution," and John Stuart Mill was said to agree. Harriet worried about French "immorality" being connected with the suffrage movement. She could have met George Sand in Paris, she wrote brother Henry, but was warned that ladies didn't receive her. Sand had left her husband and engaged in affairs, frequently seducing men. Harriet read some of her novels and concluded that the Frenchwoman personified the "animalism & atheism" of the century. Harriet thus wrote to the *Woman's Journal,* the new magazine of the NWSA's rivals, decrying any association of the American woman movement with Sand's ideas. Stanton felt called upon to respond to the woman who had nearly become her co-editor: "George Sand has done a grander work for women . . . than any woman of her day and generation; while Mrs. Stowe has been vacillating over every demand for her sex, timidly watching the weathercock of public sentiment and ridiculing the advance guard."

For her part, Harriet was "blank with astonishment" at Stanton's "envenomed response." Her failure to understand must have had to do with her lack of experience with political movements. George Sand was a feminist pioneer and, whatever her morals, Stanton could not let a hero of the movement be attacked with impunity. Here was another instance where Harriet showed where her priorities lay—Christianity over women's rights. Catharine had made the same choice when she attacked the early feminist Frances "Fanny" Wright. Wright (1795–1852), an atheist who also believed in free love, was the first woman to speak in public in the United States. Catharine described her as simultaneously masculine and whorish: with her loud voice and "great masculine person," Wright enjoyed "mingling with men in stormy debate." It seemed that Harriet was now moving away from Isabella and closer to Catharine.

In fall 1870 Catharine made an interesting decision. She agreed to act again as principal of the Hartford Female Seminary, the school she had founded almost fifty years earlier. The seminary was still unendowed and the quality of the education it offered had been declining for some time. Catharine was optimistic as usual. She wrote her publisher enthusiastically that she'd "secured fine teachers," including Harriet and Calvin, and "never saw fairer prospects of success." But everyone except Catharine and the seminary trustees must have realized the plan wouldn't work. She was now seventy and, although she showed no signs of her father's mental decline, lacked the stamina needed for the job. Being principal had worn her out when she was in her twenties.

That was why Catharine had always insisted in her educational plan on the so-called college system. That is, instead of having a principal to hire and supervise the teachers, overlook the physical plant, and take care of the finances, the teachers should be co-equal partners and share the administration of the school. In a speech she gave in December Catharine recalled that when she founded the Hartford Female Seminary all these responsibilities had devolved on her: "Ten years of such complicated labor, study, and responsibility destroyed health, as it has done for multitudes of other women, who have thus toiled unaided by any of the advantages given to [male] college teachers. Ever since that time, I have devoted my income, strength, and time to efforts for securing professional advantages of education for my sex equal to those bestowed on men." Half a century later, Catharine had to confess, women still did not have these advantages, and here she was principal again.

One of her students gave her grandnephew Lyman Beecher Stowe some recollections of Catharine during her second stint as principal. Every morning the girls would march into the auditorium to piano music. They wore small white aprons bound with green, along with artificial laurel wreathes on their heads. Miss Beecher would be standing alone on the platform singing in a quavering voice while her corkscrew curls bobbed up and down. She was dressed in "her self-made black lace dress over pink paper cambric and her self-made shoes with soft soles and velvet uppers." The pupil remembered her principal as "a strange old lady whom we both made fun of and at the same time, respected and admired. She used to give us talks on deportment and said in one such talk, 'Young ladies, when you have occasion to go on journeys in the railroad cars, do not lie back in the seat (illustrating) but sit erect and sway gently with the motion of the train.'" Other former students corroborated this recollection. They pictured her as homely looking with blue eyes and thin gray hair in curls. She taught no classes but lectured to the pupils on health and proper behavior. Apparently it wasn't enough for young ladies to sit up straight in railroad cars—they had to have all their buttons sewn on and fastened, avoid gazing in store windows, and "always move in curves," whatever that meant.

Not surprisingly, Catharine resigned in less than a year, in March 1871. She managed to enlist her cousin, Miss A. M. Beecher, to take her place. Also not surprisingly, as this had happened repeatedly in the past, her departure was shadowed by bickering over money. Catharine thought the trustees owed her about six hundred dollars, which she had paid to install a new furnace and settle debts incurred by her predecessor. The trustees begged to differ, claiming she owed *them*. This quarrel dragged on for years. Only a few months before Catharine's death John Hooker wrote to one of the seminary trustees asking him to call at his law office to settle the matter.

Catharine threatened the trustees that she would publish the story in the newspapers; she would "show the citizens of Hartford how *unjustly* they have treated their daughters in contrast to what they have done for their sons." Although Catharine never made good on her threat, she did explain in her next book why girls' schools needed to be endowed just as boys' schools were. She found when she returned as principal that the Hartford Female Seminary offered forty-four subjects of study. Though the tuition cost more than young men paid in colleges, she was still unable to retain the best teachers in so many subjects and furnish the classroom apparatus needed unless she dipped into her own salary. She concluded: "Neither Mrs. Stowe, nor myself, nor any of the most highly qualified ladies of our country, could take charge of such an institution without a sacrifice of an income counting by thousands. Will not a time come when ladies, the most highly qualified to educate their own sex, shall receive such advantages and compensation for these duties as now are exclusively given to men?"

The time would not come until the 1920s, when women also began to vote. Catharine could hardly write a paragraph, it seemed, without contrasting the treatment of women with that of men. Was she coming around to an acceptance of Isabella's new cause? Far from it. In December she participated in a debate in Boston, taking the anti-suffrage position against Mary Livermore's pro-suffrage argument (Livermore was a member of the AWSA). Catharine began by emphasizing her newer, mellower persona. She would not impugn the motives or character of her opponent, she said, introducing an interesting metaphor: just as centripetal and centrifugal forces held the physical universe in balance, the moral universe needed opposing radical and conservative elements in order to maintain a steady course. Although she, Catharine Beecher, represented the conservative element, she was willing to "meet with respect and kindness my centrifugal friend." Catharine's argument was the same practical one she had been presenting for a long time—because men had the power, the safest and most effective course for women was to try to influence and persuade them instead of seeking their own "rights." In her speech she did state more directly than ever before the class imperatives that underlay her position. If woman suffrage came to pass, there would be a huge increase of "incompetent and dangerous voters." She feared the "vast mass of ignorant women whose consciences and votes would be controlled by a foreign and domestic priesthood." One hears echoes of Lyman Beecher's going to Cincinnati to save the West from the Catholics.

Catharine believed it would be a long time before women could vote in the United States. Men would not allow it until women demanded it, and nine-tenths of American women, she claimed, did not want the vote. They would see it as an act of oppression making them neglect their own duties and assume responsibilities that belonged to men. If woman suffrage ever seemed imminent, the majority of women would organize against it. They would be joined by all the different religious institutions and by the press.

In her response to Catharine, Mary Livermore observed that her opponent had missed the main point—that women possessed both a natural and a constitutional right to vote. But Catharine had no patience with rights arguments. No one, male or female, she countered, had a right to do anything against the best good of society. That good demanded a division of labor between men and women. "If the best good of society requires women to be law-makers, judges and juries, she has a right to these offices; if it does not, she has no right to them."

No doubt Catharine and Isabella went over this same ground many times. Embarrassingly for the latter, while Catharine was publicly denying woman's right to vote, Isabella was planning the next month's NWSA lobbying convention in Washington. She knew she couldn't please Catharine, but she could keep the focus strictly on suffrage and avoid offending Harriet with any George Sand–like anti-marriage talk. Trying to control the Washington convention as closely as she had the one in Hartford, Isabella intended to eliminate the possibility of any "shocks," in Stanton's words, to her sisters. Stanton and Anthony had given her the go-ahead to organize the conference on her own. She wrote the call, which Paulina Wright Davis and Josephine Griffing co-signed; she arranged the program, invited the speakers, and assumed the financial responsibility. Indeed, this meeting would go down in history as the "Hooker Convention." It is unlikely that Stanton and Anthony knew Isabella still harbored some hope of healing the split in the movement and was writing selected congressmen that she represented no state or national society; but they did understand that she wanted the convention to focus entirely on suffrage and the need for a sixteenth amendment. No extraneous issues like marriage and divorce would be discussed, she wrote Stanton.

Stanton theoretically accepted what her new recruit was doing. "Cool, isn't it?" she wrote on this letter, as she passed it to her friend Martha Coffin Wright (Lucretia Mott's sister). "But I am so glad to get anyone to take up the burden, I say—Amen!" She wrote similarly to Josephine Griffing that Isabella thought "she could manage the cause more discreetly, more genteelly than we do, so let her take hold & try the drudgery. I am ready to rest." It was hard to maintain this attitude, however, in the face of Isabella's writing tactlessly that she could do without Stanton on the platform. Stanton exploded at this "slap in the face" and wrote Martha Wright that "So long as people pay me $75 and $100 every night, to speak on my own hook, there is no need of my talking in Conventions where my presence is not desired. I think her letter quite blunt & egoistic & somehow it hurts my self-respect."

Stanton, as the founder of the movement, was doubtless justified in feeling this way. Isabella was either forgetting or did not realize that Stanton was often the star of these conventions and attracted more supporters than she frightened away. Of all the speeches at the first Washington convention in 1869, Grace Greenwood had reported Stanton's as the best. "Her speeches are models of composition—clear, compact, elegant, and logical. She makes her points with peculiar sharpness and certainty, and there is no denying or dodging her conclusions." If Lucretia Mott was the soul of the movement and Susan B. Anthony the legs, Stanton was the mind—the "swift keen intelligence."

Stanton replied calmly that she would not come to Washington. "I did not express in *words* the *contempt* I felt at her cool impudence, but somehow *the spirit ran off the end of my pen,*" she confessed to Wright. Isabella understood that she had offended Stanton and wrote back immediately to apologize, saying she was rushed and pressured with work. She wouldn't attribute the success of the convention to her management, she said, for she understood what had been done before, "that it is the grand sweep of God's own truth, that is carrying us all along." Isabella probably thought she was mollifying Stanton, but her words simply poured oil on the fire. The anti-religious Stanton annotated this letter also for Martha Wright. In the margin by the "God's own truth" statement, she wrote, "I wonder that God shd. use such instrumentalities as Susan & me." Next to Isabella's assurance that she hadn't told any potential speakers Stanton wasn't coming, "tho' it wd. no doubt have secured some," Stanton wrote, "what a lack of delicacy to say this to me." She ended her complaint to Wright with an ironic echoing of Biblical words, "The Beecher conceit surpasses understanding."

If Isabella had explained to Stanton her fear of alienating her sisters, Stanton might have understood, but she did not explain. Isabella was to win this battle and achieve that dangerous thing—what she wanted. There would be no Elizabeth Cady Stanton at the convention to stray outside the boundaries of suffrage talk and scare people; in fact, the convention would stay focused solely on suffrage. Yet in the words of Robert Burns, "The best laid schemes o' Mice an' Men" go oft astray, and Isabella's plans were about to be upended. She would receive a greater shock than any Elizabeth Cady Stanton could have provided.

On January 10, 1871, the day before the NWSA conference was to open, Isabella learned that a stranger to the women's movement had succeeded in getting a hearing for woman suffrage before the Judiciary Committee of the House of Representatives. The NWSA leaders had tried for the past two years to obtain a hearing before this committee but had always been rejected; no woman had ever been invited to speak. The successful petitioner was a Victoria C. Woodhull from New York City. Isabella and the other NWSA leaders at the convention, Susan B. Anthony, Paulina Wright Davis, and Josephine Griffing, a suffragist from Washington, D.C., did not know

Woodhull, and the little they'd heard was not good. The past spring Victoria Woodhull and her sister Tennessee Claflin had made a splash on Wall Street when they became the first female stockbrokers. Their patron was the wealthy Cornelius Vanderbilt, who was rumored to be Tennie's lover. Victoria also had the reputation of being a "loose woman." With their stock market winnings the sisters started a journal, *Woodhull & Claflin's Weekly,* which supported a variety of radical causes and announced Woodhull as a candidate for president of the United States.

The NWSA leaders faced a dilemma: Should they ensure their respectability by shunning this Victoria Woodhull and then have to spend the morning listening to speeches while they died of suspense wondering what was happening on Capitol Hill? Or should they present a united front and support Woodhull's petition by attending the hearing? Isabella was advised to do the latter by Senator Pomeroy, with whom she was again staying, and she took his words to heart. Men could never work together in a political party, he said, if they stopped to investigate every member's antecedents and associates.

Isabella and her colleagues thus met with Woodhull for two hours. Finding her acceptably ladylike, they postponed the opening of their convention until afternoon. They quickly arranged to speak at the hearing in support of Woodhull. The press, of course, reported how the women looked and not what they said: "At the head of the class stood Mrs. Beecher Hooker—her soft, fleecy curls tied down with orthodox precision; the curling feathers of blue harmonizing with her peachy complexion. Her elegantly-fitting coat was embroidered with steel beads. . . . Susan B. Anthony snuggled close beside her, clad in a smart new dress of black silk. . . . Her spectacles clung close to her nose and she had that longing, hope-deferred look, which humanity always wears when it has been centered for half a century upon a single idea." Woodhull and her sister wore blue "business suits" with their short hair curling out from under "boyish" hats. Victoria, pale and nervous, simply read aloud her written argument in support of the memorial; initially her voice was inaudible.

The basic argument would have been new to most of the congressmen but not to the NWSA women—it was the argument introduced the year before by the Minors of St. Louis, that the Fourteenth Amendment had already enfranchised women; Woodhull thus asked Congress to make such laws as would be necessary to carry out the right guaranteed by the Constitution to the citizens of the United States to vote, without regard to sex. Isabella followed with a speech in favor of suffrage for male immigrants, as well as women, as a hedge against anarchy, for "a disenfranchised class is always a restless class." This address had obviously been composed to support a sixteenth amendment and not the Fourteenth Amendment argument (the "New Departure"). There was no time to prepare a new speech.

As the hearing ended, the Judiciary Committee promised to make a ruling before the end of January. The suffragists went excitedly to Lincoln Hall to open the convention. Isabella seated Woodhull on the platform with the leaders and, after calling the assembly to order, introduced her to the audience. Woodhull was again so nervous that she could only read her memorial; she had to grasp Isabella's arm for support to reach the podium. Then as now, observers have implied that Woodhull was faking, trying to convince the NWSA women of her modesty. One reporter stated, "Although it would seem that a Wall-street experience would fit a woman to face the worst, yet Mrs. Woodhull's heart went pit-a-pat and the blood rose and fell from her cheek as fortunes go up and down on 'change.'" In actuality, these two occasions were Victoria's first public speeches, and she reacted much as Isabella and her colleagues had. Soon she would be a practiced speaker heavily in demand.

The conventioneers responded positively to Woodhull and her idea that Congress simply needed to pass a declaratory act recognizing women's right to vote under the Fourteenth Amendment. The *History of Woman Suffrage* summarizes the convention thus:

> The third Annual National Woman's suffrage Convention . . . was an unprecedented success. Its leading spirit was Mrs. Isabella Beecher Hooker . . . [whose] zeal, activity, and amiability gave her the power to make an easy conquest wherever she carries the banner of the good cause. Her generalship in Washington marshalled hosts of new and ardent friends into the movement. . . . A good deal was said by the speakers concerning the proposed interpretation of the existing constitutional amendments. It was thus a convention with a new idea. . . . There was an air of novelty about the proceedings, indicating healthy life in the movement. The consequence was that the cause of woman's enfranchisement made a new, sudden, and profound impression at Washington.

One of Isabella's innovations was to have each of the five sessions of the convention presided over by a member of the Senate or House. It was an interesting feature, the *History* points out, to have the legislators "sitting successively in the president's chair, apparently half unconscious that it was one of greater honor than their familiar seats in the Senate." Speeches were made by Isabella herself, Olympia Brown, Susan B. Anthony, Lillie Devereux Blake, and Frederick Douglass, among others. The convention decided to drop agitation for a sixteenth amendment and concentrate solely on the New Departure. It urged women everywhere to try to register and vote; if refused, they should sue for judicial recognition of their right. The convention also established a committee to stay in Washington while Congress was in session and carry out the work. The National Woman's Suffrage and Educational Committee (NWSEC) was instructed to lobby Congress for a declaratory act and begin an educational campaign to inform women of the New Departure and their need to vote. Isabella was appointed chair and Josephine Griffing secretary; Susan B. Anthony and Paulina Wright Davis were also on the committee. Isabella would thus remain in Washington working until the end of March.

Washington was probably the best place to be. The Judiciary Committee hearing with the scandalous Woodhull as star did not go unnoticed but was reported in papers across the country. *Frank Leslie's Weekly* published a full-page woodcut of the scene. Predictably, the conservative American Woman Suffrage Association was shocked at the National's consorting with Victoria Woodhull. Her vile newspaper attacks marriage in every issue, Henry Blackwell complained to John Hooker. As for the New Departure, he hoped it would work but doubted its validity. At this point John was also dubious, and Susan B. Anthony's closest colleague, Elizabeth Cady Stanton, began to regret boycotting the Hooker Convention. What was going on in Washington? Although Stanton wanted to make use of the Minors' Fourteenth Amendment argument, she feared another plot by the Republican men. Maybe they planned to derail a sixteenth amendment by having the women concentrate solely on the New Departure and languish in the courts "where we would hang by the eyelids for a quarter of a century."

Stanton's fears, along with John Hooker's, were soon assuaged by the report of the Judiciary Committee at the end of January. The majority voted against Woodhull's memorial, arguing that Congress could not intervene in voting requirements, which were left up to the states. But the minority report by Benjamin Butler and William Loughridge of Iowa was an extensive, closely argued legal document supporting the Fourteenth Amendment interpretation. Everyone was impressed. When Isabella thanked various congressmen for their assistance as Congress adjourned, she called the minority report "our bill of rights."

One of Isabella's duties as chair of the NWSEC was to get the new women's bill of rights out to the people. The committee, meeting daily in Washington, decided that Congress might be for once in advance of the people. What was most needed was the rapid distribution of the minority report and other tracts, so that public sentiment would catch up with the New Departure. Enough pressure exerted on members of Congress, said Isabella, would make them act speedily in favor of a declaratory law. But distribution of the report required money, which the NWSEC notably lacked. Isabella came up with the idea of asking that every woman in the country who believed she had the right to vote and was willing to pledge herself to do so should send her name to the committee with one dollar to cover the expense of distributing the tracts.

Thus the Declaration and Pledge, as they were called, came into being. Isabella quoted them in her memoir:

> I opened a large volume for the signatures of women willing to sign the following declaration:
> 'Declaration and Pledge of the Women of the United States concerning their right to and use of the Elective Franchise: We, the undersigned, believing that the sacred rights and privileges of citizenship in this Republic have long been guaranteed to us by the original Constitution of the United States, and that these are now made manifest in the Fourteenth and Fifteenth Amendments, so that we can no longer refuse the solemn responsibilities thereof, do hereby pledge ourselves to accept the duties of the franchise in our several states so soon as all legal restrictions are removed.
> 'And believing that *character* is the best safeguard of national liberty, we pledge ourselves to make the personal purity and integrity of candidates for public office the *first* test of fitness.
> 'And lastly, believing in God as the Supreme Author of the first American Declaration of Independence, we pledge ourselves in the spirit of that Memorable Act to work hand in hand with our fathers, husband[s] and sons, for the maintenance of those equal rights on which our Republic was originally founded to the end that it may have what is declared to be the first condition of just government—*the consent of the governed.*'
> And during the winter hundreds of autograph signatures, on little slips of white paper, came from all parts of the country, and were pasted into the volume.

The last two paragraphs of the Pledge, on the purity of candidates and the "Supreme Author," are unmistakably of Isabella's composition. Some women were confused, in fact, wanting to sign the Declaration and refuse the Pledge. The NWSEC collected enough dollars to mail out fifty thousand copies of the minority report, the Woodhull memorial, and other arguments. Finally, after a hard-fought campaign by Isabella, Benjamin Butler agreed to allow the women to use his congressional franking privileges (free postage) in sending out tracts. Isabella wrote "Dear friend Susan," who was lecturing on the New Departure in the Midwest, about their procedures. To every woman who mailed her signature to the Declaration and Pledge they sent a printed acknowledgment, one or more tracts, and a petition to return, asking Congress for an act declaring women eligible to vote. In a short time the NWSEC was able to present Congress with petitions carrying eighty thousand signatures. Isabella was very good at the lobbying and educational work her committee engaged in, and she felt completely in her element. She told Susan that "to write the political tracts & send them to the mothers in their homes, is to preach the gospel to every creature." She was so immersed in her campaign that she couldn't help but overwork.

To some observers Isabella's labors for suffrage made her tedious. An old acquaintance of hers and Harriet's, the writer Mary Abigail Dodge, was visiting Washington in January 1871. Ever since meeting the sisters at Nook Farm in the 1850s Dodge had consistently praised Isabella, viewing her as a "great light" and following closely her women's rights career. Although Dodge was something of a feminist, believing in personal and economic independence for women, she had grown impatient with what she considered the woman movement's narrow focus on suffrage. Thus during the "Hooker Convention" she wrote a friend that "Mrs. Isabella Beecher Hooker is here fashing herself with the suffrage, and doing all that a bright, good, and beautiful woman can to make herself a bore." For her part Isabella hardly noticed her single-mindedness because she felt so close to her goal. Women would have suffrage soon, she assured her colleagues, and then they could turn to educating women to fulfill their new responsibility.

Susan B. Anthony agreed that suffrage was just around the corner. When she read the minority report, she wrote Victoria Woodhull recalling Mr. Train's prediction during the Kansas campaign that women would vote for the next president. Now his prophecy neared realization. The certainty of the women (except for Stanton, who was too wily to make predictions) that the vote was almost won is easily ridiculed. But lacking the advantage of hindsight, it was not unreasonable for them to see victory at hand. They had all been early abolitionists, and the obvious analogy was to abolition. In the 1850s the anti-slavery cause languished, held hostage to the terrible Fugitive Slave Law of 1850: the faithful felt demoralized and quarreled among themselves. No one imagined the slaves would be freed in 1863. The victory came quickly and unexpectedly, and not because a majority of the American people believed in abolition—they were led by a small vanguard of believers.

One of the signs that the abolitionists would triumph had been their increasing presence and influence in Congress after years of avoiding party politics. The suffragists saw this sign in their work over the winter of 1871. Not only had they developed a new argument, and a thoroughly presentable one based on the Constitution, but they also experienced closer relations with Congress. Even the physical separation had been bridged. Legislators sat in during the convention sessions, and the women invaded the sacred domains of the Capitol, sharing the committee room tables of the Judiciary Committee. It seemed symbolic to Isabella that her NWSEC was offered the use of the committee room of Education and Labor and later the larger Agriculture room. In her thank-you speech to the suffragists' congressional supporters, Isabella noted "the first admission of women to this Capitol as citizens having common rights with the ruling class in the use of buildings devoted to the public service." She felt that their amicable sharing of space in the Capitol should silence the "absurd charge" that men and women would cease to observe the civilities of life when they became jointly responsible for the welfare of the country.

Isabella had much to congratulate herself about in the achievements of the Hooker Convention. Not only did it advance the cause politically but it also brought Isabella the approbation of previously skeptical colleagues. Lucretia Mott, for instance, had originally thought Isabella "too green" to preside over a national convention. But she ended up writing her daughter that, although Mrs. Hooker had ignored the parliamentary rules of order, she produced a "very gratifying" meeting. Mott was struck by the grand irony of the occasion: "What a curious fact, that proper Mrs. Hooker shd. be so linked in with Mrs. Woodhull."

This linkage would not come cheap. Facts and rumors about Woodhull and her family surfaced quickly, in both New York and the Midwest, where she had formerly lived. In a recent biography of Woodhull Mary Gabriel says that the men who ran the newspapers viewed Victoria less positively when she emerged as a reformer than they had when she was simply a colorful stockbroker. The women in the drawing rooms, discussing the recent events in Washington, focused less on the new message than on the new messenger. "It was a familiar tactic for women who wanted to influence society but had no political voice—gossip was one of their only tools." The double standard was firmly ensconced. While a man's "past" was generally excused, women were held to a higher standard. As Gabriel notes,

> The married trader Jim Fisk could parade his mistress Josie Mansfield in public, or bring risque productions to his opera house, but rather than face censure he was slapped on the back and lovingly called Gentleman Jim. The *Herald* publisher James Gordon Bennett, Jr., could run naked through the countryside shouting like a madman and he was regarded as simply eccentric. William Marcy 'Boss' Tweed and his henchmen in state and city government could rob public coffers of hundreds of millions of dollars and still win reelection. But no such leniency was afforded a woman who dared leave her proper place in the domestic sphere to enter public life,

no matter how good her intentions. She had to be free from taint. Victoria was not.

Woodhull's childhood was more to be pitied than condemned. She was born Victoria Claflin, named after Queen Victoria, in an Ohio shack in 1838. Her father, "Buck" Claflin, was a petty thief and con man who drifted from town to town, and her mother, Roxanna, was a mentally unbalanced Spiritualist. Roxanna seemingly passed her talent for communing with the dead to daughters Victoria and Tennessee. When Spiritualism became a craze in the late 1840s, Buck decided to cash in. He and Roxanna traveled around with their children, exploiting them as mediums and spiritual healers. Victoria received hardly any formal education; she was beaten and probably sexually abused by her father.

As she turned fifteen, Victoria was drawn into marriage to the much older Canning Woodhull, a physician from the East who claimed to be related to the mayor of New York City. By Victoria's account, the marriage was a nightmare instead of the romantic idyll she had hoped for. Woodhull's claims were phony, he had no intention of working as a doctor or anything else, and he was an alcoholic and sexual profligate; Victoria said he spent the third night of their "honeymoon" in a house of prostitution. The Woodhulls soon had a son Byron, named for the poet. He was either born retarded, as Victoria once claimed, or fell out of a second-story window and damaged his brain, as she also explained. Victoria took her family to San Francisco and supported them by working as a "cigar girl." By the sixties they were back in the Midwest and Victoria had given birth to a healthy daughter, named Zulu Maud. She and her sister Tennie resumed their careers as spiritual healers and clairvoyants in Ohio, Indiana, and Illinois.

Many of the unsavory details that provided grist for the gossip mills came from these years: Vicky and Tennie had to leave Cincinnati under suspicion of operating a brothel, and Vicky fled Chicago when accused of fraudulent fortune-telling. Actually, the only documented evidence against the sisters involved Tennie—she was indicted for manslaughter in Illinois following one of Buck's cancer cure scams. In the public mind, though, Victoria and Tennie were virtually indistinguishable. Their behavior reinforced this impression, as the sisters dressed alike and Tennie imitated her older sister in everything. In 1865 in St. Louis Victoria met the man who would groom her to be a reformer. He was Col. James Harvey Blood, a dashing Civil War veteran and social radical. Blood supplied Victoria with some of the education she lacked, especially the anti-marriage theories that made sense of her unhappy experience.

According to the gossip, the two did/did not legally divorce their spouses and did/did not legally marry. They left St. Louis to live together and in 1868 were in Pittsburgh when Victoria had a vision. Perhaps her mentor had been teaching her about the Greeks, for a spirit guide appeared to her and wrote out his name: D-E-M-O-S-T-H-E-N-E-S. Victoria later said that the spirit of the Greek statesman instructed her to go to 17 Great James Street in New York City, where a suitable house would be vacant and ready. It was. Victoria found *The Orations of Demosthenes* waiting on a table. Then came the parts of Woodhull's life that the suffragists had more knowledge of—the meeting with Cornelius Vanderbilt, the stock brokerage, *Woodhull & Claflin's Weekly,* and the memorial to Congress.

Isabella did not have Woodhull's complete history all at once, of course. The pieces came to her gradually during the course of the year, and as they arrived she became more hard-pressed to defend Woodhull and herself for accepting Woodhull into the movement. The worst problem was not her friends or suffrage colleagues but her sisters. In February Catharine took out a page in the Hartford *Courant* to make sure no one associated her with the Hooker Convention. "I am informed that my name has appeared in some of the public prints as an advocate for woman suffrage. This is not true either of myself or of a large majority of my family and personal friends." Catharine and Harriet badgered Isabella about Woodhull; even Mary Perkins, who had recently been widowed and consoled by Isabella, joined their ranks. Isabella wrote Susan B. Anthony that she was "still praising & defending" Woodhull "though my sisters, all three, staying at Dr. Taylor's have nearly crazed me with letters imploring me to have nothing to do with her."

The latest letter was from Harriet, describing an encounter one of brother Henry's parishioners had had with Woodhull. He had met her on the night train to Washington when she was talking with a senator he knew. In the morning she asked him to breakfast with her at her hotel and proceeded to tell him her life's story—"of her first marriage—of her husband's profligacy & her having for some years lived the life of an abandoned woman." She said "she now had frequent offers of that kind but that she had formed a connection with Col. Blood & should remain constant to it." Henry's parishioner could see no good reason for Woodhull telling him all this or inviting him, as he left, to come to her room in the evening. When he encountered the senator, the senator cautioned him against spending any time with Woodhull, who was not a "proper woman." Isabella felt bound to investigate this story, which seems to have been true. Yet, as she told Anthony, the story typified gossip about Woodhull—the facts themselves were not damaging, "only *his inferences*" that a woman would not feel obliged to make.

Unfortunately, Isabella's sisters were not only bombarding her with criticism but also besieging her husband, John. They used the conventions of the time, the very ones Isabella was trying to fight against, to trap her. The idea was that the husband ought to control the wife, so that John should force her to repudiate Woodhull. John's refusal to do this earned him the contempt of his sisters-in-law. As Harriet once wrote when she was angry with Isabella, "My poor wandering sister Bell. . . . If only she had a sensible husband she might now be brought right but John ministers to the very poorest and weakest part of her nature." No doubt Harriet wanted John to behave more like her friend Susie Howard's menfolks. In 1870 Isabella had written Susie defending Stanton and Anthony's newspaper and her own choice of the NWSA over AWSA. She sympathized with Susie's difficult position in having a husband and son opposed to women's rights but suggested that she read the *Revolution* and try to think for herself. The male Howards responded immediately—and to John, not Isabella. John was thus forced to enter the controversy and defend Stanton, a woman he didn't particularly like, from charges of being a "free lover." It is a wonder that the junior Howard felt entitled to criticize women's ethics—he was the man Henry had gotten out of jail for forging Lincoln's signature in a get-rich scheme.

John Hooker was a man of principle. He knew that husbands should not be settling issues for their wives, and he could also remember the time when he turned abolitionist and well-meaning people tried to make him repudiate his new associates. But at the same time John had always craved the good opinion of his neighbors, and since his financial failures he was especially anxious; it was harder for him to stand up to criticism than it was for his wife. Isabella wrote Anthony that John was "feeble and extremely sensitive and unable to sleep under the least excitement—and he has been so harassed by my *three* sisters in N. York and by every friend we have in Hartford on my acct. that he is scarce able to exist. He defends my course everywhere—but in his own heart doubts the wisdom of it and is compelled to trust my judgment against his own." Finally, Isabella's daughters intervened: their conservative husbands deplored her feminist politics and, worse, those politics were killing their father.

Isabella continued to defend Victoria Woodhull and her own Declaration and Pledge, but she did give in to family pressure to some degree. She had originally planned to travel with Woodhull, speaking jointly with her on "A Legal and Moral View of Constitutional Equality." Woodhull would give the legal view (her memorial to Congress) and Isabella the moral (the reasons why the Bible and Jesus Christ supported women's rights). They had done this successfully at Lincoln Hall in February, introduced by Paulina Wright Davis. This time Isabella was the more nervous because of the large audience (fourteen hundred), and Victoria had to encourage her to follow her own path and call up "the spirits" to inspire and protect her. Years later Isabella remembered that speech as "the finest address I ever delivered. . . . It flowed out of my inner consciousness as if it were part of my very being." But she could not keep it up. Publicly she gave the excuse that two speeches made a program too long for one evening, but in reality she feared that her speaking with Woodhull, however exhilarating it might be, was endangering her husband's health. She told Anthony defensively that she had done her part in welcoming Woodhull to the NWSA platform and working with her in Washington.

But Isabella would not renounce her association with Victoria Woodhull even under severe pressure to do so, nor would she criticize the woman publicly. The strength of her stance is surprising considering the fact that she herself tried to silence Elizabeth Cady Stanton a few months before. In the interim she had come to regret her actions toward Stanton. She took to heart her friend Paulina Wright Davis's admonition that Stanton must be trusted. Davis maintained that neither she nor Lucretia Mott nor Olympia Brown would attend conventions if they were denied free speech. Although it was not necessary that "extraneous questions" like labor, capital, and the eight-hour workday be discussed on the platform, all topics that fit under their call, such as education and social and civil rights, should receive a fair hearing. Davis was insistent and, of course, Anthony and Brown reinforced her at the convention. Ironically, it was probably *because of* the incident with Stanton that Isabella was able to keep the principle of free speech in such clear focus. She would not again be preoccupied with respectability at the expense of principle. The strength of her adherence was that of the new convert with vision undimmed by years of compromise.

Isabella's stubborn defense of Woodhull was also fueled by a lifetime of feminist fury over the double standard. Why should Woodhull be persecuted when the sexual peccadilloes of male politicians were ignored? Susan B. Anthony put it thus: "I have *heard gossip of undue familiarity* with persons of *the opposite sex* relative to Beecher, Higginson, Butler, Carpenter, Pomeroy— and before I shall consent to an arraignment of *Woodhull* or any other *earnest woman worker* who shall come to our Platform in Washington or elsewhere— I shall insist upon the *closest investigation* into *all* the *scandals* afloat about these men." When Isabella's sisters Harriet and Mary wrote John Hooker calling Woodhull a "harlot," she took off her gloves and fought back. She reminded Harriet that she had stood by her during the Lady Byron scandal and then went for the jugular, pointing out her sisters' implicit acceptance of the double standard as the mothers of dissolute sons. "You and Mrs. Perkins each have a drinking, licentious son [Fred Stowe, Fred Perkins], and yet you know that you would be glad for them to marry the purest young girl and have tried every means to effect it hoping it might redeem them, and yet you judge Mrs. Woodhull."

When she wrote this criticism, Isabella undoubtedly had in mind the naive idealistic teenager, Victoria Claflin, being offered up to the drunken Canning Woodhull. She surely would not have written thus about Fred Stowe had she known of the tragedy in the making at the time of her letter. Fred had been fighting his alcohol addiction since the end of the war. In 1870 he had abstained for over a year and was engaged to marry a "pure young girl." Then he fell off the wagon and, ashamed of his inability to quit drinking, resolved to join the merchant marine and travel around the world. He enlisted his aunt Isabella to intercede for him to get his parents' approval. But on going ashore at San Francisco in February 1871 Fred disappeared and was never heard from again. Although the Stowes employed detectives in San Francisco, they never learned anything beyond Fred's having left the ship alive. At this point, in 1871, the family tried hard to believe that he was just too sick or too ashamed to contact them.

Fred's mother, in her quarrel with sister Isabella, was oblivious to the double standard and could see no connection between her son and that "harlot" Victoria Woodhull. Harriet thought Isabella was "infatuated" with her new colleague and went so far as to characterize the relationship as demonic possession. After all, the press referred to Woodhull as "Mrs. Satan." Harriet wrote a friend that she could not understand the secret of Woodhull's "influence over my poor sister—incredible infatuation continuing even now. I trust that God will in some way deliver her for she was and is a lovely good woman & before this witch took possession of her we were all so happy together." Today it is possible to see that Harriet had personal motives for advancing this scenario, as she was still under the shadow of the Byron controversy. Johanna Johnston, author of biographies of both Stowe and Woodhull, suggests that Stowe was trying to recapture her popularity by attacking Woodhull (the attacks started *before* Woodhull accused her brother Henry Ward Beecher of adultery). "Perhaps Mrs. Stowe was subconsciously trying to shore up her own reputation for unblemished morality with her attacks on Victoria Woodhull." It is tremendously ironic that Harriet should ascribe Isabella's defense of Woodhull to "infatuation" because that is exactly what critics implied or stated outright about Harriet's own relationship with Lady Byron—she wrote the Byron article because she had been infatuated with Lady Byron. But, unfortunately, Harriet was never able to see any of the parallels between her actions and Isabella's.

It is Harriet's view of her sister and Victoria Woodhull that has prevailed because she is the Beecher with the highest reputation to this day.

Most writers do use Harriet's word "infatuation" to describe Isabella's attitude toward Woodhull, and many employ the language of possession. Kenneth Andrews thus presents Isabella as falling "under the younger woman's spell" and being "subjected" to her. The attractiveness of the "Woodhull as witch" view is shown by the ease with which Andrew Sinclair in a standard history of the women's movement substitutes Elizabeth Cady Stanton for Isabella as Woodhull's victim. Sinclair quotes Stanton's ringing endorsement of sexual solidarity among women: "We have had enough women sacrificed to this sentimental, hypocritical prating about purity. This is one of man's most effective engines for our division and subjugation. He creates the public sentiment, builds the gallows, and then makes us hangmen for our sex. . . . If Victoria Woodhull must be crucified, let men drive the spikes and plait the crown of thorns." Then, instead of discussing Stanton's point (or the eloquence of its expression), he states that "this infatuation of Stanton with Victoria Woodhull" set back the women's movement many years.

When any evidence was produced to support the theory of Isabella's "infatuation" with Woodhull, it was usually weak. There was the February 1871 letter to Woodhull, for example, in which Isabella addressed her as "My Darling Queen." This "extreme salutation," in Johanna Johnston's view, proved "the spell that Victoria had woven over the leaders she had met in Washington." But it was not unusual for Victorian women to call each other "queen," and women christened "Victoria" and "Isabella" had a special reason for badinage based on their royal names. Similarly, when Isabella spoke of Woodhull's "wonderful magnetism," she was referring specifically to her powers as a medium and not her sex appeal; of course, Woodhull's connection with the spirits supported the view of her as witch.

Isabella was sometimes incautious in defending Victoria Woodhull, and it is fair to say that she brought some of her problems on herself. One instance was her arranging for Woodhull and her sister Catharine to meet. Isabella had concluded, quite accurately, that Woodhull's biggest detractors consisted of people who had never met her. But she went on to reason that if Catharine could talk with her "beloved queen," she would recognize her essential innocence and purity. Here Isabella's vaunted "people skills," supposedly learned through motherhood, failed her. Just about anyone else would have realized that two such strong, stubborn women with opposite views on every topic would not get along. Predictably, the meeting was a farce.

As Victoria described it, they went for a carriage ride in Central Park and Catharine began to lecture her on the folly of women challenging men's power; only well-bred women with proper antecedents could expect to persuade men to do right. The word "antecedents" was a red flag to Woodhull. She had already written Isabella that she resented people's emphasis on her

Catharine Beecher, c. 1870–1875. Courtesy Harriet Beecher Stowe Center, Hartford, Conn.

past rather than her principles—she thought woman suffrage was a "question of *Right* under the *Constitution*. I did not know it was a question of *Antecedents*." Losing her temper, Victoria pointed out the inconsistency of Catharine's attacking "free love" while her brother Henry openly practiced it. She said Catharine denied this accusation and jumped out of the carriage, screaming, "Victoria Woodhull, I will strike you for this. I will strike you dead."

This account may have been overdramatized by Woodhull, who also said she saw a band of devils with rattails hovering around Catharine's head. Nonetheless, the meeting clearly worsened the situation and led Catharine to more vituperative attacks on her brother's enemy. In her view Woodhull was either insane or the "hapless victim of malignant spirits." Isabella was hard-pressed to deal with the satanic visions of her sisters and her new colleague. Everything she or Victoria did seemed to make the conflicts worse. "[I]t is dreadful," she wrote, "this having foes in your own household—if you can escape that you can live."

8

Free Love and "Mrs. Satan," 1871–1872

IF ISABELLA WAS foolish enough to convince herself that Victoria Woodhull could win over her sisters, she was still not "infatuated" with Woodhull. She had doubts about her from the beginning, which she did not express publicly but revealed to her close colleagues. For instance, she viewed with skepticism Victoria's desire to run for president. She wrote Anthony after a meeting with Woodhull that Victoria "seemed wild only on one point—& that was her conviction that she was to be President next time & thus *ruler of the whole world*—our country being destined to lead all others." Isabella advised Victoria to keep this idea to herself. She was not prepared to back Woodhull for president because she thought the president should be of unblemished moral character and was not sure about Woodhull's. She simply intended to privately "work for her redemption if she is ensnared" and "not denounce her publicly, however guilty till the time when men guilty of the same crimes are avoided and denounced."

Isabella had also begun to suspect the situation that led most directly to the NWSA's separation from Woodhull—the influence of certain men on her ideas and behavior. Isabella wrote Mary Livermore that some man or men might be using Woodhull for their own purposes. At the time of the convention in January 1871 the NWSA women naturally thought Woodhull had composed her own memorial, but it was gradually coming out that Benjamin Butler had probably written it. (He was certainly the congressman responsible for Victoria's gaining a hearing before the Judiciary Committee.) In addition, Colonel Blood wrote much of *Woodhull & Claflin's Weekly*, along with Stephen Pearl Andrews, a radical intellectual who had joined the Woodhull entourage ("Everyone seems to condemn him—do you know him? or his antecedents?" Isabella wrote Anthony). Those antecedents again! But Isabella and her colleagues wondered if these men were as much Woodhull's "controls" as was Demosthenes. Although she was a quick study, Woodhull had little formal education. A silly letter by Isabella complaining about Woodhull's stationery as a terrible eyesore and asking her to use nicer notepaper might have been just another outbreak of gentility, as in the Stanton incident. Or Isabella could have been reacting at some level to a lack of literacy on Woodhull's part; one man who said he'd been her lover claimed she was barely literate. At any rate, Isabella and her colleagues came increasingly to believe that Woodhull was not necessarily producing her own words or even her own positions on the issues.

Some of these positions came as unpleasant surprises to the NWSA women when they read *Woodhull & Claflin's Weekly*. For Isabella, it was the *Revolution* situation all over again, only worse. One shock was the *Weekly's* support of licensed prostitution, which was complete anathema to the suffragists, who saw it as state sanction of the oppression of women. They could agree that arresting prostitutes was not the answer. The *Weekly* cleverly satirized a mass arrest on Greenwich Street, noting that when the prostitutes got out of jail, they would be magically reformed; they would now have well-paying jobs and would never go back to prostitution on Greenwich Street— "Oh, no." But state licensing was not the answer either. It had become a pet issue for Isabella since she had learned of the work of Josephine Butler in England. In the 1860s the British Parliament had passed a series of Contagious Diseases Acts providing for periodic examination of prostitutes in order to protect the health of military men. Josephine Butler was the head of the Ladies' National Association for the Repeal of the Contagious Diseases Acts (LNA). More than the American leaders, she was suited to be Isabella's idol and mentor—she came from a middle-class provincial family, was happily married to a supportive clergyman, experienced poor health, and worked for higher education and the vote for women; she was strongly religious and practiced what she preached, engaging in practical rescue work of prostitutes in Liverpool.

Isabella understood that Woodhull's disastrous first marriage had led her to back any measure that promised protection, but she was not about to abandon the Butler position for Woodhull's. She wrote Mary Livermore that the *Weekly's* stand on licensing was "intolerable to all of us." Woodhull would have to get some "prudent woman" to edit the paper if she wanted NWSA support. For the time being, in spite of their doubts, Isabella and the other NWSA leaders continued to defend Woodhull. On her way home from Washington Isabella, along with Paulina Wright Davis, visited Lucretia Mott in Philadelphia. The veteran Quaker feminist and "grand old woman" of the movement remonstrated with Woodhull over licensing but agreed that her freedom of speech should be upheld. Mott, her sister Martha Coffin Wright, and Paulina Davis all accompanied Isabella to hear Woodhull lecture in Philadelphia.

Wright told her daughter, "I think it is beautiful of Mrs. Hooker to brave all that she does from her own family and others in standing by her [Woodhull]."

As the May NWSA meeting rapidly approached, Isabella turned her attention temporarily away from Woodhull. The AWSA also intended to hold a May meeting in New York and, although Isabella had given up hope of uniting the two rival suffrage organizations permanently, she wanted to see a joint convention in order to "avoid four *dribbling* suffrage days instead of two strong ones." She enlisted the help of Caroline Severance and Mary Livermore to try to persuade the Boston leaders. Lucy Stone, however, secretly blocked the plan. She solicited letters from AWSA members to Livermore saying that they should keep clear of other organizations and reject "an affiliation with Mrs. Hooker, who is the sworn ally of Susan."

The NWSA convention was a success despite all this. The audiences were large, and they ratified the New Departure decisions made in Washington earlier in the year. Any grumblings about Victoria Woodhull's reputation were silenced by the rousing keynote address she gave on opening night. Probably written by Stephen Pearl Andrews, the speech ended dramatically: "If the very next Congress refuses women all the legitimate results of citizenship . . . we shall proceed to call another convention expressly to frame a new constitution and to erect a new government. . . . We mean treason; we mean secession. . . . We are plotting a revolution; we will overthrow this bogus Republic and plant a government of righteousness in its stead." While Victoria was galvanizing the NWSA with her vision of the future, the AWSA was timidly passing resolutions denying they were free lovers. The newspapers dubbed Victoria's speech the "Great Secession Speech" and the convention the "Woodhull Convention."

As often happened in Woodhull's life, however, any triumph on her part was soon neutralized by the antics of her large and quarrelsome family. They followed her from place to place and generally lived with and were supported by her; the family included her former husband and two children, her unsavory parents, several sisters who tended to be jealous of Victoria, their numerous children, and a brother-in-law or two. This time, just a few days after the convention, Victoria's mother took Colonel Blood to court, claiming he had tried to kill her. Woodhull's contemporary biographer Theodore Tilton was not far off when he said that "Victoria is a green leaf, and her legion of relatives are caterpillars who devour her." The family squabble was a foolish one, but danger lay in its public airing. In his testimony Blood inadvertently let slip that Dr. Canning Woodhull, Victoria's first husband, was living with the family. This news caused a sensation. Isabella interpreted it in a positive light as meaning Victoria was willing to offer charity to a man who had mistreated her, a broken-down man who was sick with his addictions and unable to care for himself (Canning Woodhull would die within the year). Victoria proved her integrity, Isabella wrote a fellow suffragist, in living up to her standard of benevolence even though "all the world should condemn and thrust at her." Almost all the world did condemn and thrust. To the prurient press Victoria was exposed as a practicing free lover living in a ménage à trois. Unfortunately, Isabella's sisters also took this view of the situation.

In May Isabella found herself and Victoria cruelly caricatured in Harriet's current novel, *My Wife and I: Or, Harry Henderson's History*, which was appearing in brother Henry's *Christian Union*. The first number had come out in November 1870 and until the next spring the serial was full of feminist ideas. Isabella no doubt influenced it, as several of her pet theories are advanced. The narrator, Harry Henderson, expresses his opinion that women and men should not be restricted to their own separate spheres of action. Women have to feel as responsible as men for the welfare of the state and men should be trained to be good husbands, equal in "purity" to women. Harry's female cousin wants the same education as her brothers. When her father pronounces the usual "What a pity she wasn't born a boy," Harry responds, "Well, let you and me do what we can . . . to bring in such a state of things in this world that it shall no longer be said of any woman that it was a pity not to have been born a man." Stowe perhaps made the narrator a male version of herself, "Harry," not "Harriet," so as to give authority to such ideas; she had just read John Stuart Mill.

Halfway into the book the tone changes radically as the feminists Audacia Dangyereyes and Stella Cerulean are introduced. Audacia bursts into Harry's office one day and invites him to her rooms for a smoke; she insists that he subscribe to her newspaper, the *Emancipated Woman*, which contains "an exposition of all the wildest principles of modern French communism." (Apparently Harriet had noticed that the first issue of *Woodhull & Claflin's Weekly* introduced a serial by the hated George Sand.) Harriet did not get Woodhull quite right—in her hoydenish behavior Audacia resembles Tennie Claflin more than the dignified Victoria, but everyone got the idea.

Readers could also recognize Audacia's patron, the respectable Mrs. Stella Cerulean, as Isabella Beecher Hooker. Some twentieth-century readers have identified Mrs. Cerulean as Elizabeth Cady Stanton, but Stowe's contemporaries would never have made that mistake. Mrs. Cerulean's two leading traits are characteristics no one could associate with Stanton—beauty and stupidity. Her good looks are emphasized to the point that one begins to suspect Harriet of being, or having been at some time, jealous of Isabella's appearance. The narrator says tartly of Mrs. Cerulean, "In common with handsome women generally, she had, during the greater part of her life, never heard anything but flattery from gentlemen, and it always agreed with her remarkably well." Though this flattery has given the woman a high opinion of herself, she is nothing but a "pretty baby." As her name "Stella" (star) "Cerulean" (sky-blue) indicates, she has her head in the clouds; in today's parlance she is an airhead. Harriet seems to have realized eventually that she was traversing the bounds of sisterly conduct in her satire of Isabella as Stella Cerulean. The character appears in only thirty pages in the middle of a nearly five hundred–page novel, though Audacia Dangyereyes is introduced again later. Nor is Mrs. Cerulean shown speaking and acting on her own; she is simply discussed by the main characters. As Lucretia Mott's niece wrote of the novel, "[T]he supposed copy of Mrs. Hooker has extremely little to do." Apparently Stowe wanted to chide her sister but not portray her as a full-fledged character.

Interestingly, Stowe has Mrs. Cerulean repeat actual arguments that Isabella used to defend her attitude toward Woodhull—for instance, the Senator Pomeroy argument that men join with anyone who will help them without regard to "antecedents." As the characters try to refute this and other arguments, their logic eventually leads them to a position diametrically opposed to the feminism of the first half of the book. Of Mrs. Cerulean, Harry's wife-to-be says, "She always thinks that she understands every-thing by intuition. I believe in my heart that she'd walk into the engine-room of the largest steamship that ever was navigated, and turn out the chief engineer and take his place if he'd let her. She'd navigate by woman's God-given instincts, as she calls them." She would keep on until she'd blown up the ship, another character chimes in. But this line of reasoning leads to the conclusion that as men have always steered the ship, they must continue to do so. So much for Stowe's "feminist" novel anticipated by Susan B. Anthony.

My Wife and I, published shortly after *Oldtown Folks,* was worlds away from the previous book. In *Oldtown Folks* Harriet introduced the super-competent Miss Nervy (short for Minerva) Randall. She is an androgynous being who excels at every household task but also reads the classics and works out problems in mathematics and surveying. In her youth Miss Nervy went on a Mediterranean voyage with her ship captain brother, who claimed she was a better mate than any man he knew. When he took ill with a fever, Miss Nervy "navigated the ship home in the most matter-of-fact way in the world." It is quite a comedown to Mrs. Cerulean's navigation by instinct. Harriet once explained her change of heart in *My Wife and I* as follows: "You think you are going to write one kind of thing, and behold! your pen travels off in an entirely different direction. Now I thought I would make this *Harry Henderson* a free-and-easy, chatty sort of story. But just as I began it, Mrs.

Stanton and all those people began making their loud talk and unsettling attacks on marriage and its sacredness, setting up new and false notions. I couldn't stand that; and so you see this story has taken a deeper hold of me than I thought it would." One might expect Woodhull to be mentioned rather than Stanton, but ever since the latter criticized her attack on George Sand, Harriet lost no opportunity to associate Stanton with free love.

Harriet's change of direction in her serial made for a rather confused novel. For instance, before Audacia Dangyereyes and Mrs. Cerulean are introduced, Harry's wife's sister Ida Van Arsdel represents feminism. In the language of the time she is a "strong minded young woman." Stowe also calls her "a serious, large-minded, large-brained woman"—Ida renounces "society" and marriage and plans to remain independent. But after Audacia enters the scene Ida seems to modulate into Catharine Beecher. Women can be granted their rights only gradually; they must be educated in public affairs before they can vote. Ida declares herself pleased that "there is no immediate prospect of the suffrage being granted to women until a generation with superior education and better balanced minds and better habits of consecutive thought shall have grown up among us." She was never in favor of granting women their rights *immediately*, she says. That might lead to terrible "disturbances" like the French Revolution.

This was exactly what Catharine had just been saying in her December 1870 debate with Mary Livermore. By the time Harriet added Audacia to her serial, Catharine had finished turning her speech into a book, *Woman Suffrage and Woman's Profession* (1871). She fleshed out her argument against woman suffrage and then devoted the remaining space to repeating her pet educational theories. However repetitive, the book did reflect the advent of Victoria Woodhull in its prefatory materials. Suddenly Catharine perceived that a national crisis was imminent. In a lengthy dedication "to the Ministers of Religion in the United States" she warns: "This *woman movement* is one which is uniting by co-operating influences, all the antagonisms that are warring on the family state. Spiritualism, free-love, free divorce, the vicious indulgences consequent on unregulated civilization, the worldliness which tempts men and women to avoid *large* families, often by sinful methods, thus making the ignorant masses the chief supply of the future majorities; and most powerful of all, the feeble constitution and poor health of women, causing them to dread maternity as—what it is fast becoming—an accumulation of mental and bodily tortures."

Catharine appealed to the clergy to help her fight these dangers, illustrating in the process her theory of the need to influence men. She becomes downright obsequious at times. "Fathers and Brethren" she calls them. "As the daughter and sister of nine ministers of Jesus Christ you will allow me to address you by those endeared names." Did she momentarily forget she had spent the past twenty years attacking the clergy in her writings? In 1860 Catharine had dedicated her book *An Appeal to the People in Behalf of Their Rights as Authorized Interpreters of the Bible* in the opposite way. She addressed it to the editors of the secular press, whom she called the people's tribunes, the defenders of liberty of conscience, freedom of speech, and "the Right of all to Interpret the Bible for themselves, unrestrained by any Ecclesiastical Power." Now she appealed to the ecclesiastical powers to promote her aims and help her "where my own strength and courage fail." One advantage of a philosophy based on principle, such as John Stuart Mill's, over Catharine's pragmatism is the greater ease in remaining consistent over a period of time.

When Catharine attacked free love, divorce, and Spiritualism in her dedication to *Woman Suffrage and Woman's Profession,* she managed not to mention Victoria Woodhull by name. Woodhull did not always return the favor. After Catharine's anti-suffrage speech in December, Victoria referred in *Woodhull & Claflin's Weekly* to "the Catherine [sic] Beechers who now clog the wheels of progress, and stand forth as the enemies of their sex . . . doing their utmost to cement the chains of their degradation, giving to man the same power over them as he possesses over his horses and dogs." Neither Catharine nor Harriet ever saw herself as an enemy of her sex. Rather, both cast themselves as woman's defenders, saving her from the dangers of the radical suffrage movement (even the AWSA was radical in their eyes).

Both sisters were willing to identify themselves with women and participate in all-female activities when they didn't see them as threatening the family. One of their last collaborative works was a pamphlet advocating the training of women as "home physicians" who would focus on preventative medicine and be paid equally with men. In 1871 Catharine and Harriet advertised a summer institute in which they would teach health courses to women, but they did not receive enough inquiries to make the project feasible. The sisters were not averse to chastising women who they felt did not properly identify with and support other women. Catharine, for instance, gave a talk in May to the "Ladies of Hartford." She made her usual pitch for an endowed women's college and provided a list of women who had given large amounts of money to endow male colleges. Why couldn't they support women instead? "Where is there a single endowment from a woman to secure a salary to a woman teaching her own proper profession?"

Also in 1871 Catharine and Harriet became involved for the first time in the emerging women's club movement, begun in 1868 when Isabella's friend Caroline Severance founded the New England Woman's Club in Boston. A month later Jane Croly, a well-known journalist, started Sorosis, the New York equivalent. Croly had undergone an experience similar to Harriet's with the *Atlantic Monthly*. The Press Club of New York had held a dinner at Delmonico's restaurant to honor Charles Dickens before his return to England. But Croly's application for a ticket was treated as a joke, and when she found out the dinner was for men only, she decided to establish her own organization.

Despite the reasons behind the genesis of this club and the New England group's being founded by Severance, the clubs were not feminist in character. Although some leading suffragists were involved—Julia Ward Howe joined Severance in Boston and Isabella Beecher Hooker became a member of Sorosis—most of the women saw these clubs as an alternative to the shockingly radical "woman movement." Croly conceived of Sorosis as a nonpolitical organization that would "promote agreeable and useful relations among women of literary and artistic tastes." Her descriptions could just as well have been written by Catharine. Not only did she and Harriet fit in well with the club's philosophy, but they were also accomplished women who could be looked up to by club members. If these clubs were not interested in changing the system, they did want to highlight women's "contributions" to society. Thus in 1871 the New England Woman's Club gave a reception to honor both Catharine and Harriet.

Isabella was feeling rather dishonored after the May NWSA conference and the appearance of Mrs. Stella Cerulean in Harriet's serial. Her sister had branded her publicly as a "gullible fool," as one writer puts it, and her sons-in-law weren't speaking to her. She was exhausted from overwork, both mental and physical. She wrote Mott's sister that she needed a vacation "even from *thinking* of these issues." Much to Isabella's relief, her niece and friend Emily Perkins Hale took her in for the month of August; Emily even assented to Isabella's condition for coming, that no one would mention even in jest the subjects of family disagreement. Isabella was nervous about visiting primarily because she would have to face her sister Mary, who after the death of Thomas Perkins lived with the Hales in Boston. She "longed, yet dreaded to meet" her. But it turned out that Mary had gone on a trip.

At the Hales' Isabella relaxed and thought up reasons for optimism. In fact, she would rather have been invited to vacation in Newport with Alice, John Day, and her granddaughter, thinking the "scrubbing" she'd received from her sons-in-law might be ending and their resentment "dying out." Besides, she tried to convince Alice (and herself?) in a letter, it was rare for husbands and mothers-in-law to get along. Emily Hale had confided in her about the "wall of coldness" that separated her mother, Mary Beecher Perkins, and her husband, Edward Everett Hale. Amid these prickly family concerns, Isabella looked forward to the end of her most controversial work. She knew she would have to help educate women to use the vote wisely, but suffrage was coming soon. When she and Stanton corresponded about the call to the January conference in Washington, Isabella wrote, "I believe that this is the last Suffrage Call to Washtn. we shall have to issue." Being more familiar with Stanton by this time, she added, "I know you will smile at this."

If Isabella was trying to convince herself that her situation was "normal" and everything was improving, she was mistaken. When she returned home from visiting the Hales, a letter awaited from Phebe Hanaford, a minister, suffragist, and AWSA member from New Haven, Connecticut. Hanaford thought Isabella was so fascinated by Victoria Woodhull that she was overlooking her disgraceful life, that is, living with two husbands and favoring the licensing of prostitution. Isabella had been "born to call others around the standard of reform" and shouldn't lessen her influence by accepting Woodhull as a suffrage leader. After Stephen Pearl Andrews published Isabella's "My Darling Queen" letter in defense of Victoria, Hanaford wrote more acidly. She rescinded her invitation to Isabella to speak in her church. Neither she nor her church trustees "owe any sort of allegiance to your 'darling queen,' the notorious mistress of Col. Blood's affections." If Isabella wanted to speak, she had to repudiate Woodhull and declare allegiance to the "Christian platform" of the American Woman Suffrage Association.

Victoria Woodhull was now being called "the Woodhull," as if she were an object. Attacks came from everywhere. In late October the Hookers' old friend and neighbor Joseph Hawley, who was now governor of Connecticut, wrote an editorial for the *Hartford Courant*, claiming he'd hesitated to denounce *Woodhull & Claflin's Weekly* because he hadn't wanted to give it free publicity. But, according to Hawley, Woodhull was demoralizing society. He had to speak out when he saw that the journal was being read by female spiritualists and suffragists who might shut their eyes to its immorality and introduce it into respectable households with young girls present.

At the same time Catharine was joining the fray once again. Woodhull had sought and received an invitation to speak in Hartford and Catharine was trying to prevent the speech from taking place. As "A Lady of Hartford," she wrote to the *Courant*, arguing that free love was contemptible and Christians should not allow such ideas to be presented in their city. This is the point at which Isabella lamented the foes in her own household. She wrote Anna Savery, the Iowa suffragist with whom she stayed on her western trip, that "the feeling on this Woodhull matter has nearly killed me. You at the West can have no conception of Connecticut phariseeism & bigotry nor of what I have suffered in consequence. . . . I am driven to death—& just now my sister Catharine is attacking Mrs. W's private character *infamously* so as to keep people from going out to hear her—the result is she will have a jam next time & last week had a good house in a stormy night. But it is dreadful this having foes in your own household—if you can escape that you can live."

As Isabella predicted, Victoria reaped a benefit from Catharine's free advertising—seven hundred Hartford citizens turned out to hear her at the Hartford Opera House. Woodhull came ready to fight. She read Catharine's letter and commented as follows: "Miss Beecher told me . . . she would strike me. She has done so, but now, instead of returning the blow, I will present her with my other cheek, with the hope that even her conscience will not smite her for speaking so unkindly of me as she has. . . . She may profess Christ, but I hope I may exceed her in living his precepts."

Woodhull's resolve to turn the other cheek did not last long. She had seen a good deal of Henry Ward Beecher during the summer of 1871; in fact, some people thought (without any compelling evidence) that they'd had a brief affair. She now wrote Henry complaining that two of his sisters "have gone out of their way to assail my character and purposes, both by the means of the public press and by numerous private letters." He should realize, she warned, that she had the "power to strike back." Apparently Henry succeeded in calling off Harriet, though he must have realized from experience that Catharine could not be muzzled. Harriet wrote a preface to the book form of My Wife and I in which she denied that any of the characters were portraits of existing people. Not that anyone would have believed by then that Audacia Dangyereyes was not Victoria Woodhull—Harriet's gesture was too little too late.

As for Victoria, she kept reaching new heights of boldness. She spoke in New York in November, soon after her Hartford talk, on "The Principles of Social Freedom." When somebody in the audience shouted out the question, "Are you a free lover?" she responded, "Yes! I am a free lover! I have an inalienable, constitutional, and natural right to love whom I may, to love as long or as short a period as I can, to change that love every day if I please!" Victoria was nothing if not dramatic. Soon after this speech Woodhull was portrayed in a cartoon by Thomas Nast in Harper's Weekly. The cartoon illustrates the demonizing of Woodhull by Harriet, Catharine, and other conservatives.

The wrangling over Woodhull made Isabella feel for the first time in her life that she might "go under," as she put it. Part of her misery came from no longer having a home of her own. The Hookers had experienced more financial reverses; among other problems they lost a thousand dollars when a man for whom John had posted bond absconded. So, on October 1, they rented out their house to Sam and Livy Clemens while the Mark Twain house was being built nearby. Isabella thus had no permanent home and "not one friend (but my husband) who is not either cold or ugly." She made this

Victoria Woodhull demonized as "Mrs. Satan." Cartoon by Thomas Nast in *Harper's Weekly*, Feb. 17, 1872.

complaint to her neighbor, Charles Dudley Warner, a man she didn't particularly care for. It was not characteristic of her to confide in him or practically beg him, as she went on to do, to publish some articles favorable to Woodhull in his Hartford *Evening Press*.

Isabella's low state is also revealed in her grateful reaction to a letter from her brother Jim and his wife, Frankie, who invited her for a visit. Now, instead of seeing Jim as a burden, Isabella felt repaid for her efforts with him: "such tender love & warm hospitality, now in the hour of my deepest need." She would go next April, she wrote daughter Mary, and have John join her there upon his return (he had escaped to Florida to stay with the Stowes in their winter home). Isabella even looked forward to her sister-in-law's "fondling ways," which she had previously found trying. Participation in the woman movement had changed her attitude toward physical affection between women. The first winter in Washington, she told Mary, she had felt uncomfortable when an NWSA woman "clung" to her, but "this last winter I just rested myself on her soft cheek & her kisses were real food & strength."

Isabella wrote this letter from New Haven, where she was visiting Hannah M. Comstock, a Connecticut colleague in the suffrage movement. She was in the midst of a speaking tour of Connecticut, visiting such towns as New London, Bridgeport, Litchfield, Meriden, Winstead, and Willimantic. A good reception in these places did much to restore Isabella's confidence. Many of the local women admired her openly, as Comstock always did, and some even supported her defense of Woodhull. She discovered, to her surprise, that she was known to ordinary women in Connecticut, women who weren't famous or active as reformers. Contacts with them reminded her of *why* she had undertaken the work that threatened to destroy her family.

At this time Isabella received a pathetic letter from a Mrs. S. H. Graves, a farmer's wife from Norfolk, Connecticut. Mrs. Graves wrote "as to a friend, for you *are* a friend to us all." She had been living in Norfolk for seventeen years with no children and only the "dreary routine of household cares" to occupy her. Her husband spent his free time at the village store while she stayed home mending his clothes. She had begged him to let her take in a child to care for, but he refused because of the expense. "Of course, such a man is bitterly opposed to 'woman's rights' and loses no opportunity for the usual sneer. I have no money and few clothes. He forbids my giving anything away, as everything is *his* and nothing mine. In short I am nothing but a housekeeper without wages, doing *all* the work of the family."

Her husband's father had just buried his fourth wife and would doubtless marry again soon because it cost too much to hire a housekeeper. Contemplating the fate of that fourth wife, who died "willingly," gave Mrs. Graves the courage to address Isabella and ask about her duty. "Now Mrs.

Hooker, please give me a little advice. Is it my duty to spend *all* my life in this way? Would it be wrong for me to go to Hartford this winter for a few weeks or to some other place where people *live?*. . . . I must get away from here for a while or go crazy. Perhaps you will say I am *already* deranged." Isabella's response has not survived, but it would be interesting to know what she advised. Was marriage so sacred that a woman without children had to immolate herself in this way? At the least, Isabella would have seen the letter as a sign that women would no longer be silent.

When she spoke in Bridgeport, she stayed with her friend Olympia Brown. Brownie was unimpressed by Woodhull but did her best to support Isabella. According to Phebe Hanaford, Brown kicked Hanaford out of her house during a "friendly call" in retaliation for Hanaford's snub of Isabella. Brownie told Isabella not to worry, that Hanaford's religion, education, and husband combined to make her mean and narrow. She said she would not attack or persecute Woodhull if she had occasion to work with her in Connecticut; she would treat her as any other co-worker. "I honor you for standing by her." Brownie gave Isabella the most sensible advice about Woodhull she had ever received. She wanted every woman to receive fair treatment and be able to speak her mind; but she suspected that Woodhull might be simply using Isabella and not truly friendly to her or the suffrage movement. She thought they shouldn't "go deeper" with her because she was not "reliable." Brownie went on to give examples of visions, predictions, and promises Victoria had made that had not turned out. Although Isabella did not entirely want to hear this, she did try to listen and steer a course between blind championship of Victoria and support of her right to free speech. It was clear that Brownie understood the principles her friend was trying to uphold and was offering her full friendship and support.

If Isabella had "not one friend" in Hartford, she thus did have supportive colleagues elsewhere in the state. She was also backed by the national leaders. Anthony wrote frequently to assure her that she understood the pressure she was under and took pride in her resistance. She encouraged Isabella to have faith in herself, the greatest requirement for a reformer, and to associate herself with the country's Founding Fathers just as Stanton and Anthony did. She knew her friend would "stand by the side of *all women* who are struggling into freedom—precisely as Jefferson and Washington stood by *all men.*" Stanton and Paulina Wright Davis were also supportive, lauding Isabella for her principled conduct.

Encouragement came from unexpected places. Edward M. Davis, Lucretia Mott's son-in-law, wrote to bless her for taking such a courageous stance on behalf of Victoria Woodhull. Martha Coffin Wright, Mott's sister and the recipient of Stanton's complaints about Isabella's excessive respectability, was completely won over by her behavior at the Washington conference after the one excluding Stanton: "Mrs. Hooker we all liked—she was full of enthusiasm and there is so much real force behind the Beecher self esteem that she commands respect. She's quite free from any arrogance of manner and the 'I am holier than thou' of her Church—liberal and generous to a surprising degree." Even Mary Livermore, an AWSA leader and vocal Woodhull detractor, praised Isabella for not withdrawing from Woodhull in Washington; if she had, she would have deserved the same rebuke Jesus Christ gave his disciples when they told him they had forbidden a man to cast out devils because he was not a follower of Christ.

In December Isabella wrote a poem that summed up her work for the year and her conviction that the "lips of women are being unsealed." The new woman's club Sorosis had asked her to speak in New York. With her regrets she sent, instead of an essay, some verses based on the Greek myth of the Sphinx, whose riddles could not be answered.

> Woman—Sphinx of the secret yet untold,
> On human wastes outlooking, sad & dumb,
> At last hears Memnon's lips of sunlit gold
> Proclaim to earth her day of honor come.
> And now her long, mute, weary non-age o'er,
> She calmly sits her own interpreter;
> Oh man!—her unsolved riddle vex no more
> With your rude guesses—'She's of Age—Ask Her.'

This poem anticipates by some thirty years Muriel Rukeyser's witty "The Myth," in which Oedipus asks the Sphinx what he did wrong that led him to his tragedy. The Sphinx replies that when he answered her famous question (what walks on four legs in the morning, two at noon, and three in the evening?) he replied "Man" but said nothing about women.

When Isabella went to Washington in January for the 1872 convention, she had another grandchild, her daughter Alice's namesake, Alice Hooker Day (born January 3). The convention also gave her a needed boost. In many ways it resembled the Washington meeting the year before, only this year Victoria Woodhull's presence came as no surprise and the stated purpose was to discuss the New Departure. Isabella presided again, and Mrs. Satan sat on the platform with Mrs. Stanton and the other leaders. Victoria had recently been elected president of the American Association of Spiritualists; her first speech was on Spiritualism. Living up to her nickname, she spoke about the denizens of the invisible sphere. The spirits had mapped out a better world to be ruled by women, Woodhull insisted, and they were making preparations to bring it about.

This speech electrified Isabella, who was leaning more and more toward Spiritualism. Her own speech was more mundane. She reported on the work of her National Woman Suffrage and Educational Committee, which had recommended that women attempt to register and vote in every election. Furthermore, "men and women should pour out money like water" to spread the word on the New Departure. Isabella thought every family in the United States should be sent a copy of the Declaration of Independence and the Constitution, "together with an argument on the fair interpretation of these documents." The convention approved another resolution demanding that Congress pass a declaratory act paving the way for women to vote under the Fourteenth and Fifteenth Amendments. In order to cover every possibility, Isabella also tried the executive route. She wrote President Grant asking for a presidential proclamation to electors instructing them to admit women to their electoral rights; she added a note to Mrs. Grant urging her to emulate the Biblical Esther and use her influence to save her people.

The lobbying activities that accompanied the convention were also much like the previous year's. This time the memorial to Congress was prepared by Stanton, Anthony, and Hooker. Isabella's contribution was a long, detailed legal argument, probably written or heavily influenced by John, supporting the idea that the Fourteenth and Fifteenth Amendments already enfranchised women. The women presented their memorial before the Judiciary Committee again. They had asked to deliver it before Congress but were turned down. This refusal was but one ominous sign that Isabella's (and the NWSA's) optimism about soon getting the vote was uncalled for. The suffragists made no advances in 1872 on the gains of their previous year in Washington. Also, a disturbing development occurred that represented a step backward. Before the convention met, a group of wives and widows of high-ranking military officers, led by "Mrs. Admiral Dahlgren" and "Mrs. General Sherman," presented their own petition to Congress. It opposed suffrage for women and argued that no "general law" affecting the condition of all women should be framed to meet "exceptional discontent." The petition was signed by over a thousand "ladies," including Isabella's enemy within, Catharine Beecher.

The NWSA made a clever and amusing response. Matilda Joslyn Gage, chair of the Committee of Arrangements, invited Dahlgren and her cohorts to debate woman suffrage at the convention. As you have publicly expressed your opposition to women voting, wrote Gage, we feel sure you will accept our invitation. In other words, she pointed out the irony in the Dahlgren group's addressing Congress when they claimed that women shouldn't act in the public sphere. When Dahlgren replied, declining to debate because of the need to preserve "female modesty," she thus had to address this paradox. She responded rather weakly that they had petitioned Congress because "the right of petition may safely be considered so common to all, and its exercise most beneficial." The conservative women had come a long way in thirty-five years—since 1837, when Catharine Beecher had argued in her *Essay on Slavery* that ladies should not petition.

It is not clear whether the conservative petition directly affected Congress's treatment (or nontreatment) of the NWSA proposals. But it doubtless had a negative effect on the association's main initiative for the year. That year, 1872, was a presidential election year. The Boston wing of the women's movement was committed to the Republican nominee, President Grant, in spite of the corruption of his administration. For one thing, the Fifteenth Amendment had not yet been ratified, and the AWSA was determined to see it through. The NWSA had no such commitments. The women attending the Washington convention decided informally that they would support whatever party adopted a woman suffrage plank. Representatives from the NWSA would be sent to all the nominating conventions. It was obvious, though, that their only bargaining chip was the promise of persuading "women," that is, the great majority of women, to support the party. If some of these women were vocally anti-suffrage, it weakened a position that was already weak because women couldn't withhold their vote from a party that displeased them. Ironically, the greatest bar to women's getting the vote was that they couldn't vote already.

Isabella still felt optimistic about gaining a suffrage plank. She wanted to support the Democrats, for she had come to think that the suffragists had to demolish the hypocritical Republican Party before they could make any progress for women. She made no secret of her views. She even told Senator Sumner, she wrote Anthony from Washington, that the NWSA was looking for honest Democrats who believed in human rights and would repudiate Republicans who were not in earnest about backing woman suffrage. The Republican senators replied that the New Departure was "worthless" and would damage the women's cause. When Anthony passed Isabella's letter on to Olympia Brown, she added a note: "It takes Mrs. Hooker to keep the 'animals' of the Washington menagerie *stirred up*." Good work at the Capitol, she wrote her colleague.

Isabella decided to devote the coming year to the election. She wrote Brownie that "My husband & *daughters* have withdrawn all opposition at last—& bid me God speed in my work if I will not invite Mrs. Woodhull into the campaign." Fortunately, Victoria was occupied with her own attempt to run for president. After Washington Isabella set up what she called her "headquarters" in New Haven, where there was less opposition to her than at Hartford. Ned remained in Hartford at his sister Mary's, and mother and son visited back and forth. Isabella claimed to Ned that she wished she could be in Florida with his father "eating sweet oranges & chatting under the trees with Aunt Hatty & Uncle Charles—instead of driving round in these dreadful March winds."

She mentioned Uncle Charles because Charles Beecher was now living in Florida also. Harriet had first tried to enlist him as a minister for the Mandarin area, provided he would convert to the Episcopalian faith. He refused but soon bought a plantation in Newport, on the Gulf Coast near Tallahassee. Charles, perhaps through Harriet's influence, was appointed state superintendent of agriculture and public instruction. Harriet was accustomed to friends and relatives from the North coming to visit and then buying land in Florida—Eunice Beecher, Henry's wife, did this as well as Charles. Some of the tourists, however, were strangers to whom Harriet Beecher Stowe's house was a sight. The owners of a local steamboat began to sell round-trip tickets from Jacksonville to Mandarin, hinting that a glimpse of Harriet might be had. According to a favorite family anecdote, one day Calvin was in his usual position reading on the veranda when the boat landed. Ordinarily the tourists tramped over the grounds peering at the house, but this day a woman stepped boldly on to the veranda and introduced herself to Calvin. "But I would have preferred to meet Mrs. Stowe," she added. "So had I, Madam," Calvin reportedly replied. "So had I a thousand times."

During winter 1872 the little structure used for school during the week and church on Sundays (Harriet taught the black Sunday school) burned down. The Stowes were pleased when the neighborhood families pledged sums of money to rebuild, for they believed in education as the key to transforming the South. Harriet occupied herself writing the sketches about life in Florida that would appear in the *Christian Union* and then constitute her next book. This was the type of writing she most enjoyed—not rushing to keep up with a long serial novel but composing at her leisure in a relaxed, informal way. She relished the opportunity to be "chatty" about everyday life. Many of the sketches were addressed to "girls," indicating Stowe's sense of writing for a less critical audience than usual. This audience would not be bored by long descriptions of birds and wildflowers or offended by the author's complaints against hunters shooting alligators for sport. Harriet eventually entitled the book *Palmetto-Leaves* after the shrub she and the twins pressed, dried, and made into fans. This title harkened back to the women-writing-for-women tradition of the 1850s when female authors adopted woodsy pseudonyms and titles. "Grace Greenwood" (Sara Clark Lippincott) contributed *Greenwood Leaves* (1850) and Harriet's friend Fanny Fern, *Fern Leaves from Fanny's Portfolio* (1853) and further series of "leaves."

In many ways the Stowes' life in Florida was idyllic. "Picnicking Up

Julington," for instance, tells of a fishing trip on Leap Year Day, February 29. The Stowe party took rowboats up Julington Creek (as wide as the Connecticut River at Hartford, Harriet says) and fished among the water lilies. They cooked the fish by digging a hole in the sand, lining it with wet lily leaves, wrapping the fish in more leaves, and starting a fire. Harriet describes other pleasure trips in 1872, but of course she still agonized over Fred's disappearance; as he had been gone for a year, there was little hope. It helped her, she wrote, "to fly from place to place, so that I cannot think continuously." But she wrote a friend's husband who had lost his son: "Oh, my dear brother, think of your blessedness by my sorrow. Where is my poor Fred? You know where Frank is, and that he is safe and blessed. I never forget my boy."

Back in the cold winds of New Haven Isabella was in her element. Sister Catharine tried to stir up some opposition, writing to her friend Leonard Bacon in New Haven. "'My soul is cast down,'" she wailed, "at the ignorance and mistaken zeal of my poor sister Bell and her coagitators—Can you not lend a helping pen to show . . . how much *moral* power is gained by taking a subordinate place." But Isabella had support in the town of her new headquarters. She started a society that held weekly meetings and worked to prepare Connecticut women to vote. Her goal and that of Olympia Brown was to encourage women to vote in small numbers in every town in Connecticut. This task entailed persuading women that they were capable of voting as well as showing them how to register and getting town registrars to accept female voters. Isabella gave many speeches encouraging women to vote and announced in the New Haven newspapers her presence at Hannah Comstock's and her willingness to provide applications to be registered. She would give all necessary assistance to those women "desiring to become electors for the first time." Her lobbying efforts with state officials seemed to be bearing fruit. A Mr. Bradley, a pro-suffrage Republican, assured her that the Republican leaders had decided to allow women to register without any opposition from them, leaving the question up to the officials of the individual towns.

Isabella also spent time writing letters and talking to delegates to the three upcoming presidential nominating conventions due to meet in the summer. There were three, not two, because a group of liberal Republicans, disgusted with the corruption of the Grant administration, had bolted the party. The Liberals would meet in May in Cincinnati, the regular Republicans in Philadelphia in June, and the Democrats in Baltimore in July. Would female delegates be received at the Liberal convention on equal terms with men? Isabella asked Benjamin Gratz Brown, who would be nominated as the vice presidential candidate. Would the Democrats include a woman suffrage plank in their platform, she inquired of Archibald Dixon, senator from Kentucky.

There was also the alternative of a new party. While Susan B. Anthony made a back-breaking speaking tour of the West, earning money to repay the debts of the defunct *Revolution*, Victoria Woodhull convinced the other leaders that the May NWSA meeting should be devoted to the formation of a new political party. The call was signed by Isabella, Matilda Joslyn Gage, Stanton and, without her knowledge, Anthony. The signers assumed that holding a political convention was a logical step in educating women for voting and party responsibilities. Suffragist Abigail Scott Duniway of Oregon, attending her first eastern convention, reported back to her newspaper that "It was the purpose of these ladies to hold a large, enthusiastic, dignified Convention, uniting many reform elements."

Anthony, however, would not go along. She considered it farcical for women, "the majority of whom do not even own our bodies to say nothing of our purses," to try to form a political party. Her distrust of Woodhull had also deepened, and she suspected Victoria of using the NWSA only to further her personal ambitions. Anthony wrote Stanton, employing her customary metaphor of the woman movement as a ship, that Woodhull "persistently means to run our craft into her port and none other. If she were influenced by *women* spirits . . . I might consent to be a mere sail-hoister for her; but as it is, she is wholly owned and dominated by *men* spirits and I spurn the control of the whole lot of them." So Anthony demanded the removal of her name from the convention call and hurried East to take charge of the meeting.

Anthony and Stanton quarreled vociferously, with Isabella taking Stanton's part in accusing their colleague of being narrow. Anthony, however, managed to control the convention by virtue of her status as an unmarried woman. Because she had remained single, she was always the suffrage leader to sign contracts and assume financial responsibility (hence her efforts to pay the *Revolution* debt). The meeting hall was rented in Anthony's name. When Woodhull announced that her People's Party was convening jointly with the NWSA, Anthony stepped forth and denied it; she had rented the hall solely for a suffrage convention, and any member of the audience who did not belong to the NWSA should leave. Woodhull and her followers walked out and managed to rent another space, Apollo Hall. She returned in the evening and tried to get the NWSA convention adjourned to meet there. Anthony again repulsed her: the association of the NWSA with Victoria Woodhull was over.

The next day Victoria's convention organized a new party, which they named the Equal Rights Party, and nominated Woodhull for president and Frederick Douglass (without his knowledge) for vice president. Of the competing NWSA meeting, Anthony wrote in her diary, "Small audience. The fiasco perfect, from calling People's Convention. Never did Mrs. Stanton do so foolish a thing. All came near being lost." She did not mention Woodhull in her diary, and years later in the *History of Woman Suffrage* the only reference is to Woodhull's 1871 memorial to Congress.

In Anthony's mind she was not repudiating or silencing Woodhull—she was simply preventing her organization from being taken over. She never publicly criticized Woodhull. The claim of a twentieth-century historian that Anthony and Stanton "denounced" Woodhull is false, though they did separate their path from hers. Isabella, characteristically viewing the whole "fiasco" in the most optimistic way, saw it as another split that would not necessarily damage the cause. There were now three organizations in the women's movement: the NWSA, the AWSA, and the Equal Rights Party. In Isabella's view these organizations could be allies and address different aspects of the issues: the AWSA would work on state suffrage and attract conservatives, the NWSA would concentrate on the New Departure and appeal to more radical women, and Woodhull's party would move beyond suffrage to deal with more diverse issues. As she wrote Stanton after the May meeting, there were now "three columns" pursuing the battle. Isabella may have preferred to be in Woodhull's column, but loyalty to Anthony and promises to her family kept her in the NWSA. She was still friendly to Woodhull. When Dr. Canning Woodhull died, she wrote Victoria to praise her kindness to him and say she felt they were sisters. She continued trying to argue Victoria out of her belief in free love, warning that men might use such a doctrine to overindulge themselves.

Much to Anthony's annoyance, Isabella was still attracted to the Equal Rights Party. I thought you felt the good Lord had "extricated you from your entanglement" with Woodhull, Anthony wrote. So how can you urge Frederick Douglass to accept the vice presidential nomination? Isabella replied that she had no intention of "cutting loose" the Equal Rights Party. She might even join them when "my dear husband is well over the Ocean, where he can't be troubled by my radicalism." John was indeed going to Europe. He tried to persuade Isabella to accompany him, which he had been doing for the past fifteen years. She always had an excuse—they should spend the money on the house, she didn't want to leave her loved ones behind. This time she had a more substantial reason not to go—she wanted to vote. She convinced John to take with him some other people who needed to get away: their daughter Mary, who was experiencing ups and downs in her marriage to Eugene Burton, and their minister, Nathaniel Burton, who needed a rest. Although Isabella missed them, she also felt relieved. She was freer to indulge in politics. Still, the first priority was to be a good neighbor. In June 1872 Mark Twain's toddler son, Langdon, died of diphtheria. Isabella's niece Lillie Warner wrote her husband that "Aunt Belle has been a great comfort" to the Clemenses. She "was with them Sat. night & has been nearly ever since, taking charge of things in her energetic & most kind way."

The month after the boy's death Isabella went to Baltimore to the Democratic convention. The Democrats were the suffragists' last hope. The Liberal Republicans had been polite to the women attending their convention and even allowed them to sit on the platform. The NWSA women were encouraged because journalist Theodore Tilton, who had been an active suffragist, was a power at the convention. But there would be no woman suffrage plank in the party platform; even Tilton made an about-face and argued that suffrage should be pursued through discussion in the media and not urged on political parties. The Liberal Republicans chose as their presidential candidate Horace Greeley, a man known to oppose political rights for women. "I hate Greeley," Isabella said of him, "as I never hated a man before in my life." Susan B. Anthony made a penetrating comment after the convention: "You see our cause is just where the anti-slavery cause was for a long time. It had plenty of friends and supporters three years out of four, but every fourth year, when a President was to be elected, it was lost sight of; then the nation was to be saved and the slave must be sacrificed. So it is with us women."

The traditional Republican convention was a slight improvement, owing primarily to the behind-the-scenes maneuvering of the AWSA. They succeeded in persuading their Republican friends to include the following statement in their platform: "The Republican party mindful of its obligation to the loyal women of America expresses gratification that wider avenues of employment have been open to women, and it further declares that her demands for additional rights, should be treated with respectful consideration." Many suffragists thought this plank seemed more of a splinter. Tilton ridiculed it as meaning the same as "Very truly yours" at the end of a letter. Isabella and Susan hoped to do better in Baltimore. They knew Greeley would be the chosen candidate but were willing to back even him with a strong woman suffrage platform plank. Isabella had been corresponding with various Democrats and had the promise of support from William Gallagher, a delegate to the convention from New Haven.

Isabella and Susan lobbied as best they could. The *Baltimore Sun* describes an interview they had in the corridor with James R. Doolittle, who was president of the convention: "Mr. Doolittle's erect and commanding figure was set off to great advantage by his elegantly-fitting dress-coat; Mrs. Hooker, tall and erect as the lord of creation she was bearding, with her abundant tresses of beautiful gray and her intellectual, sparkling eyes; Miss Anthony, the peer of both in height, with her gold spectacles set forward on a nose which would have delighted Napoleon; the two ladies attired in rich black silk—the attention of the few who lingered was at once attracted to the picture."

But if the women made a pretty picture, they were not allowed to talk on the convention floor. Doolittle did nothing, the women could not get seated on the platform, and a gag rule was invoked to stop them from addressing the convention as Gallagher had arranged. The Democrats simply adopted the candidates and platform of the Liberal Republicans. There was no woman suffrage plank. The day after the convention, a disappointed Isabella wrote out a statement of "the opinion of the suffrage ladies attending the Baltimore Convention—Miss Anthony, Mrs. Beecher Hooker and Mrs. Laura de Force Gordon." The Democratic Party rejected the opportunity to champion the rights of individuals and "hence has been attending its own funeral." Women should support the Republicans because of their platform statement, the pro–woman suffrage convictions of the candidate for vice president, Henry Wilson, and the efforts of President Grant in appointing fourteen hundred women to post office jobs.

There was thus a temporary alliance with the AWSA as the two organizations planned their activities on behalf of the Republican ticket. Isabella put her name on the list of suffragists willing to stump for Grant, though she told Henry Blackwell she would rather speak in Massachusetts and have Lucy come to Connecticut; it would be embarrassing to work against the Democrats in her home state when she had just been courting them. Although she could hardly get excited about the Grant campaign, she was enthusiastic about voting. "I mean to vote this Fall," she assured Anthony. But, warned of the women's intentions, election officials all over the country increased security. While Anthony and nineteen other Quaker women succeeded in casting their ballots in Rochester, New York, Isabella could not even enter the polling place in Hartford.

After the disappointment of the Democratic convention Isabella could have backed the Equal Rights Party instead of the Republicans. By this time, however, Woodhull's affairs were in such disarray there wasn't much party left. Again her family did her in. Unbeknown to the rest of the family, Victoria's mother, Roxanna, killed the golden goose. She sent a blackmailing letter to Cornelius Vanderbilt, causing him to withdraw his patronage. Without Vanderbilt's advice the brokerage floundered. Victoria began to run out of money and was evicted when she couldn't meet the rent on her house; *Woodhull & Claflin's Weekly* was forced to suspend publication. Victoria's jealous sister Utica made things worse by informing the authorities that Dr. Woodhull had died under suspicious circumstances. Although an autopsy cleared her of any wrongdoing, Victoria found herself attacked in the newspapers again. Speaking engagements were canceled; hotels turned the family away. By fall Victoria was so angry and desperate that during a speech to the National Association of Spiritualists, the one organization that still supported her, she suddenly felt inspired to "tell all." That is, she revealed all she knew or suspected about the sexual affairs of various prominent persons.

Unfortunately for women's rights, most of the people Woodhull named were associated in some way with the movement. For instance, she exposed the extramarital affair of Lucy Stone's husband, Henry Blackwell, with Abby Hutchinson Patton, one of the Hutchinson Family Singers. She accused Anna Dickinson of carrying on a liaison with Wendell Phillips, a married man. Phebe Hanaford, the AWSA member and minister who kept Isabella from speaking in her church, was said to practice free love. The most prominent person indicted was Isabella's brother Henry Ward Beecher, who had once been president of the AWSA. One of the Spiritualists in the convention audience later wrote that "Mrs. Woodhull's speech poured out like a stream of flame," which scorched everyone in its path.

Apparently many of those Victoria accused she had earlier tried to blackmail, yet this time her motive wasn't money. Nor did she condemn the people she named for having affairs. Their sin in her view was hypocrisy. Why should she be ruined for admitting she believed in free love when a man like Beecher lived in luxury and basked in everyone's admiration? After all, he secretly practiced what Victoria Woodhull preached. As she told the press, she criticized him not for exercising his "demanding physical nature" but for failing to do what she did, "to stand shoulder to shoulder with me and others who are endeavoring to hasten a social regeneration which he believes in." Woodhull did not rest content with her speech alone but scraped together the money for a special issue of *Woodhull & Claflin's Weekly* (November 2, 1872) that repeated the charges in print.

When Isabella wrote John in Europe about the scandal, he was shocked to hear about their friend Anna Dickinson. Why did these horrible stories have to be divulged? Like other people at the time, John worried about the effects on the movement. "When all this comes out—the H.[enry] story and that of Anna D. and Philips [sic], all woman suffragists, it will give that cause a heavy blow." He feared the scandal would "create a reaction in the public mind that will send the struggle down to another generation and postpone its triumph for thirty years." Many people thought the same. The AWSA had, of course, attacked Woodhull from the beginning (perhaps because she knew too much?) and tried to rid the movement of "side issues," like marriage and divorce, that could damage its reputation. They thought the "'Free Love' incubus" had already "done incalculable harm to the cause of woman suffrage." Perhaps so. Certainly Victoria Woodhull's personal association with the movement and the scandals she revealed did not help the cause. Ever since the pioneering British feminist Mary Wollstonecraft lived with a man without being married, the enemies of women's rights had tried to link improved status for women with a loosening of morals. Woodhull gave them plenty of material. But Eleanor Flexner argues in her classic history of the suffrage movement that the scandal did not "set the cause of woman suffrage back for many years, as has been maintained; it was no help, but there were far too many other forces pushing it forward" for the scandal to have any lasting impact.

When Woodhull made her fiery speech accusing Henry Ward Beecher of adultery, Harriet was just beginning a tour of public readings in New England. She too had taken up speaking. As usual, her finances were shaky and James Fields urged her to take advantage of the "easy money" available on the lecture circuit. But like Isabella and other suffragists when they began their women's rights careers, Harriet had no experience speaking in public and was nervous. Her first reading took place in Springfield, Massachusetts, on Friday, September 13. The audience was large and, according to the local paper, "one of the best that ever turned out, representing the most intelligent of all classes of society." Harriet, however, considered her debut a failure. She was stricken with stage fright, her voice did not carry well, and she did not hold the attention of her audience.

Rather than give up, Harriet drew inspiration from the well she had often tapped before—her father. When she arrived at the Fieldses prior to her dreaded Boston reading at the Tremont Temple, she called Annie Fields into her bedroom. She stood before the mirror, having brushed her short gray hair, which usually lay in curls around her face, straight up. Annie recalled the scene as follows: "'Look here, my dear,' she said; 'now I am exactly like my father, Dr. Lyman Beecher, when he was going to preach,' and she held up her forefinger warningly [in a typical Lyman gesture]. It was easy to see that the spirit of the old preacher was revived in her veins, and . . . when I sat with her in the ante-room waiting for the moment of her appearance to arrive, I could feel the power surging up within her. I knew she was armed for a good fight."

In Boston there was standing room only. The entrance halls were jammed with crowds that extended to the street and blocked the sidewalk. Introduced by William Lloyd Garrison, Harriet read first from *Uncle Tom's Cabin;* she usually recited comic passages with Topsy and the scenes of Little Eva's death and Eliza's escape over the ice. After an intermission she read selections from New England works, such as *Oldtown Folks* and *The Pearl of Orr's Island,* making sure to render orally the regional dialects she had pioneered in writing. Harriet's interpretation of character and use of dialect were the most praised aspects of her performance. There was still a problem with her soft voice but, at least in Boston as Annie Fields noted, "When her voice was not sufficient to make the audience hear, men and women rose from their seats and crowded round her, standing gladly, that no word might be lost."

Harriet thus lived up to the occasion, but she did not enjoy the life of a traveling lecturer any more than Isabella had. She was scheduled for forty readings and the travel was strenuous, particularly for a woman over sixty. The tour had its high points, such as the children she met named Eva and Harriet and the deaf old woman from Maine who couldn't hear the reading but came just to *see* Harriet Beecher Stowe—"I'd ruther see you than the Queen." But all in all it was lonely. She wrote Calvin, "I check off place after place as the captive the days of his imprisonment." Harriet also worried about the accusation against Henry, which struck her heart "like a knife," and about Calvin's poor health and low spirits in her absence. She teased him gently, asking him to "remain with us yet a little longer, and let us have a little quiet evening together before either of us crosses the river. My heart cries out for a home with you—our home together in Florida. Oh, may we see it again!"

At this point the Mandarin home was their only one, and it may have been concern for Calvin's health that motivated Harriet to make a quick visit to Hartford to buy another house. The Stowes had sold Oakholm in 1870. The so-called dream house had always been a sinkhole for money, and the neighborhood was rapidly deteriorating. Factories were moving closer to that part of Nook Farm, and the Park River became polluted, reverting to its original name of Hog or Meandering Swine. From 1870 to 1872 the Stowes had spent their northern summers visiting—usually Georgie in Massachusetts or Charles, who was now a Congregational minister in Saco, Maine. Now Harriet bought the Franklin Chamberlain house on Forest Street, the house now preserved as the "Harriet Beecher Stowe House." Although she described it to brother Charles as "a pretty cottage . . . near Belle," it was actually a comfortable three-story home.

In November, as Harriet finished up her tour, she was pleased to hear that Victoria Woodhull and her sister Tennie had been arrested. They were charged with sending obscene material through the mails (the issue of *Woodhull & Claflin's Weekly* that charged Henry Ward Beecher with adultery). As the U.S. district attorney was a pillar of Henry's church and the complainant also a member of the congregation, the sisters had a point when they complained about being railroaded. After spending a month in jail, Victoria decided she wanted to speak in Boston on the topic of "Moral Cowardice & Moral Hypocrisy, or Four Weeks in Ludlow Street Jail." Harriet was much more effective in preventing this speech than Catharine had been in Hartford. Instead of using the press and creating interest in Woodhull, she worked behind the scenes. She got her friends Governor Claflin and his wife (no relation to Victoria's birth family) to use their influence to deny Woodhull a city permit to speak. In a letter to Annie, Harriet gloated, reflecting that "those obscene birds" Victoria and Tennie had been turned away without any publicity. "They perfectly long to be abused in the papers & they cant [sic] get it." Harriet wrote the twins indignantly, "The impudence of those witches is incredible!" She seems to have taken the "Mrs. Satan" joke seriously and actually believed that Victoria was in league with the Devil. As she wrote Henry, she sincerely believed the wretched Woodhull was more than flesh and blood.

It may be tempting even now to see Woodhull as the devil woman who derailed the women's movement, ruining Henry's and Isabella's lives in the process. But if Woodhull hadn't blown the whistle on Henry Ward Beecher when she did, someone else probably would have done so eventually. The wronged husband, Theodore Tilton, was furiously angry at Beecher, as was one of the church trustees, Henry Bowen, whose wife had made a deathbed confession of an affair with Beecher. Isabella's family relationships may also have disintegrated to the extent they did even without Victoria Woodhull. Just as someone would probably have exposed Beecher, some other person or principle would likely have claimed Isabella's loyalty and tenacity. The real issue was not Victoria Woodhull but Isabella's devotion to women's rights in general and a single sexual standard in particular. As the editors of *The Limits of Sisterhood* conclude, "Isabella's bold defense of women's right to free speech, whatever their 'antecedents,' completed her break with the tradition of her elder sisters Catharine and Harriet. Hooker's principled stance, sustained even in the face of Woodhull's subsequent denunciation of Henry Ward Beecher, constitutes one of her most important contributions as a reformer and demonstrates her insightful grasp of the politics of sisterhood."

If Victoria Woodhull seemed the major issue to Catharine, Mary, and Harriet, she was less so to Isabella's daughters and sons-in-law. Interestingly, Mary Hooker Burton wrote a letter in 1871 defending her mother in a situation having nothing to do with Woodhull. She addressed the reporter Mary Clemmer Ames, who in a New York newspaper had ridiculed Isabella's manner in offering a prayer before the congressional hearing. Mary Burton described her mother as a "tender mother and devoted wife" who spent her time ministering to the sick and poor—in other words, a domestic "true woman" of the century: "The question of woman suffrage is little discussed in our family. My mother is content to have each one hold her own opinion. I have never heard my mother speak in public. But, knowing the woman, I know you have misrepresented both her manner and speech. Whatever she does she does with her whole heart, but that she would appear other than an earnest, womanly, modest woman, absorbed in (to her) a great cause, is impossible." In this stiffly correct letter Isabella's fault is seen as simply risking her modesty and becoming an actor on the public stage where her behavior could be misinterpreted by others. For Isabella to become an outcast, for Henry to be exposed as an adulterer, they hardly needed Mrs. Satan.

9

The Beecher-Tilton Scandal,
1872–1875

THE ACCUSATION THAT Henry Ward Beecher had an affair with Elizabeth "Lib" Tilton, one of his parishioners, did not come as news to the Beecher sisters. The gossip about Henry and various women had been circulating for years. In fact, Victoria Woodhull claimed to have heard it first at the same time she met Isabella. She said that at the Capitol, before the congressional hearing in January 1871, Benjamin Butler had instructed her to ignore any possible snubs from members of the National Woman Suffrage Association, especially from their leader, Isabella Beecher Hooker. A congressman nearby overheard this comment and remarked that a Beecher could hardly snub Mrs. Woodhull, "for I am reliably assured that Henry Ward Beecher preaches to at least twenty of his mistresses every Sunday."

As for the Beecher-Tilton affair, Lib Tilton confessed to her friend Paulina Wright Davis, who told Susan B. Anthony, Hooker, and Elizabeth Cady Stanton, who told Woodhull. Theodore Tilton also complained to Stanton about the affair. In spring 1872, even before Woodhull's announcement, the gossip was so intense that Isabella anxiously wrote Henry. His reply was disappointing. He did not deny the affair but asked for her silence: "You know my sympathy with you. Probably you and I are nearer together than any of our family. I cannot give reason now. . . . Of some things I *neither talk nor will I be talked with*. For love and sympathy I am deeply thankful. The only help that can be grateful to me or useful is silence and a silencing influence on all others. A day may come for converse. It is not now. Living or dead, my dear sister Belle, *love me*, and do not talk about me."

Isabella did keep quiet for a time, but as Milton Rugoff says, advising silence was "like recommending nonchalance in the eye of a hurricane." When Beecher was publicly accused, everyone was pressured to choose sides. Most of Henry's siblings decided to believe him innocent. Harriet admitted to her daughter that she could not even entertain the possibility of guilt. "[T]here are things which strike my *very life* and these accusations against my brother are among them. I cannot hear that subject discussed as a *possibility* open for inquiry without such an intense uprising of indignation and scorn and anger as very few have ever seen in me in these late years."

In this letter Harriet was not exaggerating her feelings in the slightest. Her relationship with Henry, who was two years younger, had always been an intense one since Harriet Porter Beecher described them at ages six and four as always hand-in-hand. They were just as close in thought and feeling; unbeknown to their stepmother, they saw themselves as neglected orphans banded together against her and the world. (Hence, as critic Janet Emig notes, the large number of unparented and abandoned children who populate Stowe's fiction. She tended to replicate in her novels the emotional relationships of her childhood.)

Harriet wrote George Eliot a long letter about Henry after the scandal was over. Although (or maybe because) the two authors never met but only corresponded, Harriet tended to express her deepest feelings in letters to the British writer. She began as follows: "It seems now but a little time since my brother Henry and I were two young people together. He was my two years' junior, and nearest companion out of seven brothers and three sisters. I taught him drawing and heard his Latin Lessons, for you know a girl becomes mature and womanly long before a boy. I saw him through college, and helped him through the difficult love affair that gave him his wife; and then he and my husband had a real German, enthusiastic love for each other, which ended in making me a wife." No doubt she meant a wife to Calvin, but the awkward phrasing of the last sentence suggests that Henry somehow made Harriet a wife, an occurrence untrue on any level but the emotional. But it was true that growing up and separating from each other created difficulties for the sister and brother. Harriet did not mention in the letter her negative feelings about Henry's wife, Eunice. While all the Beechers disliked Eunice, Harriet strongly resented her—because, says Rugoff, "she had taken Henry away."

The letter to Eliot continues with a summary of the siblings' adult lives, in which Harriet emphasizes their similar beliefs and actions—their move away from Calvinism to a more progressive theology as "Christworshipers," their fight against the Fugitive Slave Law and slavery itself. In regard to slavery, "there are those who never saw our faces that to this hour hate him and me." Henry's phenomenal popularity also created enemies, Harriet thought, in those people prone to envy. (Elsewhere she identified "the enemy" as Tilton, who was jealous of Henry's success and sought his downfall.) She concluded her letter about Henry by saying that the scandal "has drawn on my life—my heart's blood. He is myself; I know you are the kind of woman to understand me when I say that I felt a blow at him more than at myself. I, who know his purity, honor, delicacy, know that he has been

Henry Ward Beecher and Harriet Beecher Stowe, c. 1860. Courtesy Harriet Beecher Stowe Center, Hartford, Conn.

from childhood of an ideal purity. . . . Never have I known a nature of such strength, and such almost childlike innocence." "He is myself"—or as another nineteenth-century novelist, Emily Brontë, had her heroine cry in *Wuthering Heights* (1847): "I *am* Heathcliff!"

It is revealing that every time Harriet defended her brother she referred to their childhood and his "purity" as a child. She wrote one correspondent that she could not think of him as anything other than young and another that "he is more angel than brother—he is too good for me—I sit and think over all his sorrow, all the *injustice* that was at one time done him—& all his gentle childlike tenderness of heart." She thus fixed Henry eternally in childhood at a time before he was capable of committing any sexual misdeeds. The delicate boy was now a short, fat man of sixty; he weighed over two hundred pounds and had a florid face with large, sensual lips. Harriet's unrealistic view of Henry as a pure angel child is what psychologists call a "frozen image." That is to say, she froze her perceptions of her brother, "keeping the other sibling bound to an old identity—an indelible, irrevocable, unchanged and unchanging characterization of the self."

Brothers in Stowe's novels, Janet Emig points out, always come in two types—dark and fair, with all the stereotyped connotations this coloring had at the time. Thus the light-complected Augustine St. Clare in *Uncle Tom's Cabin* has an evil twin with coal-black hair and flashing black eyes. The dark brothers are Byronic heroes (or villains). Emig thinks the reason Harriet chose to write the Byron article at the time she did is because she'd heard the rumors about Henry and Lib Tilton; she had to handle her fear of the cherished fair brother's being truly a dark brother. "By isolating and embodying in Byron the wickedness of the dark brother in love with his sister, the act of bifurcation, always useful for Mrs. Stowe, had performed its most significant role: it had restored her brother to his primal innocence."

Whether or not one accepts this explanation as the unconscious motive for Harriet's exposé of Byron, it is clear that she could not be rational concerning her brother. She was unable to look dispassionately at the evidence against him or deal fairly with his accusers. The depth of her feeling for Henry explains the oddness of her demonization of Victoria Woodhull. It is odd because Harriet was a person who ordinarily went out of her way to seek balance—witness her having Uncle Tom's persecutor Simon Legree come from the North instead of the South. When she is criticized today, she is usually seen as being too conciliatory and wishy-washy, unwilling to make a strong stand. Speaking of Legree, Harriet said nothing of him or other slave-drivers that was anywhere near as extreme as her characterization of Woodhull as a witch, a prostitute, an actual devil. She was almost as vitriolic about

Elizabeth Cady Stanton, who had been an abolitionist, referring to "Mrs. Stanton & the free love roost of harpies generally."

Unfortunately, one of the "harpies" was sister Isabella, who suspected what most modern commentators have concluded: Henry was guilty of adultery and gross hypocrisy in covering it up. The evidence against Beecher was overwhelming, as the *New York Times* pointed out at the time. People who did not know Isabella or Henry well have made the suggestion that she believed him guilty because they had a bad relationship and she hated him. Henry himself contradicted this theory with his "you and I are nearer together than any of our family" statement. He may have been exaggerating in his letter to flatter Isabella and ensure her silence—he and Harriet, nearest in age, were certainly closest. Nevertheless, Isabella and Henry had always regarded each other as favorites. He had listened to her confidences growing up, and she rewarded him with an admiration he seldom received from his siblings. He had been considered one of the least promising Beecher children, but Isabella was always enthusiastic about his future as a minister. When he was starting out in Indiana, Isabella wrote John, "I think he is going somewhat in father's track & will perhaps one day come somewhere near him in eminence." An understatement, to be sure, but a prediction no one else would have made.

Isabella and Henry maintained their friendship over the years. Indeed, her doubts about him stemmed not only from the reliability of Lib Tilton's confessors but also her own observations of Henry's marriage and his social theories. She knew his marriage was grim (Eunice was often mistaken for Henry's mother, and the press nicknamed her "the Griffon," a legendary beast). When the Hookers or the Stowes stayed with the Howards in Brooklyn to avoid Eunice, Henry eagerly came to visit and seemed to dread going home. Furthermore, Henry's religious and social ideas had become progressively more liberal and permissive over the years. He had discarded the Calvinist doctrines of his father, such as original sin and the covenant of grace.

Henry's new religion was based on the love of Christ rather than the wrath of God. One no longer had to search one's soul and agonize, praying for grace. Anyone could be converted and come into the church "according to his temperament"; one needed only to hate sin and love God. Then "fired with love to God, the Christian would live according to the law of love to fellow creatures." Love, or what came to be known as "the Gospel of Love," became more and more central to Beecher. In a sermon entitled "Through Fear to Love" he postulated a kind of moral evolution (he was a believer in Darwin's theory of evolution). Morality and virtue begin in fear, but in some people fear gives way to an attraction to goodness that eventually ripens into the highest state, love. People who have evolved to this higher state and are actuated by love do right automatically and no longer require the coercive social institutions that those governed by fear still cling to.

It is only a small step to view marriage as one of these coercive institutions. Lib Tilton said Henry persuaded her that their "high religious love" was holy and did not need to be sanctified by marriage. As their love was not wrong, "it followed that any expression of that love, whether by the shake of the hand or the kiss of the lips, or even bodily intercourse . . . was not wrong." Ironically, Harriet in her novel *My Wife and I* had satirized her Woodhull character's theory as "everything ought to be love, everywhere, above and below, under and over, up and down, top and side and bottom, ought to be *love*, LOVE." But this view was as much her brother's as Woodhull's. As Altina L. Waller states in her book on the scandal: "Victoria Woodhull was entirely accurate when she claimed Beecher as a covert believer in Free Love. Woodhull simply said that all individuals had the right to decide for themselves who they would love—that no laws should govern such personal decisions. This belief coincided with Beecher's conviction that morality, fear, or law had no place in the lives of those who have reached a high religious sphere. The real difference between Woodhull and Beecher lay in the judgment of who was entitled to this freedom of choice. Woodhull was a radical because she advocated for everyone what Beecher reserved for a select few."

Belief in a double standard for Beecher behavior and the rest of humanity seems to have been in large measure a family trait. Henry's thought that his "high religious love" entitled him to break one of the Ten Commandments he urged the masses to keep was not all that different from Harriet's views on George Sand. *She* could read all of Sand's novels without harm as she "investigated" French literature, but Sand was a danger to the majority of women. Catharine thought similarly. By 1874 she was willing to concede in her *Educational Reminiscences and Suggestions* that taxpaying women should have the right to vote; yet she still opposed granting suffrage to women unlike herself, the lower-class and immigrant women.

Today's observers are not the only ones to see a parallel between Beecher's and Woodhull's philosophies. Thomas Beecher did also. With John abroad Isabella felt so alone she wrote to Tom for advice. Tom replied that he realized Woodhull "only carries out Henry's philosophy, against which I recorded my protest twenty years ago and parted (lovingly and achingly) from him, saying, 'We cannot work together.'" In following his "slippery doctrines of expediency," Henry had sacrificed his integrity. "Of the two, Woodhull is my hero, and Henry my coward." But even though Tom agreed with Isabella about Henry's probable guilt, he would do nothing. He would not come to Isabella or send Edward, as she had begged. In fact, he concluded his letter by saying, "Don't write to me." According to Tom, she could not help Henry at present and should simply keep her mouth shut and do nothing. At first glance this advice seems sound. If Isabella had taken it, she would not have been ostracized by her family and friends; her sons-in-law may not have taken action against her, and her subsequent life would have been different. But Isabella faced a genuine dilemma. There were two strong reasons why she could not in good conscience follow brother Tom's apparently sensible advice.

First, there were the women involved. Through various machinations of Henry's allies, Victoria Woodhull and her sister Tennie were kept for months in various jails, including the dreaded New York prison The Tombs. Lib Tilton was being universally reviled. In a letter to Isabella, Henry excoriated Woodhull for "the barbarity of dragging a poor, dear child of a woman into this slough." Isabella expressed a different view in her letter to her younger brother requesting advice: "Now, Tom, so far as I can see, it is he who has dragged the dear child into the slough and left her there and who is now sending another woman to prison who is innocent of all crime but a fanaticism for the truth as revealed to her, and I, by my silence, am consenting unto her death." It seemed to her that Henry was trying to "buy my silence with my love." She could not keep quiet forever, and if Henry would not speak "I cannot always stand as consenting to a lie."

The second reason Isabella felt she had to reject Tom's advice was her fear that Henry would commit suicide. She was upset by the line in his letter to her, "Living or dead, my dear sister Belle, *love me*." Living or dead? Was he thinking of killing himself, as brother George had done? Isabella grew even more alarmed when the newspapers published a letter from Henry that apologized to Tilton and went on to wish himself dead. She was right to be concerned about Henry's psychological state. Ultimately he was Tom's coward and could not summon the courage to kill himself, any more than he could to confess. Yet he threatened suicide several times in letters to his friend Frank Moulton, who acted as a "go-between," trying to soothe relations between Beecher, Tilton, and Henry Bowen. In one letter, which came to be known as the "Ragged Edge Letter," Henry offered to resign from Plymouth Church and expressed the despair Isabella suspected he was feeling beneath his cool exterior: "Nothing can possibly be so bad as the horror of great darkness in which I spend much of my time. I look upon death as sweeter-faced than any friend. . . . but to live on the sharp and ragged edge of anxiety, remorse, fear, despair, and yet to put on all the appearance of serenity and happiness, cannot be endured much longer."

Isabella thus tried to get Henry to confess. His confession would right everything—it would remove him from the unbearable hypocrisy of his situation, save him from suicide, make him share the blame with Lib Tilton, and get Victoria Woodhull out of jail. Isabella thus wrote Henry in November 1872 that she could "endure no longer." She was coming to New York to persuade him to write out a confession that she would read before his congregation. Events from then on were as farcical as a stage comedy. Henry, viewing Isabella's letter as a major threat to him, enlisted Harriet to occupy the front pew during Plymouth Church Sunday services in case Isabella suddenly appeared in the pulpit; one wonders whether the tiny Harriet was supposed to physically overpower her taller, stronger sister.

Henry also, according to Frank Moulton, came to him for advice in containing this latest disaster. Moulton thought Henry should see Isabella and gently talk her out of her plan, but Beecher said he did not want to deal with her. Edward Beecher told Henry he had visited Isabella, who seemed wildly excited. The men decided to send Tilton to Elizabeth Phelps's house, where Isabella was staying. Tilton later said that he shocked Isabella by charging her with adultery with a prominent senator when she was staying in Washington; he "left to the sound of her sobs." According to Moulton, when Tilton reported to him and Beecher the next day, "Beecher laughed, clapped his hands, and cried out, 'Bravo!'"

The Beecher men then played the card they were accustomed to producing when they had to deal with errant sisters. As they had done when Catharine insisted on defending Delia Bacon, they publicly questioned the sister's sanity. A story appeared in the New York *Tribune* stating that Henry Ward Beecher and two other family members (probably Edward and Harriet) were so worried about Mrs. Hooker's falling under the "Satanic influence" of Victoria Woodhull that they had consulted a doctor about her mental condition. Dr. Butler thought Mrs. Hooker was suffering "under a monomania superinduced by over-excitement." Mrs. Woodhull had "exercised a controlling influence over a too susceptible mind." The physician recommended that Mrs. Hooker be temporarily committed to an insane asylum.

Isabella escaped being committed, probably because the Beechers feared rousing Stanton and Anthony to her defense, but her credibility was severely damaged. Then as now, observers have seen her plan for Henry's confessing and her subsequent actions as crazy behavior. Certainly Isabella's scheme that she should read Henry's confession from his pulpit was shaped by one of her worst traits—her tendency to overdramatize situations and insert herself as the central element. In all likelihood this practice stemmed from her childhood situation as one of the youngest of many siblings competing for attention. It is also possible that Isabella had inherited a mild form of the Beecher manic depressive illness. Worry over her and Henry's dilemma may have triggered a manic state, which could be why she seemed so overexcited in New York.

The idea that Henry should confess, however, was far from crazy—it was just not expedient. Edward, who supported Henry but often seemed to believe in his guilt, counseled Isabella that if he were guilty, confession would not save him. He would fall in the world's estimation and even his own parishioners would not forgive him. Undoubtedly so, but Isabella was less interested in Henry's rank and position than his mental health and what she would have called his "soul." Emma Moulton, Frank's wife and one of the more sensible people involved in the scandal, also urged Beecher to confess. She said that Henry had told her he had repented and been forgiven by God, but she replied he should not cover up such a crime and remain in his pulpit, "living a lie."

Isabella could quote no less an authority than Henry himself on confession. A short time after the day Lib Tilton said they first had intercourse, Henry preached as follows: "The man who has been wallowing in lust, the man who has been on fire in his passions. . . . If he does the thing that is safest and best he will rise in his place and make confession. Though it be in church, and it break the order and routine of service, he will stand up and say, 'Here I am, a sinner, and I confess my sin, and I call on God to witness my determination from this hour to turn away from it.' That is the wise course, and you would think so—if it was anybody else but yourself." This was only one of several indirect confessions Henry made from the pulpit. The most startling was the Biblical text he chose for a prayer meeting at Plymouth Church at the height of the scandal. The verse reads: "Then Saul said to Jonathan, Tell me what thou hast done. And Jonathan told him, and said, I did but taste a little honey with the end of the rod that was in mine hand, and lo, I must die." It seems that even a pre-Freudian congregation would have cringed at this selection.

To Isabella's relatives and friends, her idea that Henry should confess had the fatal flaw of assuming he was guilty. No one wanted to believe it. More accurately, everyone followed Harriet in refusing to entertain the possibility of guilt. "No one" and "everyone" are scarcely exaggerated. Rugoff states flatly that "No one in Nook Farm other than Isabella believed Woodhull's story. It was simply unthinkable that the spokesman for their spiritual ideals . . . had been a lecher and a hypocrite." Harriet and Mary were furious with Isabella and shut their doors to her, as did most of her Nook Farm neighbors. This was the time when Mark Twain, perhaps forgetting Isabella's kindness when his son died, forbade his wife to see her. His sister-in-law wrote his mother, "Sam says Livy shall not cross Mrs. Hookers [sic] threshold and if he talks to Mrs. H he will tell her in plain words the reason."

Only Catharine continued to speak to Isabella because, she said, she was too old to feud with members of her family. (She did feud publicly with Woodhull, though, accusing her in the newspapers of blackmail.) Catharine's excuse of age for refusing to shun Isabella is an interesting one. Recent studies have indicated that in old age "the sibling support bond appears to intensify," and in Catharine's case this was true. Typically, the sisters had tended to support one another in a crisis; they had supported their brothers also until Isabella's defection, but when a sister needed help they tended to offer their services in person. Mary and Harriet had sometimes been distant from Catharine when they were annoyed at her, but it was new behavior to turn one's back entirely on a sister. Isabella wailed to her daughter, "Oh Alice dear why can't every body be 'in many things dissenting but still loving'?" She could not understand it. From the point in November 1872 when Henry tried to institutionalize her to the following May, Isabella was paralyzed with anguish. If she wrote any letters during that period, they have not survived. Her usual correspondents wrote anxiously, wondering why they had not heard from her. Susan B. Anthony expected her at the annual convention in Washington in January; Isabella did not show up.

John returned from Europe at the beginning of 1873 and, as usual, tried to support his wife: he set about defending her from her critics. Unfortunately, he became more a part of the problem than a part of the solution. He *did* understand why Isabella (and occasionally he himself) was being ostracized, why people couldn't simply disagree with her and continue to be loving. Isabella had broken a major, perhaps *the* major, rule of proper womanly behavior. This rule became known in the twentieth century as "Stand By Your Man." When a man was accused of wrongdoing, the role of his wife/mother/sisters/daughters was to rush to his defense and deny his guilt, whether they suspected he was guilty or not. Harriet, Mary, and Catharine were behaving correctly, while Isabella was doing the unthinkable in championing the women who had accused her brother.

Hence John came up with a defense that mitigated her transgression. She should tell people she had kept up her friendship with Woodhull in hope of influencing her not to publish the story about Henry. "This will give the appearance of self-sacrifice to your affiliation with her, and will explain your not coming abroad with me—a fact which has a very unwife-like look." To Isabella this defense had the serious problem of not being true. It did eventually convince Harriet, though, giving her a rationale for restoring relations with Isabella. In May 1873 Harriet was already softening a bit, writing daughter Eliza that she was glad the twins had reestablished relations with Isabella, even though her sister had deeply offended Harriet's sense of propriety. It was not yet time for reconciliation. "Your aunt is like many monomaniacs all right if the wrong string is not jarred but I fear that seeing me will jar it."

John's concern for appearances over truth meant that his wife's only allies who fully understood the principles she was trying to uphold were her woman suffrage colleagues. Those in Connecticut were especially sympathetic. Hannah M. Comstock, her friend in New Haven, wrote very supportive letters to "My precious friend" and "My dear precious woman" throughout the period of the scandal. At the turn of 1873 she said she wished "your dear husband & your other friends would trust your clear vision." The blame for the scandal would fall on women and not her brother, she warned Isabella. "Even the dead profligate Byron must not be spoken against by a woman— If your sister Harriet would come to your aid in this your day of trial, as you went to her with your great heart & willing hands—how much she could do for both you & your brother." Olympia Brown tried to help with John. She invited Isabella to give a sermon to her congregation in March and then sent John the favorable newspaper report. She praised him for sending Isabella affectionate letters when she was visiting and urged him to trust and believe in her. He should "be proud of a wife so loyal to truth."

Isabella's co-workers on the national level were less supportive. While they backed Isabella's position with regard to her brother, they had conflicting interests. The main concern of Stanton and Anthony was protecting Elizabeth Tilton, trying to keep her from becoming the scapegoat for the sins of the men. Ultimately, of course, they could not succeed—Hannah Comstock was right that a woman would have to pay. When the chips were down, Henry dropped his sympathetic attitude toward the poor child dragged into the slough and accused Lib of having pursued him and "thrust her affections on me unsought." The *New York Times* expressed belief in Henry's guilt but reserved its greatest censure for Lib Tilton, whom it called "degraded and worthless." One of the difficulties in trying to uphold the principle of sexual solidarity was that the interests of different women sometimes conflicted. At the end of 1872 Isabella (and Victoria Woodhull) needed Stanton and Anthony to step forward and confirm Woodhull's story about Henry; otherwise it looked as though Woodhull had fabricated it and Isabella went along because of her "infatuation." To confirm the story, however, would harm Lib Tilton, so Stanton and Anthony hid from the press as best they could.

This situation led to Isabella's violating in one way the principle she was trying to champion, against her self-interest, in other ways. She revealed to the press, in an attempt to get Stanton to speak out, that Stanton knew of the Beecher-Tilton affair and that Stanton had always been in love with her brother-in-law, Edward Bayard. The latter Stanton had confessed to Isabella "in strict confidence"—"I considered that moonlight talk as sacred as if it had been with God himself." In an unguarded moment Stanton had told Isabella her deepest secret. Several friends knew that Bayard had tried to persuade Stanton to elope with him and she had refused. But, Stanton wrote

Isabella, "to no one but you did I ever reveal the steadfastness of my affection, that instead of seeking solace elsewhere has gone out into my life work." Stanton felt that Isabella had "deeply wronged" her. She concluded sadly, "I have never yet put the least confidence in any woman that it was not betrayed."

Isabella's response to this reproach has not survived. Whatever it was, Stanton had trouble forgiving her. She continued to criticize Isabella to her friends, referring at this time to the "vague ideas floating in Mrs. Hooker's head." Stanton was uncharacteristically obtuse when it came to her colleague's struggles. She claimed to Isabella, for instance, that "I have been crucified in this matter as much as you." By the newspapers, yes—but Stanton was not being ostracized by her relatives, friends, and neighbors. Isabella may have been too embarrassed by her revelation of Stanton's secret to attend the May 1873 NWSA meeting at which she was supposed to speak. This convention was dedicated to celebrating the twenty-fifth anniversary of Seneca Falls. Isabella and John went on a short trip instead. She sent a letter apparently intended to mollify Stanton, saying she had just read the transcript of the 1848 convention for the third time and Stanton's speech at Seneca Falls had never been surpassed in the history of the country. Interestingly, she was brave enough to praise Woodhull also, but this portion of her letter was omitted from the *History of Woman Suffrage*. Her favorable reference to Woodhull upset John again.

In the summer Isabella finally made the trip to visit her brother James and his wife, Frankie. Jim was now preaching in the town of Poughkeepsie, New York, on the Hudson River. After leaving the army, he had served in brother Tom's church and then become pastor of the Congregational church in Owego, a town near Elmira. Alice Hooker had reported on a visit to the Langdons that Jim was as "handsome and as unresponsive and monosyllabic as ever." In Poughkeepsie Isabella found him as depressed as ever, even though he was liked by his congregation and made a decent salary. He and Frankie had adopted a wonderful baby named Kathy, who was "the sunshine of a house that needs a good deal of sunshine." The atmosphere was too gloomy for Isabella, who stayed less than two weeks.

On her return to Connecticut she found John in a better frame of mind. He had figured out something he could do to show his loyalty to Isabella's cause without getting further involved in the Woodhull-Beecher-Tilton mess. When Susan B. Anthony was tried in June for the "crime" of voting in the presidential election of 1872, she was victimized by a gross miscarriage of justice. The presiding judge was Ward Hunt, a Republican who had just been appointed to the U.S. Supreme Court and apparently wanted to show his gratitude to the Grant administration. Anthony and her lawyers believed he had decided her guilt in advance; after the final arguments by the prosecution and defense, he immediately produced a written opinion without leaving the bench. Judge Hunt also refused to allow Anthony to testify in her own behalf.

The worst injustice, the one John pursued and wrote an article about, was the judge's denial of a jury trial. As a criminal defendant, Anthony had the right to a trial by jury, and indeed a jury was listening to the evidence. But the jury was not given a chance to deliberate on a verdict. Judge Hunt simply directed them to find a verdict of guilty, claiming there was no question for the jury to decide. Anthony's lawyer, former Appeals Court Judge Henry R. Selden, tried to have the jury polled, but this plea was denied. John's article lambasted Judge Hunt's rulings, arguing that they represented "a very dangerous encroachment on the right of every person accused to be tried by a jury." He concluded that "it is by yielding to such encroachments that liberties are lost." John and Susan corresponded about the article, and she told him that Judge Selden considered it the best statement of the jury question he had ever seen. Unfortunately, Anthony had no legal remedies remaining. Judge Hunt had the power to deny her request for a new trial and deliberately did not order her jailed until she paid the hundred-dollar fine he had imposed; if he had, she could have taken her case to the U.S. Supreme Court. The case ended in a stalemate: Anthony would not pay the fine, and no authority pushed her to do so.

Isabella was called upon in that autumn of 1873 to defend Anthony in another matter. Sorosis, the New York women's club founded in 1868, planned to sponsor a Woman's Congress in October. Charlotte Wilbour, president of the club, sent letters to women who held "an honorable place in any of the leading reforms of the day," asking for their signatures to a call for the Congress. About a hundred women, including Isabella as a member of Sorosis and such luminaries as Sarah Grimké, Julia Ward Howe, Elizabeth Cady Stanton, Mary Livermore, and Lucy Stone, signed the call. But Susan B. Anthony never received a letter and was hurt at the omission. Isabella was not the only women's advocate who felt unsupported. Anthony wrote her that she thought she was being shunned by the Boston suffragists and by Mrs. Wilbour also. They seemed to think her verdict and sentence a disgrace and "shrink from affiliation with an adjudged criminal." Why are you and Mrs. Stanton, she asked not very diplomatically, "the two *greatest Woodhull sinners*," more respectable than I am?

Isabella's first reaction was, characteristically, to tell all and read Anthony's letter to the Congress, but fortunately she consulted Stanton and was persuaded not to. Instead she and Stanton offered a resolution at the closing session thanking Anthony for her work on behalf of women. When Henry

Blackwell omitted this resolution from newspaper accounts of the Congress, Isabella wrote him in protest. By this time Stanton seems to have forgiven Isabella for her breach of confidence. As usual, seeing each other drew them together just as writing drove them apart. Stanton sent her letter of reproach in January 1873, but after the Congress in November she wrote, "I love you better & better every time we meet."

Isabella delivered a pro-suffrage paper at the Congress, one of only two on the topic. The Congress was conceived of by many of its organizers and participants as arising in opposition to the suffragists, or as the New York *Herald* called them, "the more violent woman's rights people headed by Victoria Woodhull, Susan B. Anthony, and others of the same stripe." Charlotte Wilbour, although she believed in woman suffrage, was careful to distinguish the respectable methods of the Congress from the occasional antics of NWSA conventions. "Deliberations will be earnest and intellectual and will [be] conducted in such a calm, rational, temperate and Christian spirit as to compel the respect of the world at large."

In line with this rationale, the women at the Congress organized a new society, which they called the Association for the Advancement of Women (AAW). Given the fact that there existed an Association for the Advancement of Science, the name suggests the founders' desire for a respectable scholarly organization. The Congress was proper enough for Catharine to attend (she even became an officer of the AAW in 1875). She gave three papers, two of which she wrote alone and titled not surprisingly "Endowments for Women's Colleges" and "Of the Needs and Claims of Women Teachers." The third paper, "On the Cheering Prospects of Women," was co-written by Catharine and Harriet. If Harriet hadn't been in the Midwest on her second reading tour, the three sisters would have attended the Congress simultaneously— an embarrassing situation given that Harriet was not speaking to Isabella.

Soon after the Woman's Congress Isabella's first (and only) book was published. Her friend Hannah Comstock wrote that people were reading it in New Haven but warned tactfully that it might not be too successful. The book contained "things men are afraid of." That is, it talked about sex and advocated a single sexual standard. If her book had any influence, it was to brand Isabella in the nineteenth century as a "free lover" (the timing of publication in the midst of the Beecher scandal was certainly poor) and in the twentieth century as a prude. The volume consists of three separate parts: the article she wrote in 1867 on sex education for boys, here entitled "Motherhood"; her correspondence with John Stuart Mill; and a section on Josephine Butler's work, entitled "State Patronage of Vice." The last part is not a narrative but a compilation of extracts from writings by Butler and other opponents of the Contagious Diseases Acts in England. Isabella justifies the use of extracts in her preface, stating that nothing she could have written would have had comparable force. The result, however, was to make the book even more disjointed than it would have been if she had written her own essay. She gave this conglomeration the astonishing title of *Womanhood: Its Sanctities and Fidelities.*

The book definitely needed an editor—not just to provide a title that had some relation to the content but also to establish a single focus. Although not an excellent writer, Isabella was a competent one, and "Motherhood" is original and interesting. It could have been paired with an essay on state patronage of vice under the rubric of the need for universal sex education and a single sexual standard. Alternatively, the focus could have been on motherhood, with the strands on this subject gathered together from each of the three parts. The book was successful, though, in terms of its stated purpose—the activist one of presenting effective arguments against the state regulation of prostitution.

Isabella's concern that licensing of prostitutes might spread to the United States was not unfounded. In New York State alone, licensing bills were defeated in 1868, 1871, and 1875. St. Louis, the headquarters of the infamous Whiskey Ring, legislated regulated prostitution in 1870; opponents did not succeed in overturning it for four years. Isabella offered her services (two weeks of speaking and organizing resistance to licensing laws) to various anti-licensing leaders if she was needed. Her book was popular and appreciated in these circles, she wrote Stanton. For years she had tried to interest Stanton in Butler and anti-licensing agitation, but Stanton considered their "American issues" more important; no doubt she thought ministers and religious women could fend off licensing on their own, as indeed they did.

It may have been just as well for Isabella that *Womanhood* was not more widely read and noticed. She could hardly handle more notoriety. John was still angry over her praise of Woodhull in the May NWSA letter. Olympia Brown wrote him a sixteen-page missive while "Mrs. Hooker sits weeping by my side." She praised John for his loyalty to Isabella and his detailed review of the Susan B. Anthony trial. She also defended Isabella in the misunderstanding over the May letter, claiming that Isabella had told her at the time that she praised Woodhull's suffrage work and John hadn't objected. There was a distinction, Brownie argued, between recognizing merit in Woodhull's suffrage memorial and accepting her free love theories. Most people had yet to see that distinction. Eugene Burton still treated Isabella with contempt, and she was very anxious about Mary, who, though "delicate" in health, was pregnant for the first time. She cried out to Alice: "When your darling Kathy belongs to some-body else more than to you & when that somebody hates the very sight of you[,] for her sake & your own you wish you were dead &

safely in the land where you can watch over those you love without giving pain to anyone—then & not till then can you begin to know what this life I am trying to live is to me. God only knows how I can endure it any longer & keep the cheerful face I must keep for Mary's sake."

On November 2 Mary surprised everyone by giving birth to twins, Allen and Katherine, who weighed almost seven pounds apiece. Isabella felt relieved but still agitated over the Beecher-Tilton developments. Henry continued to deny his guilt, label Isabella insane, and persecute Victoria Woodhull. Isabella feared she would suffocate in the poisonous atmosphere. "I shall never breathe freely again," she wrote Olympia Brown, "till I am off this continent. This lying & injustice are perfectly hateful to me—& every way I am racked with heart pains." She anticipated getting off the continent, having finally agreed to go to Europe with John. He had been trying to persuade her for about fifteen years to make the European tour that was common for Nook Farm residents who needed rest or renewal. Europe was like another water cure, and most of their friends and family members had been at least once.

Isabella's favorite excuse for not going, that she couldn't bear to be separated for so long from her home and family, no longer applied—she was already separated. She also had a model in her friend Paulina Wright Davis, who was in Europe when John was there last. Davis's family had taken her abroad to escape the Beecher-Tilton scandal (she was a confidante of Lib Tilton) and regain her health. Isabella blamed her friend's illness on her being "crucified," like herself and Stanton, for defending the women involved in the Beecher-Tilton case. She feared for her own health as well as John's; in February of 1874, even with the European tour coming up, they took a short vacation to the West.

Before leaving for Europe, Isabella had one more suffrage campaign she wanted to conduct. She and Olympia Brown planned a lecture tour of Connecticut for Susan B. Anthony in late January and early February 1874. Isabella guaranteed Susan twenty-five dollars a speech over and above her expenses. As money was short for the Hookers, as usual, Isabella was nervous; when the speaking tour was a grand success, however, she broke even. She introduced Anthony and spoke herself in different towns each night. Susan's talks were so "splendid" and the response so positive she felt reassured that suffrage would soon be obtained. "The end is near," she wrote Alice.

Because she was busy arranging the Connecticut tour, Isabella did not attend the annual NWSA lobbying meeting in Washington that year. Olympia Brown was supposed to go in her place to make sure Connecticut was represented. But in a scenario that was becoming all too common in the women's movement, Brownie felt wronged and refused to go. She had surprised her friends by getting married the year before and now was pregnant.

When Stanton referred to her condition in a letter, Brownie was indignant. How could Stanton know of her affairs? She did not want to attend meetings with Stanton because she was "always unfair and always mean."

Brownie's complaint to Isabella about Stanton sounds much like Stanton's own earlier rebuke of women. She continued: "What can women do if they are constantly to attack one another in this way, only think when Mrs. Churchill wanted me to get up a lecture for her here & I wrote that I could not—she immediately jumped at the conclusion that I was about to be turned out of my church on account of Woodhul [sic] & went to circulating the story. Now Mrs. Stanton whom I have defended again and again just because I said perhaps I could not go to Washington jumps at a conclusion . . . [and] will circulate it high & low all over the land when it can only tend to injure my work & she knows it. The meanness of women toward one another does make me heart sick." Brownie then wrote Isabella a series of letters arguing that they should concentrate on local work and avoid national conventions, where the "stars" of the movement simply wanted "a great array of women to serve as background." She and Isabella should spend their time, money, and energies in Connecticut. When Isabella argued that Congress had to be pressured to act, Brownie responded that the two of them should focus on getting better congressmen elected from the state.

For the time being Isabella would act on both fronts. She wrote Stanton a long letter advising her on the upcoming May NWSA convention. Although she would be en route to Europe and could not attend, she thought the meeting should be held in a church so as to save rent money and attract religious women. She warned Stanton not to neglect the "conservative & fastidious women" but to entice them into the movement. The churches were filled with women like Isabella's sister-in-law Sarah, George's widow—conservative women holding temperance meetings. Although Isabella was not a teetotaler and initially considered the temperance workers fanatics, she and John had come to see "good purposes underneath an apparent fanaticism." She counseled Stanton to devote the meeting to the temperance theme and suggested several possible speakers. Stanton did not take this advice, though eventually the suffrage and temperance movements would be allied. On the local level Isabella busied herself raising money to help the Suffrage League, a Hartford club with her colleague Ellen Burr as president. She managed to raise the funds subscribed for the struggling league to rent a hall for their weekly meetings. Less than a week before the Hookers were planning to sail, Isabella was still collecting petitions to support a state bill that allowed women to vote in school elections.

The Mark Twain family vacated the Hooker house early, and so Isabella spent the month of April refurbishing the house for the next tenant.

She was so happy to have a home again, she hardly cared that most of the neighbors weren't speaking to her. But when Lilly Warner stopped by and described Isabella's Day grandchildren, Kathie and Allie, Isabella could hardly contain her sobs. She saw her grandchildren precious little when Alice was in town. But now Alice was at Gleason's Water Cure in Elmira and her husband did not want Isabella visiting the granddaughters in his home. "This separation from your children is *anguish* to me," she wrote Alice. The last day in Hartford, a friend took her to the Days' to say a brief goodbye to the little girls. As Isabella outlined her travel plans to Alice, she intended to stay in Europe for six months. The Hookers would tour the continent for four months, at which time John would return for the fall court session and Isabella and Ned would spend six to eight weeks longer in England. By that time, they thought, the scandal would have died down.

On May 2 the Hookers sailed from New York on the *Egypt*. They arrived in Liverpool on May 13 and went for a long drive in an open carriage. Absolutely everything was in bloom, Isabella observed, including laburnums and beautiful purple beeches. One of the first things she did in England was try to contact Josephine Butler, who lived in Liverpool. Butler was away, however, and wrote that she hoped to meet Isabella later in London; she expressed concern that the U.S. Congress would pass a bill similar to the Contagious Diseases Act. Unfortunately, Isabella was never in England at the same time as Butler and so never got to meet her idol. At the beginning of June the Hookers took off for the continent, where they left Ned with friends and made a whirlwind tour of Italy. They started in Genoa, spending a few days there and then traveling south to Pisa, Florence, and Rome. Isabella loved the harbor and gardens of Genoa and the catacombs at Rome. They visited the ruins of Pompeii and, like many another tourist, reread Bulwer-Lytton's *The Last Days of Pompeii.*

It was the art that really surprised and impressed Isabella. She had told Alice before they left that she looked forward to seeing people, rather than "landscapes or pictures," in Europe. Like many Americans of the time, she had no idea how deprived she had been artistically. Her knowledge of art lagged behind her knowledge of music. Her only real artistic education had come, ironically, from brother Henry. When he first arrived in Brooklyn to preach (in 1848), he wrote Isabella that if she would visit, he'd give her the prettiest vase in New York. She visited and he presented her with a Wedgwood vase that she considered, especially after their estrangement, one of her "chief treasures." For six weeks she and Henry had haunted the museums and galleries of New York; it was her "first introduction to art." Now, again owing to Henry in a roundabout way, she would further her artistic education.

Another pleasure of the trip was visiting sites where John, Mary, and other family members had previously been. In Bologna, for instance, a museum guard recognized John from his previous trip. From Pompeii they drove to Sorrento down the famous gorge, "down a magnificently built road, with four horses & jingling bells—the most enchanting drive I ever had in all my life." They stayed at the same hotel where sister Harriet had resided in 1859. The hostess, a large Englishwoman with a tiny Italian husband, pointed out the arbor where Harriet had written much of her novel *Agnes of Sorrento* (1862) and the rooms their neighbor Charles Dudley Warner had when he stayed there. The Hookers met up with Warner and his wife in Venice and saw the sights under their more experienced tutelage. They then took a trip on the Rhine as they made their way back to London. Isabella did not like Germany as much as Italy. "Give me the Hudson before the Rhine any day—castles or no castles," she wrote. The weather was too hot, Cologne struck her as "disagreeable," and the cathedral there seemed "dirty." From Cologne they had a "miserable" ride to Brussels to visit the lace factories. By the end of July they were back in London, soon joined by Ned.

In London a stack of mail and newspapers awaited. It was simply not possible to avoid the Beecher-Tilton scandal entirely, even if the Hookers could have contained their curiosity about what was going on at home. The scandal was front-page news in every English newspaper, and well-meaning friends sent news clips just in case. Abby Hutchinson Patton, the suffragist singer, posted envelopes full of clippings, reminding Isabella that she'd said she wanted to know the worst. Friends, acquaintances, and strangers alike wrote Isabella wondering what she knew and why she didn't assume her brother innocent. They even questioned the nineteen-year-old Ned about his mother and uncle. Isabella instructed him to say that his mother did not know the exact truth. She feared there might be some foundation for the rumors of wrongdoing, but they could be exaggerated. His Uncle Henry had lived a life devoted to others, and if he were guilty he should be forgiven. Publicly Isabella kept to this story, but privately she believed Henry to be a hypocrite. Why had he been led into temptation, she mourned to Brownie; she finally realized as never before the significance of the line in the Lord's Prayer, "Lead us not into temptation." If she were home, she would fear that her "reason itself would give way—for I feel so intensely for my brother. I cannot give him up & yet my soul revolts at his conduct beyond the power of words to describe." Unfortunately, there would be more and more evidence forthcoming as to that poor conduct.

In Brooklyn Henry Ward Beecher was being tried during July and August by his church. He and his advisers thought it looked odd not to deny the rumors, and so Henry picked six of his good friends in Plymouth Church to "investigate" the charges against him. Although the meetings of the investigating committee were supposed to be private, there were leaks from the minute the sessions started. All the newspapers were full of the committee's proceedings, reporting the witnesses who participated and their appearance, behavior, and testimony. Everyone's letters, it seemed—including Isabella's—appeared in the news. Hannah Comstock wrote her that the papers were "crazy" with the scandal: it was the biggest thing since the death of Lincoln.

Isabella's "insanity" was now paraded before the public. Tommy Shearman, one of Henry's lawyers, testified before the committee about Isabella: "I know from a private and most reliable source that for a long time she was considered out of her head . . . insane . . . deluded. She was laboring under a hallucination . . . cultivated by her intimacy and strange relationship with Victoria Woodhull. She is well known to be weak minded and to prey upon her brother." He brought up the "My Darling Queen" letter and made a new interpretation. "I cannot say it outright. The best way I can put it is that she [Isabella] had an *unnatural* affection for Mrs. Woodhull." She was not only a madwoman but a lesbian to boot!

There was yet worse news from the States than the church investigation. Daughter Mary wrote that Allen, one of her twin babies, was very ill. Unknown to the Hookers, the baby in fact had died on August 15, just before John sailed for home as had been previously planned. John heard the news when he arrived, and Isabella and Ned received a letter from Mary at the end of August in London. For the rest of her life Isabella would remember "driving the Victoria Road with Ned to keep my brain steady" and contrasting their inner turmoil with the clear blue sky above the dome of St. Paul's. On the heels of the bad news about Allen Burton came the decision of the Plymouth Church investigating committee. Henry Ward Beecher was innocent. If he was guilty of anything, it was being too generous and overlooking the vicious plots of Theodore Tilton and Frank Moulton. He had only tried to be kind to Lib Tilton, who had plagued the poor minister with her affections.

It came as no surprise, of course, that Beecher would be exonerated by his own handpicked committee. The bad news was that Tilton was so furious at the result that he filed suit in Brooklyn city court. He accused Beecher of alienating his wife's affections and demanded one hundred thousand dollars in damages. Now there would be a real trial in a real courtroom and the media circus would start all over again. The Hookers decided that Isabella and Ned should stay in Europe indefinitely instead of sailing home from England in a few weeks as they had planned. By October they were in Paris, where they stayed for seven months. Isabella would not return until after the trial was over.

To those in the know, the results of the church trial were disgusting, even if expected. Susan B. Anthony said if God started striking liars dead, Brooklyn would be full of corpses. "What a holocaust of womanhood we have had in the investigation!" exclaimed Elizabeth Cady Stanton. Lib Tilton was a pawn of the two men. Her husband would convince her to write out a confession of the adultery; Beecher would influence her to retract it; her husband would convince her to confess; and so on. It was clear that Lib would be sacrificed. Women of the National Woman Suffrage Association were dubbed "free lovers" and "human hyenas," Stanton continued, while Beecher tried to prove his own sister insane.

Stanton had an interesting economic analysis of the scandal. She predicted Beecher would beat the charges, explaining to Isabella that the publishers of Henry's latest book (*The Life of Christ*) and Plymouth Church had too much money at stake to see him sacrificed. So the blame would be "saddled upon us women." She noted that the persecution of Woodhull in the courts showed money and power behind it. The "bondholders," Stanton wrote Woodhull, "stand around Mr. Beecher, not loving truth and justice less but their own pockets more." Henry himself had become a wealthy man, unlike his father, brothers, and most ministers. He had a luxurious home in Brooklyn with so many Oriental rugs on the floor that they were often piled four deep. He collected art objects and rare books; he bought horses and country residences. During his trials Beecher calmed himself by handling the unset jewels he kept loose in his pockets. Lest his defense prove too costly, his parishioners raised his already high salary and collected one hundred thousand dollars for legal expenses.

Henry's exoneration by Plymouth Church convinced some people that he was not guilty of adultery, bringing about renewed pressure on Isabella to support him. Sister Mary had some doubts before this point, though she disapproved of Isabella's behavior. Now she was firmly in Henry's camp and in September informed John that she would never receive Isabella unless she stopped "all intercourse with Mrs. Stanton and Miss Anthony and all that set." The Chamberlins, neighbors of the Hookers and Stowes in Nook Farm, tried to mediate between the sisters. "Mediation," however, meant that Isabella would have to change her mind because the other sisters were not willing to consider that Henry might be guilty. The Chamberlins visited Isabella in Paris and analyzed the statement Henry had made in front of the church investigators. Given her reluctance to believe that Henry would swear falsely, they managed to raise "new hopes" of his innocence. Once the Chamberlins were gone, however, Isabella read other evidence and felt her hopes recede.

Numerous misunderstandings resulted from the Chamberlin visit. They told Harriet that Isabella felt wretched for having wronged Henry over the past few years. But in reality, she explained in a long letter to John, she was miserable because, guilty or innocent, *"he had so wronged me* by misleading me in every conceivable manner till I was compelled to condemn him from his own utterances both written & oral." It is interesting, she told her husband, that our friends who believe Henry innocent look upon themselves as the greatest sufferers. They have "no conception of the suffering we have been called to endure who could not indulge this belief."

The Chamberlins also caused confusion by informing people that Isabella had finally repudiated Victoria Woodhull. More letters of explanation were required. In actuality, Isabella had said she would not see Woodhull if she called on her in Paris. The reason was her desire to avoid the press. (Woodhull and her entourage were vacationing in France with money supplied by Beecher, it was rumored, to keep her from testifying in front of the Plymouth Church committee.) Communication became so convoluted Isabella had to inform John that if Harriet wrote her about the Chamberlins' report she would answer the letter and send her reply to John, keeping a copy herself. Then he could either send the letter on or return it to Paris if he thought it needed revision. It was hard to keep track of who had said what to whom. "I beg you not to repeat to any one what I said," Isabella wrote Mary Porter Chamberlin, "and if you have already done so, to qualify it by what I now say." She instructed Mary to please talk to John about other matters when she saw him, and not to reply to the letter, for she, Isabella, also was "trying to think of other things."

In Paris Isabella found many diversions. She and Ned lived on the rue Pigalle on the Left Bank. Montmartre was then more of a literary and artistic mecca than a center of nightlife; the Place Pigalle and adjoining streets were lined with artists' studios and literary cafés. The Hookers boarded in the same house with a congenial American family, the Eatons, whose son went to the Beaux Arts to take painting lessons. Every morning Isabella and Ned studied French together and then in the afternoon Ned was tutored. Isabella rented a small carriage for two francs an hour and drove all over the city until she was familiar with it. She went to the Louvre twice a week and haunted the gardens and Bois de Boulogne. She recalled Paris to her daughter Alice years later as "The clean beautiful city. It was to me a city of refuge in the days of my anguish." She could wander at will as "no one knew me to despise & condemn." Although Isabella was depressed—"sad," as she put it—the beauty of the city had a soothing influence. Isabella and Ned went to theaters and the opera at night; they heard the famous Patti sing in "The Huguenots" and listened regularly to wonderful music at the Notre Dame cathedral. Even the separation from John had its positive side, as Isabella tasted a bit of independence. She recalled later to Alice the first time she drew money from the bank in Paris without having to account for it on an everyday basis—"few men realize the comfort there is in this." It could not be said exactly that Isabella was "having a good time." In fact, the most enjoyment she got out of her European trip was writing about it to Alice fifteen years later when Alice and her family lived in Europe; Isabella would get out her old notebooks as Alice traveled and compare their reactions to various cities and works of art. But, at least before the Beecher-Tilton trial started in January 1875 (it lasted from January 11 until July 2), Paris had its comforts.

The trial immediately became a media event comparable to the affair of President Clinton in the 1990s. Reporters were allowed into the courtroom, and they analyzed every gesture of the principals in the case and every word, it seemed, of the two million words of testimony. For one hundred and twelve days the trial was front-page news. In Brooklyn crowds jammed the corridors of the courtroom and the streets outside; one day an estimated three thousand people were turned away from court. Tickets to the trial were sold on the black market for ten dollars apiece. Eventually a lottery was instituted, with the winners being given seats in the courtroom. Food vendors filled the halls and streets hawking snacks. Such a circus could not be ignored, even in Paris. As Barbara Goldsmith notes, the trial became an "obsession, a supershow, far transcending the question of innocence or guilt."

Catharine had a ringside seat at the show as she moved in with brother Edward in Brooklyn during the trial. If she harbored any doubts about Henry's innocence, she did not reveal them but gamely supported him. After Plymouth Church exonerated Henry, she penned a defense for publication in the newspapers. Mary also followed the trial closely. She became Harriet's main source of news, for Harriet, like Isabella, could not stand to be in the middle of the fray. She could just as well have written what Isabella did— that if she were near Brooklyn, her reason would give way entirely to her intense feelings for her brother. So Harriet retreated to Florida and begged Mary, "Do write me at least once a week all the scraps of news you get by being on the spot." Florida was in some ways more remote than Paris—mail, for instance, came only twice a week. Harriet wrote George Eliot that when arriving in Mandarin "I enter another life. The world recedes—I am out of it; it ceases to influence; its bustle and noise die away in the far distance." The storms and fusses carried by the "red hot hurrying newspapers" seemed only a far-off speck on the horizon.

Harriet had escaped the Beecher-Tilton scandal the previous few summers with her speaking tours and the previous few winters by busying herself in Florida—tending Calvin during an illness and visiting her brother Charles's plantation. The weather was beautiful enough to soften the "toughest old Calvinist that ever set his face as a flint." She asked Charles jokingly, "How do you think New England theology would have fared if our fathers had been landed here instead of on Plymouth Rock?" Harriet also continued to write. After *Palmetto-Leaves* she composed a popular sequel to *My Wife and I* entitled *We and Our Neighbors* (1874) and a book on women in the Bible entitled *Woman in Sacred History* (1874). The year of the trial, however, she was too on edge to write and tried to fill the hours socializing and making elaborate preparations for Easter. Like Isabella, she was only marking time until the trial ended. One of the hardest aspects of the trial for Harriet must have been the frequency with which people mentioned her Byron article as justification for the accusations against Henry—in other words, her exposé of Byron had established a precedent for the public airing of dirty laundry. By this twisted reasoning, she herself was to blame for the attack on her brother.

As Tilton and Moulton testified at the trial and the evidence against Henry piled up, Harriet grew more furious with what she saw as a Satanic plot to ruin her brother. Isabella's heart sank. She had no love for Tilton or Moulton—Tilton had threatened her with a lie (her supposed affair with a senator); Moulton had published Isabella's distraught letters to Henry, along with the other letters Henry had given him to hold. He and his wife were considered truth tellers, though, and, fortunately for Isabella, Moulton presented her in a favorable light. When asked if Beecher feared his sister Mrs. Hooker, Moulton testified that he did. She was not really a crazy woman, as she had been portrayed, but a bolder person than her brother: "Mr. Beecher's sister, the amiable, intelligent, enthusiastic, and clearheaded Mrs. Hooker, now, happily for her peace, abroad—who had become the recipient of the knowledge of the facts of Beecher's guilt, was placarded as insane . . . [because] she advised him to make a clear and full confession, in the interest of truth and justice, to rescue a woman from jail whom [sic] Mrs. Hooker believed was incarcerated for having told simply the truth."

Isabella's peace was being disturbed not only by the revelations of the trial but also by the recurrence of an old rumor. In the past Victoria Woodhull had implied that Isabella knew of her brother's behavior and approved of it. Isabella was angry but could not contradict Woodhull without adding fuel to the fire and branding her as a liar. Now Elizabeth Cady Stanton said the same thing in a newspaper. Isabella quoted the offending sentence in an angry letter to Anthony—Stanton had referred to Isabella's excellent advice to her brother to "confess his life & justify it by his theories, which *she had heard him many times enunciate.*" Although she had suspected that Henry might have a theory to justify his behavior, Isabella had never heard him enunciate it—and Stanton knew it.

It is unclear whether Stanton was consciously or unconsciously taking revenge for Isabella's revelations about her. Probably, as she herself sent Isabella the news clipping, she had intended to defend Isabella from the insanity charge and gotten carried away by her contempt for Henry and desire to underline his guilt. Every aspect of the Beecher-Tilton scandal had become for Isabella, in today's terms, a lose-lose situation. If it was galling to have people sympathize with poor Henry and call her crazy for doubting him, it was also upsetting to see the brother she loved attacked. She was most perturbed by Stanton's "cruel criticisms of him as a wilful libertine." Isabella's distance from the scene came to her aid, however. After a sleepless night, she noticed that Stanton's article was dated October 1 of the past year and thus had not been written in the midst of the trial as she had first supposed; she calmed down and contented herself with a mild letter of protest to Stanton.

It seemed that the news from the States was uniformly bad. Hannah Comstock kept Isabella up to date on the local suffrage scene in a series of warm, supportive letters. If the scandal did not have a long-term negative effect on the women's movement, it did create problems in the short run. The suffrage society in New Haven (which Olympia Brown thought Isabella's greatest accomplishment) had been strong. Now people were quitting, Comstock reported, because they were afraid of being associated with "free love"; the society was having a hard time raising money. Comstock, Brown, Ellen Burr of Hartford, and Susan B. Anthony were all working hard in Connecticut in Isabella's absence. They had two bills introduced in the legislature, one to exempt women from property taxes because they should not be taxed without representation and the other to give women the right to vote in the state. Anthony spoke for three hours at the hearing, but the bills were not favorably reported. The worst news had come in fall 1874 from the U.S. Supreme Court. The Court decided unanimously against the New Departure: the fact that women were citizens did not mean they automatically had the right to vote. This decision delivered a much greater blow to the movement than the Beecher-Tilton case could possibly have done.

In April 1875 John joined Isabella and Ned in Paris. Inwardly he was still preoccupied with the scandal, writing a series of agonized letters that month to his former pastor William Patton. "The whole matter has nearly killed me," he concluded, "& perhaps will before it is over." Outwardly he tried to be cheerful and social. He brought relatives with him, some of Isabella's favorite people—his sister-in-law, Eliza Gillette, his niece, Lilly Gillette Warner, and his cousin, Nancy Hooker Hart. They all stayed in Paris for the month. The Hookers had a "home-like fire" in their hotel suite; when the Charles Dudley Warners visited on their way to Egypt, they thought it was Nook Farm transplanted to Paris. During the summer the Hooker party left Ned to study in Paris and traveled to St. Moritz and other places in the Swiss Alps. They went to Germany and took another (more satisfactory) trip down the Rhine. Before they made their way to London, they heard that the Beecher-

Tilton trial was over. The jury had been deadlocked. They had taken over fifty ballots before the last one, which was nine to three against a verdict for Tilton. How could the jurors vote thus, the *New York Times* wondered, when the facts contradicted Beecher's explanations? The newspaper contended that "Mr. Beecher has told a dozen different stories in explanation of his letters and conduct" and every story contradicted one of the others.

Part of the answer lay in the character of the plaintiff, Theodore Tilton. Henry Ward Beecher was not being prosecuted for adultery by the State of New York, in which case the verdict may have been different. The case was a civil one in which Tilton had accused Beecher of alienating his wife's affections and asked for one hundred thousand dollars in damages. In the course of the trial many unsavory details about Tilton came out. He was an ambitious, self-involved man who was jealous of Beecher's wealth and reputation. He treated his wife worse than Beecher did his, even before he knew of her infraction, and he himself had several affairs while married. Mrs. Tilton confessed to him six years before he brought suit against Beecher; during that time he accepted money and favors from Beecher, presumably to ensure his silence. It is understandable that a jury might not want to reward Tilton's behavior with more money.

In addition, many of the jurors probably felt as Harriet did and couldn't allow themselves to even consider that the famous minister might be guilty. There was too much at stake. Clifford E. Clark Jr., one of Beecher's biographers, explains the situation thus: "The refusal to doubt Beecher's integrity is not difficult to explain when one looks at his position as a spokesman for the Victorian cultural ethos. For more than thirty years, Beecher had warned against political and economic corruption and had stressed the value of Christian ethics. . . . For those who were frightened by the rapid and chaotic social change, his views became a reference point. . . . [If Beecher were a fraud, then they] had been duped for years."

For numerous Americans an admission that Beecher might possibly be guilty was tantamount to questioning their own moral perspectives. What would become of religious values? Many of their countrypeople had the same Calvinist background as Henry and Isabella. They had seen it decline over their lifetimes, had in some cases knowingly contributed to the decline. And they were anxious about the change. If Henry's substitute for Calvinism, his positive, Christ-centered religion of love, led to lechery and hypocrisy, what would take its place? Thus Henry had to be vindicated and the Tiltons sacrificed.

After the trial Henry maintained, at least outwardly, his position of wealth and power. The price of being considered innocent, however, was to be thought weak and vulnerable in order to have been so manipulated by the Tiltons and Moultons. According to Altina L. Waller, "He was never again taken quite so seriously in political or economic matters." At the time of his death in 1887, Henry was still popular in some circles but no longer a major force in American life. By contrast, the Tiltons and Victoria Woodhull were thoroughly "ruined." Theodore was broke. He took advantage of his notoriety by lecturing in order to earn money, then slunk off to Paris. Reportedly, he occupied himself playing chess and writing bad poetry. Woodhull also became an embittered expatriate, though she managed to recoup some of her riches. At the nadir of her fortunes in 1877 she divorced Colonel Blood, renounced free love, and fled with Tennie to England. It was said that the sisters had been paid off by Cornelius Vanderbilt's son, who was facing a lawsuit over his father's will; reportedly he set them up in England to ensure that they would not testify about his father's frolics. Eventually Victoria and Tennie married wealthy men. Woodhull spent the rest of her life trying unsuccessfully to disown her past and achieve an unsullied reputation.

Such a reputation was, of course, impossible for Lib Tilton to achieve. For a while she lived quietly in Brooklyn with her mother, supporting herself by tutoring children of the Plymouth Church congregants. Three years after the trial she made a nonambiguous public confession of her and Beecher's guilt and was promptly excommunicated by the Church. She grew old "a virtual outcast," in Waller's words. She went blind and was sustained only by her daughter and a small group of Spiritualists known as the Christian Friends. When asked about Lib's final confession, Henry's response was predictable. Everyone knew Mrs. Tilton was crazy, he charged; by now she'd become a mere "unbalanced clairvoyant."

10

Spiritualism,
1875–1878

IF HENRY WARD BEECHER thought Lib Tilton an "unbalanced clairvoyant," he might as well have called his sister Isabella the same thing, for Lib's answer to the scandal was also hers. It all started after the Hookers' arrival in England when something odd happened. As Isabella recalled it to Alice years later, "When shown to our [hotel] bed room, the water pitchers, bureaus, bedsteads, chintz curtains [were] so like those of my childhood in Boston I stood trans-fixed—& the apparition of my mother, to whom I had scarcely given a thought for thirty years seemed to rise up before me, in her french [sic] calico gown & broad ruffled cap—how wonderful this law of association!" Isabella felt transported back to the time in Boston when she was only nine years old. It is hard not to see the appearance of her mother at this low point in her life as symbolic. Had brother Henry known of the vision, he might have interpreted it as the family's legacy of mental illness finally catching up with Isabella. She had tried to banish thoughts of her mother, but now Harriet Porter Beecher was back. At this point she was only a harmless "apparition"; in a few months she would return with a vengeance.

Isabella was strong enough to stand up for her own beliefs and face Henry's probable guilt—that was strong for the time. But she could not toler-ate without a crutch the implications of his fall: the depravity of human nature (had her father been right about original sin after all?) and the mockery of Christianity Henry's actions suggested. If he was, as one newspaper con-cluded, "a dunghill covered with flowers," Isabella could glimpse the dung beneath the flowers, but she couldn't live permanently with the smell. Her brother Tom could do so because he had adjusted to a very dark view of life; he had low expectations of people, and Henry simply met them. Isabella had been avoiding a dark philosophy her whole life. While she wanted "truth," as far as she could grasp it, she also had to ward off the terrible depressions of her mother and brothers. It is therefore not surprising that, while she hid from scandal in Paris, Isabella reverted in a sense to adolescence and converted to a new religion. This religion, Spiritualism, was not inconsistent with the Christianity she already believed in and also was woman-centered and optimistic. In the nineteenth century, many people became Spiritualists in order to cope with the death of a spouse or child. Isabella was reacting to the stress of the Beecher-Tilton scandal and her own ostracism by family and friends.

In her Paris hotel room her long-lost mother, Harriet Porter Beecher, suddenly appeared to her again in a vision and became her "control" or contact with the spirit world. No male Greeks for Isabella! As she later explained to her daughter Alice, she had missed her mother more and more as time went by "till in 1875 in the city of Paris suddenly my own precious showed herself to me in a mirror & undertook once more the guidance of my life." This account of missing her mother contradicts her earlier statement that she hadn't thought about her in thirty years, so it is hard to know how deeply Isabella had repressed the memory of her mother. At any rate, by the time the Hookers sailed for home in fall 1875, the repressed had returned.

Isabella was a late convert to Spiritualism, as she had been to women's rights. The Spiritualist movement sank to its low point in the 1870s; in the two previous decades it had been tremendously popular. Modern Spiritualism began at the same time and place as the women's movement—in 1848 near Rochester, New York. The young Fox sisters, Kate and Margaretta, produced strange "rappings" and claimed that spirits were communicating with them from another world. As the new religion spread throughout the country and to Europe, the rappings gradually went out of style, replaced by ouija boards with planchettes, or triangular pieces of wood said to respond to magnetic forces passing through the fingers. More and more people participated in séances held around parlor tables with men and women holding hands to form a "spirit circle." Gradually, instead of rapping out "yes," "no," or letters of the alphabet, the spirits were thought to move the planchette to spell out messages. It is difficult to calculate the number of Spiritualists because they were averse to formal organization and many people thought of themselves as "investigators" of spiritual phenomena rather than confirmed Spiritualists. Contemporary sources estimated about two million adherents of Spiritualism in 1850, growing rapidly to about seven million by 1863. The large number of deaths in the Civil War strengthened the movement as survivors tried to communicate with family members killed in battle.

Spiritualism was, of course, much more respectable then than now. The tricks of mediums were only gradually being exposed, and the idea that messages could be exchanged between this world and the next did not contradict the science of the day. If Samuel Morse could communicate instantaneously over long distances by wires, why couldn't there be a "spiritual telegraph" as well? It seemed at the time that an increasing number of forces, such as gravity and electricity, were invisible to the human eye but could be proved to exist. Besides, many prominent persons were Spiritualists. The famous abolitionists William Lloyd Garrison and Sarah Grimké were early converts, along with Robert Dale Owen, the Utopian reformer. Anna Blackwell, sister of Elizabeth and Henry, also became an advocate. Judge John Edmonds adopted Spiritualism in the 1850s and resigned his position on the New York State Supreme Court to be a full-time supporter and medium. (He was dead by 1875, but Isabella soon contacted him and persuaded him to talk to John.) There were also Spiritualist senators and representatives. It was well known that Mary Lincoln brought mediums into the White House. Of course, she could be dismissed as unbalanced, but cabinet members, senators, and Lincoln himself participated in the séances.

Some writers have claimed that Victoria Woodhull introduced Isabella to Spiritualism; the idea fits the theory that Isabella was "infatuated" with Woodhull and under her control. Catharine Beecher tended to connect Spiritualism and free love, noting the "baneful influence of spiritualism" along with the teachings of free love in destroying the stability of the family. But the Beecher family and Catharine herself had been interested in spiritual phenomena long before Woodhull or even the Fox sisters came on the scene. In the mid-1840s when she was seeking desperately to improve her health, Catharine was mesmerized (hypnotized) several times and also visited a clairvoyant in New York. Though she apparently didn't receive any significant communications from spirits, she was impressed by some of the clairvoyant's abilities. Catharine then sought a naturalistic explanation for the successes of mesmerism and spirit communication. She hypothesized in *Letters to the People on Health and Happiness* that there could be an "abnormal accumulation of nervous fluid in the brain" that gave clairvoyants such powers as moving furniture from afar or accessing the memory and knowledge of other minds. She rejected any supernatural agency and noted that "the progress of time is more and more exhibiting the folly and inconsistency of the popular delusion that brings back the spirits of departed friends to perform fantastic tricks, and to make known inane and contradictory revelations."

One place where Catharine (and the Stowes and the Hookers) learned about Spiritualism was their favorite "cure," the Drs. Taylor movement and water cure establishment in New York. Dr. George Taylor was a Spiritualist who offered séances presided over by Kate Fox (now Jencken) herself. Both Catharine and Harriet, who had also become an "investigator," attended these occasions. Fox Jencken, however, increased Catharine's skepticism. Catharine later told a friend that she had "cut up all sorts of capers" trying to mystify her. Fox Jencken and another famous medium said they'd seen a vision of

Catharine's father, who was kneeling before her offering a rose as the symbol of her purity. But this was a sentimental Victorian vision alien to the character of Lyman Beecher. Catharine reacted indignantly: "Such nonsense! When my father never in his life praised me, although he used to say that I was the best boy he had."

Harriet had once asked the living Lyman whether he thought the spirits of the dead could communicate with people who were still alive. By way of reply he told a story. Once when he was troubled and depressed he went to sleep in the bedroom where her mother had died. During the night Roxana appeared in the room and smiled upon him. Though she didn't speak, he felt his sorrows recede and awoke lighthearted in the morning. Calvin Stowe had had odd psychic experiences since childhood. He wrote about his "hallucinations" in a report for the Semi-Colon Club in Cincinnati. As a boy he had regularly talked with a spirit named Harvey and been visited by blue devils. Harriet later used much of the report almost verbatim in her novel *Oldtown Folks* (1869), which was set in Calvin's hometown.

Calvin, whom no one could accuse of being imaginative, continued to have visions as an adult. In a note to Harriet's friend George Eliot he agreed with the British novelist's dismissal of mediums but went on to suggest that there might be "some peculiarity in the nervous system, in the connecting link between soul and body," that brought some people more than others "into an almost abnormal contact with the spirit-world." Calvin and Harriet tried to communicate with their dead sons for much of their lives. After Henry Stowe drowned in 1859, Calvin felt his presence in the vibrations of an imaginary guitar. Harriet wrote her husband from Italy that she was glad. She herself had met a "very powerful medium" who brought her "strong impressions from the spiritual world, so that I feel often sustained and comforted, as if I had been near to my Henry and other departed friends."

Generally, though, Harriet distrusted mediums. She wrote her children that she shuddered to think that "our beautiful, our glorified ones should stoop lower than even to the medium of their cast-off bodies, to juggle, and rap, and squeak, and perform mountebank tricks with tables and chairs; . . . to trifle, and banter, and jest, or to lead us through endless moonshiny mazes. Sadly and soberly we say that, if this be communion with the dead, we had rather be without it. We want something a little in advance of our present life, and not below it." In many respects Harriet's attitude toward Spiritualism was similar to her attitude toward feminism. She was too interested and attracted to the theory to leave the "ism" alone (for instance, she wrote a series of articles on Spiritualism for the *Christian Union*).

Yet she could not fully accept the practitioners of the theory. Some, who appeared to be serious thinkers, she befriended and corresponded with;

there was Robert Dale Owen, for example, author of the well-known *Footfalls on the Boundary of Another World* (1860). But other Spiritualists seemed too radical, too low-class—and perhaps, like Woodhull, too much in league with the Devil. It was safer to rely on Christ as "the true bond of union between the spirit world and our souls." Thus, as with women's rights, Harriet could be quoted on either side of the divide between believer and skeptic. Characteristically, she was cautious in her public statements about Spiritualism, often criticizing its excesses, but considering her private writings most of her biographers consider her "more believer than skeptic." As Forrest Wilson notes, for thirty years Stowe "consulted 'mediums,' operated the ouija board, subscribed to spiritualist publications, [and] befriended professional spiritualists and promoted their works."

Apart from Isabella, the Beecher sibling who showed the most interest in Spiritualism was Charles. Back in 1863, at the height of the furor over the Fox sisters, he had written a report for the Congregational Association of New York and Brooklyn entitled *A Review of the "Spiritual Manifestations."* Charles believed fully in the reality of spirits and spirit communication. He claimed that all religions of the world recognized the existence of spirits; apparitions and ghosts appeared in the folklore of every culture. That is why Spiritualism had so quickly become "a household religion." Charles welcomed the revival of the Biblical belief in spirits and eagerly collected instances of spirit manifestation. By the time Isabella became a Spiritualist he was also personally interested because of the tragic loss of three of his children. His two youngest daughters had drowned, along with Edward Beecher's son, in a boating accident; his son Fred, who had been badly wounded at Gettysburg, was killed in an army skirmish against Indians in Colorado. But at the same time Charles believed in a spirit world, he also feared it. He warned that spirits could be evil as well as good and that innocent people might be "possessed" by demons.

If Isabella had not learned about Spiritualism from her family, she would have encountered it in the woman's rights movement before she met Victoria Woodhull. It was no accident that the two movements arose simultaneously in the same place. As Ann Braude notes in her book on the subject, "The two movements intertwined continually as they spread throughout the country. Not all feminists were Spiritualists, but all Spiritualists advocated woman's rights, and women were in fact equal to men within Spiritualist practice, polity, and idealogy." This was not simply a case of women being given "equal opportunity" within a structure created by and for men. Spiritualism was inherently anti-hierarchical and anti-authoritarian and many of its activities took place on women's terrain. For instance, the center of the religion was not a church but "woman's place," the home; mediumship was closely identified with femininity. As stated in the *History of Woman Suffrage*, "The only religious sect in the world . . . that has recognized the equality of woman, is the Spiritualists. They have always assumed that woman may be a medium of communication from heaven to earth, that the spirits of the universe may breathe through her lips."

This reference to Spiritualism is unusual in the *History of Woman Suffrage*. It was written by Catherine A. F. Stebbins, a Spiritualist and member of the National Woman Suffrage Association, in a chapter on woman suffrage in her native state of Michigan. The editors of the *History*, Elizabeth Cady Stanton, Susan B. Anthony, and Matilda Joslyn Gage, solicited chapters on state work. In the parts of the history they wrote themselves they seldom mentioned Spiritualism. Stanton and Gage opposed religion in general, but the three editors no doubt wanted to avoid connecting the rights of women with a movement so easily ridiculed. Twentieth-century feminists followed this lead, and thus the connections between women's rights and Spiritualism have been obscured. Actually, many nineteenth-century women's rights workers were confirmed Spiritualists, or at least serious investigators of Spiritualism. The list includes the following feminist reformers: Caroline Healey Dall, Mary Fenn Davis, Paulina Wright Davis, Abigail Scott Duniway, Eliza Farnham, Abby Kelly Foster, Frances Dana Gage, William Lloyd Garrison, Laura de Force Gordon, Sarah Grimké, Angelina Grimké Weld, Georgiana Bruce Kirby, Mary Rice Livermore, Samuel May, Thomas and Mary Ann McClintock, Frances Green McDougall, Mary Gove Nichols, Parker Pillsbury, May Wright Sewall, Catherine A. F. Stebbins, Sojourner Truth, Charlotte Fowler Wells, Charlotte B. Wilbour, Frances Willard, and Victoria Woodhull. Gordon and Wilbour worked extensively with Isabella in Washington in the years before she went to Europe; both women were mediums and had been trance speakers before they joined the women's movement.

Upon her return from Europe in fall 1875 Isabella was preoccupied with Spiritualism. One of her first actions was to visit her friend Paulina Wright Davis in Providence and participate in séances there. Although Davis was ill and could hardly function, she managed to arrange for her favorite medium to preside. Isabella felt overcome with an "abundance of revelation" from the spirits. This confusing abundance, she explained to her son Ned, combined with "the fullness of my inner life" to "shut me off from every thing else at present." She had to adjust to the constant communication of the spirits (her parents, her brother George, John's father, John's great-grandmother) and the often startling revelations of her mother. Harriet Porter Beecher told Isabella, for instance, that she had arranged her marriage to John. Isabella also wanted to learn to be a medium herself. To become a skilled medium was, like becoming a minister, one of her longtime ambitions. As recently as the few months in 1875 before she went to Europe, she had been thinking of trying to get confirmed; Olympia Brown even considered postponing her wedding until Isabella was ordained as a minister and could perform the ceremony.

But it was difficult for a woman to be officially recognized as a minister under any circumstances. The chances were slim for one who had damaged her reputation by refusing to stand by her brother and trafficking with Mrs. Satan. As Braude notes, women who became mediums assumed the authority of religious leaders: "Mediumship circumvented the structural barriers that excluded women from religious leadership. By communicating directly with spirits, mediums bypassed the need for education, ordination, or organizational recognition, which secured the monopoly of male religious leaders. While men might bar women from church councils or from theological education, human authority could not supersede that given to mediums by the spirits who spoke through them." Just as hearing the voice of God had inspired such women as Anne Hutchinson in Puritan times and Quaker Lucretia Mott in later days, the spirits empowered women.

The only matter that could begin to compete with Spiritualism for Isabella's attention was the practical question of where the Hookers would live. Their current renters were leaving, and their income was too small to allow them to live in the house on Forest Street. At least they didn't have to worry about Ned, who was in college at Boston University. During the fall and winter 1875–1876 John and Isabella stayed not far from Nook Farm with their good friends William Smith (son of their former baby nurse Anna Smith) and his wife, Virginia. Isabella was able to visit Mary and little Kate nearly every day. She searched for renters and also for boarders to provide the renters with enough income to afford the house. There had been a terrible economic crash in 1873, and the resulting depression would last the decade. Businesses failed, banks collapsed, mills and mines closed down, and factories laid off workers. Nearly everyone, including the Stowes, Victoria Woodhull, and Eugene Burton, was suffering financial embarrassment—Isabella and John were not alone in their difficulties. One of their neighbors "slit his throat" over money problems. The Hookers generously steered a potential renter to George and Lilly Warner; the Warners had to rent their house for three years and board with Lilly's parents in the Gillette house. In order to increase his income John reopened his law office in Hartford. He had given it up for a few years to concentrate solely on his court reporter job but now resumed his private practice.

Isabella's absorption in matters spiritual and material left her little time or energy for the women's movement. She had led Susan B. Anthony to think she planned to resume her work fully when she returned to the

United States. Thus Anthony wrote in fall 1875 expressing her pleasure that Isabella was back and "alive to the work." She sought advice on the movement's priorities. Where should they put their energy now? Should they have a convention in Washington in January? How could they best get the attention of Congress? The loss of their court case, *Minor v. Happersett,* had left the suffragists in a weak position. Virginia Minor, the first woman to argue that she had the right to vote under the Fourteenth Amendment, had tried, like Isabella, to vote in the 1872 election. When her vote was refused, she brought suit against a St. Louis registrar, Reese Happersett. The Missouri courts ruling against her, she appealed to the U.S. Supreme Court on the grounds that the Constitution protected her right to vote.

But the Court stated directly that the U.S. Constitution does not confer the right to vote on anyone. Yes, women were citizens, but suffrage was not co-extensive with citizenship. States had previously withheld voting rights from certain men (those who didn't own enough property, black men, criminals) and could thus deny suffrage to all women if they wished to. This meant that the quick way to gaining suffrage—reinterpretation of the Constitution—was blocked, and only the long slow ways were left. Either the laws could be changed laboriously state by state or there could be another federal amendment to the Constitution. The suffrage movement was back to the drawing board, back to the sixteenth amendment introduced years earlier. It would be forty-five years before it would be passed as the Nineteenth Amendment. Elizabeth Cady Stanton, Susan B. Anthony, and Isabella Beecher Hooker would be long dead by that time.

After suffrage was finally won, Carrie Chapman Catt (president of the National Woman Suffrage Association) summed up the work women had to do between the end of the Civil War and the passage of the Nineteenth Amendment:

> During that time they were forced to conduct fifty-six campaigns of referenda to male voters, 480 campaigns to get Legislatures to submit suffrage amendments to voters; 47 campaigns to get State constitutional conventions to write woman suffrage into state constitutions; 277 campaigns to get State party conventions to include woman suffrage planks; 30 campaigns to get presidential party conventions to adopt woman suffrage planks in party platforms, and 19 campaigns with 19 successive Congresses.
>
> Millions of dollars were raised, mainly in small sums, and expended with economic care. Hundreds of women gave the accumulated possibilities of an entire lifetime, thousands gave years of their lives, hundreds of thousands gave constant interest and such aid as they could. It was a continuous, seemingly endless, chain of activity.

The current project was a Centennial Protest planned by the NWSA for July 1876. The country was celebrating its centennial that summer with a huge fair in Philadelphia, a takeoff on the Great Exposition of London and the first event of its kind in America. The all-male Centennial Board, needing women's help to raise funds, promised them space in the main exhibit. When the time came to break this promise, the board suggested that the women construct their own building. Thus the "Woman's Pavilion" came into being. But, as Anne Farnam notes, the pavilion "represented woman's feminine domesticity only; it was filled with exhibits of embroidery, sewing, cooking and other such arts as practiced by 'ladies.'" It was simply "an after-thought," complained the *History of Woman Suffrage*, "as theologians claim woman herself to have been." The Woman's Pavilion offered "no true exhibit of woman's work."

In reaction, the NWSA decided to participate in the centerpiece of the Philadelphia fair, a Fourth of July assembly at Independence Hall. The NWSA women planned to present a Declaration of Rights for Women similar to the Seneca Falls declaration. Anthony apparently told Matilda Joslyn Gage that Isabella would help with the protest and she did work on drafting the declaration, but she disappointed Gage with her lackluster assistance in finding a headquarters in Philadelphia for women attending the fair to meet. Although she doesn't mention it in her writings of the time, Isabella would have been prevented by circumstances from playing an active role in any centennial protest. General Joseph Hawley, her friend and Hartford neighbor, had been appointed chair of the Centennial Commission. Any act on Isabella's part would have been perceived by her family and neighbors as another failure to support a man to whom she owed allegiance.

In July the NWSA women had their declaration ready, but General Hawley refused them permission to present it at the July 4 celebration. No women, of course, had been invited to speak at the event; the guest of honor was to be the emperor of Brazil, a choice many women thought inappropriate for a celebration of democracy. Hawley also refused the NWSA's request for a large number of admission tickets but, perhaps in deference to Isabella, sent five tickets to Elizabeth Cady Stanton. This act of generosity, Eleanor Flexner notes, "proved to be a mistake." On Independence Day Susan B. Anthony and four other women, at the moment the audience rose to greet the Brazilian emperor, crashed the platform and forced their declaration on the presiding senator. They then distributed copies of the document throughout the hall and, not being arrested as they had expected, adjourned to Independence Square, where Anthony read the declaration to a crowd. There was then a five-hour meeting in a nearby church. When Stanton wrote describing the event, Isabella confided to her journal her deep regret at having missed it. She would like to have heard Lucretia Mott speak at the church and the

Hutchinson Family Singers lead the group in singing her favorite hymn, "Nearer My God to Thee." As it was, Isabella made a later visit to the exposition with John and the Gillettes and was thoroughly bored.

Isabella finally got around to writing Anthony—or as she put it, the spirits finally permitted her to write—with an explanation for her lack of participation in the national movement. She told the story of her mother's appearance in Paris and said she was launched upon a new life. She believed that the second coming was near and would inaugurate an era dominated by women. Jesus Christ himself would establish a maternal government upon earth. For a time Isabella's work for women would be to listen to her inner voices and prepare for the new disposition. She was with the NWSA as much as before and wanted to keep apprised of the efforts for suffrage, but for a while she would be less active. When Anthony came to visit, Isabella wanted her to participate in a séance and only reluctantly settled for discussing suffrage.

It was not that she intended to retire from the woman movement altogether. Isabella continued to do some work, particularly at the state level. She spoke at the annual meeting of the New Haven society—never better, said Hannah Comstock—and helped John prepare a woman suffrage bill to introduce in the Connecticut Assembly. Isabella avoided attending the hearing for the bill in June 1876, telling Comstock she was sick. But when the Senate invited her specifically to speak at their hearing, she felt obligated to accept. In other words, she did only what was necessary. Organizing speaking tours of Connecticut or dreaming up new projects with Olympia Brown would have to wait; she told Brownie the same thing she told Anthony, that she was occupied entirely with the spirits.

The Hookers had rented their house to a family named Terry, then moved back to board there in May 1876. Although Isabella was delighted to be living in Ned's old rooms, her obsessions were clearly worsened by returning home. Perhaps the many echoes of the past in a house where she had lived for twenty years and brought up her children made the bygone days seem as real as the present. One of Isabella's first actions after coming home was to create a shrine to her mother, or a space to receive the spirits. In her study she arranged fresh greenery and bright scarves around a Madonna given her by sister Harriet before their estrangement. The Madonna reminded Isabella of her mother and had to substitute for a photograph or portrait, as there was no extant likeness of Harriet Porter Beecher. (This lack pained Isabella throughout her life; she always insisted that members of her family have their pictures taken regularly.)

Before decorating the room, Isabella took out the box where she kept all mementos of her mother and asked for inspiration. She was visited, she wrote, by her lost infant son, Thomas. Having grown up and become an artist in the spirit world, Thomas assisted in the arrangement of the study. He often appeared to his mother along with Joseph Haydn or his grandfather, Lyman Beecher, to whom he was very close. Isabella maintained the rest of the room as a museum of her trip to Europe. Sam and Livy Clemens, who had resumed speaking to Isabella, were so impressed by her study that they brought visitors from New York over to see it.

Upon returning home Isabella began to keep a diary that she called her "spirit journal" and modern-day commentators her "demented" diary. Knowing it could be used to ridicule her and portray her as insane, she wrote in the very first entry that the journal was strictly private, to be read only by John and the children at her death. When biographers of Mark Twain and Harriet Beecher Stowe got hold of the diary in the twentieth century, they employed it as Isabella expected. They not only made fun of her but also drew unwarranted conclusions about the Hookers' lives. Kenneth R. Andrews, for instance, in *Nook Farm: Mark Twain's Hartford Circle* (1950), made no secret of his view that a belief in either feminism or Spiritualism was a sign of insanity. He claims that John Hooker's "livelihood was curtailed by his unpopular advocacy of feminism and Spiritualism" and that his wife's causes had prevented him from being chosen as a justice of the Connecticut Supreme Court. This assertion is not footnoted, as indeed it could not be. Bad investments threatened his livelihood, and John himself said in his autobiography that he was never elected to the Supreme Court because of timing. The first vacancy on the court occurred at a time when he still wanted more experience as recorder, the second when one of his best friends desired the position; John bowed out and then the friend was defeated. Besides, Spiritualism was not unpopular at the time, even with lawyers and judges.

Isabella's diary became such a weapon against her that her descendants finally stopped granting permission for it to be quoted. It must be said, though, that the document contains much to suggest that the writer had slipped over the line between sanity and insanity. To use a more contemporary criterion for mental illness than belief in controversial causes, Isabella seemed to lose control over her behavior. It might not have been "crazy" in 1876 to communicate with one's dead son, but why couldn't she decorate a room without his assistance? The most ordinary actions required permission or confirmation from the spirits. When Isabella lost a small parcel containing a white scarf and red beads, she thought the spirits had taken it—or Harriet Porter Beecher had hidden it because she disliked the way her daughter trimmed her hat. Ironically, sister Harriet's portrayal of Isabella in *My Wife and I* as living in a dream world had come to bear some truth; as occasionally happens, art anticipated life. In spring 1876 Isabella was also experiencing alarming physical symptoms, such as severe headaches, loss of appetite, and sleeplessness. Often, she felt as though she couldn't keep her head above water; she was "like one drowning or clinging to a stray plank in mid-ocean." She had lost the ability to distract herself from pain and experienced her body and will as paralyzed.

Isabella's communication with the spirit world took several forms. There was "automatic writing," in which a spirit or spirits would give her messages to inscribe; at times her normal handwriting would give way to a strange hand. The spirits would also speak through her ("trance-speaking"). With her flair for drama, she assumed characteristic facial expressions and gestures of dead people in order to enhance the spirits' projection of themselves. Eventually she became well known for her abilities as a trance speaker and was very successful at consoling bereaved friends. Although spirit rappings were generally out of fashion in the 1870s, Isabella's "control" (her mother) often announced her presence by rappings. Isabella disapproved of noisy séances, but on sunny days she would climb out her study window to the tin roof below. There she would open her silk parasol and wait for taps to come from her mother. The spirits also sent "visions." This was Isabella's main reason for starting her spirit notebook—to record the visions that were coming to her in profusion. In May she foresaw that her granddaughter Kate Burton, who had been ill the previous winter, would die soon; unless her father changed his ways, the toddler would become the proverbial child who led the way to heaven. Naturally the family was disturbed by this prediction, though John tried to keep it from Mary and Eugene.

One of the most indefensible aspects of Isabella's communication with spirits was the self-serving nature of most of her visions and visitations. Never did she foresee death for John or Ned; no spirit ever criticized Isabella or suggested any improvement in *her* attitudes or behavior. Instead, the spirits seemed to fall all over themselves apologizing for offenses against her in life. Lyman and Harriet Porter Beecher were sorry for promulgating their Calvinist beliefs, having become more liberal in the spirit world. Thomas Perkins dropped by to say he now understood and approved the charitable impulses that made Isabella a reformer. Horace Bushnell, the Hartford minister who had recently died, apologized profusely for his lifelong opposition to woman suffrage.

Some of Isabella's visions were highly self-aggrandizing. When she wrote Elizabeth Cady Stanton that Christ would soon establish a maternal government on earth, she left out the detail that she, Isabella, would head that government; she was to be Christ's "vice regent" on earth, the personage known as "the Comforter" whom Christ had promised his disciples. She would rule personally with the aid of a group of female apostles and a cabinet of Nook Farm relatives and neighbors. Fortunately, Isabella realized what people would think of this "grand illusion," as Marie Caskey calls it, and tended to restrict it to her private writings. Her notebooks are full of lists of prospects for her cabinet; would it be too nepotistic, she wonders, to deputize John and Mary? She thought her ne'er-do-well nephew Fred Perkins would become her private secretary (probably for the reason that he had once acted as Harriet's). Because Isabella had never made a secret of her belief in a second coming during her lifetime, her family and friends were less alarmed by her messianic references than they otherwise might have been. Hardly anyone realized the personal role she expected to play in the cosmic drama to come.

Eugene Burton, however, got an inkling of his mother-in-law's visions concerning him. Isabella told Mary she'd had a dream about Eugene that the spirits had shown her was prophetic. At a time when Ned was home visiting, the three Hookers would hear a pistol shot; they would hurry to Eugene's and find him struggling with a burglar whom he had just wounded in the leg. Ned would make a tourniquet for the burglar and treat Eugene for minor injuries. (Were Eugene and the burglar one and the same? He had stolen Isabella's daughter and had been shot in the leg during the war.) Soon after the dream, in July, Eugene wrote Isabella forbidding her to enter his house again or to see his daughter under any circumstances. This was a terrible blow, of course. Isabella had long complained of restricted access to her grandchildren—she did not get to be with her granddaughters on holidays or have them stay overnight with her. One entry in the spirit journal is a long, enthusiastic description of a day when Alice brought her girls to Nook Farm for five whole hours; it was the first time they had ever eaten a meal in the Hookers' house.

Before Eugene's edict Mary could at least bring Kate over or Isabella could visit the Burton house while Eugene was at work. Now, when she tested the new state of things by appearing in the morning and asking to take Kate for a carriage ride, Mary refused. Isabella was furious with her for allowing Eugene to send the cruel letter and for upholding his decree (though Mary was having her own problems with her husband and perhaps had little influence over his behavior). The best Isabella could do was withdraw into her delusions. While Eugene focused on his daughter, she would spend more time with Mary training her for a position in the cabinet; Mary could be the assistant vice regent of Christ.

Isabella grew increasingly obsessed with the burglary drama. She had Ned show her how to make a tourniquet and persuaded him and John on several nights to sleep in their clothes in case the burglary should occur. After several false alarms Isabella determined that a certain Saturday night in September would be *the* night. She convinced John to speak with the Hartford police chief, who sent two men to watch the Burton house, and the Hookers sat up all night fully clothed. Nothing happened. In disgrace, Isabella tried to argue that she had merely mistaken the date the burglary would take place. But Ned and John, who had been very patient with her, were understandably indignant. They still half-believed in Spiritualism but insisted on her relinquishing the idea of the burglary. Isabella wrote accurately of John at that time, "Poor man he has a hard time I suppose with me." Although she had learned one lesson—that the spirits would not tell her *when* her prophetic visions would happen—Isabella was loath to give up her belief that the second coming would occur before the end of the year. She tied it more and more to her imaginings about Henry, for she also clung to her earlier idea that she would preach in Plymouth Church and Henry would confess. Harriet Porter Beecher and other spirits wanted the truth to be revealed, and so it would be at the second coming originating in Plymouth Church before the end of 1876.

As distressed as Isabella was over losing control of her life and being separated from her granddaughter Kate, there were some bright spots in her situation. Brother Tom came for a visit when he traded pulpits with the Congregational minister in Nook Farm, Joseph Twichell. Though he did not believe in Spiritualism and walked out when his first wife, Livy, spoke to him through Isabella, Tom was in general friendly and affectionate toward his sister. Family members and friends who had supported Henry showed signs of wanting to reconcile. Brother Charles agreed with her belief in a spirit world and thought the second coming was imminent; he looked for it every day, he told Isabella. While he feared her spirits might be messengers from the devil, he was willing to "agree to disagree" about Henry. Catharine arrived at the Stowes for the summer and invited Isabella over for croquet, the current fad. Isabella and Harriet thus started speaking again. The only family holdout, apart from her sons-in-law and Henry himself, was Mary Perkins. Mary still loved Isabella, Charles reported, but she would not see her unless Isabella conceded that she was wrong and Henry was innocent; Isabella would not accept that condition.

Now that the Beecher-Tilton trial was over, Harriet felt free to leave Florida early; the Stowes spent the month of May visiting Henry and the Howards in Brooklyn. Harriet did not intend to make another speaking tour in the fall. Although daughter Hatty had accompanied her to the West in 1875, taking care of packing and travel arrangements, the tour was too exhausting to be worth the money. Harriet was sixty-five, rather old for such a demanding lifestyle. Instead, she busied herself with her pen. In Florida she worked on the novel that would become *Poganuc People* (1878) and wrote a plea for the birds and animals of her adopted state. Always a protector of the environment and champion of animal rights, Harriet complained of the male tourists who crowded the boat decks and "whose only feelings amid our magnificent forests seem to be a wild desire to shoot something, and who fire at every living thing on shore, careless of maiming, wounding, or killing the living creatures." There were also the trappers of birds. "Who, now, will appear for the birds?" she asked in her article. "Who will get a protective law passed that will secure to us the song, beauty and the usefulness of these charming fellow citizens of our lovely Florida?" This was one topic on which Harriet and Isabella completely agreed.

The sisters did not get to spend much of the summer together because Harriet was called away to nurse her own wounded bird, daughter Georgiana. The mercurial Georgie was very ill during the summer of 1876. It is hard to say exactly what ailed her. Probably her manic depression was at the core of her problem, for a doctor prescribed morphine to quiet a manic state and she became addicted to the drug. She also had the Beecher-Stowe leaning toward hypochondria and a seeming tendency of her own to contract disease (she would soon have scarlet fever). Harriet captured Georgie's complex psychology in a letter to Hatty: "She is so afraid of being frightened & so depressed for fear she shall be depressed—that she does not stay alone a minute."

The next year Georgie would take the (in)famous rest cure of Dr. S. Weir Mitchell of Philadelphia. According to her cousin Fred Perkins's daughter Charlotte, Dr. Mitchell prescribed total bed rest and overfeeding for his female patients. He sent Charlotte, the budding artist and writer, home with the following advice: "Live as domestic a life as possible. Have your child with you all the time. . . . Lie down an hour after each meal. Have but two hours' intellectual life a day. And never touch pen, brush or pencil as long as you live." These instructions almost drove her insane, Charlotte Perkins Gilman wrote, and she satirized Mitchell's sexism in her short story "The Yellow Wallpaper." The doctor's rest regime did not seem to harm Georgie, but neither did it cure any of her maladies.

Isabella's reinstatement to the Nook Farm neighborhood was symbolized by an invitation to a formal lunch of Nook Farm women at Susie Warner's. This was the first such invitation Isabella had received since her return from Europe. About twenty women attended, including Livy Clemens, Mrs. Langdon, and Mary Hooker Burton. Everyone greeted Isabella cordially and, as they ate cold chicken, fried oysters, and celery salad, she thought it seemed like the pleasant social times of old. She resolved to invite some women for tea and throw an old-time holiday party at the Hooker house. But the holidays would prove very difficult, the worst Isabella had ever experienced. The Hookers ate Thanksgiving dinner with the Terrys with no children or grandchildren present. Nancy Hart, John's cousin whose husband had recently died, came from Farmington.

When Isabella took Nancy the next day to see the Mark Twain House, a tourist attraction then as now, she had "an uncomfortable interview" with Clemens. She teased him by saying she'd heard he rejected a pretty lampshade after learning it was cheap "& he was vexed and said something about things going round the neighborhood & explained that he had no knowledge or taste himself & so when an established house said a thing was good & charged a good price for it he felt sure that it was worthy of Livy & that was all he cared for. I said oh that was handsomely said but really as a matter of fact I thought one often paid a high price for a homely article under such circumstances—which he didn't seem to like & again spoke of being talked about."

It was all a joke, responded Isabella, but "his eyes flashed and he looked really angry." This clash would seem to be the result of Mark Twain's personal demons rather than Isabella's. Given her recent experiences, she would hardly understand Twain's naive expectation that he wouldn't be talked about in the neighborhood. Seeing some empty liquor bottles in the billiard room (author Bret Harte was visiting), Isabella thought they might have been drinking. She concluded, "I dread to lose the friendship of that house which is but a slender thread already I fancy." The thread was continually thinned by the machinations of one Nook Farmer who would never forgive Isabella for her role in the Beecher scandal. He was Reverend Twichell, one of Twain's best friends. Twichell seemed to generalize Isabella's actions as an attack on male clergy (and thus himself) and never lost an opportunity to downgrade her to Clemens and other Nook Farm friends.

At Christmas Eugene and Mary gathered most of the family at their house, leaving Isabella and John feeling alone and childless at the Terrys. Isabella was outwardly cheerful but inwardly close to breaking down; she felt she was living in a dream—or rather a nightmare. Fortunately, she resisted telling John she suspected the Saturday before Christmas would be the date of the Burton burglary. Again it didn't occur. Isabella exerted less self-control when it came to the Hookers' New Year's party. This was the first big social event they had hosted since before the scandal. The Terrys considerately went away, leaving the whole house at the Hookers' disposal, and they invited many of the residents of Nook Farm—Mark Twain, the Gillettes, the Hawleys, and both Warner families. The Hooker daughters came, along with Ned and his new fiancée, Martha (Mattie) Kilbourne. To Isabella, of course, the occasion promised more than a convivial evening—it was the last day of the year and thus time for the second coming to occur. She wanted to invite some Spiritualist friends to celebrate the occasion, but John expressly forbade it.

At the height of the party, when the guests were singing in the parlor,

Samuel Clemens and family, c. 1885. Courtesy The Mark Twain House, Hartford, Conn.

the Hookers' favorite medium arrived. Mrs. Roberts wore an ordinary dress unsuited to the festive occasion and was frightened by the large number of guests. Isabella took her upstairs to sit, draped in one of her own party dresses, at a table in her bedroom. When the hostess returned downstairs to help lead the singing, John was admitting two other medium friends with invitations handwritten by Isabella, a Mrs. Perry and her daughter. Mrs. Perry had also failed to dress properly, coming in a "wrapper." Another scruffy-looking medium, Dr. Williams, soon appeared and was slipped upstairs to join the ladies. The stage was set for the second coming. Isabella kept an eye on the clock as midnight approached. There were enough mediums in the house, Kenneth Andrews notes, "to body forth the Holy Ghost." But nothing happened except the only encounter of the two classes of guests. As the Mark Twains and Charles Warners came out of the parlor preparing to leave, Alice burst downstairs, saying, "Why, what is going on in your room, mother? There is the queerest looking lot up there." Isabella managed to shush her but an unhappy Dr. Williams suddenly appeared, grabbed his hat, and left in a huff, slamming the door. The Twain group took him for a coachman and congratulated Isabella on another successful party—it was just like old times at Nook Farm!

This irony provided a suitable end to the farcical New Year's Eve event. Amazingly, few of the guests ever realized what a bizarre occasion it had been. Only John Hooker knew just how far from the old times they had drifted. They had to borrow their own house to host the party because they couldn't afford to live in it; daughters Mary and Alice had to come alone because their husbands hated the Hookers; Isabella, the happy hostess of the 1850s and '60s, was such a monomaniac she had to defy her husband and secretly invite to their first post-scandal party a group of lower-class people she should have known would not feel comfortable at Nook Farm. Worse, she did not even understand the disaster that had been nearly averted. She was so deluded to suggest after the party that the Hookers continue these happy gatherings: the mediums would eventually be welcomed by the other guests, she would get a new piano, and the Church at Nook Farm she envisioned would finally come into being.

John was slow to anger, but now he was thoroughly aroused. January 1, 1877, was the lowest point of the Hookers' solid sixty-year marriage (and the few years before and after that date the general low in their relationship). John had never forgiven and forgotten the Victoria Woodhull mess; only a few weeks before the party he surprised Isabella by asserting again that she had harmed the cause of women in supporting Woodhull. For her part, Isabella scorned what she thought John's cowardice in caring so much what people would think. Now John came right out and accused Isabella of being crazy. She could no longer be trusted. But John had recently given her a weapon she could use to fight back. He and his cousin Nancy Hart had learned that their Grandfather Hooker had been insane in his old age, suffering from acute melancholia. Of course, John worried he would follow his grandfather. Before the New Year's Eve party Isabella assured him that he had inherited just a tendency, not a certainty. Now she berated him for labeling her insane—he was the pot calling the kettle black!

Isabella's spirit journal ends here. It was too frightening to contemplate a split from John after thirty-five years or the possibility that he really would go crazy as he struggled with their crumbling finances. The only subsequent entry was made the next September when the Hookers were visiting Nancy in Farmington. Isabella looked out at the beautiful hills of John's birthplace and felt nostalgic about the early years of their marriage. For a time she would swallow her hurt that her husband thought she was insane and try to support him as best she could. She gave him "magnetic rubs" for his headaches, encouraged him to exercise regularly by walking downtown to work, and helped sort out their finances and obtain legal advice.

As the Hookers wrote their lawyer, it had been "a terrible year for any body who owes anything." Friends John endorsed had failed to prosper and in some cases gone bankrupt. He still had to carry "dear old Uncle Francis" Gillette, Isabella explained to Alice, because Uncle Francis's income had shrunk to nothing when his tenants could not pay their rent. John made a salary large enough to support himself and Isabella, including two thousand dollars to save or spend going to Europe in the summer. But it took almost every dollar of his income to pay the interest on his loans. The question had become "whether out of a property that I regarded three years ago as worth at least $250,000 I shall give up all & be at ease, or carry on an exhausting struggle for five or ten years & save $100,000 out of it for my children." It was tempting to sell out at a loss to pay their debts and live on their income, but the Hookers decided to struggle on.

By this time John's debts and John's income had become jointly theirs. The good news came early in 1877 with the Connecticut legislature's passage of a women's property act. Isabella states in her memoir, "In 1870 I presented a bill to the Connecticut Legislature making husband and wife equal in property rights." This was the bill she sought Elizabeth Cady Stanton's advice about in 1869 before she'd met her in person (Stanton had been instrumental in pushing through the comprehensive Married Women's Property Act in New York). Characteristically, Stanton advised Isabella to include whatever she wanted in the bill—though the bill would fail at first, people would be educated. Stanton was right. Every year Isabella tried to get the bill passed without avail until 1876, when John's friend Richard D. Hubbard was elected governor of Connecticut. Hubbard was generally conservative, but John and Isabella persevered in making their case until he became indignant that his mother did not have the same property rights as his father. In his first message to the General Assembly he mentioned this injustice and then asked John to redraft the bill, which finally passed in 1877.

The passage of the women's property act gave Isabella a needed boost. Even her bright optimism had been dimmed a little by failure after failure in the women's rights arena—the loss of state referenda, the rejection by Congress of the sixteenth amendment, the judicial decisions against woman suffrage. Perhaps the tide was turning. Isabella and John even received two commendations. The Woman Suffrage Society of New York City passed a resolution in May 1877 thanking them for their efforts in promoting the property law. Sorosis, the women's club, adopted a similar resolution praising the Hookers for their "untiring exertions." Isabella was amused when Henry Blackwell wrote her Hartford colleague Ellen Burr wondering why Connecticut seemed to be doing better than Massachusetts. She now had a rebuttal for John's oft-repeated accusation that she had hurt the movement by supporting

Victoria Woodhull. Blackwell and Stone had rejected Woodhull from the first, so why wasn't Massachusetts forging ahead of Isabella's home state?

In spring 1877 Catharine moved from brother Edward's home in Brooklyn to brother Tom's in Elmira. She wanted to be near the Gleason Water Cure, and Julia Beecher gave her a warm welcome. Tom's wife told a friend, "I think there are worse afflictions in the world than the care of an old Christian woman who has at least tried to do good all her life and needs someone's kind attentions till the Lord calls her home." At age seventy-seven Catharine was "somewhat bowed and feeble, with a voice which was weak and quavering." Fortunately, she hadn't experienced her father's mental decline in old age. An intimate of the Thomas Beecher household recalled that she spoke easily and never had trouble finding the right words to express herself.

Of course, Catharine was still a "difficult" person. Although she had mellowed over the years, she could be uncompromising when pursuing her goals. Her grandnephew Lyman Beecher Stowe said that Andrew D. White told him of an encounter with Catharine when he was president of Cornell University and she was in her seventies. She wanted to take a particular course at Cornell and White had to inform her, "'I regret to say, Miss Beecher, that as yet, we have no courses open to women.' 'Oh, that is quite all right, Doctor White, in fact I prefer to take it with men,' she disarmingly replied." When he asked her if he could help find her lodgings in town, Catharine replied that she would stay in a certain dormitory on campus. "'But, Miss Beecher,' protested Doctor White, 'that is a dormitory for young men, it has no accommodations for ladies!' 'I have inspected the accommodations and find them entirely satisfactory,' imperturbably replied Miss Beecher, 'and as for those young men, who are of appropriate ages to be my grandsons, they will not trouble me in the least.'" According to Lyman Stowe, Catharine carried out her plan and became one of the most popular residents of the dorm. This may be another of Lyman's apocryphal stories, but it does sound like Catharine.

Her sisters were relieved to have her settled with Tom near the water cure. As Harriet expressed it in a letter to Catharine, "Too many years have passed over your head for you to be wandering like a trunk without a label." She recommended that Catharine deal with her boredom and restlessness by visiting and cheering sick people at the cure (at Edward's in Brooklyn she had occupied herself organizing the Twenty-third Ward Charity). Catharine took this advice, made new friends, and offered an early morning course of lectures at Elmira College; characteristically, she entitled the lecture series "Adaptation of Woman's Education to Home Life."

In earlier years Catharine would have been writing, but she had trouble focusing on one task for long periods of time. It was just as well for her later reputation because she'd already said everything she had to say. Her books had become repetitive. Previously she had thriftily taken large chunks of her earlier household manuals to use verbatim in later ones, but in the 1870s she started employing the same procedure with her books on education and social issues. Thus *Woman's Profession as Mother and Educator, with Views in Opposition to Woman Suffrage* (1872) was essentially the same as *Woman Suffrage and Woman's Profession*, published the year before. It had the same dedication and only two new essays. Unfortunately, *Educational Reminiscences and Suggestions* (1874) was short on reminiscences and long on suggestions. Catharine did not write autobiographically but simply recapitulated the philosophy of her previous books. The only new idea is her admission that it wouldn't be terrible for women of her class to vote. Catharine was vulnerable to the argument against taxation without representation and after years of dispute with Harriet and Isabella finally decided to compromise on the suffrage issue.

Harriet was also open to the charge of repeating herself and producing tired writing. To some extent this problem seems inevitable—after all, *Educational Reminiscences* was Catharine's twenty-eighth book, and *Poganuc People*, completed in 1877, was Harriet's thirty-fourth. She set *Poganuc People* in her native Litchfield and based the main character, Dolly Cushing, on her youthful self. The novel is pleasant and readable, offering a vivid picture of a more Puritan era; it opens in 1818, the year Connecticut disestablished Congregationalism as the state religion. *Poganuc People* can be called "tired" only in the sense that it lacks the tension and complexity of Stowe's best work— it is all polished surface. The author is frankly nostalgic and provides no underlying critique of Calvinism. Significantly, Dolly has numerous siblings who have left home and two older brothers in the household—there is no younger brother to tug on her feelings. Reviewers praised the historical accuracy of the novel, and Harriet was glad for the money.

The economic times were bad for her also—now there was the Panic of 1877 to contend with. "What a year this is," she wrote Susie Munroe, her son Charles's fiancée. Everyone's income was straitened. As to her own, "about one third has become non productive & I am only thankful that the principle is not lost—But we are all sailing close to the wind & making our expenses as small as possible." Sadly, some people had sailed too close to the wind and capsized. In the fall the family received the shocking news that William Gilman, husband of Mary Perkins's daughter Katy, was bankrupt and headed for prison. Gilman had been a prestigious lawyer, like Katy's father, and supported his family in style in Norwich, Connecticut. Caught short by the financial panic, he had forged a bank certificate and been discovered. "Your Aunt Mary is terribly overcome," Harriet wrote her son. "Katy was her darling—she never really liked her husband—& now she finds no comfort."

Eunice Beecher wrote Harriet that Katy would neither eat nor sleep and was unable to comfort herself by crying. Katy died two years later, having seemingly lost the will to live.

As 1877 wore on, Isabella gradually resumed her women's rights activities. She was more active on the state level, taking up her partnership with Olympia Brown, organizing the state meeting in October, and undertaking another speaking tour in Connecticut. The two women had also given speeches at the spring anniversary meeting of the National Woman Suffrage Association in New York; Isabella presided and invited Brownie to lead the group in prayers. Brownie tried, out of friendship, to investigate Spiritualism but did not have much success. She returned the planchette Isabella had lent her, saying she couldn't get it to move. Although many Universalists were also Spiritualists, Brownie found the new religion "a sealed book."

Both Brownie and Susan B. Anthony used the military metaphors nineteenth-century feminists were so fond of to welcome Isabella back to suffrage work. Before the New York conference Brownie wrote that she was glad Isabella was finally buckling on her armor. Anthony longed for Isabella to be "at the front of the battle again." She asked her to take charge of the January 1878 Washington meeting, along with the District of Columbia suffragist Sara Spencer. Anthony herself would not be in Washington, as she was speaking in the West. She was feeling discouraged at the results of the Colorado referendum on woman suffrage that she had gone to support. Women there had lost by the largest majority ever, she wrote Isabella, showing the folly of trying to win suffrage state by state. It was crucial for Isabella to "make a powerful attack on Congress" regarding the sixteenth amendment. As Sara Spencer wrote, "[W]e want your Beecher cannon aimed straight at the House and Senate."

Thus Isabella went to Washington at the beginning of January 1878 for one of her marathon lobbying stays—she remained there past the middle of April. Senator A. A. Sargent of California, an NWSA supporter, introduced into Congress the constitutional amendment then known as the sixteenth and eventually called the "Anthony Amendment." This measure was finally adopted in 1920 without a change of wording. It read: "The right of citizens of the United States to vote shall not be denied or abridged by the United States or by any state on account of sex." The NWSA members tried to get permission to address Congress on the amendment but were refused. Instead, Isabella, Olympia Brown, Stanton, and others spoke on behalf of the amendment in front of the Senate Committee on Privileges and Elections. Stanton put more faith in this committee than she did Isabella's prior "prayer meeting," which she boycotted, writing Anthony that God had never taken an active role in the suffrage movement. But, as it turned out, Stanton later said she had "never felt more exasperated" than in front of the Senate committee faced with the "studied inattention and contempt of the chairman, Senator Wadleigh of New Hampshire." He read the newspapers, stretched, yawned, cut his nails, and sharpened his pencil—anything to show he was not listening to the speeches. Stanton "restrained the impulse more than once to hurl my manuscript at his head."

After the hearing Isabella swallowed her pride and enlisted Wadleigh's aid in getting the NWSA arguments printed. As she had done seven years earlier, she busied herself sending out copies. Relations with the Committee on Privileges and Elections were complicated by another echo from 1871. Madeleine Dahlgren, a founder of the Anti-Woman Suffrage Society, published a letter in the *Washington Post* that she said had been written to Mrs. Hooker years before but never sent. The letter accused the suffrage workers of having loose morals and wanting to be men. Isabella responded ably and at length, sending Dahlgren a dozen copies of *Womanhood: Its Sanctities and Fidelities*. Dahlgren then memorialized the Committee on Privileges and Elections, claiming that the majority of women—"the masses of silent women"—did not want to vote. This argument was apparently more to the liking of Wadleigh and other senators, for six months later (after the "important" work was done?) they reported against the amendment.

But Isabella managed to secure hearings before other committees also. On January 30 she gave a two-hour speech on suffrage in front of the House Judiciary Committee. According to the *History of Woman Suffrage*, the room and all the hallways leading to it were jammed with people "eager to hear Mrs. Hooker." Then she persuaded some sixteen senators to invite her formally to address the Committee on Privileges and Elections again. Although the committee may have been a lost cause, numerous non-committee senators and representatives and their wives were attending the special hearing. It was held on February 22, George Washington's birthday and also Isabella's (she turned fifty-six).

According to the *Washington Post*, the committee room was packed when "Mrs. Hooker, with the fervor and eloquence of her family, reviewed all the popular arguments against woman suffrage." She then argued as follows:

> The Indian question would have been peacefully and righteously settled long ago without any standing army, if Lucretia Mott could have led in the councils of the nation, and the millions spent in fighting the Indians might have been used in kindergartens for the poor, to some lasting benefit. Down with the army, down with appropriation bills to repair the consequences of wrong-doing, when women vote. Millions more of women would ask for this if it were not for the cruelty and abuse men have heaped upon

the advocates of woman suffrage. Men have made it a terrible martyrdom for women even to ask for their rights, and then say to us, 'convert the women.' No, no, men have put up the bars. They must take them down.

Isabella's speech was notable for the amount of time she spent discussing questions only tangentially related to suffrage. According to the *Post*, she also "reviewed the Chinese question, the labor question, the subjects of compulsory education, reformation, police regulations, the social evil, and many other topics upon which men vainly attempt to legislate without the loving wisdom of mothers, sisters, and daughters." The latter phrase is no doubt a direct quotation. At the convention part of the NWSA gathering Isabella presented a paper not on woman suffrage but on the topic "A Reconstructed Police." Someone who had been reading her spirit journal would have recognized many familiar elements. The *History of Woman Suffrage* reports that the speech detailed how Isabella would run a police force if it were under her control: "Commencing with the location of the office, she proceeded with her list of feminine and masculine officers, the chief being herself."

The NWSA women, without benefit of the spirit journal, may have wondered why Isabella was suddenly interested in the police; they had no way of knowing that the list of officers coincided with her cabinet after the second coming and that the superintendent who would share power with the chief was Jesus Christ. "A Reconstructed Police" actually made sense, showing how successfully Isabella could take "crazy" ideas conceived in "madness" and translate them into practical suggestions. The police force would consist of men and women equally, and there would be matrons in charge of all station-houses. Vagrants would be fed, washed, clothed, instructed in a trade, and turned out as skilled laborers; their children would be cared for and educated.

One notable event of the NWSA convention and lobbying season was the presence of Julia Smith, an eighty-three-year-old woman from Connecticut who was attending her first national convention. Smith was a living exemplar of the seeds that could be sown in a women's rights gathering. She and her sister Abby had attended Isabella's suffrage convention in Hartford in 1869. A few years later the town of Glastonbury suddenly raised the taxes on the farm they had inherited from their father. When they went to Town Meeting to protest, they were told they could not participate or vote. On New Year's Day 1874 the tax collector seized two of their cows. Abby Smith wrote a series of letters describing the situation, which were published in the Springfield *Republican* (its editor Samuel Bowles was a friend of the Hookers' and believer in woman suffrage).

Isabella supported the Smith sisters from the beginning, contributing to their defense fund and speaking during her 1874 lecture tour about their being taxed without representation. In a pamphlet entitled *Abby Smith and Her Cows* Julia Smith stated, "Mrs. Hooker said the other day in her address at Willimantic, Conn., that Abby Smith and her cows were marching on like John Brown's soul." Since 1874 the Smiths hadn't paid their taxes and the tax collector came again. He took more cows and fifteen acres of the farm; this land, worth about two thousand dollars, was sold for a mere seventy-eight dollars and thirty-five cents. The Smith sisters became involved in a succession of lawsuits against the town, as the fame of their case spread throughout the Northeast.

In Washington in 1878 Julia Smith received, according to the *History of Woman Suffrage*, a great deal of "social attention." She was given a reception attended by "men high in political station" and people notable in art and literature. "All crowded about Miss Smith, as supported by Mrs. Hooker." Asked for a speech, Julia explained that the sisters had only two cows left, Taxey and Votey. Taxey was more aggressive than the shy Votey but soon, the sisters thought, "wherever you find Taxey there Votey will be also." From Isabella's perspective, organizing these receptions, as well as the more informal "parlor meetings," was her main NWSA duty in Washington beyond securing and attending legislative hearings.

The idea was to get congressmen of different parties, and their wives, to sponsor social gatherings at which Isabella would speak in favor of woman suffrage and any prominent suffragists attending would persuade the unconverted. Alexander Stephens, representative from Georgia, gave a reception at which Isabella targeted southern (white) women, who she felt were ripe for conversion and had been ignored by the NWSA. Senator and Mrs. Rollins sponsored a reception on Capitol Hill that turned out well. The *Washington Post* called Isabella "cultivated, refined, and convincing," possessing a "rare magnetic influence." At a suffrage benefit in a Washington church, Isabella wrote Ned, the journalist Grace Greenwood mentioned her along with Lucretia Mott, Elizabeth Cady Stanton, and Susan B. Anthony as a pioneer of woman suffrage.

These accolades helped restore Isabella's self-confidence. Although she was tired, she told her son, she felt happier than she had for a long time. Of course, she still had to contend with echoes of the past. Daughter Mary had written "frantically," begging her to come home "because somebody said something against my work here." (Didn't she realize, Isabella asked Ned bitterly, that her being home caused Mary anxiety and her, Isabella, daily suffering?) There was also the perennial problem of the women's rights advocates getting along with one another. Sara Spencer, Isabella's co-worker in Washington and chair of the NWSA's Resident Congressional Committee, had different priorities. She was active petitioning and fundraising for the sixteenth amendment while, in her view, Isabella was frittering away her time socializing.

In March Spencer sent Isabella a nasty note scribbled on one of her calling cards. The card exists now in four pieces; Isabella most likely tore it in anger when she received it. Isabella may have urged her co-worker to attend receptions, for Spencer wrote that she was a "working woman" (she and her husband ran a business college in Washington). Lately she'd had a sick baby and constant work—she couldn't spare any time for "fashionable society." As a working woman, she really needed the ballot, and she didn't care if rich women got the vote. "You are doubtless as you say very happy & so do not mean to be cruel to me, but you *are* almost beyond expression—not one feather's weight of my heavy burdens does any one ever try to lift."

This outburst obviously had more to do with Spencer's attitudes and problems than it did with Isabella. Spencer could not have known much about her colleague's situation and misperceived Isabella as a person to be envied, a rich and happy woman with an easy life (when she said she was happy, Isabella meant relatively so). If Spencer read the newspaper accounts of the receptions, her resentments would have been confirmed. These reports often sounded as though they belonged in the society pages. There are detailed descriptions of the attenders' fancy dress: they wore black velvet and diamonds, red roses and jet ornaments; a Mrs. Dr. Wallace is described, in a language perhaps meant to be English, as attired in "cuir colored gros-grain with guipure lace trimmings." Of course, most NWSA leaders realized that it took as much work to organize politicians and rich socialites for suffrage as it did to organize the poor. Thus a letter from Susan B. Anthony easily calmed Spencer down, and she was soon writing Isabella more pleasant notes. But she never shed the notion that the sociable Mrs. Hooker was filthy rich; for the next few years she wrote occasionally asking Isabella for money for the cause.

One of Sara Spencer's criticisms of her colleague when the quarrel occurred reveals an interesting feature of Isabella's thought at the time. Spencer complained to suffragist Edward M. Davis, Lucretia Mott's son-in-law, that Isabella did not fully support the sixteenth amendment. Davis wrote Isabella an angry letter asserting that if she wasn't following NWSA policy and using her influence to promote the amendment, she should resign her office in the association. Isabella responded to Davis in a long missive detailing her work with southern women and with congressmen and their wives. She claimed that her position as corresponding secretary of the organization was "merely nominal" and offered to resign if she was not allowed to "use my own judgment & follow my own conscience."

Isabella did not wax enthusiastic about the proposed sixteenth amendment. Of course she supported it, she wrote, as that was what the petitions she collected and hearings she attended were for. But she also told the Senate Committee to try other methods if they couldn't report favorably on the amendment. They could pass the Declaratory Resolution proposed in 1871 or announce that they understood the word "people" in the Constitution to include women. The federal amendment route was too slow, she argued to Davis; she wanted to be voting before an amendment could be passed. She did not want to give up the judicial route altogether. She had gone to the library of the Supreme Court and found an octavo volume of several hundred pages containing only the titles of overruled decisions. The NWSA should keep its options open, she advised Davis, for in a few years the Court might reverse its decisions against women.

In this argument Isabella was overlooking the fact that the Court decision had not been close. She had always had trouble giving up a pet idea and changing course, whether the idea was pursuit of woman suffrage through the courts or the imminence of the second coming. She still thought her brother Henry was going to kneel before her and beg her pardon (though perhaps the second coming was more likely). While Isabella worked in Washington, Lib Tilton made her final confession, asserting the truth of her affair with Beecher. Her statement did not change many minds because of her earlier vacillations when under the influence of Beecher or Theodore Tilton. Isabella, however, took this last confession as a vindication of her stance and directed Ned to read it in the newspapers. She deluded herself into thinking that she and Ned would visit Henry in Brooklyn (in actuality, either Eunice or Henry returned her letters unread).

But if she still had some unrealistic ideas, Isabella was more in control of herself when she returned from Washington than she had been when she went. Back in Hartford she started a new diary and wrote a whole week of entries with nary a mention of anyone who was not a flesh-and-blood living person. A month later, however, Isabella was communing with Disraeli, who had just died, and asking the spirits, "What next?" A pattern had been established that would last for most of her life: she would alternate between periods of practical suffrage and women's rights work, in which the spirits receded, and periods of relative inactivity in which she was preoccupied with the spirit world. Soon, even in the latter state, she would become less passive, resuming the direction of her life. Eventually any conflict she experienced between her devotion to Spiritualism and her activism for woman's rights seemed to dissolve as Spiritualism, with its egalitarian ideology, infused and helped focus Isabella's commitment to equality in her women's rights philosophy.

11

Losses,
1878–1887

IN MAY 1878 Catharine suddenly had a stroke and died. There was no prelude of illness or weakness. Just days before the attack she was writing, "I am stronger than for years" and outlining her plans to form a committee in Philadelphia to improve girls' education in health and housekeeping. Brother Tom did notice that Catharine's last days were "like a mirror fractured, each piece like the whole." He said, "She was incessantly, yet incoherently active," moving rapidly from one activity to another, from sewing to letter writing, to piano playing, to talking metaphysics. Perhaps she had a premonition of her coming death, for she wrote sister Mary that she had arranged her papers and letters, thinking all the time of the past. She was "longing to depart," she admitted. "If I pass away here I want you and Harriet to receive and divide what I leave." There was no mention of Isabella. Although Catharine had been kind to her half sister in her troubles, she reverted at the last to the deep bond she felt with Mary and Harriet as daughters of the same mother. "I pine to see you," she wrote Mary, and "What do you hear from Harriet? I wish we three could meet somewhere this Summer." Still in Florida when Catharine died, Harriet did not attend the funeral with the other sisters. She felt the loss keenly, though, addressing Mary later as her "only sister by our angelic mother."

The memorial service was held in Tom's church. It was presided over by Edward, the brother Catharine had always been closest to. As her biographer Kathryn Kish Sklar notes, he "spoke of her as she would have wished him to—with personal memories of her as a sister and a Beecher." Even the obituaries in the media mentioned her personal qualities as well as her public accomplishments. *Harper's Bazaar* sent a representative to the service or interviewed some nieces and nephews, grandnieces and grandnephews. A prospective visit from Catharine may have struck terror into the hearts of her siblings but she was warmly appreciated, the magazine noted, as an aunt and great-aunt. "She was always bright, witty, and sympathetic," said *Harper's*, "a jolly companion, and at Christmastime she was sought for. . . . She would play for the children to dance, help them get up entertainments, and write their speeches." She did have "old-fashioned notions of propriety," the article's author could not resist adding, and always expected the children to behave well.

Catharine's death was widely noted in the press. Editorials appeared in the leading newspapers of the Northeast lauding her pioneering work in the education of women. The Boston *Daily Advertiser* commented on her uniqueness: "It has been the fortune of very few women in this country to exercise a degree of influence at all comparable with that of Catharine Beecher." The *Hartford Daily Courant* stressed her amazing energy, calling her "a whole Social Science Association in permanent session." The tribute Catharine might have liked best came from the Elmira *Daily Advertiser*. The editor pointed out that a week before her death Catharine had published in his newspaper an "Appeal to the Christian Women of Elmira" (the last of numerous "appeals" throughout her life). She quoted the president of the local board of education as saying there were seventeen hundred and nineteen children in Elmira who were of school age but did not attend any school. Elsewhere Christian women had used public school buildings in off hours to teach sewing and other domestic work. Couldn't the benevolent ladies of Elmira undertake such a project of training neglected children? The Elmira editor referred to this appeal as "Miss Beecher's Legacy" and urged the women of Elmira to honor Catharine by donning her "mantle of usefulness."

As for her wider legacy, it was not entirely clear. Catharine had certainly devoted her life, as *Harper's Bazaar* pointed out, "to the elevation of her own sex and to the educational interests of the country." But with what success? She never accomplished her main goal of establishing *endowed* schools for girls and women. Nor did she leave behind one prestigious school with which her name could be forever linked, as had, for instance, Mary Lyon. For a time these failures caused Catharine Beecher's reputation to lag behind those of Lyon and other educational pioneers. Fifty years after her death, however, the tide turned and historians began to recognize the breadth of Catharine's educational efforts—that is, her influence was all the greater because she *hadn't* confined her efforts to one institution or one idea. In the history of education her role in improving the educational opportunities of women and establishing teaching as a female profession is now well recognized.

Still, Catharine is equally remembered as a conservative social thinker—an "anti" in the terms of the suffragists because she was against woman suffrage. To young people today her views on women seem hopelessly antiquated, based on the same "old-fashioned notions of propriety" as her expectations for child deportment. Yet in her youth Catharine was a radical. She refused to accept the Calvinist religion of her father and the culture surrounding it that failed to see women as worthy of education and excluded them from productive work and positions of influence. Fighting this exclusion was a brave act. Catharine's youthful rebellion was what her sisters had in mind when they memorialized her. Harriet, when she came to contribute an account of her older sister's life to *Our Famous Women* (1883), emphasized the early period; she devotes five-sixths of her sketch to the years before Catharine left the Hartford Female Seminary when she was thirty-two. Isabella later planned a memorial to "the really remarkable woman she was in those early days."

Catharine's clear vision of the ways in which women were excluded and her willingness to fight did not mean that she also saw the need for modifying the basic gender system itself—or the class and race systems of the time. As the authors of *The Limits of Sisterhood* observe, she "accepted the gender system as she found it and attempted to expand women's power within it." This approach was fundamentally flawed to a person who wanted to overturn the gender system, like Catharine's "enemy" in Woodhull days Elizabeth Cady Stanton. But Stanton also saw the conflicts and paradoxes in Catharine's position. She notes in her autobiography that when she met her at Dr. Taylor's in New York, Catharine said she opposed woman suffrage (and indeed she had acted as spoiler at National Woman Suffrage Association lobbying conventions). If there was any danger of suffrage passing she would organize against it, but as it was, "the agitation helped her work. 'It is rather paradoxical,' I said to her, 'that the pressing of a false principle can help a true one, but when you get the women all thoroughly educated, they will step off to the polls and vote in spite of you.'" As indeed they finally did.

Catharine's attempts to expand women's power also left a contradictory legacy. In some ways she strengthened women. She "helped to shape a notion of shared strength and purpose among women that has been resurgent in the contemporary women's movement." At the same time, her fear of confronting men and her blindness to class and race privilege weakened women's position. As *The Limits of Sisterhood* concludes, "Beecher's strategy for the empowering of women was fundamentally divisive and defensive—excluding more women than it included, confining women to a single sphere of action even as it aimed to enlarge their choices. In that respect, too, Catharine Beecher's legacy survives into the late twentieth century."

Coincidentally, a short time after Catharine's death Harriet came to the end of her writing career. She was sixty-seven and had doubted the year before whether she had the stamina to finish *Poganuc People*. She never expected to write another serial, she wrote her son Charles. "I hope I may be able to finish it, as I greatly desire to do so, but I begin to feel that I am not so strong as I used to be." Your mother is an old woman, she reminded him, and she "should give up writing before people are tired of reading her." She did manage to finish her last novel, although she had to stop visiting and receiving company to do it and the reviews showed that some people were already tired of reading her.

Others weren't, and in fall 1878 W. D. Howells, who had just become editor of the *Atlantic Monthly*, pleased Harriet by inviting her to contribute again. Before she left for Florida she wrote two short stories for the magazine. This was her last effort at creative writing of any length. The spark died out, as Forrest Wilson puts it, in the "languorous air of Florida." Harriet now spent her time tending to Calvin in his increasingly frequent illnesses and enjoying her outdoor life. I wish I could give you the charm of the Florida morning, she wrote her old *Atlantic* friend Oliver Wendell Holmes. "My window is wide open; it is a lovely, fresh, sunny day, and a great orange tree hung with golden balls closes the prospect from my window. The tree is about thirty feet high, and its leaves fairly glisten in the sunshine."

Isabella was also occupying herself with the care of her husband. When she returned home from the Washington lobbying season, she found him in a sorry state. John seemed feeble and was having trouble sleeping. He resented her long absence and immediately started campaigning against the possibility of her leaving him again the next winter. After Catharine's funeral he only got worse, and Isabella thought he required constant watchfulness and care on her part. She called him her "baby & husband all in one" and wondered how long she would be able to "carry" him.

The problem was a double one. On the one hand, John's dependence tired her out and kept her from the work she wanted to do. On the other, he was still very critical of her and refused to trust her judgment. As she confided to her 1878 diary, "[A]ll my life is so troubled now—*full to harassment.* . . . My husband's lack of confidence in me is a steady drawback to my happiness—he leans on me to the extent of my capacity to bear . . . insists that I am fitted for positions of immense scope, yet will not trust me to write a note—or hire a horse, and still has a vague conviction that many of our troubles about Woodhull and Henry might have been avoided if I had only followed his counsel when present, and not dared to think my own thoughts or speak my own words, while he was absent."

Isabella felt conflicted: she was tired of being patient with John yet "hungry for full companionship." The Hookers' quarrels, more frequent now than ever before, ranged from the substantive (Isabella thought John shouldn't vote for their friend Joe Hawley for senator because he opposed woman suffrage) to the trivial (John thought Ned should stop drinking coffee in the morning and regulate his bowel movements, while Isabella considered these prescriptions too rigid). There was a major argument over a cabinet photo

Isabella wanted to send a young female admirer she met in Washington. John feared the photograph made her look too young and free, like a dancing girl. She felt he was showing the "same fastidiousness" masked as good sense that "made him anxious to regulate my laughing."

When John asked Isabella if the dress in the photo was suitable for a woman her age, thus questioning her judgment in one of her areas of expertise, the quarrel escalated:

> I[sabella:] . . . [Y]ou have trespassed on my individuality just as sister Catharine on her friends, and it has been as bad for you as for me. . . .
>
> J[ohn:] On the contrary, I think the great mistake of my life is that I have been too yielding to you—I have given up more than you and where I ought to have stood my ground.
>
> I[sabella:] I am sorry to hear you say that John—very sorry, because you know it is not the exact truth—that is not what you said to John Day [in 1874, when his son-in-law hinted that Isabella ruled the household, John had written that when they disagreed she yielded five times to his one].
>
> J[ohn:] Well—I ought not to have said what I did—in defense of you, I stretched a point.
>
> I[sabella:] You lied then.
>
> J[ohn:] Yes— I think [I] have sometimes—it has been almost necessary in your defense—but it is your conduct that has created the necessity. . .
>
> I[sabella:] And the lying is worse than the trespassing, bad as that is—and this strengthens what I said of your moral deterioration.

At this point the spirits intervened on Isabella's behalf. Sister Catharine and Samuel Bowles, the Hookers' friend and editor of the Springfield *Republican* who had died earlier in the year, both "came through" to chide John. They called him "unreasonable" and "obstinate," but Isabella notes she toned down their actual language because she thought it too harsh. She was thus able to escape responsibility for her angry feelings toward her husband, which were taboo in her society ("it was hardly I, it was sister C.—she was vehemently angry with you"). She also slipped into the more comfortable role of peacemaker. As Anne Throne Margolis says, "Transforming herself once again into a mediator, she functioned not only as a 'passive' intermediary between her husband and the spirits of these two individuals . . . but also as a modifier of their outspoken and somewhat harsh 'messages.'" What John thought of being ganged up on by spirits is not known. The transparent self-serving nature of Isabella's Spiritualism cannot have hastened his acceptance of it, but at least the police were not involved this time. As for Isabella, she sank gradually into the passivity and depression of the period before she went to Washington. Should she go to Europe in the fall? She would let the spirits decide for her. No decision was forthcoming, and eventually John was the one to travel—in search of better health to water cures or to England in the summers.

In summer 1879 John took daughter Mary to London with him, leaving Isabella boarding at the Nook Farm house. She was somewhat isolated— she had no horse and could not walk to the trains on her bad ankle. But she was glad to rest and see Mary escape her miserable existence for a time. Mary's marital situation had worsened over the past few years. In the mid-1870s the Burtons had reconciled after years of quarreling over Eugene's excessive drinking and his ban on her mother; he had promised to stop drinking, though he would not let daughter Kate see her grandparents. By now he had become a confirmed alcoholic, ensconced in his "sad habit," as Isabella put it. Worse, he was violently jealous and accused Mary of having affairs with any men she met. Isabella discusses his "jealous suspicion" in her 1878 diary and observes that like her mother, daughter Mary was being accused of indulgence in "free love." In 1878 Mary tried writing a story based on her life. Isabella made fair copies for her, and her aunt Harriet promised to help with prospective publishers. She sent the manuscript to W. D. Howells, asserting that it deserved a place in the *Atlantic* and she would be personally obliged by its acceptance. Nothing came of Mary's attempt at authorship, however.

It is likely that Eugene was physically as well as emotionally abusive. The Hookers were quite circumspect in putting names to Eugene's sins, but Isabella often referred to his bullying and John wrote that Mary was "bound to a *brutal* husband who cares nothing for her." By 1883 the Burtons were separated. Given the Beecher-Hooker views about the sanctity of marriage, the reason had to be a substantial one. The usually mild-mannered John exclaimed of Eugene, "It seems as if I could shoot the scoundrel even if I had to be hung for it." Isabella noted that after the separation Eugene had "no one to bully—no one afraid of him."

Eugene lived in Middletown with his sister, while Mary took a house in Norfolk, a mountain town in the northwest corner of the state where the Hookers often summered. Eugene communicated only by postcard on business. Kate Burton, ten years old when her parents split up, went back and forth between the two. Isabella could not see Kate at all (to visit her at Norfolk might have prompted Eugene to withdraw the child from Mary), and she had to make an appointment to see her daughter Alice and her Day granddaughters. Alice had also failed to find happiness in marriage. Her husband was unfaithful and used money to control her, withdrawing it if he disapproved of her activities. At an emotional reunion of Isabella and her two daughters Mary promised to share with Alice the proceeds from her story. Isabella worried that Alice seemed so "dwarfed & narrowed," and every holiday she cried at the absence of the Day granddaughters.

The irony was not lost on Isabella that young people outside her family always seemed attracted to her. In Washington two young suffragists, Julia Holmes and Kate Trimble, lionized her. She confided to her diary that Mary confessed being jealous of Trimble and "all those girls that were so in love with me." The nineteen-year-old Trimble initiated a correspondence with Isabella when they left Washington; soon she was addressing her as "my darling mother." Young men, too, sought Isabella's friendship. Although her former confidants Robert Allen and Roswell Lamson were now married and occupied with their families, she was friendly with a Tom Beaty, whose departed mother she brought back to chat. There was also Will Gillette, her nephew and Ned's best friend from childhood. Isabella and Will remained close. In the late 1870s and early 1880s when Gillette was beginning his distinguished career as an actor (he would become famous for playing Sherlock Holmes) Isabella tried to help him by critiquing his acting and getting him loans.

The question of money was especially frustrating when it came to the young people in Isabella's family. In the early days of their marriage the Hookers seemed to have more than they knew what to do with; now they were struggling and had no money to help their children. Mary and Alice were both in need, while Ned was trying to start a career and a family. After studying at the École de Médicine in Paris during the Beecher-Tilton trial, Ned had returned to Boston University and graduated in 1877 with an M.D. He then established a practice in Hartford, specializing in homeopathic medicine. Unable to help him financially, Isabella started making a regular round of social calls in order to increase her son's clientele.

She swallowed her pride and asked Olivia Langdon for a loan of five hundred dollars. She needed it, she said, to redo the parts of the house she had looted to furnish Ned's office. She also had the expense of making a skylight window in the maids' room, as it was "not doing as we would be done by to keep servants in dark unventilated rooms." She now wanted to buy Ned a set of books for a wedding present. In September 1879 Ned married his fiancée, Martha "Mattie" Kilbourne. Though marrying was not practical financially for Ned, Isabella finally brought John around. Typically, she exaggerated her role in the marriage, writing in later years that she had chosen her son's wife for him. She did welcome Mattie, showering her with affection, as she had done with Eugene, only this time her warm feelings were returned. The two women supported each other in the years to come, Mattie accepting her mother-in-law's eccentricities and Isabella providing ready help with the children.

In the same year Harriet's Charles also married. Like Ned, he had wanted to marry earlier but had been persuaded by his parents to wait. Again like Ned, he was just beginning a distinguished career. Charley had been a typical male Beecher in his adolescence, sowing his wild oats and flirting with disbelief in God, but after his stint at sea he had settled down and gone to Harvard like a good Beecher boy. There he met Susie Munroe of Cambridge and in spring 1879 was ordained as a minister and married. His first parish lay in Stowe territory—Saco, Maine—and Harriet devoted the summer to helping settle the newlyweds in the parsonage. Harriet felt the same as Isabella about wanting to help the young couple financially. Although she was initially short, by the early '80s she was able to supplement Charley's salary by two hundred dollars a year.

For at least a decade, from the late 1870s to the late '80s, Harriet's and Isabella's lives followed a parallel course in more ways than one. The sisters had similar family situations: they felt responsible for taking care of an ailing husband and experienced their daughters more as sources of worry than support; each relied heavily on an exemplary son whose loyalty was unquestionable. Isabella, ten years younger than Harriet, continued her career as a social reformer while Harriet settled into retirement, but their psychology was much the same. If Isabella often seemed distant, living in a world beyond this one, so did Harriet. There had always been an otherworldliness about her as she suddenly withdrew into a reverie, and she had always been deeply Christian. Now, although she communicated much less than Isabella with the spirits, she focused with new intentness on the next world.

To most of her correspondents Harriet began to write of the deaths of her and Calvin's friends and associates. It gave her a dizzy feeling, she said, to think that all her old school friends were gone except for one. "I feel with you that we have come into the land of leave-taking," she wrote Dr. Holmes. But, she added, she could sometimes catch a glimpse of the "opposite shore" (she always thought of heaven as being on the opposite shore of a river). "[N]ow and then we catch a strain of music, perhaps even a gesture of recognition. They are thinking of us, without doubt, on the other side." Harriet had faith that she would eventually be reunited with the lost ones. She wrote Annie Fields in the same vein as she addressed Holmes, saying she hoped before long to join her lost sons and the companions of her youth.

If there was anything that could draw Harriet and Isabella away from their preoccupation with the "other side," it was their new grandchildren. Susie gave birth to Lyman Beecher Stowe in 1880, with Harriet arriving just in time to receive the baby from the doctor. She visited Georgie after her bout with scarlet fever the next year and then returned to Saco. Lyman, she wrote home, was an "exquisite" baby. Two years after their marriage Ned and Mattie had their first, whom they named Isabel. The birth of this namesake initiated Isabella and John into a more normal and happier experience of grandparenting than they had previously known. It made up for a lot.

Only so much of the past could be repaired, however. The first three months of 1880 Isabella spent in New York giving a round of "parlor talks." She charged five dollars for a series of six talks and a dollar for one talk; this was the paid work she had promised Mrs. Langdon she would engage in to help repay the loan. The January series focused on suffrage, but the subsequent courses of talks would branch out to include other topics. The rationale, Isabella wrote her friend Lucy Chittenden of Brooklyn, was that women needed to become better informed on public issues of the day; they had to prepare themselves either for voting on their own or, if they did not want to vote, for influencing men in the proper direction. Her proposed subjects for the March–April series were police reform, sanitary reform, jurisprudence, temperance, kindergarten and industrial schools, and prison reform.

But Isabella never got a chance to offer this course, for she was essentially kicked out of town. When she left New York to accompany John on a rare visit to his brother in Philadelphia (Isabella wanted to go to Washington, but John hated her favorite city), she received letters from Lucy Chittenden and Laura Holloway of the Brooklyn *Daily Eagle* warning her not to return to New York. The *Daily Eagle* had received some disquieting statements about Isabella saying she was hostile to her brother Henry and planned to reopen the scandal. The newspaper arranged a "truce"—they would not publish anything about Isabella if she stayed away from New York. Otherwise, Chittenden wrote John, the factions who hated Henry would use her as a pawn and "crucify" her anew with her "frank but sure to be distorted utterances as a spiritualist."

Were the people who would crucify Isabella really her brother's enemies? Or were they intermediaries acting on behalf of Henry himself? He had used Lib Tilton's Spiritualism to publicly dismiss her recent confession. Probably Isabella did not know who was threatening her. Nor did she keep a diary at that time or make references to Henry in her letters, so one cannot pinpoint her motivations for choosing New York for the parlor talks. It would be hard to believe, though, that she didn't dream of reconciliation and try to contact Henry or that he didn't feel threatened by her presence nearby. She was perfectly capable of showing up at Plymouth Church to direct his belated confession. The Hookers had recently read Nathaniel Hawthorne's *The Scarlet Letter* (1850) and marveled at the parallels between Henry and the adulterous minister Arthur Dimmesdale. They were intrigued by the refusal of Dimmesdale's congregation to believe him once he confessed. Would the same happen with Henry? Whatever Isabella's intentions in going to New York, it was not a practical move so soon after the trial. Her brother Jim wrote his wife, "I think sister Belle would have done far better to come here this winter than to be browsing around Brooklyn . . . where she will only make a nuisance of herself."

Jim went on to postulate a heritage of mental illness affecting Isabella, Tom, and himself. "I am sure that there runs a streak of insanity in our mothers [sic] three children—or rather a monomania, assuming diverse forms. I recognize it in Tom and myself. The only advantage I have is in being absolutely conscious of the fact. Tom is partially so. Belle is absolutely unconscious and is therefore the craziest of the three. However she is almost sixty. If she got well, she couldnt [sic] do much good, and if she grows worse, she cannot do much harm—and a very few years will clear us all out, and in a dozen years or so if any body should ask who were those Beechers any how, there will be nobody able to answer the question." Whether or not Jim was right about the streak of insanity, Tom would live another twenty years and Isabella twenty-five. Nor would the Beechers be forgotten.

Isabella might have been devastated about being driven from New York had she not been distracted by an exciting event. In May 1880, after years of boarding in their own home, the Hookers began keeping house again on Forest Street. This meant that Isabella was responsible for finding and taking care of boarders in order to make ends meet. The task was not a trivial one. If one family boarded for a lengthy period of time, like the Walkers did, it was fine—but there was usually a quick turnover and anxious periods when no boarders applied. During the first year, for instance, the section of the house the Hookers called "West End" had twelve different sets of boarders.

Even so, the Hookers now had control over the house and could do as much socializing as they wanted. They made up for lost time with luncheon parties, dinner parties, evening parties, birthday parties, and a succession of overnight guests. It seemed like the fifties or the period after the war and before Isabella had been ostracized. The Mark Twains and Mrs. Langdon, the Stowes, Gillettes, Warners, Hawleys, and Nathaniel Burtons gathered again at the Hookers'; even Mary and Alice came. Some of the renters were distinguished people. From July to October 1880 and occasionally thereafter the novelist Frances Hodgson Burnett boarded with the Hookers. She had not yet written her most famous books, *Little Lord Fauntleroy* (1886) and *The Secret Garden* (1911), but was collaborating on a play with Will Gillette, who spent the summer with his sister Lillie Warner. "Esmeralda," based on a Burnett short story, became her first successful play and also advanced Will's career.

Once the Hookers were settled in their house and John's health improved, Isabella resumed attending woman suffrage conventions. She stayed close to home, though, seldom venturing outside of New England. There were some notable meetings in the region in the early 1880s. In October 1880 the Woman Suffrage Jubilee took place in Worcester, celebrating the thirtieth anniversary of the first women's rights meeting to be held in Massachusetts. Isabella made a speech, along with Julia Smith Parker. The famous Connecticut tax protester had suddenly married after her sister Abby's death. It was her first marriage and she was eighty-six; she wrote the Hookers that she was just as surprised as they were. The next spring Isabella attended a rousing NWSA convention in Boston and spoke on a topic she was gradually making her own, "The Constitutional Right of Women to Vote." A Mrs. McClellan Brown was converted by this speech, as she would confess in a letter to Isabella fifteen years later.

The main point of interest at this convention was the royal reception accorded the NWSA by Massachusetts officials. The pro-woman suffrage governor John D. Long invited the women to the State House for a tour. Elizabeth Cady Stanton, the current NWSA president, had a speaking engagement elsewhere, the *History of Woman Suffrage* notes, "but Isabella Beecher Hooker and Susan B. Anthony led the way to the State House and introduced the delegates," about a hundred of them, to the governor. Isabella rather put him on the spot, saying "Speak a word to us, Governor Long, we need help. Stand here, please, face to face with these earnest women and tell us where help is to come from." Susan seconded her and repeated an old Isabella Beecher Hooker argument as she "said in low pathetic tones: 'Yes, we are tired. Sir, we are weary with our work. For forty years some of us have carried this burden, and now, if we might lay it down at the feet of honorable men, such as you, how happy we should be!'" Another honorable man, Mayor Prince of Boston, arranged for the suffragists to visit with the working women of Jordan, Marsh & Co., a large department store. Isabella again gave a speech. Like her friend Susan B. Anthony, she was very interested in working women and the current labor movements. She was also concerned with prison reform and was happy to make the visit arranged by Governor Long to the state's model women's prison at Sherborn.

After the Boston meeting the NWSA continued to invade the territory of the rival American Woman Suffrage Association with a series of seven conventions in New England. Isabella presided over the Hartford event in June. The Rev. Phebe Hanaford, having forgiven Isabella's support of Victoria Woodhull, participated in the meeting. One of the joys of the Boston and Hartford conventions for Isabella was the presence of her old friend Olympia Brown. Much to their chagrin, Brownie had been forced to leave Connecticut in 1878. Sexist members of her Unitarian Universalist congregation in Bridgeport felt that Brownie should not work once she had a husband and child. Why would she want to continue as a minister? So the congregation dismissed her. When she received a call to a church in Racine, Wisconsin, she and her family moved to the Midwest. Isabella greatly missed her colleague in Connecticut. Although she continued year after year to work for suffrage at the state level, it was never so much fun after Olympia left.

Isabella still believed that, however important the struggle for women's rights in New England, the real action was in Washington, where a federal amendment or court decision might be had. She failed to persuade John to go to Washington with her, but she went herself in January 1882 for the NWSA lobbying convention. There she gave the converse of her usual argument, perhaps reflecting her changed relationship with her husband. Instead of arguing that women's roles as wife and mother prepared them for political work, she "showed that political equality would dignify woman in home life, give added weight to her opinions on all questions, and command new respect for her from all classes of men."

The NWSA's lobbying activities were more successful than usual that year. The Senate and the House of Representatives had just appointed standing committees to "look after the interests of women," and the suffragists secured a hearing on the sixteenth amendment before the Senate committee. The first day young women and women new to the movement spoke; the second day the "old guard" took over—Isabella with Elizabeth Cady Stanton, Matilda Joslyn Gage, and Lillie Devereux Blake. The committee reported four to three in favor of submission of the amendment to the Senate. The amendment, of course, lost, but this was the first favorable majority report it had received from either house of Congress.

Thinking of John, Isabella did not run this lobbying session, nor did she stay in Washington beyond January. But even though he required his wife's presence and hated Washington, John was always willing to work in some way for women's rights. He had already made important contributions in drafting the Connecticut Women's Property bill and writing a defense of Susan B. Anthony. Soon after Isabella's return he involved himself in another battle. Mary Hall, a young woman from Hartford, had applied for admission to the Connecticut bar. She had studied law and been examined by a committee of the bar. The bar voted to admit her, subject to the opinion of the state Supreme Court, and John argued her case in front of the Court. He was severely hampered by the fact that precedent was against his client—several courts had recently decided *against* the growing number of women who wanted to be lawyers. In 1872 the Supreme Court of Illinois denied Myra Bradwell admission to the bar; she appealed to the U.S. Supreme Court, which upheld the denial. Belva Lockwood, an NWSA colleague of Isabella's in Washington, was refused admission to practice before the U.S. Supreme Court. In the neighboring state of Massachusetts Lelia Robinson was told by the Court that only the state legislature had the authority to permit women to practice law (the legislature soon passed such a statute).

While the opposing lawyers argued these precedents, John claimed that the common law and legislative history of Connecticut gave women "equal right, scope and opportunity with men whenever possible." He argued that the state constitution did not prohibit women from any public duty and pointed out that Connecticut women preached, practiced medicine, taught in public schools, and acted as executors, guardians, trustees, and overseers. Why couldn't they be lawyers too? The state licensing statute referred to "persons" who wished to practice law, and, as Isabella had argued so many times, "persons" included women. Surprisingly, John won the case. Chief Justice John Duane Park ruled that the framers of the statute could have limited "persons" to men but did not do so; they thus intended to include women. He stated broadly: "We are not to forget that all statutes are to be construed, as far as possible, in favor of equality of rights."

This decision was an important one. As Virginia G. Drachman says in her history of female lawyers, it "represented one of American women's first successes in using the judicial system to change radically their legal status." Four other states soon admitted women to the bar by judicial decision rather than legislative statute. *In re Hall* gave Isabella some supporting evidence for her preference for the judicial route in seeking woman suffrage. The pattern of relying on the legislature could be broken and an issue of women's rights decided on the grounds of equal protection of the laws. Isabella became friendly with Mary Hall during the legal case and brought her to state suffrage work. Hall became vice president of the Hartford Equal Rights Club, which was organized a few years later and included Isabella as a charter member. As a Connecticut lawyer, Hall was official but hardly equal. There was so much prejudice against a woman speaking in court that she confined herself to office work; her office staff and clientele were exclusively female. She thus functioned in her daily practice as part of the "separate sphere" the court had theoretically struck down.

In June 1882, the month after John argued the Mary Hall case, Harriet received a great honor. Houghton Mifflin Company, the publishers of the *Atlantic Monthly,* threw her a party to celebrate her seventieth birthday. Actually she wasn't seventy, but seventy-one, and the large banner at the party reading "Harriet Beecher Stowe 1812–1882" was wrong. The publishers' coyness about asking her age and Harriet's coyness in response (she said she was "at least 70") led to the mix-up. Harriet was born June 14, 1811, but for some reason Oliver Wendell Holmes insisted that her birth year was 1812. A few days before her seventy-first birthday Harriet took tea at the Hookers'; on June 14 the party took place. Despite the confusion over the date, it was an unprecedented occurrence for the *Atlantic* to honor a woman. For twenty years after the awkward dinner of 1859, where the Stowes and Harriet Prescott Spofford had been present and wine was (at least officially) restricted, the *Atlantic* dinners had been given for and by men. Arthur Gilman, a writer who attended many of these occasions and later penned a nostalgic article about them, singled out a successful dinner held in 1874 to celebrate a change in the ownership of the magazine. Twenty-eight men were present. The absence of women was highlighted when Mark Twain was asked to respond to the after dinner speeches on behalf of "the President of the United States and the Female Contributors of the *Atlantic*."

The female contributors created their own joke regarding the next dinner, which was held in 1877 to honor the poet John Greenleaf Whittier on his seventieth birthday. This time fifty-seven men gathered at the Brunswick Hotel, and the press called the company "the most notable that had ever been seen in this country within four walls." Gilman considered the "vinous offerings" just as impressive; six different wines were on the menu, "ranging from Sauterne to Burgundy, through the changes of Sherry, Chablis, 'Mumm's Dry,' Roederer Imperial, and Claret." The Whittier Birthday Dinner became famous in American literary history because of Mark Twain's feeling that the haughty Eastern writers had humiliated him by failing to laugh at his speech.

But the dinner could also be remembered for the witty protest made by the female writers, who had been excluded altogether. Each woman sent Mr. Houghton a letter the day before the dinner regretting that she wouldn't be able to attend (of course, she had never been invited!). Each woman gave a different frivolous reason for her absence—Harriet Prescott Spofford, for instance, had to study some rushes on the banks of a river. She then mentioned casually that one of the other women was about to give a dinner and start a new ladies' magazine. Each of the letter writers, who included Gail Hamilton, Helen Hunt Jackson, Rebecca Harding Davis, and Louisa May Alcott, as well as Stowe and Spofford, mentioned a different woman's name as the one who was starting a new magazine. Thus, no individual woman could be singled out as the ringleader or accused of being oversensitive to slights.

This clever protest worked. Mr. Houghton was said to "detect sarcasm" in the letters, and the publishers worried that the women actually would start their own magazine. At any rate, the all-male dinners were over. At the next seventieth birthday celebration, given as a brunch for Oliver Wendell Holmes, women constituted a third of the company. Harriet attended the brunch in December 1879 on her way to Florida for the season. She was given a prestigious seat next to Mr. Houghton, with Dr. Holmes seated on the other side. The celebration of Harriet's seventieth birthday took the form of a garden party. It was held at the estate west of Boston of her friends ex-governor of Massachusetts William Claflin and his wife (the friends who had prevented Victoria Woodhull from speaking in Boston). The number of people attending again doubled—to over two hundred. "The world and his wife came," Harriet wrote the twins, "& I shook hands with each one." For some reason the twins were not present, along with the Beecher brothers William and Tom, but everyone else from Harriet's family attended. As with Whittier's party, the guest list formed a literary who's who of the time, a veritable index to the *Atlantic Monthly*.

After two hours of socializing, the guests gathered under a tent covering some two hundred seats in front of a platform. From the platform Mr. Houghton made a tribute to Harriet and in a throwback to the early days of Catharine Beecher, when women were seen and not heard, Henry Ward Beecher responded for his sister. The speech was remembered for its wit: Henry noted that some people thought he had written *Uncle Tom's Cabin* until he wrote his novel *Norwood*—that stopped the rumor, absolutely "killed the thing dead." Harriet was probably pleased with Henry, but to a large extent the speech was more about him than about her—*his* experience reading *Uncle Tom* and *his* childhood experience of their father and sainted mother.

Following Henry's speech came the reading of poems written for Harriet—most notably by Whittier and Holmes. Dr. Holmes read Elizabeth Stuart Phelps's poem for her and Georgiana Stowe Allen's husband read her poem. Georgie's poem, which was as creditable as the other offerings, took up the theme that God wrote *Uncle Tom's Cabin*. Her mother was born "an instrument/To be played by the hand of God" in the freeing of the slaves:

> Unconscious she sweetly played,
> With music right
> And discord wrong,
> The song that *God* had made.

No doubt Harriet looked favorably on this poem, even though the effect was to reduce her own agency.

Another theme was touched upon that may have surprised guests who did not know Harriet well. Brother Edward gave a speech emphasizing her efforts on behalf of women. As W. D. Howells put it in his supplement to the *Atlantic Monthly* describing the celebration, "Rev. Edward Beecher spoke at some length of the bearing of the works of Mrs. Stowe upon the woman-suffrage question. He told of her work with the late Miss Catherine [sic] Beecher at Hartford to extend the education of women, and affirmed that the course of God's events is upward and onward to a perfect coordination of the sexes in the work of the race." Interestingly, the guests included several suffragists in addition to women writers. Along with Isabella and John were Harriet's old friend Fanny Fern and the AWSA's Henry Blackwell, Lucy Stone, and their daughter Alice Stone Blackwell.

When the poems and speeches were done, Harriet came to the front of the platform to make a brief response. Phelps, one of the *Atlantic* writers, described her appearance that day as a "memorable one. Her dignity, her repose, a certain dreaminess and aloofness of manner characteristic of her, blended gently with her look of peace and unmistakable happiness." Harriet's short speech was by far the most original one of the day and perhaps the most surprising to the guests, who all rose and remained standing while she spoke. After thanking her friends, she went on like a true social activist to talk of the present and not of the past. If anyone doubted that slavery was gone forever, they should see the freed slaves, as she did on a daily basis in the South (the population of Mandarin, Florida, in 1881 was twelve hundred, three hundred of whom were white). The black people were growing richer and happier. An "old negro friend" in the Stowes' neighborhood had a new two-story house, an orange grove, a sugar mill, and money in the bank. He told Mr. Stowe one day that he also had four horses, twenty head of cattle, and ten children—"all *mine, every one mine.*" Harriet said, "Well, now, that is a thing that a black man could not say once, and this man was sixty years old before he could say it. With all the faults of the colored people, take a man and put him down with nothing but his hands, and how many could say as much as that? I think they have done well."

One might wish for a less patriarchal example of the successes of former slaves and less emphasis on the "faults" of blacks (there being no corresponding reference to the faults of whites), but Harriet's remarks do seem a bit formulaic. They may have been a practiced response to criticisms of the freedpeople she heard everywhere—that freedpeople were lazy, lacked ambition, couldn't plan for the future, and so on. The several references to the failings of black people and the need for white people to have patience have the tone of a defensive reaction to racist assumptions by whites, which had become virulent and widespread by 1882. Harriet's speech shows that she had come to view herself as an ambassador for the freed slaves. In her mind her residence in Florida half the year was not simply an older person's respite from snow and cold, as it would become for many northerners in the twentieth century. Instead, it involved responsibilities (thus her preoccupation with church and school for the local black townspeople). To Harriet her Florida life was all of a piece with her earlier career.

Not all the guests at the seventieth birthday party remembered the event warmly. Arthur Gilman couldn't get over the deterioration he saw in the *Atlantic* dinners as women were admitted to the company. "The enlargement of the borders," he complained "was like adding water to a cup of tea. There was a suggestion of the old times, but the strength of comradeship had been weakened." (Did his editor insert "cup of tea" in place of "glass of wine"?) For some people the event had a positive influence. With almost all her family present and some of them not speaking to one another, the potential for conflict must have worried Harriet. As it turned out, Henry and Eunice avoided Isabella, but sister Mary seems to have reconciled with her at the party, ending their long estrangement. And Mary Beecher Perkins arrived at the Hookers for an extended visit less than two months later, in August 1882.

After the birthday celebration the Stowes spent time with Georgie and their grandson Freeman in Cambridge (the Allens had moved East from the Berkshires). Every day Calvin visited the Boston Public Library, where he was reading the life and diary of John Quincy Adams in a dozen volumes; he and Harriet reminisced about the long fight over slavery. They went early to Florida that fall in order to participate in an important event for Mandarin—the dedication of the Mandarin Church of Our Savior. This church had evolved from the informal Bible readings led over the years by Calvin Stowe, first in the Stowe home and then in the combination church and school building. Eventually Harriet donated land and the Stowes helped the community erect a new building. In 1880 they'd hired an Episcopal minister, C. M. Sturgess, whom Harriet thought of as "perfect." With Reverend Sturgess to look after the church, the Stowes were able to lead a lazy life.

Sometimes the weather in Florida was less than idyllic. In 1880, for instance, a late freeze reduced Harriet to tears when she saw the ruined foliage; that year the Stowes lost their income from the orange trees. The next year the house leaked before they arrived, subjecting the family to mildew. But spring 1883 was a "glorious, budding, blossoming spring," Harriet wrote, when just to breathe was a blessing. "I love to have a day of mere existence. Life itself is a pleasure when the sun shines warm, and the lizards dart from all the shingles of the roof, and the birds sing in so many notes and tones the yard reverberates; and I sit and dream and am happy, and never want to go back North, nor do anything with the toiling, snarling world again."

The world soon intruded, as it has a way of doing. In the summer Calvin, who every year seemed to grow heavier, less active, and more prone to disease, was diagnosed with a serious illness, Bright's disease. A type of nephritis, or inflammation of the kidney, Bright's disease is progressive and gradually destroys the kidneys. Calvin, who was eighty-one, would not have many years left. The winter of 1883–1884 was thus the Stowes' last in Florida. It was a happy one. Harriet wrote that Mandarin looked "gay and airy" with

Stowe family at home in Mandarin, Fla., early 1880s. Left to right: Eliza, Harriet Beecher Stowe, Charles, Calvin, Eunice Beecher, Hatty. Courtesy Harriet Beecher Stowe Center, Hartford, Conn.

its new church and rectory. She and Calvin had drawn closer in their later years when they no longer had to worry about Harriet's getting pregnant or balancing their careers and children. Harriet told Susie Howard that they had "never enjoyed each other's society more than this winter. His mind is still clear and bright, and he is competent as ever to explain a text or instruct me in the merits of a verse." But, she wrote again in the spring, she could not bring her husband to Brooklyn to visit on the way home to Hartford, as they had often done; nor was he well enough for her to leave him and come herself. People would have to make the trip to Hartford now.

One friend who came was Annie Fields, who had been in Europe at the time of the seventieth birthday celebration. She brought with her the author who had become her companion after the death of James Fields in 1881. For Sarah Orne Jewett, then thirty-five, the visit was something of a pilgrimage to the source, a chance to pay homage to the founder of local color. As Forrest Wilson puts it, Jewett "received the torch of New England realism from Harriet Beecher Stowe's hand." Jewett brought a copy of her latest novel, A Country Doctor (1884), which Harriet praised to Annie as "not only interesting & bright, but full of strong & earnest thought." Harriet invited the two women to Florida in February, for Calvin seemed much better. Ultimately, though, they couldn't go. Even if Calvin survived the trip, Harriet explained to Susie, their Mandarin house did not have the conveniences to take care of an invalid. "It was charming while Mr. Stowe was well enough to sit on the veranda and take long daily walks, but now it is safer and better that we all stay with him here." The "we all" now included Charles and his family, for in 1885 Charlie managed to secure a church in Hartford, the Windsor Avenue Congregational Church. This move allowed him to escape his contentious parishioners in Maine, help take care of his father, and start work on his mother's biography; she was already arranging her letters and papers for his use.

In January 1885 Harriet wrote Isabella the following note. The "Edward" she refers to is Isabella's son Ned Hooker, who was Calvin's doctor.

> Dear Belle
> I think more of my brothers and sisters than I ever have done before and have written to all and got replies from all but Henry [who was notorious for not answering letters]. Your letter is a comfort to me—Yesterday I asked Edward where you were and sent a message to you—I send the autograph you ask for from my poems—It is quite appropriate to the cold frozen season now that keeps me close in doors. Mr[.] Stowe sinks gradually from week to week. Edward thinks he may last months. His mind is clear and he is free from pain. We have the best of nurses and in

short we have *all* under the circumstances we could ask for. I can
scarcely believe when I see Ed's manly form and face that he came
from that little white delicate baby I once knew. He is a son to be
proud of.

    Your loving Sister

    Hatty

Isabella was indeed proud of Ned and needed him to lean on as much
as Harriet needed Charlie. The almost three years since the seventieth birthday
celebration had been a time of endings and losses for the Hookers too. By
1883 it was clear that they would not be able to keep their house; in May
they rented it again, moving out and looking for a buyer. John says in his
autobiography that he struggled unsuccessfully for several years to recover
from the financial crash of 1875–1876. "I found myself no longer able to hold
my own dwelling-house, and after a long effort to carry it, I put it into the
hands of a broker to sell." In spring 1885 the house was bought by newcomers
to Hartford, the Yosts. The Hookers lived with Ned and family during the
winters in his house on Farmington Avenue near Nook Farm. They spent the
summers vacationing or staying with John's relatives, the Harts, in Farmington.

Usually Isabella attended suffrage conventions or gave talks for part
of the year. The winter before the house was sold she gave a series of "parlor
talks" on Spiritualism in Boston. When a member of the audience asked how
her acceptance of Spiritualism had affected her religious belief, she wrote a
statement called "Confession of Faith." She said she believed in a Creator, a
first cause of all things. All creation was striving toward a higher level, and
the spirit when separated from the flesh still needed a greater power to turn
it toward holiness. "In the God of the Hebrew and the Christian, the Buddhist
and the Mahometan alike we may recognize the all-wise, tender, brooding
Mother Spirit of the Universe, under whose providential discipline, called evolution by the scientist, and foreordination and decrees by the theologian, all
souls shall at last reach their culmination." People on earth who hold communion with disembodied spirits will be "strengthened and encouraged in the
redemptive work to which we are all consecrated." They shall become more
like the great teacher Jesus of Nazareth. She still looked forward to an imminent second coming.

It was a good time for Isabella to fine-tune her religious beliefs because she was going to need her faith. Losing the house was a terrible blow,
but a worse affliction threatened. The Hookers' daughter Mary had gone into
a decline. They always worried about her health, as she seemed to grow "less

hearty" as the years went by. At first they attributed her weakness to the trials of her marriage, but escaping Eugene had actually improved her mental outlook. The problem was physical in nature, and Mary spent an increasing amount of time at water cures. She went to Dr. Jackson's Dansville cure, where her father occasionally stayed, and then to Dr. Hurd's, directed by a homeopathic physician. At the time of her fortieth birthday in August 1885 Mary was pale and sickly and had developed a severe cough. Although Isabella well knew the symptoms of tuberculosis because her mother had died of it, she tried to deceive herself as long as possible. Mary's cough was nervous, not pulmonary, she wrote Alice from vacation at Swampscott, Massachusetts; it came on only when she was overtired. She advised Alice to write Mary "diverting, cheerful letters" and everything would be fine.

By December Mary lay on her deathbed at brother Ned's. Tuberculosis, which was also known as the "white plague" and "consumption" because it seemed to consume its victims, was still as much of a scourge as when it killed Harriet Porter Beecher a half century earlier. It was a particular threat to women in youth and early middle age, who died of the disease at rates twice as high as those of men in their age group. Mary was twenty years old in 1865. Of every hundred women that age, more than five would be dead from tuberculosis by the age of thirty and more than eight by the age of fifty. In 1885 the germ theory of disease was not yet well known to the general public (it would become so in the 1890s), but Isabella knew that tuberculosis was contagious. She may have learned this from Doctor Ned or from her study of sanitation—"Woman's Work in Sanitation" was one of her speech titles in the 1880s. At any rate, she avoided kissing Mary on the lips and was later stricken with guilt that she had withheld this token of affection from her dying daughter. She devoted herself entirely to Mary's care, however. The last few weeks she spent singing her daughter's favorite hymns to her, reciting her favorite psalms and poems, and copying hymns and poems for others to deliver. Toward the end Ned gave injections of morphine and on January 20, 1886, Mary died.

If Isabella hadn't already been a Spiritualist, the calamity of losing a child would probably have converted her. It was a great comfort to have Mary coming back for a chat about the spirit world. In a way it was less painful to contemplate her death than to think of what a friend of Mary's called her "blasted life and broken heart." Mary's death seems to have confirmed John in his Spiritualism and thus brought the Hookers closer together. Earlier he was an interested "investigator" but still skeptical. Isabella's shenanigans regarding Eugene's burglar and her enlistment of the spirits on her side of marital arguments did not help. Yet two years after his daughter's death John was giving talks on Spiritualism. The ministers of Hartford asked him to address the topic at one of their meetings, and the Supreme Court judges, having heard of this successful talk, got him to repeat it at an evening gathering in the courtroom.

In the discussion of Spiritualism that he includes in his reminiscences, John says, "I started upon my investigations in utter disbelief and with a great disrelish for the whole subject." He soon found, however, that many spirit communications to him could not be accounted for by either of the two explanations advanced by anti-Spiritualists: fraud and mind reading. One of his examples is an interesting one. Having failed to sell his house, he was preparing to surrender it to the mortgagee when a friend told him she had just been to a séance and received a message for him. Governor Richard Hubbard, John's friend who had been instrumental in getting the married women's property act passed, had died recently. He came through at the séance and advised John to wait before giving up the property. That month a buyer appeared for the house. John could not explain this occurrence by fraud or mind reading, but perhaps it was mere luck. The great magician Harry Houdini would have said that he wanted too much to believe.

In any case John's embrace of Spiritualism in his and Isabella's mutual grief went a long way toward restoring the Hookers' former close relationship. A few months after Mary's death Alice questioned her father's "credulity" (for accepting Spiritualism?) in a letter, and Isabella reprimanded her. Her father was a truly "remarkable" man, she should realize; he had an unusually fine character that must be appreciated. He was by nature a poet and artist but through his study of law had also developed logical and judicial faculties. The Hookers were able to stand together to face the several deaths that followed Mary's in the next year. First, Calvin Stowe died in August 1886. He had lingered for several years after being diagnosed with the incurable Bright's disease and was anxious to "cross the river," as he and Harriet put it.

There were also unexpected deaths. In the fall Jim Beecher shocked everyone by shooting himself in exactly the same way his brother George had years ago. Jim had been persuaded by brother Henry to leave Poughkeepsie and take charge of the Plymouth Church charities. This position was unsuited to an already depressed man, and in 1882 he committed himself to the State Homeopathic Asylum for the Insane in Middletown, New York. For the next four years he bounced from institution to institution, while his wife desperately sought a cure. Frankie even consulted Isabella about Spiritualism but decided there was nothing in it to save Jim. Finally, on a trip to Elmira to visit the Gleason water cure and see brother Tom, he committed suicide.

The next winter Henry had a stroke. Isabella hurried to Brooklyn, expecting that her brother might at last apologize, but she was turned away by Eunice Beecher. She paced the sidewalk outside the Beecher house, where she was exploited for stories by reporters eager to revive the scandal. When Henry died a few days later, the papers reported that Isabella had been barred from the funeral. She had to veil herself heavily and join a procession of fifty thousand people in order to file past his coffin in Plymouth Church. Once Isabella returned to Hartford Henry's spirit appeared to her, as tearful and contrite as anyone could wish.

Harriet had to endure one more loss after Henry. In August 1887, in her presence, Georgie succumbed to her various ailments; she was only forty-four. During her vigil at Georgie's bedside Harriet wrote down the last two lines of one of her published poems: "Your joy be the reality/Our suffering life the dream." It was her Christian faith in immortality that brought Harriet through these tragedies. If she seldom conjured up the spirits of her departed family members, she focused more and more on joining them on the other side. "I have thought much lately of the possibility of my leaving you all and going home," she wrote. "I am come to that stage of my pilgrimage that is within sight of the River of Death," and she was ready. Although she suffered, sometimes in her sleep she would dream of "a vivid spiritual life" near Christ and feel on waking the "joy" she had wished her daughter.

After Calvin's death Harriet lived a quiet life in Hartford with the twins. She never went to Florida again. Instead she sold all her Mandarin properties except for the orange grove and used the money to buy Charles a parsonage near her. She asked that the Mandarin Church of Our Savior reserve a stained glass window on the river side as a memorial to Calvin (the window was delayed for lack of funds but finally completed in 1916 and dedicated to both the Stowes). Although she was now restricted to the North, Harriet lived as much outside as possible. Her neighbor Rev. Joseph Twichell in "Harriet Beecher Stowe in Hartford" attributed her good health to habits of physical exercise. Twice a day she walked for an hour or longer and between walks was "more or less out of doors." In the morning she usually walked the two miles to Charley's new house and back at "a good pace." She often left the pavement for the fields and gathered wildflowers or stopped to talk with workmen or with children playing. "A few days since," wrote Twichell, "she stopped a little girl of the writer's acquaintance who was performing the rather unfeminine feat of riding a bicycle, and had her show how she managed the mount and the dismount, etc., while she looked on laughing and applauding."

Twichell published his article in the "Authors at Home" series of *Critic* magazine. Several essays of this type appeared as people who recognized that Harriet Beecher Stowe was still alive came to pay homage. Frances Willard, the famous president of the Woman's Christian Temperance Union (WCTU), stopped by in 1887. To Willard Harriet confessed that she'd acquired the walking habit years ago at the Brattleboro Water Cure. They talked for a time and Willard recited a verse from a Stowe poem. "At this she took me by the hand, saying earnestly, 'God help you,' 'God be with you.' I kissed the dear, old, wrinkled hand that in its strength had written 'Uncle Tom's Cabin'; she gave a kind goodbye . . . and we went our ways." Willard might not have ended her account of the visit in this way had she known that the goodbye scene was familiar to others. It was Harriet's standard way of getting rid of guests she felt she had given enough time. Frances Willard also admired Isabella and had dined at the Hookers' some years before after a temperance speech in Hartford. Isabella was, like her sister, beginning to experience the phenomenon of disciples and converts. In summer 1887 she met the southern writer Grace King, who was visiting Susie and Charles Warner. The two women discussed women's rights and Spiritualism, and King described Isabella in her autobiography as "a tall, handsome woman, who talked to me about 'Woman's Rights' and converted me to her point of view."

After Mary's and the other family deaths, the bad times for the Hookers, what Isabella called their "great trials," ended. Spiritualism helped them deal with the losses and their prospects brightened. For one thing, family relationships improved and stabilized. Isabella was on friendly terms with all her remaining siblings. She and John were close again. Of course, not all relationships could be fixed. When Mary died the Hookers essentially lost their granddaughter Kate Burton as well as their daughter; Eugene allowed them no contact, even returning letters unopened. The Hookers had no legal recourse—grandparents would not have visitation rights for another century. There were compensations, however. The summer after Mary's death Ned's wife, Mattie, had their second child, Thomas. The same month that Henry died she gave birth to Joseph Hooker. Isabella and John thus had three Hooker grandchildren with whom they were close and could play the role of doting grandparents; there were no more childless holidays.

Even their relations with Alice improved when she and her family left for Europe in fall 1887. The Days would be abroad for seven years. Instead of being upset at the long separation, Isabella preferred it to the awkward situation of living close by but having to make an appointment to see Alice or her girls. Alice was an excellent letter writer, who described her doings in great detail; she agreed to write once a week. The Hookers responded with chatty joint letters. They read her letters aloud to admiring friends and neighbors and enjoyed having the relationship normalized. Did the Hookers see little of Alice and her daughters? Were the Days absent from Thanksgiving dinner? Well, they lived an ocean away.

Isabella and John even returned to their house yet another time, boarding with the Yosts, the family to whom they had sold the property. In 1887 they took the huge room they had expanded for their daughters—the room they still called "the Daughters' Room." Isabella penned a detailed description of her arrangement and decoration of the room in a long letter to Alice. As usual, she turned it into a shrine, filling it with talismanic objects connected with the dead. There was the Madonna she thought resembled her mother, the blue Wedgwood vase Henry had given her, pictures of wild roses and ferns sketched by Mary, and a bowl painted for Isabella by Hattie Hawley, who had also died in 1886. The walls were adorned with photographs of ancestors, such as Aunt Esther and Lyman Beecher, and the bureaus covered with objects Mary and Alice had been attached to—"the little wash bowl & pitcher you loved so much . . . & the white little statuette with blue ribbon round its neck that Mary loved." The next year Isabella added a large oil painting of Mary, which was done by suffragist Caroline Gilkey Rogers of Troy, New York. Isabella had met Rogers at the January 1887 NWSA lobbying convention in Washington. Although Rogers painted from a photograph and not from life, the finished product was a good enough likeness of Mary to delight and comfort Isabella.

The Yosts seemed to be the ideal landlords. John wrote Alice that the house could hardly have passed into better hands, as "Mrs. Yost makes it very homelike for us." Anxious to make friends, the Yosts encouraged John and Isabella to invite Nook Farmers to dinner. The Hookers' social life was not as frenzied as it had been when they kept house, but there were still the typical Nook Farm occasions—the Clemens's dinner for Mrs. Dickens and the children, for instance, the reception given by Charlie and Susie Warner for Joe Hawley and his new British wife, and the birthday lunch for Livy Clemens hosted by her mother. The latter event, Isabella wrote Alice, was attended by twelve "ladies," including Mrs. Chamberlin and Sarah Robinson, the daughter of her former instructor at Hartford Female Seminary. All the women were her "special friends"—as an afterthought she added, "in the olden times at least."

Now that the Hookers lived apart from Ned and his family there was constant visiting back and forth. Isabel often slept in the Daughters' Room; she spent weeks there after she came down with the chicken pox. When Mattie was ill and her cook and nurse suddenly left, Isabella filled in with the care of the baby boys. Mattie reciprocated with all the affection and praise her mother-in-law desired; she wrote Alice, "Dear mother! She has been such a comfort & bulwark of strength to me in these my most trying days." Isabella confided that sixty-five was a bit too old to be a nurse, but she loved the close contact with the children. The eight-year-old Isabel also worried about her grandmother's age. One day, Isabella wrote Alice, they were "lying in bed hugging in the morning & she said 'Oh Grandma I can't think how you can be so sweet to me—& then after a moment of thought she added—I wish tho' you were only twenty years old—(evidently realizing that I might not live as long as she did) & then added—but I should want you to *have the same face you have now, & Grandpa too.*' Isabella now had with Isabel the relationship she had longed for with her older granddaughters. Moments like this, she concluded, made life worth living.

12

The Board of Lady Managers, 1888–1893

THE YEAR 1888 was significant for both Harriet and Isabella. For one thing, the sisters were closer than they had been for forty years—ever since Harriet made her motherly visits when the young Isabella was pregnant. No longer divided by ideology, Henry, or distance, they visited and socialized at Nook Farm. Isabella read aloud Alice's letters from Europe and had Harriet over to recognize the second anniversary of Mary's death. Harriet invited Isabella to dine at her house with Charley and his wife and other relatives. Harriet enjoyed making fair copies of her poems and signing her name to them, so she did that often for the sisters to use as gifts. Although she didn't leave a record—she seldom wrote at all now, not even letters, she must have been pleased that the Hookers had developed a close friendship with some of her mother's Foote relatives. Isabella and John had long been friendly with the recently deceased Harriet Foote Hawley, Roxana's niece. Now Charlotte ("Lottie") Foote, the widow of Harriet Hawley's brother Andrew, moved in across the hall with her daughter Hattie to rent at the Yosts'. They wanted to be near another daughter, Lilly, a young woman in her late twenties who was working as a governess to the Clemens girls, helping prepare them for college. The Hookers soon became "one family with the Footes," as Isabella put it.

Isabella was busy all year with women's rights activities. First, she attended the International Council of Women in March and April in Washington. The council was the brainchild of Elizabeth Cady Stanton, who while on a European trip in 1882 had the idea of bringing together representatives from different countries to discuss their status as women. She and Susan B. Anthony decided to hold the council in 1888 to celebrate the fortieth anniversary of Seneca Falls. The planning was a huge task, as the National Woman Suffrage Association resolved to invite not only suffrage associations but also "all associations of women in the trades, professions and reforms." They had to raise twelve thousand dollars, a large sum at the time, to cover the costs of the convention. As the date approached, Stanton, who was in England visiting her daughter, began to dread the winter trip across the ocean and wrote Anthony she might not come. The pioneer of Seneca Falls, the founder of the International Council of Women, would not be present? Lucretia Mott could not fill in because she had died in 1880 (a large portrait of her would dominate the decoration of the auditorium). Anthony was incensed. "I wrote the most terrific letter to Mrs. Stanton," she confided to her diary—"terrific" in its original sense of terror-producing. "It will start every white hair on her head." Elizabeth responded with a terse cable that she was coming.

The convention opened March 25 at Albaugh's Opera House in Washington, D.C. It was the largest and most widely representative women's meeting held up to that time. Fifty-three organizations of women were represented by eighty speakers and forty-nine delegates hailing from the United States, Canada, England, Ireland, France, Italy, Denmark, Norway, Finland, and India. Susan B. Anthony welcomed the delegates and then the American pioneers of the movement. (The pioneers, thirty-six women and eight men who had been identified with the woman movement from the beginning, were later honored at a Pioneer Evening.) Finally Anthony introduced the women sitting on the platform—Lucy Stone, Frances Willard, Matilda Joslyn Gage, Isabella Beecher Hooker, Julia Ward Howe, and Clara Barton. This group, according to the *History of Woman Suffrage*, was the "most eminent galaxy of women ever assembled upon one platform."

Elizabeth Cady Stanton gave the keynote address, in which she acknowledged the advances women had made in the forty years since Seneca Falls but also pinpointed what it was that connected the women from so many different countries. She said: "Whether our feet are compressed in iron shoes, our faces hidden with veils and masks; whether yoked with cows to draw the plow through its furrows, or classed with idiots, lunatics and criminals in the laws and constitutions of the State, the principle is the same; for the humiliations of spirit are as real as the visible badges of servitude. A difference in government, religion, laws and social customs makes but little change in the relative status of woman to the self-constituted governing classes, so long as subordination in all countries is the rule of her being."

The conference lasted for a week with two sessions being held each day. The topics of the sessions varied widely, ranging from education and religion to temperance and philanthropy. Isabella gave her speech at the "Political Condition" workshop. It was entitled "The Constitutional Rights of the Women of the United States." She had first delivered this address the year before at the NWSA convention in Washington. She said she wrote most of it in 1876 for the centennial but put it away when she realized how women would be ignored. The speech summarizes the NWSA position of the early seventies—that the Constitution, properly interpreted, guarantees women the right to vote. Isabella does not rely solely on the Fourteenth Amendment here (Victoria Woodhull is not mentioned) but analyzes the preamble and several articles of the Constitution in addition. She was eminently qualified to do this. As she once pointed out, one of the advantages of having been an anti-slavery crusader was that Abolitionists had to practically memorize the Constitution. If she and John failed to teach their daughters how to choose a husband, they did hold study groups on the Constitution, going through it laboriously, article by article.

Isabella's basic method in the speech is to identify references to "the people" and argue that the people include women. She then discusses the trial of Susan B. Anthony for voting and exposes the errors, what she calls the "crime," of Judge Hunt. For Isabella this was the easiest mode of attack, for Hunt's conduct of the trial was indeed outrageous and she could rely on John's article for criticisms. Unfortunately, it was not the best mode. She does not even mention the Supreme Court decision in *Minor v. Happersett,* which put an end to the NWSA approach. In order for her analysis of the constitutional rights of women to be useful, Isabella would have had to provide some rebuttal to *Minor.* The fact that she didn't shows she was looking more to the past than the future. It was not helpful merely to assert that Judge Hunt was biased and the Constitution "actually guarantees to women the right to vote in all elections, both state and national."

But if Isabella looked more to the past than the future, the convention as a whole did not. The women established a permanent International Council of Women, which was to meet every four years. Each country had its own national council that would meet every two years. The council met in Chicago in 1893, in London in 1898, in Berlin in 1904, and so on. The convention also passed a resolution neatly summarizing the Seneca Falls demands that, in addition to suffrage, had not yet been met. This resolution stated:

> It is the unanimous voice of this International Council that all schools of theology, law, and medicine, should, in the interests of humanity, be as freely opened to women as to men, and that opportunities for industrial training should be as generally and as liberally provided for one sex as for the other. The representatives of organized womanhood in this council will steadily demand that in all avocations in which both men and women engage, equal wages shall be paid for equal work; and they declare that an enlightened society should demand, as the only adequate expression of the high civilization which it is its office to establish and maintain, an identical standard of personal purity and morality for men and women.

Isabella was enthusiastic about the council's achievements. There were even signs in Washington that all those years of lobbying conventions had not been for naught. The press reports on the council were serious and dignified; they no longer emphasized the women's clothing. Leading congressmen entertained the delegates, and President and Mrs. Grover Cleveland formally received them. Although she felt "in a state of collapse," Isabella hurried back to Hartford to prepare for a local convention to spread the good news and prepare the state society to join the national council. "Just think of it," she wrote Alice, "the mothers are coming together." In the midst of her state work, Isabella was off again in June—this time to be honored by the Woman's Club of Chicago, along with Susan B. Anthony and another woman. She and Susan then attended the Republican convention in Chicago (1888 was a presidential election year); they established headquarters in a local hotel. As in the previous election, they tried to get a suffrage plank in the party platform but were ignored.

Isabella looked forward to a needed rest in Hartford while John was taking Lottie Foote and some other people to England. He of course wanted Isabella to go along, and she of course refused to cross the ocean, especially for such a short trip. But a week before the sailing date John came down with a serious case of dysentery. As he tells the story in his *Reminiscences,* he was to leave on a Friday, and on Wednesday Isabella decided to come along and take care of him. (John includes the story in his memoirs to illustrate the truth of Spiritualism. A medium had "seen" him crossing the Atlantic with his wife; he was so certain the medium was wrong he didn't mention it to Isabella. And look what happened.) While John and the rest of the party traveled to Scotland, Isabella stayed in London and made several visits nearby; for instance, she saw some distant Hooker relatives.

One of the people she visited was Alfred Russel Wallace (1823–1913), the famous British scientist. Wallace had formulated a theory of natural selection similar to Charles Darwin's when Darwin's was in manuscript. The two naturalists communicated with each other and in 1858 issued a joint publication of the theory. Although Wallace was a distinguished scientist, he was a Spiritualist too. When on a lecture tour of the United States in 1886–1887, he met Isabella at a séance in Washington. He wrote in his memoirs that she was "a fine lecturer on social, ethical, and spiritual subjects, and was also a spiritualist and trance speaker, well known throughout America."

Visiting Wallace in his home, Isabella also hit it off with his wife. When she returned to America she concocted a scheme whereby the Wallaces would help the Hookers regain the Forest Street house. She wrote to Mrs. Wallace suggesting that the Wallaces sell their home and invest the proceeds in helping the Hookers buy back the house from the financially strapped

Yosts. Then they would all live together. Isabella would hold classes in psychology and political economy in the big parlors, and Dr. Wallace would lead in waking the American people to Spiritualism; together they would guide the reform. The Wallaces seem to have been very kind people. They chose to be flattered rather than outraged at Isabella's nerve, her failure to consider that they might not want to be uprooted from their home and culture. Wallace simply said in his autobiography that Isabella wanted them to move to America "and form a kind of home colony, being sure that she could get many advanced thinkers to join. . . . But my work was at home."

The other famous person Isabella visited in England was none other than Victoria Woodhull—or, as she was now, Mrs. John Biddulph Martin. Victoria had, as usual, landed on her feet. When she and Tennessee fled to England in 1877 (bankrolled by William Vanderbilt, it was rumored), she gave some lectures in London. At her talk on "The Human Body the Temple of God" she met Martin, a wealthy banker, who fell in love with her. His parents objected to the match, but several years later, in 1883, they were married. Victoria went to work at a brand new career—becoming respectable. She constructed a new genealogy for herself in which Buck Claflin had descended from the kings of England via Alexander Hamilton and her mother from a German family of royal blood. She repudiated her radical past, even suing the British Museum unsuccessfully for libel (they held books and pamphlets about the Beecher-Tilton trial). In an attempt to whitewash the past, Isabella's presence would be a mixed blessing because of her continuing radicalism and insistence on Spiritualism. She could and did, however, reassure John Martin that Victoria had not lied about Henry Ward Beecher. The visit was enough of a success that Victoria took Isabella the next day to see her sister. Tennie had continued to imitate Victoria and this time managed to top her achievement, marrying Francis Cook, a wealthy London businessman. Cook became a baronet the next year, giving his wife the title Lady Cook.

On her return from England Isabella found sister Harriet very sick. It is not clear exactly what her illness was, but she was barely able to sit up in bed, and everyone thought she would die. Thankful that Harriet had lasted until she returned to Hartford, Isabella sat with her every day and often spent the night. The Stowes had hired both day and night nurses, but Isabella wanted to "comfort her in her last days." She described her sister as "this sweet soul, now so near its translation to the better world." In Isabella's view, Harriet had spent her whole life "hungry for domestic affection & appreciation." The twins would not even sing her favorite hymns, the old-time Calvinist hymns that she and Isabella (and Catharine before her death) still loved. No matter how much the religion of the past had deteriorated, Isabella once noted, the old hymns were still powerful.

Isabella reported to Alice as follows:

[Harriet said] in a dreary sort of way—after I had been kissing her
forehead & stroking her hair, (which is now combed straight back
from her forehead—& this makes her look so like my father it
was difficult to think of any thing else at first)—
      'How many kisses have been wasted, because they have never
been given.'
      I said—'yes I think so—especially among women—so many
have gone hungry all their lives.'—
      'Yes—but it won't be so in the other world—it will be all
right there.'

Harriet then asked for help in "crossing the river" to Jordan.

But this was not to be. Harriet rallied and lived another eight years.
Isabella, with her typical megalomania, thought the recovery was due to her
own actions. Many Spiritualists believed they could infuse strength into a
failing person by holding their bodies, and apparently Harriet suddenly sat
up and felt better after Isabella had spent hours pressing her hands and singing hymns. Interestingly, Victoria Woodhull once said she'd brought her im-
becilic son Byron back to life by warming his cold "corpse" against her bosom.
Jesus Christ, she explained, repeated the miracle of Lazarus for her sake. Isabella felt more guilty than Christ-like about her sister's recovery. Harriet's
mind had started to fail before the illness, and afterward it was markedly
worse. She suffered from some form of dementia, possibly Alzheimer's disease, a degenerative disease of the central nervous system. She likely inherited
the gene from her father. Isabella wondered if it had been wise to revive her
when she was no longer "herself" and seemed so restless.

Soon Harriet was exhibiting typical Alzheimer's behavior such as
escaping her attendant and running away. She wandered the Nook Farm
neighborhood like a child, peering in windows, playing people's pianos, and
taking plants and flowers; she loved plucking flowers, roots and all, from the
Mark Twain greenhouse. The Clemenses had seldom socialized with Harriet
because of the age differential (she was twenty-four years older than Twain),
but they endured her unannounced visits out of admiration for her work.
Her own daughters were less tolerant. Isabella thought they had come round
during Harriet's illness and acted more affectionate, but they were terribly
embarrassed by their mother's erratic behavior once she recovered.

As Harriet's health declined, Isabella's and John's improved. John
came back from Europe renewed. He claimed he felt better than he had in
the past decade. Doctor Ned removed some polyps from Isabella's nose, restoring her sense of smell and taste. Under his supervision she began wearing

a magnetic belt to stabilize her back and a stocking on her lame leg. "I believe more & more in homeopathy," she wrote Alice. She and John still adhered to Spiritualism; John estimated that in ten years they had communicated with some four hundred and fifty spirits. But in October 1888, the same month as Harriet's near-fatal illness, Spiritualism received a serious blow. Margaretta Fox publicly confessed that she herself had produced the "spirit rappings" that started the contemporary Spiritualist movement. She made the noises by cracking her big toe. Then her sister Kate admitted to hiring a servant to rap from the basement when the sisters called on the spirits. These confessions caused a sensation, of course, and the Fox sisters wrote a book describing their fraud. (Eventually they recanted, claiming that poverty led them to make false confessions.) Isabella was upset enough to instruct Alice not to mention the Fox sisters in her letters—Alice had become a convert to Christian Science, and mother and daughter often argued the merits of the two religions.

Isabella and John remained Spiritualists for the rest of their lives despite the Fox revelations. They needed something to hold on to. They broke their only formal tie to the religion of Lyman Beecher when their minister and friend Nathaniel Burton died in 1887; after Burton's death they left the Park Church and never affiliated with another. Isabella felt that all the old "theologies have gone under & even the certainties on which they seemed founded." She discovered she could not read the old Christian standby *Pilgrim's Progress* to Isabel as she had to Mary and Alice. It was "another sorrowful thing about life," she mourned to Alice, "—this giving up old beliefs & not finding anything to take their place." Even her 1885 "Confession of Faith" had its deepening cracks and contradictions, which she revealed here and there in letters to her daughter. She expressed directly her doubts about the divinity of Jesus, implicit in the "Confession." Reason made her doubt that "Jesus was any more a son of God than other human beings are." And if there was no divine Jesus, there would be no second coming. Spiritualism had its consolations but Isabella would never be truly happy again, she admitted, until she saw Mary in the flesh. In the meantime she would pour her energies into women's rights. "I have nothing else to live for," she confessed to Alice in an undefended moment.

January 1889 found Isabella in Washington again for the NWSA lobbying convention. She had hoped to stay home and help John read proof for his court reports, but there was much to do in the nation's capital. First, she wanted to read her "Constitutional Rights of Women" paper before the U.S. Senate. Second, she wanted to make sure that women representatives were included on the planning boards for the two upcoming centennial celebrations—the centennial of the U.S. Constitution to be held in the spring and the four hundred–year anniversary in 1892 of Columbus's "discovery" of America. Her first step was to write Joe Hawley for help. Isabella's relationship with the senator had not been good for a long time because of his opposition to women's rights, and after Hattie Foote Hawley's death it further deteriorated; Hattie had always acted as peacemaker between them. Now Isabella could hardly contain "the boiling indignation of my soul" at his using his seat in Congress, where he was supposed to represent her and other Connecticut women, "to keep men as sovereigns & women as subjects forever."

Typically, Hawley did not help her with her goals, but Isabella forged ahead anyway. Although she didn't get to read her speech in front of the Senate, she did manage to have it entered into the *Congressional Record*. As for the centennial boards, she went straight to the top. President Harrison was favorably impressed by her ideas, she reported to Alice, and would "almost certainly" put at least one woman on each of the centennial boards. She also drafted a resolution, passed by the NWSA, demanding the representation of women on the boards. By April, however, when the centennial celebration of the Constitution was to begin, no woman had been invited to help with the planning.

Isabella had another reason for going to Washington, one more urgent than her speech or the centennials. Susan B. Anthony had begged her to come and help with a crisis in the affairs of the NWSA. "I must stand by her," Isabella wrote a colleague. The crisis was that the American Woman Suffrage Association had been making overtures toward uniting the two organizations, and it was now time for an NWSA decision. Understandably, the younger members of the two groups, those who hadn't been around at the time of the split in 1869, could not see any good reason for having separate associations. This was especially true given the conservative times. The women's movement was fairly respectable now, having existed for over forty years, but it didn't seem to be moving forward against its opposition. Wouldn't one large group have more impact than two small ones? Most of the veteran suffragists did not really favor union, however. Some were still motivated by personal antagonisms, and some feared the political leanings of the other group. Olympia Brown, with whom Isabella was reunited at the convention, worried that union with the AWSA would make the suffrage movement as a whole more conservative.

Isabella agreed, even though John saw the advantages of union. She feared what actually happened—that the American Association's state-by-state approach to woman suffrage would come to dominate the national approach. It seemed to her that an article by Henry Blackwell in the December *Woman's Journal* (organ of the AWSA) suggested the *Journal* would criticize and "virtually oppose the view I take in my speech, that Congress *can* settle women's right to vote as one of the 'People.'" Optimistic as usual that the end of the struggle was near, Isabella thought the two associations had no need to merge. Despite her misgivings, she agreed to represent the NWSA on the joint committee that met to iron out difficulties. The next Washington convention (1890) was held under the auspices of the National American Woman Suffrage Association (NAWSA), ending a split of twenty-one years' duration.

After her exertions in Washington Isabella embarked on an even more frenzied course of state work. She and her Connecticut colleagues had four bills in front of the legislature and she was "utterly engrossed" in pushing them through. One held that women could not be taxed until represented in government. One would strike the word "male" from the state constitution. Isabella wrote Alice that a member of the Committee on Constitutional Amendments, which had charge of the latter bill, was so impressed with her speech "that he listened to me with his mouth wide open and in the public debate last Tuesday said that Mrs. Hooker was fit to be President of the U.S." The bill lost ninety to forty-four, but Isabella thought many of the "no" voters were ashamed of the foolish arguments used to defeat it and would support the other bills. These were school suffrage and suffrage regarding the sale of liquor. School suffrage had a good chance of passing. Thanks in part to Catharine Beecher, women were now considered "natural educators," and four-fifths of the teachers in Connecticut were female. In addition, sixteen states and territories in the country had already granted school suffrage to women in some form. Why not Connecticut?

The school suffrage bill did pass the House but failed in the Senate. Isabella attributed its defeat to the machinations of the liquor dealers, who "rushed in" to quash the temperance bill and adversely affected the school bill in the Senate. The so-called temperance bill was a bold stroke—perhaps too bold—on the part of the Hookers. It gave women the right to vote regarding the licensing of the sale of liquor. As John put it forthrightly in a broadside he addressed to legislators, there was a war going on between the saloon and the home. Any citizen who wanted to "put down" liquor sales should welcome "the indispensable help of woman's vote in this contest with the liquor power." Unfortunately, the liquor dealers were making the same connection and had already announced at a national meeting their intent to oppose woman suffrage everywhere and in every form. They were less concerned about school suffrage, but the Hookers had attracted a powerful opponent with their direct attack on liquor sales.

In the midst of her lobbying and speaking activities on behalf of the four bills, Isabella was traveling to small Connecticut towns and establishing clubs for the study of political science. This was her answer to critics' objection that women were not prepared for suffrage. "I mean to have such a Club in every town in this State in the course of the year," she wrote Alice, "—then in parlor meetings women will be reading and talking about the same things and getting ready to manage town affairs as they should be managed." Men, she continued, could not even be depended on to run a village properly. "At Litchfield lately, a young teacher on her way from school through some woods, was seized by a young man of respectable family and violated twice in the same afternoon—being nearly choked to death—so much for our protectors!!" Connecticut was particularly in need of women's participation in government. After all four of her bills lost, Isabella concluded that her home state was backward and merely "living on the past."

But she had made a number of converts to the cause and deepened the commitment of some of her neighbors. She wrote Alice, "Nook Farm all well—Clemens deeply interested in W. Suff. Thinks it more important than anything else for the good of country and race he tells Lilly [Warner]—but whether he will give me the $100. I need remains to be seen. We have given $150. already—and all my time and strength and much of your father's." Isabella was not discouraged, though. Nor did she feel weak or even tired after a grueling four months of politicking. Years ago she might have been exhausted from overwork, but now she felt years younger—there was "such a sense of power within me."

She was further buoyed by a quick visit to New York. She and John attended the centennial event (which had been planned entirely by men) and the NWSA spring convention. Isabella then gave a speech at a large reception for Susan B. Anthony. She learned a valuable lesson while in New York, she wrote Alice. They visited brother Edward, who had had a leg amputated and was in the hospital. Edward was eighty-six years old, almost twenty years older than Isabella, but instead of lamenting his loss he sat up in bed and entertained his guests. He talked about "the duty of women to their country & of *man to woman* with his face all aglow." He said he wanted to live a few more years to preach to his Missionary Church and bring out a version of his works that would show the progress of religious thought in the past two decades. Isabella promised Alice that she would "take courage" from Edward's brave example and "struggle on."

The Hookers spent a wonderful summer at Nutplains, the Foote family homestead in Guilford. Their motive in going there was partly charitable. They hoped to help the Footes, who were deeply in debt, keep their land. They paid the same room and board as at the Yosts' in Nook Farm. The house seemed to Isabella full of people from the old days like Uncle Sam of Cincinnati and Roxana, her father's first wife. She wrote to sister Harriet describing her granddaughter Isabel's delight in country life and asking if Harriet had felt the same as a child visiting Nutplains. The question inspired a lucid reply from Harriet, her last letter to her sister.

August 14, 1889

My precious Sister

Having read your note *four times*, the next thing is to answer it. I *do wish* I could have been with you in your pleasant visit to Nutplains, where some of the most joyous days of my childhood were spent. All the things that you mentioned I *have done* over and over again when I was a wild free young girl. I *never got tired* of doing them. The room I slept in for the most part, was the *first right hand room* as you get to the top of the front stairs. . . . The room directly facing the head of the stairs was Aunt Harriet's [Roxana's sister] and Grandma's. [I]t had two large comfortable beds for them—I have slept with Aunt Harriet in her bed and *enjoyed* it as she always kept one so nice and warm. Then there was the colored woman Dinah was a great friend of mine and we had many frolics and capers together—she told me lots of stories and made herself very entertaining. Then there was the grave yard on Sandy Hill, the other side of the river where I often walked—I wonder if it is there now. It had a nice picket fence all round it then with a gate so I could easily get in and read the inscriptions on the grave stones. . . .

Well dear sister I see by my shortening paper that it is time for me to close. When you come back no one will welcome you more warmly than

Your loving sister Hatty

Excited by Harriet's sounding so rational, Isabella hurried to see her as soon as the Hookers returned from Guilford. Harriet could indeed recall her days at Nutplains in vivid detail, but she failed to recognize her nephew Ned Hooker. Isabella tried to draw out her memories of another beloved place, Sorrento, Italy, where she had stayed in 1860 and begun writing *Agnes of Sorrento* (Alice had just visited Sorrento). But Harriet was restless and disinterested—her recollections would only follow their own course. Not long after this visit she accosted a neighbor in the street, thinking he was Fred Stowe. Thereafter she prepared regularly for visits from her lost son. Isabella mourned her sister's decline. The publication of her biography, written by Charles Stowe, made it seem even more real that she was gone from this world. In 1890 Isabella wrote Alice that Harriet appeared at the Forest Street house every day. She sang a hymn, had a snack, and then wandered to the neighbors' houses. She was "sadly unconscious of present things—& so unlike her old self I long for her release."

When they came back to Hartford, the Hookers went in with the Footes to rent the Daughters' Room and adjoining chambers in their old home. "We feel almost like young people just going out to housekeeping," wrote Isabella. The difference from their previous stay was that they no longer boarded with the Yosts. They bought a stove and utensils for Isabella and Lottie to use in cooking. This arrangement enabled the Hookers to resume a constant round of teas, dinners, and parties, including a weekly ice cream lunch for Isabel and the grandsons. It also separated them from the Yosts, whom everyone in the household had come to dislike. Isabella complained continually to Alice about their landlords—they were inhospitable and no longer invited the neighbors over; they kept a meager table—"scant fare for a humming bird," sneered Isabella; they were letting the house and grounds deteriorate. All these failings could be attributed to the Yosts' financial troubles, but it was predictable that the Hookers would not be tolerant of people who owned the house they felt was really theirs. Either the weighty responsibility of the house or their tenants' attitude had ruined Mrs. Yost's good nature. Alice had no idea, wrote her mother, how hard it was "to live with a mean selfish woman without education or refinement & be subject to her in your own dear old home." John added a characteristic postscript to the letter—cautioning Alice not to let anyone see what her mother had written about Mrs. Yost!

The Hookers' own financial position had improved. John had sold land and paid their debts, so they could now live on his salary. Isabella's talks on Spiritualism and women's rights (she usually received twenty-five dollars plus expenses per speech) allowed her to have a monthly allowance of twenty dollars for charity. Her passion for helping the poor was no doubt part of the Beecher noblesse oblige, but in the days before social security the elderly poor had to depend on patrons and former employers. Otherwise they had to work until they dropped. A part-time maid Isabella hired in 1890 was seventy-eight years old. Her former maid Bridget, whom Isabella employed when she could, had eight children and still had to work hard every day but Sunday. Many of these older women were physically ill or depressed or both. Isabella gave Mary Downey, who had nursed Alice's daughters, half her magnetic belt and took her for rides to cheer her up. The Hookers paid for the ailing Lillie Foote to stay at the Danville water cure and looked for decent dwelling places for Mary Downey and Mary Leonard, who had been seamstress to many of Nook Farm's residents. One of the attractions of the arrangement with the Yosts was that the Marys might use the Hookers' rooms when they traveled. When she wasn't looking after her own charges, Isabella could lend a hand with other Hartford cases, for her close friend Virginia Smith served as director of the city mission (charities). Virginia was the daughter-in-law of Anna Smith, who was once nursemaid to the Hooker children and now suffered like Harriet from dementia.

In an America that was becoming increasingly polarized between the rich and the poor, as industrialists and "robber barons" made obscene fortunes off cheap labor, the Hookers took the part of the workers. Isabella denounced the brutal treatment of strikers in Chicago, which led to the Haymarket Riot of 1886. She and John thought the workers had the right to strike. As John put it in his reminiscences, "In the bitter controversy between laborers and employers my sympathies have been with the laboring class, who, I think, do not get a fair share of the product of their labor." The Hookers were not sympathetic with the anarchists, however, who were blamed for throwing a bomb in Haymarket Square. John and Isabella feared anarchy, the political theory opposed to all forms of government and state control. They preferred socialism and the ideas of Karl Marx, from which the anarchists had deviated. John argues in his memoirs that the country should have a graduated income tax and a stiff inheritance tax. The ideal system would be state ownership of land and collection of taxes by rents paid for the land. Here he was probably influenced by *Looking Backward* (1888), Edward Bellamy's wildly popular Utopian work that John and Isabella read and discussed.

The Hookers continued to be interested in the welfare of former slaves. When Alice asked if they gave to foreign missions (charities), Isabella said no because home missions were more important. The industrial colleges in the South should have all the money they could use from the North. "We invited to tea last week a Young Professor (colored) who is trying to get yearly scholarships . . . & such a story of devotion & conservative & christian [sic] industrial wisdom as he had to tell!" This man, born in Atlanta, had been educated at Yale and the Hartford Theological Seminary and then gone South to teach. He was obviously following the Booker T. Washington model of African-American progress (rise up from slavery through industrial schools) rather than the more radical course suggested by W. E. B. DuBois and Ida B. Wells (fight racism). But the Hookers had heard Washington speak in Hartford and lacked any contact with the radicals. They promised to help the professor raise money.

Isabella was also concerned about the status of the hundreds of thousands of Jews who had immigrated to the United States since 1880. She confided to Alice that the spirit of Emma Lazarus, "that sweet Jewess who has recently died in New York," came through to her when she saw Isabella reading a magazine article about her life. Lazarus was the poet whose sonnet "The New Colossus," exhorting " 'Give me your tired, your poor,' " graced the Statue of Liberty. Lazarus's spirit, Isabella thought, begged her to "work for her people, the Jews," but Isabella felt she lacked the time as Spiritualism and women's rights came first. Ironically, brother Henry had championed the Jews of Brooklyn, preaching a sermon against the anti-semitism they encountered while vacationing in the Catskills.

In February 1890 Isabella went to Washington for the first convention of the united National American Woman Suffrage Association. It was preceded by a grand celebration on February 15 recognizing the seventieth birthday of Susan B. Anthony. The birthday banquet, held at Riggs House, included two hundred guests and lasted until two o'clock in the morning. Isabella did not look forward to the NAWSA meeting, having come mainly to honor Anthony. She explained the union to Alice as stemming from the American Woman Suffrage Association's desire to take credit for the NWSA's successful work, and the Nationals' recognition that they couldn't "afford to seem discordant." But the convention impressed Isabella as proving "the superior mental and moral power of womankind." All four days were filled with magnificent oratory, with not one weak word being uttered. "Oh I am proud of my sex," she concluded. Isabella's own speech was on the Centennial of 1892, demanding the participation of women.

Elizabeth Cady Stanton delivered the opening address as newly elected president of the NAWSA. She reviewed the history of the movement for women's rights and ended with a ringing appeal for a broad platform and inclusive membership: "I think we should keep our platform as broad as Mrs. Gage and myself desire. . . . My idea of that platform is that every woman shall have a perfect right there; that she and her wrongs shall be represented in our conventions. We do not want to limit our platform to bare suffrage and nothing more. We must demand equality everywhere in Church and State. . . . We want all types and classes to come. We want all races as well as all creeds and no creeds, including the Mormon, Indian and black women."

A notable feature of the convention for Isabella was the presence of Stanton's daughter Harriot Stanton Blatch. Blatch was married to a wealthy Englishman who, Isabella couldn't resist telling Alice, "enjoys seeing her devoted to reform work in England of the most radical sort." She was a fashionable and young looking mother, Isabella continued, and also a college graduate and consummate orator. After Stanton's opening address as president of NAWSA she stood up in the box where she was sitting with Isabella and introduced her daughter to the audience. Blatch "spoke for ten minutes with admirable manner and perfect self possession." If Alice hadn't already gotten the point, Isabella concluded, "I could almost envy her such a daughter— beautiful and gifted, who will not only take up her work after she is gone but is enthusiastically with her already." (In fact, Blatch did take up her mother's work in the U.S. She returned in the early 1900s and was a force in the successful campaign for the vote.)

Isabella usually managed to conceal her disappointment in the way Alice had turned out, for she wanted to preserve a close relationship with her sole surviving daughter. She thus seldom criticized her directly. Yet Alice had, besides the example of Stanton's perfect daughter, the implicit comparison with her perfect brother Ned (luckily she and Ned got along). Ned showered his parents with attention and presented them with an approving daughter-in-law and three loving grandchildren. Isabella tried to praise Alice's husband when she heard something good of him, but she often couldn't keep her resentment at his treatment from seeping through. Nor could she stop wondering whether Alice ever did anything except travel and have a good time. "I wish you could now & then tell me of something done for somebody outside the family circle," she wrote.

If Isabella could not help mourning her lack of intimacy with Alice's daughters, she at least had some relationship with them. Eugene Burton was still returning the Hookers' letters to Kate unopened. In 1889 and '90 the struggle centered on Mary's furniture. The Hookers had stored it at Ned's and Eugene wanted it. Isabella and John wished Kate to have the furniture but feared Eugene would destroy or sell it in order to remove all traces of her mother from Kate's life. It was hard to settle this dispute when there could be no direct communication. The Hookers finally gave up and sent the furniture to Eugene's law office. Their only news of Kate came from some parents of Kate's school friends, who took pity on them.

Upon her return from Washington, Isabella went to New York to be feted at a fancy hotel by the League of Woman Suffrage. She spoke on the topic "Woman in Government" and was presented by the League with a very nineteenth-century gift—an antique mug containing hair of Charles Dickens and his parents. Hair was considered the most "alive" part of the body and Victorians often kept the locks of dead people to give away or sell; Isabella still had a large supply of Mary's hair. John was careful to inform their living daughter that the New York reception for her mother was a real honor. The Hooker marriage had gone back to being the mutual admiration society it was before the Beecher-Tilton scandal. Isabella and John constantly praised and defended each other to Alice. John's main theme was that Isabella's reform work would gain her a place in history: "The time will come when your children will be proud of being her grandchildren."

John told Alice that her mother had become an inspired speaker. This was true. Over the past seven or eight years Isabella had grown increasingly skillful at impromptu speaking. As she explained it, she had contracted to speak in 1884 before the Connecticut Agricultural Society. But when the date came around she was overwhelmed with suffrage work and had no time to write a speech. When the Society would not release her from her engagement, she had to speak off the cuff. The success of this venture raised her confidence and she began to say "my very best things" on the spur of the moment before a sympathetic audience. Being Isabella, she decided after brother Henry's death that the spirit of the great orator was taking her over during her most successful impromptu speeches.

In the summer of 1890 Isabella received another honor. As she and John vacationed in the White Mountains of New Hampshire, she was forwarded a letter from one of the Centennial Commissioners for Connecticut (i.e., men officially responsible for the Columbus quadricentennial). He nominated Isabella to represent their state on the "Board of Lady Managers" for the gigantic world's fair that was planned to honor Columbus; the men on the Commission wanted to outshine the famous Paris Exposition currently going on abroad. Isabella's campaign for the inclusion of women in the centennial planning had thus borne fruit. Not that the men were moved by a sense of justice or intended to let the women participate equally with them. Rather, the businessmen and civic leaders who headed the project found that their wives would not be shrugged off—they were already making plans and raising money for the fair. In response the men added an amendment to the Fair Bill expanding the duties of the National Commission: "And said Commission is authorized and required to appoint a Board of Lady Managers of such members and to perform such duties as may be prescribed by said Commission." Typically, when the Fair Bill came to the House of Representatives for its final hearing, this amendment was left out and had to be restored; it was omitted, the Commission said, because they considered it "of no importance whatever."

Although the women were finally included, no one seemed happy. Isabella heard that some congressmen were furious over the creation of a board of women and the women themselves, of whatever political stripe, objected to being saddled with the ridiculous name "Board of Lady Managers." A separate board was not at all what Isabella and her NAWSA colleagues had had in mind. They wanted to participate *with* the men in planning the Columbian Exposition, as it was now called; they had requested that the National Commission have some female members. They did not care to be shunted aside under the "separate but equal" doctrine. There wasn't even a real pretense of equality, as the women's board was created by and subject to the all-male commission. Isabella accepted her appointment but was skeptical from the beginning. It disappointed her, she wrote in August 1890, that Congress "makes women people subservient to men people to the very last."

By this time the city of Chicago had won a difficult battle to be the site of the Columbian Exposition. In-fighting was now going on, among the women as well as the men, for control of the planning process. Isabella went to Chicago right after her appointment to confer with one of the women's factions. This was the Queen Isabella Society, which had been formed in Chicago as early as 1889. The members were mostly professional women—doctors and lawyers—who supported suffrage and women's rights. They wanted to celebrate the achievements of a woman and settled on Queen Isabella of Castille, who enabled Columbus to make his voyage. The main goal of the Queen Isabella Society was to commission a statue of Queen Isabella that would stand on the grounds of the exposition and be officially unveiled there.

The society also sought to build a Woman's Pavilion, not to exhibit women's accomplishments (those would be included with the men's) but to serve as a clubhouse for women to use during the fair. Headquarters for the society, or the Isabellas as they were often called, were the offices of Dr. Frances Dickinson, an ophthalmologist and cousin of Susan B. Anthony. The Queen Isabella Society, having lost to the Lady Managers its bid to become the official women's group planning the exposition, at least wanted its group to dominate the board. It thus invited Isabella to visit in September, all expenses paid. They wined and dined her, and she promised the other Isabellas to help elect one of their candidates as an officer of the board.

This task turned out to be more difficult than expected. There was another women's faction in Chicago that had been planning and raising money for the fair before Chicago was chosen as its site. These women were known as the Chicago Women's Department, sometimes called the Women's Auxiliary because they saw themselves as "helpers" to the Fair Corporation, the group of men in charge of local arrangements for the fair. The women of the auxiliary did not, by and large, support woman suffrage or feminism; they were philanthropists or socialites, typically the wives of rich industrialists. The auxiliary differed from the Isabellas in its goals as well as its membership. It wanted a Woman's Building to be erected at the fair wherein women's "industries" and handiwork would be exhibited. It was less interested in gaining equality than in showing the contributions of women to charitable endeavors and the arts. (Of course, the division between women seeking equal opportunity with men and women celebrating female accomplishment still exists today.) In 1890 the women of the auxiliary had a marked political advantage over the Isabellas—their close ties to the men in charge. The auxiliary even moved into the same building as the Fair Corporation. As a historian of the exposition remarks, "This symbolic union did not augur well for the ambitions of the Isabellas."

When Isabella Beecher Hooker arrived for the first meeting of the

Board of Lady Managers in November, she met Harriet Hosmer, the sculptor whom the Isabellas had commissioned to do the statue of Queen Isabella. Hosmer lived in Rome in a colony of female artists. She had gained recognition for her statue "Zenobia," which had been exhibited in London, New York, and Boston. Isabella found Hosmer "a whole hearted strong minded woman ready to join hands with all women of brains & advanced thought." Hosmer had started work on the statue, and the Isabellas were selling shares at a dollar apiece to fund it. But the Board of Lady Managers was a different story, with the Women's Auxiliary already dominant. The male commissioners had appointed two Lady Managers from every state and territory and then thrown in an extra eight auxiliary members from Chicago.

The auxiliary thus managed to get one of their own elected president. She was Bertha Palmer, a former debutante who had married a multimillionaire. Her husband had made his fortune in dry goods and had a chunk of the Chicago lakefront filled in to create a suitable building site for the Palmer home. Bertha hosted an open house for the Lady Managers in her "palace," Isabella wrote Alice. The Palmer residence was a study in excess, boasting an eighty-foot tower reached by a spiral staircase. Bertha's bedroom was finished in ebony and gold; her dressing room contained a sunken tub shaped like a swan. Although Bertha Palmer had lived the life of a wealthy socialite and lacked any knowledge of politics or parliamentary procedure, she was no cream puff. She possessed an iron will and could lay plots far in advance to get her way, as the Isabellas would eventually discover. At the first meeting of the Lady Managers Palmer pushed through the idea of having a Woman's Building dedicated to exhibiting the work of women—just what the Isabellas did not want. But she suffered one political loss. Isabella nominated, as decided in advance, a Queen Isabella Society candidate for secretary-treasurer of the board.

As the oldest Lady Manager and an experienced speaker and attendee of large meetings, Isabella impressed many of the women. A majority of the Lady Managers, particularly those from the South, were political neophytes lacking in confidence. One woman wrote Bertha Palmer timorously that she felt herself disadvantaged because she was wholly unaccustomed to speaking in public; she felt herself "a total stranger and alone." Isabella tended to be a bit patronizing to such women, even calling the board as a whole "a kindergarten." She managed to get herself appointed head of the Committee on Permanent Organization, which was to define the structure of the board, including its rules and officers. She also succeeded in having her candidate elected secretary over Bertha Palmer's candidate.

The new secretary, Phoebe Couzins from Missouri, had a law degree and was the first woman to be appointed a U.S. Marshall. Now an Isabella, she had been a leading NWSA member for years. She was one of the women who helped Susan B. Anthony interrupt the Philadelphia centennial celebration in 1876 to present the women's Declaration of Rights. Miss Couzins shared Isabella's condescending attitude toward the board; she resented the Lady Managers' failure to realize that they owed their very existence to the pioneers for women's rights. Isabella, however, did enough personal politicking to compensate for her attitude. She took special care to befriend the southern representatives, whom she hoped to convert to woman suffrage. Although she admitted to Alice that "conservatism was the order of the day & prejudice against the strong minded very pronounced," she liked most of the women personally and found them as warm as the suffragists. Impulsively, she invited all the Lady Managers to the celebration of her golden wedding anniversary the next summer.

On August 5, 1891, the Hookers would be married for fifty years. The celebration they planned was sizable, more than comparable to sister Harriet's and Susan B. Anthony's seventieth birthday parties. Where to have it was a problem. The Forest Street home needed wallpapering, even supposing the Yosts were friendly enough to offer it, and the grounds had deteriorated too much for a lawn party. Ned's house was too small. They finally decided on the new City Mission building their friend Virginia Smith had charge of. Virginia offered to coordinate the event, and many Nook Farmers pitched in to help. Neighbors did the "elaborate decorations," which included portraits of the Beecher and Hooker ancestors. The anniversary party was not just a personal event, Isabella told Alice, but a commemoration of the two families' work for humanity. She wrote that they'd invited three thousand people. That number would seem to be a mistake, but there were one hundred and seventeen Lady Managers and the Hookers had invited other groups en masse. John put an invitation in the *Hartford Courant* and noted that "the old servants of the family will be there as guests, and the honest traders with whom we have long dealt, and their wives and children."

The day of the event hundreds, if not thousands, of people filed through the rooms of the City Mission. Isabella and John stood in a receiving line for over an hour. She dressed in her twenty-fifth anniversary silk made over; she wore as a petticoat her white muslin wedding dress skirt. One parlor was presided over by representatives of the Lady Managers, including Phoebe Couzins, and another by "distinguished woman suffragists" led by Susan B. Anthony. Anthony described the event in her diary as "a most beautiful occasion." The Equal Rights Club presented Isabella a "bride's loaf" in recognition of her being president of the Connecticut Woman Suffrage Association since 1869. John was not neglected. The Supreme Court justices came in a body to honor him, and the local press called him "the best-loved member of his

Isabella Beecher Hooker and John Hooker, 1891. Courtesy Harriet Beecher Stowe Center, Hartford, Conn.

profession in the state today." Abolitionists were represented by William Lloyd Garrison's son and Senator Joe Hawley. In the evening there was a supper, with Hawley as toastmaster, and afterward hymn singing and other music led by John Hutchinson of the Hutchinson Family Singers. Edward Beecher, now eighty-seven and sporting an artificial leg, gave the benediction. Brother Tom—"queer as ever," said Isabella—made the trip as well. (Of the Beecher siblings, Mary and Charles were also still alive but did not travel.)

The golden anniversary celebration was "the climactic event of the Hookers' last years," according to Kenneth Andrews. To Isabella it seemed bathed in a "heavenly glow." She wrote Alice after the event that John "seemed transfigured & has been serene & happy ever since." She herself felt her courage revived by all the accolades—perhaps she could accomplish something in the next ten years. The only negative was Alice's absence. Her mother couldn't resist making her suffer for it, referring to Virginia and other acolytes as her "daughters" and offering to send Alice fifty dollars if her husband wouldn't give her money for an anniversary present.

After the party the Hookers had five hundred cards and letters to answer before Isabella headed to Chicago for the second meeting of the Board of Lady Managers. She wanted to stay away, for there were dark clouds on the horizon, but her alternate could not go in her place. At the golden anniversary party Phoebe Couzins had a sorry tale to tell. Bertha Palmer had managed to oust her as secretary of the Board of Lady Managers in favor of her own candidate. This was strictly against the bylaws of the board, which specified that officers would be elected by the entire board. But Palmer had started scheming the year before and manipulated events so as to cast aspersions on Couzins's competence and honesty. Couzins reported that Palmer had altered the minutes of the last meeting, changing the bylaws to give herself control as president.

Isabella tried to support Couzins. She wrote Palmer in protest and bombarded the Lady Managers and male commissioners with letters describing the original bylaws adopted by the board. But Mrs. Palmer had her way at the September meeting. As Isabella explained to Alice, she and her namesakes could not "get justice done" for Couzins—Palmer was too powerful and the Lady Managers "a flock of sheep." Phoebe Couzins was understandably devastated. A few years after the Columbian Exposition she lay in a sanitarium crippled by anger and arthritis. She renounced her ties to the woman suffrage movement, which had previously occupied her life. Women's rights groups were just as cliquish as the Lady Managers, she thought. Girls should grow up to choose housekeeping over public affairs. "Women," she concluded bitterly, "are no better than men."

Another quarrel was simmering at the second meeting of the Board of Lady Managers. African-American women of Chicago asked Bertha Palmer to appoint a black woman to collect exhibits from "the colored women of America." When an Isabella suggested that the Chicago women's leader, Lettie Trent, be appointed to fill a vacancy on the board, Palmer balked. She feared the reaction of the southern women, one of whom averred she didn't "sit with Negroes." Further, Palmer suspected an Isabella Society plot because the five Lady Managers who Lettie Trent said were "openly committed to justice for black women" included Phoebe Couzins and Isabella Beecher Hooker. Palmer wrote that she thought the black women planned to appear before Congress and "make a strong protest against our Board, and then Mrs [sic] Hooker and Miss Couzins will enter their complaints, so that we will seem guilty of acts of wrongdoing." Eventually Lettie Trent and her followers went the way of Phoebe Couzins, as the Board of Lady Managers passed their request down to the state boards. Only one state, New York, appointed a black woman to its board and included the work of African-American women as part of its exhibits. The men did no better. Thus the Columbian Exposition, which would be nicknamed the "White City" because of its sparkling new buildings, ultimately lived down to its name.

The only thing that saved the Chicago meeting for Isabella was the royal treatment accorded her by the Queen Isabella Society. The society made her its honorary president and threw her a grand reception. She was "simply superb in her robes of *moire antique*," wrote one journalist, while another compared her oratory to her brother Henry's. She expressed her desire to see the statue of Queen Isabella, being completed in Italy by Harriet Hosmer, placed ultimately next to that of George Washington in the nation's capital. Queen Isabella was mother of the country, argued her namesake. She anticipated people's objections to the Queen's Catholicism and ties to the Inquisition by emphasizing the laudable royal desire to preserve Christianity. A Catholic newspaper quoted her as saying: "I do not sympathize with the prejudices against Isabella because she was a Catholic. What do we not owe to the Roman Catholic Church!" No doubt sister Catharine stirred in her grave at this remark.

Isabella had come a long way since the time in her childhood when she rode to Cincinnati in a wagon so her father and oldest sister could save the West from Catholicism! The older she grew, the more ecumenical she became. One of her contributions to the Columbian Exposition was a religious service she prepared for Cities' Day. "The Universal Litany" consisted of comparative selections from different scriptures. The mayor of Chicago read the Christian selections (New Testament) while Isabella interspersed quotations from other faiths—Jewish (Old Testament), Confucian, Buddhist, Hindu, and Moslem. The idea was to highlight the similarities among the various religions. As she explained, "I desired to prove by it that all religions tended toward the same ideal."

The exposition became so huge that it was not ready in 1892, the year marking the four hundredth anniversary of Columbus's voyage. Isabella, disillusioned by Mrs. Palmer's politics, made only one short trip to Chicago and tried to conduct Lady Manager business by mail. She devoted much of her time to memorializing her sisters. First, she helped plan the Hartford Female Seminary reunion, which took place in June 1892. She provided a Mrs. Holley with materials for her talk on Catharine Beecher and spoke herself about Catharine's loss of her lover and resulting determination "to think what she could do for womanhood." Isabella's assigned topic was John P. Brace and, typically, she avoided composing her own tribute by reading Harriet's, as written in their father's autobiography. In her speech Isabella referred to Harriet as if she were dead. Her sister would be with them today, she said, "only that her soul has gone up on high." The body, however, still lived down the road in Hartford. Harriet in fact posed for a bust being sculpted for the

Columbian Exposition. The sculptor, Anne Whitney of Boston, worked partly from a photograph but also spent a week with the Hookers studying her subject in person. Isabella assisted; the only way she could keep Harriet sitting quietly, she noted, was by singing her favorite hymn.

Suffrage work seemed to "creep along," Isabella wrote Alice, "—but the World's Fair will give us [women] a great lift." The Columbian Exposition finally opened on May 1, 1893. From the beginning it was an enormous success, perhaps "the most fantastic spectacle of its type ever produced on the American continent." Henry Adams, the cynical descendant of presidents, had found the Philadelphia centennial tacky but was "enchanted" by the beauty of the Chicago exhibits. The fair planners had transformed the beaches and swamps of an undeveloped park on Lake Michigan into the gleaming "White City." A network of formal lagoons and canals, all equipped with gondolas and other boats to transport visitors, surrounded a series of monumental buildings. The buildings were unified by similar materials and style of construction and a uniform cornice line. The White City was one of the grandest architectural projects ever undertaken in the United States. The city included separate major buildings to represent machinery, electricity, mining, transportation, agriculture, horticulture, fisheries, and fine arts (the latter still stands as the Chicago Museum of Science and Industry); a large number of buildings were sponsored by federal and state governments, foreign countries, and trade associations. In the bazaar and entertainment section on the Midway Plaisance stood a mammoth wheel, a glittering wonder just invented by a man named Ferris.

The scale of the venture was astonishing. The various managers of the exposition had raised and spent over thirty-three million dollars. Fortunately, the number of visitors was proportionate—about thirty million. One writer estimated at the time that if fairgoers spent just two minutes on each exhibit it would take them thirty-two years to see the entire Columbian Exposition. For some it was just too much. The midwestern author Hamlin Garland reported that his mother was stunned by the fair. "Her life had been spent among homely small things, and these gorgeous scenes dazzled her, overwhelmed her. . . . At last utterly overcome she leaned her head against my arm, closed her eyes and said, 'Take me home, I can't stand any more of it.'"

The Woman's Building, one of the twelve major buildings of the fair, was impressive in its own right. It was designed by Sophia Hayden, a twenty-one-year-old Massachusetts woman, who won the all-female architectural competition. An "enormous" building, Isabella wrote Alice, the first floor included a large exhibition hall flanked by smaller exhibit rooms; the second floor contained an auditorium, offices, and committee rooms, and the third was a roof garden that eventually included a café and "model kitchen." The journalist Kate Field, who had originally opposed a separate woman's building, wrote: "If popularity be a sign of approval, the Woman's Building outranks all others. I never entered its portals without being oppressed by an overflow of humanity. Every woman who visited the Fair made it the center of her orbit. Here was a structure designed by a woman, decorated by women, managed by women, filled with the work of women. Thousands discovered women were not only doing something, but had been working seriously for many generations."

Another popular site was the Children's Building, constructed next door to the Woman's Building with funds raised by the Board of Lady Managers. Although the building did not pretend to be an architectural showpiece, the idea behind it was progressive. Basically, it was a model day care facility demonstrating "the most healthful, comfortable, and rational system of dressing and caring for children according to modern scientific theories." Mothers could leave their children for a mere twenty-five cents and visit the fair. Of course, most mothers did not because of the newness of the idea, but about fifty to one hundred children were cared for each day.

Isabella spent most of 1893 at the Columbian Exposition: she arrived in April before it opened and left in November after it closed. Her schedule was fearsome. During the summer she did duty every day from eleven to three at the Woman's Building, presiding over the Woman's Congress. Various women had been invited to speak on a great variety of topics. The subjects ranged from Art and Assyrian Mythology to George Meredith's Novels to Woman as a Financier. Isabella had to introduce the speakers and comment on the papers. (How she managed that is unclear, though she did remind Alice that Mary had once said her mother was interested in *everything*.) When lecturers failed to show up, Isabella substituted her own speeches. Not everyone appreciated this. As one woman wrote, "old Mrs. Hooker gave an extemporaneous Suffrage speech—they say she does it everytime she can get a few minutes to talk in."

After the speeches at the Woman's Building there were committee meetings and ceremonies to open this and honor that; one day Isabella had to attend four different ceremonies. "Old Mrs. Hooker" wrote her daughter that she was so busy she wished she had a dozen bodies. In July and August the Board of Lady Managers met for the last time. There were quarrels and more quarrels. Some of the Lady Managers accused Mrs. Palmer of favoritism and fought her over who would sit on the awards juries and who would get to socialize with visiting dignitaries. As the *New York Times* reported: "The Board of Lady Managers indulged in another decidedly unpleasant wrangle today. It lasted about two hours, and in that time many unpleasant and disagreeable things were said, tears were shed, and many of the ladies gave vent to their feelings by hissing and uttering strange noises."

Besides her responsibilities at the fair, Isabella took on the supervision of two nieces, the barely grown-up twins who had been adopted by her brother Jim and his wife, Frankie. After Jim's suicide Isabella had helped Frankie start a school for girls to support herself and the children. Now she let May and Margaret stay with her at the Isabella Hotel. (After Mrs. Palmer foiled their attempt to build on the fairgrounds, the Isabellas found a site for their clubhouse and hotel two blocks from the entrance.) The twins later resided at the Woman's Dormitory a mile away; Isabella got them jobs waiting on tables in order to earn their board. May and Margaret reported to their mother that Aunt Belle was "just a love" but seemed tired and had seen little of the fair. After the Board of Lady Managers adjourned, John came to Chicago and the Hookers rented a place for themselves and the Beecher daughters so they could all attend the exposition.

Isabella was disappointed that the statue of the Spanish queen had still not arrived in Chicago. It was expected as late as June 1893, when Harriet Hosmer set sail from Italy with the plaster cast. Hosmer expected to cast it in bronze but lost faith in the Isabella Society when they failed to raise enough money. She thus took the plaster statue to San Francisco for a small fair. There it disappeared, and its present whereabouts is still a mystery. The Isabellas thus fell short of their original goals for the Columbian Exposition: they had no pavilion within the fairgrounds, and they had no statue of the queen, failing to make her a viable symbol of the fair. Instead, Bertha Palmer virtually became the queen herself. On the last day of the fair the Lady Managers who had remained on site called a meeting to unveil the portrait of Mrs. Palmer they had commissioned. (Isabella boycotted the meeting in protest— she now described Palmer as "treacherous" and "a vindictive woman eaten up with vanity.") The portrait shows a Bertha Palmer looking twenty years younger in a full-length gown of filmy white material. She wears a crown and carries a jeweled gavel that resembles a scepter. The speaker introducing the portrait called her "Our Queen."

If the Isabellas fell short of their specific goals, however, they succeeded in a larger sense. As their honorary president had predicted, the Columbian Exposition gave women a great lift. The humorist Marietta Holley in *Samantha at the World's Fair* (1893) has her protagonist exclaim, "The wimmen managers wuz the first wimmen that wuz ever officially commissioned by Congress, and never have wimmen swung out so, or, to be poetical, never have they cut so wide and broad a swath on the seedy old fields of Time, as they do to this Fair." A male historian of the fair notes that at Chicago in

1893, "the symbols and actuality of womanhood were everywhere." Perhaps the symbols reflected the Gibson Girl more than the ancient queen. Maybe they could not receive the full approval of the Isabella Society, but there was no repeat of the 1876 centennial, where women were conspicuous only by their absence. Women were not an afterthought in Chicago—they "swung out." In a final irony, history enacted the Isabellas' revenge on Bertha Palmer. Palmer became a victim of the phenomenon whereby historians collapse all women's achievements into those of the most famous woman of the time. Thus the credit for women's prominence at the 1893 World's Fair has often been given not to Bertha Palmer but to the arch-feminist Susan B. Anthony!

13

The Last of the Beechers,

1893–1907

ISABELLA PLANNED TO STAY in Chicago past the end of the World's Fair to help dismantle the Woman's Building. But John, who had gone home after the performance of his wife's "Universal Litany," came down with pneumonia and called her back to Hartford. He thought he might die. "I hope when my hour comes," he wrote Alice, "I shall be at home & that your mother will be living & by my bedside." John soon recovered and in January 1894 retired from his job. At seventy-seven he had been for some years the oldest lawyer in Connecticut. Around the time of his retirement he developed what Isabella called a "hypochondriacal derangement." Without work to distract him he reacted to the slightest illness by collapsing entirely. Soon John had a real ailment. During the national bicycle craze he was run over by a bike and suffered a broken hip.

His wife was not at all happy to be back at Nook Farm. An incident had occurred the past year that reminded Isabella of the treatment of Phoebe Couzins by the Lady Managers and, inevitably, of her own trials during the Beecher-Tilton scandal. Virginia Smith had run afoul of the Hartford selectmen and been forced to resign as city missionary. In her zeal to get infants out of poorhouses and adopted into good homes she made the selectmen look bad and was accused of "baby farming on a large scale." Isabella was disgusted at the way the local newspapers and the ministers, including her old enemy Joseph Twichell, repudiated Virginia without hearing her side of the story. Charles Dudley Warner refused to listen to Isabella's defense and said he would have nothing to do with "that woman." Isabella wrote Alice that "our circle of true friends has been sorrowfully narrowed" and "Hartford is spoiled for me." If it hadn't been for Ned and his family, she and John would have moved to another city. Isabella had never forgotten her neighbors' ostracism of her twenty years earlier; in letters to Alice she would occasionally burst out with "How could they? How could they?" Nook Farm had lost its charm, she wrote, and all that saved it were the Gillettes—George and Lillie

Gillette Warner, Aunt Eliza (who would die in two weeks), and her son Will Gillette. Will had lost his young wife to a ruptured appendix and looked to Isabella for sympathy and advice on his plays.

Unfortunately, Isabella's usual outlet for frustrations in her personal life—suffrage work—was blocked to some extent on the national level. After the first convention of the united National American Woman Suffrage Association (NAWSA) in 1890, she continued to attend the Washington conventions. In 1891 she delivered a paper entitled "Woman in Politics and Jurisprudence." The theme was a familiar one. As the *History of Woman Suffrage* put it, "she showed the necessity in politics and in law of a combination of the man's and the woman's nature, point of view and distinguishing characteristics." The next year Isabella was back, working hard and receiving one of the greatest honors bestowed on her by her colleagues (though she probably didn't realize it at the time). She was chosen to accompany the three brightest stars of the nineteenth-century women's movement—Elizabeth Cady Stanton, Susan B. Anthony, and Lucy Stone—in speaking before the Senate Committee on Woman Suffrage. The *History* noted that "Four of the greatest women this nation ever produced addressed this committee." Stanton quoted from the speech that would become her most famous, "The Solitude of Self," and Isabella elaborated her familiar complaint about the law making sons their mothers' rulers and thus teaching them disrespect.

For the women involved, the hearing before the Senate committee was the high point of their careers. The year 1892 marked Stanton's and Stone's last appearances at a national suffrage convention: Stone died in 1893, and Stanton worked in other venues. Anthony and Hooker would increasingly be on the losing side of NAWSA debates. The political strategies of the women who had once belonged to the American Woman Suffrage Association were winning out, as Isabella and Olympia Brown had predicted they would. The former AWSA suffragists were generally more conservative and favored the state-by-state approach over the national one to gaining suffrage. In 1892 they began to discuss holding the annual convention in cities other than Washington. A disgusted Isabella wrote Stanton that all they did at Washington was "put our old Prest. [president] on the shelf [Stanton was replaced as president] & decide that as we couldn't afford to hold two Conventions in a year—the one at Washington must be omitted & the different States have the honor." The next year Alice Stone Blackwell made a formal motion to that effect, which passed despite Anthony's protests.

Olympia Brown's reaction to the NAWSA change of emphasis was to call a meeting in Chicago, which Isabella attended. The women formed the Federal Suffrage Association in order to work toward a change in the U.S. Constitution. Isabella noted that the country was large and "women cannot get too many Associations before the public to urge their demands for full and equal suffrage." The founders divided the United States into four districts longitudinally in order to assure the cooperation of northern and southern women in each district. Isabella went so far as to contact Victoria Woodhull Martin, who was in Chicago with her husband, and ask the best method of reviving her Fourteenth Amendment argument. Mrs. Martin was not interested. The Federal Suffrage Association made sure there were suffragists to testify in Washington at congressional hearings, but it never became large or particularly influential. Historians of the suffrage movement point out that after 1893, when NAWSA began to convene away from Washington, neither the House nor the Senate gave woman suffrage a favorable committee report. The Susan B. Anthony amendment was pretty much dead until 1913.

Isabella's relationships with her old colleagues followed much the same pattern as they had in the 1870s. While she and Brownie and Anthony worked together without effort, she just as easily ruffled Stanton's feathers. Stanton reverted to her old practice of annotating Isabella's letters. In response to the idea that she'd been "put on the shelf" by the NAWSA, Stanton wrote, "I was not laid on the shelf. I resigned because I really did not wish to be President any longer. I had been chosen two years in succession by a large majority, should have been again had I chosen to accept the nomination." When Isabella suggested to Brownie that Stanton be made president of the Federal Suffrage Association, Stanton wrote that she wouldn't accept an office in any organization. Isabella, as in the past, was blissfully unaware that she had annoyed her colleague. She stayed with Stanton in December 1892 when she went to New York to speak at the Pilgrim Mothers' Dinner. (This was a dinner modeled after the Pilgrim Fathers' Dinners that had been held for years; it was sponsored by the New York City Woman Suffrage League, of which Lillie Devereux Blake was president. Livy Clemens also attended the dinner.) Far from undervaluing Stanton as her tactlessness might suggest, Isabella was full of praise in her letters to Alice. She said that whenever she looked at Stanton she thought, "What a wonderful human being you are!"

Isabella and Susan B. Anthony saw more of each other in the early nineties than they had in a long time. Not only did they attend each other's anniversary events (Susan's seventieth birthday, Isabella's golden wedding), but they also paid each other working visits. Anthony came to Hartford to cheer on the state suffrage association. During her stay she accompanied Isabella to sister Harriet's for hymn singing. When Isabella visited Anthony, the Rochester newspapers interviewed them. "Women Will Soon Vote: At Least Mrs. Isabella Beecher Hooker Says They Will" was the headline of one article. Isabella rode her favorite hobbyhorse, contending that the U.S. Supreme

Court would soon recognize women's right to vote as guaranteed by the Constitution.

The two suffragists emphasized the successes of the movement—the refusal of Wyoming to become a state unless admitted with equal suffrage, the fact that twenty-six states now allowed women to vote on school matters. But at the Democratic convention of 1892, which Isabella and Susan attended together, they encountered the same old broken promises as they had in times past. Although they were allowed to address the resolution committee, arguing for a woman suffrage plank in the platform, they were prevented from speaking to the convention as a whole. According to one of Anthony's biographers, "Mrs. Hooker remained alone in the convention until 2 o'clock in the morning, hoping to get a chance to address that body. She had not been fooled as many times as Miss Anthony, who returned to the hotel and went to bed." No woman suffrage plank appeared in the platform.

Isabella and Susan agreed on most issues. Their one area of contention was Spiritualism, which Anthony firmly rejected. She and Stanton would now and then exchange sarcastic comments about the "vague ideas floating in Mrs. Hooker's head" (Stanton). Isabella still tried to entice her colleagues to participate in séances and speculate about the afterlife. Anthony finally addressed the topic directly in a letter. She had no knowledge of "the before and the after," she explained, and no desire or time to learn about the invisible realms. "I know this seems very material to you, and yet to me it is wholly spiritual, for it is giving time and study rather to making things better in the *between*, which is really all that we can influence."

During the 1890s, Isabella drew closer to one of Anthony's friends, Frances Willard. She had known Willard for some time as a suffragist and seen her rise to a position of power and prestige as head of the Woman's Christian Temperance Union (WCTU); in 1890 the WCTU had a hundred times the membership of the NAWSA. Isabella pronounced herself "in love with Frances Willard" and sometimes attended her WCTU meetings. She was invited to sit on the platform yet could not speak or join the society because she was not a "prohibitionist," in her terms. In other words, she was not a teetotaler and did not believe in banning alcohol entirely. Isabella felt that this requirement was "narrow" and even "bigoted." In spite of being Fred Stowe's aunt and Eugene Burton's mother-in-law, she had little knowledge of addiction. She advocated temperance in its dictionary definition of moderation and would have liked to join the movement. She complained that she should have been "eagerly welcomed to the ranks."

With another possibility for activism blocked, Isabella turned after the fair to state suffrage work. In 1894 she held regular luncheons for the executive board of the state society and concentrated on teaching the work to her young vice presidents. "My suffrage work is booming," she reported. Soon she was printing fifty thousand copies of an equal rights tract to circulate in every town in Connecticut. When in June the Equal Rights Club of Hartford decorated the graves of former suffrage workers (the Smith sisters, Nathaniel Burton, and others), Isabella gave the invocation and address. According to a newspaper report, she "spoke with the old-time enthusiasm and fervor." School suffrage finally passed in 1893 after several years of effort. But all the other attempts to extend partial suffrage to women failed year after year—municipal suffrage, right to vote for presidential electors, right of taxpaying women to vote on money questions. Usually a bill would pass one branch of the state legislature, raising the hopes of Isabella and her colleagues, and then fail in the other branch. It was hard and frustrating work.

In 1895 Isabella had the more pleasant task of presenting a marble bust of sister Harriet to the Hartford Public Library. This was the bust sculpted by Anne Whitney for the Columbian Exposition. Connecticut had a large and impressive exhibit of the writings of Connecticut women in the Woman's Building. Some one hundred and fifty authors, including Catharine Beecher and Isabella Beecher Hooker, were represented in the prize-winning exhibit. The Connecticut women highlighted the writings of Harriet Beecher Stowe. Featured in a special mahogany cabinet were treasures lent by the Stowe children: a very rare copy of the first printing of *Uncle Tom's Cabin* as originally bound; forty-two translations of the novel in such languages as Armenian, Welsh, and Dutch; a complete set of Stowe's works bound in calfskin. Virginia Smith had the idea of commissioning the bust to stand next to the book cabinet. She raised the thousand dollars for the sculptor's fee solely from women and children in Connecticut cities and towns. The bust was a great success, apparently well appreciated by the Stowe family. The surviving children and grandchildren attended the ceremony at the library, along with many Hookers and Nook Farm neighbors.

The first stanza of Harriet's favorite hymn, "The Christian Pyre," finally came to pass. It went:

> Happy soul, thy days are ended.
> All thy mourning days below;
> So, by angel guards attended,
> To the sight of Jesus go.

Harriet died in 1896 just after her eighty-fifth birthday. Her family was at her bedside, including Isabella, who had long promised to be present when her sister "crossed the river." There was a simple funeral service at the Forest Street home before Harriet was buried beside Calvin in Andover, Massachusetts. The manager of her lecture tours, J. B. Pond, described the funeral to his friend Mark Twain in Europe. Mr. Twichell conducted the service, he noted; most of the distinguished people of Hartford and "all of your old neighbors" attended. Susy Clemens, visiting Nook Farm while her father lectured in Europe, was also present.

Few of Harriet's old friends were left to attend her services or write about her—only Annie Fields and Sarah Orne Jewett. Pond continued, "The familiar poet-friends, and men of letters, she has outlived; even Mrs. Gov. Claflin, of Boston, died on the 13th of May last. Mrs. [Henry Ward] Beecher, in her eighty-fifth year, accompanied me. She is quite feeble. Mrs. Hooker was at the funeral, but she and Mrs. Beecher did not meet,—a very pathetic condition of affairs." Of Harriet's other siblings, Edward and his wife had died the year before. Charles was present at the burial service with his daughter, but Thomas and Mary were invalids and could not attend. Pond wrote Twain that Mary Perkins lived only minutes away in Hartford with one of her children. She had deteriorated physically and was deaf but had "an intellect as brilliant and sparkling as ever." Pond called on her and learned that she hadn't seen Harriet in eight years—she preferred to remember her sister as she was in earlier times.

The rest of the world concurred. The obituaries in the newspapers and magazines of the day had an air of surprise about them, as though the authors thought Stowe had died long ago. They often damned her with faint praise and dismissed the novels after *Uncle Tom's Cabin* as "third rate." By contrast, Susan B. Anthony tried to claim her for the women's movement. In a letter to the *Outlook* she quoted from Stowe's *House and Home Papers* ("Every woman has rights as a human being first, which belong to no sex"), ignoring the satire of feminists in *My Wife and I*. She stretched the truth in arguing that "Mrs. Stowe was ever in full accord with her illustrious sister, Mrs. Isabella Beecher Hooker, one of the ablest and most persistent advocates of equal rights." No doubt Harriet would have preferred the floral tribute of Boston African Americans, who left a wreath on her grave from "Uncle Tom's children," or the poetic tribute of Paul Laurence Dunbar.

One of the first black writers to gain national fame, Dunbar (1872–1906) expressed the majority late nineteenth-century African-American view of Stowe just as surely as Frederick Douglass voiced the slaves' reaction when he called Harriet's great novel "the *master book* of the nineteenth century." (Or just as surely as James Baldwin, in his attack on racial stereotyping in *Uncle Tom's Cabin*, expressed the twentieth-century view.) Dunbar, whose parents had been slaves, wrote the following sonnet:

Harriet Beecher Stowe
She told the story, and the whole world wept
        At wrongs and cruelties it had not known
        But for this fearless woman's voice alone.
        She spoke to consciences that long had slept:
Her message, Freedom's clear reveille, swept
        From heedless hovel to complacent throne.
        Command and prophecy were in the tone,
        And from its sheath the sword of justice leapt.
Around two peoples swelled a fiery wave,
        And both came forth transfigured from the flame.
        Blest be the hand that dared be strong to save,
And blest be she who in our weakness came—
        Prophet and priestess! At one stroke she gave
        A race to freedom, and herself to fame.

After Harriet's death Isabella had an unpleasant run-in with the Stowe family. Harriet had set up a trust fund for the twins, who were now sixty, but it did not yield enough income by 1896 to maintain the Forest Street house. Isabella, trying to help, published a plea for support in the local newspapers. She claimed the twins had been consulted first, but Eliza and Hattie felt humiliated and sent in a retraction; they were "far from needing assistance," they said. Isabella's fundraising schemes, however well-meaning, tended to be on the crass side. She wrote a fifteen-page summary of Harriet's life—"A Brief Sketch of the Life of Harriet Beecher Stowe"—and had it printed. On the last page she advertised a souvenir teaspoon she had designed in her sister's memory. "The spoon has on the handle the head of Mrs. Stowe, with representations of Little Eva and of Topsy, and in the bowl Uncle Tom sitting by his cabin." If this weren't enough, a facsimile of Stowe's autograph was engraved on the back of the handle. One could buy the teaspoon at any Hartford jewelry store for one dollar and seventy-five cents.

Harriet's passing in effect marked the end of the literary colony at Nook Farm. Only a few weeks later Mark Twain's daughter Susy contracted spinal meningitis and died in her old home. This was only the first of the losses that would embitter Clemens in his old age and assure his never returning to the Hartford residence. Even the Hookers gave up the struggle to live in the house they once owned on Forest Street. Following Harriet's death they rented a small house on the edge of Nook Farm; by the end of 1897 they bought it. A historian of Nook Farm notes that "the era of Nook Farm as a little community of active authors and social reformers ended in the late 1890s." Appropriately, the last work written by an original resident of the area was John Hooker's autobiography, *Some Reminiscences of a Long Life* (1899).

The Hookers' loss of their dream of regaining the Forest Street house was not as painful as it could have been. In their new, more modest establishment they began to receive letters and visits from their Day granddaughters, Kathy and Allie. Early in the 1890s John Day softened his opposition to Isabella for some unstated reason (her official appointment as Lady Manager, the accolades the Hookers received at their golden anniversary?). Isabella was thrilled to hear from Alice that "your husband has really spoken kindly of me to his daughters." She began to write the girls directly, sending articles and news of her activities. By this time, they were actually young women, Kathy twenty-two and Allie twenty. They had spent their adolescence in Europe, which no doubt seemed to them the sole reason for their distance from their grandparents.

When the Days returned to the United States in 1894 and settled in New York, Kathy and Allie made frequent visits to Connecticut. In 1897 the Hookers actually attended a banquet with Alice and John Day and had "a cozy time." When Day died in 1899, any possible obstacle to the close relationship Isabella craved with her granddaughters was removed. Ironically, the Day girls, on whom she had exerted little direct influence, turned out more like her than their fashion-plate mother. They were fiercely independent and dedicated to obtaining the best possible education. Kathy studied at the Atelier Moderne in Paris and painted in the Neo-Impressionist manner. Later in life she earned two master's degrees, one in psychology and one in history. She became a power in Hartford restoration, saving the Mark Twain and Harriet Beecher Stowe houses and establishing the Stowe-Day foundation and library.

Allie entered the Boston Cooking School after the Days returned to the United States but then switched to Bryn Mawr, graduating in 1902. She also did graduate work, studying at New York University and Columbia. Like her mother and grandmother, she married a lawyer, but she maintained an active public career for twenty-five years. Alice Day Jackson first "became active in organizations having as their object the improvement of labor conditions" and then served as an officer of the Consumers' League of New York and the National Consumers' League. Her grandmother would have been pleased that she joined the Women's City Club and was president of the League of Women Voters in her New York district.

Isabella was impressed by her granddaughters' ambitions and the efforts of women in general to improve their education. She wrote an article, "Are Women Too Ignorant?," which was published in 1898 as a suffrage leaflet by the NAWSA organ the *Woman's Journal*. In preparation for writing the article, she asked Thomas Wentworth Higginson for a copy of the letter she had sent him forty years before praising his essay on women's education and bemoaning her lack. She still remembered the catalyst to her career in the women's movement. (Higginson also remembered the letter, though he couldn't find it. He recalled specifically her comments on the sacrifices made to send boys, but not girls, to college.)

She had recently conversed with a young woman, Isabella began her essay, who thought women should be educated about public affairs before being allowed to vote. It would be "dreadful to double the ignorant vote." The article was an attempt to refute the idea that women were ignorant. First, there was the changed situation in formal education. Isabella cited statistics from the National Commissioner of Education showing that fifty-five percent of students above the elementary school level were female. Second, she argued, older women were educating themselves through the burgeoning club movement. Society women had founded innumerable literary, scientific, and political clubs throughout the country, and the number of benevolent societies and organizations to aid schools and poor scholars was rapidly growing.

But Isabella wanted to emphasize in her article "the education that the so-called lower classes are giving themselves." She gave two examples of Hartford clubs she had been invited to speak to: a "society of colored women" working to found a state home for aged African Americans and a "Ladies' Benevolent Society" founded by Catholic working women. The latter group had quickly grown to four hundred members. When women began to work on social issues, Isabella thought, there should be no question of their voting in ignorance. She concluded: "Let us take courage, dear sisters, and not allow ourselves to be deluded by the fear that we are not sufficiently educated to take part in public affairs. Responsibility is all the education we need to-day, and when put to the test we shall not be found wanting."

In the same year Isabella wrote "Are Women Too Ignorant?" Elizabeth Cady Stanton proposed a radically different answer. She told the Senate Committee on Woman Suffrage in 1898 that the proper response to fears of women doubling the ignorant vote was: "Abolish the ignorant vote." In other words, Congress should pass a law requiring educated suffrage. She pointed out the unfairness of the situation where "thousands from every incoming steamer go practically from the steerage to the polls," while educated women are turned away. Women suffered under a "foreign yoke." In states where constitutional amendments were proposed to enfranchise women, the immigrant vote always opposed woman suffrage. Isabella's friend Olympia Brown, now living in Wisconsin, reported that the great majority of immigrants were male and in the last state election "foreign" voters had outnumbered the "American." Every new influx of foreigners reduced women's chances. When we are told, Brown fulminated, "that loyal women, pioneer women, the descendants of the Pilgrim Fathers, are not even to ask for the right of suffrage lest the Scandinavians should be offended, it is time to rise in indignation and ask, Whose country is this? Who made it? Who have periled their lives for it?" Brown, like Stanton, was outraged that women remained "the political inferiors of all the riff-raff of Europe that is poured upon our shores. It is unbearable. There is no language that can express the enormous injustice done to women."

The language Brown and Stanton expressed certainly betrayed them. The invidious contrast of the Pilgrim Fathers and the riffraff from foreign countries has led to the current denigration of the women's attitudes as "nativist" and "classist," while the injustice done to them is ignored. It is interesting, however, that Isabella never used this language or subscribed to her friends' views, in either her public writings or her letters and journals. One might assume that she had. No one had more pride of ancestry—there was not only the larger-than-life Lyman Beecher but also Thomas Hooker. She took every opportunity to tell people that her husband was descended from the founder of Connecticut.

Isabella thus qualified as a Pilgrim Mother, but she did not go on about "riff-raff." Although she wanted to hear Brown's numbers and was concerned about immigrant men's strengthening male domination, she felt that the more quickly immigrants got the franchise, the better. Their exercise of the vote would educate them and increase their faith in democracy, providing a hedge against anarchy. "There are those who say we have too many votes already. No, we have not too many. On the contrary, to take away the ballot even from the ignorant and perverse is to invite discontent, social disturbance, and crime." The New World would prove that the Old World government by the few was wrong "by inviting every newcomer to our shore to share our liberties." The real danger of mass immigration, thought Isabella, was that the greed of the robber barons would push the immigrants to armed revolt. When the Homestead Steel workers were fired on by orders of Andrew Carnegie, she wrote: "Only think of Carnegie with his 30-odd millions grudging his faithful workmen the trifle that would help them to lay by a mite for a rainy day, and preparing hot steam and rifles to protect his works."

Ironically, though Isabella did not contrast her high Beecherdom and Hookerdom with the low-class status of immigrant male voters, others in the movement did. The contrast itself began to seem her most useful contribution to the new, more conservative NAWSA. Isabella attended the association's annual convention in 1898 because it was held in Washington, D.C., and marked the fiftieth anniversary of the Seneca Falls convention. She thought her offering would be the address she had prepared on "United States Citizenship," giving a history of the suffragists' efforts to get the Constitution reinterpreted; many of the younger women attending did not even know about

Susan B. Anthony's trial for voting illegally back in 1872. But according to the *History of Woman Suffrage,* Isabella's speech could not be heard and the audience started getting "very fidgety." Anthony came forward and told them they should be content just to sit back and look at Mrs. Hooker: "She is always a commanding presence on the stage." On this evening, with her silver gray dress and whitening curls, "she was a picture which would delight an artist."

Isabella would not remain a silent image at the podium. Tossing aside her manuscript, she explained that "I never could give a written speech, but Susan insisted that I must this time." She then spoke "clearly and forcibly with her old-time power." When the talk was over, though, Anthony enforced her point. She rose and put her arm around Isabella, forming a "tableau." Isabella then kissed Susan, who said: "To think that such a woman, belonging by birth and marriage to the most distinguished families in our country's history, should be held as a subject and have set over her all classes of men, with the prospect of there being added to her rulers the Cubans and the Sandwich Island Kanakas. Shame on a government that permits such an outrage!"

The 1898 NAWSA meeting was the last national suffrage convention Isabella would attend, though she did not realize it at the time. She planned to go in 1900, now that the convention was being held in Washington in alternate years only. She spent November 1899 getting her latest petitions signed and finishing her speech on the "Duty of Woman Citizens." As it turned out, her "statesmanlike paper" had to be read by her friend Mary Seymour Howell of New York. Because John was sick, Isabella stayed home, missing both the NAWSA meeting, the last with Susan B. Anthony as president, and the subsequent celebration of Anthony's eightieth birthday.

John's illness was not his customary hypochondria that came on when his wife wanted to take a suffrage trip. In fact, he was in good spirits, enjoying the visits of his children and grandchildren and feeling relieved that he'd finished his autobiography the year before. But he was feeble and seldom ventured outside. (Isabella wrote in the middle of March that neither of them had left the house since before Christmas.) John had grown deaf and was continually bothered by indigestion and sleeplessness at night. Isabella wrote Allie Day that she didn't know how long her "delicate" grandpa would last—she hoped they could "keep him" for another year. John himself predicted that he would live until the Hookers' sixtieth anniversary (August 5, 1901) and then "go quickly."

In spring 1900 Isabella suddenly lost all her remaining siblings. Mary and Tom died on the same day, she in Hartford and he in Elmira; Charles followed a few weeks later. Mary's death was perhaps the greatest shock, though she was the oldest at age ninety-five. She had convinced everyone she would live to be a hundred. Lyman Beecher Stowe recalled that when his great aunt was "training for this century run," she wouldn't let people talk with her longer than five minutes for fear they would tire her out. Even though she fell short of her goal, Mary had witnessed most of the changes of the nineteenth century. She liked to say that in youth she was known as Lyman Beecher's daughter; in middle age she was Harriet Beecher Stowe's sister; in old age she'd become Edward Everett Hale's mother-in-law.

After hearing about the deaths of Mary and Tom, Susan B. Anthony wrote Isabella a letter of condolence. You're the only one left of your father's large family, aren't you? she asked. In reality, Charles was still alive when Anthony wrote, but Isabella would soon be the only remaining child of Lyman Beecher. As she entitled her 1905 magazine article, she'd become "The Last of the Beechers." She now had more friends and relatives "on the other side" than left in life. When Isabella conducted her morning sessions communicating with the spirits, there was often a crowd present. In her 1901 diary she mixes the living and the dead indiscriminately. As Eliza Stowe (living) arrives for a visit, Susy Clemens (dead) comes too. John Hooker (living) wanders in reading the *Hartford Courant* while its former editor Charley Warner (dead) talks about music.

John's end was near, Isabella realized sadly. Throughout January 1901 she felt an "increasing overshadowing sense of his near departure." As his stomach pains and coughing fits grew worse, Ned gave him morphine. He died on February 12 at age eighty-four. He did not quite make it to his sixtieth wedding anniversary, but he died as he wished—at home with Isabella nearby. She was at first disoriented by the loss of the man who had been at the center of her life for so long. He had been for the most part a loyal and loving partner. He stood by her side during their "great trials" and made important contributions to the cause of women's rights; it was John who drafted the Connecticut women's property law, served as an officer of the state suffrage association, and provided the analysis of Susan B. Anthony's trial. He taught Isabella the intricacies of the U.S. Constitution. Although he never became a minister as sister Catharine had wanted, he upheld moral standards while the certainties of the old religion waned. Sometimes these moral standards may have been too conventional (as in his wholesale rejection of Victoria Woodhull without meeting her), but more often they were not. The same good instincts that had made John an abolitionist carried through to the end.

Isabella was smart enough to know, even if she hadn't had her daughters' husbands and some of her friends to compare him with, that she had been lucky in her choice of spouse. John's departure left a permanent empty space. She panicked at the idea of living in the house alone and for a time required either Alice or Kathy to stay with her; there were also Lillie Foote and the Hookers' servant Mary Casey (daughter-in-law Mattie was in Europe). By April Isabella had rallied, writing Kathy Day to apologize for her earlier dependence. She no longer felt so lonely, she said. She had come to think of John as off on a long journey that filled him with delight. He wrote such happy letters she could not wish him back. Of course, by this time Isabella was communing with his spirit as though he were still alive.

Immediately after John's death, Isabella confided to her diary that she might give up woman suffrage and "make spiritualism my chief purpose in life." Maybe she was too sunk in her spirit world or felt unable to continue state work without her longtime supporter. Whatever the case, she soon changed her mind. At the end of March the state suffrage organization had Carrie Chapman Catt, the new president of the NAWSA, come to speak. (Catt, an excellent organizer, would be at the helm when suffrage was won in 1920.) Isabella revived to host a dinner for Catt and accompany her to the state legislature's hearing on municipal suffrage. On their way to the Capitol the "stunning old lady," as Catt viewed her, rehearsed her speech. In front of the committee Isabella's "opening sentences came out clearly, splendidly phrased, leading on to the main argument, then suddenly she faltered; she had lost the continuity. She became confused, broke off abruptly and introduced Mrs. Catt." Before giving her own speech, Catt finished Isabella's argument as she had heard it rehearsed, even trying to use "the Beecher words she had so admired." A state suffrage worker wrote Isabella afterward that she'd been "heroic in putting aside your sorrow and thinking of how to advance suffrage."

During the summer a bigger opportunity for advancing suffrage presented itself. Isabella wrote Kathy from Norfolk that the spirits wanted her to rest up and prepare for important work in the future. She thought it might be the proposed Connecticut constitutional convention, which would begin in January 1902. She hoped this was the work, "for if there is any subject that I fully comprehend & love to talk about it is Constitutions—State & National." Isabella had been discouraged about the state situation for some time. As she wrote Olympia Brown, they might have been able to "drag old Connecticut into line" if Brownie had stayed. But now Isabella was "absolutely alone." The few remaining workers had no money or influence, and there wasn't a single good speaker left in the state.

The constitutional convention afforded the best chance in years to expunge the word "male" from the state constitution once and for all. Isabella thus set to work preparing a memorial for the Connecticut Woman Suffrage Association (CWSA) to present to the convention. The CWSA, she reminded the delegates, had been formed in 1869 and had been trying for over thirty years to get the constitution changed to allow women to vote. "In furtherance of this object we have printed and circulated more than 200,000 tracts . . . and have submitted bills to every legislature since 1869 asking for some form of woman suffrage." She wrote as though the CWSA were still a force, not mentioning that its membership had declined to fifty people.

The failure of the CWSA bills Isabella attributed to the legislatures' refusal to let suffragists address either house in general session. Thus only legislators interested in the question would attend their committee hearings. Those "bitterly prejudiced" against woman suffrage stayed away and then voted the bills down. Isabella felt that the present convention was not properly constituted because women hadn't been consulted regarding its makeup and hadn't been allowed to vote for the delegates. But the convention could redeem itself by allowing women to address it and by giving them a part of the hall and a committee room for discussion and storage of their documents.

To her memorial Isabella attached "an argument thereon," a revised form of the essay she had written for the NAWSA in 1898. Entitled "United States Citizenship: Its Origin and Growth," the essay summarized the events she saw as key in attempts to democratize American government. She started with Thomas Hooker, who rebelled against the authoritarian government of the Massachusetts Bay Colony and suggested a "general council chosen by all" to rule Connecticut. She conceded that Hooker probably didn't mean to include women in the "all," but in 1848 women met at Seneca Falls to demand an equal place in government. Isabella revisited the Fourteenth and Fifteenth Amendments, the NWSA convention of 1871, and her Declaration and Pledge. She then devoted several pages to Susan B. Anthony's trial, concluding that the constitutional convention could rectify the injustice done to women and replace Connecticut's male oligarchy with a true democracy. She asked the convention to strike the word "male" from the voting qualifications and add a new section: "The right of citizens of the State of Connecticut to vote and hold office shall not be denied or abridged on account of sex."

Isabella introduced the memorial in January 1902 but made little progress with it. The delegates seemed "very stupid men" who opposed her at every opportunity. As final decisions would not be made until later in the year, she took a break from lobbying at the end of February. The occasion was her eightieth birthday, February 22, 1902. She held an open house at her home from morning to evening that day. By putting a notice in the local newspapers, Isabella invited friends and neighbors and all the ministers and teachers of the city to call on her. She wrote her niece May Beecher, one of the twins she had entertained at the Columbian Exposition, that the party was to honor John and his ancestor Thomas Hooker as well as the Beechers.

She wanted all Lyman Beecher's grandchildren to be there or to send a message. Would May please invite Henry's family?

The latter wish went unfulfilled, of course, but the birthday gathering bore witness to Isabella's continuing ecumenicism. Her grandnephew Lyman Beecher Stowe described it thus:

> In spite of a driving snowstorm which became a blizzard, a steady stream of people called from ten in the morning until ten at night. There were the great and the near great, old and young, rich and poor, educated and uneducated, suffrage leaders, cranks and freaks. Among the callers was the Roman Catholic Bishop of the city who took especial pleasure in paying his tribute to this daughter of Lyman Beecher—that redoubtable enemy of his church. There were, too, the leading Jewish rabbis and Negro preachers, and the Irish Mayor of the city who at Mrs. Hooker's request made a speech. In short, it was a typical Beecher gathering—nothing polite nor select about it, but entirely consistent with Isabella Beecher Hooker's motto: 'The world is my country; to do good is my religion.'

According to Lyman Stowe, by the time the last caller left, Isabella's children and remaining relatives were about to drop from exhaustion. They asked her solicitously how she was doing after twelve straight hours of conversation. She "replied brightly, 'Oh, I'm all right. I'm going to hop into bed now and try and get caught up in my reading.'" She had a huge pile of magazines to get through that she'd been too busy to read. One hopes that she had canceled some of the twenty-eight magazine subscriptions the Hookers had when John was still alive.

The Beecher energy and Hooker tolerance may have carried Isabella through her birthday marathon, but they didn't make it any easier to change people's minds. When she returned to the constitutional convention, she found the delegates just as stubborn as before. By May they hadn't acted on any of her requests. Perhaps because they weren't all politicians, they didn't find it necessary to be as polite as the legislators she usually lobbied. On behalf of the Connecticut Woman Suffrage Association, Isabella received the strongest rebuff she had ever gotten. Not only did the delegates refuse to let her address the convention, but they also declined to grant the CWSA a hearing in front of the committee to which their memorial was referred. In a previously unheard-of move, they disdained to receive copies of the memorial and argument that Isabella had printed by the thousand. She had overspent her allowance for nothing and was forced to ask Kathy Day to pay room and board during her customary summer visit. "I have done spending money in suffrage work," she declared bitterly.

Essentially Isabella was done with suffrage work. No one thought it unreasonable to retire at age eighty, and her treatment by the constitutional convention was a crushing blow. That "horrid convention," she wrote, ended all hope of her living to vote or see the women of her native state assume the "responsibilities of citizenship." Yet Isabella could not quit altogether. Being a Beecher, she could hardly let one of her writings go unread. She thus distributed her memorial and argument as widely as she could and asked the help of organizations, such as the Connecticut Children's Aid Society, to circulate it. She helped present a municipal suffrage bill to the Connecticut legislature and as late as fall 1904 attended the annual state woman suffrage convention. She remained president of the CWSA until 1905.

But work that was costly or strenuous was out. Isabella wrote Clara B. Colby, a western suffragist who was secretary of the Federal Suffrage Association, to rescind an invitation to come to Connecticut. She'd asked her in a "burst of zeal," she explained, yet "it would take three months to galvanize this stupid old state" and she had promised her children and grandchildren to take time off. "My health gave way under the Constitutional Convention & I am very slowly recovering." She would like to work in Washington next winter, she concluded. That was not to be. The attitudes in the national capital toward suffrage were not much better than in Hartford. Besides, Isabella felt unappreciated by the new united suffrage movement. Since the Columbian Exposition, she wrote Colby in another letter, she had been "ignored and never treated with the old time courtesy and appreciation of the value of my devoted service." She was the only officer of the NAWSA who was a Lady Manager, but someone else had been asked to give the official word on the fair. She was "snubbed," she complained, "instead of being congratulated and honored." If she had been physically stronger and felt her old optimism about gaining suffrage, Isabella would probably have overcome her resentment at being forgotten in Washington. As it was, she stayed home.

Ironically, one of the women who took Isabella's place at the NAWSA conventions—she and not Isabella spoke at the Senate hearing on woman suffrage in 1904—was a relative, her grandniece Charlotte Perkins Gilman. Charlotte was the daughter of the ne'er-do-well Frederick Beecher Perkins and thus the granddaughter of Mary Beecher Perkins. Before her groundbreaking *Women and Economics* (1898), Charlotte was known primarily as a feminist poet. Isabella and John wrote her, praising the poetry. In 1894 they planned to visit her in California but ended up having to cancel their trip. As Charlotte did not return East to live until after 1900, she and Isabella never got to know each other well. Olympia Brown inquired about her in

1901 and Isabella replied, "As to Mrs[.] Perkins Gilman she is all right—a noble woman of large gifts who has had a history that can[']t be put into print." Charlotte divorced her first husband, allowing their daughter to live part of the time with him. Recently she had married her cousin Houghton Gilman, son of Mary's daughter Catherine. A world-weary Isabella advised Brownie that Charlotte might not be able to do much in the movement except write books, for "the world will not pardon peculiarities—and you may not be able to carry her without injuring your own usefulness."

It has been said that Isabella missed an opportunity to mentor a "daughter" who would follow in her footsteps, as Harriot Stanton Blatch and Alice Stone Blackwell followed in Stanton's and Stone's. Isabella's "cobwebs of prejudice" (against divorce, against a woman undertaking a career at the expense of mothering) kept her from transmitting her legacy through Gilman. Certainly these prejudices stopped her from pursuing a closer relationship with her grandniece, but by the time the two women met as adults Charlotte's ideas deviated sharply from Isabella's. Even though both women were feminists, Gilman did not glorify motherhood, nor did she believe in a philosophy of rights. She thought more like Catharine Beecher in many ways. She would have heralded Catharine's view that people possess only the "rights" that benefit society as a whole. If Gilman's great-aunts influenced her at all beyond their having adopted public work as "world-servers," it was in their (Catharine's and to some extent Harriet's) preoccupation with improving health and reorganizing domestic space. In a review of Harriet's biography Gilman said she saw both glory and pathos in Stowe's life—"glory that such transcendent genius should have burned in the heart of a woman, adding to her fulness of womanhood the wide glory of service to humanity; and pathos, deep to bitterness, in seeing this great world-servant burdened and broken by the necessity of being a house-servant as well."

If Isabella and her grandniece had become better acquainted, the rationalist Gilman might not have been able to tolerate Isabella's fascination with the spirit world. In the last two years of her life Isabella did what she'd often threatened earlier: she gave up her various causes and devoted herself entirely to Spiritualism. Sometimes she would hire her favorite medium, Mrs. Lazzaro, for days at a time and she and Lillie and Lottie Foote would have a marathon session. Most of her letters became catalogs of the spirits' visits. Enemies, such as her sons-in-law, came to beg forgiveness (Eugene Burton died in 1904). Charles Dickens wrote a story through Isabella. A young-looking sister Catharine brought her lost fiancé, Alexander Fisher, and reminisced with Lillie Foote about the old days at Nutplains.

In her last years Isabella was less tolerant of skeptics than she had previously been. When her friend George Warner complained about her preoccupation with Spiritualism, she chided him for his "ignorance." She sniped at her daughter's belief in Christian Science, even though she and Alice had agreed not to discuss religion. They didn't want to quarrel. Isabella distrusted Mary Baker Eddy, whom she saw as mercenary and egocentric. She also disliked Alice's certainty that Christian Science was the "true" religion. It was good to seek, she reminded Alice, but "we must not allow ourselves to think for a moment that we alone have sought & found." Kathy Day played mediator between her mother and grandmother. In 1905 Isabella assured her that she wasn't trying to shake her mother's faith but in fact envied her "absolute certainties." Probably Kathy's intimacy with her grandmother in her final years stemmed in part from her status as an "investigator" of Spiritualism. She did not reject Isabella's beliefs wholesale, as did her mother and sister Allie, and even joined her grandmother in séances.

When Kathy was traveling in Japan in 1905, Isabella wrote her that she'd had Mark Twain and his only remaining daughter, Clara, to dinner at her house. Her old neighbor was "a most fascinating man—both in aspect & speech & never so much as now." They got into a discussion of the Russo-Japanese War and then Twain grew "positively garrulous in response to my asking him to repeat his story of wireless transference of thought as given to your grandpa & me in 1874." The dinner was such a success that Isabella forgot their previous run-ins and invited him to meet Mrs. Lazzaro for a séance. But while Twain believed in mental telepathy, he had no use for Spiritualism. He expressed his skeptical attitude to a mutual friend, who passed it on to Isabella. She wrote Twain haughtily, accusing him of demanding tests before he would open his mind. He was obviously not prepared to commune with the spirits, and she thus withdrew her invitation. She enclosed a pamphlet on Spiritualism, which he tore in half in a rage.

Isabella's small brick "cottage" on Marshall Street was, like the old Forest Street house, full of shrines to the departed. One end of the spacious dining room was dedicated to the Hookers and the other end to the Beechers. There were a recently discovered oil portrait of Lyman Beecher, paintings by Harriet, and a detailed parchment map of the United States drawn by Catharine at age fourteen. In her living room Isabella had placed photographs of Stanton and Anthony and a facsimile copy of the Declaration of Independence. When Isabella received a greeting card from Victoria Woodhull Martin, she sent her a copy of her memorial to the constitutional convention and noted that she'd recently found an 1871 photograph of Victoria in her desk. She put it beside her bust of Harriet Beecher Stowe, she wrote, in the parlor that she had filled with the pictures of noble women. How Harriet's spirit felt about this sacrilege she didn't say. Presumably all was forgiven in the Spirit World, and even Henry accepted the fact that she displayed a bust of

Left to right: Alice Hooker Day, Isabella Beecher Hooker, Katharine Day, c. 1896–1902. Courtesy Harriet Beecher Stowe Center, Hartford, Conn.

him too. Her psychic powers had greatly enlarged, she wrote Woodhull, so that she could easily contact relatives on the other side with no other medium present.

Isabella had finally resigned herself to not becoming the Comforter during her lifetime. She had misunderstood the timing, she thought, as in the case of Eugene's burglary. She would eventually be the Comforter but not until after her death. Isabella also had to accept the fact that she would never vote. Other women would soon be able to join the body politic, she predicted. That was the "great comfort" of her old age, she wrote in her memoir "The Last of the Beechers," which was published in *Connecticut Magazine* in 1905. But, still, the "degradation" of her political classification with "minors, criminals, and idiots" was hard to bear. It aroused within her "a storm of indignation" that shook her "very soul of souls."

The sad truth that the indefatigable suffragist Susan B. Anthony would never cast a legal vote seemed particularly unjust. Anthony's eighty-fifth birthday was celebrated at the 1906 NAWSA convention in Baltimore. Isabella did not attend the celebration, as she no longer traveled outside of Connecticut. She could only send a letter of congratulations and hold a dinner with some Hartford suffragists to honor the occasion. A month later Anthony died. As NAWSA women across the nation held memorial services, Isabella's relationship with her beloved colleague was not forgotten. At the Kentucky service, for instance, the women constructed a makeshift altar with a portrait of Anthony surrounded by photos of Elizabeth Cady Stanton, Lucy Stone, and Isabella Beecher Hooker.

If other people remembered Isabella's service to the movement more than she gave them credit for, it was still frustrating to be a relic instead of an activist. According to Lyman Beecher Stowe, she and her namesake granddaughter had the following conversation the year of Anthony's death:

> Isabella: I can't stand all the suffering in the world!
> Isabel: Well, grandmother, you have the satisfaction of knowing
>   you have always done more than your share to relieve it.
> Isabella: That's the point. As long as I could help, I could stand
>   it, but now that I can no longer help, I can't stand it!

Lyman Stowe also reported that Isabella said to her granddaughter, "Isabel, I don't ask you to keep the Ten Commandments—you probably will anyway—but if I ever catch you being bored I'll disown you." She was still interested in everything and embraced new inventions. She had wanted a telephone for five years before she got one in 1901: "what a wonderful invention the phone is," she exclaimed. On the other hand, Isabella had become, in her words, a "serious invalid." Her bad ankles made it hard to walk, she was often nauseous, and her rheumatism worsened all the time (she thought she had contracted it working in the Woman's Building at the World's Fair). All in all, she was a "feeble dependent being," she wrote Lilly Foote.

Besides her friends Lilly Foote and Lilly Warner and her children and grandchildren, Isabella had the perfect nurse and companion during her last year. She was a poverty-stricken widow, Cynthia Fuller, who had worked in the suffrage movement and was also a Spiritualist and medium. Isabella busied herself in her last few months making plans for Mrs. Fuller to continue suffrage work. She also tried to arrange for her to act as an intermediary between Isabella, after her death, and her still-living colleagues. Ironically, Isabella's last letter (or at least the last to be preserved) was to the colleague who almost destroyed her, Victoria Woodhull Martin. Writing in September 1906, she addressed Woodhull as her dear friend and confessed to feeling sorrowful that she couldn't have continued working with her because of her connection with brother Henry. But soon, perhaps, Isabella could help her with her work from the other side through Mrs. Fuller. She clearly realized that she didn't have long to live. She was extremely frail and longing to be released, she concluded. She had not solved the "mystery of death" any more than she had ended the rule of patriarchy. A reformer to the last, Isabella once wrote that she could not appreciate the "wisdom" of death—"why it could not have been made a blessed transition instead of a sorrowful change."

Isabella stayed alive to see the next year begin but did not make it to her eighty-fifth birthday. She at least got her wish as to manner of death— at home with her dear ones close and "in a quiet, orderly way." She had a stroke on January 13, 1907, and died on the 25th. "Last of Beecher Family Is Dead," announced the Hartford Courant on its front page, followed by "Would Have Been 85 on Feb. 22—Famed for Her Labors for Equal Rights for Women." The obituary included her picture and claimed she had inherited her full share of the "ability and originality" that characterized the Beecher family. Or, put less positively, she was eccentric. The family had "ideas and convictions" and if these were unpopular or "took an acute form," the Beechers persevered. They "followed no paths but made their own." The Courant detailed Isabella's work for women's rights by quoting extensively from her memoir in Connecticut Magazine. They ended with praise for her benevolence and charitable ministrations in the city of Hartford.

In sum, the obituary was more flattering than Isabella would have expected from her least favorite newspaper. She had hated it for a long time because of its anti-feminist stand and refusal to publicize her women's rights activities. The next day the editors reverted to type, showing their truer colors in an editorial entitled simply "Mrs. Hooker." Hartford remembered all three of Lyman Beecher's daughters, the editors said (leaving out Mary). Catharine taught school in the city; Harriet lived in Hartford a third of a century and died in her Nook Farm house; Isabella was a resident for over fifty years. But in middle age the youngest sister got "wrapped up" in an unfortunate cause. The *Courant* holds the opinion that Dr. Bushnell held, the editors explained—that is, the late Horace Bushnell, the famous Hartford minister, believed that women's rights was an unnatural reform. (Bushnell's spirit had, of course, appeared to Isabella to apologize for this mistaken view.) The *Courant* editors thus preferred to recall Mrs. Hooker's earlier Nook Farm years—her open door and fine hospitality, her "unfailing kindliness." The feminist Isabella Beecher Hooker she had become was something else again.

Isabella's funeral was held January 28 at her home. Coincidentally her niece Hatty Stowe died of a stroke that same day. A Unitarian minister presided at the service assisted by Isabella's nephew Charles Stowe. Another nephew, Mary's son Charles Perkins, served as honorary pallbearer, as did Mark Twain. In spite of their tense relationship, Twain had more generous words for Isabella than the *Hartford Courant* did. On March 1 he wrote in his *Autobiography*, "The Beecher talent is all gone now; the last concentration of it went out of the world with Isabella Beecher Hooker. . . . [She] threw herself into the women's rights movement among the earliest, some sixty years ago [actually thirty-five], and she labored with all her splendid energies in that great cause all the rest of her life; as an able and efficient worker she ranks immediately after those great chiefs, Susan B. Anthony . . . [and] Elizabeth Cady Stanton." Isabella and her colleagues were "brave women" who besieged the legislatures of the land and started a revolution. He concluded dramatically, "They broke the chains of their sex and set it free."

If this is how Isabella would have liked to be remembered, it was not the last word. A year later she was again on the front page of the *Courant*. The headlines read: "Mrs. Hooker's Talks With Spirits. . . . Dr. Hooker Tells of His Mother's Wills. Examination of Mrs. Powers Leads the Lawyers Up to Family Troubles." Mrs. Powers was the married name of Isabella's estranged granddaughter Kate Burton. She was a shadow who came back to haunt her grandmother in death as she did in life. Kate challenged Isabella's will, made in November 1904, which left Kate a thousand dollars to spend in remembrance of her grandfather. She wanted this will declared invalid in favor of the one the Hookers had made in 1900 before John's death. That will gave Kate a legacy of ten thousand dollars.

What had happened between 1900 and 1904? In 1900 the Hookers thought that eventually, once Eugene Burton could no longer interfere, Kate would be reconciled with them. In October 1904 Eugene died. Four of Isabella's closest family members, her son Ned and granddaughter Isabel and her daughter Alice and granddaughter Kathy, testified as to what occurred next. Isabella sent Kate Burton a telegram, placing herself at Kate's service, and Ned's wife, Mattie, wrote a friendly letter. Isabella expected Kate to communicate with them and when this didn't happen decided to change her will. No doubt her expectation was irrational. She hadn't been allowed to see Kate since Mary's death in 1886. Eugene had thus had almost twenty years to turn his daughter against her grandparents. That damage was not going to be undone in a month.

But Isabella's children and other grandchildren encouraged her to decrease Kate's legacy. As Alice testified, she believed her mother ought to leave her estate to those who were "kind and loving" to her in life. Kathy Day said she wondered why her grandmother hadn't changed the will before, considering the "repeated insults" she had received from the Burtons. Kathy testified to her grandmother's hurt at not being invited to Kate's wedding and referred to a "cold" letter Isabella had received from Kate about a year after Eugene's death and a few weeks after her first stroke. Kate wrote that she wanted to be just to the dead and say that her father never asked her to promise she wouldn't communicate with her mother's family after his death. (Translation: the long silence was her own doing.) She expressed no concern for Isabella's health, only that she hoped she was enjoying the autumn weather.

It would seem that the evidence of Kate's hostility toward the Hookers and the united front of the family against her claim would have been persuasive. But her lawyers cleverly cast a different spin on the story. They portrayed Isabella as either too old or too insane (as evidenced by her truck with spirits) to have known what she was doing when she changed her will. She was a dupe. Whenever possible, Kate's lawyers presented advanced age and lunacy as interchangeable. For instance, they ridiculed Isabella for worrying about her thinning hair and consulting the spirit of a doctor about how to restore it. The villains who exerted "undue influence" on the foolish old lady to change her will were, alternatively, the spirits or her son Dr. Hooker. Incredibly, Ned was made to seem a greedy rich man who plotted to keep Kate away from his mother in order to steal her ten thousand dollars. His evil sister Alice Day helped him with the plot (although Alice refused any money under either of the wills). Kate's lawyers agreed that one of the "sad spectacles" in the courtroom was "the presence of Mrs. Day, whose husband died leaving her $500,000 which she looks upon as a mere bagatelle. She comes up from her Fifth avenue [sic] home, and assists her brother to keep the money away from this [poor] girl."

One of the biggest problems in presenting a clear case for the jury was the agreement of the lawyers for both sides not to expose the quarrel between Isabella Hooker and Eugene Burton. Kate would have hesitated to open the door to attacks on her father's alcoholism and misogyny. The Hookers needed to make sure that Victoria Woodhull would not be brought into the picture; they had enough to contend with in Isabella's spirit communications. But without any history of the family relationships the jury had no way to choose between the scenarios presented by the lawyers. Although the judge instructed them that no evidence had been presented linking Isabella's decision to spirit influence, the jury bought the poor-girl-rejected-by-her-rich-family story and overturned the will. In the process Isabella's name was further tarnished and those of her children dragged in the dirt.

All three Beecher sisters who had public careers experienced the nearly universal drop in reputation that occurs with famous people after their death. In addition, they were victims of the special fate reserved for achieving women after 1920. In a reaction to women gaining the vote—perhaps a backlash—women's accomplishments were denigrated or forgotten for several decades. Women like Catharine or Harriet who in life stood shoulder to shoulder with men in their professions were gradually relegated to secondary status. Horace Mann became the innovator in education while Catharine was ignored. Harriet's novels could not be mentioned in the same breath as Hawthorne's or Melville's; her work was "propaganda" while theirs was "art."

There were also more individual reasons for the sisters' loss of prominence. Catharine, for instance, could not be associated with any one prestigious school that continued to exist in the way that Mary Lyon could be linked with Mt. Holyoke. The Catharine Beecher philosophy of domesticity would have resonated with the public in the 1950s, but no one knew to read her books. Although Harriet's *Uncle Tom's Cabin* had never been entirely forgotten, new generations of African Americans scorned romantic racialism and demanded true equality. They saw Harriet's Christian hero as a toady to whites and gave a new, pejorative meaning to "Uncle Tom." Stowe's New England novels were simply overlooked.

Not until the second wave of the women's movement, beginning in the late 1960s, did Catharine and Harriet regain their stellar reputations. Catharine Beecher was finally recognized for her contributions to women's health and women's education, including her influential plan to make women teachers and send them West. Her glorification of domesticity and emphasis on women's moral superiority were seen as doctrines having a powerful effect on the ethos of the time. As for Harriet Beecher Stowe, she remained the leading female novelist of nineteenth-century America and took her place as a writer worthy to be considered alongside the *Atlantic Monthly* men. *Uncle Tom's Cabin* came to be seen as a great novel and a conscious artistic creation despite its flaws. Stowe's role as initiator of the New England local-color tradition was also restored to view. New biographies signaled and at the same time helped further the rehabilitation of Harriet's and Catharine's fame.

In the case of Isabella, this restoration process did not occur, although her papers were collected early on. Kathy Day eventually accomplished her grandmother's goal of a Beecher-Hooker memorial when she established the Stowe-Day Memorial Library and Historical Foundation in Nook Farm. But the Hooker papers were initially used, in books such as Kenneth Andrews's *Nook Farm* (1950), to brand Isabella a crank, if not a downright lunatic. Her relationship with Victoria Woodhull and adherence to Spiritualism have made many subsequent writers uncomfortable. Furthermore, her very devotion to woman suffrage has delayed the recognition of her work. In the early days of the women's movement, when the contributions of women such as Catharine and Harriet were being reevaluated, suffrage was downplayed. Women's accomplishments had been equated with suffrage for too long, it was thought. Women who came after Elizabeth Cady Stanton and Susan B. Anthony were widely criticized for having narrowed their aspirations to suffrage instead of concentrating on other rights. Of course, this view was simplistic, ignoring the early feminists' varied activities, such as their work for property rights and representation of women in national events like the Columbian Exposition. But it did take another twenty-five years for attention to be paid to the so-called secondary echelon of suffragists (that is, those who were not Stanton or Anthony).

A final estimate of Isabella Beecher Hooker's importance to the women's movement will have to await more detailed accounts of the other workers in the "second echelon." Still, her contributions were considerable, especially for someone who did not take up a career until her late forties. She was the single most important women's rights worker in nineteenth-century Connecticut. She established the state equal rights and suffrage organizations, converted women like the Smith sisters, raised and spent large sums of money, brought in nationally known speakers, and shepherded the women's property bill through the legislature. Isabella's continual legislative lobbying, both in Hartford and in Washington, prepared the legislatures for women's final push for suffrage.

On the national level she exerted her greatest influence during her Washington winters. It was Isabella who kept a constant eye on the federal solution and did the groundwork for the route that younger suffragists would finally take to victory. Susan B. Anthony always recognized the significance of the efforts pioneered largely by Isabella in the national capital. At the turn of the century she wrote a younger colleague about the necessity of securing hearings before congressional committees. She stressed "the far reaching importance of our Hearings before the committees, of the publication of the speeches by the Government, and the sending out of the speeches under the frank of the Members to the friends in the several States of the Union. I have always believed, and never more strongly than now, that the educational work done by these hearings was farther reaching and did quite as much good work in the rural districts as the holding of meetings in each."

It could be argued that Isabella was perhaps *too* focused on Washington—on lobbying Congress and distributing widely the pro-suffrage speeches. She seemed unable to change with the times. In the new century she was still pushing her central theories, those with which she had originally entered the movement. Isabella interrupted her memorial to the Connecticut constitutional convention, for example, to bring in the superiority of motherhood argument. Men kept telling her, she said, that there would always be war. She replied with her old insistence on mother power—"we mothers are fast coming to the fixed resolve that we will bring no more sons into the world to cut each other's throats. Where then will the fighters come from?"

Isabella also seemed fixated on the theories and tactics of the early 1870s, if she wasn't fixated on Victoria Woodhull personally. She took every possible opportunity to discuss the Constitution and the idea that its Fourteenth Amendment gave women (as citizens) the right to vote. Congress had only to pass a declaratory act asserting this as their opinion—or the suffragists should try again to take the judicial route. To the younger women this argument may have seemed bewildering and antiquated, yet they did need to hear it.

Isabella's characteristic stubbornness also had its virtues. Her preoccupation with the Constitution offered a needed reminder of democratic ideals in the conservative years of the late nineteenth and early twentieth centuries. Her grandniece Charlotte Perkins Gilman was more in tune with the times as she adapted feminism to the social Darwinist, racialist, and other inegalitarian theories of the era. Pro-suffrage arguments increasingly became arguments of "expediency," to use Aileen Kraditor's term, instead of justice. In other words, society needed women to vote: women would clean up politics; women would attack and solve the problems of the cities. Like most suffragists, Isabella sometimes argued from expediency. Her "mother power" theory is one example: mothers would presumably vote for pacifist ends. But what women would or wouldn't *do* with the vote was not the most important thing. When Isabella reverted repeatedly to the Constitution, harping on its references to "the people" and the rights and duties of citizens, she brought into prominence the principles on which the country was founded. Women should be part of the body politic because that was just and fair. As Isabella argued of the immigrants who were flocking to the United States, the tendency of democracy as expressed in the Constitution was to teach and make responsible, not to exclude.

This concept of democracy was perhaps Isabella's most important contribution to the women's movement—the idea that "women could grow in stature only if responsibility were placed upon them." If possession of the ballot would save the immigrants from anarchy and turn them into productive citizens, it would do the same for women. Isabella once addressed the Judiciary Committee of the House of Representatives as follows: "If you cannot live in safety with irresponsible men in your midst, how can you live with irresponsible women? Much more, how can you grow into the stature of . . . perfect legislators, except your mothers are instructed on these great subjects you are called to legislate upon, that they may instruct you in their turn! You do not know anything so well as what your mothers have taught you; but they have not taught you political economy. . . . No man or woman studies a subject profoundly except he or she is called upon to act upon it." Once women were granted suffrage, they would quickly grow to stand by men's side in public life.

In this passage Isabella mixes two of her key ideas, the importance of mothers and the educative powers of responsibility. The ideology of motherhood was, of course, part of the times—part of the very context in which Isabella lived. Her sisters shared it. Elizabeth Ammons says of Harriet and Isabella, "Both women associated Christ with women, defined the coming Milennium [sic] in matrifocal terms, and look to feminine values as the foundation for ethical revolution in America." She could just as well have added Catharine, who was the teacher of matrifocal values in the Beecher family. But the idea that women needed suffrage to learn responsibility was more original. As early as 1866, Henry Ward Beecher had spoken of women's "duty," rather than their "right," to vote. Isabella probably adopted the kernel of her belief from her brother, but she developed the idea further; instead of setting women in opposition to the flood of male immigrants as her colleagues did, she made them parallel seekers of responsibility for government.

Ironically, the woman who had entered the suffrage movement from expediency in her search for a midlife career and rose to leadership on the basis of her family name became a passionate advocate for equality. As such, she may be a more attractive model for the young women of today than others who lived a century ago. Her attack on the double standard was far too radical for her time—many proponents of women's rights barely understood it themselves. Isabella's support of Victoria Woodhull against her own brother and in the face of vehement opposition from her family was the bravest thing she did. To those who were looking on at the time it may have seemed a foolhardy act, a negative exemplar. Adherence to principle brings public humiliation and ostracism, other women may have concluded. While Isabella's sisters ultimately forgave her, her sons-in-law did not, leading to tragic consequences in her life. But with the benefit of hindsight a morally courageous stance can be admired. If mothers stopped preparing their sons for war, Isabella argued, war would disappear. Similarly, if women refused to make exceptions to their principles for husbands, sons, and brothers, the double standard would collapse. Isabella Beecher Hooker was indeed eccentric, perhaps at times insane. But if every woman had adopted her principles and adhered to them as strongly as she did, the rule of patriarchy would have come to an end.

Abbreviations

AHD   Alice Hooker Day

AUTO   *The Autobiography of Lyman Bee-cher*, ed. Barbara M. Cross. 2 vols. Cambridge: Belknap Press of Harvard University Press, 1961 [orig. 1864].

CB   Catharine Beecher

Fiche   Refers to microfiche number in IBHP, below

HBS   Harriet Beecher Stowe

HW   *History of Woman Suffrage*, ed. Elizabeth Cady Stanton, Susan B. Anthony, and Matilda Joslyn Gage. 4 vols. Rochester, N.Y.: Susan B. Anthony, 1881, 1886, 1902, 1922.

IBH   Isabella Beecher Hooker

IBH-Mem   Isabella Beecher Hooker. "The Last of the Beechers: Memories on My Eighty-Third Birthday," *Connecticut Magazine*, 9 (Spring 1905), 286–298.

IBHP   *The Isabella Beecher Hooker Project: A Microfiche Edition of Her Papers*, ed. Anne Throne Margolis. Millwood, N.Y.: KTO Microform, 1979.

IBHP-G   Guide/Index to IBHP, above. Hartford: Stowe-Day Foundation, 1979.

JH   John Hooker

LIMITS   *The Limits of Sisterhood: The Beecher Sisters on Women's Rights and Woman's Sphere*, ed. Jeanne Boydston, Mary Kelley, and Anne Margolis. Chapel Hill: University of North Carolina Press, 1988.

S-D   Harriet Beecher Stowe Center, Hartford, Connecticut

SCH   Schlesinger Library, Radcliffe Institute, Harvard University

Notes

CHAPTER 1. Calvinist Childhoods

page
1   "tall, fair and lovely": Milton Rugoff, *The Beechers*, p. 4.
2   "entered into my character": AUTO, vol. 1, p. 85.
2   "Thou little immortal!": Ibid., p. 87.
2   "to feel the confidence": Kathryn Kish Sklar, *Catharine Beecher*, p. 3.
2   "that passionate love": LIMITS, p. 28.
3   "with a border": AUTO, vol. 1, p. 86.
3   "What she saw": Ibid., p. 94.
3   "ludicrous," "By this intellectual": Ibid., pp. 98, 104.
4   "at a period when babies": HBS, *Poganuc People*, p. 8.
4   "Roxana became pure": Forrest Wilson, *Crusader in Crinoline*, p. 32.
4   "an outlandish, threadbare": Marie Caskey, *Chariot of Fire*, p. 11.
5   "I was about six": AUTO, vol. 1, p. 267.

5   "a fine-looking," "She is twelve": Ibid., p. 273.
6   "family malaise," "violent": Rugoff, *The Beechers*, p. 13.
6   "finely chiseled": Caskey, *Chariot of Fire*, p. 17.
6   "the first in acute": AUTO, vol. 1, p. 353.
6   "addressing her conscience": Ibid.
6   "ruined hopes," "Oh, Edward," "When I look": LIMITS, pp. 31–32.
7   "vaguely unhappy": Caskey, *Chariot of Fire*, p. 17.
7   "there is the strongest": IBH to JH, Sept. 7, 1843 (Fiche 5).
7   "Puritan penitentiary": Robert Ingersoll, quoted in Paxton Hibben, *Henry Ward Beecher*, p. [14].
7   "take him by the nose": AUTO, vol. 2, p. 88. A disciple of Lyman's once described him on all fours playing "riding horse" with two children on his back. "He would run horse fashion, trot, gallop, stop, run back, kick up, throw the riders, and then run away, with all the children after him screaming with delight." James C. White, *Personal Reminiscences*, p. 21.
8   "victory will be achieved": AUTO, vol. 2, p. 12.
8   "new, airy," "This soil": Ibid., pp. 42–43.
8   "Oh, my dear son": AUTO, vol. 1, p. 341.
9   "drudgery," "has as it were": LIMITS, p. 36.
9   "It was the proudest": AUTO, vol. 1, p. 399.
9   "first juvenile": IBH-Mem, p. 286.
10 "my own father": IBH to JH, Sept. [22?], 1843 (Fiche 5).
10 Isabella also: From summer 1831 to summer 1832. See letters to her from her mother in the Joseph K. Hooker Collection, S-D.
10 "as the church": Rugoff, *The Beechers*, p. 77. "Jug" was a double pun, referring also to the jugs of rum that, unbeknown to Lyman, had been stored by a merchant in the church basement; the jugs burst in the fire.
11 "going over," "If we gain": AUTO, vol. 2, p. 167.
11 "very beautiful": Ibid., p. 200.
11 "Noah, and his wife": Ibid., p. 208.
12 "We went to Philadelphia": IBH-Mem, p. 286.
12 "the most inconvenient": Quoted in Wilson, *Crusader in Crinoline*, p. 109.
12 "attended all," "general discontent," "the wearied, anxious look": Elizabeth Cady Stanton, *Eighty Years and More*, pp. 133, 147–148.
13 "the magnificent," "to climb to," "once when a great flock": IBH-Mem, pp. 286–289. Many autobiographies of feminists contain recollections of climbing trees as a girl. See Barbara A. White, "Three Feminist Mother-Daughter Pairs," p. 287.
13 "with a quiet fervor": IBH-Mem, p. 286.
14 "to turn over," "my school": LIMITS, p. 50.
14 "an exuberant," "replete with moral oxygen": AUTO, vol. 2, p. 231.
14 "rhapsodic tribute," "theological indoctrination," "bilious fever": Rugoff, *The Beechers*, p. 139.
14 This letter: AUTO, vol. 2, pp. 310–312.
15 "the United States Constitution," "I date": IBH-Mem, p. 289.
15 "found all in a flurry": AUTO, vol. 2, p. 246.
15 "for he loved," "I can see him now": IBH-Mem, p. 288.
16 "to have a voice," "Surely you": Sarah and Angelina Grimké, *The Public Years*, p. 197.
16 "he-goat men": AUTO, vol. 2, p. 260.
17 "I looked so quiet": Ibid., p. 265.
17 "[W]ell do I remember": IBH-Mem, p. 289.
17 Although Lyman hinted, "Constitutionally," "shivered": AUTO, vol. 2, pp. 265, 275.
18 "The next morning": AUTO, vol. 1, p. 267.
18 the older boys reacted: see, for instance, AUTO, vol. 2, p. 277.

18 "She was polished": Quoted in William C. Beecher and Samuel Scoville, *Biography of Henry Ward Beecher*, p. 66.

18 "that was the last": IBH-Mem, p. 289.

18 "Forbidden": IBH to JH, Aug. 8, 1844 (Fiche 5).

18 "a shadow life," "sexual love": Rugoff, *The Beechers*, p. 160.

19 "haunted with": IBH to JH, July 18, 1852 (Fiche 11).

19 "I have cried": IBH to Esther M. Beecher, Feb. 26, 1842 (Fiche 4). Apparently the letter was lost, although Isabella had saved school compositions from that time. She wished her husband John could have read the letter.

19 "as her representative": Ibid.

19 "fine looking woman": CB to Mary Cogswell, May 29, 1837, Beecher-Stowe Collection, SCH.

19 "never loved or trusted": HBS to CB, Aug. 27, 1858, Beecher-Stowe Collection, SCH.

19 Isabella continued to attend: The chronologies in LIMITS and IBHP-G claim that she moved to Hartford to live with Mary in 1835, returned to Cincinnati in 1836 or 1837, and then went again to Hartford in 1838. But internal evidence of her school compositions, dated 1835 to 1837, indicates they were written in Cincinnati; nor is she listed as a student in the Hartford Female Seminary catalogs until 1838. Isabella herself contributed to the misunderstanding. She wrote in her memoir that "At sixteen I was sent back to New England, on account of the death of my mother," but this is misleading. Her mother died when she was thirteen, and she traveled to New England at age sixteen. It was "on account of the death of my mother" only in the sense that Isabella thought her stepmother wanted her to leave home.

20 "where from joy": IBH, "Now Oft Let Me Wander" [1835] (Fiche 87).

20 "It is out of the question": Mary Dutton to CB, [1835, between Dec. 21 and Dec. 23], Acquisitions, S-D.

20 "Catharine's school," "Tell Catharine," "cousin": Sklar, *Catharine Beecher*, pp. 131, 117.

20 "Monday morning," "prosaical people": IBH, "Journal of a School Girl" [1836–1837] (Fiche 88).

21 "all I suffered": CB to Mary Dutton, May 21, 1838, Collection of American Literature, Beinecke Rare Book and Manuscript Library, Yale University.

21 "There's not a vital": LIMITS, pp. 99–100.

21 "At fifteen," "At sixteen and a half": Ibid., p. 100.

22 "filling the place": IBH to JH, Feb. 7, 1841 (Fiche 1).

22 "When the children," "affecting speech": Edward F. Hayward, *Lyman Beecher*, pp. 94–95.

22 "[A] greater evil": Lyman Beecher, *Letters*, pp. 90–91.

22 "Cate has neither conscience": LIMITS, p. 14. For more on Catharine's manipulations, see Sklar, *Catharine Beecher*, p. 170.

22 "as a kind of live": Rugoff, *The Beechers*, p. 289.

23 "sucked into the vortex": AUTO, vol. 1, p. 390.

23 "only thro' a determined": LIMITS, p. 100.

23 "she was conveniently": Rugoff, *The Beechers*, p. 280.

23 "He valued boys": Doris Faber, *Love and Rivalry*, p. 3.

24 Literary critics have always complained: see, for instance, Gamaliel Bradford, "Harriet Beecher Stowe," pp. 84–94.

24 "bare bones," "with the flesh": LIMITS, p. 100.

24 "I should be ashamed": AUTO, vol. 1, p. 384.

CHAPTER 2. Marriage and Motherhood

25 "exerting a very": HBS, IBH, and George Beecher to Lyman and Lydia Beecher, July 3, [1837] (Fiche 2).

25 "very genteel," "quite the gentleman," "as quiet as": Angelina Grimké, Diary, July 8, 1831, Weld-Grimké Papers, Clement Library, University of Michigan.

27 "two girls and a man": Esther M. Beecher to HBS, July 7, 1837, Beecher-Stowe Collection, SCH.

27 "Oh what a sister": LIMITS, p. 90.

27 "sacred," "charming": IBH-Mem, p. 286.

27 "all at once": IBH to Robert Allen, Feb. 4, 1868 (Fiche 38).

27 "rendered the goodness": Lyman Beecher to IBH, Mar. 3, 1838, Joseph K. Hooker Collection, S-D.

28 "who was a rare": JH, Some Reminiscences, p. 10.

28 "aged father": IBH to JH, Dec. 2, 1839 (Fiche 1).

28 "where now the postage": JH, Some Reminiscences, p. 17.

28 "the few &": IBH to JH, Dec. 18, 1840 (Fiche 1).

29 "There are certain": Calvin Stowe to HBS, Sept. 29, [1844], Beecher-Stowe Collection, SCH.

29 "This is a": IBH to JH, Nov. 9, 1839 (Fiche 1).

29 "Bell is formed": LIMITS, p. 339.

29 "susceptible": IBH to JH, Nov. 9, 1839 (Fiche 1).

30 "long been accustomed": IBH to JH, June 12, 1841 (Fiche 6).

30 "You will have troubles": Quoted in Edward Hayward, Lyman Beecher, p. 106.

30 "You have never stood": Charles Beecher to IBH, Nov. 18, 1839, Joseph K. Hooker Collection, S-D.

30 "Nobody writes": Charles Beecher to IBH, Nov. 14, 1839, Joseph K. Hooker Collection, S-D.

30 "I was made": HBS to George Beecher, Feb. 20 [1830?], Acquisitions, S-D.

31 "Every young man": IBH to JH, Oct. 21, 1839 (Fiche 1).

31 "clashing views": CB to JH, Nov. 27, 1839, Joseph K. Hooker Collection, S-D.

31 "We have both erred": IBH to JH, Sept. 25, 1839 (Fiche 2).

32 Isabella started backtracking: It is thus not true that Isabella resented John's failure to become a minister, as Marie Caskey states in Chariot of Fire, p. 105.

32 "immolation": IBH to JH, July [14], 1841 (Fiche 4).

32 "angel," "for her part": Caskey, Chariot of Fire, p. 107.

32 "are such": IBH to JH, Mar. 16, 1841 (Fiche 3).

33 " 'Is that the justice": Lyman Beecher Stowe, Saints, Sinners and Beechers, p. 345.

33 "putting Lucy": Quoted in Andrea Moore Kerr, Lucy Stone, p. 84.

33 "cease to be Hatty," "duty of submission," "I don't know": LIMITS, pp. 51, 90.

34 "Poor thing": CB to Mary Beecher Perkins, IBH, and Esther M. Beecher, Oct. 22, 1837, Beecher-Stowe Collection, SCH.

35 "I also have made": LIMITS, p. 67.

35 "wrote to get money": Joan D. Hedrick, Harriet Beecher Stowe, p. 121.

35 "You must be," "drop the E.": LIMITS, p. 69.

35 "Nutplains," "love affair": Hedrick, Harriet Beecher Stowe, pp. 15–16.

36 "interest in," "to it I owe": IBH-Mem, p. 291.

36 "too much one," "I never": IBH to JH, Sept. [19], 1843 (Fiche 5).

36 "ridiculed": IBH to JH, Dec. 25, 1844 (Fiche 6).

37 "universal disregard": JH, Some Reminiscences, pp. 22–23.

37 "the wise procedure": IBH, "Shall Women Vote? A Matrimonial Dialogue," in On Common Ground, p. 75.

37 "surreptitiously laid": Ibid.

38 "perfect happiness," "How I thank": JH to IBH, Dec. 20, 1844, IBH Collection, S-D.

38 "little," "the progress," "I talked": IBH to JH, Dec. 30, 1842 (Fiche 4).

38 "hopeless," "absolutely nothing": Ibid.
38 "wounded": IBH to JH, Sept. 6, 1843 (Fiche 5).
38 "smug self-congratulation": Hedrick, *Harriet Beecher Stowe*, p. 235.
38 "It is amusing": IBH to JH, June 20, 1852 (Fiche 10).
39 "How strange": JH to IBH, Dec. 20, 1844, IBH Collection, S-D.
39 "public woman," "I could not": LIMITS, p. 341.
39 "When [s]he grows": Alfred Adler, *What Life*, p. 147.
39 "her reformist," "firstborn": Frank J. Sulloway, *Born to Rebel*, p. 154, p. 171.
39 "empathize," "find a valued": Ibid., pp. 70, 353.
40 "that breast": IBH to JH, Jan. 2, 1843 (Fiche 4).
40 "Joe beat his": IBH to JH, May 28, 1845 (Fiche 6).
41 "Mrs. Hooker": Quoted in Caskey, *Chariot of Fire*, p. 107.
41 "No one publicly": Milton Rugoff, *The Beechers*, p. 203.
41 "shook my whole": AUTO, vol. 2, p. 371.
41 "She was an expert": Kathryn Kish Sklar, *Catharine Beecher*, p. 186.
42 "My dear Sister": Thomas Beecher to IBH, Jan. 9, 1843, Joseph K. Hooker Collection, S-D.
42 "wayward," "under *home influences*": IBH to JH, Feb. 7, 1841 (Fiche 1).
42 "put both hands": AUTO, vol. 2, p. 381.
42 "Father got here": Henry Ward Beecher to Eunice Bullard Beecher, Nov. 11, 1844, Beecher-Scoville Family Papers, Sterling Memorial Library, Yale University.
43 One of Stowe's biographers: Hedrick, *Harriet Beecher Stowe*, p. 49.
43 "I will if I live": LIMITS, p. 156.
43 "darling": IBH to JH, Sept. 24, 1845 (Fiche 6).
43 "vividly remembered": IBH to JH, Oct. 11, 1864 (Fiche 28).
44 "the first text-book": Benjamin R. Andrews, "Miss Catherine [sic] Beecher," p. 214.
44 "the mother writes," "the greatest work": CB, *A Treatise*, pp. 13–14.
44 "If it were not for these maiden": LIMITS, p. 118.
44 "holy life": IBH, Journal, Dec. 7, 1845 (Fiche 89).
45 "has *in some things*": LIMITS, p. 90. My italics.
45 "preclude other": IBH to JH, Apr. 8, 1840 (Fiche 2).
45 "I almost wish": IBH to Esther M. Beecher, Aug. 22, 1846 (Fiche 6).
45 "as sweet": IBH, Journal, Nov. 11, 1847 (Fiche 89).
45 "obstinate fit," "I never whipped": IBH to JH, Mar. 29, 1847 (Fiche 8).
45 "lack of government," "unsteady": CB, *Treatise*, p. 225. For Lyman's views, see AUTO, vol. 2, p. 312.
45 "It pains me," "I started up": LIMITS, p. 94.
46 "troubled": Caskey, *Chariot of Fire*, p. 108. Another writer, trying to show that Isabella was a woman of "uncontrollable passions," says she "savagely beat" Mary with the brush. Barbara Goldsmith, *Other Powers*, p. 197.
46 "The literal fact," "everlasting jealousy": IBH, Journal, Mar. 21, 1851 (Fiche 89).
47 "the rock on": LIMITS, p. 93.
47 "much anxiety": IBH to JH, July 4, 1852 (Fiche 11).
47 "my poor dear": IBH to JH, June 10, 1852 (Fiche 10).
47 "your experience": IBH to HBS, July 31, 1849 (Fiche 8).
48 "My Charley": LIMITS, p. 93.
48 "I am perfectly": IBH to JH, Feb. 15, 1847 (Fiche 7).
48 "I do hate" "cross," "I abate": IBH to JH, June [4], 1857 (Fiche 14).
50 "imprudence," "I am," "various brothers": CB, *Truth Stranger than Fiction*, pp. 237, 272, 284.
50 "it did my heart": HBS to CB [1850 or 51], Beecher-Scoville Family Papers, Sterling Memorial Library, Yale University.

50 "series of sketches": Quoted in Hedrick, *Harriet Beecher Stowe*, p. 208.

50 "the time is come": LIMITS, pp. 156–157.

51 "would have been as foul": Thomas Beecher to IBH, Sept. 16, 1853, Joseph K. Hooker Collection, S-D.

51 "rude, ungoverned": Nathan Lord to Lyman Beecher, June 6, 1845, Beecher-Stowe Collection, SCH.

51 "He is an odd fish," "Jim has just": IBH to JH, July 18, 1852 (Fiche 11).

CHAPTER 3. In the Wake of *Uncle Tom's Cabin*

53 "loathesome," "whose touch": LIMITS, p. 159.

53 "vile wretch": Quoted in Thomas F. Gossett, *Uncle Tom's Cabin*, p. 189.

54 "Mrs. Stowe betrays": [William Gilmore Simms], review of *A Key to Uncle Tom's Cabin*, p. 226.

54 "How could a plain": Forrest Wilson, *Crusader in Crinoline*, p. 283.

54 "At one step": Henry Wadsworth Longfellow, *Life of*, p. 233.

54 "So you want": Quoted in *The Oxford Harriet Beecher Stowe*, p. 71.

54 "She dropped": Annie Fields, Ed., *Life and Letters of Harriet Beecher Stowe*, p. 163.

55 "marked the climax": Robert Merideth, *The Politics of the Universe*, p. 147.

55 "Edward, you've": Lyman Beecher Stowe, *Saints, Sinners and Beechers*, p. 149.

55 "another book": LIMITS, p. 350.

55 "The fact": IBH to JH, July 4, 1852 (Fiche 11).

56 "Harriet found": Wilson, *Crusader in Crinoline*, p. 296.

56 "forever *conscious*," "At first": IBH to JH, June 26, 1852 (Fiche 10).

56 "romp," "wild": IBH to JH, June 25, 1852 (Fiche 10).

57 Harriet tried: She later confessed to one of Garrison's sons that she was at first "dreadfully afraid" of his father. See Wendell Phillips Garrison and Francis Jackson Garrison, *William Lloyd Garrison*, p. 401.

57 "Louisa would": Harriet A. Jacobs, *Incidents in the Life of a Slave Girl*, p. xix.

57 "Slavery is terrible," "petted," "Mrs. Stowe thinks": Ibid., pp. 77, 235, xix.

58 "After that": HBS to Calvin Stowe, Oct. 10, 1856, quoted in Charles E. Stowe, *Life of Harriet Beecher Stowe*, p. 279.

58 "An important reformation": Quoted in Mae Elizabeth Harveson, *Catharine Esther Beecher*, p. 250.

59 "to establish *endowed*": LIMITS, p. 250.

59 "woman's true profession": CB, *The Evils Suffered by American Women and American Children: The Causes and the Remedy* (New York: Harper & Bros., 1846), p. 10.

59 "I considered": HBS to Lyman Beecher and Henry Ward Beecher, Sept. 9, 1851, Beecher-Scoville Family Papers, Sterling Memorial Library, Yale University.

60 "curious thread": JH, *Some Reminiscences*, p. 171.

60 "like a little society": Ibid. For a useful map of Nook Farm, see Joseph S. Van Why, *Nook Farm*, p. 5.

61 "Montgomery, the Irishman," "stand up": IBH, Journal, Jan. 8, 1854 (Fiche 90).

61 "Victorian aspirations": Rugoff, *The Beechers*, p. 285.

62 "holy," "What a fool!": IBH, Journal, Feb. 13, 1853 (Fiche 92).

62 "I took": IBH, Journal, Jan. 10, 1852 (Fiche 91).

62 "christocentric": Marie Caskey, *Chariot of Fire*, p. 167.

62 "had no business": Quoted in Stuart C. Henry, *Unvanquished Puritan*, p. 279.

62 "task": Quoted in Rugoff, *The Beechers*, p. 91.

63 "vast array": CB, *Common Sense*, p. xi.

63 "I have only stepped": LIMITS, pp. 248–249.
63 "Henry was the only": Quoted in IBH to JH, July 17, 1857 (Fiche 15).
64 "I am cold": Quoted in Charles E. Stowe, *Life of Harriet Beacher Stowe*, pp. 340–341.
64 "These hard old": HBS, *The Minister's Wooing*, p. 25.
64 "a powerfully built," "'Why, de Lord": Ibid., pp. 111, 347.
64 "absorbed in": IBH to AHD, Mar. 6, 1865 (Fiche 31).
66 "so stupefied": IBH, Journal, Apr. 9, 1855 (Fiche 92).
66 "poor little unfledged": IBH, Journal, Apr. 29, 1855 (Fiche 92).
66 "my health": IBH, Journal, May 26, 1855 (Fiche 93).
66 "Alice was": IBH, Journal, May 13, 185[6] (Fiche 93).
66 in New York City: See Catharine Clinton, *The Other Civil War*, p. 32.
66 "the influx": LIMITS, p. 250.
67 "but not Bridget," "her good": IBH to JH, June 27, 1860 (Fiche 24).
67 "her father's," "if she lives": IBH, Journal, Aug. 14, 1850 (Fiche 89).
67 "Sometimes I": IBH Journal, Apr. 11, 1851 (Fiche 89).
68 "[M]y soul": IBH, Journal, Apr. 18, 1852 (Fiche 90).
68 "every thing": IBH, Journal, July 13, 1851 (Fiche 89).
68 "the same old story," "The little darling": IBH, Journal, Nov. [26], 1863 (Fiche 94).
69 "I never saw girls": Mary Beecher Perkins to Thomas Perkins, [Jan. after the 10th, 1857], Katharine S. Day Collection, S-D.
69 "in the regular way": IBH, Journal, Feb. 26, 1865 (Fiche 94).
69 "a very": IBH, Journal, Dec. 11, 1851 (Fiche 90).
70 All the women's rights: For further discussion of their attitudes toward education, see Barbara A. White, "Three Feminist Mother-Daughter Pairs," p. 276.
70 "Siamese": IBH to JH, May 16, 1857 (Fiche 14).
70 "I do": IBH to JH, Oct. 16, 1853 (Fiche 12).
70 "a sad state," "If your health": Calvin Stowe to HBS, June 30, 1846, Acquisitions, S-D.
70 "In the end": Mary Kelley, "At War with Herself," p. 33.
71 "severe": IBH to JH, Apr. 18, 1857 (Fiche 13).
71 "Oh my": IBH to JH, Jan. 24, 1860 (Fiche 16).
71 "You mentioned": IBH, "Shall Women Vote?," p. 76.
72 "alas!": LIMITS, p. 100.
72 "that it is right": [Thomas Wentworth Higginson], "Ought Women to Learn the Alphabet?" p. 149.
72 "the *women* who," "mean safety": Thomas Wentworth Higginson to IBH, Feb. 19, 1859 (Fiche 133).
72 "the mythification": Hedrick, *Harriet Beecher Stowe*, p. 289.
73 "should have": Ibid.
73 "quietly dressed": Thomas Wentworth Higginson, *Letters and Journals*, p. 108.
73 "a visible awkwardness," "suffused": Thomas Wentworth Higginson, *Cheerful Yesterdays*, pp. 178–179.
74 "what maturity": IBH, "Shall Women Vote?" p. 72.
74 "they have less talent": LIMITS, p. 60.
74 "the conservators," "to secure a *liberal*": CB, *The True Remedy*, pp. 28, 52.
74 "posts of honor": Ibid., p. 232.
74 the work of housewives: For a sampling of quotations from CB on the importance of women's domestic pursuits, see Margaret Farrand Thorp, "Woman's Profession—Catharine E. Beecher," pp. 54–55.
75 "I am *not* nothing!": Lyman Beecher Stowe, *Saints, Sinners and Beechers*, p. 134.
75 "Is it claimed," "remunerative," "rushing": CB, *The True Remedy*, pp. 231–232.
76 "taking all these": IBH, "Shall Women Vote?" pp. 71–72.

76 "radical": Thomas Wentworth Higginson to IBH, Mar. 4, 1860 (Fiche 133).
76 "To do great": Ibid.
76 "the opinion of an anonymous": Ibid.
76 "Ironically": Anne Throne Margolis, "A Tempest Tossed Spirit," in IBHP-Guide, p. 16.
76 "useless": IBH to JH, June 19, 1860 (Fiche 20).

CHAPTER 4. Water Cure and Civil War

77 "At four": CB, *Letters to the People*, pp. 117–118. Elizabeth Blackwell, the first American woman doctor, described her treatment at Priessnitz's clinic in her *Pioneer Work*, pp. 129–132.
77 "It is such": IBH to JH, Apr. 28, 1860 (Fiche 17).
78 "obeyed the laws," "the great advantage": CB, *Letters*, pp. 113, 126.
78 "*Milwaukee, Wis.,*" "Residence": Ibid., pp. 148–149.
79 "I have seen": Ibid., p. 127.
79 "but whether the cure": IBH, Journal, Sept. 26, 1855 (Fiche 93).
80 "sympathy for the special": Kathryn Kish Sklar, "All Hail to Pure, Cold Water," p. 67.
80 "the chronic diseases": Quoted in Evelyn Giammichele and Eva Taylor, "Elmira Water Cure," p. 1539. For more on the Gleasons, see Jane B. Donegan, "Hydropathic Partners," chap. 3 in her "*Hydropathic Highway*," pp. 39–61. The Elmira Water Cure is also discussed in Susan E. Cayleff, *Wash and Be Healed*, pp. 102–105 and *passim*.
80 "monthly has": IBH to JH, May 19, 1860 (Fiche 18).
80 "there was quite": IBH to JH, June 19, 1860 (Fiche 20).
80 "The neck & mouth," "with instruments": Ibid.
81 "pernicious customs": CB, *Letters*, p. 107.
81 "a dress which": Mary Abigail Dodge, *Gail Hamilton's Life in Letters*, vol. 1, p. 84.
81 "for the physical freedom," "Heigh! Ho!": Elizabeth Cady Stanton, *Eighty Years*, p. 202.
82 "the burden of": IBH to Mary Hooker, June 20, 1860 (Fiche 21).
82 She had injured: Isabella recalled the carriage accident in detail 40 years later. She wrote Alice: "It is just 40 years since it [her ankle] began to ache & is now stiffer than ever." IBH to AHD, Oct. 6, 1889 (Fiche 67).
82 "Catarrh": Quoted in Giammichele and Taylor, "Elmira Water Cure," p. 1539.
82 "poor food": IBH to JH, June 1, 1860 (Fiche 19).
82 "They put them," "chew & chew": IBH to JH, June 13, 1860 (Fiche 20).
83 "notions": Marie Caskey, *Chariot of Fire*, p. 113.
84 "double capacity": IBH to JH, Apr. 28, 1860 (Fiche 17).
84 "But if No. 1": IBH to AHD, May 7, 1860 (Fiche 17).
84 "[Y]ou have so long": Ibid.
84 "Your character": IBH to Mary Hooker, May [19], 1860 (Fiche 18).
85 "true Yankees," "too pragmatical": Thomas K. Beecher to IBH, July 27, 1845, Joseph K. Hooker Collection, S-D.
85 "He is very": IBH to JH, Apr. 28, 1860 (Fiche 17).
85 "modify": IBH to JH, May 26, 1860 (Fiche 18).
85 "it is funny": IBH to JH, June 24, 1860 (Fiche 21).
86 "one of the best men": Ibid.
86 "sweet young girl," "Oh dear—how blind": IBH to JH, July 15, 1860 (Fiche 23).
86 "mental excitement": Rachel B. Gleason, *Talks to My Patients*, p. 14.
86 "bilious": IBH to JH, Aug. 8, 1860 (Fiche 24).
86 "to live for others": IBH to Mary Hooker, Aug. 15, 1860 (Fiche 24).
87 "the treadmill": IBH to JH, June 24, 1860 (Fiche 21).

87 "I have a pleasure": Annie Fields, Ed., *Life and Letters of Harriet Beecher Stowe*, p. 285.
87 "pioneered the women's": Josephine Donovan, *New England Local Color Literature*, p. 50.
88 "the most charming": Quoted in Charles Edward Stowe, *Life of Harriet Beecher Stowe*, p. 327.
88 "Who could write": Fields, *Life and Letters*, p. 286.
88 "little dreaming": Forrest Wilson, *Crusader in Crinoline*, p. 470.
88 "Lincoln supper": IBH, Journal, Jan. 6, 1866 (Fiche 94).
88 "a Maine logger": JH to IBH, May 21, 1860, IBH Collection, S-D.
88 "he is honest": Ibid.
89 "a slave hound," "I know": Quoted in John Niven, *Connecticut for the Union*, p. 27.
89 "insidious temptation": IBH to President Lincoln, November 1861 (Fiche 25).
90 "I am going to Washington": Fields, *Life and Letters*, p. 262.
90 "I *must* see Fred": HBS to Hatty Stowe, Nov. 4, 1862, Beecher-Stowe Collection, SCH.
90 "Sister Hattie": Mary Beecher Perkins to IBH, nd [1856], Joseph K. Hooker Collection, S-D.
90 "a good hearted weak": HBS to Calvin Stowe, Nov. 16, 1862, Katharine Day Collection, S-D.
90 "an old goose": IBH to JH et al., Nov. 20, [1862] (Fiche 26).
91 "He looked perfectly": IBH to JH, Dec. 2, [1862] (Fiche 26).
91 "infected": IBH to JH, Nov. 30, 1862 (Fiche 26).
91 "For once": IBH to JH, Dec. 2, [1862] (Fiche 26).
91 "her highness": IBH to Mary Hooker, Nov. 19, 1862 (Fiche 25).
92 "[t]he contraband," "slow, solemn," "I never heard": IBH to JH, Dec. 2, [1862] (Fiche 26).
92 "Yes I think," "magnificent," "imposing": IBH to JH, Dec. 1, 1862 (Fiche 26).
92 "we perfectly screamed": Hatty Stowe to Eliza Stowe, Dec. 3, 1862, Beecher-Stowe Collection, SCH.
92 "I must tell you": IBH to JH, Dec. 2, [1862] (Fiche 26).
92 "an old battered": Ibid.
93 "I will say": Ibid.
93 "save the original": Ibid.
93 "We are so helpless": IBH to JH, Nov. 25, [1862] (Fiche 26).
93 "to home": Charles E. Stowe and Lyman Beecher Stowe, *Harriet Beecher Stowe*, p. 203.
93 "So this is": Ibid.
93 "I think": IBH to JH, Dec. 2, [1862] (Fiche 26). Isabella's letter to John about the Lincoln meeting also clears up other questions, such as those raised by F. Lauriston Bullard in his "Abraham Lincoln and Harriet Beecher Stowe." He speculates about the date of the interview, guessing Nov. 25 rather than the Dec. 2 established by Isabella. Bullard also discusses the possibility of Stowe's having seen Lincoln twice because Henry Ward Beecher wrote a Lincoln biographer in 1886 that Harriet repeated to him the president's premonition that he wouldn't survive the war; it was assumed that Lincoln made the remark near the end of the war. Isabella's account shows that his prediction occurred during the Dec. 2, 1862, interview.
95 "Mrs. Stowe!" "this woman," "Thus in great triumph": Wilson, *Crusader in Crinoline*, p. 487.
95 "The old oak": Quoted in ibid., p. 491.
95 "an unpremeditated": AUTO, vol. 2, p. 419.
95 "full of bright": HBS to [Hatty, Eliza, and Georgiana Stowe], Jan. 17, 1863, Beecher-Stowe Collection, SCH.
95 "Tom got him": IBH to JH, Mar. 10, 1863 (Fiche 27).
96 "out of his," "Jim loathes," "with his last": IBH to JH, [March 1863] (Fiche 27).
96 "very blue": IBH to JH, Mar. 13, 1863 (Fiche 27).

96 "real comfort," "He is too excitable," "loved & petted": IBH to JH, [1863] (Fiche 26).
96 "fearfully excited": IBH to JH, Mar. 10, 1863 (Fiche 27).
97 "as a drama": Milton Rugoff, *The Beechers*, p. 454.
97 "let Belle tamper": Thomas K. Beecher, copied by IBH in IBH to Henry Ward Beecher, Apr. 20, 1863 (Fiche 27).
97 "talk less nonsense": Quoted in Rugoff, *The Beechers*, p. 458. Frankie discusses their experience in detail in Frances Beecher Perkins, "Two Years with a Colored Regiment."
97 "reduces them": Quoted in Ira Berlin, Joseph P. Reidy, and Leslie Rowland, Eds., *Freedom's Soldiers*, p. 113.
98 "I am glad": IBH to Mary Hooker, July 5, 1860 (Fiche 22).
98 "son," "his *four* children": IBH, Journal, Christmas 1864 (Fiche 94).
99 "I am living": IBH to JH, Mar. 12, 1864 (Fiche 29).
99 "We will put," "led 4500": Ibid.
100 "a jewel of a woman": IBH to Mary Hooker, Mar. 8, [1864] (Fiche 28).
100 "[W]hen I read that book": Fields, *Life and Letters*, p. 274.

CHAPTER 5. The Gilded Age

101 "Aunt Catherine [sic]": Charlotte Perkins Gilman, *The Living*, p. 12.
101 "He has been": HBS, "Chimney Corner," *Atlantic Monthly*, 16 (August 1865), p. 233.
101 "little book": Quoted in Milton Rugoff, *The Beechers*, p. 360.
102 "Tell Mrs. Fields": Annie Fields, Ed., *Life and Letters of Harriet Beecher Stowe*, p. 293.
102 "Aunt Harriet": Gilman, *The Living*, p. 16.
102 "made bird-like": Caroline M. Severance, *The Mother of Clubs*, p. 121.
102 "a poor drooping": HBS to Hatty and Eliza Stowe, Aug. 14, 1859, Beecher-Stowe Collection, SCH.
103 "gay old": IBH to AHD, Jan. 20, 1867 (Fiche 33).
104 "Bridget's": IBH, Journal, Apr. 12, 1867 (Fiche 95).
104 "Here were gathered": Severance, *The Mother of Clubs*, p. 121.
104 "serene & beautiful": IBH to AHD, Jan. 27, 1865 (Fiche 30).
104 "my *poor husband*": IBH to JH, May 15, 1860 (Fiche 18).
104 "If I had": IBH to JH, July 28, 1860 (Fiche 23).
104 "covered sleigh": IBH, Journal, Feb. 26, 1865 (Fiche 94).
105 "The luxury": Kenneth R. Andrews, *Nook Farm*, p. 101.
105 "immediately go": HBS to James T. Fields, Oct. 18, [1866], Fields Papers, Henry E. Huntington Library.
105 "took over the world": Rugoff, *The Beechers*, p. 360.
106 "enjoy Henry": IBH to JH, Mar. 30, 1865 (Fiche 31).
106 "Hatty & Eliza": Frances Foote Godkin to Katherine Rockwell, nd [c. Dec. 1863], Foote Collection, S-D.
106 "[T]he energy": HBS to Hatty, Eliza, and Georgiana Stowe, Oct. 5, 1863, Beecher-Stowe Collection, SCH.
106 Harriet had been trained: Joan D. Hedrick, *Harriet Beecher Stowe*, p. 298.
106 "rich & handsome," "a certain infelicity," "old-fashioned notions": IBH, Journal, Feb. 26, 1865 (Fiche 94).
107 "Adams' stock," "such dangerous": IBH to Robert Allen, June 24, 1867 (Fiche 35).
107 "Poor Hattie": IBH to JH, Oct. 16, 1864 (Fiche 29).
108 "harmless," "I never was happier": IBH to AHD, July [13], 1867 (Fiche 36).
109 "little twinges": IBH to Robert Allen, July 28, 1868 (Fiche 39).
109 "He is tired": IBH to AHD, Sept. 22, 1867 (Fiche 36).

109 "childish prejudice": IBH to Robert Allen, Apr. 1, 1868 (Fiche 38).

110 "[S]o the argument": IBH to AHD, Feb. 16, 1867 (Fiche 34).

110 "I felt," "I never knew," "One whole long": IBH to AHD, Sept. 22, 1867 (Fiche 36).

110 "That function": Elizabeth Cady Stanton, *Elizabeth Cady Stanton*, vol. 2, p. 270.

110 curing sick babies: This image would become as conventional for maternal feminists as climbing trees in childhood would be in feminist memoirs. In an article on Isabella, her Connecticut colleague Ella Burr McManus describes the exact same behavior on Isabella's part, noting that she saw Isabella calm a wailing baby on a train.

110 "the temptation": William O'Neill, *Everyone Was Brave*, p. 34.

111 "sacred": IBH to Robert Allen, Oct. 23, 1867 (Fiche 37).

111 "our intimacy": IBH to AHD, Mar. 27, 1867 (Fiche 35).

111 "round & plump": IBH to AHD, Apr. 18, 1867 (Fiche 35).

112 "I think it is not love," "I have nothing": IBH to AHD, [September 1867?] (Fiche 36).

112 "filled with desires": IBH, Journal, Dec. 30, 1866 (Fiche 94).

112 "we are growing": IBH to AHD, Mar. 2, 1865 (Fiche 31).

112 "Oh Mother": AHD to IBH, Feb. 24, 1867, IBH Collection, S-D.

112 "resort to keeping": IBH to AHD, Mar. 27, 1867 (Fiche 35).

112 "overcome the spirit," "It is surprising": IBH, Journal, Dec. 8, 1867 (Fiche 95).

113 "beautiful girl": Mark Twain to Jane Lampton Clemens and Pamela A. Moffett, Jan. 8, 1868, in *Mark Twain's Letters*, vol. 2, p. 144.

113 "I wish you would": IBH to AHD, [Jan. 8, 1867] (Fiche 33). The year attributed to this letter by S-D is incorrect. It should be 1868.

113 "At the hospitable": "Mark Twain on His Travels," San Francisco *Alta California*, Mar. 3, 1868, p. 1.

113 "walk mighty straight": Mark Twain to Mary Mason Fairbanks, Jan. 24, 1868, in *Mark Twain's Letters*, vol. 2, p. 166.

113 "Samuel L. Clemens": IBH, Autograph Album, Jan. 24, 1868 (Fiche 96).

113 "humiliated": Mark Twain to Olivia L. Langdon, Mar. 6, 1869, in *Mark Twain's Letters*, vol. 3, p. 140.

114 "do in the world": IBH to AHD, Jan. 28, 1867 (Fiche 33).

114 "to become a Doctor": IBH, Journal, Oct. 29, 1867 (Fiche 95).

114 "quite a society belle," "brought contempt": IBH to Robert Allen, Apr. 14, 1868 (Fiche 38).

114 "all manners": IBH to Robert Allen, Aug. 18, 1868 (Fiche 40).

114 "seeing you glide": IBH to AHD, May [13], 1868 (Fiche 38).

115 "my new mamma": IBH to Robert Allen, May 29, 1868 (Fiche 39).

115 "that argument": Forrest Wilson, *Crusader in Crinoline*, p. 518.

115 "I live in a great centre": HBS to James Parton, Feb. 6, 1868, Fanny Fern Papers, Smith College.

116 "New England life": HBS to James T. Fields, [February 1864], Fields Papers, Henry E. Huntington Library.

116 "that simple": HBS, *Oldtown Folks*, p. 421.

116 "golden calf": Ibid., p. 110.

117 "Now I know": Charles Beecher to Henry Ward Beecher, Apr. 12, 1857, Beecher-Scoville Family Papers, Sterling Memorial Library, Yale University.

117 "Aunt Catharine": Lyman Beecher Stowe, p. 121.

117 "[Y]ou habitually," "you really": IBH to CB, [c. 1869] (Fiche 40).

118 "injudicious": IBH to CB, Apr. 17, 1860 (Fiche 16).

118 "Edward, do come": Lyman Beecher Stowe, *Saints, Sinners and Beechers*, p. 121.

118 "When I had a home": LIMITS, p. 352.

119 "united petition," "very much sooner," "the ballot never": CB and HBS, *The American Women's Home*, p. 468.

119 "I am deep": IBH to Robert Allen, Nov. 28, 1868 (Fiche 40).

119 "grows more": IBH to AHD, [Jan. 10, 1867] (Fiche 33).

120 "the speaker who," "we found": IBH-Mem, p. 293.

120 "always uses": IBH to AHD, Feb. 4, 1867 (Fiche 33).

120 "It was she": IBH-Mem, pp. 293–294.

120 "slept with," "I am enjoying": IBH to AHD, Feb. 4, 1867 (Fiche 33). For discussion of this typical language, see Carroll Smith-Rosenberg, "The Female World of Love and Ritual," pp. 1–29.

120 "snuggle": Susan B. Anthony to Anna E. Dickinson, Mar. 18, 1868, Anna E. Dickinson Papers, Manuscript Division, Library of Congress.

121 "stout and a judge": IBH to Mary Hooker Burton, Feb. 13, 1867 (Fiche 34).

121 "The truth is," "shut my teeth": IBH to AHD, Feb. 16, 1867 (Fiche 34).

121 "Women are feebly," "inordinate": IBH, Womanhood, p. 13.

121 "a case of criminal," "is just as": Ibid., pp. 19–20.

122 "I have heard": Ibid., pp. 24–25.

122 "more probable," "theory of": Ibid., p. 22.

122 a twentieth-century writer: Andrews, Nook Farm, p. 141.

123 In any case she was unwilling: Isabella explains this in a letter to her brother Henry which is included in Plymouth Church and Its Pastor, p. 508.

123 "take care of young," "all my time," "old fogies": IBH to Robert Allen, May 16, 1867 (Fiche 35).

123 "much approved": IBH to AHD, [Feb. 15, 1866] (Fiche 32).

124 "[T]hey were totally," "this was the Negro's": Eleanor Flexner, Century of Struggle, pp. 145–146.

124 "I am so relieved": IBH to Robert Allen, June 29, 1867 (Fiche 35).

124 Harriet Taylor: for discussion of her authorship, see John M. Robson, The Improvement of Mankind, pp. 50–68.

125 "being irritated," "Mrs. Blackwell": IBH to AHD, July 14, 1867 (Fiche 36).

125 "I do see the gulf": Quoted in Katherine Devereux Blake and Margaret Louise Wallace, Champion of Women, p. 77.

125 "charming," "black lace," "Grinfill": Ibid., pp. 74–76.

CHAPTER 6. Suffrage Arguments

127 "a habit": IBH, A Mother's Letters, p. 17.

127 "I am not": Ibid.

127 "another demonstration": IBH to JH, May 20, 1860 (Fiche 18).

128 "they are cut": LIMITS, p. 101.

128 "power and glory": Jean V. Matthews, Women's Struggle for Equality, p. 135.

128 "[N]othing could be": IBH, A Mother's Letters, p. 25.

128 "You know a little," "Thus encouraged": IBH to Robert Allen, Apr. 1, 1868 (Fiche 38).

129 "make its own," "my daughters": Ibid.

129 woman movement: I use the term "woman movement" or "woman's movement" because this was how it was referred to in the nineteenth century. Our foremothers also said "woman suffrage," not "women suffrage." Henceforth, I will use the term "women's movement" only when referring to the entire movement, 1848 to the present.

129 "an orator": IBH to Robert Allen, Nov. 28, 1868 (Fiche 40).

129 "beautiful and charming": Karen F. Stein, "Paulina Kellogg Wright Davis," vol. 1, p. 475.

129 "I met Paulina": IBH-Mem, p. 294.

130 "fallen in love": IBH to Edward Hooker, Nov. 17, 1868 (Fiche 40).

130 "a few weeks": IBH-Mem, p. 295.
130 "Oh if the women": Susan B. Anthony to IBH, June 11, 1869 (Fiche 114).
132 "form a society": Elizabeth Cady Stanton, *Eighty Years*, p. 83.
132 "always pushing": Ibid., p. 165.
132 "While I have been mourning": IBH-Mem, p. 295.
132 "a noble woman," "the most intense," "I have handled": LIMITS, p. 197.
132 "She is," "I am obliged": Ibid., p. 198.
133 "Lucy Stone": IBH to Robert Allen, Nov. 28, 1868 (Fiche 40).
133 "repudiated the principles": HW, vol. 2, p. 381.
133 "With us, the matter": Ibid., p. 382.
133 "but not because": Ibid.
133 "will, of course, advocate," "I will be thankful": Ibid., pp. 381, 383–384.
134 "the first national": Ellen Carol DuBois, *Feminism and Suffrage*, p. 190.
134 Robert E. Riegel: Robert E. Riegel, "The Split," pp. 487–493.
136 "sick unto death": *The Selected Papers of Elizabeth Cady Stanton and Susan B. Anthony*, Ed. Patricia G. Holland and Ann D. Gordon, vol. 2, p. 421.
136 "fallen in love," "peculiar": IBH to Caroline Severance, Aug. 27, [1869] (Fiche 41).
137 "was quick," "Lucy has hurt": LIMITS, pp. 198–199.
137 Kathleen Barry argues: *Susan B. Anthony*, pp. 180–181.
137 in November 1869: Barry, p. 181, mistakenly says 1870, but IBH's summarizing letter to Susan Howard is dated Jan. 2, 1870. IBH's notes on her conversation with Blackwell may be found at the end of Fiche 98.
137 "that Mr. Train": IBH to Susan Howard, Jan. 2, 1870 (Fiche 43).
138 "I could hardly," "but I cannot think": Ibid.
138 "realize anew": Ibid.
138 "the spirit of love," "*speak* of Mrs.": LIMITS, p. 198.
139 "*since that break*": IBH to Susan Howard, Jan. 2, 1870 (Fiche 43).
139 "The truth is": LIMITS, p. 199.
139 "state affairs": IBH to Caroline Severance, Aug. 27, [1869] (Fiche 42).
141 "bring out the fastidious": LIMITS, p. 199.
141 "dignity," "authorship": Ibid., pp. 277, 270.
141 "1. The right": Ibid., p. 269.
142 "I think that a State": Ibid., p. 268.
142 "ideology": Ibid., p. 260.
142 "precisely similar," "neither privacy": HBS, "The Woman Question," p. 520.
142 "bring with them kelp": LIMITS, p. 267.
142 "They owe them": Ibid., p. 261.
142 "the record," "what a true woman": Ibid., p. 262.
143 "hold her tongue": "Injurious Works," p. 347.
143 "the spirit of caste": IBH, Letter to *Nation*, p. 391.
143 "a series," "literary": "Mrs. Stowe's," p. 437.
143 "culminating": Josephine Donovan, *New England*, p. 62.
143 "labored": Joan D. Hedrick, *Harriet Beecher Stowe*, p. 344.
144 "dreamy little female," "no male personage": "Mrs. Stowe's," p. 437.
144 "Rudeness": HBS to E. L. Godkin, draft, [Summer 1869], Beecher-Stowe Collection, SCH.
144 "objective," "sentimentalist," "like nothing": [Henry James], "Dallas Galbraith," pp. 330–331.
144 "fritters away": HBS, "How Shall I Learn," p. 56.
144 "fine, subtle": [Mary Abigail Dodge] Gail Hamilton, *Country Living*, p. 188.
145 "all the barbarous": HW, vol. 1, pp. 825–826.
145 "In 1870": IBH-Mem, p. 295.

145 "We are busy": Quoted in Edward Wagenknect, *Harriet Beecher Stowe*, p. 97.
145 "doctrine of Stuart Mills": LIMITS, p. 255.
146 "John Stuart Mill says": HBS, "What Is," p. 568.
146 "It has wholly converted": HBS to Fanny Fern, July 25, [1869], Fanny Fern Papers, Smith College.
146 "Yes I do": LIMITS, p. 278.
146 "comparative endowment," "moral advantage": Ibid., p. 194.
146 "But I do not": Ibid., p. 196.
147 "what injury": IBH to Mary Rice Livermore, Nov. 15, 1869 (Fiche 41).
147 "[A]s Susan": IBH to Henry B. Blackwell, Dec. [1], 1869 (Fiche 41).
147 "dress, manners": Elizabeth Cady Stanton to IBH, Sept. 23, 1869 (Fiche 137).
147 "Mrs. Hooker wrote each": Quoted in Alma Lutz, *Created Equal*, pp. 182–183.
148 "This practical organizing": IBH-Mem, p. 295.
148 "If such women": HW, vol. 3, p. 323.
149 "*you* are the only": Susan B. Anthony to IBH, Jan. 12, 1870 (Fiche 115).
149 "I really have": Susan B. Anthony to IBH, [Dec. 1869] (Fiche 114).
149 "if *Cash will*," "We are through": Stanton and Anthony, *Selected Papers*, pp. 255–257.
150 Harriet remembered: She also recalled her father's lament at Byron's dying without having "done something for Christ." AUTO, vol. 1, p. 393.
150 "romantic friendship": Josephine Donovan, "Harriet Beecher Stowe's Feminism," p. 150.
150 "I left you": Annie Fields, Ed., *Life and Letters of Harriet Beecher Stowe*, p. 236.
151 "a symbol of," "I consider Lady": Donovan, "Harriet Beecher Stowe's Feminism," p. 150.
151 "it would be sure": Quoted in Alex L. Murray, "Harriet Beecher Stowe on Racial Segregation in the Schools," p. 518.
151 "deluded," "craving for notoriety": Jean W. Ashton, *Harriet Beecher Stowe*, pp. 29–36.
152 "the abominations": Elizabeth Cady Stanton, "The Moral of the Byron Case," p. 1.
152 "men have the physical," "They cannot be forced": CB, *Woman Suffrage*, p. 17.
152 "The establishing": Elizabeth Cady Stanton, *Elizabeth Cady Stanton*, vol. 2, p. 124.
152 "since we cannot": IBH, "Happy New Year," p. 10.
153 "I have all": HBS to Henry Ward Beecher, nd [c. 1870], Beecher-Scoville Family Papers, Sterling Memorial Library, Yale University.
153 "my opportunity," "I should avoid": IBH to Susan Howard, Jan. 2, 1870 (Fiche 43). As Anne Farnam notes, most suffragists used military terms to describe their work, but Isabella made use of religious language and imagery. She "spoke constantly in terms of preaching sermons, of regeneration, conversion, and salvation." "Woman Suffrage as an Alternative to the Beecher Ministry," p. 73.

CHAPTER 7. "Foes in Your Own Household"

154 "sinking turn": HBS to Hatty and Eliza Stowe, nd (postmarked Aug. 16), [1869], Beecher Stowe Collection, SCH.
154 "a fall": Mary B. Graff, *Mandarin on the St. Johns*, p. 48.
154 "hut": Annie Fields, Ed., *Life and Letters of Harriet Beecher Stowe*, p. 339.
154 "being chatelaine": James C. Austin, *Fields of the Atlantic Monthly*, p. 297.
155 "even Higginson": Susan B. Anthony to IBH, Dec. 17, 1869 (Fiche 114).
155 "infamous assumption": HW, vol. 2, p. 418.
155 "the fifth commandment": Ibid., p. 415.
156 "Yesterday morning": Ibid., p. 425.
156 "Olympia Brown": Ibid.

156 "then very beautiful," "rare moral courage," "I have learned more": Olympia Brown, *Acquaintances Old and New*, pp. 89–90.

156 the second woman: Dana Greene calls Brown the "first denominationally ordained female minister" because the ordination of Lucy Stone's friend and later sister-in-law, Antoinette Brown [Blackwell], in 1853 "did not meet the requirements of the Congregational denomination." Olympia Brown, *Suffrage and Religious Principle*, p. 13.

156 "I do so long," "the liberty," "patiently dumb": IBH to Elisabeth Gillette Warner, Mar. 19, 1870 (Fiche 43).

158 "a kind of ladies'": HW, vol. 2, p. 400.

159 "terrible sufferer": IBH to Robert Allen, May 15, 1870 (Fiche 43).

159 "excitable state": HBS to Mary Beecher Perkins, Oct. 11, [1870], Helen D. Perkins Collection, S-D.

159 "first lady-in-waiting": Fields, *Life and Letters*, p. 324.

159 "so you will": Elizabeth Cady Stanton and Susan B. Anthony, *Selected Papers*, pp. 359–360.

160 "barbarous": Eugene Benson, "George Sand and the Marriage Question," *Revolution*, July 7, 1870, pp. 1–2.

160 "animalism": HBS to Henry Ward Beecher, nd [June? 1870], Beecher-Scoville Family Papers, Sterling Memorial Library, Yale University.

160 "George Sand": Stanton, "A Word about George Sand," p. 169.

160 "blank with astonishment": Quoted in Joan D. Hedrick, *Harriet Beecher Stowe*, p. 373.

160 "great masculine," "mingling with men": LIMITS, p. 236.

160 "secured fine," "never saw fairer": CB to "Jack" [John R. Howard], Aug. 19, 1870, Katharine S. Day Collection, S-D.

161 "Ten years": CB, *Woman Suffrage*, p. 34.

161 "her self-made," "a strange old": Quoted in Lyman Beecher Stowe, *Saints, Sinners and Beechers*, pp. 133–134.

161 "always move": Quoted in Mae Elizabeth Harveson, *Catharine Esther Beecher*, p. 231.

161 "show the citizens": CB to S. J. Andrews, Mar. 14, 1873, Hartford Female Seminary Papers, Connecticut Historical Society.

162 "Neither Mrs. Stowe": CB, *Woman's Profession*, p. 41.

162 "meet with respect": CB, *Woman Suffrage*, p. 4.

162 "incompetent," "vast mass": Ibid., pp. 11–12, 205.

163 "If the best": Ibid., p. 205.

163 "Cool, isn't," "But I am": IBH to Elizabeth Cady Stanton, Nov. 25, 1870 (Fiche 44). Garrison Family Papers, Sophia Smith Collection.

163 "she could": Elizabeth Cady Stanton to Josephine Griffing, Dec. 1, 1870, in Elizabeth Cady Stanton and Susan B. Anthony, *Papers of Elizabeth Cady Stanton and Susan B. Anthony*, Ed. Patricia G. Holland and Ann D. Gordon, vol. 14, p. 1122.

163 "slap," "[s]o long as": Elizabeth Cady Stanton to Martha Coffin Wright, Dec. 27, 1870, in Stanton and Anthony, *Papers*, vol. 14, p. 1160.

164 "Her speeches are," "swift": HW, vol. 2, pp. 360–361.

164 "I did not express": Elizabeth Cady Stanton to Martha Coffin Wright, Dec. 30, 1870, in Stanton and Anthony, *Papers*, vol. 14, p. 1177.

164 "that it is the grand," "I wonder that," "what a lack," "The Beecher conceit": IBH to Elizabeth Cady Stanton, Dec. 29, 1870 (Fiche 44). Garrison Family Papers, Sophia Smith Collection.

165 "At the head," "business suits": *The Press—Philadelphia*, Jan. 13, 1871, p. 6.

165 "a disenfranchised": HW, vol. 2, p. 460.

166 "Although it would seem": *The Press—Philadelphia*, Jan. 13, 1871, p. 6.

166 "The third Annual": HW, vol. 2, p. 442.

166 "sitting successively": Ibid.

167 "where we would hang": Elizabeth Cady Stanton to Victoria Woodhull, Feb. 20, 1871, in Stanton and Anthony, *Papers*, vol. 15, p. 418.

167 "our bill": HW, vol. 2, p. 490.

168 "I opened a large": IBH-Mem, p. 297.

168 "Dear friend Susan," "to write the political": LIMITS, pp. 205–206.

169 "great light": Dodge, *Gail Hamilton's Life*, vol. 2, p. 643.

169 "Mrs. Isabella": Ibid., p. 671.

170 "the first admission," "absurd charge": HW, vol. 2, p. 489.

170 "too green," "very gratifying," "What a curious": Lucretia Coffin Mott, *Selected Letters*, pp. 451–455.

170 "It was a familiar," "The married trader": Mary Gabriel, *Notorious Victoria*, pp. 88–89.

172 "I am informed": *Hartford Courant*, Feb. 1, 1871.

172 "still praising": LIMITS, p. 206.

172 "of her first marriage," "She now had," "only his *inferences*": IBH to Susan B. Anthony, Mar. 11, 1871 (Fiche 44).

173 "My poor wandering": LIMITS, p. 291.

173 "feeble and extremely": Ibid., p. 209.

174 "the finest address": IBH to Victoria Woodhull Martin, Feb. 4, 1889 (Fiche 63).

174 "I have *heard gossip*": Susan B. Anthony to Martha Coffin Wright, Mar. 21, 1871 (Fiche 116). This letter is accompanied by Anthony's note asking Wright to pass it on to IBH. The first part of the letter is in the Stanton papers at the Library of Congress and is printed in Stanton and Anthony, *Selected Papers*, pp. 426–427.

174 "harlot": HBS and Mary Beecher Perkins to JH, Mar. 2, 1871, IBH Collection, S-D.

174 "You and Mrs.": Quoted in Barbara Goldsmith, *Other Powers*, p. 370.

175 "influence over my": HBS to Mary Claflin, [Dec. 24, 1872], copy, S-D.

175 "Perhaps Mrs. Stowe": Johanna Johnston, *Mrs. Satan*, p. 97.

176 "under the younger woman's": Kenneth R. Andrews, *Nook Farm*, p. 36.

176 "We have had enough," "this infatuation": Quoted in Andrew Sinclair, *The Better Half*, p. 192.

176 "extreme salutation": Johnston, *Mrs. Satan*, p. 91.

176 "wonderful magnetism": LIMITS, p. 207.

178 "question of *Right*": Ibid., p. 208.

178 "Victoria Woodhull,": *Woodhull & Claflin's Weekly*, May 17, 1872, p. 15. See an account of their meeting in Goldsmith, *Other Powers*, p. 270.

178 "hapless victim,": Quoted in Robert Shaplen, *Free Love and Heavenly Sinners*, p. 132.

178 "[I]t is dreadful": IBH to Anna Savery, Nov. 12, 1871 (Fiche 46).

CHAPTER 8. Free Love and "Mrs. Satan"

179 "seemed wild," "work for her": LIMITS, pp. 206–207.

179 "Everyone seems to condemn": IBH to Susan B. Anthony, Mar. 11, 1871 (Fiche 44).

180 "Oh, no": "Policemen and Prostitutes," *Woodhull & Claflin's Weekly*, Apr. 29, 1871, p. 10.

180 "intolerable," "prudent": IBH to Mary Rice Livermore, Mar. 17, [1871] (Fiche 45).

181 "I think": LIMITS, p. 302.

181 "avoid four": IBH to Susan B. Anthony, Mar. 11, 1871 (Fiche 44).

181 "an affiliation": Lucy Stone and Henry B. Blackwell, *Loving Warriors*, p. 239.

181 "If the very next": Victoria C. Woodhull, "A Lecture on Constitutional Equality," pp. 31–32.

181 "Victoria is a green": Quoted in Barbara Goldsmith, *Other Powers*, pp. 288–289.

182 "all the world": LIMITS, p. 312.

182 "What a pity": HBS, *My Wife and I*, p. 121.

182 "an exposition": Ibid., p. 257.

182 "In common," "pretty baby": Ibid., pp. 235–236, 263.

183 "[T]he supposed copy": LIMITS, p. 302.

183 "She always thinks": HBS, *My Wife and I,* pp. 263–264.

183 "navigated the ship": HBS, *Oldtown Folks,* p. 427.

183 "You think you are": As recalled in John Raymond Howard, *Remembrance of Things Past.*

184 "strong minded," "a serious," "there is no immediate," "disturbances": HBS, *My Wife and I,* pp. 221, 235, 261, 264.

184 "to the Ministers," "This *woman movement*": CB, *Woman Suffrage,* p. 3.

184 "Fathers and Brethren," "As the daughter": Ibid.

185 "the Right of all": CB, *An Appeal to the People,* p. 2.

185 "where my own": CB, *Woman Suffrage,* p. 5.

185 "the Catherine [sic]": Victoria Woodhull, "Editorial," *Woodhull & Claflin's Weekly,* Jan. 14, 1871, p. 10.

185 "home physicians": Kathryn Kish Sklar, *Catharine Beecher,* p. 268.

185 "Where is there": CB, *Woman's Profession,* p. 118.

186 "promote agreeable": Jane Cunningham Croly, *Sorosis,* p. 8. For more on Croly and Sorosis, see Karen J. Blair, *The Clubwoman as Feminist,* pp. 22–54.

186 "gullible fool": Goldsmith, *Other Powers,* p. 295.

186 "even from *thinking*": IBH to Martha Coffin Wright, July 23, 1871 (Fiche 45). Garrison Family Papers, Sophia Smith Collection.

186 "longed, yet dreaded," "scrubbing": IBH to AHD, Aug. 16 [1871] (Fiche 46).

186 "scrubbing," "dying out," "wall of coldness": Ibid.

187 "I believe that this": IBH to Elizabeth Cady Stanton, Oct. 18, 1871 (Fiche 46).

187 "born to call," "owe any sort": Phebe Hanaford to IBH, Aug. 9, 1871 (Fiche 133).

187 "the feeling on this": IBH to Anna Savery, Nov. 12, 1871 (Fiche 46).

188 "Miss Beecher told": Quoted in Emanie Sachs, *"The Terrible Siren,"* p. 125.

188 in fact, some: Lois B. Underhill, *The Woman Who Ran for President,* p. 158. Underhill agrees that Beecher and Woodhull had an affair, giving as evidence the late hours at which they met that summer—hardly a convincing proof.

188 "have gone out," "power to strike": Charles F. Marshall, *The True History of the Brooklyn Scandal,* p. 358.

188 "Are you a free": Victoria C. Woodhull, "A Speech on the Principles of Social Freedom," p. 23.

188 "go under," "not one friend": IBH to Charles Dudley Warner [1871 after Nov. 1st] (Fiche 46).

190 "such tender," "fondling ways," "clung," "this last winter": IBH to Mary Hooker Burton, [c. 1870] (Fiche 42). The content suggests the letter was actually written in November 1871.

190 "as to a friend," "dreary routine," "Of course, such a man": LIMITS, p. 204.

190 "willingly," "Now Mrs. Hooker": Ibid.

191 "friendly call": Phebe Hanaford to IBH, Aug. 9, 1871 (Fiche 133).

191 "I honor you," "go deeper," "reliable": Olympia Brown to IBH, Dec. 9, 1871 (Fiche 123).

191 "stand by the side": Susan B. Anthony to IBH [June 1871] (Fiche 116).

192 "Mrs. Hooker": LIMITS, p. 302.

192 "lips of women": Ibid., p. 310.

192 "Woman—Sphinx": IBH to Alice C. Fletcher, Dec. 8, 1871 (Fiche 46).

193 "[m]en and women," "together with": HW, vol. 2, p. 497.

193 "general law," "exceptional discontent": Ibid., p. 495. The petition first appeared in the May 1871 issue of *Godey's Lady's Book,* signed by 19 women, including Catharine Beecher. Additional signatures were requested, and the document was presented to Congress

late in the year. HW estimates 1,000 signatures, but those favoring the petition reported 5,000 names. See Susan E. Marshall, *Splintered Sisterhood*, pp. 20–23.

193 "female modesty," "the right": Ibid.

194 "worthless," "It takes": IBH to Susan B. Anthony, Jan. 21, 1872 (Fiche 47).

194 "My husband," "headquarters": IBH to Olympia Brown, Feb. 14, 1872 (Fiche 47).

195 "eating sweet oranges": IBH to Edward Hooker, Mar. 7, 1872 (Fiche 47).

195 "But I would": Forrest Wilson, *Crusader in Crinoline*, p. 585.

196 "to fly," "Oh, my dear": Annie Fields, Ed., *Life and Letters of Harriet Beecher Stowe*, p. 33

196 "'My soul'": LIMITS, p. 257.

196 "desiring to become": IBH, "To the Women of New Haven," Unidentified news clipping
in letter to Edward Hooker, Mar. 7, 1872 (Fiche 47).

197 "It was the purpose": Abigail Duniway, quoted in Helen Krebs Smith, *The Presumptuous
Dreamers*, p. 127.

197 "the majority of whom": Susan B. Anthony to Lillie Devereux Blake, May 14, 1872, in
Elizabeth Cady Stanton and Susan B. Anthony, *Papers of Elizabeth Cady Stanton and Susan
B. Anthony*, vol. 16, p. 98.

197 "persistently means": Elizabeth Cady Stanton and Susan B. Anthony, *The Selected Papers
of Elizabeth Cady Stanton and Susan B. Anthony*, p. 485.

197 "Small audience": Ibid., p. 493.

198 The claim of a twentieth-century: Altina L. Waller, *Reverend Beecher and Mrs. Tilton*, p. 4.

198 "three columns": LIMITS, p. 209.

198 "extricated you": Susan B. Anthony to IBH, May 19, 1872 (Fiche 117).

198 "cutting loose," "my dear": IBH to Susan B. Anthony, May 26, 1872, copy enclosed in
IBH to J. L. Sands and George R. Allen, May 24, 1872 (Fiche 47). Garrison Family Papers, Sophia Smith Collection. This letter alone is enough to refute Kathleen Barry's assertion that Isabella was a "disciple" of Anthony (p. 199). There are also Isabella's independent character and her careful investigation of the movement before joining the
NWSA. Barry's contention that "Isabella Hooker typified the second generation of the
women's movement" is also questionable. Although she started out more conservative,
Isabella was closer to the earlier generation in some ways (e.g., in her abolitionism)
and gradually developed a "radical analysis of male power" (p. 201). Kathleen Barry,
Susan B. Anthony.

198 "Aunt Belle," "was with them": Elisabeth Gillette Warner to George H. Warner, quoted
in Susan K. Harris, *The Courtship of Olivia Langdon and Mark Twain*, p. 148.

199 "I hate Greeley": IBH to "Friend Carrington," [1872] (Fiche 46).

199 "You see our": Quoted in Israel Kugler, *From Ladies to Women*, p. 108.

199 "The Republican," "Very truly": Ibid., p. 111.

199 "Mr. Doolittle's": Quoted in Ida Husted Harper, *The Life and Work of Susan B. Anthony*,
vol. 1, p. 417.

200 "the opinion," "hence has been": IBH, "Baltimore Conclusion," [July 10, 1872] (Fiche 99).

200 "I mean to vote": IBH to Susan B. Anthony, May 26, 1872, copy enclosed in IBH to J. L.
Sands and George R. Allen, May 24, 1872 (Fiche 47).

201 "Mrs. Woodhull's speech": Quoted in Barbara Goldsmith, *Other Powers*, p. 335.

201 "demanding," "to stand": Victoria C. Woodhull, "Victoria C. Woodhull's Complete and
Detailed Version," pp. 9–10.

201 "When all this," "create a reaction": JH to IBH, Oct. 31, 1872, IBH Collection, S-D.

201 "'Free Love' incubus": *Woman's Journal*, May 18, 1872.

202 "set the cause": Eleanor Flexner, *Century of Struggle*, p. 158.

202 "one of the best": Fredrick Trautmann, "Harriet Beecher Stowe's Public Readings in
New England," p. 283.

202 "'Look here, my dear'": Fields, *Life and Letters*, p. 345.

202 "When her voice": Ibid., p. 346.

203 "I'd ruther see you": Wilson, *Crusader in Crinoline*, p. 580.

203 "I check off": HBS to Calvin Stowe, Nov. 24, 1872, in Charles E. Stowe, *Life of Harriet Beecher Stowe*, p. 497.

203 "like a knife": Wilson, *Crusader in Crinoline*, p. 579.

203 "remain with us": Fields, *Life and Letters*, pp. 346–347.

203 "a pretty cottage": Ibid., p. 352.

203 "those obscene birds," "They perfectly": HBS to Annie Fields, Dec. 25, 1872, Fields Papers, Henry E. Huntington Library.

204 "The impudence": HBS to Hatty and Eliza Stowe, Dec. 19, 1872, Beecher-Stowe Collection, SCH.

204 "Isabella's bold": LIMITS, p. 196.

204 "tender mother," "The question": Quoted in John Hooker, *Some Reminiscences of a Long Life*, p. 345.

CHAPTER 9. The Beecher-Tilton Scandal

205 "for I am reliably": Victoria C. Woodhull, "Victoria C. Woodhull's Complete and Detailed Version," p. 10.

205 "You know my sympathy": Charles F. Marshall, *The True History of the Brooklyn Scandal*, p. 334.

205 "like recommending": Milton Rugoff, *The Beechers*, p. 490.

205 "[T]here are things": LIMITS, p. 289.

206 Janet Emig notes: Janet A. Emig, "The Flower in the Cleft," p. 229.

206 "It seems now": Annie Fields, Ed., *Life and Letters of Harriet Beecher Stowe*, p. 362.

206 "she had taken": Rugoff, *The Beechers*, p. 267.

206 "Christ-worshipers," "there are those," "has drawn on": Fields, *Life and Letters*, pp. 362, 366. She thought Henry was also hated because people still hated Christ; in proportion as Henry "makes Christianity aggressive on sin they are malignant and spring joyfully on him when their time comes." Fields, *Life and Letters*, p. 328.

208 "he is more angel": HBS to [Elizabeth Lyman], nd, copy, S-D.

208 "frozen image," "keeping the other": Stephen P. Bank and Michael E. Kahn, *The Sibling Bond*, p. 73.

208 "By isolating": Emig, "The Flower in the Cleft," p. 235.

209 "Mrs. Stanton & the free": HBS to [Mary Claflin], Aug. 22, 1874, copy, S-D.

209 People who did not: Even recent historians have made this mistake. Noel Gerson, for example, offers the bizarre argument that since childhood, the much younger Isabella had been jealous of the close relationship between Harriet and Henry and wanted to take her revenge on them. Gerson, *Harriet Beecher Stowe*, p. 36.

209 "I think he is": IBH to JH, Dec. 2, 1839 (Fiche 1).

209 "the Griffon": Barbara Goldsmith, *Other Powers*, p. 417.

209 "according to his": Quoted in Clifford E. Clark Jr., *Henry Ward Beecher*, p. 134.

209 "fired with love": Marie Caskey, *Chariot of Fire*, p. 380.

210 "high religious love": Marshall, *True History*, p. 116.

210 "it followed that": *Tilton vs. Beecher*, vol. 3, p. 819.

210 "everything ought to be": HBS, *My Wife*, p. 267.

210 "Victoria Woodhull": Altina L. Waller, *Reverend Beecher and Mrs. Tilton*, pp. 116–117.

210 "only carries," "slippery," "Of the two," "Don't write": Marshall, *True History*, p. 335.

211 "the barbarity": Ibid., p. 333.

211 "Now, Tom," "buy my silence," "I cannot always": Ibid., pp. 333–334.

211 "Nothing can possibly": Ibid., p. 361. The whole of this "Ragged Edge Letter" is reproduced in Richard Wightman Fox, *Trials of Intimacy*, p. 351.
212 "endure no longer": Marshall, *True History*, p. 337.
212 "left to the sound," "Beecher laughed": Quoted in Barbara Goldsmith, *Other Powers*, pp. 357–358.
212 "Satanic influence," "under a monomania," "exercised a controlling": Ibid., p. 358.
213 "living a lie": Quoted in Robert Shaplen, *Free Love and Heavenly Sinners*, p. 235.
213 "The man who": *Tilton vs. Beecher*, vol. 3, p. 960.
213 "Then Saul said": 1 Sam. 14:43.
213 "No one in Nook": Rugoff, *The Beechers*, p. 576.
213 "Sam says Livy": Mark Twain and Mary E. Clemens to Jane Lampton Clemens and Pamela A. Moffett, *Mark Twain's Letters*, vol. 5, p. 230.
214 "the sibling support": Ann Goetting, "The Developmental Tasks of Siblingship," p. 712.
214 "Oh Alice dear": IBH to AHD, May 21, 1873 (Fiche 48).
214 "This will give": Marshall, *True History*, p. 336.
214 "Your aunt is": LIMITS, p. 288.
215 "My precious friend," "your dear husband," "Even the dead": Hannah M. Comstock to IBH, Dec. 31, 1872, and June 19, 1873 (Fiche 127).
215 "be proud": Olympia Brown to JH, Mar. 18, 1873 (Fiche 124).
215 "thrust her affections": Marshall, *True History*, p. 525.
215 "degraded": *New York Times*, July 3, 1875, p. 7.
215 "in strict confidence," "to no one," "deeply wronged," "I have never": Elizabeth Cady Stanton to IBH, June 21, [1873] (Fiche 139).
216 "vague ideas floating": Elizabeth Cady Stanton, *Elizabeth Cady Stanton*, vol. 2, p. 142.
216 "I have been crucified": LIMITS, p. 303.
216 "handsome and": AHD to IBH, Jan. 31 [1867?], IBH Collection, S-D.
216 "the sunshine of": IBH to AHD, June 20, 1873 (Fiche 48).
217 "a very dangerous," "it is by": JH, *Some Reminiscences*, p. 170.
217 "an honorable place": Quoted in Ruth Bordin, *Frances Willard*, p. 70.
217 "shrink from affiliation," "the two *greatest*": Susan B. Anthony to IBH, Oct. 13, 1873 (Fiche 118).
218 "I love you": Elizabeth Cady Stanton to IBH, Nov. 3, 1873 (Fiche 140).
218 "the more violent": *New York Herald*, Oct. 16, 1873.
218 "Deliberations will be": Sorosis minutes quoted in Karen J. Blair, *The Clubwoman as Feminist*, p. 45.
218 "things men are": Hannah M. Comstock to IBH, Nov. 11, 1873 (Fiche 127).
219 For years: See IBH to Elizabeth Cady Stanton, Mar. 13, 1874 (Fiche 50). For an account of licensing attempts in the United States, see David J. Pivar, *Purity Crusade*, pp. 50–77.
219 "Mrs. Hooker sits": Olympia Brown to JH, Mar. 18, 1873 (Fiche 124).
219 "When your darling": IBH to AHD, Sept. 1, 1873 (Fiche 49).
220 "I shall never": IBH to Olympia Brown, Nov. 8, 1873 (Fiche 49).
220 "crucified": IBH to AHD, Mar. 1, 1874 (Fiche 49).
220 "splendid," "The end": IBH to AHD, Jan. 28, 1874 (Fiche 49).
221 "always unfair": Olympia Brown to IBH, Jan. 6, 1874 (Fiche 124).
221 "What can women": Ibid.
221 "stars," "a great array": Olympia Brown to IBH, [Jan.? after 6, 1874?] (Fiche 125).
221 "conservative & fastidious," "good purposes": IBH to Elizabeth Cady Stanton, Mar. 13, [1874] (Fiche 50).
222 "This separation from": IBH to AHD, Mar. 23, 1874 (Fiche 50).
222 "landscapes or pictures": IBH to AHD, Mar. 1, 1874 (Fiche 49).
222 "chief treasures," "first introduction": JH and IBH to AHD, Sept. 19, 1889 (Fiche 66).
223 "down a magnificently": IBH to AHD, Feb. 5, 1889 (Fiche 63).

223 "Give me the Hudson," "disagreeable," "dirty," "miserable": IBH to Edward Hooker, July 21, 1874 (Fiche 50).

223 "reason itself": IBH to Olympia Brown, Aug. 28, 1874 (Fiche 50).

224 "crazy": Hannah M. Comstock to IBH, Aug. 6, 1874 (Fiche 127).

224 "I know from," "I cannot say": New York Daily Graphic, Aug. 21, 1874.

224 "driving the Victoria": IBH to AHD, Aug. 1, 1893 (Fiche 79).

225 "What a holocaust," "free lovers," "human hyenas": Chicago Tribune, Sept. 18, 1874.

225 "saddled upon us": LIMITS, p. 303.

225 "bondholders": Quoted in Johanna Johnston, Mrs. Satan, p. 220.

225 "all intercourse with": LIMITS, p. 298.

225 "new hopes": Ibid., p. 321.

226 "he had so wronged," "no conception": Ibid., p. 322.

226 "I beg you," "trying to think": Ibid., p. 323.

226 "The clean beautiful," "no one knew": JH and IBH to AHD, Nov. 18, 1889 (Fiche 67).

226 "sad," "few men realize": IBH to AHD, Dec. 13, 1887 (Fiche 58).

227 "obsession": Goldsmith, Other Powers, p. 412.

227 "Do write me": LIMITS, p. 289.

227 "I enter another," "red hot hurrying": Fields, Life and Letters, p. 336.

227 "toughest old Calvinist," "How do you": Ibid., p. 351.

228 "Mr. Beecher's sister": Marshall, True History, p. 502.

228 "confess his life": IBH to Susan B. Anthony, Feb. 18, 1875 (Fiche 51).

229 "cruel criticisms": Ibid.

229 "The whole matter": JH to William Patton, Apr. 23, 1875, Manuscripts 91093, Folder A at the Connecticut Historical Society, Hartford, Connecticut.

229 "home-like fire": IBH and JH to AHD, Jan. 10, 1888 (Fiche 58).

230 "Mr. Beecher": New York Times, July 2, 1875, p. 7.

230 "The refusal to doubt": Clifford E. Clark Jr., Henry Ward Beecher, p. 225.

230 "He was never": Waller, Reverend Beecher, p. 148.

230 "a virtual outcast": Ibid., p. 145.

230 "unbalanced clairvoyant": Quoted in Shaplen, Free Love, p. 267.

CHAPTER 10. Spiritualism

232 "When shown": IBH and JH to AHD, Nov. 23, 1887 (Fiche 57).

232 "a dunghill": Quoted in Johanna Johnston, Mrs. Satan, p. 235.

233 Spiritualism: I use a capital "s" to remind myself and readers that Spiritualism should be considered, historically, a particular type of religion, like Catholicism or Episcopalianism, rather than a form of mental illness or folly.

233 "till in 1875": IBH to AHD, Aug. 22, 1889 (Fiche 66).

233 Contemporary sources: In 1869 HBS estimated that there were between four and five million Spiritualists in the United States. The occasion for this estimate was her urging Osgood & Fields to advertise Oldtown Folks in the Spiritualist journal, The Banner of Light (Joan D. Hedrick, Harriet Beecher Stowe, p. 346).

234 "baneful influence": LIMITS, p. 251.

234 "abnormal accumulation," "the progress of time": CB, Appendix to Letters, pp. 26-27.

234 "cut up," "Such nonsense!": Quoted in Kathryn Kish Sklar, Catharine Beecher, p. 272.

235 "some peculiarity": Quoted in Forrest Wilson, Crusader in Crinoline, p. 574.

235 "very powerful": Annie Fields, Ed., Life and Letters of Harriet Beecher Stowe, pp. 253.

235 "our beautiful": Ibid., 309.

236 "the true bond": Ibid., p. 310.

236 "more believer," "consulted": Wilson, *Crusader in Crinoline*, p. 436.
236 "a household," "possessed": Charles Beecher, *A Review*, p. 94.
236 "The two movements": Ann D. Braude, *Radical Spirits*, p. 3.
237 "The only religious": HW, vol. 3, p. 530.
237 The list: The kernel of this list appears in Robert E. Riegel, *American Feminists*, p. 191. Braude questions whether Stanton, Anthony, and Gage "intentionally excluded" Spiritualism from their history of the women's movement or whether they were simply unfamiliar with it. They could not have been unfamiliar because of their association with Isabella, as well as Paulina Wright Davis and Victoria Woodhull (*Radical Spirits*, p. 81).
237 "abundance of revelation," "the fullness": JH and IBH to Edward Beecher Hooker, Feb. 20, 1876 (Fiche 51).
238 "Mediumship circumvented": Braude, *Radical Spirits*, p. 84.
238 "slit his throat": IBH to Edward Beecher Hooker, Jan. 16, 1876 (Fiche 52).
239 "alive to the work": Susan B. Anthony to Olympia Brown, Nov. 3, 1875 (Fiche 119).
239 "During that time": Carrie Chapman Catt and Nettie Rogers Shuler, *Woman Suffrage and Politics*, p. 108.
240 "represented woman's feminine": Anne Farnam, "Isabella Beecher Hooker as a Woman Suffragist," p. 74.
240 "an after-thought," "no true exhibit": HW, vol. 3, p. 54.
240 "proved to be": Eleanor Flexner, *Century of Struggle*, p. 174.
242 "spirit journal," "demented": Wilson, *Crusader in Crinoline*, p. 600.
242 "livelihood was curtailed": Kenneth R. Andrews, *Nook Farm*, p. 126.
243 "like one drowning": Quoted in Milton Rugoff, *The Beechers*, p. 584. The ban on the "demented" diary may not still hold, but out of sympathy with the family's dismay at critics' treatment of Isabella, I do not quote directly from it.
243 "vice regent," "the Comforter": Ibid.
244 "grand illusion": Marie Caskey, *Chariot of Fire*, p. 320.
245 "Poor man": Quoted in Andrews, *Nook Farm*, p. 58.
246 "whose only feelings," "Who, now, will": HBS, "Protect the Birds," pp. 33–34.
246 "She is so afraid": HBS to Hatty Stowe, Aug. 15, 1876, Beecher-Stowe Papers, SCH.
246 "Live as domestic": Charlotte Perkins Gilman, *The Living*, p. 95.
247 "an uncomfortable," "& he was vexed": Quoted in Andrews, *Nook Farm*, p. 86.
247 "his eyes flashed," "I dread to lose": Quoted Ibid., pp. 86–87.
248 "wrapper," "to body forth," "Why, what is": Ibid., p. 60.
249 "magnetic rubs": Copy, JH to Mr. Hascall, Apr. 15, 1877, in IBH to AHD, Apr. 17, 1877 (Fiche 53).
250 "a terrible year": Ibid.
250 "dear old Uncle": IBH to AHD, Apr. 17, 1877 (Fiche 53).
250 "whether out": Copy, JH to Mr. Hascall, Apr. 15, 1877, in IBH to AHD, Apr. 17, 1877 (Fiche 53).
250 "In 1870": IBH-Mem, p. 295.
250 "untiring exertions": Sarah E. Fuller to IBH and JH, May 28, 1877 (Fiche 131).
251 "I think there": LIMITS, p. 353.
251 "somewhat bowed": Mae Elizabeth Harveson, *Catharine Esther Beecher*, p. 237.
251 " 'I regret' ": Lyman Beecher Stowe, *Saints, Sinners and Beechers*, p. 129.
251 " 'But, Miss' ": Ibid., p. 130.
251 "Too many years": LIMITS, p. 353.
252 The author: Charles H. Foster argues persuasively that Stowe's "primary point" is to "win in imagination her father's approval for her 'signing off' to Anglicanism." *The Rungless Ladder*, p. 240.

252 "What a year," "about one third": HBS to Susie Munroe, July 23, 1878, Beecher-Stowe Collection, SCH.

252 "Your Aunt Mary": HBS to Charles Stowe, Oct. 8, 1877, Beecher-Stowe Collection, SCH. William and Katy Perkins Gilman were the parents of Houghton Gilman, Charlotte Perkins Gilman's second husband.

253 "a sealed book": Olympia Brown to IBH, June 26, [1875–1876?], (Fiche 125).

253 "at the front": Susan B. Anthony to IBH, Dec. 6, 1876 (Fiche 119).

253 "make a powerful": Susan B. Anthony to IBH, Nov. 11, 1877 (Fiche 119).

253 "[W]e want": Sara Spencer to IBH, Nov. 18, 1877 (Fiche 136).

253 "prayer meeting": Ellen Carol DuBois, "The Limitations of Sisterhood," p. 162.

254 "never felt more," "studied inattention," "restrained": HW, vol. 3, p. 93.

254 "the masses of silent women": Ibid., p. 101.

254 "eager to hear": Ibid., pp. 103–104.

254 "Mrs. Hooker," "The Indian question": Ibid., p. 105.

255 "reviewed the Chinese," "Commencing": Ibid., pp. 105–106, 73.

256 "Mrs. Hooker said": Julia E. Smith, Abby Smith and Her Cows, p. 30.

256 "social attention," "men high," "All crowded," "wherever": HW, vol. 3, p. 98.

256 "cultivated": Ibid., p. 99.

256 "frantically": IBH to Edward Beecher Hooker, Apr. 15, 1878 (Fiche 54).

257 "working," "fashionable," "You are": Sara Spencer to IBH [March 1878] (Fiche 136).

257 "cuir colored": HW, vol. 3, p. 99.

257 "merely nominal," "use my": IBH to Edward M. Davis, Mar. 31, 1878 (Fiche 53).

CHAPTER 11. Losses

259 "I am stronger": "Catharine E. Beecher," p. 372.

259 "like a mirror": Lyman Beecher Stowe, Saints, Sinners and Beechers, p. 136.

259 "longing to depart," "I pine": LIMITS, pp. 354–355.

259 "only sister": HBS to Mary Beecher Perkins, [July 1887], Beecher-Stowe Collection, SCH.

259 "spoke of her": Kathryn Kish Sklar, Catharine Beecher, p. 273.

259 "She was always": "Catharine E. Beecher," p. 373.

260 "It has been": Boston Daily Advertiser, May 13, 1878.

260 "a whole Social Science": Hartford Daily Courant, May 13, 1878.

260 "Miss Beecher's," "mantle": Elmira Daily Advertiser, May 13, 1878.

260 "to the elevation": "Catherine E. Beecher," p. 371.

261 "the really remarkable": IBH to AHD, Apr. 11, 1892 (Fiche 77).

261 "accepted the gender": LIMITS, p. 232.

261 "the agitation": Elizabeth Cady Stanton, Eighty Years, p. 264.

261 "helped to shape," "Beecher's strategy": LIMITS, p. 232.

261 "I hope I may," "should give up": Annie Fields, Ed., Life and Letters of Harriet Beecher Stowe, p. 372.

262 "languorous air": Forrest Wilson, Crusader in Crinoline, p. 606.

262 "My window": Fields, Life and Letters, p. 373.

262 "baby & husband," "carry": IBH, Diary, Sept. 1, 1878 (Fiche 105), and Oct. 2, 1878 (Fiche 106).

262 "[A]ll my life": LIMITS, p. 325.

262 "hungry for full companionship": Ibid.

263 "same fastidiousness": IBH, Diary, Nov. 19, 1878 (Fiche 106).

263 "[Y]ou have trespassed": LIMITS, p. 326.

263 "unreasonable": IBHP-G, p. 39.

263 "it was hardly I": LIMITS, p. 326.
263 "Transforming herself": Anne Throne Margolis, Ed., *The Isabella Beecher Hooker Project*, p. 39.
264 "sad habit": IBH, Diary, Oct. 10, 1878 (Fiche 106).
264 "jealous suspicion": IBH, Diary, Sept. 3, 1878 (Fiche 105).
264 "bound to a *brutal* [my italics]," "It seems as if": JH to IBH, IBH Collection, Sept. 23, 1884, S-D.
264 "no one to bully": JH and IBH to AHD, Aug. 11, 1885 (Fiche 56).
265 "dwarfed & narrowed": IBH, Diary, Oct. 10, 1878 (Fiche 106).
265 "all those girls": IBH, Diary, Nov. 27, 1878 (Fiche 106).
265 "my darling mother": Kate Trimble to IBH, Nov. 21, 1878 (Fiche 141).
265 "not doing as we": IBH, Diary, Oct. 10, 1878 (Fiche 106).
266 "I feel with you," "opposite shore," "[N]ow and then": Fields, *Life and Letters*, p. 373.
267 "exquisite": HBS to Calvin, Hatty, and Eliza Stowe, June 27, 1881 Beecher-Stowe Collection, SCH.
267 "frank but sure": Lucy B. Chittenden to JH, Mar. 25, 1880 (Fiche 126).
268 "I think sister": James C. Beecher to Frances Beecher, Mar. 20, [ca. 1879], James C. Beecher Family Papers, SCH.
268 "I am sure": Ibid.
269 "but Isabella," "Speak a word," "said in low pathetic": HW, vol. 3, pp. 194–195.
270 Brownie should not: See IBH, "Notes Regarding Universalist Church Trial Against Olympia Brown," [1874–1878] (Fiche 113).
270 "showed that political": HW, vol. 3, p. 226.
270 "look after the interests": Ibid.
271 "equal right," "We are not": Quoted in Virginia G. Drachman, *Sisters in Law*, pp. 30–32. She attributes this argument to George McManus, whom she has arguing for Hall. Actually, McManus and George Collier argued against Hall, as John notes in his *Some Reminiscences*, p. 146.
271 "represented one": Ibid., p. 33.
271 "at least 70," "the President": Arthur Gilman, "Atlantic Dinners," pp. 656, 651.
272 "the most notable," "vinous offerings": Ibid., p. 652.
272 "detect sarcasm": J. C. Derby, *Fifty Years Among Authors*, p. 283. For further discussion of the protest, see Susan Coultrap-McQuin, *Doing Literary Business*, pp. 2–6.
273 "The world": HBS to Hatty and Eliza Stowe, June 20, 1882, Beecher-Stowe Collection, SCH.
273 "killed the thing": Arthur Gilman, "Atlantic Dinners," p. 656.
273 "an instrument": [W. D. Howells], "The Birthday Garden Party," p. 9.
273 "Rev. Edward Beecher": Ibid., p. 10.
274 "memorable one": Elizabeth Stuart Phelps, *Chapters from a Life*, p. 138.
274 "old negro," "Well, now": [W. D. Howells], "The Birthday Garden Party," p. 10.
275 "The enlargement": Arthur Gilman, "Atlantic Dinners," p. 657.
275 "perfect": Fields, *Life and Letters*, p. 387.
275 "glorious, budding," "I love to have": Ibid.
275 "gay and airy," "never enjoyed": Ibid., p. 388.
277 "received the torch": Wilson, *Crusader in Crinoline*, p. 623.
277 "not only interesting": HBS to Annie Fields, Sept. 24, 1884, James Thomas Fields Collection, Henry E. Huntington Library.
277 "It was charming": Fields, *Life and Letters*, p. 389.
277 "Dear Belle": LIMITS, p. 355.
278 "I found myself": JH, *Some Reminiscences*, p. 256.
278 "In the God," "strengthened": IBH, "Confession of Faith," *Connecticut Magazine* 9 (Spring 1905): p. 305.

278 "less hearty": IBH to Robert Allen, Oct. 23, 1867 (Fiche 37).

279 "diverting": IBH to AHD, Aug. 11, 1885 (Fiche 56).

279 Of every hundred women: Barbara Ehrenreich and Deirdre English, *Complaints and Disorders*, p. 19.

279 "blasted life": Francis A. Walker to IBH, Jan. 7, 1890 (Fiche 142).

280 "I started": JH, *Some Reminiscences*, p. 262.

280 "credulity," "remarkable": IBH to AHD, June 5, 1886 (Fiche 56).

281 "Your joy": HBS, manuscript, "The Other World," Aug. 5, 1887, Joseph K. Hooker Collection, S-D.

281 "I have thought," "I am come," "a vivid," "joy": Fields, *Life and Letters*, p. 390.

281 "more or less," "a good pace," "A few days": Joseph H. Twichell, "Mrs. Harriet Beecher Stowe," p. 301.

282 "At this she": Frances E. Willard, "Harriet Beecher Stowe," p. 288.

282 "a tall, handsome": Grace King, *Memories of a Southern Woman*, p. 77.

282 "great trials": IBH to AHD, Aug. 4, 1889 (Fiche 86a).

283 "the little wash": IBH to AHD, Dec. 1, 1887 (Fiche 57).

283 "Mrs. Yost": IBH and JH to AHD, Nov. 23, 1887 (Fiche 57).

283 "special friends": IBH to AHD, Dec. 9, 1887 (Fiche 57).

283 "Dear mother!": IBH and Martha Kilbourne Hooker to AHD, Nov. 14, 1887 (Fiche 57).

283 "lying in bed": JH and IBH to AHD, Jan. 15, 1889 (Fiche 63).

CHAPTER 12. The Board of Lady Managers

285 "one family": IBH to AHD, Dec. 31, 1887 (Fiche 58). For a Foote genealogy, see the autobiography of the most famous Foote, Mary Hallock Foote, the artist wife of Andrew's younger brother, Arthur: *A Victorian Gentlewoman*, inside cover. Thanks to Melody Graulich for reminding me of this source.

285 "all associations": HW, vol. 4, p. 125.

286 "I wrote the most," "It will start": Quoted in Kathleen Barry, *Susan B. Anthony*, p. 285.

286 "most eminent": HW, vol. 4, p. 136.

286 "Whether our feet": Ibid., pp. 133–134.

287 "crime," "actually guarantees": IBH, *The Constitutional Rights*, pp. 13, 1.

287 "It is the unanimous": HW, vol. 4, pp. 136–137.

288 "in a state": IBH to AHD, Apr. 10, 1888 (Fiche 60).

288 "Just think": IBH to AHD, Apr. 18, 1888 (Fiche 60).

288 "a fine lecturer": Alfred Russel Wallace, *My Life*, p. 122.

289 "and form": Ibid., pp. 122–123.

289 "comfort her": IBH to AHD, Oct. 5, 1888 (Fiche 58).

289 "this sweet soul," "hungry for": IBH to Charlotte Foote, Oct. 10, 1888 (Fiche 58).

290 "[Harriet said] in a dreary": Ibid.

291 "I believe": IBH to AHD, Feb. 13, 1889 (Fiche 63).

291 Margaretta Fox: For a discussion of the confessions, see Ruth Brandon, *The Spiritualists*, p. 228.

291 "theologies have": IBH to AHD, Nov. 7, 1890 (Fiche 72).

291 "another sorrowful": IBH to AHD, Dec. 29, 1891 (Fiche 76).

291 "Jesus was any": IBH to AHD, Jan. 7, 1890 (Fiche 68).

291 "I have nothing": IBH to AHD, June 9, 1889 (Fiche 65).

292 "the boiling": IBH to AHD, July 10, 1889 (Fiche 65).

292 "almost certainly": IBH to AHD, Jan. 30, 1889 (Fiche 63).

292 "I must stand": IBH to William Lloyd Garrison Jr., Jan. 14, 1889 (Fiche 62). Garrison Family Papers, Sophia Smith Collection.

292 "virtually oppose": Ibid.
293 "utterly": IBH to AHD, Apr. 12, 1889 (Fiche 64).
293 "that he listened": LIMITS, p. 217.
293 "rushed in": IBH to AHD, June 9, 1889 (Fiche 65).
293 "put down," "the indispensable": JH, "Shall Women Be Allowed to Vote upon the Sale of Liquor and in School Matters?" May 6, 1889 (Fiche 64).
294 "I mean," "At Litchfield": LIMITS, p. 217.
294 "living on": IBH to AHD, Apr. 12, 1889 (Fiche 64).
294 "Nook Farm": LIMITS, p. 217.
294 "such a sense": IBH to AHD, Mar. 5, 1889 (Fiche 63).
294 "the duty of women," "take courage," "struggle on": IBH to AHD, May 3, 1889 (Fiche 64).
295 "My precious:" LIMITS, p. 356.
295 "sadly unconscious": IBH to AHD, Jan. 16, 1890 (Fiche 68).
296 "We feel almost": IBH to AHD, Oct. 15, 1889 (Fiche 67).
296 "scant fare": IBH to AHD, Aug. 4, 1889 (Fiche 86a).
296 "to live with": Ibid.
297 "In the bitter controversy": JH, Some Reminiscences, p. 228.
297 "We invited": JH and IBH to AHD, July 2, 1890 (Fiche 71).
297 "that sweet Jewess": IBH to AHD, Oct. 30, 1888 (Fiche 61).
297 "work for her people": IBH to AHD, Nov. 21, 1888 (Fiche 61).
298 "afford to seem": IBH to AHD, Feb. 13, 1890 (Fiche 68).
298 "the superior mental," "Oh I am proud": LIMITS, pp. 218–219.
298 "I think we should": HW, vol. 4, p. 165.
298 "enjoys seeing": LIMITS, p. 219.
298 "spoke for ten," "I could almost envy": Ibid.
299 "I wish you": IBH to AHD, Aug. 7, 1892 (Fiche 77).
299 "The time": JH and IBH to AHD, Mar. 19, 1890 (Fiche 69).
300 "my very best": IBH to AHD, Dec. 18, 1888 (Fiche 62).
300 "And said Commission," "of no importance": Jeanne Madeline Weimann, The Fair Women, pp. 32–33.
300 "makes women people": IBH to AHD, Aug. 9, 1890 (Fiche 71).
301 "This symbolic union": Weimann, The Fair Women, p. 30.
302 "a whole hearted": IBH to AHD, Dec. [5], 1890 (Fiche 72).
302 "palace": Ibid.
302 "a total stranger," "kindergarten": Quoted in Weimann, The Fair Women, pp. 49–51.
303 "conservatism was": IBH to AHD, Dec. [5], 1890 (Fiche 72).
303 "elaborate decorations": Kenneth R. Andrews, Nook Farm, p. 220.
303 "the old servants": John Hooker, Some Reminiscences, p. 177.
303 "distinguished woman suffragists": Ibid.
303 "a most beautiful": Quoted in Ida Husted Harper, The Life and Work, vol. 2, p. 709.
303 "the best-loved member": JH, Some Reminiscences, p. 173.
304 "queer as ever": IBH and JH to AHD, Apr. 18, 1891 (Fiche 74).
304 "the climactic event": Andrews, Nook Farm, p. 221.
304 "heavenly glow," "seemed transfigured": IBH to AHD, Aug. 17, 1891 (Fiche 74).
305 "get justice done," "a flock of sheep": IBH to AHD, Sept. 21, 1891 (Fiche 75).
305 "Women": Weimann, The Fair Women, p. 101.
305 "the colored women," "sit with Negroes": Ibid., pp. 103–104.
305 "openly committed," "make a strong": Ibid., p. 110.
306 "simply superb," "I do not sympathize": "Mrs. Isabella Beecher-Hooker," Boston Pilot, Oct. 3, 1891, p. 5. Isabella was also quoted as saying of the Virgin Mary, "And why

should we scruple at the honors paid to her who bore a Divine Son for the redemption of man?" Apparently the divinity of Christ depended on Isabella's argument of the moment.

306 "I desired to prove": IBH-Mem, p. 298.

306 "to think what," "only that her soul": IBH, "John Pierce Brace," pp. 25–26.

307 "creep along": IBH to AHD, Jan. 27, 1892 (Fiche 76).

307 "the most fantastic": John G. Cawelti, "America on Display," p. 334.

307 "enchanted": Patricia O'Toole, The Five of Hearts, p. 265.

307 One writer estimated: Kate Brannon Knight, History of the Work, p. 43.

307 "Her life had been": Hamlin Garland, A Son, p. 460.

307 "enormous," "model": IBH to AHD, Sept. 21, 1891 (Fiche 75).

308 "If popularity": Quoted in Weismann, The Fair Women, p. 277.

308 "the most healthful": Weismann, The Fair Women, p. 332.

308 "old Mrs. Hooker": Quoted in ibid., p. 568.

308 "The Board of Lady": "Lady Managers Disagree," New York Times, Aug. 6, 1893, p. 5.

309 "just a love": May Beecher and Margaret Beecher to Frances Beecher Perkins, July 26, 1893, James C. Beecher Family Papers, SCH. Frances was now Beecher Perkins because after James's suicide she married the divorced Frederick Perkins, Mary's oldest son and Charlotte Perkins Gilman's father.

309 There it disappeared: A mural painted by Mary Cassatt for the Woman's Building also disappeared and has never been found. See Weimann, The Fair Women, pp. 591–593.

309 "treacherous": JH and IBH to AHD, Oct. 12, 1893 (Fiche 79).

309 "a vindictive woman": IBH to JH, Aug. 16, 1893 (Fiche 79).

309 "Our Queen": Mary K. Eagle, Ed., Congress of Women, p. 817.

309 "The wimmen managers": Marietta Holley, Samantha at the World's Fair, p. 257.

310 "the symbols and actuality": Cawelti, "America on Display," p. 339.

CHAPTER 13. The Last of the Beechers

311 "I hope when my hour": JH and IBH to AHD, Nov. 18, 1893 (Fiche 79).

311 "hypochondriacal derangement": IBH to AHD, July 4, 1894 (Fiche 81).

311 "baby farming": IBH, "Charges Refuted," Rochester Democrat and Chronicle, Aug. 8, 1892 (Fiche 77).

311 "that woman," "our circle of true," "Hartford is spoiled,": IBH to AHD, Nov. 28, 1893 (Fiche 79).

311 "How could they?": IBH to AHD, July 25, 1892 (Fiche 77).

312 Will had lost: For a discussion of Will's relationship with the Hookers at this time, see Doris E. Cook, Sherlock Holmes, pp. 35–36.

312 "she showed the necessity": HW, vol. 4, p. 179.

312 "Four of the greatest": Ibid., p. 189.

312 "put our old Prest.": IBH to Elizabeth Cady Stanton, Apr. 26, 1892, Olympia Brown Collection, SCH.

312 "woman cannot get": Federal Suffrage Association, p. 2.

313 Isabella went so far: She did meet with Victoria's husband, John Martin, who typed notes of their interview on May 13, 1892 (see Fiche 77 for a copy). No doubt Martin prepared the notes and had Isabella sign them so he could protect Victoria from the charge that her accusation of Henry Ward Beecher was false. Still, there was much cloak and dagger in the whole transaction.

313 "I was not": IBH to Elizabeth Cady Stanton, Apr. 26, 1892, Olympia Brown Collection, SCH.

313 "What a wonderful": IBH to AHD, Dec. 27, 1892 (Fiche 78).
313 "Women Will Soon Vote": Rochester *Democrat and Chronicle*, Aug. 6, 1892, p. 1 (Fiche 77).
314 "Mrs. Hooker remained": Ida Husted Harper, *The Life and Work*, vol. 2, p. 725.
314 "vague ideas": Elizabeth Cady Stanton to Antoinette Brown Blackwell, June 10, 1873, in Stanton and Blatch, vol. 2, p. 142.
314 "the before," "I know": Harper, *The Life and Work*, vol. 2, p. 899. The disagreement does not mean, of course, that "Mrs. Hooker never liked either Mrs. Stanton or Miss Anthony very much," as Robert Riegel contends in *American Feminists*, p. 143. Isabella and Susan were friends, although they did not always agree, and she and Stanton were at worst ambivalent about each other.
314 "in love with Frances": IBH to AHD, Mar. 11, 1891 (Fiche 73).
314 "prohibitionist": IBH to JH, Nov. 14, 1891 (Fiche 75).
314 "narrow," "eagerly welcomed": IBH to Katharine Seymour Day, Nov. 14, 1892 (Fiche 78).
315 "My suffrage work": JH and IBH to AHD, May 26, 1894 (Fiche 80).
315 "spoke with the old-time": Unidentified clipping, Edna Burr Scrapbook, Connecticut State Library.
315 Featured in a special mahogany: The Stowe exhibit was so extensive, Kate Brannon Knight devoted some forty pages to describe it in her book on the work of Connecticut women at the Columbian Exposition.
315 "Happy soul": "What Interested Mrs. Stowe," Hartford *Times*, May 25, 1894 (Fiche 80).
316 "all of your old": J. B. Pond to Mark Twain, July 3, 1896, quoted in Kenneth R. Andrews, *Nook Farm*, p. 219.
316 "The familiar poet-friends," "an intellect": Ibid.
316 "third rate": "Harriet Beecher Stowe," *Spectator*, July 4, 1896, p. 3.
316 "Every woman has rights," "Mrs. Stowe was ever": Susan B. Anthony, "Miss Anthony on Mrs. Stowe," p. 213.
316 "the *master book*": Quoted in Josephine Donovan, *"Uncle Tom's Cabin,"* p. 17.
317 "Harriet Beecher Stowe": Paul Laurence Dunbar, "Harriet Beecher Stowe," p. 61. The Baldwin article is "Everybody's Protest Novel."
317 "far from needing": Hartford *Daily Courant*, Aug. 13, 1897, p. 6. Charles Dudley Warner mentions the twins' "mortification" in a letter to Annie Fields, Sept. 19, 1897, James Thomas Fields Collection, Henry E. Huntington Library.
317 "The spoon has": IBH, *A Brief Sketch*, p. 16.
317 "the era of Nook Farm": Joseph S. Van Why, *Nook Farm*, p. 63.
318 "your husband has": IBH to AHD, Oct. 27, 1892 (Fiche 78).
318 "a cozy time": IBH to Katharine Seymour Day, Jan. 27, 1897 (Fiche 81).
318 "became active": "Jackson, Alice Hooker Day," p. 130.
319 "dreadful to double": IBH, "Are Women Too Ignorant?" p. 1.
319 "the education," "society of colored women," "Ladies," "Let us take courage": Ibid., pp. 1–2.
319 "Abolish the ignorant," "thousands from every," "foreign yoke": HW, vol. 4, p. 317.
319 "that loyal women," "the political inferiors": Ibid., pp. 148–49. See also Olympia Brown, "United States Citizenship" in *Suffrage and Religious Principle*, pp. 121–130.
320 "There are those," "by inviting every": HW, vol. 4, pp. 115–116.
320 "Only think of Carnegie": IBH to AHD, July 25, 1892 (Fiche 77).
321 "very fidgety," "She is always," "she was a picture": HW, vol. 4, p. 296.
321 "I never could give," "clearly and forcibly": Ibid.
321 "tableau," "To think that such": Ibid.
321 "statesmanlike paper": Ibid., p. 358.
321 "delicate": IBH to Alice Day Jackson, Jan. 23, 1900 (Fiche 83).
321 "keep him": IBH to AHD, Mar. 2, 1900 (Fiche 83).

321 "go quickly": JH and IBH to Frances Beecher Perkins, Jan. 22, 1899 (Fiche 82).

322 "training for this": Lyman Beecher Stowe, Saints, Sinners and Beechers, p. 152.

322 "increasing overshadowing": IBH, Diary, Jan. 31, 1901 (Fiche 110).

323 "make spiritualism": IBH, Diary, Feb. 20, 1901 (Fiche 110).

323 "stunning old lady," "opening sentences," "the Beecher words": Quoted in Mary Gray Peck, Carrie Chapman Catt, pp. 117–118.

323 "heroic in putting": I. S. Koons to IBH, Apr. 26, 19[01] (Fiche 133).

323 "for if there": IBH to Katharine Seymour Day, July 2, 1901 (Fiche 84).

323 "drag old Connecticut," "absolutely": IBH to Olympia Brown, Jan. 22, 1899 (Fiche 82).

324 "In furtherance": IBH, "Memorial of the Connecticut Woman Suffrage Association," p. 3 (Fiche 85).

324 "bitterly prejudiced": Ibid., p. 5.

324 "general council," "The right of citizens": Ibid., pp. 5, 21.

324 "very stupid men": IBH to Katharine Seymour Day, Jan. 12, 1902 (Fiche 84).

325 "In spite of": Lyman Beecher Stowe, Saints, Sinners and Beechers, p. 353. The motto is borrowed from the American Revolution hero Thomas Paine.

325 "replied brightly": Ibid.

326 "I have done": IBH to Katharine Seymour Day, [1902?] (Fiche 84).

326 "horrid convention": Ibid.

326 "responsibilities": IBH-Mem, p. 298.

326 "burst of zeal," "My health gave way": IBH to Clara B. Colby, June 23, 1903 (Fiche 85).

326 "ignored and never treated," "snubbed": LIMITS, p. 331.

327 "As to Mrs[.]," "the world will not": Ibid., p. 358.

327 "cobwebs of prejudice": Jennifer Rafferty, "Charlotte Perkins Gilman," p. 14.

327 "world-servers": Charlotte Perkins Gilman, The Living, p. 3.

327 reorganizing domestic space: For a discussion of this issue, see Valerie Gill, "Catharine Beecher and Charlotte Perkins Gilman," pp. 17–24.

327 "glory that such": Charlotte Perkins Gilman, review of The Life of Harriet Beecher Stowe, p. 197.

328 "ignorance": IBH to George H. Warner, May 30, 1900 (Fiche 86a).

328 "we must not": IBH to AHD, Sept. 23, 1900 (Fiche 83).

328 "absolute certainties": IBH to Katharine Seymour Day, July 27, 1905 (Fiche 85).

328 "a most fascinating," "positively garrulous": IBH to Katharine Seymour Day, Aug. 13, 1905 (Fiche 85).

328 tore in half: According to Frederick Anderson, editor of the Mark Twain Papers, Sept. 21, 1977 (Target for Fiche 85).

330 "great comfort": IBH-Mem, p. 295.

330 "degradation," "a storm of indignation": Ibid.

330 At the Kentucky service: Sara Hunter Graham, "The Suffrage Renaissance," p. 175.

330 "I can't stand": Lyman Beecher Stowe, Saints, Sinners and Beechers, p. 353.

330 "Isabel, I don't": Ibid., p. 352.

330 "what a wonderful": IBH to AHD, Katharine Seymour Day, and Alice Day Jackson, May 27, 1901 (Fiche 83).

331 "serious invalid": IBH to Victoria Woodhull Martin, Sept. 14, 1906 (Fiche 86).

331 "feeble dependent": IBH to Lilly Gillette Foote, Sept. 5, [1906] (Fiche 86).

331 "mystery of death," "wisdom": IBH to AHD, Oct. 15, 1889 (Fiche 67).

331 "in a quiet": IBH to JH, May 26, 1860 (Fiche 18).

331 "Last of Beecher," "ability," "ideas and convictions," "followed no paths": "Last of Beecher Family Is Dead," Hartford Courant, Jan. 25, 1907, p. 1.

332 "wrapped up," "unfailing kindliness": "Mrs. Hooker," Hartford Courant, Jan. 26, 1907, p. 8.

332 "The Beecher talent," "brave women," "They broke": Quoted in Laura E. Skandera-Trombley, Mark Twain, p. 141.

332 "Mrs. Hooker's Talks": "Mrs. Hooker's Talks with Spirits," *Hartford Courant*, Mar. 20, 1908, p. 1.

333 "kind and loving," "repeated," "cold": "Arguments Next in Hooker Will Case," *Hartford Courant*, Mar. 25, 1908, p. 13.

333 "undue influence," "sad spectacles": "Mrs. Hooker's Will Set Aside by Jury," *Hartford Courant*, Mar. 26, 1908, p. 2.

335 "the far reaching importance": Susan B. Anthony to Rachel Foster Avery, May 12, 1899, in Elizabeth Cady Stanton, *Papers of Elizabeth Cady Stanton and Susan B. Anthony*, vol. 39, p. 855.

336 "we mothers": IBH, "Memorial," p. 12.

336 "expediency": Aileen S. Kraditor, *The Ideas of the Woman Suffrage Movement*, p. 52. For further discussion of the anti-egalitarian ideologies of the time, see Suzanne M. Marilley, *Woman Suffrage*, pp. 159–162.

337 "women could grow": Andrews, *Nook Farm*, p. 138.

337 "If you cannot live": IBH, "Remarks of Mrs. Hooker," p. 30.

337 "Both women associated": Elizabeth Ammons, "Heroines in *Uncle Tom's Cabin*," p. 163.

337 "duty": Henry Ward Beecher, *Woman's Duty*.

Bibliography

Primary Works

MANUSCRIPT COLLECTIONS

Beinecke Rare Book and Manuscript Library, Yale University, New Haven, Conn.
Collection of American Literature
Clement Library, University of Michigan, Ann Arbor, Mich.
Weld-Grimké Papers
Connecticut Historical Society, Hartford, Conn.
Hartford Female Seminary Papers
Connecticut State Library, Hartford, Conn.
Frances E. Burr Scrapbooks
Papers of the Conn. Woman Suffrage Association, 1869–1921
Henry E. Huntington Library, San Marino, Calif.
James T. Fields Papers
Manuscript Division, Library of Congress, Washington, D.C.
Anna E. Dickinson Papers
Joshua R. Giddings and George Washington Julian Papers
Harriet Foote Hawley Papers
Joseph Roswell Hawley Papers
Whitelaw Reid Family Papers
Schlesinger Library, Radcliffe Institute, Harvard University, Cambridge, Mass.
James C. Beecher Family Papers
Beecher-Stowe Collection
Olympia Brown (Willis) Papers
Charlotte Perkins Gilman Papers
Harriet Goodhue Hosmer Papers
Sophia Smith Collection, Smith College, Northampton, Mass.
Fanny Fern Papers
Garrison Family Papers
Sterling Memorial Library, Yale University, New Haven, Conn.
Beecher-Scoville Family Papers
Harriet Beecher Stowe Center, Hartford, Conn.
Acquisitions
Katharine S. Day Collection
Foote Collection
Isabella Beecher Hooker Collection
IBHP
Joseph K. Hooker Collection
Helen D. Perkins Collection

NEWSPAPERS AND WEEKLY JOURNALS

San Francisco *Alta California*
Hartford Courant
Nation

The Press-Philadelphia
Revolution
Woman's Journal
Woodhull & Claflin's Weekly

BOOKS BY THE BEECHERS (LYMAN AND HIS CHILDREN)

The Autobiography of Lyman Beecher. Ed. Barbara M. Cross. 2 vols. Cambridge: Belknap Press of
    Harvard University Press, 1961 [orig. 1864].
Beecher, Catharine. *An Appeal to the People on Behalf of Their Rights as Authorized Interpreters of the*
    Bible. New York: Harper & Bros., 1860.
————. *Common Sense Applied to Religion, or the Bible and the People.* New York: Harper & Bros.,
    1857.
————. *Educational Reminiscences and Suggestions.* New York: J. B. Ford, 1874.
————. *The Evils Suffered by American Women and American Children: The Causes and the Remedy.*
    New York: Harper & Bros., 1846.
————. *Letters to the People on Health and Happiness.* New York: Harper & Bros., 1855.
————. *A Treatise on Domestic Economy.* 1841. Reprint. New York: Schocken Books, 1970.
————. *The True Remedy for the Wrongs of Women.* Boston: Phillips, Sampson, 1851.
————. *Truth Stranger than Fiction: A Narrative of Recent Transactions Involving Inquiries in Regard to*
    the Principles of Honor, Truth and Justice which Obtain in a Distinguished American University.
    New York: Printed for the Author, 1850.
————. *Woman Suffrage and Woman's Profession.* Hartford, Conn.: Brown and Gross, 1871.
————. *Woman's Profession as Mother and Educator, with Views in Opposition to Woman Suffrage.*
    Philadelphia: George Maclean, 1872.
Beecher, Catharine, and Harriet Beecher Stowe. *The American Women's Home, or Principles of*
    Domestic Science. New York: J. B. Ford, 1869.
Beecher, Charles. *A Review of the "Spiritual Manifestations".* New York: G. P. Putnam, 1853.
Beecher, Henry Ward. *Woman's Duty to Vote.* New York: American Equal Rights Association,
    1867.
Beecher, Lyman. *Letters of the Rev. Dr. Beecher and Rev. Mr. Nettleton on the "New Measures".* New
    York: G. & C. Carvill, 1828.
Fields, Annie, Ed. *Life and Letters of Harriet Beecher Stowe.* Boston: Houghton, Mifflin, 1898.
Hooker, Isabella Beecher. *Are Women Too Ignorant?* Boston: Woman's Journal, 1898. Woman
    Suffrage Leaflet, vol. 7, no. 3.
————. *A Brief Sketch of the Life of Harriet Beecher Stowe.* Hartford, Conn.: Privately printed, 1896.
————. "Confession of Faith, April 14, 1885." *Connecticut Magazine* 9 (Spring 1905): p. 305.
————. *The Constitutional Rights of the Women of the United States: An Address Before the*
    International Council of Women, Washington, D.C., March 30, 1888. Hartford, Conn.: Case,
    Lockwood & Brainard, 1900.
————. "Happy New Year." *Revolution*, Jan. 6, 1870, pp. 10–11.
————. "John Pierce Brace." In *Hartford Female Seminary Reunion, June 9, 1892*, pp. 25–31.
    Hartford, Conn.: Case, Lockwood & Brainard, 1892.
————. "The Last of the Beechers: Memories on My Eighty-Third Birthday." *Connecticut*
    Magazine 9 (Spring 1905): pp. 286–298.
————. Letter to *Nation*, Nov. 12, 1868, pp. 391–392.
————. "The McFarland-Richardson Tragedy." *Revolution*, Dec. 16, 1869, pp. 376–377.
————. "Memorial of the Connecticut Woman Suffrage Association to the Constitutional
    Convention Assembled in Hartford, Connecticut, Jan. 1, 1902, and an Argument
    Thereon." Fiche 85.
————. *A Mother's Letters to a Daughter on Woman Suffrage.* Hartford, Conn.: Connecticut

Woman Suffrage Association, 1870. First published anonymously in *Putnam's Monthly*, November, December 1868.

———. "Remarks of Mrs. Hooker before the Judiciary Committee of the House of Representatives, at Washington, in January 1871." Hartford, Conn.: Case, Lockwood & Brainard, 1900.

———. "Shall Women Vote? A Matrimonial Dialogue." In *On Common Ground: A Selection of Hartford Writers*. Ed. Alice DeLana and Cynthia Reik, pp. 68–79. Hartford, Conn.: Stowe-Day Foundation, 1975.

———. "The Universal Litany." *Connecticut Magazine* 9 (Spring 1905): p. 306.

———. *Womanhood: Its Sanctities and Fidelities*. Boston: Lee and Shepard, 1873.

The Isabella Beecher Hooker Project: A Microfiche Edition of Her Papers. Ed. Anne Throne Margolis. Millwood, N.Y.: KTO Microform, 1979.

The Limits of Sisterhood: The Beecher Sisters on Women's Rights and Woman's Sphere. Ed. Jeanne Boydston, Mary Kelley, and Anne Margolis. Chapel Hill: University of North Carolina Press, 1988.

Stowe, Harriet Beecher. "Catherine [sic] E. Beecher." In *Our Famous Women: An Authorized Record of the Lives and Deeds of Distinguished American Women of Our Times*. Ed. Elizabeth Stuart Phelps (Ward), pp. 75–93. 1883. Reprint. Freeport, N.Y.: Books for Libraries Press, 1975.

———. "Chimney Corner." *Atlantic Monthly*, 16 (August 1865): pp. 233–237.

———. "How Shall I Learn to Write?" *Hearth and Home*, Jan. 16, 1869, p. 56.

———. *The Minister's Wooing*. New York: Derby and Jackson, 1859.

———. *My Wife and I: Or, Harry Henderson's History*. Boston: Houghton, Mifflin, 1871.

———. *Oldtown Folks*. Boston: Fields, Osgood, 1869.

———. *The Oxford Harriet Beecher Stowe Reader*. Ed. Joan D. Hedrick. New York: Oxford University Press, 1999.

———. *Poganuc People*. Boston: Houghton, Mifflin, 1878.

———. "Protect the Birds." *Semi-Tropical*, 3 (January 1877): pp. 33–34.

———. "What Is and What Is Not the Point in the Woman Question." *Hearth and Home*, Aug. 28, 1869, pp. 568–569.

———. "The Woman Question." *Hearth and Home*, Aug. 7, 1869, pp. 500–521.

Secondary and Other Works

Adams, John P. *Harriet Beecher Stowe: Updated Edition*. Boston: Twayne, 1989.

Adler, Alfred. *Understanding Human Nature*. London: George Allen & Unwin, 1928.

———. *What Life Should Mean to You*. London: George Allen & Unwin, 1932.

Ammons, Elizabeth. "Heroines in *Uncle Tom's Cabin*." *American Literature* 49 (May 1977): pp. 116–179.

Andrews, Benjamin R. "Miss Catherine [sic] Beecher, the Pioneer in Home Economics." *Journal of Home Economics* 4 (June 1912): pp. 211–222.

Andrews, Kenneth R. *Nook Farm: Mark Twain's Hartford Circle*. Cambridge: Harvard University Press, 1950.

The Annual Catalogue of the Hartford Female Seminary. Hartford: P. B. Gleason, 1838 and 1839.

Anthony, Susan B. "Miss Anthony on Mrs. Stowe." *Outlook*, Aug. 1, 1896, p. 213.

Ashton, Jean W. *Harriet Beecher Stowe: A Reference Guide*. Boston: G. K. Hall, 1977.

Austin, James C. *Fields of the Atlantic Monthly: Letters to an Editor, 1861–70*. San Marino, Calif.: Huntington Library, 1953.

Baldwin, James. "Everybody's Protest Novel." *Partisan Review* 16 (June 1949): pp. 578–585.

Bank, Stephen P., and Michael E. Kahn. *The Sibling Bond*. New York: Basic, 1982.

Barry, Kathleen. *Susan B. Anthony: A Biography of a Singular Feminist*. New York: New York University Press, 1988.

Beecher, William C., and Samuel Scoville. *A Biography of Henry Ward Beecher*. New York: C. L. Webster, 1888.

"Beecherism and Its Tendencies." *Catholic World* 12 (January 1871): pp. 433–450.

Benson, Eugene. "George Sand and the Marriage Question," *Revolution*, July 7, 1870, pp. 1–2.

Berlin, Ira, Joseph P. Reidy, and Leslie S. Rowland, Eds. *Freedom's Soldiers: The Black Military Experience in the Civil War*. Cambridge: Cambridge University Press, 1998.

Blackwell, Elizabeth. *Pioneer Work in Opening the Medical Profession to Women*. New York: E. P. Dutton, 1895.

Blair, Karen J. *The Clubwoman as Feminist: True Womanhood Redefined, 1868–1914*. New York: Holmes & Meier, 1980.

———. "Jane Cunningham Croly." In *American Women Writers: A Critical Reference Guide*. Ed. Lina Mainiero, vol. 1, pp. 422–424. New York: Frederick Ungar, 1979.

Blake, Katherine Devereux, and Margaret Louise Wallace. *Champion of Women: The Life of Lillie Devereux Blake*. New York: Fleming H. Revell, 1943.

Bordin, Ruth. *Frances Willard: A Biography*. Chapel Hill: University of North Carolina Press, 1986.

Bradford, Gamaliel. "Harriet Beecher Stowe." *Atlantic Monthly* 122 (July 1918): pp. 84–94.

Brandon, Ruth. *The Spiritualists: The Passion for the Occult in the Nineteenth and Twentieth Centuries*. New York: Alfred A. Knopf, 1983.

Braude, Ann D. *Radical Spirits: Spiritualism and Women's Rights in Nineteenth-Century America*. Boston: Beacon Press, 1989.

Brown, Olympia. *Acquaintances Old and New among Reformers*. Milwaukee: S. E. Tate, 1911.

———. *Suffrage and Religious Principle: Speeches and Writings of Olympia Brown*. Ed. Dana Greene. Metuchen, N.J.: Scarecrow Press, 1983.

Bullard, F. Lauriston. "Abraham Lincoln and Harriet Beecher Stowe." *Lincoln Herald* 48 (June 1946): pp. 11–14.

Bynum, W. F. *Science and the Practice of Medicine in the Nineteenth Century*. Cambridge: Cambridge University Press, 1994.

Caskey, Marie. *Chariot of Fire: Religion and the Beecher Family*. New Haven, Conn.: Yale University Press, 1978.

"Catharine E. Beecher," *Harper's Bazaar*, June 8, 1878, pp. 371–373.

Catt, Carrie Chapman, and Nettie Rogers Shuler. *Woman Suffrage and Politics: The Inner Story of the Suffrage Movement*. New York: Charles Scribner's Sons, 1923.

Cawelti, John G. "America on Display: The World's Fairs of 1876, 1893, 1933." In *The Age of Industrialism in America: Essays in Social Structure and Cultural Values*. Ed. Frederic Cople Jaher, pp. 317–363. New York: Free Press, 1968.

Cayleff, Susan E. *Wash and Be Healed: The Water-Cure Movement and Women's Health*. Philadelphia: Temple University Press, 1987.

Chester, Giraud. *Embattled Maiden: The Life of Anna Dickinson*. New York: G. P. Putnam's Sons, 1951.

Clark, Clifford E., Jr. *Henry Ward Beecher: Spokesman for a Middle-Class America*. Urbana: University of Illinois Press, 1978.

Clinton, Catherine. *The Other Civil War: American Women in the Nineteenth Century*. New York: Hill and Wang, 1984.

Cook, Doris E. *Sherlock Holmes and Much More, or Some of the Facts about William Gillette*. Hartford, Conn.: Connecticut Historical Society, 1970.

Coultrap-McQuin, Susan. *Doing Literary Business: American Women Writers in the Nineteenth Century*. Chapel Hill: University of North Carolina Press, 1990.

Croly, Jennie Cunningham. *Sorosis: Its Origins and History*. New York: J. J. Little, 1886.

Davis, Paulina W. *A History of the National Woman's Rights Movement for Twenty Years, 1850–1870.* New York: Source Book Press, 1970 [orig. 1871].

Derby, J. C. "Harriet Beecher Stowe." In *Fifty Years Among Authors, Books, and Publishers.* New York: G. W. Carleton, 1884.

Dodge, Mary Abigail [Gail Hamilton, pseud.]. *Country Living and Country Thinking.* Boston: Ticknor and Fields, 1863.

———. *Gail Hamilton's Life in Letters.* Ed. H. Augusta Dodge, 2 vols. Boston: Lee & Shepard, 1901.

Donegan, Jane B. *"Hydropathic Highway to Health": Women and Water Cure in Antebellum America.* Westport, Conn.: Greenwood Press, 1986.

Donovan, Josephine. "Harriet Beecher Stowe's Feminism." *American Transcendental Quarterly* 48–49 (Summer 1982): pp. 141–157.

———. *New England Local Color Literature: A Women's Tradition.* New York: Frederick Ungar, 1983.

———. *"Uncle Tom's Cabin": Evil, Affliction, and Redemptive Love.* Boston: Twayne, 1991.

Drachman, Virginia G. *Sisters in Law: Women Lawyers in Modern American History.* Cambridge: Harvard University Press, 1998.

DuBois, Ellen Carol. *Feminism and Suffrage: The Emergence of an Independent Women's Movement in America, 1848–1869.* Ithaca, N.Y.: Cornell University Press, 1978.

———. "The Limitations of Sisterhood: Elizabeth Cady Stanton and Division in the American Suffrage Movement, 1875–1902." In *Woman Suffrage & Women's Rights.* New York: New York University Press, 1998.

———. "Taking the Law into Our Own Hands: *Bradwell, Minor,* and Suffrage Militance in the 1870's." In *One Woman, One Vote: Rediscovering the Woman Suffrage Movement.* Ed. Marjorie Spruill Wheeler, pp. 81–98. Troutdale, Ore.: New Sage Press, 1995.

Dunbar, Paul Laurence. "Harriet Beecher Stowe." *Century* 57 (November 1898): p. 61.

Eagle, Mary K., Ed. *Congress of Women Held in the Women's Building, World's Columbian Exposition, Chicago, 1893.* Chicago: W. B. Conkey, 1894.

Ehrenreich, Barbara, and Deirdre English. *Complaints and Disorders: The Sexual Politics of Sickness.* Old Westbury, N.Y.: Feminist Press, 1973.

Elsmere, Jane Shaffer. *Henry Ward Beecher: The Indiana Years, 1837–1847.* Indianapolis: Indianapolis Historical Society, 1973.

Emig, Janet A. "The Flower in the Cleft: The Writings of Harriet Beecher Stowe." *Bulletin of the Historical and Philosophical Society of Ohio* 21 (October 1963): pp. 223–238.

Faber, Doris. *Love and Rivalry: Three Exceptional Pairs of Sisters.* New York: Viking Press, 1983.

Farnam, Anne. "Isabella Beecher Hooker: 'Shall Women Be Allowed to Vote upon the Sale of Liquor and in School Matters?'" Connecticut Historical Society *Bulletin* 36 (April 1971): pp. 41–51.

———. "Isabella Beecher Hooker as a Reformer: Or a Quest for Personal Power." Master's thesis. University of Connecticut, 1970.

———. "Isabella Beecher Hooker as a Woman Suffragist: A Centennial Frame of Reference." *Connecticut Review* 5 (October 1971): pp. 70–82.

———. "Woman Suffrage as an Alternative to the Beecher Ministry." In *Portraits of a Nineteenth Century Family: A Symposium on the Beecher Family.* Ed. Earl A. French and Diana Royce, pp. 71–97. Hartford, Conn.: Stowe-Day Foundation, 1976.

Federal Suffrage Association: Its Origin and Constitution. Np, 1892.

Flexner, Eleanor. *Century of Struggle: The Woman's Rights Movement in the United States.* Rev. ed. Cambridge: Harvard University Press, 1975.

Foote, Mary Hallock. *A Victorian Gentlewoman in the Far West: The Reminiscences of Mary Hallock Foote.* Ed. Rodman W. Paul. San Marino, Calif.: Huntington Library, 1972.

Foster, Charles H. *The Rungless Ladder: Harriet Beecher Stowe and New England Puritanism.* Durham, N.C.: Duke University Press, 1954.

Foster, John T., Jr., and Sarah Whitmer Foster. *Beechers, Stowes, and Yankee Strangers: The Transformation of Florida*. Gainesville: University Press of Florida, 1999.

Fox, Richard Wightman. *Trials of Intimacy: Love and Loss in the Beecher-Tilton Scandal*. Chicago: University of Chicago Press, 1999.

Gabriel, Mary. *Notorious Victoria: The Life of Victoria Woodhull, Uncensored*. Chapel Hill, N.C.: Algonquin Books of Chapel Hill, 1998.

Garland, Hamlin. *A Son of the Middle Border*. New York: Macmillan, 1914.

Garrison, Wendell Phillips, and Francis Jackson Garrison. *William Lloyd Garrison, 1805–1879*. Boston and New York: Houghton, Mifflin, 1889 [orig. 1885].

Gerson, Noel. *Harriet Beecher Stowe: A Biography*. New York: Praeger, 1976.

Giammichele, Evelyn, and Eva Taylor. "Elmira Water Cure: Silas and Rachel Gleason and Their 'Tavern for the Sick.'" *Chemung Historical Journal* 12 (December 1966): pp. 1535–1541.

Gill, Valerie. "Catharine Beecher and Charlotte Perkins Gilman: Architects of Female Power." *Journal of American Culture* 2 (Summer 1998): pp. 17–24.

Gilman, Arthur. "Atlantic Dinners and Diners." *Atlantic Monthly* 100 (November 1907): pp. 646–657.

Gilman, Charlotte Perkins. *The Living of Charlotte Perkins Gilman: An Autobiography*. 1935. Reprint. Madison: University of Wisconsin Press, 1990.

———. Review of *The Life of Harriet Beecher Stowe* by Charles E. Stowe and Lyman Beecher Stowe, *Forerunner* 2 (July 1911): pp. 196–197.

Gleason, Rachel B. *Talks to My Patients: Hints on Getting Well and Keeping Well*. New York: M. L. Holbrook, 1895 [orig. 1887].

Goetting, Ann. "The Developmental Tasks of Siblingship over the Life Cycle." *Journal of Marriage and the Family* 48 (November 1986): pp. 703–714.

Goldsmith, Barbara. *Other Powers: The Age of Suffrage, Spiritualism, and the Scandalous Victoria Woodhull*. New York: Alfred A. Knopf, 1998.

Goodsell, Willystine. *Pioneers of Women's Education in the United States: Emma Willard, Catherine [sic] Beecher, Mary Lyon*. New York: McGraw-Hill, 1931.

Gossett, Thomas F. *Uncle Tom's Cabin and American Culture*. Dallas, Tex.: Southern Methodist University Press, 1985.

Graff, Mary B. *Mandarin on the St. Johns*. Gainesville: University of Florida Press, 1953.

Graham, Sara Hunter. "The Suffrage Renaissance: A New Image for a New Century, 1896–1910." In *One Woman, One Vote: Rediscovering the Woman Suffrage Movement*. Ed. Marjorie Spruill Wheeler, pp. 157–178. Troutdale, Ore.: New Sage Press, 1995.

Griffith, Elisabeth. *In Her Own Right: The Life of Elizabeth Cady Stanton*. New York: Oxford University Press, 1984.

Grimké, Sarah, and Angelina Grimké. *The Public Years of Sarah and Angelina Grimké: Selected Writings, 1835–1839*. Ed. Larry Ceplair. New York: Columbia University Press, 1989.

Guide/Index to the Isabella Beecher Hooker Project. Hartford, Conn.: Stowe-Day Foundation, 1979.

Hamand, Wendy F. "'No Voice from England': Mrs. Stowe, Mr. Lincoln, and the British in the Civil War." *New England Quarterly* 61 (March 1988): pp. 3–24.

Harper, Ida Husted. *The Life and Work of Susan B. Anthony*. 2 vols. Indianapolis: Bowen, Merrill, 1898–1908.

"Harriet Beecher Stowe." *Spectator*, July 4, 1896, p. 3.

Harris, Susan K. *The Courtship of Olivia Langdon and Mark Twain*. Cambridge: Cambridge University Press, 1996.

Harveson, Mae Elizabeth. *Catharine Esther Beecher*. New York: Arno Press, 1969 [orig. 1932].

Hayward, Edward F. *Lyman Beecher*. Boston: Pilgrim Press, 1904.

Hedrick, Joan D. *Harriet Beecher Stowe: A Life*. New York: Oxford University Press, 1994.

Henry, Stuart C. *Unvanquished Puritan: A Portrait of Lyman Beecher.* Grand Rapids, Mich.: William
B. Eerdmans, 1973.

Hibben, Paxton. *Henry Ward Beecher: An American Portrait.* New York: George H. Doran, 1927.

Higginson, Thomas Wentworth. *Cheerful Yesterdays.* Boston: Houghton, Mifflin, 1898.

———. *Letters and Journals, 1846–1906.* Ed. Mary Thacher Higginson. Boston: Houghton,
Mifflin, 1921.

[Higginson, Thomas Wentworth]. "Ought Women to Learn the Alphabet?" *Atlantic Monthly* 3
(February 1859): pp. 137–150.

Holley, Marietta. *Samantha at the World's Fair.* New York: Funk & Wagnalls, 1893.

Holley, Mrs. Alexander H. "Catharine Beecher." In *The Hartford Female Seminary Reunion, June 9,
1892,* pp. 17–24. Hartford, Conn.: Case, Lockwood & Brainard, 1892.

Hooker, John. "Shall Women Be Allowed to Vote upon the Sale of Liquor and in School
Matters?" May 6, 1889.

———. *Some Reminiscences of a Long Life.* Hartford, Conn.: Belknap & Warfield, 1899.

Hopkins, Vivian C. *Prodigal Puritan: A Life of Delia Bacon.* Cambridge: Belknap Press of Harvard
University Press, 1959.

Howard, John Raymond. "Harriet Beecher Stowe: A Sketch." *Outlook,* July 25, 1896, pp. 138–143.

———. *Remembrance of Things Past: A Familiar Chronicle of Kinsfolk and Friends Worth While.* New
York: Thomas Y. Crowell, 1925.

Howe, Julia Ward. *Reminiscences, 1819–1899.* Boston and New York: Houghton, Mifflin, 1900.

[Howells, W. D.] "The Birthday Garden Party to Harriet Beecher Stowe." *Atlantic Monthly*
Supplement 50 (August 1882): pp. 1–16.

"Injurious Works and Injurious Criticism." *Nation,* Oct. 29, 1868, pp. 346–347.

Jablonsky, Thomas J. *The Home, Heaven and Mother Party: Female Anti-Suffragists in the United
States, 1868–1920.* Brooklyn, N.Y.: Carlson Publishing, 1994.

"Jackson, Alice Hooker Day." In *National Cyclopaedia of American Biography,* vol. 21, p. 130. New
York: J. T. White, 1931.

Jacobs, Harriet A. *Incidents in the Life of a Slave Girl.* Ed. Jean Fagan Yellin. Cambridge, Mass.:
Harvard University Press, 1987 [orig. 1861].

[James, Henry.] "Dallas Galbraith." *Nation,* Oct. 22, 1868, pp. 330–331.

Johnston, Johanna. *Mrs. Satan.* New York: G. P. Putnam's Sons, 1967.

Kelley, Mary. "At War with Herself: Harriet Beecher Stowe as Woman in Conflict within the
Home." *American Studies* 19 (1978), pp. 23–40.

Kerr, Andrea Moore. *Lucy Stone: Speaking Out for Equality.* New Brunswick, N.J.: Rutgers
University Press, 1992.

King, Grace. *Memories of a Southern Woman of Letters.* New York: Macmillan, 1932.

Knight, Kate Brannon. *History of the Work of Connecticut Women at the World's Columbian
Exposition.* Hartford, Conn.: Case, Lockwood & Brainard, 1898.

Korobkin, Laura Hanft. *Criminal Conversations: Sentimentality and Nineteenth-Century Legal Stories of
Adultery.* New York: Columbia University Press, 1998.

Kraditor, Aileen S. *The Ideas of the Woman Suffrage Movement, 1890–1920.* New York: W. W.
Norton, 1981 [orig. 1965].

Kugler, Israel. *From Ladies to Women: The Organized Struggle for Women's Rights in the Reconstruction
Era.* Westport, Conn.: Greenwood Press, 1987.

Lockwood, Allison. *Passionate Pilgrims: The American Traveler in Great Britain, 1800–1914.* New
York: Cornwall, 1981.

Longfellow, Henry Wadsworth. *Life of Henry Wadsworth Longfellow with Extracts from His Journals
and Correspondence.* Ed. Samuel Longfellow. 2 vols. Boston: Ticknor and Co., 1886.

Lutz, Alma. *Created Equal: A Biography of Elizabeth Cady Stanton, 1815–1902.* New York: John Day,
1940.

Margolis, Anne Throne. "A Tempest Tossed Spirit: Isabella Beecher Hooker and Woman

Suffrage." In *Guide/Index to The Isabella Beecher Hooker Project*, pp. 9–45. Hartford, Conn.: Stowe-Day Foundation, 1979.

Marilley, Suzanne M. *Woman Suffrage and the Origins of Liberal Feminism in the United States, 1820–1920*. Cambridge, Mass.: Harvard University Press, 1996.

Mark Twain's Letters. Vol. 2, 1867–1868. Ed. Harriet Elinor Smith and Richard Bucci. Berkeley: University of California Press, 1990. Vol. 3, 1869. Ed. Victor Fischer and Michael B. Frank. Berkeley: University of California Press, 1992. Vol. 5, 1872–1873. Ed. Lin Salamo and Harriet Elinor Smith. Berkeley: University of California Press, 1997.

Marshall, Charles F. *The True History of the Brooklyn Scandal: Being a Complete Account of the Trial of the Rev. Henry Ward Beecher, of Plymouth Church, Brooklyn, Upon Charges Preferred by Theodore Tilton, Including All the Original Letters, Documents and Private Correspondence, with Biographies of the Leading Actors in the Great Drama*. Philadelphia: National Publishing, 1874.

Marshall, Susan E. *Splintered Sisterhood: Gender and Class in the Campaign against Woman Suffrage*. Madison: University of Wisconsin Press, 1997.

Matthews, Jean V. *Women's Struggle for Equality: The First Phase, 1828–1876*. Chicago: Ivan R. Dee, 1997.

McManus, Ella Burr. "Home Life of Isabella Beecher Hooker." *Connecticut Magazine* 9 (Spring 1905): pp. 299–302.

Meredith, Robert. *The Politics of the Universe: Edward Beecher, Abolition and Orthodoxy*. Nashville, Tenn.: Vanderbilt University Press, 1968.

Meyer, Ellen G. "Isabella Beecher Hooker, Catharine Beecher: An Attempt to Find as Women Their Place in Society." Unpublished paper, Connecticut Historical Society, June 2, 1977.

Miller, Francis Trevelyan. "An Appreciation [of Isabella Beecher Hooker]." *Connecticut Magazine* 9 (Spring 1905): pp. 302–304.

Mintz, Steven. *Prison of Expectations: The Family in Victorian Culture*. New York: New York University Press, 1983.

Mott, Lucretia Coffin. *Selected Letters*. Ed. Beverly Wilson Palmer. Urbana: University of Illinois Press, 2002.

"Mrs. Isabella Beecher-Hooker." Boston *Pilot*, Oct. 3, 1891, p. 5.

"Mrs. Stowe's 'Oldtown Folks,'" *Nation*, June 3, 1869, pp. 436–438.

Murray, Alex L. "Harriet Beecher Stowe on Racial Segregation in the Schools." *American Quarterly* 12 (Winter 1960): pp. 518–519.

Nichols, Carole. *Votes and More for Women: Suffrage and After in Connecticut*. New York: Haworth Press, 1983.

Niven, John. *Connecticut for the Union: The Role of the State in the Civil War*. New Haven, Conn.: Yale University Press, 1965.

Noun, Louise R. *Strong-Minded Women: The Emergence of the Woman-Suffrage Movement in Iowa*. Ames: Iowa State University Press, 1969.

O'Neill, William. *Everyone Was Brave: A History of Feminism in America*. Chicago: Quadrangle Books, 1971.

O'Toole, Patricia. *The Five of Hearts: An Intimate Portrait of Henry Adams and His Friends, 1880–1918*. New York: Clarkson Potter, 1990.

Peck, Mary Gray. *Carrie Chapman Catt: A Biography*. New York: H. W. Wilson, 1944.

Perkins, Frances Beecher. "Two Years with a Colored Regiment." *New England Magazine* 17 (January 1898): pp. 533–543.

Phelps, Elizabeth Stuart. *Chapters from a Life*. Boston and New York: Houghton Mifflin, 1896.

Pivar, David J. *Purity Crusade: Sexual Morality and Social Control, 1868–1900*. Westport, Conn.: Greenwood Press, 1973.

Plymouth Church and Its Pastor, or Henry Ward Beecher and His Accusers. Ed. J. E. P. Doyle. Hartford, Conn.: Park, 1874.

Pugh, Evelyn. "John Stuart Mill, Harriet Taylor, and Women's Rights in America." *Canadian Journal of History* 13 (1978): pp. 423–442.

Rafferty, Jennifer. "Charlotte Perkins Gilman, the Beecher Sisters, and Hartford Origins." Paper presented at the National Women's Studies Association annual meeting, Washington, D.C., June 1993.

Riegel, Robert E. *American Feminists.* Lawrence: University of Kansas Press, 1963.

———. "The Split of the Feminist Movement in 1869." *Mississippi Valley Historical Review* 49 (December 1962): pp. 485–496.

Robinson, Harriet H. *Massachusetts in the Woman Suffrage Movement.* Boston: Roberts Bros., 1881.

Robson, John M. *The Improvement of Mankind: The Social and Political Thought of John Stuart Mill.* Toronto: University of Toronto Press, 1968.

Rugoff, Milton. *The Beechers: An American Family in the Nineteenth Century.* New York: Harper & Row, 1981.

Sachs, Emanie. *"The Terrible Siren": Victoria Woodhull.* New York: Harper & Bros., 1928.

Severance, Caroline M. *The Mother of Clubs: Caroline M. Seymour Severance.* Ed. Ella Giles Ruddy. Los Angeles: Baumgardt Publishing, 1906.

Shaplen, Robert. *Free Love and Heavenly Sinners: The Story of the Great Henry Ward Beecher Scandal.* New York: Alfred A. Knopf, 1954.

Shklar, Judith N. *American Citizenship: The Quest for Inclusion.* Cambridge, Mass.: Harvard University Press, 1991.

[Simms, William Gilmore.] Review of *A Key to Uncle Tom's Cabin. Southern Quarterly Review* n.s. 7 (July 1853): p. 226.

Sinclair, Andrew. *The Better Half: The Emancipation of the American Woman.* New York: Harper & Row, 1965.

Skandera-Trombley, Laura E. *Mark Twain in the Company of Women.* Philadelphia: University of Pennsylvania Press, 1994.

Sklar, Kathryn Kish. "All Hail to Pure, Cold Water!" *American Heritage* 26 (December 1974): pp. 64–69, 100–101.

———. *Catharine Beecher: A Study in American Domesticity.* New York: W. W. Norton, 1976.

Smith, Helen Krebs. *The Presumptuous Dreamers: A Sociological History of the Life and Times of Abigail Scott Duniway, 1834–1871.* Lake Oswego, Ore.: Smith, Smith and Smith, 1974.

Smith, Julia E. *Abby Smith and Her Cows.* 1877. Reprint. New York: Arno Press, 1972.

Smith-Rosenberg, Carroll. "The Female World of Love and Ritual: Relations between Women in Nineteenth-Century America." *Signs* 1 (Autumn 1975): pp. 1–26.

Squire, Belle. *The Woman Movement in America.* Chicago: A. C. McClung, 1911.

Stanton, Elizabeth Cady. *Eighty Years and More: Reminiscences, 1815–1897.* 1898. Reprint. New York: Schocken Books, 1971.

———. *Elizabeth Cady Stanton as Revealed in Her Letters, Diary and Reminiscences.* Ed. Theodore Stanton and Harriot Stanton Blatch. 2 vols. New York: Harper & Bros., 1922.

———. "The Moral of the Byron Case." *Independent,* Sept. 9, 1869, p. 1.

———. "A Word about George Sand." *Revolution,* Sept. 15, 1870, p. 169.

Stanton, Elizabeth Cady, and Susan B. Anthony. *Papers of Elizabeth Cady Stanton and Susan B. Anthony.* Ed. Patricia G. Holland and Ann D. Gordon. Wilmington, Del.: Microfilm, 1991. Guide and Index to the Microfilm, 1992.

———. *The Selected Papers of Elizabeth Cady Stanton and Susan B. Anthony.* Ed. Ann D. Gordon. 2 vols. New Brunswick, N.J.: Rutgers University Press, 1997, 2000.

Stanton, Elizabeth Cady, Susan B. Anthony, and Matilda Joslyn Gage, Eds. *History of Woman Suffrage.* 4 vols. Rochester, N.Y.: Susan B. Anthony, 1881, 1886, 1902, 1922.

Stein, Karen F. "Paulina Kellogg Wright Davis." In *American Women Writers: A Critical Reference Guide.* Ed. Lina Mainiero, vol. 1, pp. 476–478. New York: Frederick Ungar, 1979.

Stone, Lucy, and Henry B. Blackwell, *Loving Warriors: Selected Letters, 1853–1893*. Ed. Leslie Wheeler. New York: Dial Press, 1981.

Stowe, Charles Edward. *The Life of Harriet Beecher Stowe*. Boston: Houghton, Mifflin, 1890 [orig. 1889].

Stowe, Charles Edward, and Lyman Beecher Stowe. *Harriet Beecher Stowe: The Story of Her Life*. Boston: Houghton, Mifflin, 1911.

Stowe, Lyman Beecher. *Saints, Sinners and Beechers*. Indianapolis: Bobbs-Merrill, 1934.

Sulloway, Frank J. *Born to Rebel: Birth Order, Family Dynamics, and Creative Lives*. New York: Pantheon, 1996.

Talcott, Mary K. "Historical Sketch of the Seminary." In *The Hartford Female Seminary Reunion, June 9, 1892*, pp. 1–16. Hartford, Conn.: Case, Lockwood & Brainard, 1892.

Thorp, Margaret Farrand. "Woman's Profession—Catherine E. Beecher." In *Female Persuasion: Six Strong-Minded Women*, pp. 11–55. New Haven, Conn.: Yale University Press, 1949.

Tilton vs. Beecher: Action for Criminal Conversation. 3 vols. New York: McDivitt, Campbell, 1875.

Trautmann, Fredrick. "Harriet Beecher Stowe's Public Readings in New England." *New England Quarterly* 47 (June 1974): pp. 279–289.

Twichell, Joseph H. "Mrs. Harriet Beecher Stowe in Hartford." *Critic*, Dec. 18, 1886, pp. 301–302.

Tyler, Alice Felt. "Isabella Beecher Hooker." *Notable American Women, 1607–1950: A Biographical Dictionary*. Ed. Edward T. James, pp. 212–214. Cambridge: Belknap Press of Harvard University Press, 1973.

Underhill, Lois B. *The Woman Who Ran for President: The Many Lives of Victoria Woodhull*. Bridgehampton, N.Y.: Bridge Works, 1995.

Van Why, Joseph S. "Crusaders of the Pen & Podium: Henry Ward Beecher, Thomas K. Beecher, and Other Family Members." In *Portraits of a Nineteenth-Century Family: A Symposium on the Beecher Family*. Ed. Earl A. French and Diana Royce, pp. 97–127. Hartford, Conn.: Stowe-Day Foundation, 1976.

———. *Nook Farm*. Ed. Earl A. French. Hartford, Conn.: Stowe-Day Foundation, 1975.

Wagenknect, Edward. *Harriet Beecher Stowe: The Known and the Unknown*. New York: Oxford University Press, 1965.

Wallace, Alfred Russel. *My Life: A Record of Events and Opinions*. 2 vols. London: Chapman & Hall, 1905.

Waller, Altina L. *Reverend Beecher and Mrs. Tilton: Sex and Class in Victorian America*. Amherst: University of Massachusetts Press, 1982.

Weimann, Jeanne Madeline. *The Fair Women*. Chicago: Academy Press, 1981.

White, Barbara A. "Three Feminist Mother-Daughter Pairs in the Nineteenth- and Early Twentieth-Century United States." In *Generations*, pp. 274–287. Ed. Devoney Looser and E. Ann Kaplan. Minneapolis: University of Minnesota Press, 1997.

White, James C. *Personal Reminiscences of Lyman Beecher*. New York: Funk & Wagnalls, 1882.

Willard, Frances E. "Harriet Beecher Stowe at Home." *Chautauqua* 8 (February 1888): pp. 287–288.

Willard, Frances E., and Mary A. Livermore, Eds. "Mrs. Isabella Beecher Hooker." In *American Women: Fifteen Hundred Biographies*, vol. 1, pp. 390–392. New York: Mast, Crowell & Kirkpatrick, 1897.

Wilson, Forrest. *Crusader in Crinoline: The Life of Harriet Beecher Stowe*. Philadelphia: J. B. Lippincott, 1941.

Woodhull, Victoria. "A Speech on the Principles of Social Freedom [1871]," "Complete and Detailed Version of the Beecher-Tilton Affair [1872]," and "A Lecture on Constitutional Equality [1871]." In *The Victoria Woodhull Reader*. Ed. Madeleine B. Stern. Weston, Mass.: M & S Press, 1974.

Index

Revolution 130, 135, 148, 152, 153, 173, 180
  Beecher editorship of 149, 150
  debt 197
  offices 158
  Sand article 159
Rugoff, Milton 6, 14, 18
  on George Beecher 41
  on Beecher-Tilton scandal 205, 213
  on IBH 23, 97
  on HBS 101, 206

Sand, George 54, 159, 160, 163, 182, 184, 210
Scarlet Letter, The (Nathaniel Hawthorne) 67, 267
second coming 241, 245, 247, 291
Semi-Colon Club 14, 235
Seneca Falls
  anniversaries 285, 320
  1848 meeting 12, 75, 100, 124, 132, 139, 216, 324
  pioneers of 186
  resolutions 287
  women speaking at 158
Severance, Caroline 99–100, 102, 104, 119, 120, 121, 123, 132
  and AWSA 135, 136
  IBH visits 129
  IBH writes 138, 139, 181
  religion 137
  and speaking 158
  and women's club movement 185, 186
Shakespeare, William 83, 95
"Shall Women Vote? A Matrimonial Dialogue" (IBH) 71, 73, 76, 128
"Sinners in the Hands of an Angry God" (Jonathan Edwards) 2, 63
sixteenth amendment 155, 166, 167, 239, 253, 257, 270, 313
Sklar, Kathryn Kish 2, 41, 80, 259
slavery
  battle over at Lane Seminary Beecher position on 15, 16, 37
  CB essay on 16
  Fugitive Slave Law 50, 55, 169, 206
  Hookers' view of 37
  M. F. Hubbard and 3
  rights of slaves 16
  See also abolitionism
Smith, Abby 255, 256, 269
Smith, Anna (HBS servant) 35, 48, 66
Smith, Anna (IBH servant) 45, 66, 238, 297

Smith, Julia. *See* Parker, Julia Smith
Smith, Virginia 238, 296, 303
Smith sisters 35, 255, 256, 269, 335
Some Reminiscences of a Long Life (JH) 27, 317
Sorosis 125, 185, 186, 192, 217, 250
Spencer, Sara 253, 256, 257
Spiritualism 171, 184, 185, 192, 193, 235, 247, 289
  advocates of 234, 288
  James Beecher and 280
  critics of 242, 245
  history of 233, 236
  setback to 291
  Lib Tilton and 231
  and Victoria Woodhull 290
Spofford, Harriet Prescott 73, 272
Springfield *Republican* 255, 263
Stanton, Edwin M. 96, 97
Stanton, Elizabeth Cady ix, 33, 72, 156, 182, 191, 239, 335
  advocates educated suffrage 319
  and AERA 133
  autobiography 12, 13, 81
  and Beecher-Tilton scandal 205, 212, 215, 225, 228, 229
  biography 132
  and Bloomer dress 81
  and Centennial Protest 240
  class 125
  defense of George Sand 160
  education of daughters 69
  at Hartford convention 147
  at Hooker convention 163, 164, 167
  IBH letters to 243
  and International Council of Women 285
  letters to IBH 143
  life in Boston 12
  life in Seneca Falls 13
  Lucy Stone view of 135, 138
  meets IBH 119, 126, 130, 136
  and NWSA 134, 148, 269
  oratory 158, 312
  as president of NAWSA
  quarrel with IBH 163–164
  radicalism of 100
  relationships with
    Susan B. Anthony 197, 330
    CB 261
    daughter Harriot Stanton Blatch 286, 299, 327
    Olympia Brown 221